Programming for the Internet of Things:
Using Windows 10 IoT Core and Azure IoT Suite

Dawid Borycki

PUBLISHED BY

Microsoft Press
A division of Microsoft Corporation
One Microsoft Way
Redmond, Washington 98052-6399

Library of Congress Control Number: 2016959963

ISBN: 978-1-5093-0206-2

Printed and bound in the United States of America.

1 17

Microsoft Press books are available through booksellers and distributors worldwide. If you need support related to this book, email Microsoft Press Support at *mspinput@microsoft.com*. Please tell us what you think of this book at *https://aka.ms/tellpress*.

This book is provided "as-is" and expresses the author's views and opinions. The views, opinions and information expressed in this book, including URL and other Internet website references, may change without notice.

Some examples depicted herein are provided for illustration only and are fictitious. No real association or connection is intended or should be inferred.

Microsoft and the trademarks listed at *https://www.microsoft.com* on the "Trademarks" webpage are trademarks of the Microsoft group of companies. All other marks are property of their respective owners.

Acquisitions Editor: Devon Musgrave
Editorial Production: Polymath Publishing
Technical Reviewer: Chaim Krause
Copy Editor: Traci Cumbay
Layout Services: Shawn Morningstar
Indexing Services: Kelly Talbot Editing Services
Proofreading Services: Corina Lebegioara
Cover: Twist Creative • Seattle

Contents

Introduction

Lately, the Internet of Things (IoT), big data, machine learning, and artificial intelligence have become very hot topics. *IoT* is defined as the global network of interconnected devices. These devices can be as small as implantable continuous glucose monitors or wearables, or as big as credit card–sized computers, like the Raspberry Pi. As the number of such devices continues to grow, the amount of data they generate will rapidly increase—and new technological challenges will appear.

The first of these challenges relates to storage. Small devices have physical constraints that do not allow them to store big datasets. Second, big data exceeds the computational capabilities of traditional algorithms and requires different, statistical-based approaches. These are provided by machine learning, a branch of artificial intelligence. Hence, IoT, big data, machine learning, and artificial intelligence are tightly related concepts. Typically, devices are end-points, which send data over the network to the cloud, where data is stored and processed to get new, previously unavailable insights. These insights may help to understand and optimize processes monitored by smart devices.

While this description may sound fascinating, the number of new technologies you need to learn to start implementing custom IoT solutions might seem daunting. Fortunately, Microsoft created Windows 10 IoT Core and Azure IoT Suite, which enable you to program custom IoT solutions fairly quickly. Their functionality is limited only by your imagination. In this book, you will find numerous projects presented in a step-by-step manner. By completing them, you not only obtain the fundamentals of device programming, but you will also be ready to write code to revolutionize devices and robots, which can do the work for you!

This book helps you to master IoT programming in three main parts. Each contains a suitable level of detail and explains how to prepare your development environment, read data from sensors, communicate with other accessories, build artificial vision, build motors, build hearing systems, and incorporate machine learning and artificial intelligence into your device. This book also shows you how to set up remote telemetry and predictive maintenance like Azure IoT solutions and to build custom IoT solutions from scratch.

Audience and expected skills

This book is devoted to students, programmers, engineers, enthusiasts, designers, scientists and researchers who would like to use their existing programming skills to start developing software for custom devices and sensors and also use the cloud to store, process, and visualize remote sensor readings.

I assume the reader knows fundamental aspects of C# programming and is experienced in Windows programming. Therefore, no special discussion is devoted to C# or to programming fundamentals. I do not assume any previous knowledge of audio and image processing, machine learning, or Azure. These topics are explained in detail.

Tools and required hardware

Throughout this book, I use Windows 10 and Visual Studio 2015/2017 as the development environment. Most of the hardware components I use are from the Microsoft IoT Pack for Raspberry Pi, provided by Adafruit Industries. Any additional hardware elements like cameras, add-on boards for Raspberry Pi, communication adapters, or motors will be described in chapters dealing with the particular topic.

Organization of this book

This book is divided into the following three parts:

- Part I: Essentials

- Part II: Device programming

- Part III: Azure IoT Suite

In Part I, I explain the fundamentals of embedded programming and discuss how they differ from desktop, web, and mobile app programming. I also show how to configure the programming environment and write "Hello, world!"–like projects on the Windows 10 IoT Core. Additionally, I describe several fundamental concepts regarding the UWP threading model and XAML markup for declaring the UI. Most experienced developers can skip elements of this part that they are already well-versed in and proceed to the second part.

Part II contains chapters related to device programming with Windows 10 IoT Core and the UWP. I first show you how to acquire data from multiple sensors and control a device. Subsequently, I explain how to acquire and then process signals from a microphone and a camera. Then, I show you how to use various communication protocols, including serial communication, Bluetooth, Wi-Fi, and AllJoyn, to enable your IoT module to communicate with other devices. I also show you how to control motors and use Microsoft Cognitive Services and Azure Machine Learning to make your device really smart and intelligent.

Part III is devoted to the cloud. I show you how to use two preconfigured Azure IoT solutions for remote device telemetry and predictive maintenance. In the last chapter, I present a detailed process of building a custom IoT solution from scratch. This shows the essence of IoT programming, in which data from remote sensors is transferred to the cloud, where it is stored, processed, and presented. Moreover, I explain how to report abnormal sensor readings directly to the mobile app running on Windows 10.

This material is supplemented by six appendixes, which show how to blink an LED with Visual Basic and JavaScript (Appendix A), present HDMI modes of the Raspberry Pi (Appendix B), explain bit encoding (Appendix C), describe code-sharing strategies (Appendix D), introduce Visual C++/Component Extensions (Appendix E), and show how to set up Visual Studio 2017 for IoT development (Appendix F). These appendixes are available online here: *https://aka.ms/IoT/downloads*.

Conventions

The following conventions are used in this book:

- **Boldface** type is used to indicate text that you type.

- *Italic* type is used to indicate new terms and URLs.

- Code elements appear in a monospaced font.

About the companion content

I have included companion code to enrich your learning experience. The companion code for this book can be downloaded from the following page:

https://aka.ms/IoT/downloads

You may also download the code from GitHub here:

https://github.com/ProgrammingForTheIoT

The source code is partitioned into subfolders that correspond to particular chapters and appendixes. To improve book readability, in many places, I refer to the companion code rather than showing the full listing, so it is good to have the companion code open while reading this book.

Acknowledgments

This book would not exist without the support of Devon Musgrave, who enthusiastically responded to my book proposal and provided initial comments along with writing guidance.

I'm grateful to Chaim Krause for thoroughly checking every single project discussed in this book and finding all—even the smallest—issues. I'm also very indebted to Kraig Brockschmidt, who comprehensively peer-reviewed every chapter. His wide experience and valuable comments significantly improved the quality of this book. Finally, thanks to Traci Cumbay for her excellent work as copy editor.

Many thanks to Kate Shoup for managing the book's production. I also thank Kim Spilker for shepherding this book to its completion.

Finally, special thanks go to my wife Agnieszka and daughter Zuzanna for their continuous support and patience, shown to me during the writing of this book.

Errata and book support

We have made every effort to ensure the accuracy of this book and its companion content. Any errors that have been reported since this book was published are listed on our Microsoft Press site at:

https://aka.ms/IoT/errata

If you find an error that is not already listed, you can report it to us through the same page.

If you need additional support, email Microsoft Press Book Support at *mspinput@ microsoft.com*.

Please note that product support for Microsoft software is not offered through the addresses above.

We want to hear from you

At Microsoft Press, your satisfaction is our top priority and your feedback our most valuable asset. Please tell us what you think of this book at:

https://aka.ms/tellpress

The survey is short, and we read every one of your comments and ideas. Thanks in advance for your input!

Stay in touch

Let's keep the conversation going! We're on Twitter: @MicrosoftPress.

PART I

Essentials

The first part of this book covers basic aspects of programming for the Internet of Things (IoT) using Windows 10 IoT Core. Chapter 1, "Embedded devices programming," defines embedded devices, describes their role, and shows how such devices compose the IoT. It explains why embedded programming is challenging and how it differs from desktop, web, and mobile programming.

In Chapter 2, "Universal Windows Platform on devices," I introduce the Universal Windows Platform (UWP) and Windows IoT Core and show you the advantages and limitations of using these tools for rapid software development for embedded devices. I show you how to install and configure a development environment and implement a "Hello, world!" project for the Windows IoT device using selected programming models available on the UWP.

Chapter 3, "Windows IoT programming essentials," dives into asynchronous programming—one of the key aspects for IoT programming. I show you the difference between headed and headless modes, and I characterize the IBackgroundTask interface and asynchronous programming patterns for UWP apps. In this chapter, I also discuss timers and thread synchronization.

Chapter 4, "User Interface design for headed devices," runs through the most important aspects of designing a user interface (UI) for headed Windows IoT Core devices using XAML. These include controls used to define UI layout (Grid, StackPanel, RelativePanel), control styling and formatting, events, and data binding.

CHAPTER 1

Embedded devices programming

Embedded devices work as the control units of a broad range of tools including house accessories, car engines, robots and medical devices. These control units use specially designed software to exchange data with sensors of any kind. Embedded devices apply sophisticated algorithms to sensor data to monitor, control, and automate the specific process. This chapter defines embedded devices, discusses their role, and shows the possibilities that arise from connecting such smart devices. It also describes the structure of embedded devices, their programming aspects, and the common problems and challenges they can present.

What is an embedded device?

An *embedded device* (*ED*) is a special-purpose computing system for automating a specific process. Unlike a general-purpose computer, which has a fairly standard set of peripherals (input/output devices for display, storage, communication), an ED is designed for a specific purpose. As a consequence, input and output devices of an ED can be far different from those in general-purpose computers. An ED can be fully functional without a keyboard or a monitor; as you can easily imagine, using your laptop or desktop without such fundamental components would be impossible.

Though specialized and general-purpose computers differ by peripherals, their core parts are similar: a central processing unit (CPU or microprocessor) and memory. The microprocessor executes the computer program, which consists of the instructions fetched from memory. Procedures executed by the CPU then control the dedicated hardware. Such a combination of an ED and hardware is called an embedded system.

Special-purpose firmware

In contrast to a typical computing system, an ED is usually dedicated to controlling particular hardware; hence, its form factor and processing capabilities are tailored to the special system. In particular, an ED does not necessarily have to run multiple programs at the same time. Instead, an ED runs specially designed software, called firmware. The firmware functionality is usually not generic and performs tasks devised to the particular hardware. Typically, firmware is loaded to the device in the factory or by the maker during development.

You see an example of firmware specificity in microwave ovens. An embedded device built into a microwave controls the time and heating temperature of the food based on user input provided through the key pad or touch screen. Unlike a keyboard, which is essentially the same for any general-purpose computer, microwave input components strongly differ among devices. Thus the ED of the particular microwave manufacturer cannot be generalized to all microwave ovens. Furthermore, different ovens are equipped with distinct intrinsic sensors and electronic components. Hence, each model has its own specific firmware, adjusted to the hardware capabilities and the system's purpose.

The lifecycle of the firmware loaded to an embedded device is quite different from typical applications of computer systems. The program stored in ED memory is activated whenever the device is switched on and works as long as the device is powered. During this time, firmware communicates with sensors and also input/output (I/O) devices using peripherals. These peripherals constitute interfaces between intrinsic parts of an ED and its environment. Most common peripherals include the following:

- Serial Communication Interface (SCI)

- Serial Peripheral Interface (SPI)

- Inter-Integrated Circuit (I^2C)

- Ethernet

- Universal Serial Bus (USB)

- General Purpose Input/Output (GPIO)

- Display Serial Interface (DSI)

Typically, an ED does not require a full-size display. In the extreme case, an ED can even have just a single-pixel display, composed of a single LED used as an indicator. Color or blinking frequency of such an LED can communicate errors or encode monitored values.

Microcontroller memory

Very often, an embedded device has to be accommodated in a very small housing and be power-efficient. To save space and resources, CPU, memory, and peripherals are integrated into a single chip, which is called the microcontroller.

The microcontroller's memory is divided into two main parts: Read Only Memory (ROM), which stores the firmware, and Random Access Memory (RAM), which stores variables used by the software components. ROM memory is non-volatile and can be modified using additional developer tools and (or) a programmer. Non-volatile memory is required to instantly load firmware as soon as the ED is powered up. For example, when you power up your wireless router, it begins execution of the firmware stored in ROM, while your connection settings, including credentials, frequency band, and Service Set Identifier (SSID) are managed in RAM (typically they are loaded from some non-volatile memory to RAM, after the device's boot).

This memory configuration resembles the scenario used in other computer systems, in which ROM stores the special program, known as the basic input/output system (BIOS) or the Unified Extensible Firmware Interface (UEFI). Typically, the BIOS runs immediately after the computer is turned on, and it initializes hardware and loads the operating system, which then creates processes (program instances) and their threads.

ED memory is also supplemented by additional non-volatile storage, termed Electrically Erasable Programmable ROM (EEPROM). Writing to EEPROM is very slow; its main purpose is to store device calibration parameters, which are restored to RAM after a power loss. The data stored in EEPROM depends on the applications and the device type but usually contains calibration parameters used for converting the raw data acquired from sensors into values representing physical parameters such as temperature, humidity, geolocation, or device orientation in three-dimensional space. EEPROM serves as the basis for flash memory, which is used in modern memory sticks and solid state drives (SSD). These newer designs offer much faster speeds than EEPROMs. Figure 1-1 shows a summary of memory types.

FIGURE 1-1 Different purposes require different types of memory.

EEPROM memories usually are designed to store larger amounts of data. Accessing data in large sets can be slow, especially for I/O operations. Hence, to improve I/O, processors also use memory registers —quickly accessible locations for small amounts of fast memory. Registers are especially important for microcontrollers because they control peripherals, as I describe later in this chapter.

Depending on the application, the performance, capabilities, and peripherals may significantly differ among devices. For example, the processing performance of an ED controlling a car engine must be much higher than that of a microcontroller embedded in the simple consumer electronic gadget, like a media receiver. The proper and error-free control of the vehicle is much more critical than that of an electronic gadget.

Embedded devices are everywhere

Embedded devices are everywhere, and are often so hidden that we don't even notice their existence. In the automotive world, numerous internal and external sensors within the vehicle's modules constantly monitor intrinsic systems. Data from these detectors is transferred through peripherals to an appropriate ED, which continually analyzes this input to keep track of the vehicle traction, control the engine, or display an external temperature or vehicle's location, among other functions. In the financial sector, embedded devices control units of the automated teller machines (ATM) to enable a bank customer to make a financial transaction automatically. Healthcare screening devices are also managed by embedded devices that control the position of a light beam to noninvasively produce an image of the human body or deliver information about diseases. Intelligent buildings, weather stations, and security devices are equipped with specially designed microcontrollers that acquire data from sensors or images from cameras; they then inspect them using digital signal and image-processing techniques to monitor temperature or humidity, detect unauthorized access, or optimize resource usage.

Embedded devices are becoming an important component of the personal healthcare systems. Wearable embedded devices containing heart-rate and blood pressure sensors or even noninvasive glucose monitoring systems can continuously read health parameters, process them in real-time, and transfer this data to the wearer's doctor. These wearable EDs may significantly improve diagnosis and treatment by providing detailed information about the wearer's health status.

Embedded devices simplify energy usage monitoring through remote reading from power meters. Information coming from embedded devices controlling regulatory drivers can optimize power distribution.

Small, form-factor, smart devices are not limited to serious applications. They can also provide a lot of joy. Kinect and HoloLens are prominent examples of devices that have business and fun applications. Kinect is a motion controller, equipped with movement sensors and cameras to recognize complex gestures and track people; you might know it from Xbox computer games. HoloLens further advances these developments by providing augmented reality to significantly enhance perception. The core elements of both Kinect and HoloLens are multiple sensors and cameras that analyze the environment and process input from voice, gesture, or gaze.

Primarily, embedded devices act as artificial intelligence systems that automate everyday actions performed by people to make our lives easier and better. An ED takes data as an input, processes it, makes decisions, and implements control algorithms and corrective procedures. They not only automate specific processes but can predict manufacturing failures, diseases, accidents, or weather.

An ED can easily detect sensor readings that exceed thresholds set by the programmer and perform predictive analysis and even preventive maintenance ranging from saving food from being overheated to preventing a car engine from being damaged. Because microchips can now efficiently run very advanced software that implements sophisticated control and diagnostic algorithms, an ED can perform process automation and predictive analysis that significantly reduces the risk of using a particular system, diminish process cost and time, and improve efficiency.

A lot of applications for embedded devices already exist, but many more unexplored possibilities are easy to imagine, as are the advantages of building new devices. Many of these arise from the possibility of connecting smart devices into the advanced networks of hardware units.

Connecting embedded devices: the Internet of Things

ARPANET, the Internet predecessor, was created to enhance the potential of isolated general-purpose computer systems. Connecting workstations accelerated communication and data sharing. Moreover, new software versions could be quickly distributed among connected computers, and computations could be run in parallel on multiple systems. These advantages quickly proved very useful and were translated to public networks, which later became the one global system of interconnected computer networks—the Internet. Nowadays, the Internet is one of the fundamental elements helping people to communicate, share files, distribute information, and automate and simplify many everyday processes. In short, the power of general-purpose computers was enormously amplified when they became inter-connected via the Internet.

A similar idea produced the Internet of Things (IoT), the network of distributed embedded devices. EDs are very useful in isolated systems, but their power is enhanced tremendously when they're connect-ed into a global detection or monitoring system that includes many hardware units. This connectivity yields a lot of advantages, because the large amount of data can provide invaluable information about the status of a given business process or monitored system. Data analysis can then lead to completely new conclusions unavailable by using a single smart device or sensor or by monitoring the given pro-cess manually.

In a sense, IoT is the world of various connected devices, which acquire data from sensors and then distribute this information among other computer systems, either desktop or mobile, by using local or global communication networks. Depending on the nature of the application, you can benefit from IoT with just one ED—or billions. The number, type, and capabilities of devices in the IoT grid can be tailored to particular requirements, processes, or systems. But new devices aren't always necessary; IoT can be composed of existing devices and sensors, as in the case of the MyDriving app (*http://aka.ms/ iotsampleapp, https://channel9.msdn.com/Shows/Visual-Studio-Toolbox/MyDriving-Sample-Application*).

IoT devices are becoming the crucial part of automation and robotics because of rapid technologi-cal advances in data transfer rates, sensor and device miniaturization, and microcontrollers that can process large amounts of data using advanced control and diagnostic algorithms. Although a single IoT device can process readings from connected sensors and perform appropriate actions, that device can't always store large amounts of data. Moreover, analysis of the information coming from many IoT devices becomes challenging, especially in the case of large IoT grids.

Current and future IoT applications rely not only on the embedded device itself but also on the ability to extract invaluable insights from data acquired using that device. Connecting smart devices yields new possibilities and brings new challenges in terms of processing and analyzing large amounts of data. Every device may be integrated with different sensors and thus use distinct communication protocols. Combining smart devices requires sophisticated acquisition, storage, and processing ap-proaches in which data coming from different devices is unified and processed using statistical models on the shared system.

Such a centralized processing unit performs advanced analysis and turns untapped data into clear, readable reports by exposing the uniform interface for presenting, accumulating, and filtering acquired and processed data. Therefore, IoT is usually composed of a central storage and processing system, which gives users the ability to connect their devices and easily process, and more importantly, understand data coming from those smart units. This functionality is delivered by the Microsoft Azure IoT Suite, which I describe in detail in Part III, "Azure IoT Suite."

Figure 1-2 shows an example of the Microsoft Azure IoT Suite as the central management system for IoT devices integrated with different sensors.

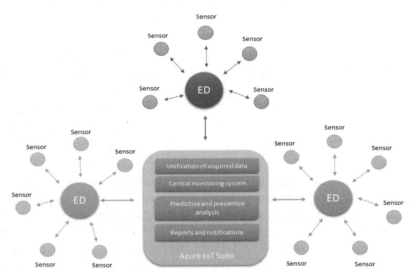

FIGURE 1-2   In an IoT, data coming from various sensors connected to distinct embedded devices (ED) is transferred to the central, cloud-based system.

To put it in its most basic terms, the *things* in IoT means devices and sensors of any kind, while the *Internet* refers to the centralized system that connects and manages those devices. That system further processes untapped data coming from sensors using business intelligence techniques to generate clean and readable information, which in turn simplifies decision-making, enables predictive and preventive analysis, and automates many business processes.

Electric energy usage provides a practical example of how IoT simplified business process. First, the electromechanical meters were replaced by electronic meters (embedded devices) that not only measure electric energy usage and provide clearer display but can also record other parameters to support time-of-day billing or prepayment meters. Electronic meters greatly enhanced measurements of electric energy usage; however, manual sensor readings were still required—until electric energy meters were connected to obtain readings remotely and store them in the central processing system. As a result, power stations automatically acquire and process data not only for billing purposes but also to optimize electric energy distribution, maintain the network, or predict malfunctions.

Fundamentals of embedded devices

How does software executed by the CPU interact with peripherals to acquire data from sensors and communicate with other devices? It requires several hardware and software concepts.

From the hardware point of view, the microcontroller is connected to peripherals through physical connectors, exposed as pins on the external casing. (See Figure 1-3.) The process is independent of the particular transmission protocol and medium used to transfer data (e.g., wires, fibers, or free-space communication channels) and works like this:

1. Wired connections between the microcontroller and peripherals carry electrical signals that encode bits of information as physical quantities such as the voltage or current.

2. These physical observables are converted to digital values using appropriate analog-to-digital converters.

3. Digital values are converted back to physical quantities before being sent to peripherals using digital-to-analog converters.

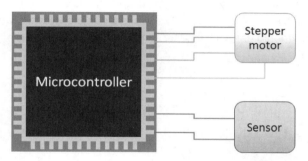

FIGURE 1-3 Peripherals are connected to the microcontroller pins.

Software accesses received binary data (read operation) and knows how to send data to peripherals (write operation). In general, the digital representation of signals received from peripherals is distributed among the devices using the data bus. Proper data distribution requires an address bus, which carries information about physical locations of binary data in physical memory. In general, there are two ways of reading and writing data to peripherals using data and address buses. These are defined as the port-mapped and memory-mapped I/O.

- In the port-mapped I/O, the CPU uses separate address buses for addressing data in local memory and in peripherals. Special read/write instructions transfer data between the microcontroller and peripherals. (See Figure 1-4.) From the hardware point of view, having separate address buses simplifies addressing. However, from the software point of view, accessing the peripherals using port-mapped I/O is quite complicated because it not only requires reading or writing data to memory registers but also requires appropriate I/O instructions for receiving and sending binary data from and to a peripheral.

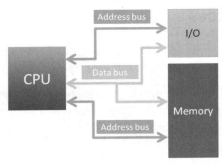

FIGURE 1-4 In port-mapped I/O, two separate address buses point to physical locations in memory and peripherals; memory and I/O devices have to be accessed separately.

■ Memory-mapped I/O reserves some part of the RAM memory for communication, so firmware virtually accesses I/O devices in the same way it accesses memory registers—with a single address bus. (See Figure 1-5.) This approach naturally simplifies software. However, using a single address bus to control memory and peripherals transfers software complications to a lower level. More sophisticated schemas are therefore required for address decoding and encoding. In addition, the amount of memory available to the user is slightly decreased. On the Windows desktop platform, you can check the amount of such hardware-reserved memory using Task Manager. (See Figure 1-6.)

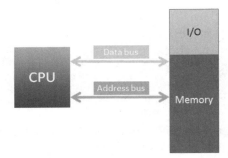

FIGURE 1-5 In memory-mapped I/O, a single address bus points to physical locations in memory and peripherals; additional I/O instructions become unnecessary.

Registers are the building blocks of the RAM memory, and—depending on the microcontroller type—may contain 8, 16, 24, 32, or 64 bits. Some of these registers in the amount defined by the microcontroller's manufacturer are designed to exchange data between a processor and peripherals and thus decrease the amount of RAM memory for the user. (Refer to Figure 1-6.) Each bit of such specially designed register is mapped to the physical I/O ports, which constitute the physical pins of the microcontroller.

The logical bit values assigned to the particular pin are controlled by the voltage level or current intensity, which define their off (0) and on (1) states. Because these pins are mapped to memory registers, any voltage level or current changes are automatically reflected into the memory registers.

Thus, firmware accesses the data received from the peripheral by reading an appropriate memory register, identified by its address, pointing to its location in the memory. Data is sent back to the peripheral in the same way—that is, by modifying values stored in registers. This process requires conversion between physical quantity such as voltage or current and binary representation.

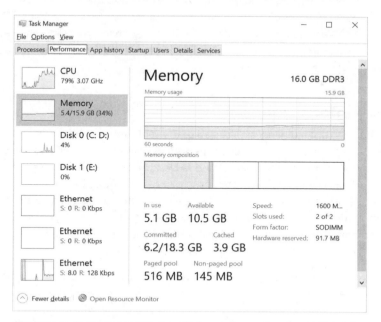

FIGURE 1-6   In computer systems, which use memory-mapped I/O, hardware-reserved memory decreases total memory available for applications; in this example, hardware uses approximately 92 MB.

In some circumstances, the approach may slow down overall memory access, because converting and transferring physical signals between CPU and peripherals can be slower than the intrinsic mechanism used by RAM. Moreover, some memory is reserved for communication and is not accessible to the user. Using port-mapped I/O, in which physical pins are not mapped to the memory registers, can sometimes be preferable. CPU uses additional commands to send requests and receive answers from the peripherals. The data transferred is stored in a separated address space but requires additional physical pins for initiating communication. The particular communication approach depends on the microcontroller manufacturer. Programmers need to know the address of memory registers associated with the particular peripheral and communication protocol. (See Chapter 6, "Input and output.")

The software of the embedded device does not need to constantly read values from registers to get an updated state of the sensor. Instead, the firmware can be automatically informed whenever an appropriate event occurs. For this purpose, microcontrollers use interrupts, which are the signals generated whenever pins change their physical state. The CPU executes an interrupt handler, which is a software function associated with a given interrupt. This allows firmware to react to external events without endlessly reading register values. Such reactive programming is similar to the event-based approach known in high-level application programming. In such a case, every user request or action, like pressing a button, generates an event that in turn runs the associated event handler. The logic implemented within this procedure responds to the user request.

Embedded device programming vs. desktop, web, and mobile programming

Although embedded systems are programmed using the same languages and similar tools as desktop, web, and mobile apps are, ED coding requires direct interaction with hardware elements. Hence, ED programming differs from desktop, web, and mobile coding. There are also many similarities, however. Specific comparisons in terms of user interface, hardware abstraction layer, robustness, resources, and security are discussed below.

Similarities and user interaction

The idea behind interrupts and interrupt handling is quite similar to events and event handling in desktop and mobile programming. However, each technology uses distinct nomenclature, which closely matches internal aspects of the particular programming scope. In desktop and mobile applications, events are related to any user action, like pressing a button or scrolling lists. Any action of this kind generates an event, which can be processed by methods called event handlers. Events can be also triggered by hardware or system-related issues to indicate, for example, low battery level, loss of wireless connection, or connection/disconnection of an external device. Event handlers can be used to respond to any user action or occurrence triggered by the hardware or the operating system.

Similarly, in Model-View-Controller applications, developed for mobile (Android, iOS) or web platforms (ASP.NET), every user action or query incoming from other applications or services is defined as the request or action. Every request is processed by the request-handler module, which maps the particular action to the appropriate method of the class, implementing the controller. The latter interprets a request, updates the state (model) of the application, and produces the corresponding response by presenting a view.

Thus, in all cases, the software responds to user requests or external signals and processes them to take an appropriate action or produce a corresponding response. However, in desktop, web, and mobile programming, these requests are mostly generated by the user; IoT interrupts are usually generated by external signals related to sensors (electrical signals). Thus, embedded device programming differs from desktop, web, and mobile programming by the source that generates events. This doesn't mean that an ED doesn't respond to user requests at all. IoT devices can be equipped with input systems like touch screens, by which users configure an ED. Hence, IoT may also implement a user interface (UI).

In subsequent chapters, to distinguish two possible sources of events, I will refer to interrupts whenever I deal with sensors and to events whenever I discuss methods handling user requests generated through a UI.

Hardware abstraction layer

At first glance, some aspects of ED programming are similar to desktop, web, and mobile application-development techniques, but more key differences than similarities exist. These differences come mostly from the fact that typical high-level programming doesn't require low-level interaction with the hardware.

Because hardware-related aspects are implemented within the operating system or hardware drivers, they typically aren't accessed directly by the programmer.

The common computer or smartphone is an advanced version of an ED. Internal functions of mobile and desktop systems are based on the same concepts as an IoT device. Namely, the CPU communicates with peripherals using similar techniques. Software developers implicitly use them during software development tasks such as accessing files on the hard drive, sending serialized data over a network, or simply displaying messages on the screen.

Conventional computer systems, however, are standardized and use operating systems that implement a hardware abstraction layer. Programming frameworks and convenient application programming interfaces significantly simplify the process of software development by providing a large number of implemented algorithms, data structures, and functions for performing common operations.

ED programming is similar to writing device drivers, which map hardware operations to operating system functions. However, ED software not only provides such an intermediate layer but also controls hardware units. ED development means combining the roles of hardware, drivers, OS, and application into one piece of firmware, so the boundaries are more blurred.

In general-purpose computer systems, the hardware abstraction provides a unified layer, which allows customers to buy any kind of keyboard, mouse, display, storage, and so on, without worrying about their underlying differences. For ED development, you can virtually work with any kind of device without any intermediate layer.

Robustness

Computing devices embedded in car safety systems, electronic stability programs (ESPs) offer a good example of ED robustness. ESP controls a vehicle's stability by detecting loss of traction. It analyzes data coming from various hardware units sensing the speed and acceleration of the car's wheels. The data analysis required to predict understeer or oversteer can be very complex. This task requires constant data processing and noise-issue handling.

In real-world applications, sensor readings can be affected by noise arising from intrinsic electronical circuits due to some fundamental physical effects. Therefore, the sensor readings may vary in time. The programmer must take these noise effects into account, usually by accumulating readings over time and processing them using statistical measures, like mean or median. Depending on the application, such processing may require more advanced control algorithms to filter incorrect readings and to provide steady and predictable control of the hardware units. This is especially important for safety-critical applications. For this reason, the firmware should be robust and error-free in order to quickly respond to rapidly changing and noise-affected sensor readings.

For specific applications (like ESP), the IoT software needs to be optimized to act very fast, because sometimes a few milliseconds' delay may play a very crucial role, while in the case of typical desktop, web or mobile applications, such a delay will be probably unnoticed by the user.

Resources

IoT devices are frequently very small to fit into the body of the system they control or monitor. Embedded devices can be as small as a coin or credit card, which means they typically have limited storage and processing power in comparison to typical computers or smartphones. The software controlling the embedded device has to use hardware resources responsibly, without wasting memory and CPU time. This issue is also crucial for high-level programming, but it may not be as important for typical computer systems, which come equipped with large amounts of memory and huge processing capabilities.

Security

As Figure 1-3 shows, data transferred between peripherals and CPU could be accessed by monitoring physical pin signals. This way of reverse engineering your ED could utilize an oscilloscope, although that's unlikely since it requires physical access to your device. On the other hand, when you connect your ED to the network, especially a wireless network, the probability of your data being intercepted increases significantly.

Security is an important issue for any type of programming, but IoT devices connected to wireless networks are most prone to loss of data. For this reason, you need to secure data transferred over a network using cryptography algorithms.

Connected EDs process and collect sensitive data and control critical hardware. Often, they are directly exposed to cyber-attacks—for example, through the Internet connection. Therefore, the so-called *Security of Things* becomes a very important issue.

The data collected by connected EDs includes private information. For example, home-automation electronics track your daily habits—when you leave and come back from your house, TV channels you watch, and so on. It also tracks what images your security cameras capture. And of course, it has the access codes for various devices. Therefore, if home automation is not properly secured, all this data can be stolen. Worse, it could be used to take control of your house or to spy on you. There is also a danger of an attacker remotely taking control of IoT devices that run on your car. For instance, attacker could disable your braking or steering system while you are driving.

These two examples prove how important Security of Things is. You can secure your IoT system by adopting proper filtering and by validating and encrypting transferred data. Further, you must check the internal consistency of the filesystem and other components of the IoT system.

Benefits of the Windows 10 IoT Core and Universal Windows Platform

Several problems arise when programming IoT devices—and can quickly discourage you from developing software for smart devices. These problems are typically due to the following issues:

- Having to use native tools, compiler chains, and programming environments provided by microcontroller manufacturers

- Low-level programming languages and tools

- Debugging difficulties

- The lack of patterns and best practices

- Narrow community

- UI development using cross-platform libraries and tools

- Broad range of sensors and hardware units to control

- Having to secure communication protocols by writing cryptography algorithms from scratch

Windows 10 IoT Core and the Universal Windows Platform (UWP) solve these problems. The former is the most compact version of Windows 10 and is tailored for IoT needs, while the latter is the API for accessing Windows 10 functions and thus simplifies embedded programming.

The UWP provides you a unified API and set of programming tools, which are exactly the same as you probably already use for your web, mobile, or desktop programming. UWP programming tools follow the *write once run everywhere* paradigm. Such an approach provides programming tools and technologies that enable you to write the application by using the single programming language and environment, and then deploy your app to multiple devices, ranging from IoT, through smartphones, and up to desktop and enterprise servers. By using the same tool set you can target additional platforms.

The UWP also implements many comprehensive algorithms and functions that

- Simplify access to sensors

- Perform robust calculations

- Write advanced functionalities with minimal code

- Extensively query your data

- Secure data transfer using cryptography algorithms

- Support many other IoT applications, like signal and image processing, programming artificial intelligence, and interacting with central processing systems, which unify your untapped data and turn them into readable reports

Finally, the UWP can be accessed using several high-level and popular programming languages including C# and JavaScript, which significantly simplifies your software development process. The UWP provides a set of UI controls that can be seamlessly integrated into software for IoT devices. This turns the problematic native-based development of firmware into a cheerful experience of building software for smart, connected devices.

Windows 10 IoT Core and a broad range of UWP functionalities described in subsequent chapters of this book allow you to quickly develop applications for IoT, prepare proof-of-concept solutions, and yield a unique opportunity to build and program custom devices whose functionality is limited only by the maker's imagination.

Summary

This chapter provided theoretical information. It discussed the most important concepts behind IoT, which you typically do not think of when developing software for desktop, web, or mobile platforms. I pointed out several common challenges that embedded programmers must tackle. I also presented how Windows 10 IoT Core and Azure IoT Suite can help you develop IoT solutions.

CHAPTER 2

Universal Windows Platform on devices

IoT devices typically do not have a full-size display, which could be used for the type of output that comes from a typical "Hello, world!" starter application. Instead, IoT devices have only a few LEDs or pixels—or, in the extreme case, just a single LED or pixel—to display information. So, in the world of embedded programming we say "Hello" by turning an LED on and off.

In this chapter, I show you how to use the UWP interfaced through C#, and C++ to trigger the LED. I use these two languages only, because in this book all apps will be implemented using C#. C++ will be used later to implement the Windows Runtime Component, interfacing native code.

I first define Windows 10 IoT Core and guide you through the installation and configuration processes of all the required software and hardware components. I then explain an electronic LED circuit assembly. After you've had your hands on the code, I show you useful tools and utilities for remote device management and accessing its contents.

What is Windows 10 IoT Core?

Windows 10 IoT Core is a compact version of Windows 10 designed and optimized for embedded devices. Windows 10 IoT Core implements the platform, hardware, and software abstraction layers, which simplifies the process of application development for IoT devices. Until recently this area was exclusively reserved for rare and native programming technologies. However, thanks to Windows 10 IoT Core, every high-level software developer can now code embedded devices by using the Universal Windows Platform programming interfaces available for all Windows 10 platforms.

Hardware, platform, and software abstraction layers implemented within Windows 10 IoT Core are composed of the native drivers, which can be accessed using any of the UWP programming languages, including C#, C++, Visual Basic, or JavaScript. Windows 10 IoT Core also supports the Python and Node. js runtimes. Therefore, you can easily access microcontroller interfaces, capabilities using high-level programming languages. Most of the low-level stuff—which typically forces you to use archaic or low-level programming constructs—is thankfully performed within Windows 10 IoT Core.

The power of Universal Windows Platform for devices

All Windows 10 platforms use a common base, implementing a unified kernel and a common application model. The Universal Windows Platform contains a unified application programming interface available for every UWP device. As a result, an application developed using this core part can run on any Windows 10 device, including desktop, mobile, tablet, HoloLens, Xbox, Surface Hub, and IoT devices. However, the core parts of Windows and its API do not contain some specific features designed exclusively for one particular platform or another. This is because some hardware platforms provide features not available on other devices. For example, IoT devices can control certain custom sensors that aren't available on desktop or mobile devices. The implementation of all programming interfaces in the core part of the UWP would be redundant, so, to target platform specificity, the UWP delivers software development kit (SDK) extensions designed for particular device families (enabling access to features available exclusively on the IoT platform, for example). Figure 2-1 shows the relationship between the core part of the UWP and SDK extensions.

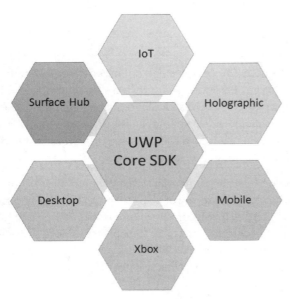

FIGURE 2-1 To access features specific for a particular device family you can reference an appropriate SDK extension: IoT, Holographic, Mobile, Xbox, Desktop, and Surface Hub.

The important advantage of the UWP is that even when an extension SDK is referenced by a UWP project, the application can still be deployed to the platforms that do not support the particular extension set. Conditional compilation is not required. However, a programmer still needs to ensure that an application does not access features that are unavailable. To check whether a particular API is available for the current platform, use static methods of the `ApiInformation` class, defined in the `Windows.Foundation.Metadata` namespace. The following code can be used to check if a particular type, `Windows.Phone.Devices.Power.Battery`, is present. It produces `false` when the code is run on the desktop platform and `true` if the app utilizing this code is run on Windows Phone.

```
var typeName = "Windows.Phone.Devices.Power.Battery";
var canIReadBatteryLevelOfMyWindowsPhone = Windows.Foundation.Metadata.
    ApiInformation.IsTypePresent(typeName);
System.Diagnostics.Debug.WriteLine("Can I access a battery level of my Windows
Phone: " + canIReadBatteryLevelOfMyWindowsPhone);
```

Because of the common, unified programming interfaces available on every Windows 10 device and the abstraction layer that exempts developers from writing their own native drivers (for example, for mapping memory registers), Windows 10 IoT Core also delivers software development kits available for other UWP devices. IoT developers can easily perform various programming tasks, such as creating rich and adaptive user interfaces, handling gesture and voice input, and connecting the device to web and cloud services, just to name a few.

Such an approach has several advantages over other solutions. First, Windows 10 IoT Core programmers can benefit from functionality already implemented within the core part of the Universal Windows Platform. This shortens development time and significantly increases software capabilities. Second, UWP apps can target novel prototype devices, running Windows 10 IoT Core. Finally, an app can be monetized through the same distribution channel (that is, Windows Store).

Windows 10 IoT Core is a great tool for rapid prototype development. However, native solutions can be preferable in some scenarios. That doesn't mean Windows 10 IoT Core and the UWP are not fully functional for IoT development, but that for exceptional cases, e.g., extremely time-critical applications, you'd want to avoid the additional processing time for transferring signals and data between additional layers provided by Windows 10 IoT Core. In such cases, you'd use native tools and reduce usability and flexibility for performance increases.

Tools installation and configuration

Let's make sure you've got all the software tools you'll need for this book. Here are the required elements.

- A development PC with Windows 10 installed and enabled developer mode
- Visual Studio 2015 (Update 1 at least) as the integrated development environment
- Windows IoT Core project templates
- Windows 10 IoT Core Dashboard
- IoT device

Windows 10

Application development for Windows IoT Core requires a PC controlled by Windows 10, version 10.0.10240 or higher. Windows 10 installation is straightforward, and for this reason I don't describe it in detail here.

If Windows 10 is already installed on your development PC, you should verify its version—and upgrade if necessary. To verify the system version run winver from a command prompt or by searching for it in the start menu. (See Figure 2-2.)

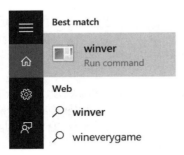

FIGURE 2-2   The winver application will tell you the build number of Windows 10 on your machine.

After verifying the Windows version, enable developer mode on the development PC. You can do so by using the Windows Settings application, which can be executed by searching for it in the Start menu (as winver). To enable developer mode, go to the **Update & Security** section of the settings and select **Developer Mode** on the **For Developers** tab, as you see in Figure 2-3.

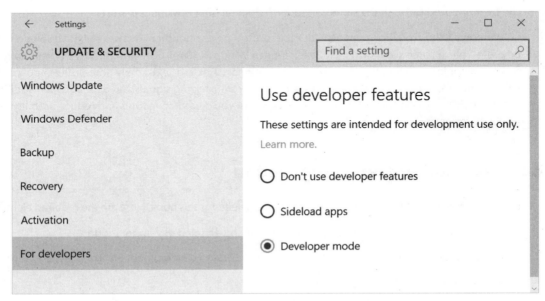

FIGURE 2-3   Enable developer mode in Windows 10 through Update & Security within Settings.

Visual Studio 2015 or later

Your Windows IoT Core development PC should also include Visual Studio 2015 Update 1 (or later) as the integrated development environment. It's available for download at *https://www.visualstudio.com/vs/* in three different versions: Community, Professional, and Enterprise. The first version is free, and the other two require licenses but can be used for free within an evaluation period. In this book, I am using Visual Studio 2015 Community. In Appendix F, "Setting up Visual Studio 2017 for IoT development," I also show how to setup Visual Studio 2017 RC for IoT (UWP) development. Aspects presented in this book are compatible with Visual Studio 2017 RC.

The installation process of Visual Studio 2015 is automatic. However, the SDK for the Universal Windows Platform might not be included in the default Visual Studio 2015 installation. Therefore, during Visual Studio 2015 installation, make sure that the **Tools and Windows 10 SDK** check box under the **Windows and Web Development** node is selected, as shown in Figure 2-4.

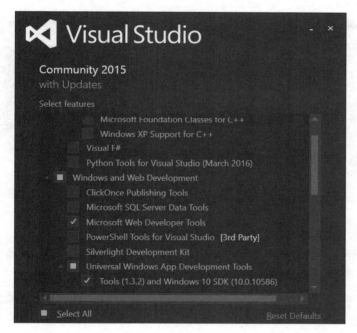

FIGURE 2-4   The Universal Windows App Development Tools are required for Windows IoT Core development. This figure shows the installer of the Visual Studio 2015 Community Update 2 with Universal Windows App Development Tools in version 1.3.2 and the Windows 10 SDK in version 10586.

Windows IoT Core project templates

Microsoft provides additional project templates designed for developing IoT applications without a user interface of any form. These are the so-called headless apps—in contrast to headed apps with the UI. I tell you more about the headless apps in Chapter 3, "Windows IoT programming essentials."

The IoT project templates for headless apps can be installed as an extension to Visual Studio 2015 by following these steps:

1. In Visual Studio 2015, go to **Tools > Extensions and Updates**.

2. In the Extensions and Updates dialog box, expand the **Online** node and in the search box at the top right of the dialog box, type **IoT**.

3. In the search results, find **Windows IoT Core Project Templates**, as shown in Figure 2-5, and click the **Download** button. This will start the download process for the templates.

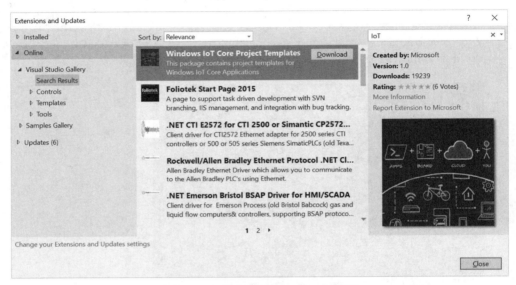

FIGURE 2-5   The Extensions and Updates dialog box in Visual Studio 2015.

4. After the project templates are downloaded, the Visual Studio Extension (VSIX) Installer will display a license terms screen. Click **Install**.

5. The Installer will confirm that the extension has been successfully installed. Click **Close**, and restart Visual Studio 2015.

Windows 10 IoT Core Dashboard

After installing Visual Studio 2015, you need to download and install the Windows 10 IoT Core Dashboard. This application helps set up new—and manage and configure existing—Windows 10 IoT Core devices connected to the local network, available both to the development PC and your IoT devices.

First, download the installer for the dashboard from *http://bit.ly/iot_dashboard*. Then run the installer file you just downloaded, and click **Install** on the first security warning dialog box that appears. This will start the download and installation process for the dashboard, and you'll see an Installing Windows 10 IoT Core Dashboard dialog box, after which another security warning might be displayed.

(Click **Run** if this second warning appears.) When the dashboard is installed and ready for use, you'll see its welcome screen, shown in Figure 2-6.

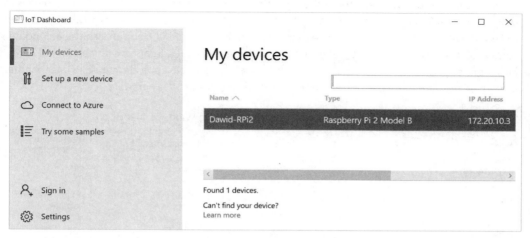

FIGURE 2-6 The Windows 10 IoT Core Dashboard showing the list of discovered IoT devices. Note that the My Devices list will be most likely empty at this stage.

Device setup

Now that you have all the necessary software components for your development environment, let's set up an IoT device.

Windows 10 IoT Core Starter Pack for Raspberry Pi 2 and Pi 3

While I was writing this chapter, Windows 10 IoT Core was available for four development boards (see Table 2-1 for a comparison):

- Raspberry Pi 2 (RPi2)

- Raspberry Pi 3 (RPi3)

- MinnowBoard MAX

- Qualcomm DragonBoard 410c

I decided to use the first of these because it was available within the Starter Pack for Windows 10 IoT, prepared by Adafruit (*http://bit.ly/iot_pack*). This pack offers a very convenient way to start IoT programming, since it contains all the necessary tools and verified, compatible components to assemble prototype circuits and develop software for Windows IoT devices. This is very important, especially in the early stage of development, because in case of any troubleshooting you can eliminate basic problems related to some of the hardware components like wires, LEDs, or sensors. Of course, you don't have to use the Starter Pack for RPi2. You can always get the RPi2 and other components separately.

However, you need to ensure that your hardware elements are compatible with the RPi2 and Windows 10 IoT Core. You can find the Microsoft-verified list of Windows 10 IoT Core compatible hardware components (like micro SD cards, sensors, and so on) at *http://bit.ly/iot_compatibility_list*. This remark is especially important when you want to use a different micro SD card. In that case you would need at least a class 10 micro SD card. Note that instead of the Starter Pack for RPi2, you can also use an updated version of this pack containing the RPi3. However, the latter is not equipped with an internal ACT LED. This requires you to use an external LED circuit to run a few sample apps, described in later chapters. Moreover, the Starter Pack for RPi3 does not contain an external Wi-Fi module.

TABLE 2-1   Selected features of development boards supporting Windows 10 IoT Core

Board	Raspberry Pi 2	Raspberry Pi 3	MinnowBoard MAX	Qualcomm DragonBoard 410c
Architecture	ARM	ARM	x64	ARM
CPU	Quad-core ARM® Cortex® A7	Quad-core ARM® Cortex® A8	64-bit Intel® Atom™ E38xx Series SoC	Quad-core ARM® Cortex® A53
RAM	1 GB	1 GB	1 or 2 GB	1 GB
On-board WiFi	-	+	-	+
On-board Bluetooth	-	+	-	+
On-board GPS	-	-	-	+
HDMI	+	+	-	+
USB ports	4	4	2	2
Ethernet port	+	+	+	+

Besides the RPi2 (or RPi3), the Microsoft IoT Pack for Raspberry Pi 2/3, as shown in Figure 2-7, contains the following components, wires and sensors:

- Raspberry Pi 2/3 Case—housing for the Raspberry; detailed instructions for inserting a board into the case can be found at *http://bit.ly/rpi_case*

- 5V 2A Power Supply with micro-USB cable

- Solderless Breadboard—required for circuit assembly

- Ethernet cable

- USB Wi-Fi module

- 8 GB micro SD card with Windows IoT Core (16 GB card in the case of RPi3)

- Male/Male jumper wires

- Female/Male jumper wires

- Two potentiometers

- Three tactile switches

- Ten resistors

- One capacitor

- Six LEDs

- One photocell

- Temperature and barometric sensor

- Color sensor

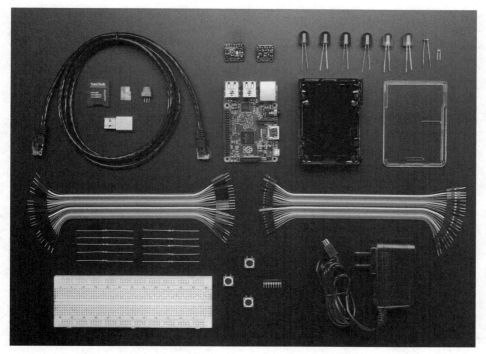

FIGURE 2-7   Contents of the Starter Pack for Windows 10 IoT Core on Raspberry Pi 2. A pack containing Raspberry Pi 3 is very similar. Source: *http://www.adafruit.com*.

You will use some of the above components to assemble the circuit, which is composed of the LED and resistor and will be controlled by the Windows universal app. However, before doing that, you will deploy Windows 10 IoT Core to the RPi2 (or RPi3) device and perform its basic configuration. Windows 10 IoT Core is already preloaded to the micro SD card, which comes with the Windows 10 IoT Starter Pack, but I prefer to describe the Windows 10 IoT Core installation and deployment because the IoT Starter Pack may not include the newest build of Windows 10 IoT Core. Also, you may need to deploy Windows 10 IoT Core if your micro SD card needs to be replaced.

Windows 10 IoT Core installation

The easiest way to install Windows 10 IoT Core on the RPi2 (or RPi3) is through the IoT Dashboard. The wizard available on the Set Up a New Device tab of the IoT Dashboard fully automates this process after you insert one of the compatible micro SD cards into the PC's card reader. Subsequently, select the device type, type in your device name (I set it to "Dawid RPi-2") and new administrator password, choose the Wi-Fi network connection (if available), accept the software license terms, and click **Download and Install**. (See Figure 2-8.) The IoT Dashboard will start flashing your SD card. The current progress will be displayed, as shown in Figure 2-9. The Deployment Image Servicing and Management tool will apply the Windows 10 IoT Core image to the SD card. (See Figure 2-10.) The IoT Dashboard will then display the confirmation screen that looks like Figure 2-11.

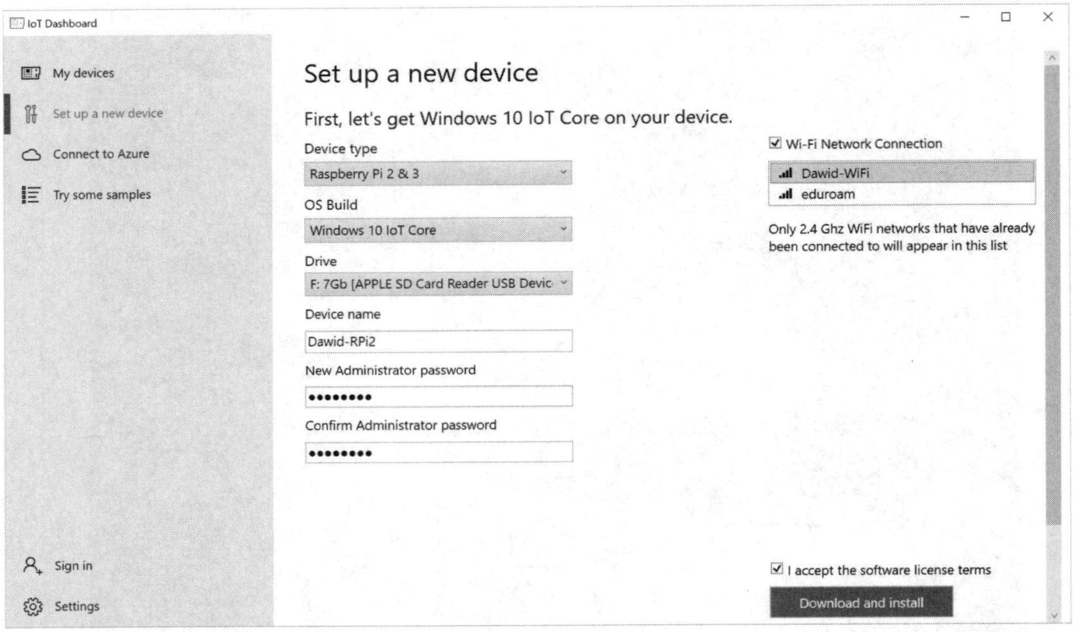

FIGURE 2-8   Setting up a new Windows 10 IoT Core device.

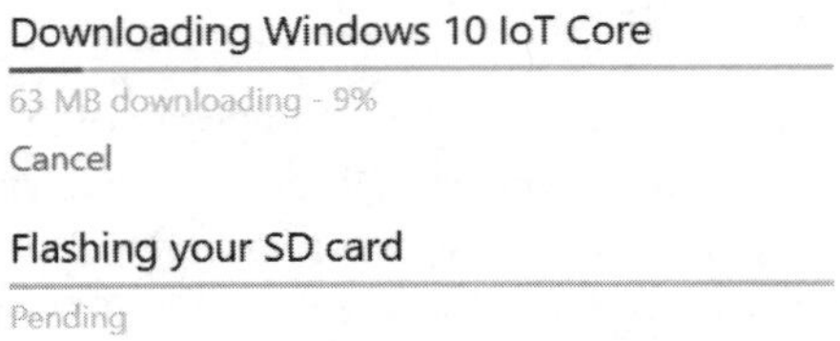

FIGURE 2-9   SD card preparation.

FIGURE 2-10 Deployment Image Servicing and Management tool is applying the Windows 10 IoT Core image to the SD card.

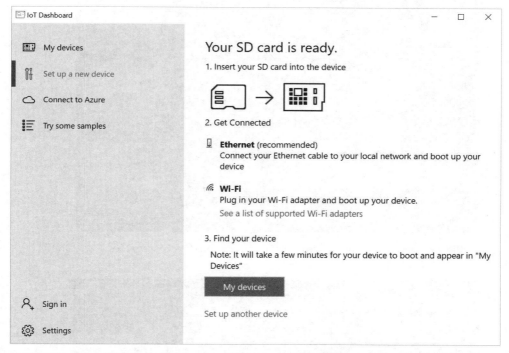

FIGURE 2-11 The IoT Dashboard shows successful image deployment by displaying the confirmation screen with subsequent instructions.

Configuring the development board

You see the top and the bottom views of the Raspberry Pi 2 Model B V 1.1, which are in Figure 2-12 and Figure 2-13, respectively. The main part of the board is the Broadcom BCM2836 chip, integrating the 900 MHz quad-core ARM Cortex-A7 CPU and VideoCore IV 3D graphics core with 1 GB of RAM memory. Raspberry Pi 2 is equipped with the following ports:

- 4 USB type A ports

- 1 micro-B USB port for power purposes

- 1 Local Area Network (LAN) adapter

- 1 HDMI port

- 1 3.5 mm audio jack and composite video (A/V)

- 40 GPIO pins

- 1 micro SD card slot, located at the back surface of the board (see Figure 2-13)

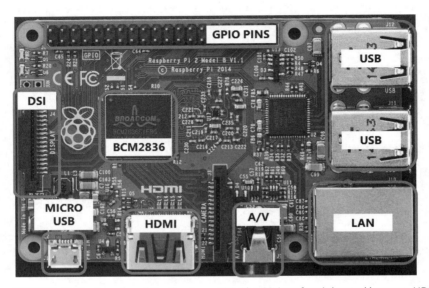

FIGURE 2-12 The top view of the Raspberry Pi 2. The CSI interface is located between HDMI and A/V ports.

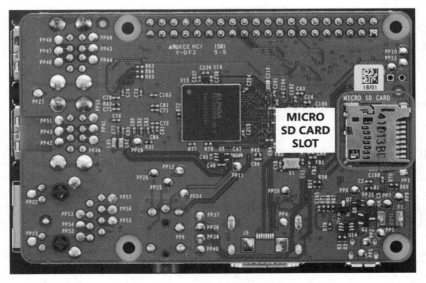

FIGURE 2-13 The bottom view of the Raspberry Pi 2.

The Raspberry Pi 2 and Pi 3 also include a Camera Serial Interface (CSI) and a Display Serial Interface (DSI). However, when I was writing this chapter, the DSI interface was not supported by Windows 10 IoT Core.

In order to prepare and run the RPi2 (or RPi3), complete the following procedure:

1. Insert the micro SD card with Windows 10 IoT Core into the Raspberry Pi 2 SD card slot.

2. Plug in the 5V 2A micro-B USB power supply to the board. The RPi2 will boot Windows 10 IoT Core automatically, which may take a minute or two.

3. Connect the Ethernet cable to the same local network as the development PC or plug the USB Wi-Fi module into one of the Raspberry's type A USB ports.

The RPi2 board is now ready. To proceed, you need to run the IoT Dashboard and go to the **My Devices** tab. The IoT Dashboard will automatically discover available IoT devices as shown in Figure 2-14. Note that if you choose the Wi-Fi connection during installation (refer to Figure 2-8), your IoT device will be automatically connected to this network. Also, be patient when booting your device for the first time. It may take longer. If your IoT device is still unavailable, you need to restart the RPi2 or RPi3 by reconnecting the power supply.

My devices

Name ∧	Type	IP Address	Settings	OS
Dawid-RPi2	Raspberry Pi 2 Model B	172.20.10.3	✎	10.0.14393.0

Search

FIGURE 2-14   The list of discovered IoT devices.

Hello, world! Windows IoT

With all the software tools installed and configured, and the IoT device in place, you can now write your first embedded UWP application: a "Hello, world!" app that toggles the LED connected to the RPi2 (or RPi3) through the electronic circuit.

Circuit assembly

To control an LED, you first need to assemble an electrical circuit. You can do so by connecting one of the LEDs delivered with the Windows 10 IoT Core Starter Pack for RPi2 (or RPi3) to the appropriate GPIO pins of the IoT device. For development boards, physical pins of the microcontroller are typically available through the pin expansion header to simplify solderless pin connection. (Refer to Chapter 1, "Embedded devices programming," and Figure 1-3 for more information.) The expansion header is physically connected to microcontroller pins by traces on the printed circuit board (PCB). You can visually inspect these traces by analyzing the RPi2 board or an appropriate PCB design.

LED, resistor, and electronic color codes

Every LED has a specified operating current required to power the LED, but you need to be careful to not exceed the maximum threshold value lest you destroy the LED. Input current to the LED circuit is regulated by a resistor. The recommended resistance is usually described in the LED manufacturer's datasheet.

The LEDs available within the Windows 10 IoT Core Starter Pack are low power, so you'll use a 560 Ohm (Ω) resistor to limit the current flow. The resistors contained in the Starter Pack for Windows 10 IoT Core are encoded using the 4-digit color code, consisting of four vertical color stripes, called bands. The first three bands encode the actual resistance, and the last one, which is usually spaced from the other bands, denotes the resistance tolerance, i.e., any deviation from the value declared by the manufacturer.

The resistance value is encoded using two significant figures (first and second band) and the multiplier (third band). Table 2-2 shows you the meaning of each band color. The resistor in your Starter Pack with color code green-blue-brown-gold has a resistance of $R = 56 \times 10^1 = 560\ \Omega$ with a tolerance ΔR of $\pm 5\%$. Similarly, the color code brown-black-orange-gold represents the following values: $R = 10 \times 10^3 = 10\ k\Omega$ and $\Delta R = \pm 5\%$. For more details, see *http://bit.ly/ electronic_color_code*.

TABLE 2-2   Electronic resistance color codes

Color	Significant figure value	Multiplier	Tolerance
Black	0	10^0	Does not apply
Brown	1	10^1	±1%
Red	2	10^2	±2%
Orange	3	10^3	Does not apply
Yellow	4	10^4	±5%
Green	5	10^5	±0.5%
Blue	6	10^6	±0.25%
Violet	7	10^7	±0.1%
Gray	8	10^8	±0.05%
White	9	10^9	Does not apply
Gold	Does not apply	10^{-1}	±5%
Silver	Does not apply	10^{-2}	±10%
None	Does not apply	Does not apply	±20%

The longer leg of an LED is called anode (positive charge), and the shorter leg is a cathode (negative charge). Because the electric charge flows from the positive to the negative leg, the resistor should be connected to the longer leg of the LED. You subsequently connect the resistor and the shorter LED leg to the GPIO pins of the RPi2. You can use either of two configurations for controlling the LED using a microcontroller: the logical active-low and active-high states.

Active-low and active-high states

The GPIO pins can possess the logical (digital) values of 0 (or low) or 1 (or high). The first one typically corresponds to a voltage of 0 V or less, while the second represents a voltage level above some threshold. In practice, an analog voltage signal is susceptible to noise. Accordingly, a signal randomly oscillates around low or high values. To ensure that an analog voltage signal represents valid low and valid high logic levels, pull-down (for low state) and pull-up (for high state) resistors are used. Thus, you have two options to induce the carrier flow through the LED:

- **Active-low state** Connect the longer LED leg through the resistor to the power supply pin with the voltage of 3.3 V and the second LED leg to the GPIO pin. When the GPIO pin is driven to a low state, current flows from the power pin through the resister to the LED.

- **Active-high state** Connect the LED's cathode to the ground (GND), and the anode to a GPIO pin. A GPIO pin driven into a high state induces the carrier flow.

Raspberry Pi 2 pinout

Before you configure an LED circuit in the active-low or active-high state, you need to familiarize yourself with the RPi2 pinout, which exposes the peripherals through a 40-pin expansion header; refer to Figure 2-12 and see Figure 2-15. Each pin of this header is numbered, starting from 1. Pins with odd numbers are located in the top header row. This means that the pin number 1 is located in the bottom left corner of the header (first element in the second header row), while the pin number 2 is located right above pin number 1. Consequently, the 40th pin sits in the far right end of the first header row.

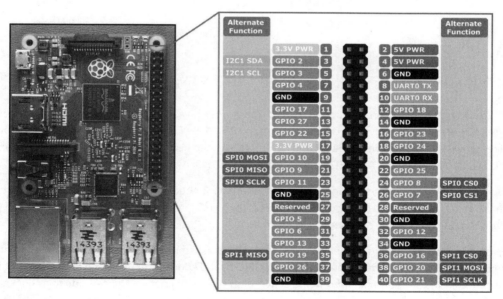

FIGURE 2-15 Pin mappings of the Raspberry Pi 2. Source: Windows Dev Center (*http://windowsondevices.com*). You can find an interactive version of this diagram at *http://pinout.xyz/*.

All the physical pins of the Raspberry Pi 2 can be divided into six groups, assigned to the following expansion header pins:

- 3.3V power pins: 1, 17

- 5V power pins: 2, 4

- I²C bus pins: 3, 5

- Ground (GND) pins: 6, 9, 14, 20, 25, 30, 34, and 39

- SPI bus pins: 19, 21, 23, 24, and 26

- Manufacturer-reserved pins: 8, 10, 27 and 28

Additionally, 17 GPIO pins are available to the user. Table 2-3 summarizes their numbers and initial states (right after the boot).

TABLE 2-3 GPIO ports assignment of the Raspberry Pi 2

Header pin	GPIO number	Initial state	Header pin	GPIO number	Initial state
7	4	Pull up	31	6	Pull up
11	17	Pull down	32	12	Pull down
12	18	Pull down	33	13	Pull down
13	27	Pull down	35	19	Pull down
15	22	Pull down	36	16	Pull down
16	23	Pull down	37	26	Pull down
18	24	Pull down	38	20	Pull down
12	25	Pull down	40	21	Pull down
29	5	Pull up			

Two additional GPIO ports, 35 and 47, control the status of two LEDs located on the RPi2 board. These LEDs are located above the DSI interface of the RPi2. (See Figure 2-12.) The GPIO port 35 controls the red power LED (PWR), while the second controls the green LED (ACT). In this chapter, I use an external LED only. Note that the ACT LED is unavailable on the RPi3.

As Figure 2-15 shows, several pins can have an alternate function. For example, header pins 2 and 5 (GPIO 2 and 3, respectively) can also provide access to the I²C interface. The section "Using C# and C++ to turn the LED on and off" delves into this issue.

According to the RPi2 pinout, the active-low state can be assembled by wiring the shorter leg of an external LED to pin 29 on the expansion header (GPIO 5) and connecting the longer LED through the resistor to pin 1 (3.3 V power supply). In the active-high state, you connect the cathode to a GPIO pin.

Note that the LED can be powered without writing the actual software. You can connect the second LED leg to one of the GND pins. The LED will be turned on immediately, and the RPi2 will simply act as a 3.3 V battery.

In the active-high configuration, the shorter leg of the LED can be connected to ground, e.g., header pin 6. The longer LED leg is then connected to the resistor and the GPIO pin, with an initial state of 0 (pull down). Then the LED is powered by driving the selected GPIO port to an active-high state.

Solderless breadboard connection

The Starter Pack for Windows 10 IoT Core contains the breadboard, which supports prototype wiring of electronic elements and does not require soldering. This breadboard is composed of two power rails on both sides and also contains 610 tie points, arranged in an array; see the bottom part of Figure 2-7. Each row of this array is labeled by a capital letter A through J, and the columns are numbered starting from 0. These labels help to localize tie points on the breadboard.

To assemble the LED circuit in an active-low state, you bend both legs of the resistor and use two female/male jumper cables. Figure 2-16 shows a connection diagram, which I made using the open-source tool Fritzing. (Download it at fritzing.org.) Table 2-4 shows you the breadboard-header map, and Figure 2-17 shows the actual connection.

FIGURE 2-16   An active-low state LED circuit visualization using a fritzing diagram.

TABLE 2-4 Sample connection map for an active-low LED circuit

Component	Leg or connector	Breadboard tie point location	Header pin
LED	Shorter leg	Row: F, Column: 30	-
	Longer leg	Row: F, Column: 31	-
Resistor	First leg	Row: H, Column: 31	-
	Second leg	Row: H, Column: 35	-
First jumper cable (purple in Figure 2-16 and in Figure 2-17)	Male connector	Row: J, Column: 35	-
	Female connector	-	1 (or 17)
Second jumper cable (yellow in Figure 2-16 and in Figure 2-17)	Male connector	Row: J, Column: 30	-
	Female connector	-	29 (or pins 7, 31 for pull-up initial state)

FIGURE 2-17 Real assembly of an active-low state LED circuit.

Typically, for the active-low state, you want to choose the GPIO pin, which is initially in a pull-up state. This ensures that the current flow is disabled when you access the port. Conversely, in the active-high state, you use the GPIO ports, which are in a pull-down state when the IoT device is powered up and the carrier's flow is disabled. Such alternative (active-high) circuit assembly can be configured as shown in Figure 2-18, Table 2-5, and Figure 2-19. Compare this configuration with an active-low state.

FIGURE 2-18 An active-high state LED circuit visualization using a fritzing diagram (compare with Figure 2-16).

TABLE 2-5 Sample connection map for an active-high LED circuit

Component	Leg or connector	Breadboard tie point location	Header pin
LED	Shorter leg	Row: F, Column: 30	-
	Longer leg	Row: F, Column: 31	-
Resistor	First leg	Row: H, Column: 31	-
	Second leg	Row: H, Column: 35	-
First jumper cable (purple in Figure 2-18 and in Figure 2-19)	Male connector	Row: J, Column: 35	-
	Female connector	-	37 (or any other GPIO port with pull-down initial state, e.g., pins 11, 12)
Second jumper cable (yellow in Figure 2-18 and in Figure 2-19)	Male connector	Row: J, Column: 30	-
	Female connector	-	9 (or any other GND, e.g., pins 6, 14)

FIGURE 2-19 Real assembly of an active-high state LED circuit.

Using C# and C++ to turn the LED on and off

You are now ready to write the UWP app that will power an LED that's connected in the active-low configuration. You can accomplish this task with any of several programming models available on the UWP. You can implement the logic layer of the application by using any of the following:

- C#

- C++

- Visual Basic

- JavaScript

Depending on the language, the user interface can be declared using XAML for C#, C++, and Visual Basic or using HTML/CSS for JavaScript. In this section I use C# and C++. Examples for Visual Basic and JavaScript can be found in Appendix A, "Code examples for controlling LED using Visual Basic and JavaScript."

C#/XAML

Follow these steps to write the first UWP app for the Windows IoT device using C#/XAML programming languages:

1. Open VS 2015 (or later) and go to **File > New > Project**.

2. In the new New Project dialog box:

  a. Type **Visual C#** in the search box, as shown in Figure 2-20.

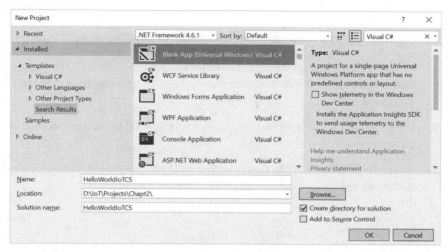

FIGURE 2-20 A New Project dialog box of Visual Studio 2015. The Blank App (Universal Windows) project template for Visual C# is selected.

  b. Select the **Visual C# Blank App (Universal Windows)** project template.

  c. Change the project name to **HelloWorldIoTCS** and click the **OK** button.

  d. In the New Universal Windows Project dialog box, set **Target Version** and **Minimum Version** to **Windows 10 (10.0; Build 10586)**. (See Figure 2-21.) The new blank project has been created.

FIGURE 2-21 The New Universal Windows Project dialog box of Visual Studio 2015 lets you configure the target and minimum supported version of Windows 10.

Target and minimum platform versions

Target platform versions specify the UWP API available to your app. The higher the value, the more updated API you can use. Similarly, the minimum platform version specifies the minimum UWP version on which your app can run.

Note In subsequent chapters, if not stated otherwise, I will set the target version to Windows 10 (10.0; Build 10586).

3. Open the Solution Explorer by clicking **View > Solution Explorer**.

4. In the Solution Explorer, expand the **HelloWorldIoTCS** node, and then right-click the **References** option. From the context menu select **Add Reference**. A Reference Manager window appears.

5. In the Reference Manager window, go to the **Universal Windows** tab and then click the **Extensions** tab.

6. Select the **Windows IoT Extensions for the UWP** check box, as shown in Figure 2-22, and then close Reference Manager by clicking the **OK** button.

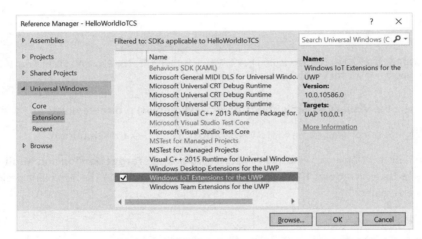

FIGURE 2-22 A Reference Manager of the HelloWorldIoTCS project. The Windows IoT Extensions for the UWP check box is selected.

7. Using the Solution Explorer, open the **MainPage.xaml.cs** file and modify its contents according to Listing 2-1.

LISTING 2-1 An LED is driven using GpioController

```
using System.Threading.Tasks;
using Windows.Devices.Gpio;
using Windows.UI.Xaml.Controls;
using Windows.UI.Xaml.Navigation;

namespace HelloWorldIoTCS
{
```

```
public sealed partial class MainPage : Page
{
    private const int gpioPinNumber = 5;
    private const int msShineDuration = 5000;

    public MainPage()
    {
        InitializeComponent();
    }

    protected override void OnNavigatedTo(NavigationEventArgs e)
    {
        base.OnNavigatedTo(e);

        BlinkLed(gpioPinNumber, msShineDuration);
    }

    private GpioPin ConfigureGpioPin(int pinNumber)
    {
        var gpioController = GpioController.GetDefault();

        GpioPin pin = null;
        if (gpioController != null)
        {
            pin = gpioController.OpenPin(pinNumber);
            if (pin != null)
            {
                pin.SetDriveMode(GpioPinDriveMode.Output);
            }
        }

        return pin;
    }

    private void BlinkLed(int gpioPinNumber, int msShineDuration)
    {
        GpioPin ledGpioPin = ConfigureGpioPin(gpioPinNumber);

        if(ledGpioPin != null)
        {
            ledGpioPin.Write(GpioPinValue.Low);

            Task.Delay(msShineDuration).Wait();

            ledGpioPin.Write(GpioPinValue.High);
        }
    }
}
```

8. Under the **Project** menu go to **HelloWorldIoTCS Properties**.

9. In the HelloWorldIoTCS Properties dialog box, go to the **Debug** tab (see Figure 2-23) and do the following:

   a. From the **Platform** drop-down list, select **ARM**.

   b. In the **Start Options** group, select **Remote Machine** from a **Target Device** drop-down list, and then click the **Find** button. Your IoT device will appear under the Auto Detected expander as shown in Figure 2-24. If it does not appear, you need to provide its name or IP address manually. You can obtain these values through the Windows 10 IoT Core Dashboard. (See Figure 2-14.)

   c. Click the **Select** button and close the project properties window.

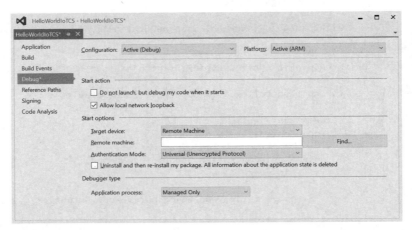

FIGURE 2-23   The Debug tab of the project properties window. Note that you need to select Active (ARM) from the Platform drop-down list.

FIGURE 2-24   IoT device discovery.

10. Above Visual Studio 2015, locate the configuration toolbar, which is shown in Figure 2-25. Using the drop-down list, set the configuration to **Debug**, the platform to **ARM**, and the debugging target to **Remote Machine**.

FIGURE 2-25 Configuration toolbar.

11. Run the app. Use the **Start Debugging** option of the **Debug** menu or click the **Remote Machine** button in the configuration toolbar.

After you perform the above procedure, the UWP app will be automatically deployed to the RPi2 device and then executed. Subsequently, the LED will shine for 5 seconds. You can break the application execution at any time by clicking **Debug > Stop Debugging**.

Several aspects of the above solution require additional attention. Notice, first, that the HelloWorldIoTCS project is composed of the following elements:

- **project.json** This file specifies project dependencies, frameworks, and runtimes as JSON objects. Each entry of dependencies comprises the name-version pair of the NuGet package. By default, there is only one such package: Microsoft.NETCore.UniversalWindowsPlatform. Under the frameworks collection you specify the frameworks that your project targets. For the UWP, you use the uap10.0 framework (the Universal App Platform). Runtimes contain the list of runtime identifiers (RIDs). In general, you can use any value specified here: *http://bit.ly/runtimes*. But for the UWP project template we used, there are only Windows 10 RIDs, and you do not need other RIDs to complete examples developed in this book. You will need other RIDs when developing cross-platform .NET Core apps—for example, ASP.NET Core MVC web apps or web services.

- **Package.appxmanifest** This is an application manifest file. This XML file contains the information necessary to publish, display, and update an application, and it defines the capabilities, functionality, and application requirements.

- **Assets folder** This contains the project assets.

- **App.xaml and App.xaml.cs files** These implement the App class.

- **MainPage.xaml and MainPage.xaml.cs** These implement the main (default) view of the application.

The default implementation of the App class, generated automatically, displays the view implemented in the MainPage class. The MainPage class derives from the Page class and implements the default application view using two files: MainPage.xaml and MainPage.xaml.cs. MainPage.xaml declares the user interface, while MainPage.xaml.cs implements the logic associated with the view. Hence, MainPage.xaml.cs is commonly referred to as the *code-behind*.

Chapter 3, "Windows IoT programming essentials," explains a mechanism of navigation between views and an entry point of the UWP IoT apps. For now, I turn your attention to the MainPage.xaml.cs only, because the application logic is included in this file only. Moreover, the current application implements an empty UI, which does not contain any visual elements.

Within the `MainPage` class, given in Listing 2-1, I declared two constant fields: `gpioPinNumber` and `msShineDuration`. The first one defines the pin number of the GPIO port used to control the LED state, while the second determines how long an LED will shine. In this example I assume that the LED circuit is assembled according to Table 2-4. Therefore, the `gpioPinNumber` was assigned the value of 5.

The procedures responsible for shining the LED are implemented within the `BlinkLed` method. This is called under the overridden implementation of the `Page.OnNavigatedTo` event handler. In the `BlinkLed` method two logical parts can be distinguished. The first one invokes the `ConfigureGpioPin` method, which acquires the reference to the default GPIO controller of the IoT device. An abstract representation of this object is the `Windows.Devices.GpioController` class.

The `GpioController` class exposes several members, designed to simplify interfacing the GPIO peripherals. In particular, the static method `GetDefault` returns the default GPIO controller of the embedded device. I use this method in Listing 2-1 to get an access to the RPi2 GPIO controller. After obtaining an instance of the `GpioController` class representing a default GPIO controller, the selected GPIO port is opened by calling an `OpenPin` method. A successful call to this method returns an instance of the `GpioPin` class, being an abstract representation of the GPIO port.

The most general version of the `OpenPin` method accepts two input arguments. The first one (`pinNumber`) indicates the GPIO pin number, while the second (`sharingMode`) defines the sharing mode of the GPIO port. This sharing mode is defined by one of the values of the `Windows.Devices.Gpio.GpioSharingMode` enumeration. Namely, this type exposes two values: `Exclusive` and `SharedReadOnly`. In an exclusive mode, the programmer may either write to or read from the GPIO port, while in the second case, the write operations are not allowed. In the shared mode, the programmer may use several instances referencing the same GPIO port. This is impossible if the GPIO pin is accessed in an exclusive mode. In such a case, subsequent attempts to open the GPIO port will cause an exception.

The second version of the `OpenPin` method, used in Listing 2-1, expects the GPIO pin number only, and opens the GPIO pin in an exclusive mode.

The instance method `SetDriveMode` of the `GpioPin` class is subsequently used to switch the GPIO to the output mode. The available GPIO drive modes are represented by values implemented within the `GpioPinDriveMode` enumeration.

After configuring the GPIO drive mode, all you need to do is to set the GPIO port to the low state. This will induce the current flow through the LED circuit. The LED circuit will be powered as long as the control GPIO pin is set to the high state. This happens automatically after a delay, specified using the `msShineDuration` member of the `MainPage` class. The delay is implemented using the `Delay` static method of the `Task` class, which I tell you more about in Chapter 3.

When the LED is connected to the RPi2 in an active-high state, the above procedure progresses differently. Namely, to turn on an LED you drive the GPIO pin to the high state and subsequently write a low value to disable current flow. The `BlinkLed` method takes the form from Listing 2-2, and according to Table 2-3, you would need to update the value of `gpioPinNumber` to 26.

```
private void BlinkLed(int gpioPinNumber, int msShineDuration)
{
    GpioPin ledGpioPin = ConfigureGpioPin(gpioPinNumber);

    if(ledGpioPin != null)
    {
        ledGpioPin.Write(GpioPinValue.High);

        Task.Delay(msShineDuration).Wait();

        ledGpioPin.Write(GpioPinValue.Low);
    }
}
```

By default, the GPIO ports available to the user are either in the pull-up or pull-down input mode; see Table 2-3. These modes correspond to the logically active (pull-up) or inactive (pull-down) input GPIO ports, which are represented as GpioPinDriveMode.InputPullUp and GpioPinDriveMode.InputPullDown, respectively.

When you configure a physical pin with alternate functions as the GPIO, then you cannot access these alternate functions without releasing the instance of the GpioPin by calling a Dispose method.

A final note is devoted to the Windows IoT extensions for the UWP. By referencing them, you get access to a GPIO-specific—or more generally, an IoT-specific—API of the UWP. If you right-click Windows IoT Extensions for the UWP entry in the Solution Explorer, you will find the location of this SDK. In this case, the default Visual Studio installation, the Windows IoT extensions for the UWP 10.0.10586 reside in the following folder:

%ProgramFiles(x86)%\Windows Kits\10\Extension SDKs\WindowsIoT\10.0.10586.0

After opening this folder, you will find an Include\winrt subfolder. It contains the set of generated interface definition language (IDL) and C++ header files. For instance, windows.devices.gpio.idl and windows.devices.gpio.h are provided to access low-level OS features for interfacing GPIO, which we implicitly used in the preceding example. This analysis shows that you can use C++ to access low-level Windows APIs. The next section shows how C++ can be used to implement the LED blinking functionality, where a delay is implemented using the Sleep function of the Windows API. Moreover, Chapter 8, "Image processing," shows how you can use C++ to implement Windows Runtime Components for native code interfacing. You can find a detailed discussion of C++ and Windows Runtime Components in articles by Kenny Kerr in the MSDN magazine at *http://bit.ly/cpp_winrt*.

C++/XAML

In this section I will show you how to implement the C++ application, which controls the LED circuit. Follow these steps:

1. Create a new project using VS 2015 by going to **File > New > Project**.

2. In the New Project dialog box (see Figure 2-26):

    a. Type **Visual C++** in the search box.

    b. Select the **Blank App (Universal Windows)** project template and set **Target** and **Minimum Versions** to **Windows 10 (10.0; Build 10586)**. (See Figure 2-21.)

    c. Change the project name to **HelloWorldIoTCpp** and click the **OK** button.

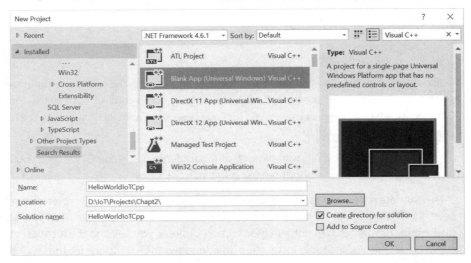

FIGURE 2-26   The New Project dialog box of Visual Studio 2015. The Blank App (Universal Windows) for Visual C++ project template is highlighted.

3. Add a reference to **Windows IoT Extensions for the UWP**. You can do that just as you did in the previous section. (See Figure 2-22.)

4. Modify **MainPage.xaml.h** according to the code snippet in Listing 2-3.

```
LISTING 2-3   MainPage class declaration

#pragma once

#include "MainPage.g.h"

using namespace Windows::UI::Xaml::Navigation;
using namespace Windows::Devices::Gpio;

namespace HelloWorldIoTCpp
```

```
{
    public ref class MainPage sealed
    {
    public:
        MainPage();

    protected:
        void OnNavigatedTo(NavigationEventArgs ^e) override;

    private:
        const int pinNumber = 5;
        const int msShineDuration = 2000;

        GpioPin ^ConfigureGpioPin(int pinNumber);
        void BlinkLed(int ledPinNumber, int msShineDuration);
    };
}
```

5. In the MainPage.xaml.cpp file, insert the code block from Listing 2-4.

LISTING 2-4   MainPage implementation

```
#include "pch.h"
#include "MainPage.xaml.h"

using namespace HelloWorldIoTCpp;
using namespace Platform;

MainPage::MainPage()
{
    InitializeComponent();
}

void MainPage::OnNavigatedTo(NavigationEventArgs ^e)
{
    __super::OnNavigatedTo(e);

    BlinkLed(pinNumber, msShineDuration);
}

GpioPin ^MainPage::ConfigureGpioPin(int pinNumber)
{
    auto gpioController = GpioController::GetDefault();

    GpioPin ^pin = nullptr;

    if (gpioController != nullptr)
    {
        pin = gpioController->OpenPin(pinNumber);
```

```
            if (pin != nullptr)
            {
                pin->SetDriveMode(GpioPinDriveMode::Output);
            }
        }

        return pin;
    }

    void MainPage::BlinkLed(int ledPinNumber, int msShineDuration)
    {
        GpioPin ^ledGpioPin = ConfigureGpioPin(ledPinNumber);

        if (ledGpioPin != nullptr)
        {
            ledGpioPin->Write(GpioPinValue::Low);

            Sleep(msShineDuration);

            ledGpioPin->Write(GpioPinValue::High);
        }
    }
```

6. Compile and deploy an app to the IoT device:

   a. Open the HelloWorldIoTCpp properties window and navigate to the **Debugging** tab under the **Configuration Properties** node.

   b. Select **ARM** from the **Platform** drop-down list.

   c. Choose **Remote Machine** from the **Debugger** tab to launch a drop-down list.

   d. Change **Authentication Type** to **Universal (Unencrypted Protocol)**, and find your IoT device using the **<Locate...>** option under the **Machine Name** drop-down list. (See Figure 2-27.)

   e. Click the **Apply** button and close the project properties window.

7. Run the app.

As in the previous section, the app will automatically deploy to the IoT device and execute. The application implements the same functionality—i.e., it shines the LED for a specified amount of time, determined by the value of the msShineDuration member; see Listing 2-3.

The main difference between C++ and C# implementations is that the default application view, i.e. MainPage, is now implemented within three (C++) instead of just two (C#) files. Namely, a C++ project includes MainPage.xaml, MainPage.xaml.h, and MainPage.xaml.cpp. The first file, MainPage.xaml, defines the UI, while the other two implement the logic (code-behind). The header file, MainPage.xaml.h, contains the declaration of the MainPage class, whose definition is stored in MainPage.xaml.cpp.

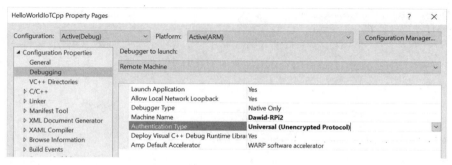

FIGURE 2-27 The Remote Machine configuration for a C++ Universal Windows project.

Additional symbols (e.g. ^), which are related to the Component Extensions (CX) of the C++ language, allow access to the objects from the Universal Windows Platform programming interface and are explained in Appendix E, "Visual C++ component extensions."

By using C++ as the programming language, you get access not only to the UWP API but also to the low-level Windows API. In particular, in Listing 2-4, to implement a delay between subsequent calls to the method `Write` of the `GpioPin` class, I used the `Sleep` function, declared in the Windows API.

Useful tools and utilities

Very often an embedded device works in a remote location. To remotely manage such a device you can use several tools and utilities, including Device Portal and Windows IoT Remote Client. Moreover, you can associate the Secure Shell (SSH) connection and manage the device by using the command line. To access files stored on the device's SD card, you can use File Transport Protocol (FTP). In this section, I show you how to use Device Portal and Windows IoT Remote Client, and how to connect to the Windows 10 IoT Core device using the free FTP and SSH clients.

Device Portal

Device Portal is a web-based utility that enables you to configure an IoT device, install or uninstall its applications, display the active processes, and update Windows 10 IoT Core. Basically, Device Portal is the layer that exposes functionality, which you typically access in the desktop version of Windows 10 through the Task Manager or Control Panel. Naturally, not all functions of Task Manager and Control Panel are available in Device Portal—only those related to Windows 10 IoT Core. Simply, Device Portal lets you remotely manage your device. Interestingly, a very similar Device Portal is available for holographic platforms (HoloLens), and even for desktop Windows 10 (starting with its Anniversary Edition).

To access Device Portal you use the IoT Dashboard. Go to the **My Device** list and right-click your IoT devices. Then, as shown in Figure 2-28, select the **Open in Device Portal** option from the context menu. Device Portal will open in the default browser and ask you to provide credentials (see Figure 2-29). Type **administrator** for the login, and for the password, provide a value you previously configured during Windows 10 IoT Core installation through the IoT Core Dashboard.

FIGURE 2-28 Context menu of the IoT device in the IoT Dashboard.

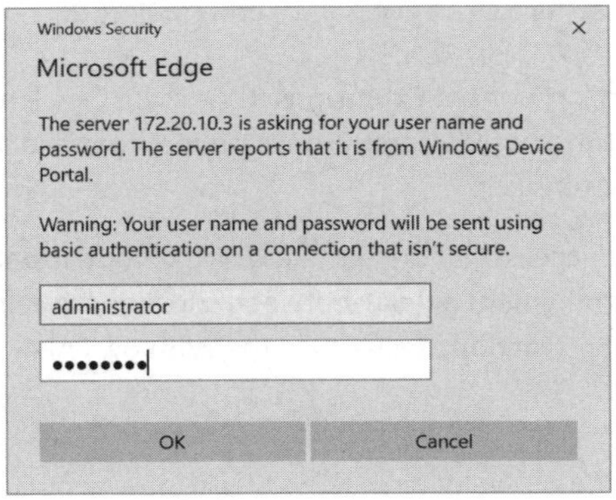

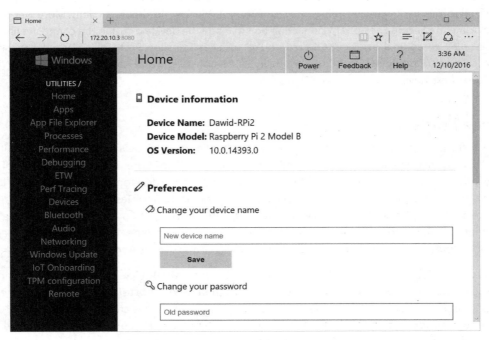

FIGURE 2-29 Windows Device Portal login screen.

FIGURE 2-30 The Home tab of the Windows Device Portal.

After successful login to Device Portal, you will see the screen shown in Figure 2-30. By default, it displays the Home tab. It contains basic information about your device and enables you to configure device preferences, like name, password, and display settings. I encourage you to navigate among the tabs of the Device Portal to see what is available there. We will use specific functions of the Device Portal later.

Windows IoT Remote Client

Starting from the Windows 10 IoT Core Anniversary Edition build, you can remotely control your IoT device using the Windows IoT Remote Client. This is a tiny app that you install on your development PC, tablet, or phone from the Windows Store. When you set up the connection using Remote Client between a PC, tablet, or phone and the IoT device, the IoT device will transmit its current screen to the Windows IoT Remote Client app. In this way you can preview your UWP apps running on the remote IoT device from another UWP device (desktop or mobile).

To set up such a connection, you first need to enable Windows IoT Remote Server using Device Portal. As shown in Figure 2-31, all you need to do is to select the **Enable Windows IoT Remote Server** check box on the Remote tab. Then, you simply run the Windows IoT Remote Client, where you either choose your device from the drop-down list or type its IP address (see Figure 2-32). After clicking the **Connect** button, you will see an IoT device screen, as shown in Figure 2-33.

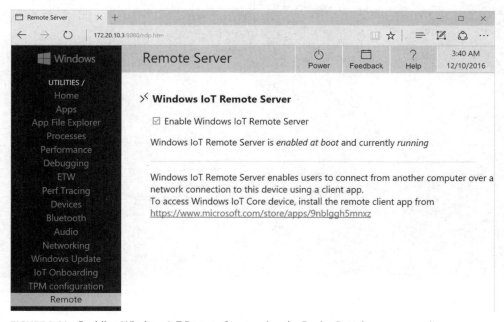

FIGURE 2-31   Enabling Windows IoT Remote Server using the Device Portal.

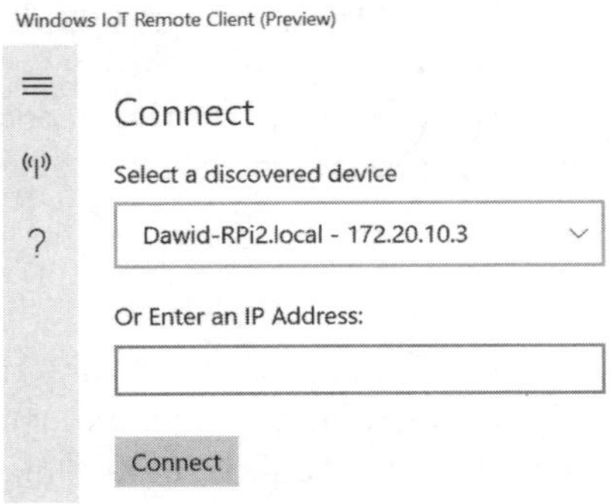

Connect

Select a discovered device

Dawid-RPi2.local - 172.20.10.3 ⌄

Or Enter an IP Address:

Connect

FIGURE 2-32   Connecting to the remote IoT device using Windows IoT Remote Client.

FIGURE 2-33   Windows IoT Remote Client showing the default Windows 10 IoT Core headed app running on the Raspberry Pi 2 Model B.

Note that Windows IoT Remote Client works similarly to remote desktop clients you're familiar with. So you can use the input devices of your desktop PC (keyboard and mouse) or mobile (touchscreen) to control remote IoT apps. This offers a very convenient way of testing your apps without the need of hooking up the physical input devices to the IoT device.

SSH

You can use the Putty application to associate an SSH connection. Putty is one of the most popular SSH Windows clients. You can download this lightweight application-executable tool from *http://www.putty.org/*.

Follow these steps to connect to your Windows 10 IoT Core using the Putty terminal:

1. Download and run the Putty SSH client.

2. In the main Putty window, shown in Figure 2-34, enter a hostname (or an IP address) of your IoT device and then click **Open**.

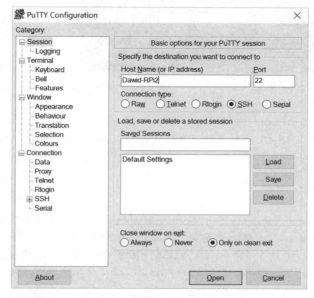

FIGURE 2-34 The Putty application.

3. A security warning appears. Click the **Yes** button.

4. Enter your credentials.

5. List the SD card content by typing the following commands (see Figure 2-35):

```
cd C:\

dir
```

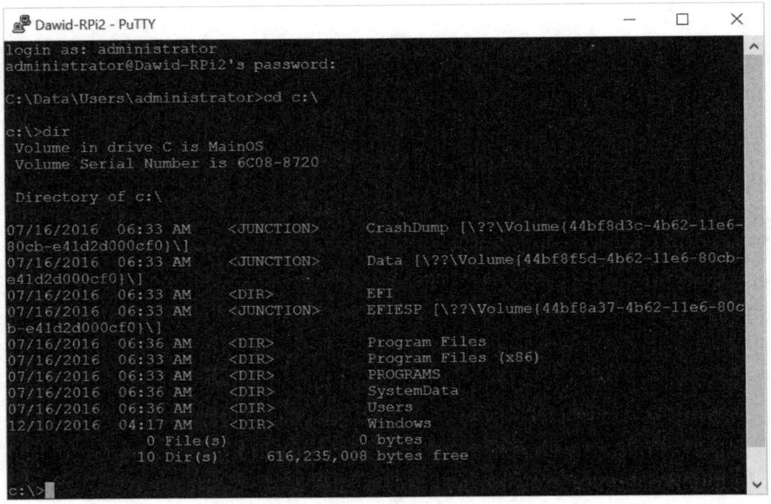

FIGURE 2-35 Folder structure of the Windows 10 IoT Core device obtained using the SSH client application.

While connected to Windows 10 IoT Core using the SSH protocol, you can use similar commands to those in the desktop command prompt. For example, to display a list of active processes, you can type **tlist**. To investigate network connections, you can use the **netstat** utility.

FTP

By default, the FTP server is disabled on Windows 10 IoT Core. To enable it, you can use the SSH connection, where you run the following command: **start c:\Windows\System32\ftpd.exe**. This will start the FTP server. You confirm that this server is running by typing **tlist | more**. This command displays the list of active processes. Press the spacebar to go to the next page of this list or **Enter** to show the next line.

You can stop the FTP server anytime by typing **kill <PID>**, where <PID> is the process identifier. It is displayed in the process list on the left of the process name.

To establish the FTP connection with your IoT device, you need an FTP client application. Here, I am using WinSCP, which is the free FTP/SFTP client for Windows. You can download it from: *https://winscp. net/eng/download.php*.

After you install and run this application, you see the configuration screen (see Figure 2-36). Using this dialog box, perform the following steps:

1. Select **FTP** from the **File Protocol** drop-down list.

2. Provide the IP address (hostname) and connection credentials of the embedded device running Windows 10 IoT Core. Use **administrator** as a login; for the password, use the value you configured previously using the IoT Dashboard.

3. Click the **Login** button to connect to the IoT device.

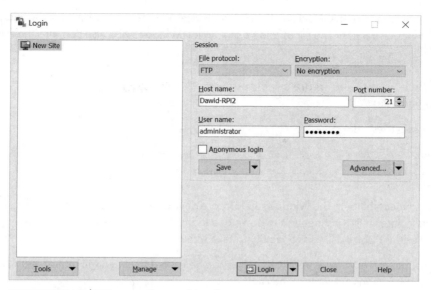

FIGURE 2-36 An FTP connection configuration.

4. During the connection process, a security warning appears. Confirm it by clicking the **Yes** button.

5. The contents of the IoT device SD card appear (See Figure 2-37.)

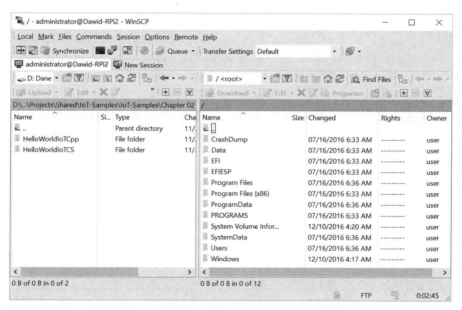

FIGURE 2-37 Contents of the SD card of a Windows 10 IoT Core device.

The folder structure of the Windows 10 IoT Core device resembles a typical folder arrangement of a desktop Windows version. The list of folders of a typical Windows disk also contains the following elements:

- EFI
- Program Files
- Program Files (x86)
- Users
- Windows

Remote connectability to the Windows 10 IoT Core device lets you transfer files. For example, you can easily associate an FTP connection to download log files, which can store sensor readings, device status, etc. For this book, I use this capability to take screenshots and transfer them to my PC.

Note also that in the WinSCP application, files can be copied between the remote and local machines using the options available in the Files menu.

Summary

This chapter explored two programming technologies for developing UWP apps for Windows 10 IoT Core. The examples implemented above prove that the UWP offers a convenient way to implement software for smart devices.

Depending on the language you choose, extra capabilities show up. For example, using C++ gives you access not only to the UWP programming interface but to low-level Windows APIs.

Using C++ for embedded software development has an additional advantage. Namely, you can easily integrate the UWP with native libraries. This can be very useful in scenarios that require interfacing the legacy code, such as existing native C/C++ libraries. You can explore this possibility further in Chapter 8, "Image processing."

Windows IoT programming essentials

R aspberry Pi 2 and Pi 3 are equipped with High-Definition Media Interface (HDMI), designed for transferring audio and video data. Therefore, you can connect RPi2 or RPi3 to any external display compatible with HDMI. This gives you the ability to develop applications with user interfaces such that the untethered data received from sensors is processed in the background and then visualized using XAML or HTML/CSS controls.

The Universal Windows Platform (UWP) packs plenty of API and language-specific extensions for performing background operations. However, developing multithreaded applications brings additional complications. For example, you can't get access to UI elements from background threads without employing thread-synchronization techniques.

In this chapter, I first show you how to configure an RPi2/RPi3 HDMI interface, and then characterize the headed and headless modes of Windows 10 IoT devices. The main difference between headed and headless mode is that headless apps do not have a UI of any kind. Furthermore, as I show in this chapter, headed and headless apps use different entry points and so are executed by the OS in different manners. In particular, headless apps run as background tasks.

I also describe the most common classes for worker thread creation, management, and synchronization. That information is important later when you implement an interactive application for recurrent LED blinking.

The aim of this chapter is not to fully describe the threading model of the .NET Framework UWP applications but to explain the most common threading aspects. If you're interested in more details about the .NET Framework threading model, check out the book *CLR via C#* by Jeffrey Richter.

Connecting Raspberry Pi 2 to an external display and boot configuration

Hooking up your RPi2 to an external display is straightforward. You connect the HDMI interface of RPi2 using an appropriate cable to a monitor or TV before turning on the RPi2. That last point is important, since the Broadcom microcontroller can disable the HDMI interface when the HDMI cable is disconnected.

After you've connected the external display, resolution and screen parameters adjust automatically, and you see the familiar Windows 10 logo on the attached screen. However, if the resulting screen is furrowed, you might need to change the boot configuration of your RPi2. This configuration is stored in the config.txt file on the microSD card. The default contents of config.txt appear below:

```
gpu_mem=32                      # set ARM to 480Mb DRAM, VC to 32Mb DRAM
framebuffer_ignore_alpha=1      # Ignore the alpha channel for Windows.
framebuffer_swap=1              # Set the frame buffer to be Windows BGR compatible.
disable_overscan=1              # Disable overscan
init_uart_clock=16000000        # Set UART clock to 16Mhz
hdmi_group=2                    # Use VESA Display Mode Timing over CEA
arm_freq=900
arm_freq_min=900
force_turbo=1
```

To adjust the display configuration, update the value of hdmi_group from 2 to 1 or add an additional setting, hdmi_mode, and set its value according to screen resolutions supported by your display. Appendix B, "Raspberry Pi 2 HDMI modes," lists available values for hdmi_mode. You can also change the screen resolution and orientation using the Device Portal Display Resolution and Display Orientation drop-down lists in the Home tab, shown in Figure 3-1. However, if it turns out your device does not wake up after you change the display settings (due to incompatible configuration), you can always restore it by editing config.txt.

FIGURE 3-1 The Display Settings section of the Home tab in the Device Portal.

You can employ a boot configuration of RPi2 to change other device parameters. In particular, gpu_mem allows you to set the amount of RAM (in megabytes) reserved for the graphics unit of the Broadcom microcontroller, while init_uart_clock configures the frequency of the universal asynchronous receiver/transmitter interface (UART).

I do not describe other configuration modes in detail since my goal is to point out to you that a config.txt file can be used to solve potential problems with display configuration.

Headed and headless modes

Windows 10 IoT Core is configured in the headed mode by default. In this mode, applications have the user interface (UI). In particular, upon RPi2 startup, an interactive app is executed. (See Figure 3-2.) It displays basic device parameters, like name, IP address, and OS version. It also allows you to configure the device and even run sample applications available on the Tutorials tab.

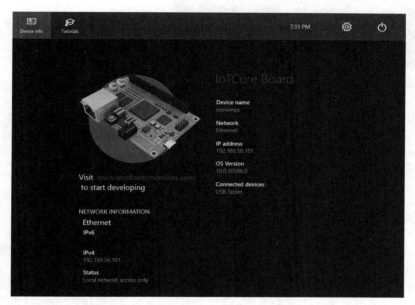

FIGURE 3-2   The Windows 10 IoT Core default app. This illustration was prepared by virtualizing the Windows 10 IoT Core for x86 architecture. In the case of a physical RPi2 device, the icon in the top left corner would be different.

In the headed mode, the standard UWP UI stack processing is active. Because it requires extra UI stack processing, you may want to save system resources by switching Windows 10 IoT Core into the headless mode. In headless mode, the IoT applications work as background tasks and do not call upon the UI. Although the apps are non-interactive, you can still access the UWP programming interface.

Windows 10 IoT Core does not allow the user to switch between the UI applications at runtime. Only one single UI app can be launched at a time. In contrast, many background (headless) applications can run in the background, even if the smart device is configured to work in the headed mode.

Headed and headless modes of Windows 10 IoT Core can be configured using the SSH connection (see Chapter 2, "Universal Windows Platform on devices") and the `setbootoption` command. This command has two arguments, headed or `headless`, which set the appropriate device mode. For example, in order to configure an IoT device for the headed mode (see Figure 3-3), follow these steps:

1. Connect to a device using SSH. (Refer to the "Useful tools and utilities" section in Chapter 2.)

2. Type **setbootoption headless**.

3. Reboot your device by typing **shutdown /r /t 0**. Alternatively, you can restart the device using the Device Portal or default startup app—i.e., by clicking the **Restart** button in the top-right corner; refer to Figure 3-2.

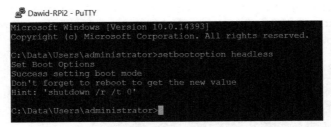

FIGURE 3-3   IoT device mode configuration using the setbootoption command line tool.

In general, you use headed mode for IoT devices equipped with a display or when you write a Universal Windows app. Otherwise, for scenarios targeting an IoT platform only, and when your app has to run continuously, choose the headless mode. Headed mode can be beneficial when you test your app on the development PC. For this reason, I generally use headed mode.

Headless applications

Background headless applications written using C# or C++ (and Visual Basic; see Appendix A, "Code examples for controlling LED using Visual Basic and JavaScript") are implemented within the type, derived from the IBackgroundTask interface. This interface exposes a single Run method, which is the entry point for such headless IoT applications. This concept is similar to the Main method of the Program class, the default entry point of headed apps. However, the background task is automatically re-started by Windows 10 IoT Core whenever it exits or crashes.

The upcoming sections show you how to implement LED blinking sample applications using the IoT project templates for C# and C++. I compare them to sample apps developed in Chapter 2.

C#

Let's start with the C# programming language. In this case the background app implementation proceeds as follows:

1. Bring up the New Project dialog box of VS 2015.

2. In the New Project dialog box:

   a. Type **IoT** in the search box.

   b. Select the **Visual C# Background Application (IoT)** project template.

   c. Change the project name to **IoTBackgroundAppCS**, as shown in Figure 3-4.

3. Reference Windows IoT Extensions for the UWP. Follow steps 4–6 of the "C#/XAML" section in Chapter 2.

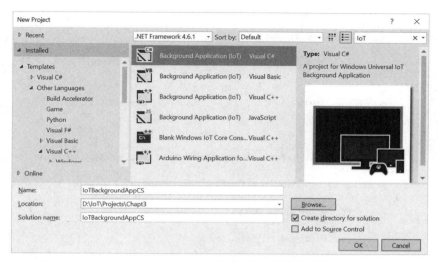

FIGURE 3-4 New Project dialog box of Visual Studio 2015 with Background Application (IoT) Visual C#
project template highlighted.

4. Using Solution Explorer, open the **StartupTask.cs** file and modify it according to Listing 3-1.

LISTING 3-1 C# Windows 10 IoT Core background application

```csharp
using System.Threading.Tasks;
using Windows.ApplicationModel.Background;
using Windows.Devices.Gpio;

namespace IoTBackgroundAppCS
{
    public sealed class StartupTask : IBackgroundTask
    {
        private const int gpioPinNumber = 5;
        private const int msShineDuration = 5000;

        public void Run(IBackgroundTaskInstance taskInstance)
        {
            BlinkLed(gpioPinNumber, msShineDuration);
        }

        private GpioPin ConfigureGpioPin(int pinNumber)
        {
            var gpioController = GpioController.GetDefault();

            GpioPin pin = null;

            if (gpioController != null)
            {
                pin = gpioController.OpenPin(pinNumber);
```

```
            if (pin != null)
            {
                pin.SetDriveMode(GpioPinDriveMode.Output);
            }
        }

        return pin;
    }

    private void BlinkLed(int gpioPinNumber, int msShineDuration)
    {
        GpioPin ledGpioPin = ConfigureGpioPin(gpioPinNumber);

        if (ledGpioPin != null)
        {
            while(true)
            {
                SwitchGpioPin(ledGpioPin);
                Task.Delay(msShineDuration).Wait();
            }
        }
    }

    private void SwitchGpioPin(GpioPin gpioPin)
    {
        var currentPinValue = gpioPin.Read();

        GpioPinValue newPinValue = InvertGpioPinValue(currentPinValue);

        gpioPin.Write(newPinValue);
    }

    private GpioPinValue InvertGpioPinValue(GpioPinValue currentPinValue)
    {
        GpioPinValue invertedGpioPinValue;

        if (currentPinValue == GpioPinValue.High)
        {
            invertedGpioPinValue = GpioPinValue.Low;
        }
        else
        {
            invertedGpioPinValue = GpioPinValue.High;
        }

        return invertedGpioPinValue;
    }
  }
}
```

5. Deploy the app to your IoT device using steps 9–10 of the "C#/XAML" section from Chapter 2.

The above code, responsible for blinking the LED, is similar to the code you used in the headed counterpart of the IoTBackgroundAppCS app—the HelloWorldIoTCS project. However, the execution model is much simpler because it leaves out most of the unnecessary functionality. Moreover, all the implementation is contained within a single class; to achieve an analogous result using the standard UWP project template, we actually used three classes: `Program`, `App` and `MainPage`. (See the "An entry point of the headed application" section later in this chapter.)

In principle, the application logic for controlling the LED using the headless app could be exactly the same as in the HelloWorldIoTCS project. But, to avoid code duplication, I have extended the previous example in the following way. First, I employed the `Read` method of the `GpioPin` class to get the current value of the GPIO pin. Then I inverted this value and wrote it to the GPIO port to either disable or enable current flow, depending on the previous state.

I used two methods to implement this functionality: `InvertGpioPinValue` and `SwitchGpioPin`. The latter, together with a delay statement, exists within an infinite while loop. Hence, the LED is continuously switched between on and off states.

C++

Visual C++ project templates not only allow you to write a background headless IoT application, but also let you use the Arduino Wiring API. Let's investigate these possibilities, starting with the background app.

Background application

You implement the Windows Universal IoT background application using C++ similarly to the C# used in the previous section. Follow these steps:

1. Use the New Project dialog box to create a new background application IoTBackgroundAppCpp using the Visual C++ Background Application (IoT) project template. You can find this template as shown in Figure 3-4.

2. Reference Windows IoT Extensions for the UWP.

3. Open the StartupTask.h file and modify the declaration of the StartupTask class as in Listing 3-2.

4. Go to StartupTask.cpp, and using Listing 3-3, update the definition of the `StartupTask` class.

5. Deploy the app to your IoT device using the procedure described in steps 6 and 7 of the "C++/ XAML" section of Chapter 2.

LISTING 3-2   Declaration of the StartupTask class

```
#pragma once
#include "pch.h"

using namespace Windows::Devices::Gpio;

namespace IoTBackgroundAppCpp
```

```
{
    [Windows::Foundation::Metadata::WebHostHidden]
    public ref class StartupTask sealed : public Windows::ApplicationModel::
        Background::IBackgroundTask
    {
    public:
        virtual void Run(Windows::ApplicationModel::Background::
        IBackgroundTaskInstance ^taskInstance);

    private:
        const int pinNumber = 5;
        const int msShineDuration = 2000;

        GpioPin ^ConfigureGpioPin(int pinNumber);
        void BlinkLed(int ledPinNumber, int msShineDuration);
        void SwitchGpioPin(GpioPin ^gpioPin);
        GpioPinValue InvertGpioPinValue(GpioPinValue currentPinValue);
    };
}
```

LISTING 3-3 StartupTask class definition

```
#include "pch.h"
#include "StartupTask.h"

using namespace IoTBackgroundAppCpp;
using namespace Platform;
using namespace Windows::ApplicationModel::Background;

void StartupTask::Run(IBackgroundTaskInstance ^taskInstance)
{
    BlinkLed(pinNumber, msShineDuration);
}

GpioPin ^StartupTask::ConfigureGpioPin(int pinNumber)
{
    auto gpioController = GpioController::GetDefault();

    GpioPin ^pin = nullptr;
    if (gpioController != nullptr)
    {
        pin = gpioController->OpenPin(pinNumber);

        if (pin != nullptr)
        {
            pin->SetDriveMode(GpioPinDriveMode::Output);
        }
    }

    return pin;
}
```

```cpp
void StartupTask::BlinkLed(int ledPinNumber, int msShineDuration)
{
    GpioPin ^ledGpioPin = ConfigureGpioPin(ledPinNumber);

    if (ledGpioPin != nullptr)
    {
        while (true)
        {
            SwitchGpioPin(ledGpioPin);

            Sleep(msShineDuration);
        }
    }
}

void StartupTask::SwitchGpioPin(GpioPin ^gpioPin)
{
    auto currentPinValue = gpioPin->Read();

    GpioPinValue newPinValue = InvertGpioPinValue(currentPinValue);

    gpioPin->Write(newPinValue);
}

GpioPinValue StartupTask::InvertGpioPinValue(GpioPinValue currentPinValue)
{
    GpioPinValue invertedGpioPinValue;

    if (currentPinValue == GpioPinValue::High)
    {
        invertedGpioPinValue = GpioPinValue::Low;
    }
    else
    {
        invertedGpioPinValue = GpioPinValue::High;
    }

    return invertedGpioPinValue;
}
```

The C++ background application developed in this section works exactly the same as the app developed in the previous section. Namely, the LED is repeatedly switched on or off, depending on the current value of the GPIO pin used to drive the LED circuit.

Note that the C++ project templates provide additional opportunities. Apart from the Background Application (IoT) project template, the programmer can use two additional project templates. These are:

- **Blank Windows IoT Core Console Application**   This generates a simple console application with the main function composing the entry point. The structure of this project looks exactly like the typical native-based solution for embedded programming.

- **Arduino Wiring Application for Windows IoT Core**   This project template allows you to use existing Arduino applications directly in the Windows 10 IoT Core applications.

The Arduino Wiring Application for Windows IoT Core project template can be of special interest when performance is an issue or if you are familiar with the Arduino platform. Essentially, the Arduino Wiring project template uses direct memory access, which increases performance at the cost of security. Moreover, the Arduino Wiring API simplifies the porting of existing Arduino-based solutions to Windows 10 IoT Core for RPi2 (or RPi3) and MinnowBoard MAX boards. Existing libraries and solutions can be directly copied to the source code of the Windows 10 IoT Core application generated using an appropriate project template. Many existing libraries for Arduino can now be used on the Windows 10 IoT Core platform.

Arduino wiring application

Follow these steps to build the C++ application using the Arduino Wiring Application for Windows IoT Core project template:

1. Bring up the New Project dialog box.

2. Select **Visual C++ Arduino Wiring Application for Windows IoT Core**. Refer to Figure 3-4.

3. Change the project name to **ArduinoWiringApp** and click the **OK** button to close the New Project dialog box.

4. In Solution Explorer view, double-click **ArduinoWiringApp.ino** and edit its contents according to Listing 3-4.

LISTING 3-4   Controlling the LED circuit using Arduino Wiring Application for Windows IoT Core

```cpp
const uint8_t pinNumber = GPIO5;
const int msShineDuration = 500;

void setup()
{
    pinMode(pinNumber, OUTPUT);
}

void blinkLED()
{
    int currentPinValue = digitalRead(pinNumber);
    int newPinValue = !currentPinValue;

    digitalWrite(pinNumber, newPinValue);
}

void loop()
{
    blinkLED();

    delay(msShineDuration);
}
```

5. Change the device controller driver to **Direct Memory Mapped Driver**:

    a. Log in to the Device Portal.

    b. Navigate to the **Devices** tab. (See Figure 3-5.)

    c. Select **Direct Memory Mapped Driver** from the Default Controller Driver drop-down list.

    d. Reboot your device to enable these changes to take effect. (See Figure 3-6.)

FIGURE 3-5 Devices tab of the Device Portal.

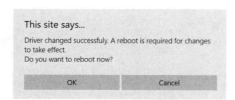

FIGURE 3-6 Reboot confirmation dialog box.

6. After the device is restarted, deploy an app to your IoT device using the procedure described in steps 6–7 of the "C++/XAML" section of Chapter 2.

Basically, the Arduino Wiring app you just created consists of two elements:

- `setup` function
- `loop` function

The `setup` function is invoked only on startup, so you can use it to perform the initial board configuration—e.g., to configure the GPIO pin drive mode to output. The `loop` function is invoked repeatedly to execute an actual LED circuit control. It does so by using two functions, `digitalRead` and `digitalWrite`, which work analogously as corresponding methods of the `GpioPin` class. Specifically, `digitalRead` obtains the current value of the GPIO pin, while `digitalWrite` updates the value of the pin.

More formally, the code from Listing 3-4 is called the *sketch file*. Methods defined there are invoked within the StartupTask class (StartupTask.cpp file). StartupTask implements a Run method, which as shown in Listing 3-5 first makes a call to the setup method and then repeatedly invokes the loop function within the infinite loop.

LISTING 3-5   StartupTask of ArduinoWiringApp

```
using namespace Windows::ApplicationModel::Background;

// These functions should be defined in the sketch file
void setup();
void loop();

namespace ArduinoWiringApp
{
    [Windows::Foundation::Metadata::WebHostHidden]
    public ref class StartupTask sealed : public IBackgroundTask
    {
    public:
        virtual void Run(Windows::ApplicationModel::Background::
            IBackgroundTaskInstance^ taskInstance)
        {
            auto deferral = taskInstance->GetDeferral();

            setup();
            while (true)
            {
                loop();
            }

            deferral->Complete();
        }
    };
}
```

ArduinoWiringApp uses C programming conventions. Therefore, every function has to be declared on top of subsequent statements that use that function. Accordingly, in Listing 3-4, the blinkLED function was defined before the loop function. Otherwise, the code of ArduinoWiringApp would not compile.

By comparing source code from Listing 3-4 with implementations of previous examples, you see that the Arduino Wiring application allows you to significantly simplify the number of statements necessary to control an LED circuit.

An Arduino Wiring application created using the Arduino Wiring Application for Windows IoT Core project template includes the header file pins_arduino.h, which implements pin-number mappings for RPi2 and MinnowBoard MAX. By default, the project compiles for the RPi2 board. In order to change this behavior, you can use either _M_IX86 or _M_X64 preprocessor directives or simply change the platform to x86 or x64. Note that the GPIO5 declaration in Listing 3-4 comes from pins_arduino.h.

At the end of the pins_arduino.h file, the following declaration appears:

```
static const uint8_t LED_BUILTIN = 41;
```

You can use the above mapping to drive the green LED of the RPi2 board. I encourage you to modify the sample applications in this chapter to control the built-in LED instead of using a custom LED circuit. You should simply use a LED_BUILTIN constant for Arduino Wiring or a GPIO number of 47 in other cases (C#, C++).

A pins_arduino.h file resides under the External Dependencies subfolder of ArduinoWiringApp and is part of the Microsoft.IoT.Lightning SDK. Specifically, this package contains the set of providers that you can use to interface on-board controller buses through the Direct Memory Mapped Driver (DMAP). We used this possibility here to drive the GPIO pin to blink the LED.

The Microsoft.IoT.Lightning SDK also provides more header files. For instance, ArduinoCommon.h declares an OUTPUT constant:

```
const UCHAR DIRECTION_OUT = 0x01;
#define OUTPUT DIRECTION_OUT
```

Interestingly, the Microsoft.IoT.Lightning SDK can be also installed as the NuGet package to the C# project. Then you can use the Lightning providers instead of the default bus providers class to increase performance at the cost of reduced security. I'll show you how to use the Microsoft.IoT.Lightning SDK in Chapter 10, "Motors."

Summary

Several aspects of background applications for Windows 10 IoT Core are worth noting. Most important, C#, C++, and Visual Basic background applications are implemented in the same way as the background tasks for regular Windows Runtime (WinRT) or UWP apps—i.e., they derive from the IBackgroundTask interface. This interface implements a single Run method, which can be interpreted as the analogue of either the static Main method of the Program class or the main function in C programming. Hence, the Run method of the class, deriving from the IBackgroundTask interface, constitutes the entry point of the background application. Such applications are automatically re-started by Windows 10 IoT Core whenever they crash or exit. Such a mechanism ensures that background applications run continuously and independently.

An entry point of the headed application

As in other Windows versions, Windows 10 IoT Core creates a process whenever a user or the operating system runs an application—in headed or headless mode. That process is defined as an instance of the application. At this stage, the operating system assigns to the process the hardware and software resources required to run the application—that is, the memory, processor time, access to the file system, and so on. Windows also creates the first thread of the process. This thread, which is usually defined as the main or UI thread, begins the app execution from the entry point. You just saw that an entry point of headless apps is the Run method.

In general, the entry point for the UWP application depends on the programming language used for the app development and also on the IoT device mode. For headed IoT devices, the entry point shares the same structure as UWP apps for other platforms—desktop or mobile. As you see later in this section, the entry point for XAML applications is the static `Main` method of the `Program` class, while WinJS (HTML) apps for this purpose employ an anonymous JavaScript function; see Appendix A.

C#/XAML

The entry point of C#/XAML UWP applications is generated automatically by Visual Studio 2015 and stored in the App.g.i.cs file (C#), which you can find in the $(ProjectDir)\obj\$(PlatformName)\ $(Configuration) folder, where $(ProjectDir), $(PlatformName) and $(Configuration) are the Visual Studio macros for build commands.

The first one, `$(ProjectDir)`, contains the absolute path to the project directory, while the second, `$(PlatformName)`, depends on the active solution platform. Finally, the last one, `$(Configuration)`, specifies the solution configuration. The values of `$(PlatformName)` and `$(Configuration)` can be modified using the Configuration Manager window of the current solution (see Chapter 2).

In the case of the C++ apps, the entry point is implemented in two files: App.g.h and App.g.hpp. Both reside under the folder $(ProjectDir)\Generated Files.

I discuss the default entry point for C#/XAML applications using the HelloWorldIoTCS app, which was developed in the previous chapter. The default implementation of App.g.i.cs for this project appears in Listing 3-6. This file consists of two classes: the static `Program` class and partial implementation of the App class. However, the actual entry point is the static `Main` method of the `Program` class.

The declaration of the `Main` method contains a single statement, which calls the static `Start` method of the `Application` class. The latter, which is declared in the `Windows.UI.Xaml` namespace, provides a mechanism for app activation, app lifetime management, app resources, and unhandled exception detection. In particular, the static `Start` method initializes an application and allows it to instantiate the `Application` class using `ApplicationInitializationCallback`. This callback is invoked during the app initialization. The instance of `ApplicationInitializationCallback` can be passed by using an argument of the `Application.Start` method.

LISTING 3-6   Default entry point of the C# UWP application

```
namespace HelloWorldIoTCS
{
#if !DISABLE_XAML_GENERATED_MAIN
    /// <summary>
    /// Program class
    /// </summary>
    public static class Program
    {
```

```
            [global::System.CodeDom.Compiler.GeneratedCodeAttribute(
                "Microsoft.Windows.UI.Xaml.Build.Tasks"," 14.0.0.0")]
            [global::System.Diagnostics.DebuggerNonUserCodeAttribute()]
            static void Main(string[] args)
            {
                global::Windows.UI.Xaml.Application.Start((p) => new App());
            }
        }
#endif

    partial class App : global::Windows.UI.Xaml.Application
    {
        [global::System.CodeDom.Compiler.GeneratedCodeAttribute(
            "Microsoft.Windows.UI.Xaml.Build.Tasks"," 14.0.0.0")]
        private bool _contentLoaded;
        /// <summary>
        /// InitializeComponent()
        /// </summary>
        [global::System.CodeDom.Compiler.GeneratedCodeAttribute(
            "Microsoft.Windows.UI.Xaml.Build.Tasks"," 14.0.0.0")]
        [global::System.Diagnostics.DebuggerNonUserCodeAttribute()]
        public void InitializeComponent()
        {
            if (_contentLoaded)
                return;

            _contentLoaded = true;
#if DEBUG && !DISABLE_XAML_GENERATED_BINDING_DEBUG_OUTPUT
            DebugSettings.BindingFailed += (sender, args) =>
            {
                global::System.Diagnostics.Debug.WriteLine(args.Message);
            };
#endif
#if DEBUG && !DISABLE_XAML_GENERATED_BREAK_ON_UNHANDLED_EXCEPTION
            UnhandledException += (sender, e) =>
            {
                if (global::System.Diagnostics.Debugger.IsAttached)
                    global::System.Diagnostics.Debugger.Break();
            };
#endif
        }
    }
}
```

In the case of the automatically generated entry point, the app is activated using the App class, which derives from the Application class. You find the default implementation of the App class in the code-behind of App.xaml. Thus, depending on the programming language, the App class is declared in App.xaml.cs (C#) or App.xaml.h and App.xaml.cpp (C++).

A partial declaration of the App class also resides in the corresponding App.g.* files, which include the definition of the `InitializeComponent` method. Basically, the method is composed of two elements:

- An exception handler for any detected unhandled exceptions that occur during runtime

- An event handler for managing data binding errors; see Chapter 4, "User interface design for headed devices"

The default declaration of the `InitializeComponent` method as well as the automatic generation of the `Program.Main` method can be suppressed or modified by using appropriate preprocessor directives in the Conditional Compilation Symbols text box of the Build tab in the Project properties window, shown in Figure 3-7. In particular, by declaring a DISABLE_XAML_GENERATED_MAIN directive, you can suppress the generation of the default `Main` method. As a consequence, the project would not compile due to the following error: CS5001: Program does not contain a static 'Main' method suitable for an entry point. To overcome this problem, you can write your own `Main` method or re-enable the automatic generation of a default entry point.

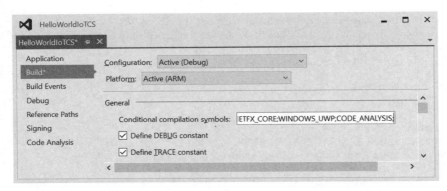

FIGURE 3-7   Conditional compilation symbols for the C# UWP application.

I conducted this discussion using a C# UWP sample application. However, the general structure of the automatically generated code for C++ UWP applications is the same. Appropriate files containing entry points differ by keywords of the programming languages, but the semantics are the same. For this reason, I describe the default App class for the C# programming language only.

The content of the App.xaml.cs file, which contains the declaration of an App class, appears in Listing 3-7. Analyze the structure of this implementation to understand the execution flow of the XAML applications you developed in Chapter 2. You need to understand what happens right after the application is run and what kind of steps invoke the `OnNavigatedTo` method, in which you actually run the code for controlling the LED circuit.

LISTING 3-7   Automatically generated implementation of the App class

```
using System;
using Windows.ApplicationModel;
using Windows.ApplicationModel.Activation;
```

```csharp
using Windows.UI.Xaml;
using Windows.UI.Xaml.Controls;
using Windows.UI.Xaml.Navigation;

namespace HelloWorldIoTCS
{
    sealed partial class App : Application
    {
        /// <summary>
        /// Initializes the singleton application object.  This is the first line of
        /// authored code executed, and as such is the logical equivalent of main() or
        /// WinMain(). </summary>
        public App()
        {
            this.InitializeComponent();
            this.Suspending += OnSuspending;
        }

        /// <summary>
        /// Invoked when the application is launched normally by the end user.  Other
        /// entry points will be used such as when the application is launched to open a
        /// specific file.  </summary>
        /// <param name="e">Details about the launch request and process.</param>
        protected override void OnLaunched(LaunchActivatedEventArgs e)
        {

#if DEBUG
            if (System.Diagnostics.Debugger.IsAttached)
            {
                this.DebugSettings.EnableFrameRateCounter = true;
            }
#endif

            Frame rootFrame = Window.Current.Content as Frame;

            // Do not repeat app initialization when the Window already has content,
            // just ensure that the window is active
            if (rootFrame == null)
            {
                // Create a Frame to act as the navigation context and navigate to the
first page

                rootFrame = new Frame();

                rootFrame.NavigationFailed += OnNavigationFailed;

                if (e.PreviousExecutionState == ApplicationExecutionState.Terminated)
                {
                    //TODO: Load state from previously suspended application
                }

                // Place the frame in the current Window
                Window.Current.Content = rootFrame;
            }
```

```
            if (e.PrelaunchActivated == false)
            {
                if (rootFrame.Content == null)
                {
                    // When the navigation stack isn't restored navigate to the first page,
                    // configuring the new page by passing required information as a
                    // navigation parameter
                    rootFrame.Navigate(typeof(MainPage), e.Arguments);
                }
                // Ensure the current window is active
                Window.Current.Activate();
            }

        /// <summary>
        /// Invoked when Navigation to a certain page fails
        /// </summary>
        /// <param name="sender">The Frame which failed navigation</param>
        /// <param name="e">Details about the navigation failure</param>
        void OnNavigationFailed(object sender, NavigationFailedEventArgs e)
        {
            throw new Exception("Failed to load Page " + e.SourcePageType.FullName);
        }

        /// <summary>
        /// Invoked when application execution is being suspended. Application state is
        /// saved without knowing whether the application will be terminated or resumed
        /// with the contents of memory still intact.
        /// </summary>
        /// <param name="sender">The source of the suspend request.</param>
        /// <param name="e">Details about the suspend request.</param>
        private void OnSuspending(object sender, SuspendingEventArgs e)
        {
            var deferral = e.SuspendingOperation.GetDeferral();
            //TODO: Save application state and stop any background activity
            deferral.Complete();
        }
    }
}
```

The App class in Listing 3-7 contains the parameterless constructor, which makes a call to the InitializeComponent method (defined in the App.g.i.cs file). Then this constructor attaches the handler to the Suspending event. The latter is invoked when the application is suspended. In general, the app can be suspended by the user or the operating system. In either case, the Suspending event can be used, for instance, to save the current application state or release exclusive resources. The state of the application can be further restored using the Resuming event of the Application class or within the OnLaunched method. This method is called upon every time the application is started by the user.

An automatically generated version of the OnLaunched method initializes the Frame class and then uses its Navigate method to display the view implemented within the MainPage class. This invokes the MainPage.OnNavigatedTo event, which you used in Chapter 2 to blink an LED.

The first argument of the Frame.Navigate method is the type derived from the Page class. Every view of the XAML UWP applications is implemented in this way. Hence, you can freely change the argument of the Frame.Navigate method to display a different view, which can be implemented by deriving from the Page class. I delve into the methods of view design in Chapter 4.

Asynchronous programming

Headed applications may need to continuously display results of the background operations—for example, to display values acquired from various sensors. In order to implement such an application, you can use asynchronous programming patterns available for UWP apps. Before going into details, I describe the fundamental aspects of threads and the UWP threading model for C# applications. From now, most of the sample applications are implemented using C#.

Worker threads and thread pool

The main application thread can create additional threads, defined as worker threads. In IoT programming, you generally use worker threads to obtain sensor readings because an operation may be delayed. For example, this might happen in cases of disrupted communication, such as when the user interface, which is controlled by the main thread, is blocked waiting for a response from the sensor. By using worker threads, you ensure that the UI is responsive to user requests.

To simplify the initiation of asynchronous operations using worker threads written in C# and Visual Basic, .NET Framework provides a task-based asynchronous pattern (TAP). The central point of this pattern is the Task class, declared in the System.Threading.Tasks namespace.

In the TAP pattern, an asynchronous operation can be started in one of two ways:

- By instantiating the Task class with an argument representing the code to execute and invoking the Start method

- By using the Task.Run static method

In either case, the asynchronous operation is enqueued in the thread pool, which is the set of worker threads pre-created when Windows 10 is started. Accordingly, to execute the operation in the background, you can also use the static method RunAsync of the ThreadPool class. The latter is declared in the Windows.System.Threading namespace.

I show you next how to write the sample application, which will simulate sensor readings. These readings will be implemented as an asynchronous operation, which will be executed using the Task and ThreadPool classes. Follow these steps:

1. Create the new Visual C# application, ThreadingSample, using the Blank App (Universal Windows) project template.

2. Go to the MainPage.xaml file and modify its content according to Listing 3-8.

LISTING 3-8   Declaration of the user interface of the MainPage view

```xml
<Page
    x:Class="ThreadingSample.MainPage"
    xmlns="http://schemas.microsoft.com/winfx/2006/xaml/presentation"
    xmlns:x="http://schemas.microsoft.com/winfx/2006/xaml"
    xmlns:local="using:ThreadingSample"
    xmlns:d="http://schemas.microsoft.com/expression/blend/2008"
    xmlns:mc="http://schemas.openxmlformats.org/markup-compatibility/2006"
    mc:Ignorable="d">

    <Page.Resources>
        <Style TargetType="Button">
            <Setter Property="Margin"
                    Value="10" />
            <Setter Property="HorizontalAlignment"
                    Value="Center" />
        </Style>

        <Style TargetType="StackPanel">
            <Setter Property="HorizontalAlignment"
                    Value="Center" />
            <Setter Property="VerticalAlignment"
                    Value="Top" />
            <Setter Property="Orientation"
                    Value="Vertical" />
        </Style>
    </Page.Resources>

    <StackPanel Background="{ThemeResource ApplicationPageBackgroundThemeBrush}">
        <Button x:Name="TaskButton"
                Click="TaskButton_Click"
                Content="Asynchronous operation (Task)" />

        <Button x:Name="ThreadPoolButton"
                Click="ThreadPoolButton_Click"
                Content="Asynchronous operation (ThreadPool)" />

        <Button x:Name="TimerButton"
                Click="TimerButton_Click"
                Content="Start Timer" />

        <Button x:Name="ThreadPoolTimerButton"
                Click="ThreadPoolTimerButton_Click"
                Content="Start ThreadPoolTimer" />
    </StackPanel>
</Page>
```

3.   In the MainPage.xaml.cs file, insert the statements depicted in Listing 3-9.

LISTING 3-9 Code-behind of the MainPage view

```csharp
using System;
using System.Diagnostics;
using System.Threading;
using System.Threading.Tasks;
using Windows.System.Threading;
using Windows.UI.Xaml;
using Windows.UI.Xaml.Controls;

namespace ThreadingSample
{
    public sealed partial class MainPage : Page
    {
        private Random randomNumberGenerator = new Random();
        private const int msDelay = 200;

        private const string debugInfoPrefix = "Random value";
        private const string numberFormat = "F2";
        private const string timeFormat = "HH:mm:fff";

        public MainPage()
        {
            InitializeComponent();
        }

        private void GetReading()
        {
            Task.Delay(msDelay).Wait();
            var randomValue = randomNumberGenerator.NextDouble();

            string debugString = string.Format("{0} | {1} : {2}",
                DateTime.Now.ToString(timeFormat),
                debugInfoPrefix,
                randomValue.ToString(numberFormat));

            Debug.WriteLine(debugString);
        }

        private void TaskButton_Click(object sender, RoutedEventArgs e)
        {
            var action = new Action(GetReading);
            Task.Run(action);

            // or alternatively:
            // Task task = new Task(action);
            // task.Start();
        }

        private async void ThreadPoolButton_Click(object sender, RoutedEventArgs e)
        {
            var workItemHandler = new WorkItemHandler((arg) => { GetReading(); });
```

```
                await ThreadPool.RunAsync(workItemHandler);
        }

        private void TimerButton_Click(object sender, RoutedEventArgs e)
        {

        }

        private void ThreadPoolTimerButton_Click(object sender, RoutedEventArgs e)
        {

        }
    }
}
```

The user interface of the ThreadingSample app is composed of four buttons. Use the **Asynchronous Operation (Task)** and **Asynchronous Operation (ThreadPool)** buttons to initiate asynchronous operations. The event handler attached to the first button uses the Task class, while the second button invokes the background work using the static RunAsync method of the ThreadPool class.

In either case, the asynchronous operation simulates the reading from the sensor. To this end, I use a random number generator and a delay that mimics the lag time before the particular sensor sends a response. The value of a randomly generated number is subsequently displayed in the Output window of Visual Studio 2015. (See Figure 3-8.)

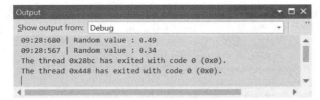

FIGURE 3-8   The output window of Visual Studio 2015 shows the results generated by the ThreadingSample app.

You use the other two buttons declared in the MainPage view in the next section.

Timers

Many IoT applications require continuous monitoring of a specific process such that data from sensors has to be acquired and processed in the background at specified intervals. Timers offer a convenient method for performing such periodic operations. The UWP includes two classes implementing timers. These are the Timer class, declared in the System.Threading namespace, and the ThreadPoolTimer class, declared in the Windows.System.Threading namespace.

To supplement the ThreadingSample app by logic to simulate periodic sensor readings, modify the MainPage.xaml.cs file as follows:

1. Supplement the definition of the `MainPage` class by the private members from Listing 3-10 and the methods in Listing 3-11.

LISTING 3-10 Members of the MainPage class for timers management

```
private const string timerStopLabel = "Stop";
private const string timerStartLabel = "Start";

private TimeSpan timeSpanZero = TimeSpan.FromMilliseconds(0);
private TimeSpan timeSpanDelay = TimeSpan.FromMilliseconds(msDelay);

private Timer timer;
private ThreadPoolTimer threadPoolTimer;

private bool isTimerActive = false;
private bool isThreadPoolTimerActive = false;
```

LISTING 3-11 Imitated sensor readings using timers

```
private void InitializeTimer()
{
    if(timer != null)
    {
        return;
    }
    else
    {
        var timerCallback = new TimerCallback((arg) => { GetReading(); });

        timer = new Timer(timerCallback, null, Timeout.InfiniteTimeSpan, timeSpanDelay);
    }
}

private void UpdateButtonLabel(Button button, bool isTimerActive)
{
    if(button != null)
    {
        var buttonLabel = button.Content as string;
        if(buttonLabel != null)
        {
            if(isTimerActive)
            {
                buttonLabel = buttonLabel.Replace(timerStartLabel, timerStopLabel);
            }
            else
            {
                buttonLabel = buttonLabel.Replace(timerStopLabel, timerStartLabel);
            }

            button.Content = buttonLabel;
        }
```

```csharp
        }
    }

    private void UpdateTimerState()
    {
        if(isTimerActive)
        {
            // Stop Timer
            timer.Change(Timeout.InfiniteTimeSpan, timeSpanDelay);
        }
        else
        {
            // Start Timer
            timer.Change(timeSpanZero, timeSpanDelay);
        }

        isTimerActive = !isTimerActive;
    }

    private void StartThreadPoolTimer()
    {
        var timerElapsedHandler = new TimerElapsedHandler((arg) => { GetReading(); });

        threadPoolTimer = ThreadPoolTimer.CreatePeriodicTimer
            (timerElapsedHandler, timeSpanDelay);
    }

    private void StopThreadPoolTimer()
    {
        if(threadPoolTimer != null)
        {
            threadPoolTimer.Cancel();
        }
    }

    private void UpdateThreadPoolTimerState()
    {
        if (isThreadPoolTimerActive)
        {
            StopThreadPoolTimer();
        }
        else
        {
            StartThreadPoolTimer();
        }

        isThreadPoolTimerActive = !isThreadPoolTimerActive;
    }
```

2. In the constructor of the `MainPage` class, insert the bolded statement in Listing 3-12.

LISTING 3-12 Timer initialization

```
public MainPage()
{
    InitializeComponent();

    InitializeTimer();
}
```

3. Finally, update definitions of the `TimerButton_Click` and `ThreadPoolTimerButton_Click` event handlers according to Listing 3-13.

LISTING 3-13 Timers activation

```
private void TimerButton_Click(object sender, RoutedEventArgs e)
{
    UpdateTimerState();

    UpdateButtonLabel(sender as Button, isTimerActive);
}

private void ThreadPoolTimerButton_Click(object sender, RoutedEventArgs e)
{
    UpdateThreadPoolTimerState();

    UpdateButtonLabel(sender as Button, isThreadPoolTimerActive);
}
```

Several aspects of the above solution require additional comments. Specifically, when the application starts, the instance of the `Timer` class is initialized using the `InitializeTimer` method; see Listing 3-12. This method instantiates the `Timer` class using a constructor, which has four arguments:

- The first argument, `callback`, allows you to set the callback function, which is invoked periodically.

- The second argument of the `Timer` class passes additional arguments to the callback function.

- The third parameter, `dueTime`, sets the delay time before the callback function is executed.

- The last argument, `period`, specifies the interval at which the callback function is invoked.

The instance of the `Timer` class does not have any public members for starting and stopping the timer. Therefore, the `Timer` class is initialized with an infinite time interval (`Timeout.InfiniteTimeSpan`) of the dueTime parameter. To start the timer, I dynamically change the dueTime value to 0 by using the `Change` method of the `Timer` class instance; see the `UpdateTimerState` method from Listing 3-11. As a result, the `GetReading` method is invoked periodically at 200 ms intervals. When the timer is active, the Output window displays randomly generated numbers, as you see in Figure 3-9. To stop the timer, you set the dueTime back to `Timeout.InfiniteTimeSpan`.

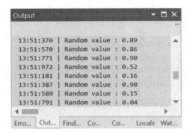

FIGURE 3-9 Periodic background operations executed using the `Timer` class.

You can achieve analogous functionality by using the `ThreadPoolTimer` class. To instantiate this class, you can use a static method, `CreatePeriodicTimer`. In the simplest case, it accepts two arguments: `handler` and a `period`. The first argument, `handler`, indicates the callback function, which is invoked periodically with a time delay specified by a `period` argument. The timer, created using `CreatePeriodicTimer`, starts invocation of the callback function immediately and can be stopped by calling the `Cancel` method of an instance of the `ThreadPoolTimer` class; see the `StopThreadPool-Timer` method from Listing 3-11.

Again, you can't dynamically modify the value of a `period` parameter. A new instance of `Thread-PoolTimer` is created every time the `StartThreadPoolTimer` method is invoked.

In real-world applications, you probably want to display the sensor readings on the screen. Include this functionality in the ThreadingSample app by performing the following changes:

1. Open the MainPage.xaml file and update its content according to Listing 3-14.

LISTING 3-14 MainPage.xaml of the ThreadingSample project

```
<Page
    x:Class="ThreadingSample.MainPage"
    xmlns="http://schemas.microsoft.com/winfx/2006/xaml/presentation"
    xmlns:x="http://schemas.microsoft.com/winfx/2006/xaml"
    xmlns:local="using:ThreadingSample"
    xmlns:d="http://schemas.microsoft.com/expression/blend/2008"
    xmlns:mc="http://schemas.openxmlformats.org/markup-compatibility/2006"
    mc:Ignorable="d">
```

```xml
<Page.Resources>
    <Style TargetType="Button">
        <Setter Property="Margin"
                Value="10" />
        <Setter Property="HorizontalAlignment"
                Value="Center" />
    </Style>

    <Style TargetType="StackPanel">
        <Setter Property="HorizontalAlignment"
                Value="Center" />
        <Setter Property="VerticalAlignment"
                Value="Top" />
        <Setter Property="Orientation"
                Value="Vertical" />
    </Style>

    <Style TargetType="ProgressBar">
        <Setter Property="Height"
                Value="20" />
        <Setter Property="Margin"
                Value="5" />
        <Setter Property="Foreground"
                Value="Orange" />
    </Style>
</Page.Resources>

<StackPanel Background="{ThemeResource ApplicationPageBackgroundThemeBrush}">
    <Button x:Name="TaskButton"
            Click="TaskButton_Click"
            Content="Asynchronous operation (Task)" />

    <Button x:Name="ThreadPoolButton"
            Click="ThreadPoolButton_Click"
            Content="Asynchronous operation (ThreadPool)" />

    <Button x:Name="TimerButton"
            Click="TimerButton_Click"
            Content="Start Timer" />

    <Button x:Name="ThreadPoolTimerButton"
            Click="ThreadPoolTimerButton_Click"
            Content="Start ThreadPoolTimer" />

    <ProgressBar x:Name="ProgressBar" />
</StackPanel>
</Page>
```

2. In the MainPage.xaml.cs file, modify the GetReading method from Listing 3-9, as you see in Listing 3-15.

LISTING 3-15   Timers activation

```
private void GetReading()
{
    Task.Delay(msDelay).Wait();
    var randomValue = randomNumberGenerator.NextDouble();

    string debugString = string.Format("{0} | {1} : {2}",
        DateTime.Now.ToString(timeFormat),
        debugInfoPrefix,
        randomValue.ToString(numberFormat));

    Debug.WriteLine(debugString);

    ProgressBar.Value = Convert.ToInt32(randomValue * 100);
}
```

3. Deploy and run the app.

Introducing the above changes to the ThreadingSample app adds the ProgressBar control to the MainPage view; see Listing 3-14. It also modifies the definition of the GetReading method, shown in Listing 3-15, such that a randomly generated value is used to configure the value displayed using the ProgressBar control.

When the application is launched and the GetReading function is invoked, the ProgressBar control will reflect the currently generated random value. However, after you run the app, an exception is thrown at some point. This exception informs you that "The application called an interface that was marshalled for a different thread."

The above problem arises because of specific aspects of the UWP threading model, in which every UI element is created and controlled by the main thread. Although the main thread can either start new or use pre-created worker threads for performing background operations, the worker threads cannot update the UI elements directly. Instead, the worker threads have to send the appropriate requests to the main thread.

Worker threads synchronization with the UI

In the headed mode, the main thread controls the user interface. Every request of the UI updates made by calls from the worker threads are sent to the main thread, which then updates the UI state. For this reason, the main thread is also called the user interface thread.

You can synchronize the worker threads with the UI thread by using one of the following classes: CoreDispatcher, SynchronizationContext or DispatcherTimer.

CoreDispatcher

The CoreDispatcher class implements the mechanism for processing control messages and dispatching the events. There is a single CoreDispatcher running all the time to manage every control of the headed application. You can access the instance of the CoreDispatcher class by using the public Dispatcher property of the DependencyObject class. The latter is the central part of the XAML property system and thus many types of control properties derive from the DependencyObject class.

Follow these steps to access CoreDispatcher and use its members to safely (in the sense of multi-threading) update the property Value of ProgressBar control in the ThreadingSample application:

1. Import the Windows.UI.Core namespace. Include the following statement in the header of the MainPage.xaml.cs file:

   ```
   using Windows.UI.Core;
   ```

2. In the MainPage class, define the DisplayReadingValue method; see Listing 3-16.

LISTING 3-16 Thread-safe procedure for setting control properties

```
private async void DisplayReadingValue(double value)
{
    if(Dispatcher.HasThreadAccess)
    {
        ProgressBar.Value = Convert.ToInt32(value);
    }
    else
    {
        var dispatchedHandler = new DispatchedHandler(() => {
            DisplayReadingValue(value); });

        await Dispatcher.RunAsync(CoreDispatcherPriority.Normal, dispatchedHandler);
    }
}
```

3. Modify the definition of the GetReading method (shown in Listing 3-9) according to Listing 3-17.

LISTING 3-17 Displaying imitated sensor reading within the ProgressBar control

```
private void GetReading()
{
    Task.Delay(msDelay).Wait();
    var randomValue = randomNumberGenerator.NextDouble();

    string debugString = string.Format("{0} | {1} : {2}",
        DateTime.Now.ToString(timeFormat),
        debugInfoPrefix,
        randomValue.ToString(numberFormat));

    Debug.WriteLine(debugString);
```

```
        //ProgressBar.Value = Convert.ToInt32(randomValue * 100);

        DisplayReadingValue(randomValue * 100);
    }
```

The CoreDispatcher class has the RunAsync member. It allows you to enqueue the selected operation such that it will be invoked on the UI thread. In Listing 3-16, I use the RunAsync method to update the Value property of the ProgressBar control. To check whether the UI element can be updated directly or through the UI thread, an instance of CoreDispatcher exposes the public, read-only property HasThreadAccess. If DisplayReadingValue is called by the UI thread, HasThreadAccess is true, so the given control can be updated directly. In contrast, when a worker thread invokes the DisplayReading-Value method, the HasThreadAccess property of the CoreDispatcher class instance is false. Hence, the DisplayReadingValue executes the RunAsync method of the CoreDispatcher class instance.

The RunAsync method accepts two arguments: priority and agileCallback. The first one is used to configure the importance of an action, specified using the agileCallback parameter. The priority can have one of the values of the CoreDispatcherPriority enumeration: Idle, Low, Normal, or High. In the code block from Listing 3-16, I set the priority to Normal, whereas for the agileCallback parameter I pass an anonymous function, which invokes the DisplayReadingValue method. As a result, the UI thread invokes DisplayReadingValue again. This time, however, Dispatcher.HasThreadAccess is true (because DisplayReadingValue is invoked on the UI thread), so the ProgressBar.Value property can be updated safely. Consequently, the imitated sensor readings are displayed in the main app view after you press any of the available buttons; see the orange bar in Figure 3-10.

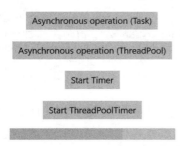

FIGURE 3-10   A fragment of the MainPage view, showing the changes of the values displayed using the ProgressBar control.

SynchronizationContext

The CoreDispatcher class synchronizes access to the UI elements. Every UI request sent from worker threads is enqueued and invoked sequentially. There is yet another way to implement such synchronization. This solution employs the SynchronizationContext class, declared in the System.Threading namespace.

Basically, SynchronizationContext is an alternative to CoreDispatcher. You can use them interchangeably, solely depending on your preference. You will probably find the SynchronizationContext preferable if you have worked previously with the Windows Forms apps.

In the next example, I modify the source code of the ThreadingSample app to use SynchronizationContext for thread-safe updates of the ProgressBar control:

1. In the MainPage.xaml.cs file, declare the private member of type SynchronizationContext and initialize this variable in the MainPage constructor, as you see in Listing 3-18.

LISTING 3-18 Obtaining a reference to an instance of the SynchronizationContext class

```
private SynchronizationContext synchronizationContext;

public MainPage()
{
    InitializeComponent();

    InitializeTimer();

    synchronizationContext = SynchronizationContext.Current;
}
```

2. Supplement the definition of the MainPage class by a method, according to Listing 3-19.

LISTING 3-19 Thread-safe access to control properties by using synchronization context

```
private void DisplayReadingValueUsingSynchronizationContext(double value)
{
    var sendOrPostCallback = new SendOrPostCallback((arg) =>
    {
        ProgressBar.Value = Convert.ToInt32(arg);
    });

    synchronizationContext.Post(sendOrPostCallback, value);
}
```

3. Finally, modify a GetReading function (see Listing 3-17) according to Listing 3-20.

LISTING 3-20 Displaying imitated sensor reading using synchronization context

```
private void GetReading()
{
    Task.Delay(msDelay).Wait();
    var randomValue = randomNumberGenerator.NextDouble();

    string debugString = string.Format("{0} | {1} : {2}",
```

```
            DateTime.Now.ToString(timeFormat),
            debugInfoPrefix,
            randomValue.ToString(numberFormat));

    Debug.WriteLine(debugString);

    //ProgressBar.Value = Convert.ToInt32(randomValue * 100);

    //DisplayReadingValue(randomValue * 100);

    DisplayReadingValueUsingSynchronizationContext(randomValue * 100);
}
```

After you deploy and launch the app, you see that the app performs as it did before. The only difference is that for thread synchronization I used the SynchronizationContext class, which offers an alternative way for thread-safe UI access from the functions of worker threads.

You can obtain a reference to this context by using the static property Current of the SynchronizationContext class. After obtaining an instance of the SynchronizationContext class, you can invoke any operation on the UI thread by using the Send or Post methods. The syntax of the two is exactly the same. Namely, the Send and Post methods accept two arguments: d of type SendOrPostCallback and state of type object. The first one specifies the method to be invoked, while the state parameter is used to pass additional arguments to that callback.

The only difference between the Send and Post methods is that the first one dispatches the callback synchronously, while the Post method does it asynchronously.

DispatcherTimer

The DispatcherTimer class implements a periodic timer integrated with the dispatcher associated with the main thread dispatcher. As a result, periodic callbacks are invoked on the UI thread, so the synchronization techniques described in the two previous sections become unnecessary. However, the whole callback is invoked on the UI thread, so it cannot include the long operations, which can eventually block the UI.

The DispatcherTimer class is discussed in the example you will explore in the next section.

Blinking the LED using DispatcherTimer

This section shows you how to implement an interactive Windows 10 IoT Core application that controls the built-in green ACT LED of the RPi2 device and displays whether this LED is switched on or off. You'll declare the UI, consisting of a button, a slider, and an ellipse. The button starts and stops the asynchronous operation for controlling the LED, the slider enables the configuration of the LED blinking frequency, and the color of the ellipse reflects the current state of the LED. Namely, the background of the ellipse will be gray when the LED is switched off, and red when it's on.

Perform the following steps to implement an interactive UWP app for controlling the LED of an RPi2 device:

1. Create the new project BlinkyApp using the Visual C# Blank App (Universal Windows) project template.

2. Reference Windows IoT Extensions for the UWP.

3. Open the MainPage.xaml file and declare the user interface using Listing 3-21.

LISTING 3-21   Main view declaration

```xml
<Page
    x:Class="BlinkyApp.MainPage"
    xmlns="http://schemas.microsoft.com/winfx/2006/xaml/presentation"
    xmlns:x="http://schemas.microsoft.com/winfx/2006/xaml"
    xmlns:local="using:BlinkyApp"
    xmlns:d="http://schemas.microsoft.com/expression/blend/2008"
    xmlns:mc="http://schemas.openxmlformats.org/markup-compatibility/2006"
    mc:Ignorable="d">

    <Page.Resources>
        <Thickness x:Key="DefaultMargin">10</Thickness>

        <Style TargetType="Ellipse">
            <Setter Property="Margin"
                    Value="{StaticResource DefaultMargin}" />
            <Setter Property="Height"
                    Value="100" />
            <Setter Property="Width"
                    Value="150" />
        </Style>

        <Style TargetType="Button">
            <Setter Property="Margin"
                    Value="{StaticResource DefaultMargin}" />
            <Setter Property="HorizontalAlignment"
                    Value="Center" />
        </Style>

        <Style TargetType="Slider">
            <Setter Property="Margin"
                    Value="{StaticResource DefaultMargin}" />
            <Setter Property="Minimum"
                    Value="100" />
            <Setter Property="Maximum"
                    Value="5000" />
            <Setter Property="StepFrequency"
                    Value="100" />
        </Style>
```

```xaml
            <Style TargetType="TextBlock">
                <Setter Property="Margin"
                        Value="{StaticResource DefaultMargin}" />
                <Setter Property="HorizontalAlignment"
                        Value="Center" />
                <Setter Property="FontSize"
                        Value="20" />
            </Style>
        </Page.Resources>

        <StackPanel Background="{ThemeResource ApplicationPageBackgroundThemeBrush}">
            <Button x:Name="MainButton"
                    Click="MainButton_Click" />

            <Ellipse x:Name="LedEllipse" />

            <Slider x:Name="Slider"
                    ValueChanged="Slider_ValueChanged"/>

            <TextBlock Text="{Binding Value, ElementName=Slider}" />
        </StackPanel>
    </Page>
```

4. Modify the content of the MainPage.xaml.cs file according to Listing 3-22. (The GPIO pin number used here corresponds to the built-in ACT LED of the Raspberry Pi 2. Note that this example is not compatible with Raspberry Pi 3, since it does not have the ACT LED. You will need an external LED circuit for that.)

LISTING 3-22 Logic of the BlinkyApp

```csharp
using System;
using Windows.Devices.Gpio;
using Windows.UI;
using Windows.UI.Xaml;
using Windows.UI.Xaml.Controls;
using Windows.UI.Xaml.Controls.Primitives;
using Windows.UI.Xaml.Media;

namespace BlinkyApp
{
    public sealed partial class MainPage : Page
    {
        private const int ledPinNumber = 47;

        private GpioPin ledGpioPin;
        private DispatcherTimer dispatcherTimer;

        private const string stopBlinkingLabel = "Stop blinking";
        private const string startBlinkingLabel = "Start blinking";
```

```
public MainPage()
{
    InitializeComponent();

    ConfigureGpioPin();
    ConfigureMainButton();
    ConfigureTimer();
}

private void ConfigureMainButton()
{
    MainButton.Content = startBlinkingLabel;

    MainButton.IsEnabled = ledGpioPin != null ? true : false;
}

private void UpdateMainButtonLabel()
{
    var label = MainButton.Content.ToString();

    if (label.Contains(stopBlinkingLabel))
    {
        MainButton.Content = startBlinkingLabel;
    }
    else
    {
        MainButton.Content = stopBlinkingLabel;
    }
}

private void ConfigureGpioPin()
{
    var gpioController = GpioController.GetDefault();

    if (gpioController != null)
    {
        ledGpioPin = gpioController.OpenPin(ledPinNumber);

        if (ledGpioPin != null)
        {
            ledGpioPin.SetDriveMode(GpioPinDriveMode.Output);
            ledGpioPin.Write(GpioPinValue.Low);
        }
    }
}

private void Slider_ValueChanged(object sender,
    RangeBaseValueChangedEventArgs e)
{
    var msDelay = Convert.ToInt32(Slider.Value);
    dispatcherTimer.Interval = TimeSpan.FromMilliseconds(msDelay);
}
```

```csharp
        private void ConfigureTimer()
        {
            dispatcherTimer = new DispatcherTimer();
            dispatcherTimer.Tick += DispatcherTimer_Tick;
        }

        private void DispatcherTimer_Tick(object sender, object e)
        {
            Color ellipseBgColor;
            GpioPinValue invertedGpioPinValue;

            var currentPinValue = ledGpioPin.Read();

            if (currentPinValue == GpioPinValue.High)
            {
                invertedGpioPinValue = GpioPinValue.Low;
                ellipseBgColor = Colors.Gray;
            }
            else
            {
                invertedGpioPinValue = GpioPinValue.High;
                ellipseBgColor = Colors.LawnGreen;
            }

            ledGpioPin.Write(invertedGpioPinValue);
            LedEllipse.Fill = new SolidColorBrush(ellipseBgColor);
        }

        private void UpdateTimer()
        {
            if(dispatcherTimer.IsEnabled)
            {
                dispatcherTimer.Stop();
            }
            else
            {
                dispatcherTimer.Start();
            }
        }

        private void MainButton_Click(object sender, RoutedEventArgs e)
        {
            UpdateTimer();

            UpdateMainButtonLabel();
        }
    }
}
```

When you deploy and run BlinkyApp to your IoT device, you can dynamically control the blinking frequency by using a `Slider` control.

To periodically switch the LED on or off, BlinkyApp uses a `DispatcherTimer` class. This class can be instantiated by using a parameterless constructor. Set the callback function by using the `Tick` event; see the `ConfigureTimer` method from Listing 3-22. After the timer is started, the callback function is periodically invoked at the intervals specified by the `Interval` property. In the above example, the `Interval` property is set using the `Slider` control; note the `Slider_ValueChanged` function from Listing 3-22.

In the above example, the callback function (`Tick` event handler) changes the GPIO pin value and also updates the ellipse background to reflect the current LED state. The dispatcher timer is integrated with the UI thread, so the `Ellipse` control can be safely updated (in the thread safety sense).

Periodic asynchronous operations implemented using the `DispatcherTimer` class can be started and stopped by using `Start` and `Stop` members. Such an interface is more convenient than the one exposed by the `Timer` and `ThreadPoolTimer` classes.

Summary

This chapter was devoted to essential aspects of Windows 10 IoT Core programming. I started the discussion with headed and headless device modes, describing the entry points for UI and background applications. I showed the sample usage of the Arduino Wiring API for controlling the LED of the RPi2. Furthermore, I described the fundamentals of asynchronous programming in terms of IoT devices. You'll see these aspects again in Chapters 5–14.

CHAPTER 4

User interface design for headed devices

Chapter 3, "Windows IoT programming essentials," shows you how applications developed for headed devices running Windows 10 IoT Core can be interactive. That means you can build the user interface for exchanging data and messages with the user. In particular, the UI can be used to control the smart device and to present sensor readings in a concise and pictorial way using standard or custom UWP controls. Access these controls by using XAML (C#, C++, or VB apps) or HTML (JavaScript apps) markup.

This chapter covers all the details of building a UI with XAML, including the visual designer, XAML namespaces, controls, styles, layouts, events, and data binding. If you've already worked with XAML in other contexts, such as WPF or UWP apps, feel free to skip ahead to Chapter 5, "Reading data from sensors." Just know that there are a few bits here relevant specifically to IoT and UWP only:

- IoT device preview in the visual designer

- RelativePanel layout

- Adaptive and state triggers

- Compiled data binding

UI design of UWP apps

Throughout this chapter, I build several sample apps to present XAML capabilities in terms of designing a UI for UWP apps. This description is not only limited to IoT headed devices but can be used for other UWP devices. The headed applications built previously were based on the Universal Windows project template. As a result, these apps can be executed on any device running Windows 10. You can explore this possibility by executing the BlinkyApp on the local machine. Follow these steps:

1. Open the BlinkyApp project in Visual Studio 2015.

2. Navigate to the configuration toolbar and change the platform to either the x86 or x64 architecture, depending on your system architecture (32-bit or 64-bit).

3. Using the drop-down list of the configuration toolbar, change the target device to **Local Machine**.

4. Run the app.

After you perform the preceding operations, BlinkyApp is executed on the local machine. However, the Start Blinking button, as shown in Figure 4-1, is inactive. This is because the desktop environment does not give you access to any of the GPIO controllers; the static `GetDefault` method of the `GpioController` class returns `null`.

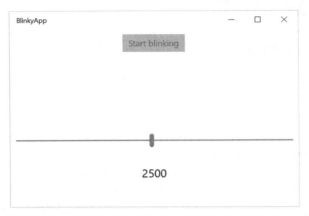

FIGURE 4-1   BlinkyApp executed on the Windows 10 desktop platform.

Although you cannot use the local machine to test functionality related to the IoT hardware, you can still use the development PC to design and test the user interface. In this example, you can change the slider position to verify that a number displayed in the TextBlock control changes appropriately. I took the screenshots of the sample applications created in this chapter using a local machine.

Visual designer

Visual Studio 2015 enables you to create a UI using the *visual designer,* which lets you manually design the UI by dragging the controls from a toolbox to the canvas representing the app page. You can update the appearance of the controls as well as the page itself by using the Properties window, or you can modify the controls by editing the XAML markup. Every change made using the Properties window is automatically reflected in the XAML markup—and vice versa. Therefore, the visual designer allows you to preview the appearance of the page; you don't need to execute an app.

To see how this works, create a new project named HeadedAppDesign using a Visual C# Blank App (Universal Windows). After the project is created, double-click **MainPage.xaml** in the Solution Explorer to bring up the designer view you see in Figure 4-2.

By default, the designer view is divided into two panes: design and XAML. The first one shows the page (left part of Figure 4-2), while the second allows you to edit the XAML markup. The design pane contains an additional device toolbar, which you see in Figure 4-3. You can use the device toolbar to configure the page preview. The drop-down list lets you choose the screen size of the virtual preview device. Two buttons next to the drop-down list control the screen orientation (landscape or portrait).

The button on the far right of the toolbar activates the modal device settings window, in which you configure the theme of the virtual device. You can use the device toolbar to fully control the appearance of your views on various devices. This is especially useful when you design UWP apps, targeting devices equipped with different screens.

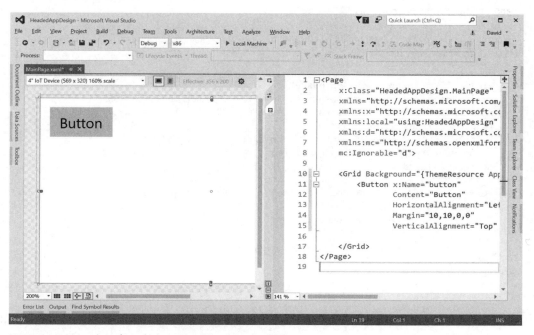

FIGURE 4-2   User interface design using Visual Studio 2015.

FIGURE 4-3   Use the device toolbar to preview your page on virtual devices with different displays.

The toolbox, which you activate by clicking the **Toolbox** option from the **View** menu, lists all available XAML controls. (See Figure 4-4.) You can drag any of the controls available in the toolbox to the page. Try it by dragging a button on the page; the XAML markup will be automatically updated and will look similar to what is used in Listing 4-1.

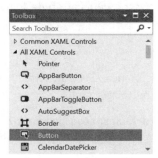

FIGURE 4-4   Toolbox contains a list of available XAML controls.

Note, first, that the XAML declarations have a hierarchical structure with only one root element, which may have one or more descendants. In Listing 4-1, the root element is the Page object. This object constitutes a container for the other UI elements. The Page element can have only a single child object, which is usually a control responsible for defining the view layout, e.g., Grid or StackPanel. Each can host multiple controls.

LISTING 4-1   MainPage declaration

```
<Page
    x:Class="HeadedAppDesign.MainPage"
    xmlns="http://schemas.microsoft.com/winfx/2006/xaml/presentation"
    xmlns:x="http://schemas.microsoft.com/winfx/2006/xaml"
    xmlns:local="using:HeadedAppDesign"
    xmlns:d="http://schemas.microsoft.com/expression/blend/2008"
    xmlns:mc="http://schemas.openxmlformats.org/markup-compatibility/2006"
    mc:Ignorable="d">

    <Grid Background="{ThemeResource ApplicationPageBackgroundThemeBrush}">
        <Button Content="Button"
                HorizontalAlignment="Left"
                Margin="10,10,0,0"
                VerticalAlignment="Top" />
    </Grid>
</Page>
```

A declaration of the root element contains several xmlns attributes. As is the case for the XML, they import and bind namespaces.

XAML namespaces

In the theory of programming, a namespace is a way of organizing the elements of the source code, such as declarations and definitions of classes, structures, variables, and enumerations. Namespaces allow you to organize the code into collections of related purposes and to control their scope to avoid name conflicts.

In XAML and XML, namespaces are qualified by a prefix, which follows the xmlns attribute. In particular, the attribute

```
xmlns:local="using:HeadedAppDesign"
```

imports a namespace HeadedAppDesign and maps it to a prefix local:. Hence, every UI element declared in the HeadedAppDesign namespace can be accessed by using the local: prefix.

As an example, follow these steps to define the class overriding the default Button element by introducing the following changes in the HeadedAppDesign project:

1. Add the MyButton.cs file by clicking the **Add Class** option in the **Project** menu.

2. In the Add New Item dialog box that appears, select the **Class** element, and type **MyButton.cs** in the text box. (See Figure 4-5.)

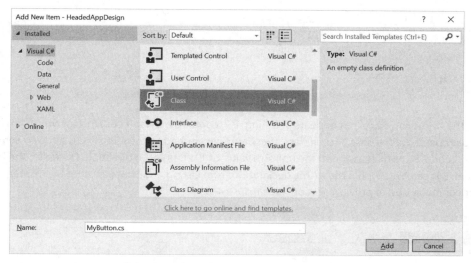

FIGURE 4-5   New Item dialog box of Visual Studio 2015.

3. Modify the content of the MyButton.cs file according to Listing 4-2.

```
LISTING 4-2   UI element definition
using Windows.UI.Xaml;
using Windows.UI.Xaml.Controls;

namespace HeadedAppDesign
{
    public class MyButton : Button
    {
        private const string defaultContent = "My content";
        private const double defaultMargin = 10.0;

        public MyButton()
        {
            Content = defaultContent;
            Margin = new Thickness(defaultMargin);
        }
    }
}
```

4. Update the MainPage.xaml file as shown in Listing 4-3.

```
<StackPanel Background="{ThemeResource ApplicationPageBackgroundThemeBrush}">
    <Button x:Name="DefaultButton"
            Content="Button"
            HorizontalAlignment="Left"
            Margin="10,10,0,0"
            VerticalAlignment="Top" />

    <local:MyButton />
</StackPanel>
```

The MyButton class, as it appears in Listing 4-2, contains a default constructor, which is used to set two properties of the base Button class. These are Content and Margin. The first is set to My content, and the second, Margin, is assigned the uniform value of 10 along each direction. Declaring the instance of the MyButton class within the XAML declaration from Listing 4-3 drives another My Content button to appear in the device preview section. (See Figure 4-6.)

FIGURE 4-6   Device preview, showing an additional button declared using a local prefix.

After compiling the project, you see that the MyButton control, declared in Listing 4-2, appears in the toolbox. Visual Studio automatically recognized this definition as the new UI element. So, if you want to add another instance of the MyButton control, you can do so by dragging the MyButton control onto the particular page. Check this yourself; the additional MyButton instance isn't used in this chapter.

Listing 4-3 shows you how to use XAML namespaces to declare UI elements. Notice that, apart from the local qualifier, the default UWP view declaration (see Listing 4-1) also contains the following namespace bindings: d:, mc:, and x:.

The namespace bound to the d: prefix contains declarations that support visual designer tools (the prefix d: comes from the designer namespace). Design-related declarations can be ignored during a runtime. Specify this by using the mc:Ignorable attribute. The mc: prefix is an acronym of markup compatibility. Accordingly, the objects declared in the corresponding namespace support the XAML files, parsing mechanism.

The namespace bound to the x: prefix contains the most frequently used elements. In particular, the default UWP page XAML declaration uses the following objects from the x: namespace:

- **x:Class**   This defines the class, implementing a code-behind associated with the XAML declaration.

- **x:Name**   This sets the unique name identifying the object. This attribute accesses the element from a code-behind or other XAML declarations—for example, for data-binding purposes, which I explain later in this chapter.

Note that the default declaration of the Page element includes the xmlns attribute, which does not have any prefix. This attribute imports the default core XAML namespace.

Control declaration, properties, and attributes

The declaration of every object in XAML, much like in HTML and XML markup, is composed of a pair of tags. The opening tag consists of the element name surrounded by angle brackets, while the closing tag has an additional slash before the closing bracket. Set the Content property of the control by typing a value between an opening and closing tag, as shown in Listing 4-4.

LISTING 4-4   Button declaration
```
<Button>Internet of Things</Button>
```

In order to set the value of other control properties, you can supplement the opening tag with appropriate attributes. Listing 4-5 shows the declaration of the Button control, in which the font size is set to 22 px.

LISTING 4-5   Font size configuration using an opening tag attribute
```
<Button FontSize="22">Internet of Things</Button>
```

The opening tag can have multiple attributes, like FontSize, Foreground, and Content properties of the Button. (See Listing 4-6.)

LISTING 4-6   Multiple attributes of the opening tag
```
<Button FontSize="22"
        Foreground="White"
        Content="Internet of Things"></Button>
```

Shorten the declaration from Listing 4-6 further as shown in Listing 4-7. Such shortened syntax is not appropriate when the control contains child elements (e.g., see the StackPanel declaration in Listing 4-3).

LISTING 4-7   Shortened Button declaration
```
<Button FontSize="22"
        Foreground="White"
        Content="Internet of Things" />
```

In the declarations from Listing 4-5, Listing 4-6, and Listing 4-7, control properties use inline attributes. Alternatively, you can modify the control properties by using the property element syntax, in which the visual appearance of the UI element is defined using nested XAML tags. Listing 4-8 shows an example of this syntax.

LISTING 4-8   Property element syntax

```
<Button>
    <Button.FontSize>22</Button.FontSize>
    <Button.Foreground>White</Button.Foreground>
    <Button.Content>Internet of Things</Button.Content>
</Button>
```

At first glance, the property element syntax seems to be much more complicated than the attribute syntax. However, the property element syntax is the only way to modify the properties of the complex type—those that cannot be represented by a single literal. The property and attribute syntaxes can be combined but are not interchangeable.

In Listing 4-9 I show the declaration in which the attribute syntax configures a font size, the foreground, and the content of a button, while the property element syntax changes the background to a linear color gradient.

Add a definition from Listing 4-9 to the MainPage.xaml file, right below a declaration of `<local:MyButton />`. The new button looks like the one in Figure 4-7. The font color becomes white, and the button background is filled with several gradients.

LISTING 4-9   Simultaneous usage of the attribute and property element syntax

```
<Button FontSize="22"
        Foreground="White"
        Content="Internet of Things">
    <Button.Background>
        <LinearGradientBrush StartPoint="0,0"
                             EndPoint="1,0">
            <GradientStop Color="Yellow"
                          Offset="0.0" />
            <GradientStop Color="Red"
                          Offset="0.25" />
            <GradientStop Color="Blue"
                          Offset="0.75" />
            <GradientStop Color="LimeGreen"
                          Offset="1.0" />
        </LinearGradientBrush>
    </Button.Background>
</Button>
```

Internet of Things

FIGURE 4-7   Appearance of the button declared using statements from Listing 4-9.

You probably wonder how you can quickly get to know all the properties available for a particular control. The answer is straightforward: The list of all control properties and their values is available from the Properties window. You can access this dialog box by clicking the **Properties Window** option of the Visual Studio's **View** menu. After activating the Properties window, you can either click the given control in the device preview section of the visual designer or the corresponding declaration of the XAML code. The properties list of the button declared in Listing 4-9 looks like the one in Figure 4-8. The background property reflects the actual value of the button depicted in Figure 4-7. You can use the Properties window to modify any of the available control properties. I encourage you to update the selected properties and verify that the XAML markup is automatically adjusted.

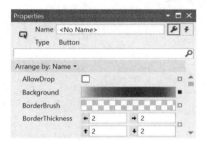

FIGURE 4-8   The properties window displaying the attribute values of the button declared in Listing 4-9.

UI design using visual tools is very convenient, especially early in your experience with XAML. You may also prefer it when you configure complex properties. But as you gain experience you will likely favor manual markup editing, because it offers a much faster way of defining the UI. You can simply move selected parts of the markup by copying and pasting selected areas of the code. Visual elements can be instantiated within the code-behind, and the procedures implemented in the code-behind can be employed to dynamically modify control properties.

Styles

The previous section defines control properties independently using appropriate attributes. This approach is suitable when the UI contains only one control of the specific type and each attribute has unique values. However, if the XAML tags share the same attribute values, then duplication of the attribute declarations increases the markup complexity and hampers the code maintenance, because the same changes have to be made in several declarations. Naturally, such control declarations violate a basic programming principle: *do not repeat yourself* (*DRY*) or *duplication is evil* (*DIE*).

To enable XAML declarations' reusability and attribute sharing across controls, UWP implements the Style class. The latter is declared in the Windows.UI.Xaml namespace and lets you define the property setters, which can be shared between instances of a type implementing specific control.

Style declaration must contain the TargetType attribute, which determines the type of the target control. An attempt to apply a style to an incompatible control type would raise an exception of type Windows.UI.Xaml.Markup.XamlParseException.

Style declaration

Style is typically declared within the *resource collection*—the set of reusable definitions, including styles. The scope of the resource collection can be limited to a control, a view, or the application.

All objects in the resource collection are uniquely identified by the value assigned to their x:Key attribute. In the case of styles, you do not need to specify an x:Key attribute. Such a style declaration will become anonymous and will be implicitly applied to all matching controls within a given resource scope.

In Listing 4-10, I show the sample declaration of an anonymous style that targets controls of type Button and is embedded in the resource collection of the MainPage.

LISTING 4-10 Style declaration

```
<Page.Resources>
    <Style TargetType="Button">
    </Style>
</Page.Resources>
```

You can also create styles dynamically from the code-behind. For instance, Listing 4-11 presents the C# version of the style declaration from Listing 4-10. As shown, the style declared in the code-behind can be explicitly applied to a control only by assigning the appropriate value to the Style property of an instance of the class implementing that control. (See Listing 4-12.) Listing 4-11 contains the rest of the MainPage class implementation. Note that to make the code in this listing compile, you need to set the XAML object name to DefaultButton, as shown in Listing 4-3.)

LISTING 4-11 Dynamic style construction

```
using Windows.UI.Xaml;
using Windows.UI.Xaml.Controls;

namespace HeadedAppDesign
{
    public sealed partial class MainPage : Page
    {
        private Style coloredButtonStyle = new Style(typeof(Button));

        public MainPage()
        {
            InitializeComponent();
        }
    }
}
```

LISTING 4-12 Constructor of the MainPage class depicting the dynamic style assignment

```
public MainPage()
{
    InitializeComponent();
```

```
        DefaultButton.Style = coloredButtonStyle;
}
```

Style definition

The style definition is a collection of `Setter` class instances (property setters). Each of them can set a given control property by changing the `Property` and `Value` attributes of the `Setter` class instance. You use the `Property` attribute to select the target control property and then set its target value using the `Value` attribute. Each style definition can have as many property setters as necessary. Listing 4-13, in which an Internet of Things button declaration was simplified, highlights a sample style definition of the style declared in Listing 4-10. Now, only the `Content` property is set inline.

Listing 4-13 also shows an updated declaration of the MainPage.xaml of the HeadedAppDesign project. When you make these changes in your local project, the visual appearance of all the buttons will be updated accordingly.

LISTING 4-13 Style definition consists of the list of property setters

```
<Page x:Class="HeadedAppDesign.MainPage"
    xmlns="http://schemas.microsoft.com/winfx/2006/xaml/presentation"
    xmlns:x="http://schemas.microsoft.com/winfx/2006/xaml"
    xmlns:local="using:HeadedAppDesign"
    xmlns:d="http://schemas.microsoft.com/expression/blend/2008"
    xmlns:mc="http://schemas.openxmlformats.org/markup-compatibility/2006"
    mc:Ignorable="d">

    <Page.Resources>
        <Style TargetType="Button">
            <Setter Property="BorderThickness"
                    Value="0.5" />
            <Setter Property="BorderBrush"
                    Value="Black" />
            <Setter Property="FontSize"
                    Value="22" />
            <Setter Property="Margin"
                    Value="10,10,0,0" />
            <Setter Property="Foreground"
                    Value="White"/>
            <Setter Property="Background">
                <Setter.Value>
                    <LinearGradientBrush EndPoint="1,0"
                                         StartPoint="0,0">
                        <GradientStop Color="Yellow"
                                      Offset="0" />
                        <GradientStop Color="Red"
                                      Offset="0.25" />
                        <GradientStop Color="Blue"
                                      Offset="0.75" />
                        <GradientStop Color="LimeGreen"
                                      Offset="1" />
```

```
                    </LinearGradientBrush>
                </Setter.Value>
            </Setter>
        </Style>
    </Page.Resources>

    <StackPanel Background="{ThemeResource ApplicationPageBackgroundThemeBrush}">
        <Button x:Name="DefaultButton"
                Content="Button"
                HorizontalAlignment="Left"
                Margin="10,10,0,0"
                VerticalAlignment="Top" />

        <local:MyButton />

        <Button Content="Internet of Things" />

    </StackPanel>
</Page>
```

To achieve a similar result by using code-behind procedures, you would need a little bit more coding. Listing 4-14 shows the MainPage.xaml.cs file with the necessary changes. You can check the effect of this code by running the app, since it does not affect the appearance (in the design pane) of the first button at all. The latter has assigned the anonymous style, so in the design pane of Visual Studio you see the same formatting as was applied to the Internet of Things button. (It is the same type as the first button.) After you run the app, the code-behind applies coloredButtonStyle to the control named DefaultButton, so its visual appearance is changed and will look analogous to Figure 4-9.

LISTING 4-14 Style definition in the code-behind

```
using Windows.UI;
using Windows.UI.Xaml;
using Windows.UI.Xaml.Controls;
using Windows.UI.Xaml.Media;

namespace HeadedAppDesign
{
    public sealed partial class MainPage : Page
    {
        private Style coloredButtonStyle = new Style(typeof(Button));

        public MainPage()
        {
            InitializeComponent();

            SetStylePropertySetters();

            button.Style = coloredButtonStyle;
        }
```

```
private void SetStylePropertySetters()
{
    coloredButtonStyle.Setters.Add(new Setter(BorderThicknessProperty, 0.5));
    coloredButtonStyle.Setters.Add(new Setter(BorderBrushProperty, Colors.Black));
    coloredButtonStyle.Setters.Add(new Setter(FontSizeProperty, 20));
    coloredButtonStyle.Setters.Add(new Setter(ForegroundProperty, Colors.White));
    coloredButtonStyle.Setters.Add(new Setter(MarginProperty,
        new Thickness(10, 10, 0, 0)));
    coloredButtonStyle.Setters.Add(new Setter(BackgroundProperty,
        GenerateGradient()));
}

private LinearGradientBrush GenerateGradient()
{
    var gradientStopCollection = new GradientStopCollection();

    gradientStopCollection.Add(new GradientStop()
    {
        Color = Colors.Yellow,
        Offset = 0
    });

    gradientStopCollection.Add(new GradientStop()
    {
        Color = Colors.Orange,
        Offset = 0.5
    });

    gradientStopCollection.Add(new GradientStop()
    {
        Color = Colors.Red,
        Offset = 1.0
    });

    return new LinearGradientBrush(gradientStopCollection, 0.0);
}
}
}
```

FIGURE 4-9 The effect of dynamic (top button; see Listing 4-14) and static (bottom button; see Listing 4-13) style application.

Although the anonymous style, defined in Listing 4-13, will automatically be applied to every `Button` object declared within the `MainPage` of the HeadedAppDesign application, the property setters can be overridden under the particular button declaration. For example, when you add a declaration highlighted in Listing 4-15 to the MainPage.xaml file, a new button with a font size of 12 px and a fixed width of 190 px will be created.

LISTING 4-15   Overriding a style under the control declaration

```
<StackPanel Background="{ThemeResource ApplicationPageBackgroundThemeBrush}">
    <Button x:Name="DefaultButton"
            Content="Button"
            HorizontalAlignment="Left"
            Margin="10,10,0,0"
            VerticalAlignment="Top" />

    <local:MyButton />

    <Button Content="Internet of Things" />

    <Button Content="Windows 10 IoT Core"
            FontSize="12"
            Width="190" />
</StackPanel>
```

You may now be wondering how to restore the default formatting of the buttons added to the main view of the HeadedAppDesign project. You do it by changing the style declaration from Listing 4-13 to make a style non-anonymous. In other words, you explicitly set a style identifier. The unique identifier for style and other resources is configured by the value assigned to the Key attribute defined in the namespace bound to the `x:` prefix. Listing 4-16 shows such a modified declaration of a button style declared in the `MainPage` resources. After you make this change, all the properties of every button will be restored to the default values.

LISTING 4-16   Style declaration supplemented by the unique identifier

```
<Style TargetType="Button"
       x:Key="ColoredButtonStyle">
```

Supplementing the style declaration with a unique identifier turns that style into a non-anonymous set of property setters. Unlike the anonymous style, it has to be explicitly assigned to the given control by using the `Style` property (Listing 4-12 and Listing 4-14) or the XAML markup extensions.

But wait—how do you apply the style to the given control? By appropriately referencing the style. You do this by using specific markup extensions, which are discussed under the next section.

StaticResource and ThemeResource markup extensions

The XAML processor, during the UI declaration parsing, converts the literal attribute values into primitive or complex types. To disable or modify such default parsing, the XAML introduces a concept of markup extensions. These objects are declared by using the curly brackets and instruct the XAML processor to handle the attribute value in a non-standard way.

Several markup extensions are implemented in the core and default XAML namespaces. For control formatting, we should distinguish two: {StaticResource} and {ThemeResource}. {StaticResource} indicates the object declared in the resource collection and is typically used to assign a set of property setters to the control. The second markup extension, {ThemeResource}, works like {StaticResource} but it defines theme-dependent property setters. The style may be automatically adjusted to the theme settings used by the particular Windows 10 device. For example, different button backgrounds can be applied in the Light and Dark color themes.

To present the sample usage of {StaticResource} and {ThemeResource} markup extensions, I modify the MainPage declaration in Listing 4-17. This declaration supplements the resources of MainPage with the ResourceDictionary class, consisting of ColoredButtonStyle and two theme-dependent resource dictionaries. These collections contain declarations of the objects used to set the Foreground and Background properties of the Button control by using the {ThemeResource} markup extension. The XAML processor automatically resolves the current theme and applies the corresponding properties to the given button. Remember, you can change the current theme of the designer preview using a device toolbar. (Refer to Figure 4-3.) For this purpose, you use the **Theme** drop-down list of the Device Preview Settings dialog box. (See Figure 4-10.)

FIGURE 4-10 Device preview theme configuration.

LISTING 4-17 XAML markup extensions for declaring and applying theme-dependent property setters

```
<Page x:Class="HeadedAppDesign.MainPage"
      xmlns="http://schemas.microsoft.com/winfx/2006/xaml/presentation"
      xmlns:x="http://schemas.microsoft.com/winfx/2006/xaml"
      xmlns:local="using:HeadedAppDesign"
      xmlns:d="http://schemas.microsoft.com/expression/blend/2008"
      xmlns:mc="http://schemas.openxmlformats.org/markup-compatibility/2006"
      mc:Ignorable="d">

    <Page.Resources>
        <ResourceDictionary>
            <ResourceDictionary.ThemeDictionaries>
                <ResourceDictionary x:Key="Light">
```

```xml
            <Color x:Key="ForegroundColor">White</Color>

            <LinearGradientBrush x:Key="ColoredLinearGradientBrush"
                                 EndPoint="1,0"
                                 StartPoint="0,0">
                <GradientStop Color="Yellow"
                              Offset="0" />
                <GradientStop Color="Red"
                              Offset="0.25" />
                <GradientStop Color="Blue"
                              Offset="0.75" />
                <GradientStop Color="LimeGreen"
                              Offset="1" />
            </LinearGradientBrush>
        </ResourceDictionary>
        <ResourceDictionary x:Key="Dark">
            <Color x:Key="ForegroundColor">Yellow</Color>

            <LinearGradientBrush x:Key="ColoredLinearGradientBrush"
                                 EndPoint="1,0"
                                 StartPoint="0,0">
                <GradientStop Color="LimeGreen"
                              Offset="0" />
                <GradientStop Color="Blue"
                              Offset="0.25" />
                <GradientStop Color="Red"
                              Offset="0.75" />
                <GradientStop Color="Yellow"
                              Offset="1" />
            </LinearGradientBrush>
        </ResourceDictionary>
    </ResourceDictionary.ThemeDictionaries>

    <Style TargetType="Button"
           x:Key="ColoredButtonStyle">
        <Setter Property="BorderThickness"
                Value="0.5" />
        <Setter Property="BorderBrush"
                Value="Black" />
        <Setter Property="FontSize"
                Value="22" />
        <Setter Property="Margin"
                Value="10,10,0,0" />
        <Setter Property="Foreground"
                Value="{ThemeResource ForegroundColor}" />
        <Setter Property="Background"
                Value="{ThemeResource ColoredLinearGradientBrush}" />
    </Style>
    </ResourceDictionary>
</Page.Resources>

<StackPanel Background="{ThemeResource ApplicationPageBackgroundThemeBrush}">
    <Button x:Name="DefaultButton"
            Content="Button"
```

```
                HorizontalAlignment="Left"
                Margin="10,10,0,0"
                VerticalAlignment="Top" />

        <local:MyButton />

        <Button Content="Internet of Things"
                Style="{StaticResource ColoredButtonStyle}"/>

        <Button Content="Windows 10 IoT Core"
                FontSize="12"
                Width="190"
                Style="{StaticResource ColoredButtonStyle}"/>
    </StackPanel>
</Page>
```

The app can also request a color theme during the initialization; you can either update the content of App.xaml, as you see in Listing 4-18, or set the requested theme in the App class constructor, defined in the App.xaml.cs file (see Listing 4-19). You cannot change the theme of an application during a run-time. Trying to do so throws an exception of type System.NotSupportedException.

LISTING 4-18   Requested theme can be set using the attribute of the Application tag

```
<Application
    x:Class="HeadedAppDesign.App"
    xmlns="http://schemas.microsoft.com/winfx/2006/xaml/presentation"
    xmlns:x="http://schemas.microsoft.com/winfx/2006/xaml"
    xmlns:local="using:HeadedAppDesign"
    RequestedTheme="Dark">
</Application>
```

LISTING 4-19   Developers can request a theme programmatically during app initialization (App.xaml.cs), provided it was not already set in the App.xaml file (XAML declaration; see Listing 4-18)

```
public App()
{
    InitializeComponent();
    Suspending += OnSuspending;

    RequestedTheme = ApplicationTheme.Light;
}
```

Finally, the style is assigned to a control by using the {StaticResource} markup extension (see the bottom part of Listing 4-17), and the default view of HeadedAppDesign in a Light and Dark color theme (see Figure 4-11).

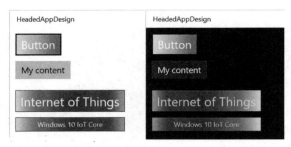

FIGURE 4-11 Theme-dependent control styling.

Visual states and VisualStateManager

During the testing of the HeadedAppDesign project, you probably noted that the buttons, when clicked, undergo a visual change. A short animation plays, and the background and foreground are altered. Moreover, the button is slightly displaced from its original position. Such dynamic modification of the control properties informs the user that a particular action was taken, preventing him from clicking a button again. You can use this approach to inform the user that a sensor reading is approaching critical or abnormal values. The color of the indicator may change depending on the signals received from the sensors attached to the IoT device. Sensor readings can show several visual states with different property setters.

Visual states can be defined inside the control template by setting the Template property to an instance of the ControlTemplate class. In general, this class defines the visual structure of the XAML controls. Visual states are represented by the instances of type VisualState. The latter can be composed of the Storyboard class instance or the set of property setters. The former defines the control animation, while the latter is a collection of the instances of the Setter class. Usually, the property setters look similar to the style definition because the animations are effectively done by temporal formatting adjustments. However, the property setters of a visual state are configured through the Target instead of the Property attribute. In general, the ControlTemplate class may consist of several XAML controls. If so, property setters may be associated with different XAML objects. The syntax for identifying these elements reads as: ControlName.TargetProperty, where ControlName is set through the x:Name attribute and TargetProperty denotes the control attribute, which will be updated by the property setter.

After the visual states are defined, they can be activated using the static method GoToState of the VisualStateManager class. Alternatively, you can write custom classes, which update the values of selected control properties or switch styles from the code-behind due to actions taken by the user or changes in external signals. You can also use the adaptive and state triggers, which I discuss in the next section.

Now I present sample definitions of the control's visual states and the usage of the selected methods of the VisualStateManager class. Here is the list of changes required to be introduced in the HeadedApp-Design project:

1. Modify the ColoredButtonStyle definition as shown in Listing 4-20.

LISTING 4-20   Visual states are defined within the control template

```xml
<Style TargetType="Button"
       x:Key="ColoredButtonStyle">
    <Setter Property="BorderThickness"
            Value="0.5" />
    <Setter Property="BorderBrush"
            Value="Black" />
    <Setter Property="FontSize"
            Value="22" />
    <Setter Property="Margin"
            Value="10,10,0,0" />
    <Setter Property="Foreground"
            Value="{ThemeResource ForegroundColor}" />
    <Setter Property="Background"
            Value="{ThemeResource ColoredLinearGradientBrush}" />
    <Setter Property="Template">
        <Setter.Value>
            <ControlTemplate TargetType="Button">
                <Grid x:Name="RootGrid"
                      Background="{TemplateBinding Background}">
                    <VisualStateManager.VisualStateGroups>
                        <VisualStateGroup x:Name="CommonStates">
                            <VisualState x:Name="Normal" />

                            <VisualState x:Name="PointerOver">
                                <VisualState.Setters>
                                    <Setter Target="RootGrid.Background"
                                            Value="{ThemeResource ForegroundColor}" />
                                    <Setter Target="ContentPresenter.Foreground"
                                            Value="{ThemeResource
                                                    ColoredLinearGradientBrush}" />
                                </VisualState.Setters>
                            </VisualState>

                            <VisualState x:Name="Pressed">
                                <Storyboard>
                                    <SwipeHintThemeAnimation ToHorizontalOffset="5"
                                                             ToVerticalOffset="0"
                                                             TargetName="RootGrid" />
                                </Storyboard>
                            </VisualState>
                        </VisualStateGroup>
                    </VisualStateManager.VisualStateGroups>
                    <ContentPresenter x:Name="ContentPresenter"
                                      BorderBrush="{TemplateBinding BorderBrush}"
                                      BorderThickness="{TemplateBinding BorderThickness}"
                                      Content="{TemplateBinding Content}"
                                      Padding="{TemplateBinding Padding}"
                                      HorizontalContentAlignment=
                                          "{TemplateBinding
                                                  HorizontalContentAlignment}"
                                      VerticalContentAlignment=
                                          "{TemplateBinding VerticalContentAlignment}" />
```

```
            </Grid>
          </ControlTemplate>
        </Setter.Value>
    </Setter>
</Style>
```

2. Update the part of the MainPage declaration between the StackPanel tags according to Listing 4-21. (Note in the listing that the name of the first button was changed.)

LISTING 4-21   Declarations of buttons of the MainPage

```
<Button x:Name="GoToStateButton"
        Content="Change visual state"
        HorizontalAlignment="Left"
        Margin="10,10,0,0"
        VerticalAlignment="Top"
        Click="GoToStateButton_Click" />

<local:MyButton />

<Button x:Name="IoTButton"
        Content="Internet of Things"
        Style="{StaticResource ColoredButtonStyle}" />

<Button x:Name="Windows10IoTCoreButton"
        Content="Windows 10 IoT Core"
        FontSize="12"
        Width="190"
        Style="{StaticResource ColoredButtonStyle}" />
```

3. Open the MainPage.xaml.cs file and define two private members and update the default constructor of the MainPage class, as shown in Listing 4-22.

LISTING 4-22   Additional private fields of the MainPage class and its updated constructor

```
private const string pointerOverVisualStateName = "PointerOver";
private const string normalVisualStateName = "Normal";

public MainPage()
{
    InitializeComponent();

    SetStylePropertySetters();

    GoToStateButton.Style = coloredButtonStyle;
}
```

4. Include the methods from Listing 4-23 in the definition of the MainPage class.

LISTING 4-23 Visual state swapping using the VisualStateManager

```
private void GoToStateButton_Click(object sender, RoutedEventArgs e)
{
    SwapButtonVisualState(IoTButton);
    SwapButtonVisualState(Windows10IoTCoreButton);
}

private void SwapButtonVisualState(Button button)
{
    string newVisualState = pointerOverVisualStateName;

    if(button.Tag != null)
    {
        if(button.Tag.ToString().Contains(pointerOverVisualStateName))
        {
            newVisualState = normalVisualStateName;
        }
        else
        {
            newVisualState = pointerOverVisualStateName;
        }
    }

    VisualStateManager.GoToState(button, newVisualState, false);

    button.Tag = newVisualState;
}
```

Several aspects of the preceding solution deserve further comment. The button template of Colored-ButtonStyle defines a visual state group of the name CommonStates. This group consists of three visual states: Normal, PointerOver, and Pressed. The Normal visual state does not include any property setters. It just reverts any control formatting changes made by two other visual states. The PointerOver visual state defines two property setters, which swap the Foreground and Background properties, while the Pressed visual state plays the animation implemented in the SwipeHintThemeAnimation class. This animation is configured to shift the button by 5 px toward the right border of the MainPage window. This happens every time the button is clicked. The direction and the amount of button translation are configured using the ToHorizontalOffset and ToVerticalOffset attributes of the SwipeHintTheme-Animation class. SwipeHintThemeAnimation, as well as other XAML library animations, is defined in the Windows.UI.Xaml.Media.Animation namespace. Although XAML animations are not described here, feel free to check them by replacing SwipeHintThemeAnimation with types whose names end with Animation. You can find these classes using the Object Browser. (See Figure 4-12.) Activate this window by using the View/Object Designer option, and then type **Animation** in the search box.

Going back to the example code, the IoTButton and Windows10IoTCoreButton go into the PointerOver visual state when the mouse pointer falls within the bounding rectangles of these controls or when a Change Visual State button is clicked. In the PointerOver visual state, the Background property of the RootGrid is set to the ForegroundColor theme resource, while the Foreground of the ContentPresenter is set to the ColoredLinearGradientBrush theme resource. You see the effect of these changes in Figure 4-13.

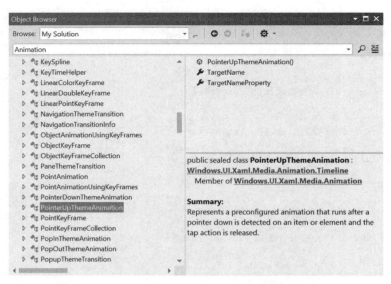

FIGURE 4-12 Object Browser showing the list of classes whose names contain Animation.

FIGURE 4-13 Visual states of ColoredButtonStyle.

You can employ the control templates to alter the visual structure of XAML controls. Use this feature to implement rounded buttons or text box indicators. Typically, these controls are rectangular, but you can modify them by using the control templates. Listing 4-24 shows the style definition, which contains the control template for ellipsis buttons. Associating EllipsisButtonStyle with Windows10IoTCore-Button will give you the result you see in Figure 4-14.

FIGURE 4-14 A rounded button created by extending the ColoredButtonStyle and using the control template.

The `EllipsisButtonStyle` was defined by inheriting the set of property setters from the `Colored-ButtonStyle`. In XAML, styles can be extended by using the `BasedOn` attribute of the `Style` tag (Listing 4-24). Such an extended style inherits property setters declared in the style determined by the value of the `BasedOn` attribute. The new style may, however, locally override property setters of the parent style.

LISTING 4-24 Extending definition of the ColoredButtonStyle by changing the visual structure of the button

```
<Style x:Key="EllipsisButtonStyle"
       TargetType="Button"
       BasedOn="{StaticResource ColoredButtonStyle}">
    <Setter Property="Template">
        <Setter.Value>
            <ControlTemplate TargetType="Button">
                <Grid Margin="10">
                    <Ellipse Fill="{TemplateBinding Background}"
                             Margin="-10" />
                    <ContentPresenter HorizontalAlignment="Center"
                                      VerticalAlignment="Center" />
                </Grid>
            </ControlTemplate>
        </Setter.Value>
    </Setter>
</Style>
```

Adaptive and state triggers

Visual states of the control can be activated by the adaptive and state triggers. The first, implemented in the `AdaptiveTrigger` class, turns on the indicated visual state, when the width or height of the app window is equal to or larger than the specified value. The adaptive trigger is typically used to adjust the application page to the screen size.

Listing 4-25 shows the modified version of the `ColoredButtonStyle` definition, in which the adaptive trigger was associated with a `LayoutChanged` visual state. This state is activated when the height of the application window is equal to or larger than 350 px. In such a case the corresponding button is rescaled by 115%. The property `RenderTransform` is assigned an instance of the `ScaleTransform` class. The latter implements a scale transform, which can be parameterized by four attributes: `ScaleX`, `ScaleY`, `CenterX`, and `CenterY`. The `ScaleX` and `ScaleY` define the scaling coefficients—the values used to multiply the current width (`ScaleX`) and height (`ScaleY`) of the given visual element. `CenterX` and `CenterY` properties specify the point of the center of the scale operation. By default, `CenterX` = `CenterY` = 0. This location, as in typical computer visual applications, corresponds to the upper-left corner of the XAML control. The effect of the adaptive trigger implemented in Listing 4-25 is presented in Figure 4-15.

LISTING 4-25 A button is rescaled when the window height is equal to or larger than 350 px

```
<Style TargetType="Button"
       x:Key="ColoredButtonStyle">
```

```
// This part is unchanged with respect to Listing 4-20

<Setter Property="Template">
    <Setter.Value>
        <ControlTemplate TargetType="Button">
            <Grid x:Name="RootGrid"
                  Background="{TemplateBinding Background}">
                <VisualStateManager.VisualStateGroups>
                    <VisualStateGroup x:Name="CommonStates">
                        <VisualState x:Name="Normal" />

                        <VisualState x:Name="PointerOver">
                            <VisualState.Setters>
                                <Setter Target="RootGrid.Background"
                                        Value="{ThemeResource ForegroundColor}" />
                                <Setter Target="ContentPresenter.Foreground"
                                        Value="{ThemeResource
                                        ColoredLinearGradientBrush}" />
                            </VisualState.Setters>
                        </VisualState>

                        <VisualState x:Name="Pressed">
                            <Storyboard>
                                <SwipeHintThemeAnimation ToHorizontalOffset="5"
                                                         ToVerticalOffset="0"
                                                         TargetName="RootGrid" />
                            </Storyboard>
                        </VisualState>

                        <VisualState x:Name="LayoutChanged">
                            <VisualState.Setters>
                                <Setter Target="RootGrid.RenderTransform">
                                    <Setter.Value>
                                        <ScaleTransform ScaleX="1.15"
                                                        ScaleY="1.15" />
                                    </Setter.Value>
                                </Setter>
                            </VisualState.Setters>

                            <VisualState.StateTriggers>
                                <AdaptiveTrigger MinWindowHeight="350" />
                            </VisualState.StateTriggers>

                        </VisualState>

                    </VisualStateGroup>

                </VisualStateManager.VisualStateGroups>

                // This part is identical as in Listing 4-20

            </Grid>
        </ControlTemplate>
```

```
            </Setter.Value>
        </Setter>
</Style>
```

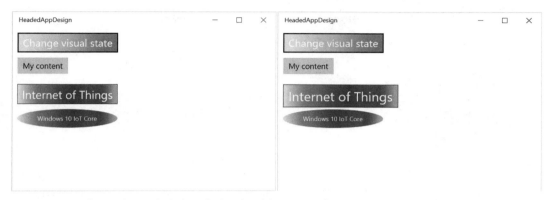

FIGURE 4-15 A button is rescaled when the height of the app window reaches the value of 350 px.

A state trigger is activated by a custom conditional declaration, which can be defined using the IsActive property of an instance of the StateTrigger class. To show a sample usage of this mechanism, I supplement the declaration of the MainPage of the HeadedAppDesign project with the CheckBox control. Subsequently, I link the IsActive property of the StateTrigger with the IsChecked property of the CheckBox control. So the state trigger is activated whenever the CheckBox control is checked.

You see XAML declarations implementing such functionality in Listing 4-26, and the effect of these modifications in Figure 4-16.

LISTING 4-26 State trigger associated with the Translated visual style

```
<StackPanel Background="{ThemeResource ApplicationPageBackgroundThemeBrush}">
    <VisualStateManager.VisualStateGroups>
        <VisualStateGroup>
            <VisualState x:Name="Translated">
                <VisualState.Setters>
                    <Setter Target="GoToStateButton.RenderTransform">
                        <Setter.Value>
                            <TranslateTransform X="100" />
                        </Setter.Value>
                    </Setter>
                </VisualState.Setters>

                <VisualState.StateTriggers>
                    <StateTrigger IsActive="{Binding IsChecked,
                                             ElementName=StateTriggerCheckBox}" />
                </VisualState.StateTriggers>
            </VisualState>
        </VisualStateGroup>
    </VisualStateManager.VisualStateGroups>
```

```
    // This part is the same in Listing 4-21

    <CheckBox x:Name="StateTriggerCheckBox"
              Content="Is state trigger active?"
              Margin="10"/>
</StackPanel>
```

FIGURE 4-16 The CheckBox control activates the state trigger, which toggles a button into a visual state named Translated.

The XAML declarations from Listing 4-26 define the new visual state, named Translated. In this visual state, the GoToStateButton is displaced along the horizontal direction by 100 px. I used the instance of the TranslateTransform class. It implements the affine transform, which moves the visual element by an offset, represented as a two-element vector [X, Y]. Entries of this translation vector are set using the X and Y attributes of the TranslateTransform class. (See Listing 4-25.)

The Translated visual state was defined under the VisualStateManager associated with the StackPanel control. In this case, the control template is not needed. However, the visual state applies to the particular StackPanel control only.

The state trigger, associated with the Translated visual state, is activated whenever the State-TriggerCheckBox is checked. In XAML, such functionality can be achieved using a data binding technique, in which control properties are linked using the {Binding} markup extension. I further discuss this mechanism later in this chapter.

Resource collections

The scope of every style declared in previous examples was limited to the current page. In general, styles (or in broader sense, resources) can be scoped at the control, page, or application level. Moreover, styles can be shared among different applications by storing them as resource dictionaries in files ending with the .xaml extension.

Control scope

To define the style scoped at the control level, use the XAML property element syntax and embed the declarations between the opening and closing tags implemented in the Resources or Style classes. To show an example, I will supplement the MainPage declaration with a Rectangle control, as shown in

Listing 4-27. The corresponding markup consists of two elements: resources and an anonymous style. The resources section defines two constants of type double, which are used in the style definition to set the width and height of the rectangle. The anonymous style is declared as a child of the Rectangle control, so in that case there is no need to configure the style identifier. The style is automatically applied to that Rectangle control. There are no other rectangles within that scope.

```
LISTING 4-27   Control-scoped resources declaration
<Rectangle>
    <Rectangle.Resources>
        <x:Double x:Key="RectWidth">100</x:Double>
        <x:Double x:Key="RectHeight">100</x:Double>
    </Rectangle.Resources>
    <Rectangle.Style>
        <Style TargetType="Rectangle">
            <Setter Property="Fill"
                    Value="Orange" />
            <Setter Property="Width"
                    Value="{StaticResource RectWidth}" />
            <Setter Property="Height"
                    Value="{StaticResource RectHeight}" />
        </Style>
    </Rectangle.Style>
</Rectangle>
```

The resources scoped at the page-level use the control-scoped resources, because Page is also a control. However, it usually hosts other controls, so the resources declared within a page-scope are also available for child controls, which the initial examples regarding buttons showed.

Application scope

The application-scoped resources are defined in an App.xaml file under the Application.Resources tag. For instance, you can move the page-scoped declarations from MainPage.xaml to App.xaml as you see in Listing 4-28. Every page of the HeadedAppDesign project can then reference ColoredButtonStyle and EllipsisButtonStyle.

After moving resources to the App.xaml file, styles do not appear in the design pane until you need to rebuild the project; you can do so by using the Rebuild option from the Build menu.

```
LISTING 4-28   Declaration of the resources scoped at the application level
<Application
    x:Class="HeadedAppDesign.App"
    xmlns="http://schemas.microsoft.com/winfx/2006/xaml/presentation"
    xmlns:x="http://schemas.microsoft.com/winfx/2006/xaml"
    xmlns:local="using:HeadedAppDesign">

    <Application.Resources>
        <ResourceDictionary>
```

```
        // This part does not change with respect to Listing 4-24 and Listing 4-25
      </ResourceDictionary>
    </Application.Resources>
</Application>
```

Importing resources

The resources—that is, control styles, templates, and other XAML object definitions—can be shared across different UWP applications by using the merged dictionaries, which can be defined by using the attribute `MergedDictionaries` of an instance of the `ResourceDictionary` class.

As a next example, I move the definition of the style `EllipsisButtonStyle` to a dictionary declared in a separate file. I merge this dictionary with the XAML declarations from the App.xaml file. This task consists of the following steps:

1. Bring up the Add New Item dialog box using the option **Add New Item** of the **Project** menu.

2. In the Add New Item dialog box, go to the **Visual C#/XAML** tab, then select the **Resource Dictionary** item, and in the Name text box type **MyDictionary.xaml**. (See Figure 4-17.)

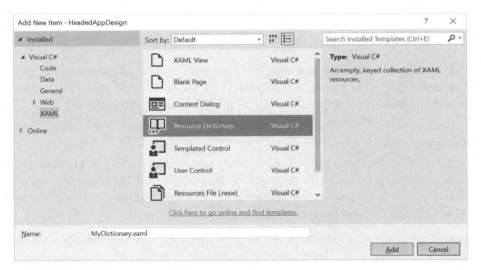

FIGURE 4-17   Adding a resource dictionary.

3. Click the **Add** button. MyDictionary.xaml is added to the HeadedAppDesign project.

4. Modify the content of MyDictionary.xaml, according to Listing 4-29.

LISTING 4-29   The content of the MyDictionary.xaml file

```
<ResourceDictionary
    xmlns="http://schemas.microsoft.com/winfx/2006/xaml/presentation"
    xmlns:x="http://schemas.microsoft.com/winfx/2006/xaml"
```

```
xmlns:local="using:HeadedAppDesign">

<Thickness x:Key="DefaultMargin">10</Thickness>
<Thickness x:Key="NegativeMargin">-10</Thickness>

<Style x:Key="EllipsisButtonStyle"
       TargetType="Button"
       BasedOn="{StaticResource ColoredButtonStyle}">
    <Setter Property="Template">
        <Setter.Value>
            <ControlTemplate TargetType="Button">
                <Grid Margin="{StaticResource DefaultMargin}">
                    <Ellipse Fill="{TemplateBinding Background}"
                             Margin="{StaticResource NegativeMargin}" />
                    <ContentPresenter HorizontalAlignment="Center"
                                      VerticalAlignment="Center" />
                </Grid>
            </ControlTemplate>
        </Setter.Value>
    </Setter>
</Style>
</ResourceDictionary>
```

5. In the App.xaml file, replace the definition with an import of MyDictionary.xaml (see Listing 4-30).

LISTING 4-30   Importing resources from a file

```
<Application
    x:Class="HeadedAppDesign.App"
    xmlns="http://schemas.microsoft.com/winfx/2006/xaml/presentation"
    xmlns:x="http://schemas.microsoft.com/winfx/2006/xaml"
    xmlns:local="using:HeadedAppDesign">

    <Application.Resources>
        <ResourceDictionary>
            // This part does not change with respect to Listing 4-27

            <!--<Style x:Key="EllipsisButtonStyle"
                   TargetType="Button"
                   BasedOn="{StaticResource ColoredButtonStyle}">
                <Setter Property="Template">
                    <Setter.Value>
                        <ControlTemplate TargetType="Button">
                            <Grid Margin="10">
                                <Ellipse Fill="{TemplateBinding Background}"
                                         Margin="-10" />
                                <ContentPresenter HorizontalAlignment="Center"
                                                  VerticalAlignment="Center" />
                            </Grid>
                        </ControlTemplate>
                    </Setter.Value>
```

```
                </Setter>
            </Style>-->

        <ResourceDictionary.MergedDictionaries>
            <ResourceDictionary Source="MyDictionary.xaml" />
        </ResourceDictionary.MergedDictionaries>
      </ResourceDictionary>
    </Application.Resources>
</Application>
```

Naturally, the visual appearance of controls in the main page of the HeadedAppDesign project does not change. This example shows you that merged dictionaries offer a convenient way of sharing resources across applications and help to organize and isolate XAML files with respect to platform type or localization.

Accessing resources from the code-behind

Resources declared in XAML, either at the control-, page- or application-level scope, can be accessed from the code-behind procedures. Each resource is identified by its key (the value of the x:Key attribute) and can be accessed by using the appropriate instance of the ResourceDictionary class. Resources declared at the control- and page-level scope can be accessed using the Resources property of the control. The instance of ResourceDictionary, which stores resources scoped at the application level, is available through the Application.Current.Resources property.

We will adapt this mechanism in the HeadedAppDesign project to dynamically swap styles of the instance of the MyButton control. I thus introduce the following changes in the HeadedAppDesign application:

1. Define the OrangeButtonStyle XAML object under the Resources tag of the Page object declared in the MainPage.xaml file (Listing 4-31).

LISTING 4-31 OrangeButtonStyle definition

```
<Page.Resources>
    <Style x:Key="OrangeButtonStyle"
            TargetType="Button">
        <Setter Property="Background"
                Value="Orange" />
        <Setter Property="BorderBrush"
                Value="OrangeRed" />
        <Setter Property="BorderThickness"
                Value="2" />
        <Setter Property="FontSize"
                Value="26" />
    </Style>
</Page.Resources>
```

2. Extend the declaration of the MyButton control by using the Click attribute (Listing 4-32).

> **LISTING 4-32** Assigning an event handler
>
> ```
> <local:MyButton Click="MyButton_Click" />
> ```

3. Define the three methods from Listing 4-33 in the MainPage class (MainPage.xaml.cs).

> **LISTING 4-33** Procedures for retrieving an object from the resource collection, and also for style swapping
>
> ```csharp
> private Style GetStyleFromResourceDictionary(ResourceDictionary
> resourceDictionary, string styleKey)
> {
>     Style style = null;
>
>     if(resourceDictionary != null && !string.IsNullOrWhiteSpace(styleKey))
>     {
>         if(resourceDictionary.ContainsKey(styleKey))
>         {
>             style = resourceDictionary[styleKey] as Style;
>         }
>     }
>
>     return style;
> }
>
> private void SwapStyles(Button button)
> {
>     // Application-scoped resource
>     var coloredButtonStyle = GetStyleFromResourceDictionary(
>         Application.Current.Resources, "ColoredButtonStyle");
>
>     // Page-scoped resource
>     var ellipsisButtonStyle = GetStyleFromResourceDictionary(
>         Resources, "OrangeButtonStyle");
>
>     Style newStyle;
>     if (button.Style == coloredButtonStyle)
>     {
>         newStyle = ellipsisButtonStyle;
>     }
>     else
>     {
>         newStyle = coloredButtonStyle;
>     }
>
>     button.Style = newStyle;
> }
>
> private void MyButton_Click(object sender, RoutedEventArgs e)
> {
> ```

```
            MyButton myButton = sender as MyButton;

            if(myButton != null)
            {
                SwapStyles(myButton);
            }
        }
```

To safely get an instance to the object declared within the resource collection, I implemented a GetStyleFromResourceDictionary helper method. It accepts two arguments: an instance of the ResourceDictionary collection and the style identifier. The GetStyleFromResourceDictionary method checks whether the arguments are correct and then verifies that a given resource collection contains a specified style. If so, a reference to that object is returned.

Subsequently, the GetStyleFromResourceDictionary helper function is employed within the SwapStyles method to get styles identified by the ColoredButtonStyle and OrangeButtonStyle keys. The first one is scoped at the application level, so you look for it in the Application.Current. Resources collection. The OrangeButtonStyle object is defined in the resources of the MainPage. Therefore, you access this collection using a Resources property.

After the styles are read from the resources, use them to set the value of the Style property of the instance of the MyButton control. To see this working, you need to run the app and click the MyButton (My Content label) control several times. (See Figure 4-18.)

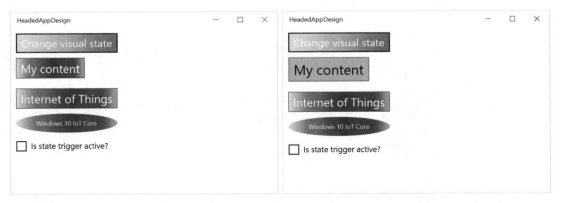

FIGURE 4-18 Dynamic style swapping from the code-behind. The visual appearance of the My content button changes after the button is clicked; compare the visual styles of the My content button on the two panels.

Default styles and theme resources

When the Style property of a given control is not set explicitly, the XAML controls use the default definitions for styles and theme resources. These default definitions can be found in two files: generic.xaml and themeresources.xaml. These files reside under the following folder of the Windows 10 SDK:

DesignTime\CommonConfiguration\Neutral\UAP\<SDK version>\Generic

The placeholder <SDK version> looks like 10.0.10586.0. Typically, the preceding folder exists under the Program Files (x86)\Windows Kits\10 path.

Interestingly, the definitions stored under the generic.xaml and themeresources.xaml files can be overridden or exploited to construct new styles. For instance, you can override the ApplicationPage-BackgroundThemeBrush theme resource by updating the ThemeDictionaries collection, whose original declaration is given in Listing 4-17, according to Listing 4-34. Consequently, the Background property of the StackPanel will change appropriately. You can check this by running the app or reviewing the design pane. I recommend you verify that the page background also follows the color theme.

LISTING 4-34   Overriding ApplicationPageBackgroundThemeBrush

```
<ResourceDictionary.ThemeDictionaries>
    <ResourceDictionary x:Key="Light">
        // As in Listing 4-17
        <SolidColorBrush x:Key="ApplicationPageBackgroundThemeBrush"
                         Color="LightGoldenrodYellow" />
    </ResourceDictionary>
    <ResourceDictionary x:Key="Dark">
        // As in Listing 4-17
        <SolidColorBrush x:Key="ApplicationPageBackgroundThemeBrush"
                         Color="DarkSlateGray" />
    </ResourceDictionary>
</ResourceDictionary.ThemeDictionaries>
```

Layouts

In principle, XAML controls can be positioned relative to each other by appropriate configuration of the Margin attribute. However, arranging controls using this method cannot guarantee a correct UI display on different screens. To solve this issue, XAML provides several controls for automatic layout. These include: StackPanel, Grid, and RelativePanel.

I have used StackPanel and Grid controls several times already. Here, I briefly summarize their usage and also introduce the RelativePanel control, which you can use to define adaptive UI layouts, or views that respond to dynamic changes of the window size in order to optimally arrange visual elements on the screen. In web programming, such adaptive layout changes are known as responsive web design.

StackPanel

StackPanel arranges child controls such that they are aligned in a horizontal or vertical line. This alignment orientation is configured using the Orientation attribute. By default, the orientation is Vertical.

The StackPanel controls can be nested, so you can use multiple instances of these controls to build a table consisting of child controls. To illustrate this, create a new blank UWP C# project, named Layouts.StackPanel and declare the MainPage as shown in Listing 4-35. These declarations arrange nine TextBlock controls in the array, consisting of three rows and three columns, so your view will look like the one you see in Figure 4-19.

LISTING 4-35 Nesting the StackPanel controls

```xml
<Page
    x:Class="Layouts.StackPanel.MainPage"
    xmlns="http://schemas.microsoft.com/winfx/2006/xaml/presentation"
    xmlns:x="http://schemas.microsoft.com/winfx/2006/xaml"
    xmlns:local="using:Layouts.StackPanel"
    xmlns:d="http://schemas.microsoft.com/expression/blend/2008"
    xmlns:mc="http://schemas.openxmlformats.org/markup-compatibility/2006"
    mc:Ignorable="d">

    <Page.Resources>
        <Style TargetType="StackPanel">
            <Setter Property="HorizontalAlignment"
                    Value="Center" />
            <Setter Property="VerticalAlignment"
                    Value="Center" />
            <Setter Property="Background"
                    Value="{ThemeResource ApplicationPageBackgroundThemeBrush}" />
        </Style>

        <Style TargetType="TextBlock">
            <Setter Property="FontSize"
                    Value="40" />
            <Setter Property="Margin"
                    Value="20" />
        </Style>
    </Page.Resources>

    <StackPanel>
        <StackPanel Orientation="Horizontal">
            <TextBlock Text="A" />
            <TextBlock Text="B" />
            <TextBlock Text="C" />
        </StackPanel>

        <StackPanel Orientation="Horizontal">
            <TextBlock Text="D" />
            <TextBlock Text="E" />
            <TextBlock Text="F" />
        </StackPanel>

        <StackPanel Orientation="Horizontal">
            <TextBlock Text="G" />
            <TextBlock Text="H" />
            <TextBlock Text="I" />
        </StackPanel>
    </StackPanel>
</Page>
```

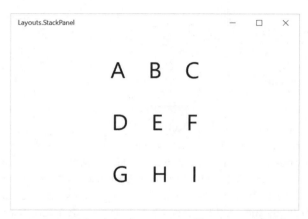

FIGURE 4-19 Visual elements arranged in an array using the StackPanel controls.

Grid

The Grid control represents the layout that allows you to arrange controls in a tabular form. The default Grid is composed of one row and one column. You can change this configuration by using two attributes: RowDefinitions and ColumnDefinitions. They constitute the collections of the RowDefinition and ColumnDefinition objects that allow you to define the properties of each row and column of the Grid. In particular, the number of elements of RowDefinitions and ColumnDefinitions specify the number of rows and columns, respectively. Moreover, each RowDefinition can be used to configure the Height property of the row. Similarly, the ColumnDefinition class contains the Width attribute for controlling the horizontal dimension of the column. The Height and Width attributes can be configured absolutely, relatively, or automatically.

To absolutely set the dimensions of the grid's rows and columns, you assign the numeric value (given in pixels) to the attributes Height and Width of the RowDefinition and ColumnDefinition, respectively. The corresponding cell of the Grid will have a fixed size. In this case, the child control, which has dimensions larger than the size of the cell, would be clipped. To automatically adjust the size of the Grid cell to the content's dimensions, you can set the Height and Width properties to Auto.

Dimensions of the particular row and column of the Grid control can be also adjusted relatively to other declarations of RowDefinition and ColumnDefinition for the given Grid. For this purpose, use the * symbol. It instructs the XAML parser that the particular row or column should use the remaining view area. For example, if the Grid contains two rows of fixed Height, say 150 px, and the screen height is equal to 400 px, then a third row, for which Height was set to *, would have a width of 100 px (400 − [2 × 150]), assuming the Grid is spanned onto the whole screen.

Specifically, the symbol * can be preceded by a numeric value. It has an effect on the view if dimensions of at least two rows or columns are parameterized in this way. In such a case, the available space is divided into appropriate fractions. For example, the declaration from Listing 4-36 divides a Grid control into two rows. The first one takes ¾, while the second uses ¼ of the available screen area.

LISTING 4-36 Relative configuration of the height of the row in the Grid control

```
<Grid.RowDefinitions>
    <RowDefinition Height="3*" />
    <RowDefinition Height="*" />
</Grid.RowDefinitions>
```

To summarize the preceding discussion, create a new blank UWP C# project named Layouts.Grid and modify the Page declaration according to Listing 4-37. Doing so creates the app view you see in Figure 4-20. Notice in the figure that the center column takes half of the available width, while each of the external columns use a quarter of the width. The height of the first row is fixed, so it does not change when you resize the window. The height of the last row, which is spanned across three columns, adjusts automatically to its content. Accordingly, the height of the last row changes after you change the size of the child control—for instance, the font size.

LISTING 4-37 Absolute, relative, and automatic row and column definitions of the Grid control

```
<Page
    x:Class="Layouts.Grid.MainPage"
    xmlns="http://schemas.microsoft.com/winfx/2006/xaml/presentation"
    xmlns:x="http://schemas.microsoft.com/winfx/2006/xaml"
    xmlns:local="using:Layouts.Grid"
    xmlns:d="http://schemas.microsoft.com/expression/blend/2008"
    xmlns:mc="http://schemas.openxmlformats.org/markup-compatibility/2006"
    mc:Ignorable="d">

    <Page.Resources>
        <Style TargetType="TextBlock">
            <Setter Property="FontSize"
                    Value="40" />
            <Setter Property="Padding"
                    Value="20" />
            <Setter Property="TextAlignment"
                    Value="Center" />
            <Setter Property="VerticalAlignment"
                    Value="Center" />
        </Style>

        <Style TargetType="Border">
            <Setter Property="BorderThickness"
                    Value="10" />
        </Style>

        <Style x:Key="InnerBorder"
               TargetType="Border">
            <Setter Property="BorderThickness"
                    Value="0,10,0,10"/>
        </Style>
    </Page.Resources>
```

```
    <Grid Background="{ThemeResource ApplicationPageBackgroundThemeBrush}">
        <Grid.RowDefinitions>
            <RowDefinition Height="150" />
            <RowDefinition Height="*" />
            <RowDefinition Height="Auto" />
        </Grid.RowDefinitions>

        <Grid.ColumnDefinitions>
            <ColumnDefinition Width="*" />
            <ColumnDefinition Width="2*" />
            <ColumnDefinition Width="*" />
        </Grid.ColumnDefinitions>

        <Border BorderBrush="Orange">
            <TextBlock Text="A" />
        </Border>

        <Border BorderBrush="Orange"
                Grid.Column="1"
                Style="{StaticResource InnerBorder}">
            <TextBlock Text="B" />
        </Border>

        <Border BorderBrush="Orange"
                Grid.Column="2">
            <TextBlock Text="C" />
        </Border>

        <Border BorderBrush="GreenYellow"
                Grid.Row="1"
                Grid.Column="0">
            <TextBlock Text="D" />
        </Border>

        <Border BorderBrush="GreenYellow"
                Grid.Row="1"
                Grid.Column="1"
                Style="{StaticResource InnerBorder}">
            <TextBlock Text="E" />
        </Border>

        <Border BorderBrush="GreenYellow"
                Grid.Row="1"
                Grid.Column="2">
            <TextBlock Text="F" />
        </Border>

        <Border BorderBrush="LightCoral"
                Grid.Row="2"
                Grid.ColumnSpan="3">
            <TextBlock Text="Spanned row" />
        </Border>
    </Grid>
</Page>
```

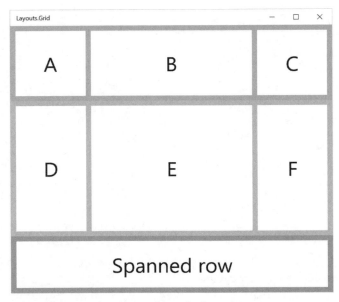

FIGURE 4-20 UI elements positioned using `Grid`.

You can now inspect the effect of the declarations from Listing 4-37 by changing the size of the app window. For instance, the height of the first and third rows does not change when you resize the window. This is because the height of the first row is fixed to 150 px, while the third row automatically adjusts to the dimension of the child controls. In this example, the third row contains a `TextBlock` control, so the only way to change the third row height is to modify the font size. On the other hand, the height of the middle row changes when you resize the app window. The middle row fills all available space between the first and third rows.

While resizing the app window, you can also note that the width of each column is adjusted automatically. However, the width fractions used by each column stay the same.

RelativePanel

`RelativePanel` implements the container for controls, in which child elements can be positioned relatively to each other. To this end the `RelativePanel` class implements a number of attributes that specify how the particular child control is aligned with respect to other visual elements embedded in the instance of the `RelativePanel` class.

The relative control positioning, when combined with adaptive and state-style triggers, becomes similar to responsive web design, in which the arrangement of the visual elements adjusts dynamically to the size of the application window.

I will now show an example layout declaration based on such a design by creating the new blank UWP C# project named Layouts.RelativePanel and declaring the `MainPage`, as shown in Listing 4-38. Listing 4-38 declares the page consisting of the three squares: red, orange, and yellow—each 200 × 200 px.

Initially, the red and orange squares form a horizontal line, while the yellow square is below the red one. That layout was achieved using the instance of the `RelativePanel` class, which hosts squares. To force the XAML parser to position the orange square next to the red one, I used the `RelativePanel.RightOf` attribute. Similarly, the `RelativePanel.Below` attribute was employed to position the yellow square below the red square.

LISTING 4-38 RelativePanel enables relative positioning of the child controls

```xml
<Page
    x:Class="Layouts.RelativePanel.MainPage"
    xmlns="http://schemas.microsoft.com/winfx/2006/xaml/presentation"
    xmlns:x="http://schemas.microsoft.com/winfx/2006/xaml"
    xmlns:local="using:Layouts.RelativePanel"
    xmlns:d="http://schemas.microsoft.com/expression/blend/2008"
    xmlns:mc="http://schemas.openxmlformats.org/markup-compatibility/2006"
    mc:Ignorable="d">

    <Page.Resources>
        <Style TargetType="Rectangle">
            <Setter Property="Width"
                    Value="200" />
            <Setter Property="Height"
                    Value="200" />
        </Style>
    </Page.Resources>

    <RelativePanel Background="{ThemeResource ApplicationPageBackgroundThemeBrush}">
        <VisualStateManager.VisualStateGroups>
            <VisualStateGroup x:Name="CommonStates">
                <VisualState x:Name="OneLineLayout">
                    <VisualState.StateTriggers>
                        <AdaptiveTrigger MinWindowWidth="600" />
                    </VisualState.StateTriggers>

                    <VisualState.Setters>
                        <Setter Target="YellowSquare.(RelativePanel.AlignTopWithPanel)"
                                Value="True" />
                        <Setter Target="YellowSquare.(RelativePanel.RightOf)"
                                Value="OrangeSquare" />
                    </VisualState.Setters>
                </VisualState>
            </VisualStateGroup>
        </VisualStateManager.VisualStateGroups>

        <Rectangle x:Name="RedSquare"
                   Fill="Red"/>

        <Rectangle x:Name="OrangeSquare"
                   Fill="Orange"
                   RelativePanel.RightOf="RedSquare"/>
```

```
            <Rectangle x:Name="YellowSquare"
                       Fill="Yellow"
                       RelativePanel.Below="RedSquare" />
    </RelativePanel>
</Page>
```

When the width of the window becomes equal to or larger than 600 px, the adaptive trigger activates the OneLineLayout visual state. In this state, the yellow square is placed next to the orange square by setting the RelativePanel.AlignTopWithPanel property to true and the RelativePanel.RightOf to OrangeSquare.

You can see the effect of such dynamic control rearrangement in Figure 4-21. Note that to dynamically adjust the view layout to respond to changes in window size requires no logic. These adjustments are performed automatically, and everything is declared within the view. Consequently, the UI developer can design user experiences (UX) independently of the code-behind programmer. This, in turn, helps to separate roles in the project, and the UI/UX programmer can design views for different platforms with virtually no need to know IoT.

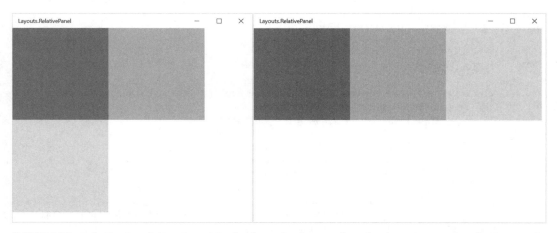

FIGURE 4-21 RelativePanel, together with adaptive style triggers, allows for dynamic control rearrangement in order to respond to app window size changes.

Events

An event, defined within a class, constitutes the mechanism of informing other application components (sometimes called listeners) of the occurrence of a specific situation. In the case of views, events are usually employed to notify listeners about actions taken by the user such as clicking a button, selecting an item from a drop-down list, or selecting a check box. In IoT applications, events are typically employed to send notifications about the status of background operations.

Events can be understood as the messages sent from the sender (provider), generating an event to the listener. Successful communication between the provider and the listener requires an appropriate interface. The listener should know what kind of messages it will receive from the sender.

This mechanism uses the delegate type, which corresponds to pointers to functions in C/C++. Basically the delegate declaration specifies the signature of a method, compatible with the particular event—the structure of the message.

The delegate declaration for the `Click` event of the `Button` control appears in Listing 4-39. This delegate matches methods, which do not return values and accept two arguments: `sender` of type `object` and `e` of type `RoutedEventArgs`. The first represents the provider raising an event, while the second transfers information about the event (event arguments).

The code snippet from Listing 4-39 also shows that, in general, the delegate declaration consists of the access modifier (`public`, `private`, `protected`, `internal`, or `protected internal`), the `delegate` keyword, and a signature, composed of a return data type, a name, and a method's formal parameter list.

LISTING 4-39 Declaration of the RoutedEventHandler delegate

```
public delegate void RoutedEventHandler(System.Object sender, RoutedEventArgs e);
```

Event handling

Events can be handled by associating with them the special methods known as event handlers. These functions implement a logic, which responds to notifications generated by providers. In many of the preceding sections I have used events, usually to handle button clicks. Event handlers were wired with corresponding events using XAML attributes. However, other aspects of events and event handling were omitted—until now.

Typically, the class, which raises an event, passes to the event handler additional information, which conforms to a delegate declaration. In terms of controls, the additional data includes an instance of the object that raises an event (`sender`) and an instance of the class that contains additional data characterizing an event. For example, the KeyUp event of the `TextBox` control sends to the listener an instance of the KeyRoutedEventArgs class, declared in the `Windows.UI.Xaml.Input` namespace. The instance of this class has a Key member, which stores an information about the key pressed by the user.

To explore this mechanism, I implement another UWP headed application using the following schema:

1. Create the new Blank App (Universal Windows) project, named EventsSample.

2. Modify the MainPage.xaml file according to Listing 4-40.

LISTING 4-40 Main view definition of the EventsSample application

```
<Page
    x:Class="EventsSample.MainPage"
    xmlns="http://schemas.microsoft.com/winfx/2006/xaml/presentation"
    xmlns:x="http://schemas.microsoft.com/winfx/2006/xaml"
```

```xml
        xmlns:local="using:EventsSample"
        xmlns:d="http://schemas.microsoft.com/expression/blend/2008"
        xmlns:mc="http://schemas.openxmlformats.org/markup-compatibility/2006"
        mc:Ignorable="d">

        <Page.Resources>
            <Thickness x:Key="DefaultMargin">10,5,10,10</Thickness>

            <Style TargetType="TextBox">
                <Setter Property="Margin"
                        Value="{StaticResource DefaultMargin}" />
            </Style>

            <Style TargetType="Button">
                <Setter Property="Margin"
                        Value="{StaticResource DefaultMargin}" />
            </Style>

            <Style TargetType="ListBox">
                <Setter Property="Margin"
                        Value="{StaticResource DefaultMargin}" />
            </Style>
        </Page.Resources>

        <Grid Background="{ThemeResource ApplicationPageBackgroundThemeBrush}">
            <Grid.RowDefinitions>
                <RowDefinition Height="Auto" />
                <RowDefinition Height="*" />
            </Grid.RowDefinitions>

            <StackPanel>
                <TextBox x:Name="IoTTextBox"
                         KeyUp="IoTTextBox_KeyUp" />
                <Button x:Name="ClearButton"
                        Content="Clear list"
                        Click="ClearButton_Click" />
            </StackPanel>

            <ListBox x:Name="IoTListBox"
                     Grid.Row="1" />
        </Grid>
    </Page>
```

3. Update the MainPage class (MainPage.xaml.cs) definition as shown in Listing 4-41.

LISTING 4-41   MainPage class of the EventsSample application

```csharp
using Windows.UI.Xaml;
using Windows.UI.Xaml.Controls;
using Windows.UI.Xaml.Input;
```

```
namespace EventsSample
{
    public sealed partial class MainPage : Page
    {
        public MainPage()
        {
            InitializeComponent();
        }

        private void ClearButton_Click(object sender, RoutedEventArgs e)
        {
            IoTListBox.Items.Clear();
        }

        private void IoTTextBox_KeyUp(object sender, KeyRoutedEventArgs e)
        {
            IoTListBox.Items.Add(e.Key.ToString());
        }
    }
}
```

After executing the EventsSample app, information about every character typed in the TextBox control is displayed as a list item. (See Figure 4-22.) This was achieved by reading the value of the Key property of the instance of KeyRoutedEventArgs. The latter property is of the enumeration type VirtualKey, which consists of 170 elements that represent each keystroke.

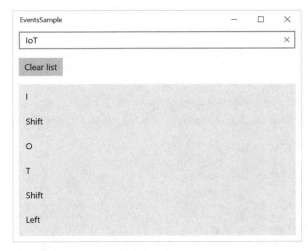

FIGURE 4-22 The list of keystrokes.

In the preceding example, the event handlers are associated with controls by using XAML attributes. Alternatively, the method can be coupled with an event from the code-behind by using the += operator. An event handler can be disassociated at any time with a use of the -= operator. This possibility is presented in the following example:

1. Complement `Page.Resources` with the style defined in Listing 4-42.

LISTING 4-42   Style definition for the CheckBox control

```
<Style TargetType="CheckBox">
    <Setter Property="IsChecked"
            Value="True" />
    <Setter Property="Margin"
            Value="{StaticResource DefaultMargin}" />
</Style>
```

2. Modify the `StackPanel` declaration of `MainPage` according to Listing 4-43.

LISTING 4-43   CheckBox declaration

```
<StackPanel>
    <TextBox x:Name="IoTTextBox" />
        <!--KeyUp="IoTTextBox_KeyUp" />-->

    <Button x:Name="ClearButton"
            Content="Clear list"
            Click="ClearButton_Click" />

    <CheckBox x:Name="KeyUpEventActiveCheckBox"
              Content="Is KeyUp event active?"
              Checked="KeyUpEventActiveCheckBox_Checked"
              Unchecked="KeyUpEventActiveCheckBox_Checked" />
</StackPanel>
```

3. Extend a definition of the `MainPage` class with the methods from Listing 4-44.

LISTING 4-44   Dynamic association and disassociation of the event handlers

```
private void KeyUpEventActiveCheckBox_Checked(object sender, RoutedEventArgs e)
{
    CheckBox checkBox = sender as CheckBox;

    bool isChecked = IsCheckBoxChecked(checkBox);

    if (isChecked)
    {
        IoTTextBox.KeyUp += IoTTextBox_KeyUp;
    }
    else
    {
        IoTTextBox.KeyUp -= IoTTextBox_KeyUp;
    }
}


private bool IsCheckBoxChecked(CheckBox checkBox)
```

```
{
    bool isChecked = false;

    if (checkBox != null)
    {
        if (checkBox.IsChecked.HasValue)
        {
            isChecked = checkBox.IsChecked.Value;
        }
    }

    return isChecked;
}
```

After compiling and executing the EventsSample app, the KeyUp event of the TextBox control will be handled if the CheckBox control is checked. Note that I removed the attribute KeyUp from the declaration of the TextBox control. It follows that associating an event handler using += adds an extra method, which is invoked whenever the particular event is raised. Therefore, the KeyUpEventActive-CheckBox_Checked method would be called twice. To avoid such a situation, I removed the KeyUp attribute of the TextBox control.

In Listing 4-43, the same event handler was associated with two events: Checked and Unchecked. This was possible since both events use the same delegate declaration—KeyEventHandler. (See Listing 4-45.) In the other words, the structure of the message sent from the provider to a listener is the same for both events.

LISTING 4-45   Declaration of the KeyEventHandler delegate

```
public delegate void KeyEventHandler(System.Object sender, KeyRoutedEventArgs e);
```

Event handlers and visual designer

Associating methods with events using XAML attributes requires a priori knowledge of the event name. This can be difficult, especially when you want to use an untypical event. Use the Properties window, which is shown in Figure 4-8, to find what you need.

The Properties window shows the list of properties and the list of events raised by the particular control. To activate the list of events for the given control, you simply click the lightning bolt icon, which appears in the top right corner of the Properties window. Figure 4-23 shows you the result. In this mode, you can see the list of all events and the corresponding event handlers. If you double-click one of the empty text boxes, Visual Studio automatically generates an empty definition of the method handling the selected event. You can check this independently using any event you want.

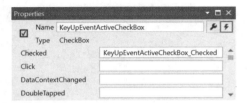

FIGURE 4-23 Events of the CheckBox control.

Event propagation

XAML view definitions possess a hierarchical structure. Hence, events raised by XAML controls can be propagated to parent controls. This mechanism is defined as event routing and can be adapted for handling events of child controls using an event handler associated with the parent control. In the declarations of most event delegates, the type name of the second argument contains the Routed component (see Listing 4-45).

Here's an example of how event routing may influence the interactivity of headed IoT apps. I modify the EventsSample app as follows:

1. Open the MainPage.xaml file and then update the Grid control definition according to Listing 4-46.

LISTING 4-46 Updated definition of the MainPage of the EventsSample project

```xaml
<Grid Background="{ThemeResource ApplicationPageBackgroundThemeBrush}"
    Tapped="Grid_Tapped">
    <Grid.RowDefinitions>
        <RowDefinition Height="Auto" />
        <RowDefinition Height="*" />
    </Grid.RowDefinitions>

    <StackPanel>
        <TextBox x:Name="IoTTextBox" />

        <StackPanel Orientation="Horizontal">
            <Button x:Name="ClearButton"
                    Content="Clear list"
                    Click="ClearButton_Click" />

            <AppBarButton Icon="Globe"
                          Tapped="AppBarButton_Tapped"/>
        </StackPanel>

        <CheckBox x:Name="KeyUpEventActiveCheckBox"
                  Content="Is KeyUp event active?"
                  Checked="KeyUpEventActiveCheckBox_Checked"
                  Unchecked="KeyUpEventActiveCheckBox_Checked" />
    </StackPanel>
```

```
        <ListBox x:Name="IoTListBox"
                 Grid.Row="1" />
</Grid>
```

2. In the MainPage.xaml.cs, supplement the definition of the MainPage class by using the four methods from Listing 4-47.

LISTING 4-47 Tracking an event route by displaying type names of controls participating in the event routing process

```
private void Grid_Tapped(object sender, TappedRoutedEventArgs e)
{
    DisplayEventRoute(sender, e.OriginalSource);
}

private void AppBarButton_Tapped(object sender, TappedRoutedEventArgs e)
{
    IoTListBox.Items.Add("AppBarButton tapped event");
}

private void DisplayEventRoute(object sender, object originalSource)
{
    string routeString = string.Empty;

    routeString = "Sender: " + GetControlTypeName(sender);
    routeString += ", original source: " + GetControlTypeName(originalSource);

    IoTListBox.Items.Add(routeString);
}

private string GetControlTypeName(object control)
{
    string typeName = "Unknown";

    if(control != null)
    {
        typeName = control.GetType().Name;
    }

    return typeName;
}
```

I supplemented the UI of the EventsSample app by declaring the AppBarButton with a globe icon. This control has an associated event handler for the Tapped event, which is raised when the user clicks a control using a pointer or touch gesture (in the case of touch-enabled IoT devices). To horizontally align the AppBarButton with a button of Clear label, I used an additional StackPanel control. The declaration of the Grid control was extended by the Tapped attribute in order to associate the Grid_Tapped event handler with the Tapped event.

The method `Grid_Tapped` displays the type name of the controls participating in the event routing. Namely, it adds to the list box a string that consists of the type name of the control sending the event information and the type name of the original event source, i.e., the actual control that raised the event.

After launching the app, you can notice that clicking the `AppBarButton` fires the Tapped event. As a result, the literal `AppBarButton tapped event` is displayed in the list box. However, in Figure 4-24 you see that an additional item is added to the list box. This element presents the event route. It means that clicking the globe icon raised the Tapped event of both the `AppBarButton` and `Grid` controls. The Tapped event was propagated from the child (`AppBarButton`) to a parent control (`Grid`).

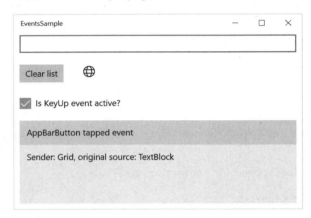

FIGURE 4-24   Event propagation.

Note that the list box shows a `TextBlock` as the control type of the control raising the event. This is because the default template of the `AppBarButton` control defined in the generic.xaml consists of the `TextBlock`.

The event propagation to the parent control can be disabled. To inform the runtime that an event is handled and should not be propagated to the parent control, you can set the `Handled` property of the `TappedRoutedEventArgs` to `true`, as shown in Listing 4-48.

LISTING 4-48   Disabling event routing

```
private void AppBarButton_Tapped(object sender, TappedRoutedEventArgs e)
{
    IoTListBox.Items.Add("AppBarButton tapped event");
    e.Handled = true;
}
```

Declaring and raising custom events

Custom events are declared as members of the code-behind classes. In particular, in the case of C# an event declaration is composed of the field access modifier, an event keyword, a delegate type, and an event name. Additionally, the event declaration can be supplemented with the following keywords: `static`, `virtual`, `sealed`, or `abstract`. The meaning of these keywords is the same as in the case of other class members and classes. Namely, events marked as `static` can be used without instantiating a class, while the `virtual` keyword specifies that derived classes can override the event. This is not possible if the event is marked as `sealed`. Any `abstract` events have to be implemented by derived types.

In IoT programming, events can be used to report a progress or status of the background operation. In the next example, I simulate such a background operation by implementing a Task, which generates a random number and passes it to listeners through the custom event. Here is the list of changes required to implement the EventsSample app:

1. Bring up the Add New Item dialog box by clicking the **Add Class** option in the **Project** menu.

2. Type **RandomNumberEventArgs.cs** in the Name text box of the Add New Item dialog box. Close the dialog box by clicking the **Add** button. A new file will be added to the project. Edit it according to Listing 4-49.

LISTING 4-49   Definition of the custom class used to pass data to the event listener

```
using System;

namespace EventsSample
{
    public class RandomNumberEventArgs : EventArgs
    {
        private Random r = new Random();

        public double Value { get; private set; }

        public RandomNumberEventArgs()
        {
            Value = r.NextDouble();
        }
    }
}
```

3. Open the MainPage.xaml.cs file and import two namespaces: `System` and `System.Threading.Tasks` by placing the following procedures in the file header:

```
using System;
using System.Threading.Tasks;
```

4. Supplement the definition of the `MainPage` class with the members and methods from Listing 4-50.

LISTING 4-50   Raising and handling of the custom event

```
private const int msDelayTime = 500;
public event EventHandler<RandomNumberEventArgs> RandomNumberGenerated = delegate
{ };

private async void MainPage_RandomNumberGenerated(object sender,
    RandomNumberEventArgs e)
```

```
{
    await Dispatcher.RunIdleAsync((a) => { IoTListBox.Items.Add(e.Value); });
}

private void RaiseCustomEventButton_Click(object sender, RoutedEventArgs e)
{
    Task.Run(() => {
        Task.Delay(msDelayTime).Wait();

        RandomNumberGenerated(this, new RandomNumberEventArgs());
    });
}
```

5. Update the default constructor of the MainPage class as shown in Listing 4-51.

LISTING 4-51   Associating an event handler with the custom event

```
public MainPage()
{
    InitializeComponent();

    RandomNumberGenerated += MainPage_RandomNumberGenerated;
}
```

6. Finally, in the MainPage.xaml file insert a Button declaration from Listing 4-52 just below the markup defining the AppBarButton.

LISTING 4-52   Button declaration for activating simulated background operation

```
<Button x:Name="RaiseCustomEventButton"
        Content="Raise custom event"
        Click="RaiseCustomEventButton_Click" />
```

In general, the event declaration can use arbitrary delegates. However, in the declarations from Listing 4-50, I used the EventHandler delegate. It simplifies the event declaration by providing delegates that conform to the UWP API. Namely, these delegates hold a reference to a method, which does not return any value and accepts two arguments. The first one is used to pass to the listener an instance of the class representing the provider. The second argument contains an instance of the class storing additional event data. In the preceding example (Listing 4-50), additional data is composed of the randomly generated number, which is passed using an instance of the RandomNumberEventArgs class. The latter derives from the type EventArgs.

In general, passing a single value does not require declaring a new class. However, it is good practice to package a value into a class. Such an approach helps you further maintain and extend the source code.

The random value is generated in the background after a fixed delay, which emulates a finite time required by the sensor to read data. After that delay, I raise the RandomNumberEvent by simply invoking the associated delegate. Additionally, I send to the listeners the instance of the MainPage class and the new instance of the RandomNumberEventArgs. The randomly generated number is stored in the Value member of an instance of the RandomNumberEventArgs class.

Normally, you are obligated to check whether any listener is attached to the event before you can invoke a delegate. To this end, you can write the following conditional statement:

```
if (RandomNumberGenerated != null)
{
    RandomNumberGenerated(this, new RandomNumberEventArgs());
}
```

However, in Listing 4-50, I assigned an empty delegate to the event. This ensures that RandomNumberGenerated event always has the associated event handler, although this default handler does not do anything. Therefore, the preceding verification is not required.

Interestingly, C# 6.0 introduces a feature that simplifies delegate invocation. You can check whether a delegate has an associated event using the null-conditional operator (?.) like so:

```
RandomNumberGenerated?.Invoke(this, new RandomNumberEventArgs());
```

Custom events are consumed by listeners in exactly the same way as regular events—namely, by linking an event with an appropriate handler. (See Listing 4-50.) In this example, the custom event RandomNumberGenerated is associated with the MainPage_RandomNumberGenerated method. So, after you run the app and click the Raise Custom Event button, the randomly generated value is displayed in the ListBox control with a half-second delay.

Data binding

Data binding is the technique for linking two properties—the source and the target—such that the target property is automatically updated whenever the source property changes. This *one-way binding* releases the developer from the necessity of writing logic for rewriting values from the source to the target property.

Data binding can be also configured to operate in a bidirectional mode (*two-way binding*). In this case, any changes to the target property also update the source property. There is also a *one-time binding*, in which the target property is updated just once, after the first modification of the source property.

In terms of UI design, data binding simplifies the process of event handling and presenting data to the user. Namely, the data received from the sensors can be stored in the class properties and bound to the UI such that controls displaying sensor readings are automatically updated. On the other hand, you do not need to hook up the special event handlers, which aim only at reading values entered by the user. They can be bound to the appropriate properties. Consequently, the amount of code-behind is reduced.

In several of the preceding examples I have used one-way binding to link two control properties. Here, I describe this technique in more detail and discuss converters and binding UI elements to class members.

Binding control properties

You can link two control properties using a {Binding} markup extension, which is declared in the Windows.UI.Xaml.Data namespace. The Binding class, implementing the {Binding} markup extension, possesses several public properties. The most important is the Path property, which indicates the source property of the data binding association. The value assigned to the ElementName property sets the source control, while the FallbackValue property can be used to set up a value that's displayed when the XAML parser is unable to obtain a value through data binding. The Mode property indicates the binding direction, described by one of the values of the BindingMode enumeration: OneTime (for one-time binding), OneWay (for one-way binding), or TwoWay (for two-way binding).

To illustrate the use of the Binding class attributes, create a new project, DataBinding, using a Blank App (Universal Windows) template. The declaration of the MainPage (MainPage.xaml) of this app is given in Listing 4-53.

LISTING 4-53   One-way and two-way data binding of control properties

```
<Page
    x:Class="DataBinding.MainPage"
    xmlns="http://schemas.microsoft.com/winfx/2006/xaml/presentation"
    xmlns:x="http://schemas.microsoft.com/winfx/2006/xaml"
    xmlns:local="using:DataBinding"
    xmlns:d="http://schemas.microsoft.com/expression/blend/2008"
    xmlns:mc="http://schemas.openxmlformats.org/markup-compatibility/2006"
    mc:Ignorable="d">

    <Page.Resources>
        <Thickness x:Key="DefaultMargin">20</Thickness>

        <Style TargetType="Slider">
            <Setter Property="Margin"
                    Value="{StaticResource DefaultMargin}" />
        </Style>

        <Style TargetType="TextBox">
            <Setter Property="Margin"
                    Value="{StaticResource DefaultMargin}" />
            <Setter Property="MaxWidth"
                    Value="100" />
            <Setter Property="FontSize"
                    Value="25" />
            <Setter Property="TextAlignment"
                    Value="Center" />
        </Style>
```

```
        <Style TargetType="TextBlock">
            <Setter Property="Margin"
                    Value="{StaticResource DefaultMargin}" />
            <Setter Property="HorizontalAlignment"
                    Value="Center" />
            <Setter Property="FontSize"
                    Value="40" />
        </Style>
    </Page.Resources>

    <StackPanel Background="{ThemeResource ApplicationPageBackgroundThemeBrush}">
        <Slider x:Name="MsDelaySlider" />

        <TextBox Text="{Binding Value, ElementName=MsDelaySlider, Mode=TwoWay,
            FallbackValue=0}"/>

        <TextBlock Text="{Binding Value, ElementName=MsDelaySlider}"/>
    </StackPanel>
</Page>
```

After running the DataBinding app and moving the Slider control, other UI elements, particularly the TextBox and TextBlock controls, are updated automatically. This effect, illustrated in Figure 4-25, is accomplished using a one-way data binding. On the other hand, the Text property of the TextBox control is bound to the Value attribute of the Slider control using a two-way binding. Hence, the value presented by a Slider control is updated automatically whenever a user enters a new numeric value to the TextBox control. While running this example, take into account that the TextBox control informs listeners about the value change after it loses the focus. This means that you need to take the pointer out of the TextBox control by clicking a tab or tapping (clicking) somewhere in the app window.

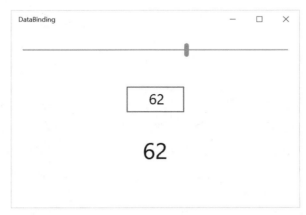

FIGURE 4-25   Data binding: TextBlock and TextBox controls are updated automatically when a user moves a slider along the track.

Note that the Path property is the default attribute of the {Binding} markup extension, and thus you are not required to explicitly write an assignment of the Path attribute. Namely, the declaration of the data binding can read as

```
<TextBlock Text="{Binding Value, ElementName=MsDelaySlider}"/>
```

instead of

```
<TextBlock Text="{Binding Path=Value, ElementName=MsDelaySlider}"/>
```

Converters

In the preceding section, I showed you that a data binding mechanism automatically converts the value stored in the Value attribute of the Slider control, which is of type double, to its string representation that is accepted by the Text properties of the TextBox and TextBlock controls. This also works in the opposite direction, i.e. string values entered into TextBox are converted to numeric values. Such a default converter may not always be feasible, especially for converting values of custom or complex types.

The XAML data-binding engine allows you to specify a custom converter using a Converter attribute of the {Binding} markup extension. A class-implementing custom converter should implement the IValueConverter interface. The latter consists of two methods: Convert and ConvertBack. By implementing these methods, you can modify data passed through the data-binding link. The Convert method is called when the data is transferred from the source to the target property, while the ConvertBack method is invoked as the value passes from the target to the source property. Naturally, the ConvertBack method is called only when data binding is setup in the two-way mode.

In this section, I show you how to implement NumericToMsDelayConverter, which supplements the numerical value with the ms suffix. Subsequently, we use this converter to display values in the TextBlock control. This procedure consists of the following steps:

1. Using the Add New Item dialog box, add to the project a NumericToMsDelayConverter.cs, and modify its content according to Listing 4-54.

LISTING 4-54   Converter definition
```
using System;
using Windows.UI.Xaml.Data;

namespace DataBinding
{
    public class NumericToMsDelayConverter : IValueConverter
    {
        private const string msSymbol = "ms";

        public object Convert(object value, Type targetType,
            object parameter, string language)
        {
            return string.Format("{0} {1}", value, msSymbol);
        }

        public object ConvertBack(object value, Type targetType,
            object parameter, string language)
        {
```

```
            throw new NotImplementedException();
        }
    }
}
```

2. Declare the `NumericToMsDelayConverter` in the App.xaml file as shown in Listing 4-55.

LISTING 4-55   Declaration of custom converter as a static resource

```
<Application
    x:Class="DataBinding.App"
    xmlns="http://schemas.microsoft.com/winfx/2006/xaml/presentation"
    xmlns:x="http://schemas.microsoft.com/winfx/2006/xaml"
    xmlns:local="using:DataBinding"
    RequestedTheme="Light">

    <Application.Resources>
        <local:NumericToMsDelayConverter x:Key="NumericToMsDelayConverter" />
    </Application.Resources>
</Application>
```

3. Use the `NumericToMsDelayConverter` in the declaration of the `TextBlock` control. (See Listing 4-53.) The updated declaration of this control is given in Listing 4-56.

LISTING 4-56   Using a custom converter during data binding

```
<TextBlock Text="{Binding Value,
            ElementName=MsDelaySlider,
            Converter={StaticResource NumericToMsDelayConverter}}" />
```

When you run the app, the data passed using a binding is transferred through the `NumericToMs-DelayConverter`. Accordingly, the value of the `Slider` control is converted to its text representation. Moreover, the ms suffix is attached to the resulting string. `NumericToMsDelayConverter` is used in the one-way binding, so the `ConvertBack` method is not implemented here.

Binding to the fields

Control properties can be also bound to the fields of the code-behind classes. You can define such a link using the `{x:Bind}` markup extension, which works a lot like the `{Binding}` markup extension, but there's an important difference between the two: the binding, declared using `{x:Bind}`, is compiled with the code-behind. For this reason, any typos are resolved during the compilation and not at runtime as in the case of the `{Binding}` markup extension.

Moreover, `{Binding}` requires you to bind the control property to the `DataContext` field of the Page class. In contrast, `{x:Bind}` allows any of the code-behind objects to act as the binding source.

In this section, I associate the MsDelay property of the MainPage with the label (TextBlock control) of the UI declaration. The value of MsDelay will be incremented in the background, and the current value will be displayed in the TextBlock control. The described functionality requires the following modifications of the DataBinding project:

1. Modify the MainPage.xaml.cs as shown in Listing 4-57.

LISTING 4-57 Notification about changes of the property bound to the UI are sent using events

```
using System;
using System.ComponentModel;
using System.Runtime.CompilerServices;
using System.Threading.Tasks;
using Windows.UI.Xaml;
using Windows.UI.Xaml.Controls;

namespace DataBinding
{
    public sealed partial class MainPage : Page, INotifyPropertyChanged
    {
        private int msDelay;

        public int MsDelay
        {
            get
            {
                return msDelay;
            }
            private set
            {
                msDelay = value;
                OnPropertyChanged();
            }
        }

        public event PropertyChangedEventHandler PropertyChanged = delegate { };

        public MainPage()
        {
            InitializeComponent();
        }

        public void OnPropertyChanged([CallerMemberName] string propertyName = "")
        {
            PropertyChanged(this, new PropertyChangedEventArgs(propertyName));
        }

        private async void Button_Click(object sender, RoutedEventArgs e)
        {
            Button button = sender as Button;

            if (button != null)
            {
                button.IsEnabled = false;
```

```
                    await BackgroundAction();

                    button.IsEnabled = true;
                }
            }

            private Task BackgroundAction()
            {
                const int msDelay = 50;
                const int iterationsCount = 100;

                return Task.Run(async () =>
                {
                    for (int i = 1; i <= iterationsCount; i++)
                    {
                        await Dispatcher.RunIdleAsync((a) => { MsDelay = i; });

                        Task.Delay(msDelay).Wait();
                    }
                });
            }
        }
    }
```

2. Update the XAML declaration of the MainPage (MainPage.xaml file) according to Listing 4-58.

LISTING 4-58   Declaration of the compiled binding

```
<StackPanel Background="{ThemeResource ApplicationPageBackgroundThemeBrush}">
    <Slider x:Name="MsDelaySlider" />
    <TextBox Text="{Binding Path=Value, ElementName=MsDelaySlider, Mode=TwoWay,
FallbackValue=0}" />

    <!--<TextBlock Text="{Binding Value, ElementName=MsDelaySlider,
        Converter={StaticResource NumericToMsDelayConverter}}" />-->

    <TextBlock Text="{x:Bind MsDelay, Converter={StaticResource
        NumericToMsDelayConverter}, Mode=OneWay}" />

    <Button Content="Run task"
            Click="Button_Click" />
</StackPanel>
```

When you run the app and click a Run Task button, the underlying background operation starts. It changes the value of the MsDelay property from 1 to 100. As a result, the label of the MainPage displays the current value of the MsDelay property. (See Figure 4-26.)

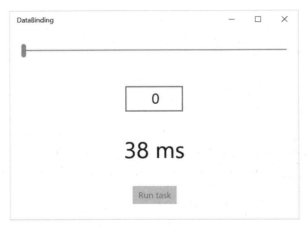

FIGURE 4-26 The label is updated by changing the property value from the code-behind.

Because the MsDelay property is changed by a background thread, you need to ensure that the UI element is accessed by the main thread. So, the MsDelay is updated through a Dispatcher class.

Each declaration containing the {x:Bind} markup extension is compiled. This means that the XAML declarations responsible for updating the UI are automatically turned into C# code, which together with other C# statements are subsequently transformed into a binary file. The intermediate C# code containing compiled binding can be found under the intermediate obj folder. You can find there the file <PageName>.g.cs, where <PageName> corresponds to the view name. In the case of the DataBinding app, this file is MainPage.g.cs. If you open this file, you can find the methods responsible for updating the Text property of the TextBlock control according to the MsDelay attribute. These methods look like Listing 4-59. You see that this code simply updates the Text property of the TextBlock control using the NumericToMsDelayConverter defined previously. In particular, you see that the automatically generated C# code, as you'd expect, invokes the Convert method of the NumericToMsDelayConverter class.

LISTING 4-59 Compiled binding

```
private void Update_(global::DataBinding.MainPage obj, int phase)
{
    this.bindingsTracking.UpdateChildListeners_(obj);
    if (obj != null)
    {
        if ((phase & (NOT_PHASED | DATA_CHANGED | (1 << 0))) != 0)
        {
            this.Update_MsDelay(obj.MsDelay, phase);
        }
    }
}

private void Update_MsDelay(global::System.Int32 obj, int phase)
{
    if((phase & ((1 << 0) | NOT_PHASED | DATA_CHANGED)) != 0)
```

```
    {
        XamlBindingSetters.Set_Windows_UI_Xaml_Controls_TextBlock_Text(this.obj3,
            (global::System.String)this.LookupConverter("NumericToMsDelayConverter").
            Convert(obj, typeof(global::System.String), null, null), null);
    }
}
```

If you go further, you can easily notice that the `Update_` method from Listing 4-59 makes a call to the `UpdateChildListeners_` instance method of the `MainPage_obj1_BindingsTracking` class. This class implements a listener that consumes messages propagated using the `INotifyPropertyChanged` interface, which consists of the single event `PropertyChanged`. This event is invoked to inform the UI about changes of the properties participating in the data binding.

By analyzing the definition of the `UpdateChildListeners_` method —see Listing 4-60—you can see that this function associates the `PropertyChanged_` handler with the `PropertyChanged` event. The `PropertyChanged_` method invokes the `Update_MsDelay` method from Listing 4-59.

LISTING 4-60 Data binding uses events to receive notifications about property changes
```
public void UpdateChildListeners_(global::DataBinding.MainPage obj)
{
    MainPage_obj1_Bindings bindings;
    if(WeakRefToBindingObj.TryGetTarget(out bindings))
    {
        if (bindings.dataRoot != null)
        {
            ((global::System.ComponentModel.INotifyPropertyChanged)bindings.dataRoot).
                PropertyChanged -= PropertyChanged_;
        }
        if (obj != null)
        {
            bindings.dataRoot = obj;
            ((global::System.ComponentModel.INotifyPropertyChanged)obj).PropertyChanged
            += PropertyChanged_;
        }
    }
}

public void PropertyChanged_(object sender,
    global::System.ComponentModel.PropertyChangedEventArgs e)
{
    MainPage_obj1_Bindings bindings;
    if(WeakRefToBindingObj.TryGetTarget(out bindings))
    {
        string propName = e.PropertyName;
        global::DataBinding.MainPage obj = sender as global::DataBinding.MainPage;
        if (global::System.String.IsNullOrEmpty(propName))
        {
            if (obj != null)
```

```
        {
            bindings.Update_MsDelay(obj.MsDelay, DATA_CHANGED);
        }
    }
    else
    {
        switch (propName)
        {
            case "MsDelay":
            {
                if (obj != null)
                {
                    bindings.Update_MsDelay(obj.MsDelay, DATA_CHANGED);
                }
                break;
            }
            default:
                break;
        }
    }
}
}
```

In order to inform the UI about updates of the `MsDelay` property, I implemented the `INotify-PropertyChanged` interface by defining an event `PropertyChanged` in the `MainPage` class. (See Listing 4-57.) This event is fired whenever a set accessor of the `MsDelay` property is used. As a result, the listener of `MainPage_obj1_BindingsTracking` consumes this information and appropriately updates the `TextBlock` control.

In Listing 4-58, I explicitly set the `Mode` of the `{x:Bind}` markup extension to `OneWay`. By default, a binding declared using the `{x:Bind}` markup extension works as the one-time binding, so the `Text` property would be updated only once. In contrast, for the one-way binding associated using the `{Binding}` markup extension, you are not required to explicitly set the `Mode` attribute, since it is `OneWay` by default. This comment is especially important if you worked previously with the `{Binding}` markup. You may probably need to change some of your habits after switching to `{x:Bind}`.

Binding to methods

If you set the target and minimum platform versions to the Windows 10 Anniversary Edition (10.0; Build 14393), you can bind control properties to methods. You can use this mechanism to bind multiple control properties because UWP does not support multi-value binding as WPF does. This section shows how to extend the DataBinding app to calculate a sum of two slider values using binding to methods:

1. Open the DataBinding properties dialog box, click the **Application** tab, and change the Target Version and Min Version settings to **Windows 10 Anniversary Edition (10.0; Build 14393)**, as shown in Figure 4-27. When you do, a pop-up dialog box appears, informing you that a project must be closed and reopened to update these settings. Accept this to proceed.

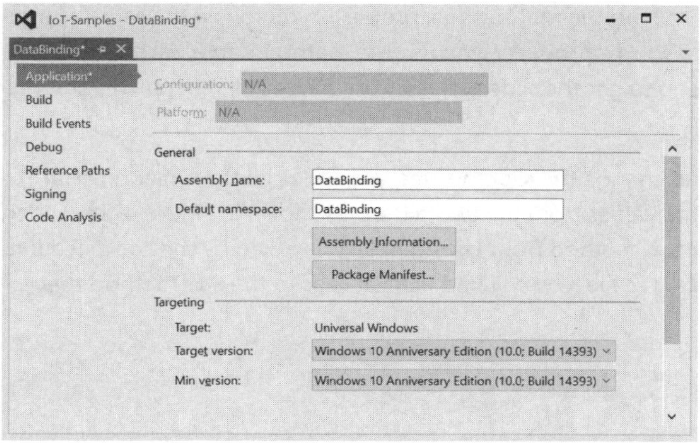

FIGURE 4-27 Configuring the target and minimum version.

2. Open the MainPage.xaml file and extend the `StackPanel` declaration as shown in Listing 4-61.

LISTING 4-61 Binding the property value to the method

```
<StackPanel Background="{ThemeResource ApplicationPageBackgroundThemeBrush}">
    <Slider x:Name="MsDelaySlider" />

    <Slider x:Name="SecondSlider" />

    <TextBox Text="{Binding Path=Value, ElementName=MsDelaySlider, Mode=TwoWay,
        FallbackValue=0}" />

    <!--<TextBlock Text="{Binding Value, ElementName=MsDelaySlider,
        Converter={StaticResource NumericToMsDelayConverter}}" />-->
    <TextBlock Text="{x:Bind MsDelay,
        Converter={StaticResource NumericToMsDelayConverter}, Mode=OneWay}" />

    <TextBlock Text="{x:Bind Sum(MsDelaySlider.Value, SecondSlider.Value),
        Mode=OneWay}" />

    <Button Content="Run task"
            Click="Button_Click" />
</StackPanel>
```

3. In MainPage.xaml.cs, implement a new method, shown in Listing 4-62, below the definition of `BackgroundAction` (refer to Listing 5-47).

LISTING 4-62 A simple summing function, bound to the UI

```
private string Sum(double val1, double val2)
{
    return "Sum: " + (val1 + val2).ToString();
}
```

As shown in Listing 4-61, to bind the method to a property, you follow the same approach as used before. However, instead of a source property, you use the method name. All method arguments are passed as in the C# code. Here, to get the slider values, I use named slider controls and then access their `Value` property.

When you run the app and change the slider values, you will note that an additional `TextBlock` control displays the sum of the values from the two sliders (as shown in Figure 4-28). Whenever you change the slider position, a `Sum` method from Listing 4-62 is invoked by the compiled binding. If you now revisit the MainPage.g.cs file, you will find explicit calls to the `Sum` method there.

FIGURE 4-28 Additional text block displays a sum of values set by two sliders.

Summary

In this chapter I described methods for constructing the UI for headed IoT devices (and also for the UWP apps). I covered a broad range of aspects, starting from visual designer, control declarations, and resources, continuing through layouts and adaptive triggers, and ending with data binding. These topics are of great importance for designing the UI and show the great power of XAML in terms of UI design.

Note that XAML allows you to embed fundamental logic inside the UI declaration. Common tasks like property rewriting should not be contained in the code-behind. Instead, the corresponding binding should be defined. Definitions of the control's visual appearance can be contained in XAML resources. Subsequently, the visual states can be triggered using the adaptive state triggers or static methods of the `VisualStateManager` class. Basically, you should tend to separate the logic from the UI as much as possible and, as a result, your UI and logic can be developed in parallel by different group members. Moreover, such an approach improves the portability of your app, because XAML is also employed to design the UI of the cross-platform applications developed using Xamarin.Forms. This topic is covered in the book *Creating Mobile Apps with Xamarin.Forms* written by Charles Petzold.

Device programming

Part I showed you the fundamentals of IoT programming. Part II uses these fundamentals to explore the capabilities of the UWP and Windows 10 IoT Core in relation to device programming for sensor reading, controlling a device using buttons or a joystick, connectivity, audio, and image processing. Chapter 5, "Reading data from sensors," is dedicated to sensors, which can be used to implement robot senses. I describe useful classes for performing operations on bits and bytes (`BitConverter` and `BitArray`) to serialize and transfer data, and I show how to read and interpret data from a broad range of sensors measuring temperature, humidity, barometric pressure, acceleration, and magnetic field.

In Chapter 6, "Input and output," I describe hardware interrupts and methods for controlling a device using buttons and a joystick, combining these elements with an LED array to implement simple I/O devices for the IoT. Chapter 7, "Audio processing," presents the speech synthesis and recognition capabilities of Windows IoT Core. I describe the fundamentals of sound waves and several audio processing routines in the frequency domain to calculate the spectrum of the audio signal. The spectrum will be subsequently divided into bands and displayed on the LED array. These functionalities implement the sample application, in which LEDs blink in rhythm with music.

Chapter 8, "Image processing," covers the machine vision applications. I show you how to implement a vision system consisting of a USB camera, UWP face detection, and tracking procedures. I show you how to build a custom image-processing app, in which images acquired from a USB camera will be processed to find and recognize various objects.

Chapter 9, "Connecting devices," is devoted to connectivity. I present a broad range of interfaces for IoT device connectivity, showing you how to implement sample applications that enable devices to talk to each other by using wired and wireless communication modules.

Chapter 10, "Motors," presents the fundamentals of motor control, which you'll use to smoothly control motors for adaptive device control or, more generally, to build movable IoT devices, including robots.

In Chapter 11, "Device learning," I show how to incorporate artificial intelligence in your IoT device using Microsoft Cognitive Services and Azure Machine Learning solutions. Specifically, I explain how to implement an app capable of recognizing human emotions and how to implement a custom anomaly detector. So, you'll learn how to make intelligent, autonomous IoT devices.

CHAPTER 5

Reading data from sensors

Modern sensors are manufactured as microelectromechanical systems (MEMS), in which very small intrinsic elements are deflected due to changes in a specific physical observable value— temperature, pressure, position in space, and so on. These changes are typically reported using electric signals, which are then transferred to appropriate electronics, which in turn process and interpret data to a form that is human-readable.

Obtaining data from sensors typically consists of reading raw byte values from appropriate memory registers. Thus, understanding raw data representation and organization is crucial for proper interpretation of information received from sensors. IoT software extensively uses low-level manipulations on bits, bytes, data types, bit shift operations, and so on.

I start this chapter with background information on how you typically handle low-level bit and byte operations using bitwise, bit shift operators, and some handy classes like BitConverter and BitArray. You'll use this knowledge to obtain and interpret values received from various sensors of the Sense HAT add-on board for the RPi2 and RPi3.

The Sense HAT add-on board you see in Figure 5-1 is equipped with several sensors, including: thermometer, barometer, magnetometer, gyroscope, and accelerometer. These sensors are manufactured by STMicroelectronics (STM), and are controlled in a very similar way. Namely, to control them you need to set particular bit values of specific memory register bytes. This is important, because several STM sensors by default are in the power-safe mode, in which their functioning is limited to save power. Therefore, to turn on sensors into a regular, operating mode you need to set appropriate bits.

FIGURE 5-1   Sense HAT add-on board for Raspberry Pi 2 and Pi 3. This board is attached to the Raspberry Pi using a 40-pin header. Courtesy of *http://www.adafruit.com*.

After you configure a sensor, you need to appropriately convert raw byte arrays to human-readable numbers, which correctly represent physical values being monitored. This may require several conversion steps using device-specific calibration parameters, which you can also obtain from the sensor's memory.

These aspects are explained here so that at the end of this chapter you will achieve the functionality depicted in Figure 5-2. Consequently, after reading this chapter, you can start building your own environmental or more sophisticated monitoring systems.

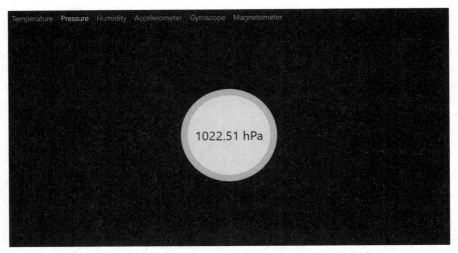

FIGURE 5-2 Barometric pressure reading acquired from the LPS25H sensor of the Sense HAT add-on board.

Bits, bytes, and data types

When you implement high-level applications you usually do not think in terms of bits and bytes. Rather, you work with larger data types (for example, integers, floats, strings), which you use as your building blocks for abstract classes that represent particular domain objects and processes you are automating with your software. At this point, you usually do not really have to take care of how the particular bits and bytes are organized in the memory.

However, in the IoT world, data is packed such that every single bit is utilized. This helps to minimize the amount of information transferred between a sensor and a microcontroller, or between various IoT devices. Therefore, you need to carefully extract information from byte arrays, including the proper data order, so you finally obtain the correct value representing a physical variable being monitored by your IoT device.

In subsequent sections I will show how to do that using bitwise operators and classes implemented by the UWP. If you feel you need to get a quick reminder about bits, bytes, and data type organization, you can refer to Appendix C, "Bits, bytes, and data types," in which those concepts are explained. Moreover, in that appendix I also cover the hexadecimal numeral system. This can be found useful, since IoT sensor documentation is usually based on such numeric representation. If you are already familiar with these concepts, you are good to go to the next section.

Decoding and encoding binary data

In the IoT world the data transmitted between sensors and microcontrollers is encoded using bits, so each byte can carry up to eight pieces of information. To decode this data you can use the bitwise operations or methods of the `BitConverter` and `BitArray` classes. Here, I am presenting both of these approaches since if you look up a particular problem's solution, the answer will be typically given in terms of bitwise and shift operators rather than based on the `BitConverter` and `BitArray` classes. However, these classes provide a robust solution for bit and byte operations, and thus can significantly shorten the development time and improve readability of your code. So, it is beneficial to know how `BitConverter` and `BitArray` look under the hood. But again, if you are already familiar with these concepts, feel free to jump to the "Sense HAT add-on board" section.

Bitwise operators

There are four common bitwise operations: conjunction & (AND), alternative | (OR), exclusive OR ^ (XOR), and complement ~ (NOT). These operators are used to quickly manipulate bits composing a particular variable.

The bitwise complement is a unary operator. That is, it expects a single operand and inverts every bit of the variable. For example, the bitwise complement of 0010 1110 is 1101 0001.

Bitwise AND, OR, and XOR operators require two operands, and the results produced by these operators are given in Table 5-1. Namely, the AND (&) bitwise operator yields 1 when both operand bits have the value of 1 and yields 0 otherwise. The OR (|) bitwise operator yields 1 whenever one of the two operands is set. And the XOR (^) bitwise operator outputs 0 when the operands are the same and 1 if they are different.

TABLE 5-1   Non-unary bitwise operators

Bit 1	Bit 2	& (AND)		(OR)	^ (XOR)
0	0	0	0	0
0	1	0	1	1
1	0	0	1	1
1	1	1	1	0

All the preceding bitwise operators, except a complement, are also supplemented by the following shorthand operators: &=, |=, and ^=. These work the same as the operators described in Table 5-1 but can be used to shorten procedures in which you need to perform a particular bit operation followed by the assignment, as presented in Listing 5-1.

LISTING 5-1   A method showing the usage and results of the shorthand bitwise operators

```
private void BitwiseOperators()
{
    byte a = 0;  // Binary: 0000
```

```
    byte b = 5;  // Binary: 0101
    byte c = 10; // Binary: 1010

    c |= a; // c = 10 (Binary: 1010)
    c ^= b; // c = 15 (Binary: 1111)
    c &= b; // c =  5 (Binary: 0101)
}
```

Shift operators, bit masking, and binary representation

Bitwise operations are also supplemented by shift operators: << and >>. These operators shift bits of the expression to the left (<<) or right (>>) by the specified number of bit places. The single shift effectively multiplies (<<) or divides (>>) a number by 2. Listing 5-2 shows a few examples of shift operations and their output. Note that shifting a value of 0 does not do anything because none of the bits is initially set.

LISTING 5-2 Sample usage of bit shift operators

```
private void BitShiftOperators()
{
    byte a = 0;  // Binary: 0000 0000
    byte b = 4;  // Binary: 0000 0100
    byte c = 8;  // Binary: 0000 1000

    int bitShiftResult;

    bitShiftResult = a << 1; // bitShiftResult =  0 (Binary: 0000 0000)
    bitShiftResult = b >> 1; // bitShiftResult =  2 (Binary: 0000 0010)
    bitShiftResult = c << 2; // bitShiftResult = 32 (Binary: 0010 0000)
}
```

Shift operations in combination with bitwise operators are typically used to create bit masks. In particular, a bit mask can be applied to a variable using an & bitwise operator to find whether a specific bit is set. This might seem like one of many academic problems you solved during your programming classes or tutorials. Actually, in the IoT world, you use shift and bitwise operators to determine whether the particular sensor or a board function is on or off, to combine bytes into larger datatypes, or to convert sensor readings to meaningful values.

Bits can be ordered in two different ways: starting from the most significant bit (MSB) or from the least significant bit (LSB). This ordering is important because it is tightly related to decoding the bit collection to a meaningful value. (See Appendix C for further details.) It is also required to appropriately configure a device. In technical documentation, binary representation typically starts with the MSB. Moreover, such bit ordering is generated by the ToString method of the Convert class (defined in the System namespace).

Let's now use the System.Convert.ToString method to find a binary representation of a 16-bit integer. For this purpose, I could write a simple console app, consisting of the one method for converting a decimal value into the binary string. Rather than doing that, I will take a different path. Namely, I will write the headed UWP app, which will use data binding, and an appropriate converter for determining binary representation. The idea is to show how you can incorporate data binding mechanisms, which you typically use for your high-level UWP, WinRT, or WPF apps to implement IoT software.

In general, in the high-level apps that consume web services or database records, you use data binding to diminish the amount of procedures that simply rewrite property values. Moreover, you use converters for extracting and displaying selected information only.

In the IoT software you can use exactly the same tools, though your converters look "more low-level". This is the beauty of the UWP, since your source code looks "very high-level", and you can use all your favorite programming patterns. However, some specific aspects (like converters, and some logic) are tailored to the particular "low-level" needs of your sensors, detectors, cameras, or IoT end-points, in short.

Let's get back to the point and implement the mentioned algorithm for extracting bit values. Here is a detailed procedure for implementing this on the UWP platform:

1. Create the new UWP blank app BinaryRepresentation.

2. Add to the project a new file ShortToBinaryConverter.cs, and modify it according to Listing 5-3. (Note that this mechanism is similar to the one you use for the typical high-level UWP or WinRT apps you wrote previously.)

LISTING 5-3   Binary representation of a 16-bit signed integer is retrieved using a converter

```
using System;
using Windows.UI.Xaml.Data;

namespace BinaryRepresentation
{
    public class ShortToBinaryConverter : IValueConverter
    {
        public object Convert(object value, Type targetType,
            object parameter, string language)
        {
            string result = string.Empty;

            if (value != null)
            {
                short inputValue;
                if (short.TryParse(value.ToString(), out inputValue))
                {
                    const int bitCount = 16;

                    result = System.Convert.ToString(inputValue, 2);
                    result = result.PadLeft(bitCount, '0');
                }
            }

            return result;
        }
```

```
        public object ConvertBack(object value, Type targetType,
            object parameter, string language)
        {
            throw new NotImplementedException();
        }
    }
}
```

3. Update the `MainPage` definition of the BinaryRepresentation app as shown in Listing 5-4.

LISTING 5-4 User interface definition of the BinaryRepresentation app

```xml
<Page
    x:Class="BinaryRepresentation.MainPage"
    xmlns="http://schemas.microsoft.com/winfx/2006/xaml/presentation"
    xmlns:x="http://schemas.microsoft.com/winfx/2006/xaml"
    xmlns:local="using:BinaryRepresentation"
    xmlns:d="http://schemas.microsoft.com/expression/blend/2008"
    xmlns:mc="http://schemas.openxmlformats.org/markup-compatibility/2006"
    mc:Ignorable="d">

    <Page.Resources>
        <Thickness x:Key="DefaultMargin">5</Thickness>

        <x:Double x:Key="DefaultFontSize">28</x:Double>

        <x:Double x:Key="DefaultTextBoxWidth">150</x:Double>

        <local:ShortToBinaryConverter x:Key="ShortToBinaryConverter" />

        <Style TargetType="TextBlock">
            <Setter Property="Margin"
                    Value="{StaticResource DefaultMargin}" />
            <Setter Property="VerticalAlignment"
                    Value="Center" />
            <Setter Property="FontSize"
                    Value="{StaticResource DefaultFontSize}" />
        </Style>

        <Style TargetType="TextBox">
            <Setter Property="Margin"
                    Value="{StaticResource DefaultMargin}" />
            <Setter Property="FontSize"
                    Value="{StaticResource DefaultFontSize}" />
            <Setter Property="Width"
                    Value="{StaticResource DefaultTextBoxWidth}" />
        </Style>
    </Page.Resources>

    <StackPanel Background="{ThemeResource ApplicationPageBackgroundThemeBrush}">
        <StackPanel Orientation="Horizontal">
```

```
            <TextBlock Text="Enter a value: " />
            <TextBox x:Name="TextBoxInputValue" />
        </StackPanel>

        <TextBlock Text="Binary representation (MSB): " />
        <TextBlock Text="{Binding Text, ElementName=TextBoxInputValue,
            Converter={StaticResource ShortToBinaryConverter}}" />
    </StackPanel>
</Page>
```

The UI is composed of three labels (TextBlock controls) and one text box. You can use the text box to enter the number you wish to convert to the binary representation. The result of this operation is displayed in one of the labels. Note that the resulting value is data-bound to the text box, so all the logic is implemented within the appropriate converter. An actual code-behind (MainPage.xaml.cs) has only the default content. Refer to Figure 5-1 for a visual representation of the UI.

To limit the length of numbers in a binary representation I allow the user to convert 16-bit signed integers only. This conversion is implemented using data binding and a converter, the definition of which is given in Listing 5-3. This ShortToBinaryConverter class uses a System.Convert.ToString method. You can use this method to get not only the binary representation of the particular variable, but also its octet and hexadecimal form. To change the numeral system radix, you can use the second argument of the System.Convert.ToString method, using one of the following values: 2 (binary), 8 (octet), 10 (decimal), or 16 (hexadecimal).

For binary number representation, System.Convert.ToString outputs the string without leading zeros. To restore them, I pad the resulting string with zeros, so the output looks as shown in Figure 5-3. This figure depicts the binary representation of two values: 255 and 21845. The first one is represented by eight ones and eight zeros, while the binary representation of the latter comprises alternating ones and zeros. The smallest index is assigned to the MSB. Therefore, the string containing a binary representation starts with the MSB.

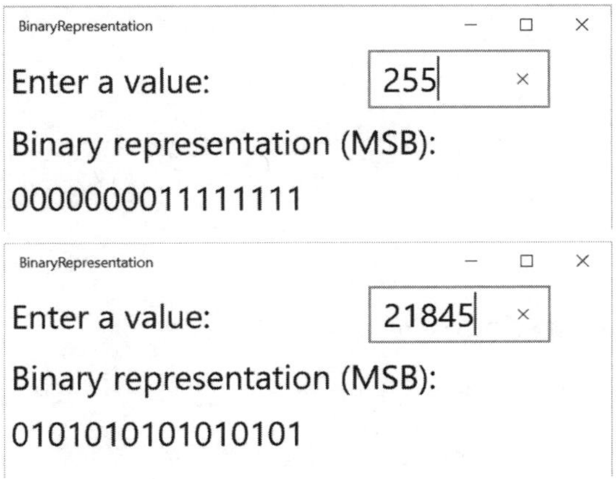

FIGURE 5-3 Binary representation of 16-bit signed integers starting with the most significant bit.

How can you get the LSB representation? By either reversing the string or writing your own method for querying bits. The former can be done using the Reverse method from System.Linq, while the latter can be implemented using the bitwise AND operator together with shift operators as shown in Listing 5-5. Namely, you shift a value of 1 by a specified number of places to create a bit mask and then apply this mask to the analyzing value using a bitwise & operator. The result of this operation is either 1 (if the bit is set) or 0 (otherwise).

LISTING 5-5 Querying bits using a bitwise operator and a bit mask created with a bit shift

```
private string IsBitSet(short value, int position)
{
    return (value & (1 << position)) > 0 ? "1" : "0";
}
```

You can now utilize this approach in the BinaryRepresentation app. To this end, update the Convert method of the ShortToBinaryConverter class as shown in Listing 5-6.

LISTING 5-6 Binary representation determined by querying bits using a binary mask

```
public object Convert(object value, Type targetType, object parameter, string language)
{
    var result = string.Empty;

    if (value != null)
    {
        short inputValue;
        if (short.TryParse(value.ToString(), out inputValue))
        {
            const int bitCount = 16;

            // result = System.Convert.ToString(inputValue, 2);
            // result = result.PadLeft(bitCount, '0');

            for (int i = 0; i < bitCount; i++)
            {
                result += IsBitSet(inputValue, i);
            }
        }
    }

    return result;
}
```

Additionally, in MainPage.xaml, change the last TextBlock definition as follows:

```
<TextBlock Text="Binary representation (LSB):" />
```

After you re-run the app, you may note that binary representation now starts with the LSB, as shown in Figure 5-4.

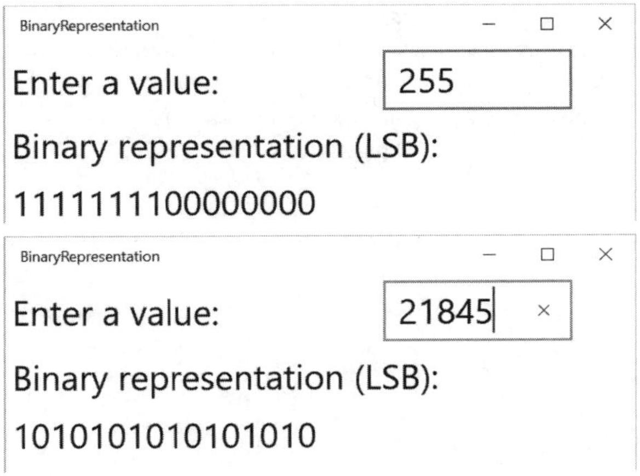

FIGURE 5-4 Binary representation of 16-bit signed integers using LSB-first bit ordering. Bit order is reversed with respect to Figure 5-3.

Naturally, using a bit mask to find the LSB-first bit ordering is not very efficient. It's better to reverse the output of the System.Convert.ToString method. However, the use of bit masks is more general. Bit masks can be also used for setting and clearing particular bit values. In particular, to set the value of the bit at a given position to 1, you follow the same scheme as shown in the method IsBitSet from Listing 5-5—just replace an & operator by |. (See Listing 5-7.) Consequently, to clear the bit (set its value to 0), you use & together with binary negation (~) as shown in Listing 5-8.

LISTING 5-7 Setting a bit using bitwise and bit shift operators

```
private static int SetBit(int value, int position)
{
    return value | (1 << position);
}
```

LISTING 5-8 Clearing a bit value

```
private static int ClearBit(int value, int position)
{
    return value & ~(1 << position);
}
```

Let's now incorporate methods from Listing 5-7 and Listing 5-8 in the BinaryRepresentation app to manipulate bit values of the input 16-bit integer. To this end, replace the declaration of the outer StackPanel by the declarations from Listing 5-9, and subsequently update MainPage.xaml.cs according to Listing 5-10. The input integer value that you typed in the text box is bitwise manipulated in the code-behind using the data bound properties. The resulting binary representation of the OutputValue is then displayed in the view. As you can see, everything is without using event handlers. Then, after you re-run the app, you can manipulate particular bits of the input integer, as shown in Figure 5-5.

LISTING 5-9 Updated UI declaration introduces additional text boxes that allow you to set and clear bits at the particular index

```xml
<StackPanel Background="{ThemeResource ApplicationPageBackgroundThemeBrush}">
    <Grid>
        <Grid.RowDefinitions>
            <RowDefinition Height="Auto" />
            <RowDefinition Height="Auto" />
            <RowDefinition Height="Auto" />
        </Grid.RowDefinitions>

        <Grid.ColumnDefinitions>
            <ColumnDefinition Width="*" />
            <ColumnDefinition Width="*" />
        </Grid.ColumnDefinitions>

        <!--First row-->
        <TextBlock Text="Enter a value:" />
        <TextBox Text="{x:Bind InputValue, Mode=TwoWay}"
                    Grid.Column="1" />

        <!--Second row-->
        <TextBlock Text="Bit to set:"
                    Grid.Row="1" />
        <TextBox Text="{x:Bind BitToSet, Mode=TwoWay}"
                    Grid.Row="1"
                    Grid.Column="1" />

        <!--Third row-->
        <TextBlock Text="Bit to clear:"
                    Grid.Row="2" />
        <TextBox Text="{x:Bind BitToClear, Mode=TwoWay}"
                    Grid.Row="2"
                    Grid.Column="1" />
    </Grid>

    <TextBlock Text="Binary representation (LSB):" />
    <TextBlock Text="{x:Bind OutputValue, Converter={StaticResource
        ShortToBinaryConverter}, Mode=OneWay}" />
</StackPanel>
```

LISTING 5-10 Updating MainPage.xaml.cs

```csharp
using System.ComponentModel;
using System.Runtime.CompilerServices;
using Windows.UI.Xaml.Controls;

namespace BinaryRepresentation
{
    public sealed partial class MainPage : Page, INotifyPropertyChanged
    {
```

```csharp
public event PropertyChangedEventHandler PropertyChanged = delegate { };

public short BitToSet
{
    get { return bitToSet; }
    set { SetBit(value); }
}

public short BitToClear
{
    get { return bitToClear; }
    set { ClearBit(value); }
}

public short InputValue
{
    get { return inputValue; }
    set { OutputValue = inputValue = value; }
}

public short OutputValue
{
    get { return outputValue; }
    set
    {
        outputValue = value;
        OnPropertyChanged();
    }
}

private const int shortBitLength = 16;

private short bitToSet;
private short bitToClear;
private short inputValue;
private short outputValue;

public MainPage()
{
    InitializeComponent();
}

private void OnPropertyChanged([CallerMemberName] string propertyName = "")
{
    PropertyChanged(this, new PropertyChangedEventArgs(propertyName));
}

private void SetBit(short position)
{
    if(position >= 0 && position <= shortBitLength)
    {
        OutputValue |= (short)(1 << position);
```

```
                bitToSet = position;
            }
        }

        private void ClearBit(short position)
        {
            if (position >= 0 && position <= shortBitLength)
            {
                OutputValue &= (short)~(1 << position);
                bitToClear = position;
            }
        }
    }
}
```

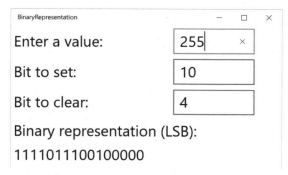

FIGURE 5-5 Initial value of 255 (1111 1111 0000 0000) is modified by setting the bit at index 10, and clearing the bit at index 4. So the final value is 1263 (1111 0111 0010 0000).

Why did I guide you through all these steps? I wanted to explicitly show that developing headed IoT apps using Windows 10 IoT Core follows the same patterns as you most probably already know from developing apps for desktop or mobile Windows platforms. Accordingly, programming the UI/UX layers of the IoT headed apps using Windows 10 IoT Core and the UWP is very similar to UWP programming. However, as you can see, you face more low-level specific aspects of programming than you typically do during your mobile and desktop app development.

Byte encoding and endianness

After getting familiar with bitwise and shift operators, let's now have a look at another two important concepts: byte encoding and endianness. These two play an important role when you work with data types occupying more than 8 bits. Such objects can be viewed as the byte arrays that are often used to transmit information over the network or to store data in memory. The transmitted or read data needs to be interpreted on the endpoint. This can be also done using shift and bitwise operators. For instance, to convert two bytes into the unsigned 16-bit integer, you can use the code given in Listing 5-11.

LISTING 5-11 Byte array to ushort conversion

```
var data = new byte[] { 65, 127 };
var result = (ushort)(data[0] | data[1] << 8);
```

The preceding conversion shifts the second byte by eight positions to the left, and then calculates the bitwise alternative with the first byte. Naturally, this can be generalized to 32-bit and 64-bit integers. Listing 5-12 contains the example for converting the four-element byte array to `uint`:

LISTING 5-12 Byte array to uint conversion assuming little-endianness

```
const int offset = 8;
var data = new byte[] { 65, 127, 1, 13 };
uint result = data[0];

for(int i = 1; i < data.Length; i++)
{
    result |= (uint)(data[i] << i * offset);
}
```

In general, the result of the preceding operations depends on the byte order—that is, the endianness. Bytes are ordered from the most significant (containing the MSB) to the least significant one. However, the former can be positioned in the first (farthest to the left) or last (farthest to the right) element of the byte array. The first case is referred to as the big-endian, while the second byte sequence order is defined as the little-endian. The most and least significant bytes are also denoted as high and low byte, respectively. For example, if you receive the 2 byte array {0, 255} and convert it to ushort using the code from Listing 5-11, you will get 65280, because the last byte (255) is assumed to be most significant. In contrast, in the big-endian format, the first byte (0) is assumed to be most significant as in decimal numbers, where digits are ordered from the most to the least significant values. We first have millions, then thousands, and so on. Therefore, in the big-endian format, the received array should be interpreted as 255 instead of 65280.

The endianness naming convention (big- and little-endian) might be confusing. Here, *big* and *little* are related to memory addresses. In the little-endian format, byte significance increases with increasing memory addresses. The last element of the byte array is stored in the memory cell with the smallest address. In the big-endian format, byte significance decreases with increasing memory addresses. Hence, the last byte is stored in the memory cell with the largest address.

The endianness depends on the system's architecture and thus may differ between IoT devices. The proper interpretation of the byte array requires knowledge of this ordering. You typically determine endianness from the sensor or device's specification. In Listing 5-11 and Listing 5-12, I assumed that the byte sequence follows the little-endianness. In the case of the big-endianness, the conversion should be performed in an opposite order as shown in Listing 5-13. Alternatively, you can reverse the input array.

```
const int offset = 8;
var data = new byte[] { 65, 127, 1, 13 };
int lastElementIndex = data.Length - 1;
var result = data[lastElementIndex];

for (int i = 0; i < data.Length; i++)
{
    result |= (uint)(data[i] << (lastElementIndex - i) * offset);
}
```

BitConverter

Byte array conversion is a typical, and as you will see later, important task when you need to read data from sensors or to communicate with other devices. Converting byte arrays is important because unless you use additional libraries, the data you read from a sensor's memory or receive from a remote device is a raw byte stream. To interpret this data, you need the specification of a communication protocol for the sensor or device you are going to interface. Then, according to these specs, you write the byte array parser, which transforms a raw byte stream into meaningful information—for example, temperature or humidity values, commands, and so on.

To simplify and automate byte conversion, the UWP implements the System.BitConverter class. The BitConverter class exposes several public methods that accept a byte array and convert it to an integral, floating point number, or a character. Listing 5-14 depicts the code snippet, which converts the four-byte array to the unsigned 32-bit integer. So, rather than using bit shift operators and bit masks, you can invoke one method, which does the conversion for you.

LISTING 5-14   Byte array conversion using the BitConverter class

```
var data = new byte[] { 65, 127, 1, 13 };
var result = System.BitConverter.ToUInt32(data, 0);
```

In Listing 5-14 I used the ToUInt32 static method of the BitConverter class. It accepts two arguments. The first one is the byte array, while the second, startIndex, is used to indicate the index of the byte array at which conversion begins. You typically use this parameter while you read and then convert long byte streams. So the conversion can be done within a loop, in which you appropriately change the startIndex argument of the static BitConverter methods.

The BitConverter class can be also used to check for the device's endianness. This information can be retrieved by reading a value stored in the IsLittleEndian field. For instance, if you received a byte array from the big-endian machine and your code is running on the little-endian CPU, the definition of your conversion method will look like the one presented in Listing 5-15. As you can see, before converting the byte array, I first check for the endianness, and reverse the input array if necessary. For this reversion, I used the extension Reverse method, which is defined in the System.Linq namespace.

LISTING 5-15 Byte array obtained from the big-endian machine is reversed before conversion

```
var data = new byte[] { 13, 1, 127, 65 }; // Assumption: big-endian format

if (BitConverter.IsLittleEndian)
{
    data = data.Reverse().ToArray();
}

var result = System.BitConverter.ToUInt32(data, 0);
```

The code presented in Listing 5-15 is only valid for a byte array containing a single unsigned integer. If your input array contains multiple byte-encoded numbers, then you need to isolate them before reversion and conversion. In such cases, you can use the static Copy method of the Array class, and proceed as shown in Listing 5-16. In this code snippet, after verifying argument values, I first copy the four bytes from the provided array, starting from the specified index, and subsequently perform the array-to-UInt32 conversion using the BitConverter class.

LISTING 5-16 Appropriate four bytes are isolated from the input array before performing the conversion to the unsigned 32-bit integer

```
public static uint GetUInt32(byte[] value, int startIndex)
{
    const int uintLength = 4;

    // Verify value argument
    if (value == null)
    {
        throw new ArgumentNullException();
    }

    // Verify startIndex
    if (startIndex < 0 || startIndex > value.Length - uintLength)
    {
        throw new ArgumentOutOfRangeException();
    }

    var singleIntegerBuffer = new byte[uintLength];

    Array.Copy(value, startIndex, singleIntegerBuffer, 0, uintLength);

    if (BitConverter.IsLittleEndian)
    {
        singleIntegerBuffer = singleIntegerBuffer.Reverse().ToArray();
    }

    return BitConverter.ToUInt32(singleIntegerBuffer, 0);
}
```

Another important member of a `BitConverter` class is the `GetBytes` method. It retrieves byte representation of a variable of the simple type, so it works in opposition to procedures explained previously.

The sample code presenting how to get the byte representation of the integer value is shown in Listing 5-17. There, I simply calculate the difference between two constant values, representing maximum values of the `ulong` and `uint` data types. The resulting value is of type `ulong`, and therefore spans over eight bytes. Four of them are 0's, while the others are 255, so after converting them back to `ulong` you will get 18446744069414584320; see Appendix C.

LISTING 5-17   Retrieving byte representation of the unsigned 64-bit integer

```
var bytes = System.BitConverter.GetBytes(ulong.MaxValue - uint.MaxValue);
for(int i = 0; i < bytes.Length; i++)
{
    System.Diagnostics.Debug.WriteLine(bytes[i]);
}
```

BitArray

The UWP also delivers the `System.Collections.BitArray` class, which is a convenient representation of the bit collection. Each element of this collection is represented as a Boolean variable. An instance of `BitArray` can be created using a byte array. Then, the resulting `BitArray` instance comprises the collection of bits representing the particular input array of bytes. Each element of this collection is the logical value corresponding to the bit value at the particular position.

We can now use the functionality of the `BitConverter` and `BitArray` classes to modify the definition of the `ShortToBinaryConverter` class previously used in the BinaryRepresentation app to find the binary representation of a signed 16-bit integer. The corresponding implementation is presented in Listing 5-18. It is worthwhile to compare that definition with the original version of `ShortToBinaryConverter` using the `IsBitSet` method from Listing 5-5. As you can see, now instead of using bitwise operators to check the logical bit value, I can simply check the Boolean value of the `BitArray` element at the specific index. Moreover, to get the byte array of the unsigned 16-bit integer, I used the `GetBytes` method of the `BitConverter` class.

LISTING 5-18   Binary representation is extracted using the methods of the BitConverter and BitArray classes

```
using System;
using System.Collections;
using Windows.UI.Xaml.Data;

namespace BinaryRepresentation
{
    public class ShortToBinaryConverter : IValueConverter
    {
        public object Convert(object value, Type targetType,
            object parameter, string language)
        {
            string result = string.Empty;
```

```csharp
            if (value != null)
            {
                short inputValue;
                if (short.TryParse(value.ToString(), out inputValue))
                {
                    //const int bitCount = 16;

                    //result = System.Convert.ToString(inputValue, 2);
                    //result = result.PadLeft(bitCount, '0');

                    //for (int i = 0; i < bitCount; i++)
                    //{
                    //    result += IsBitSet(inputValue, i);
                    //}

                    var bytes = BitConverter.GetBytes(inputValue);
                    var bitArray = new BitArray(bytes);

                    for (int i = 0; i < bitArray.Length; i++)
                    {
                        result += BoolToBinaryString(bitArray[i]);
                    }
                }
            }

            return result;
        }

        public object ConvertBack(object value, Type targetType,
            object parameter, string language)
        {
            throw new NotImplementedException();
        }

        private string IsBitSet(short value, int position)
        {
            return (value & (1 << position)) > 0 ? "1" : "0";
        }

        private string BoolToBinaryString(bool value)
        {
            return value ? "1" : "0";
        }
    }
}
```

An instance of the BitArray class also exposes several members for performing bitwise operations. These include Not, And, Or, and Xor methods, which implement a bitwise complement (NOT), conjunction (AND), alternative (OR), and exclusive alternative (XOR), respectively (refer to Table 5-1). You can use these methods to alternatively implement the same functionality as presented in Listing 5-1. Namely, in Listing 5-19, I show the complete code snippet for performing bitwise alternative, exclusive alternative, and conjunction using the appropriate methods of the BitArray class. First, I instantiated three BitArray classes. Subsequently, I consecutively invoked Or, Xor, and And methods. They correspond to |, ^, and & bitwise operators. Afterwards, I debug the numeral and binary values of the bits comprising the BitArray classes. To obtain an actual value of the bit-encoded byte, I used the CopyTo method of the BitArray class. This automatically decodes bits to bytes. Finally, I obtain a binary representation using the Convert.ToString method, so the BitArrayBitwiseManipulation method from Listing 5-19 outputs the following values to the console (Output window of Visual Studio):

```
10 (Binary: 1010)
15 (Binary: 1111)
5 (Binary: 101)
```

LISTING 5-19   Bitwise operations using the BitArray class

```
public static void BitArrayBitwiseManipulation()
{
    byte a = 0;  // Binary: 0000
    byte b = 5;  // Binary: 0101
    byte c = 10; // Binary: 1010

    // Create bit arrays
    var aBitArray = new BitArray(new byte[] { a });
    var bBitArray = new BitArray(new byte[] { b });
    var cBitArray = new BitArray(new byte[] { c });

    // Bitwise alternative
    cBitArray.Or(aBitArray);
    DebugBitArrayValue(cBitArray);

    // Bitwise exclusive alternative
    cBitArray.Xor(bBitArray);
    DebugBitArrayValue(cBitArray);

    // Bitwise conjunction
    cBitArray.And(bBitArray);
    DebugBitArrayValue(cBitArray);
}

private static byte GetByteValueFromBitArray(BitArray bitArray)
{
    var buffer = new byte[1];

    // Perform conversion
    ((ICollection)bitArray).CopyTo(buffer, 0);

    return buffer[0];
}

private static void DebugBitArrayValue(BitArray bitArray)
{
    var value = GetByteValueFromBitArray(bitArray);
```

```
    var binaryValue = Convert.ToString(value, 2);

    var debugString = string.Format("{0} Binary: {1}", value, binaryValue);

    System.Diagnostics.Debug.WriteLine(debugString);
}
```

In addition, the BitArray class implements the Set method, which you can use to update the bit value at the particular position—for example, cBitArray.Set(3, true);. We thus conclude that BitArray together with BitConverter simplify typical bit and byte array manipulations by providing an additional higher-level API. It would be ideal if BitConverter would implement an extra method, capable of converting BitArray to the appropriate numeral values. However, one can always implement an appropriate set of extension methods himself or herself.

Sense HAT add-on board

We now use all the preceding information to read data from sensors available on the Sense HAT add-on board for the RPi2 and RPi3. Sense HAT was specially designed for the Astro PI project, in which two Raspberry Pi computers are utilized to measure various environmental and dynamical properties of the International Space Station.

The Sense HAT is equipped with an 8x8 array of colored LEDs, a five-button joystick, and several sensors for monitoring temperature, pressure, humidity, inertia, and the magnetic field. The Sense HAT can be connected to RPi2 using a 40-pin GPIO extension port and can communicate with Raspberry Pi 2 (or 3) using the I²C interface. The Sense HAT has its own microcontroller, which serves as the proxy for accessing particular board components, including sensors, LED array, and joystick.

In the next few sections, I will show how to configure Sense HAT sensors, and how to obtain and interpret data provided by them.

User interface

Before writing the actual code for sensor interaction, I prepared the application's user interface (see Figure 5-2) such that data received from each Sense HAT sensor can be displayed using the custom control on a separate tab. To force the dark color theme, I set the RequestedTheme attribute of the Application tag to Dark.

The custom control implements the rounded text block control with a yellow background and orange border. You can find the complete implementation of this control in the companion code (Chapter 05/SenseHat/Controls/RoundedTextBlock.xaml). Note that hereafter, instead of showing the full code listings, I will refer to the companion code whenever the full listings are not required.

The tabular control in the UWP is implemented within a Pivot class, and each tab is represented as the PivotItem.

Next, I defined the generic `Vector3D` class (see the companion code in Chapter 05/SenseHat/Helpers/Vector3D.cs), which stores components of three-dimensional vectors. As you will see later, this structure is used to represent readings obtained from the accelerometer, gyroscope, and the magnetometer in a more concise way.

Subsequently, I implemented the `SensorReadings` class (see the companion code in Chapter 05/SenseHat/Sensors/SensorReadings.cs), which aims at storing values obtained from each sensor. Public properties of the `SensorReadings` class, as shown in Listing 5-20, are one-way bound to the UI, so we do not need to manually set control properties to update the UI. The fields of an instance of the `SensorReadings` class are bound to the UI and formatted using converters (see the companion code in Chapter 05/SenseHat/Converters), declared in the application-scoped resource dictionary. Every sensor reading is presented using a separate tab of the `Pivot` control. Therefore, the user can use swipe or mouse to navigate between tabs. You can find the complete implementation of the SenseHat UI in the companion code. (See Listing 5-21. Converters are used to format numeral values such that they are supplemented by appropriate physical units.)

LISTING 5-20   MainPage declaration

```
<Page
    x:Class="SenseHat.MainPage"
    xmlns="http://schemas.microsoft.com/winfx/2006/xaml/presentation"
    xmlns:x="http://schemas.microsoft.com/winfx/2006/xaml"
    xmlns:local="using:SenseHat"
    xmlns:controls="using:SenseHat.Controls"
    xmlns:d="http://schemas.microsoft.com/expression/blend/2008"
    xmlns:mc="http://schemas.openxmlformats.org/markup-compatibility/2006"
    mc:Ignorable="d">

    <Pivot Background="{ThemeResource ApplicationPageBackgroundThemeBrush}">
        <PivotItem Header="Temperature">
            <controls:RoundedTextBlock Text="{x:Bind sensorReadings.Temperature,
            Mode=OneWay, Converter={StaticResource TemperatureToStringConverter}}" />
        </PivotItem>

        <PivotItem Header="Pressure">
            <controls:RoundedTextBlock Text="{x:Bind sensorReadings.Pressure,
            Mode=OneWay, Converter={StaticResource PressureToStringConverter}}" />
        </PivotItem>

        <PivotItem Header="Humidity">
            <controls:RoundedTextBlock Text="{x:Bind sensorReadings.Humidity,
            Mode=OneWay, Converter={StaticResource HumidityToStringConverter}}" />
        </PivotItem>

        <PivotItem Header="Accelerometer">
            <controls:RoundedTextBlock Text="{x:Bind sensorReadings.Accelerometer,
            Mode=OneWay, Converter={StaticResource LinearAccelerationToStringConverter}}" />
        </PivotItem>
```

```
        <PivotItem Header="Gyroscope">
            <controls:RoundedTextBlock Text="{x:Bind sensorReadings.Gyroscope,
            Mode=OneWay, Converter={StaticResource AngularSpeedToStringConverter}}" />
        </PivotItem>

        <PivotItem Header="Magnetometer">
            <controls:RoundedTextBlock Text="{x:Bind sensorReadings.Magnetometer,
            Mode=OneWay, Converter={StaticResource MagneticFieldToStringConverter}}" />
        </PivotItem>
    </Pivot>
</Page>
```

LISTING 5-21 Application-scoped converter declarations

```
<Application
    x:Class="SenseHat.App"
    xmlns="http://schemas.microsoft.com/winfx/2006/xaml/presentation"
    xmlns:x="http://schemas.microsoft.com/winfx/2006/xaml"
    xmlns:local="using:SenseHat"
    xmlns:converters="using:SenseHat.Converters"
    RequestedTheme="Dark">

    <Application.Resources>
        <converters:TemperatureToStringConverter x:Key="TemperatureToStringConverter" />
        <converters:PressureToStringConverter x:Key="PressureToStringConverter" />
        <converters:HumidityToStringConverter x:Key="HumidityToStringConverter" />
        <converters:LinearAccelerationToStringConverter
            x:Key="LinearAccelerationToStringConverter" />
        <converters:AngularSpeedToAccelerationConverter
            x:Key="AngularSpeedToAccelerationConverter" />
        <converters:MagneticFieldToStringConverter x:Key="MagneticFieldToStringConverter" />
    </Application.Resources>
</Application>
```

As you can see, the source code of the SenseHat app is organized into subfolders. Such a procedure helps you to organize your solution and isolate specific functionalities. In Visual Studio 2015 you create such project folders in the Solution Explorer using the Add/New Folder option from the project's context menu. You can activate this menu by right-clicking the project name in the Solution Explorer. Then, any code file added to such a project's folder is automatically filled with the namespace block, which has the form of <ProjectName>.<FolderName>, where <ProjectName> and <FolderName> stand for the name of your project (for example, SenseHat) and the folder name (for example, Sensors), respectively. For example, code files in the Sensors subfolder are automatically assigned the namespace of SenseHat.Sensors.

It should be also pointed out that in Listing 5-20, and Listing 5-21 I use custom XAML namespace prefixes: xmlns:controls and xmlns:converters. They allow me to refer to objects declared in the following C# namespaces: SenseHat.Controls (RoundedTextBlock control) and SenseHat.Converters (data binding value converters).

Temperature and barometric pressure

Let's now get the temperature and barometric pressure values using an LPS25H sensor of the Sense HAT add-on board. The LPS25H sensor is the compact sensor, manufactured by STM. This sensor allows you to monitor (sample) temperature and pressure with the maximum frequency of 25 Hz (that is, every 40 milliseconds).

The pressure sensing element of LPS25H consists of the MEMS in which a micro-sized membrane is deflected when the external pressure is applied. The deflection induces a piezo resistance, which in turn is converted into an analog voltage. Subsequently, a voltage level is translated using an analog-to-digital converter, and the resulting digital value is stored in the sensor's memory. Since pressure depends also on the temperature, LPS25H contains another MEMS element for measuring this physical quantity to provide accurate barometric pressure readings.

In general, both pressure and temperature values can be accessed through the I²C or SPI serial interfaces by reading values stored in the appropriate registers. This requires the knowledge of the register mapping, which can be found in the LPS25H datasheet at *http://bit.ly/pressure_sensor*.

However, the Sense HAT add-on board is equipped with an additional Atmel ATtiny88 microcontroller, which acts as the layer for accessing sensors, an LED array, and a joystick. RPi2 and RPi3 can only communicate with Atmel ATtiny88 using an I²C interface.

The functionality of exchanging data through an I²C peripheral is implemented in the `I2cDevice` class, defined in the `Windows.Devices.I2c` namespace of the Windows IoT Extensions for the UWP. The `I2cDevice` class does not implement any public constructors. So, to get an instance of that class to associate a connection with a sensor, you use the static method `FromIdAsync` of the `I2cDevice` class. It expects two arguments: the device identifier and an instance of the `I2cConnectionSettings` class. The first one is obtained by enumerating the available I²C interfaces. This can be done using a `FindAllAsync` method of the `DeviceInformation` class, defined in the `Windows.Devices.Enumeration` namespace. Each of the available I²C devices is identified by its address, which is passed through an instance of the `I2cConnectionSettings` class. You do this by using the second argument of the `FromIdAsync` method.

Let's write a helper class for obtaining an instance of the `I2cDevice` class using the physical sensor address. According to the preceding scheme we first set up the connection settings and then enumerate available devices to find the one that matches the given address. The complete implementation of this class, stored in the I2cHelper.cs file of the SenseHat app, is shown in Listing 5-22.

LISTING 5-22 Definition of the I2cHelper class

```
using System;
using System.Linq;
using System.Threading.Tasks;
using Windows.Devices.Enumeration;
using Windows.Devices.I2c;

namespace SenseHat.Helpers
{
```

```
    public static class I2cHelper
    {
        public static async Task<I2cDevice> GetI2cDevice(byte address)
        {
            I2cDevice device = null;

            var settings = new I2cConnectionSettings(address);

            string deviceSelectorString = I2cDevice.GetDeviceSelector();

            var matchedDevicesList = await DeviceInformation.
                FindAllAsync(deviceSelectorString);
            if(matchedDevicesList.Count > 0)
            {
                var deviceInformation = matchedDevicesList.First();

                device = await I2cDevice.FromIdAsync(deviceInformation.Id, settings);
            }

            return device;
        }
    }
}
```

After obtaining an instance of the `I2cDevice` class we can start transferring data between a micro-controller and a sensor. In I²C serial communication, data is transferred in a binary format as a byte array. Therefore, the `I2cDevice` class exposes several members for reading and writing byte arrays to and from sensors. This set of methods includes `Read`, `Write`, and `WriteRead`. The first and the second methods are used to read and write a byte array from the given register, while the `WriteRead` method performs a read operation followed by writing data to the register. `WriteRead` is a shortcut method, because typically, you want to send a request to the sensor, and then read the response using the same register address.

Reading and writing data from STM sensors follows the same scheme. Since other sensors of the Sense HAT add-on board are also manufactured by STM, I will implement the helper class, which will simplify the process of reading data from 8-bit registers, and will also automate conversion of byte arrays to 16-bit, and 32-bit signed integers. The definition of this class is given in Listing 5-23 (see the companion code at Chapter 05/SenseHat/Helpers/RegisterHelper.cs).

LISTING 5-23 Helper class for performing common register operations

```
using System;
using System.Linq;
using Windows.Devices.I2c;

namespace SenseHat.Helpers
{
    public class RegisterHelper
    {
```

```csharp
public static byte ReadByte(I2cDevice device, byte address)
{
    Check.IsNull(device);

    // Write buffer contains the register address
    var writeBuffer = new byte[] { address };

    // Read buffer is a single-element byte array
    var readBuffer = new byte[1];

    device.WriteRead(writeBuffer, readBuffer);

    return readBuffer.First();
}

public static void WriteByte(I2cDevice device, byte address, byte value)
{
    Check.IsNull(device);

    var writeBuffer = new byte[] { address, value };

    device.Write(writeBuffer);
}

public static short GetShort(I2cDevice device, byte[] addressList)
{
    const int length = 2;

    Check.IsLengthEqualTo(addressList.Length, length);

    var bytes = GetBytes(device, addressList, length);

    return BitConverter.ToInt16(bytes.ToArray(), 0);
}

public static int GetInt(I2cDevice device, byte[] addressList)
{
    const int minLength = 3;
    const int maxLength = 4;

    Check.IsLengthInValidRange(addressList.Length, minLength, maxLength);

    var bytes = GetBytes(device, addressList, maxLength);

    return BitConverter.ToInt32(bytes.ToArray(), 0);
}

private static byte[] GetBytes(I2cDevice device, byte[] addressList, int totalLength)
{
    var bytes = new byte[totalLength];

    for (int i = 0; i < addressList.Length; i++)
```

```
        {
            bytes[i] = ReadByte(device, addressList[i]);
        }

        if (!BitConverter.IsLittleEndian)
        {
            bytes = bytes.Reverse().ToArray();
        }

        return bytes;
    }
  }
}
```

The code snippet from Listing 5-23 shows how to use `Write` and `WriteRead` methods of the `I2c-Device` class to obtain single bytes stored in the particular registers of an I²C device. As you can see, in the `RegisterHelper` class I am using methods of the `BitConverter` class to convert byte arrays to integral data types. Moreover, the argument validation is performed using a helper Check class. It is implemented in the following file of the companion code: Chapter 05/SenseHat/Helpers/Check.cs. Note that this class will be used in many other projects as the helper. Particular implementations of the Check class may vary between projects.

The next step is to ensure that connection with the STM sensor is established and the sensor is properly initialized. This can be done by reading the WHO_AM_I register at the address of 0x0F using the ReadByte static method of the `RegisterHelper` class. If everything goes correctly, a sensor will return the value of 0xBD.

However, before going further an important aspect of STM sensors should be explained. Namely, according to the LPS25H datasheet, this module (and other sensors, which we will use in this chapter) by default is in the power-down control mode. In this mode, the sensor will not return actual readings. We need first to turn the sensor on. To this end, we must set the proper value in the control register. The latter consists of the unsigned byte, in which each bit is responsible for basic sensor configuration. (See Figure 5-6 and page 25 of the sensor datasheet.) In particular, the last bit (MSB) controls the sensor mode (power-down or active mode), bits on position 4-6 control the output data rate (ODR), while the bit of index 2 controls the block data update (BDU).

Bit index	0	1	2	3	4	5	6	7
Function	SPI Interface Mode	Reset AutoZero	Block Data Update (BDU)	Interrupt Circuit	Output Data Rate (ODR)			Power-down (PD)

FIGURE 5-6 Bit-encoding of the LPS25H control register. Only the BDU, ODR, and PD bits are used, since communication is performed using the I²C bus, and we do not use interrupts nor reset the vauto zero function.

To turn on the sensor, we need to set the MSB of the control register to 1—that is, turn the sensor from the power-down into an active-mode. Next, we can configure the BDU and ODR.

The BDU configures the way internal sensing module updates the register. For BDU = 0, the sensing module continuously updates registers with temperature and pressure values. So the low and high bytes are updated at different times. Consequently, when you read the register during an update, you may get an incorrect value. To disable such continuous updates, the BDU is recommended to have a value of 1.

The ODR defines the sensor refresh (sampling) rate—that is, how often a module will measure the pressure and the temperature. ODR bit configuration is shown in Table 5-2. Note that, contrary to STM datasheets, I am using the LSB bit ordering. This is due to the fact that such ordering corresponds to the convention used in the BitArray class. Namely, the first element of the BitArray collection is the LSB at index 0.

TABLE 5-2   Output data rate configuration for the LPS25H module

Register bit index			Refresh rate [Hz]
4 (ODR0)	5 (ODR1)	6 (ODR2)	
0	0	0	One-shot
1	0	0	1
0	1	0	7
1	1	0	12.5
0	0	1	25

There are also three other functions, configured using the control register. These are: SPI Interface Mode (bit at index 0), Reset AutoZero (bit at index 1), and Interrupt Circuit (bit at index 3). The first one, SPI Interface Mode, lets you configure the SPI Mode. However, since we use the I^{2}C interface, we leave the SPI Mode at the default value. The second control bit, Reset AutoZero, is used to reset the reference pressure, which is used for sensor readings calibration. Again, we do not re-calibrate the sensor manually, and leave the Reset AutoZero bit at its default value (that is, 0). Lastly, Interrupt Circuit allows you to enable interrupts whenever the new sensor reading is available.

Here, we will only configure the PD, BDU, and ODR of the control register, and preserve the default values of the other bits. To simplify the control register configuration, I implemented another helper class, TemperatureAndPressureSensorHelper. See its fragment in Listing 5-24. You can find the full code of this class in the companion code (Chapter 05/SenseHat/Helpers/TemperatureAndPressureSensor-Helper.cs).

LISTING 5-24   Control register configuration using the BitArray class

```
public static byte ConfigureControlByte(
    BarometerOutputDataRate outputDataRate = BarometerOutputDataRate.Hz_25,
    bool safeBlockUpdate = true, bool isOn = true)
{
    var bitArray = new BitArray(Constants.ByteBitLength);
```

```
    // BDU
    bitArray.Set(bduIndex, safeBlockUpdate);

    // ODR
    SetOdr(outputDataRate, bitArray);

    // Power-down bit
    bitArray.Set(pdIndex, isOn);

    return ConversionHelper.GetByteValueFromBitArray(bitArray);
}
```

TemperatureAndPressureSensorHelper has one public member, ConfigureControlByte. The latter method has three arguments: outputDataRate, safeBlockUpdate, and isOn. The first argument is of the custom enumeration type BarometerOutputDataRate. It defines five members; see the bottom part of Listing 5-25. These values correspond to the ODR configuration given in Table 5-2, and are used to set the sensor sampling rate.

Two other arguments of the ConfigureControlByte method set the BDU (safeBlockUpdate) and PD (isOn). As you can see, the definition of ConfigureControlByte uses a high-level API provided by the BitArray class and other methods described earlier. In particular, to change the particular bit value, I used the Set method of the BitArray class instance.

The private SetOdr method is implemented in a similar manner. (See Listing 5-25.) Namely, depending on the ODR selected using one of the values of the BarometerOutputDataRate enumeration, I instantiate a three-element array of Boolean variables. This array reflects the logical states of the ODR bits. Subsequently, I assign these values to the BitArray collection using the helper method SetBitArray-Values implemented in the ConversionHelper class. (See Listing 5-26.)

LISTING 5-25   Barometric sensor sampling rate configuration

```
private static void SetOdr(BarometerOutputDataRate outputDataRate, BitArray bitArray)
{
    bool[] odrBitValues;

    switch (outputDataRate)
    {
        case BarometerOutputDataRate.OneShot:
            odrBitValues = new bool[] { false, false, false };
            break;

        case BarometerOutputDataRate.Hz_1:
            odrBitValues = new bool[] { true, false, false };
            break;

        case BarometerOutputDataRate.Hz_7:
            odrBitValues = new bool[] { false, true, false };
            break;
```

```
        case BarometerOutputDataRate.Hz_12_5:
            odrBitValues = new bool[] { true, true, false };
            break;

        case BarometerOutputDataRate.Hz_25:
        default:
            odrBitValues = new bool[] { false, false, true };
            break;
    }

    ConversionHelper.SetBitArrayValues(bitArray, odrBitValues, odrBeginIndex, odrEndIndex);
}

public enum BarometerOutputDataRate
{
    OneShot, Hz_1, Hz_7, Hz_12_5, Hz_25
}
```

LISTING 5-26 A helper method for setting elements of the BitArray collection

```
public static void SetBitArrayValues(BitArray bitArray, bool[] values,
    int beginIndex, int endIndex)
{
    Check.IsNull(bitArray);
    Check.IsNull(values);

    Check.IsPositive(beginIndex);
    Check.LengthNotLessThan(bitArray.Length, endIndex);

    for (int i = beginIndex, j = 0; i <= endIndex; i++, j++)
    {
        bitArray[i] = values[j];
    }
}
```

I implemented the skeleton, SensorBase class (see the companion code at Chapter 05/SenseHat/
Sensors/SensorBase.cs), which simplifies such operations as reading the WHO_AM_I register and setting control register values. The Sensor-Base class has one public property, IsInitialized, which is
used to check whether the sensor has been properly initialized—that is, if the WHO_AM_I register has
the expected value. Moreover, SensorBase contains four protected, overridable members: device,
sensorAddress, whoAmIRegisterAddress, and whoAmIDefaultValue. The first is used to store the
reference of the I2cDevice class. The second stores the sensor address—that is, the address of the
actual I²C device, which is used to access the particular sensor. All the sensor addresses can be retrieved
from the interactive diagram available at *http://pinout.xyz/pinout/sense_hat*. Finally, two last private
members, whoAmIRegisterAddress and whoAmIDefaultValue, are used to set the WHO_AM_I register
address and the value for the particular sensor. Accordingly, sensorAddress, whoAmIRegisterAddress,
and whoAmIDefaultValue have their protected access modified, and thus can be overridden in the
particular class implementing the abstraction layer for each STM sensor.

In addition, the `SensorBase` class implements the public `Initialize` method, which associates the I²C connection, reads the WHO_AM_I register, and then configures the control register using the `Configure` method. (See Listing 5-27.) Note that this procedure is performed only once if the sensor is not initialized. As you can see, the base definition of the `Configure` method is empty. We will override this method individually for each sensor.

LISTING 5-27   Selected methods of the base class representing the physical STM sensor

```
public async Task<bool> Initialize()
{
    if (!IsInitialized)
    {
        device = await I2cHelper.GetI2cDevice(sensorAddress);

        if (device != null)
        {
            IsInitialized = WhoAmI(whoAmIRegisterAddress, whoAmIDefaultValue);

            if (IsInitialized)
            {
                Configure();
            }
        }
    }

    return IsInitialized;
}

protected bool WhoAmI(byte registerAddress, byte expectedValue)
{
    byte whoami = RegisterHelper.ReadByte(device, registerAddress);

    return whoami == expectedValue;
}

protected virtual void Configure(){ }
```

Let's start with the barometric sensor first. The full implementation of the class `TemperatureAnd-PressureSensor`, being the abstract LP25SH sensor representation, is given in the companion code: Chapter 05/SenseHat/Sensors/TemperatureAndPressureSensor.cs. The `TemperatureAndPressure-Sensor` implements the constructor, which sets the protected members of the base class, and overrides the base `Configure` method. (See Listing 5-28.)

LISTING 5-28   Initialization and configuration of the temperature and pressure sensor

```
public TemperatureAndPressureSensor()
{
    sensorAddress = 0x5C;
```

```
    whoAmIRegisterAddress = 0x0F;
    whoAmIDefaultValue = 0xBD;
}

protected override void Configure()
{
    CheckInitialization();

    const byte controlRegisterAddress = 0x20;
    var controlRegisterByteValue = TemperatureAndPressureSensorHelper.ConfigureControlByte();

    RegisterHelper.WriteByte(device, controlRegisterAddress, controlRegisterByteValue);
}
```

The central part of the TemperatureAndPressureSensor class comprises two public methods: Get-Temperature and GetPressure. These methods are based on the previously developed helper classes, so as shown in Listing 5-29, the implementation is clean and concise. Reading the temperature from the LP25SH sensor is performed by obtaining two bytes from appropriate registers and then turning them into a single 16-bit integer, which is later rescaled to degrees Celsius.

LISTING 5-29 Implementation of GetTemperature and GetPressure

```
public float GetTemperature()
{
    CheckInitialization();

    // Register address list
    const byte tempLowByteRegisterAddress = 0x2B;
    const byte tempHighByteRegisterAddress = 0x2C;

    // Read low, and high bytes and convert them to 16-bit signed integer
    var temperature = RegisterHelper.GetShort(device,
        new byte[] { tempLowByteRegisterAddress, tempHighByteRegisterAddress });

    // Convert to physical units [degrees Celsius]
    return temperature / tempScaler + tempOffset;
}
```

As shown in Listing 5-29, to get the temperature value I read two bytes from the registers of the following addresses: 0x2B and 0x2C. Subsequently, these values are turned into a signed 16-bit integer. The resulting raw number must be converted into a physically significant value given in degrees Celsius. To this end, I used the following equation:

$$T = \frac{t}{480} + 42.5$$

where t is the raw value obtained from the sensor's memory, and the constant values are stored as private members of the TemperatureAndPressureSensor class.

The pressure reading is obtained in a similar manner. (See Listing 5-30. Pressure is obtained by reading three bytes, turning them into a 32-bit signed integer, and converting them to a physically significant unit.) The raw barometric pressure p is stored using three bytes in the registers of the following addresses: 0x28, 0x29, and 0x2A. Values obtained from these registers are converted to a 32-bit signed integer, which is then translated to hectopascals (hPa) using the following relation:

$$P = \frac{p}{4096}$$

where the constant scaler is stored in the pressureScaler private field of the TemperatureAndPressureSensor class.

LISTING 5-30   Obtaining the pressure reading

```
public float GetPressure()
{
    CheckInitialization();

    // Register address list
    const byte pressureLowByteRegisterAddress = 0x28;
    const byte pressureMiddleByteRegisterAddress = 0x29;
    const byte pressureHighByteRegisterAddress = 0x2A;

    // Read registers and convert resulting values to a 32-bit signed integer
    var pressure = RegisterHelper.GetInt(device, new byte[] {
        pressureLowByteRegisterAddress,
        pressureMiddleByteRegisterAddress,
        pressureHighByteRegisterAddress });

    // Convert to physical units [hectopascals, hPa]
    return pressure / pressureScaler;
}
```

Let's now put things together, and display barometric sensor readings in the UI. To this end, in the MainPage.xaml.cs file, we initialize the TemperatureAndPressureSensor class, and then begin continuous sensor reading. (See Listing 5-31.) Additionally, within the MainPage class, I defined the helper private method BeginSensorReading. I use this method to run continuous sensor reading acquisition with the specified delay times. In the case of the barometric sensor used in this section, the sampling rate was set to 25 Hz. Therefore, the GetTemperature and GetPressure methods of the TemperatureAndPressureSensor class are invoked every 40 milliseconds.

LISTING 5-31   Displaying the values of temperature and barometric pressure

```
using System;
using SenseHat.Sensors;
using Windows.UI.Xaml.Controls;
using Windows.UI.Core;
using System.Threading.Tasks;
```

```
namespace SenseHat
{
    public sealed partial class MainPage : Page
    {
        private SensorReadings sensorReadings = new SensorReadings();

        private TemperatureAndPressureSensor temperatureAndPressureSensor =
            new TemperatureAndPressureSensor();

        public MainPage()
        {
            InitializeComponent();

            InitSensors();
        }

        private async void InitSensors()
        {
            // Temperature, and pressure sensor
            if (await temperatureAndPressureSensor.Initialize())
            {
                BeginTempAndPressureAcquisition();
            }
        }

        private void BeginTempAndPressureAcquisition()
        {
            const int msDelayTime = 40;

            BeginSensorReading(async () =>
            {
                // Get, and display sensors readings
                await Dispatcher.RunAsync(CoreDispatcherPriority.Normal, () =>
                {
                    sensorReadings.Temperature = temperatureAndPressureSensor.
                        GetTemperature();
                    sensorReadings.Pressure = temperatureAndPressureSensor.GetPressure();
                });
            }, msDelayTime);
        }

        private void BeginSensorReading(Action periodicAction, int msDelayTime)
        {
            Task.Run(() =>
            {
                while (true)
                {
                    periodicAction();
                    Task.Delay(msDelayTime).Wait();
                }
            });
        }
    }
}
```

After compiling and running the app, you will see the temperature and pressure values, as shown in Figure 5-2 and Figure 5-7.

To check whether the barometric pressure really works, you can compare your readings with local weather station reports. To verify if a temperature sensor functions properly, you can cover the Sense HAT with your hand. You should then notice that the temperature increases. Please keep in mind that the temperature value obtained by the Sense HAT may differ from your room temperature. This is because sensor readings may be affected by the temperature of the RPi2 or RPi3, which may be higher than room temperature, especially after a device has been warmed up.

FIGURE 5-7 Temperature reading of the LPS25H sensor.

In Figure 5-8 I plotted the time course of the recorded temperature after a short puff on the Sense HAT add-on board. A temperature peak is clearly visible. Here is where the science comes into play. Very often, the IoT processing module must continuously monitor physical quantities to detect any abnormalities arising due to external conditions. In this section, we implemented such continuous acquisition and will learn how to detect external disturbances in Chapter 11, "Device learning."

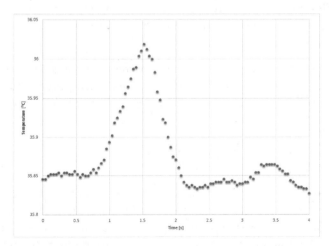

FIGURE 5-8 Temperature time course recorded using an IoT device.

As a final note for this section, let me point out that most of the implementation time was devoted to building helper classes for performing bit manipulations and byte array conversions. Given those helpers, the definition of the `TemperatureAndPressureSensor` class is very clear and contains only the logic specific to that particular sensor. Therefore, in the next sections we will use our base implementations to handle readings from other sensors of the Sense HAT add-on board.

Relative humidity

The Sense HAT humidity sensor is composed of the STM HTS221 module (*http://bit.ly/humidity_sensor*). This sensing module uses the polymer dielectric planar capacitor as a relative humidity sensing element.

In general, the data acquisition from that sensor proceeds similarly as in the case of LPS25H. We first need to read the WHO_AM_I register, then configure the ODR, and finally turn on the active device mode using the control register. In this case the address and the default value of the WHO_AM_I register are 0x0F and 0xBC, respectively. The byte stored in the control register of address 0x20 is composed of the bit controlling the power state (bit at index 7), the BDU (bit at index 2), and the ODR (the first and the second bit). Specifically, the ODR configuration is given in Table 5-3.

TABLE 5-3 Output data rate configuration for the HTS221 module

Register bit index		Refresh rate [Hz]
0 (ODR0)	1 (ODR1)	
0	0	One-shot
1	0	1
0	1	7
1	1	12.5

To configure the control register I wrote another helper class: `HumiditySensorHelper` (see the companion code at Chapter 05/SenseHat/Helpers/HumiditySensorHelper.cs). The implementation of this class is parallel to `TemperatureAndPressureSensorHelper`. There are only a few slight differences in handling the ODR. Therefore, a detailed description of this class is omitted.

Subsequently, after configuring the sensor, reading the raw humidity value h_r proceeds similarly as in the previous section. Namely, one needs to read values from the 0x28 and 0x29 registers and then convert them into a 16-bit signed integer. However, conversion to relative humidity, $H_\%$ (which is reported by weather stations), requires linear interpolation:

$$H_\%(h_r) = \left(\frac{h_1 - h_0}{t_1 - t_0}\right)(h_r - t_0) + t_1$$

Coefficients h_0 and h_1 are stored as unsigned 8-bit integers in two registers: 0x30 and 0x31. According to the sensor datasheet, after you obtain these values, you need to divide them by 2. Subsequently, you need to read registers 0x36, 0x37 and 0x3A, 0x3B to obtain the values of the t_0 and t_1 coefficients, respectively. These are signed 16-bit integers, so for this purpose, we can use the `GetShort` method of the `RegisterHelper` class. The full implementation of the algorithm for gathering the h_0, h_1, t_0, and t_1 coefficients is contained within the private member `GetHumidityScalers` of the `HumiditySensor` class. (See Listing 5-32 and the HumiditySensor.cs file of Chapter 05/SenseHat/Sensors.)

LISTING 5-32 Retrieving interpolation coefficients from the humidity sensor memory

```
private void GetHumidityScalers()
{
    CheckInitialization();

    const byte h0RegisterAddress = 0x30;
    const byte h1RegisterAddress = 0x31;

    const byte t0LowByteRegisterAddress = 0x36;
    const byte t0HighByteRegisterAddress = 0x37;

    const byte t1LowByteRegisterAddress = 0x3A;
    const byte t1HighByteRegisterAddress = 0x3B;

    const float hScaler = 2.0f;

    humidityScalerH0 = RegisterHelper.ReadByte(device, h0RegisterAddress) / hScaler;
    humidityScalerH1 = RegisterHelper.ReadByte(device, h1RegisterAddress) / hScaler;

    humidityScalerT0 = RegisterHelper.GetShort(device,
        new byte[] { t0LowByteRegisterAddress, t0HighByteRegisterAddress });
    humidityScalerT1 = RegisterHelper.GetShort(device,
        new byte[] { t1LowByteRegisterAddress, t1HighByteRegisterAddress });
}
```

Linear interpolation coefficients do not change during runtime. Therefore, as shown in Listing 5-33, I invoke the `GetHumidityScalers` method only once within the `Configure` method of the `Humidity-Sensor` class.

LISTING 5-33 Interpolation coefficients are gathered after configuring the control register

```
protected override void Configure()
{
    CheckInitialization();

    const byte controlRegisterAddress = 0x20;
    var controlRegisterByteValue = HumiditySensorHelper.ConfigureControlByte();

    RegisterHelper.WriteByte(device, controlRegisterAddress, controlRegisterByteValue);

    GetHumidityScalers();
}
```

Next, we can retrieve the humidity by reading bytes stored in the registers at the addresses of 0x28 and 0x29. Similarly, as in the previous section, such functionality is based on the appropriate methods of the `RegisterHelper` class. (See Listing 5-34.)

```
public float GetHumidity()
{
    CheckInitialization();

    const byte humidityLowByteRegisterAddress = 0x28;
    const byte humidityHighByteRegisterAddress = 0x29;

    var rawHumidity = RegisterHelper.GetShort(device,
        new byte[] { humidityLowByteRegisterAddress, humidityHighByteRegisterAddress });

    return ConvertToRelativeHumidity(rawHumidity);
}

private float ConvertToRelativeHumidity(short rawHumidity)
{
    var slope = (humidityScalerH1 - humidityScalerH0) / (humidityScalerT1 - humidityScalerT0);

    return slope * (rawHumidity - humidityScalerT0) + humidityScalerH0;
}
```

Finally, to display the relative humidity, we only have to instantiate the HumidityAndTemperature-Sensor class and begin humidity acquisition in the same manner as we did in the previous section. (See Listing 5-35.) Then, after re-running the SenseHat app, it will display the relative humidity in the appropriate tab. (See Figure 5-9.)

LISTING 5-35   Relative humidity acquisition

```
private HumidityAndTemperatureSensor humidityAndTemperatureSensor =
    new HumidityAndTemperatureSensor();

private async void InitSensors()
{
    // Temperature and pressure sensor
    if (await temperatureAndPressureSensor.Initialize())
    {
        BeginTempAndPressureAcquisition();
    }

    // Humidity
    if (await humidityAndTemperatureSensor.Initialize())
    {
        BeginHumidityAcquisition();
    }
}

private void BeginHumidityAcquisition()
{
    const int msDelayTime = 80;
```

```
    BeginSensorReading(async () =>
    {
        // Get, and display humidity sensor readings
        await Dispatcher.RunAsync(CoreDispatcherPriority.Normal, () =>
        {
            sensorReadings.Humidity = GetHumidity();
        });
    }, msDelayTime);
}
```

The HTS221 sensor also allows you to measure temperature. This proceeds similarly to what I showed earlier, so I encourage you to implement that functionality independently using the module's datasheet.

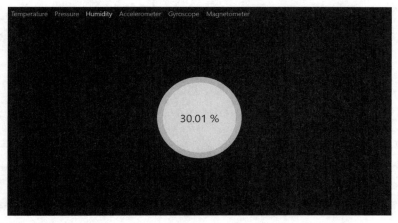

FIGURE 5-9 Relative humidity value gathered using the HTS221 sensor of the Sense HAT add-on board.

Accelerometer and gyroscope

The accelerometer and the gyroscope of the Sense HAT are components of the STM LSM9DS1 sensing module (*http://bit.ly/inertial_sensor*). This sensor uses the inertial motion of the object of a known mass to measure its linear acceleration (accelerometer) and angular speed (gyroscope).

The LSM9DS1 is manufactured using MEMS technology, so the object is mounted on micro springs. The module movement causes an object to displace. By measuring this movement in time, the acceleration and speed are determined. The resulting values are encoded by the electrical signals, which are converted to a digital representation and stored in appropriate registers. So, as before, the acceleration and speed values are obtained by reading relevant values from the sensor's memory.

According to the LSM9DS1's data sheet, to get simultaneous readings from the accelerometer and the gyroscope, we need to use two control registers: 0x10 (CTRL_REG1_G) and 0x20 (CTRL_REG6_XL). First, we need to write a power-down command (a value of 0x00) to the CTRL_REG6_XL register. Second, we configure the ODR of CTRL_REG1_G. In this case the ODR bits occupy positions 5-7, and their meaning is given in Table 5-4. Again, ODR configuration is implemented within the helper class `InertialSensor-Helper` (see the companion code at Chapter 05/SenseHat/Helpers/InertialSensorHelper.cs).

Here, I will use the refresh rate of 238 Hz, so the `Configure` method of the `InertialSensor` class takes the form depicted in Listing 5-36, so the value written to CTRL_REG1_G is 0000 0001 (that is, 0x80). To measure linear acceleration and angular speed simultaneously, two control registers are configured. First, CTRL_REG6_XL is set to 0x00; then I use CTRL_REG1_G to set the sampling rate to 238 Hz.

TABLE 5-4 Output data rate and power down configuration for the LSM9DS1 module

Register bit index			Refresh rate [Hz]
5 (ODR0)	6 (ODR1)	7 (ODR2)	
0	0	0	Power down
1	0	0	14.9
0	1	0	59.5
1	1	0	119
0	0	1	238
1	0	1	476
0	1	1	952

LISTING 5-36 The Configure method of the InertialSensor class

```
protected override void Configure()
{
    CheckInitialization();

    // Write power-down to 6XL register
    const byte controlRegister6XlAddress = 0x20;
    const byte controlRegister6XlByteValue = 0x00;

    RegisterHelper.WriteByte(device, controlRegister6XlAddress, controlRegister6XlByteValue);

    // Enable gyroscope and accelerometer
    const byte controlRegister1GAddress = 0x10;
    var controlRegister1GByteValue = InertialSensorHelper.ConfigureControlByte();

    RegisterHelper.WriteByte(device, controlRegister1GAddress, controlRegister1GByteValue);
}
```

The LSM9DS1 measures the acceleration along three axes: longitudinal (X), lateral (Y), and normal (Z). For angular speed measurements, these axes are denoted as roll (R), pitch (P), and yaw (Y_w). To represent acceleration readings along each axis, I am using the generic `Vector3D` class. (See Listing 5-37.) This class is an abstract representation of three element vectors. Each component of such vectors corresponds to the particular axis along which the sensor measures the linear acceleration and angular speed.

```
namespace SenseHat.Helpers
{
    public class Vector3D<T> where T : struct
    {
        public T X { get; set; }
        public T Y { get; set; }
        public T Z { get; set; }

        public override string ToString()
        {
            return string.Format("{0} {1} {2}", X, Y, Z);
        }
    }
}
```

Given the Vector3D class, an actual sensor reading of linear acceleration proceeds as follows. (See Listing 5-38). First, raw measurements along X, Y, and Z axes are gathered from six memory registers. Their memory location is pointed by the following addresses: 0x28 and 0x29 (X), 0x2A and 0x2B (Y), and 0x2C and 0x2D (Z). Next, each pair of those bytes is turned into a signed 16-bit integer, which is subsequently appropriately rescaled.

LISTING 5-38 Sensor reading of linear acceleration

```
public Vector3D<float> GetLinearAcceleration()
{
    var xLinearAccelerationRegisterAddresses = new byte[] { 0x28, 0x29 };
    var yLinearAccelerationRegisterAddresses = new byte[] { 0x2A, 0x2B };
    var zLinearAccelerationRegisterAddresses = new byte[] { 0x2C, 0x2D };

    var xLinearAcceleration = RegisterHelper.GetShort(device,
        xLinearAccelerationRegisterAddresses);
    var yLinearAcceleration = RegisterHelper.GetShort(device,
        yLinearAccelerationRegisterAddresses);
    var zLinearAcceleration = RegisterHelper.GetShort(device,
        zLinearAccelerationRegisterAddresses);

    return new Vector3D<float>()
    {
        X = xLinearAcceleration / linearAccelerationScaler,
        Y = yLinearAcceleration / linearAccelerationScaler,
        Z = zLinearAcceleration / linearAccelerationScaler
    };
}
```

The linear acceleration returned by the sensor is given in the units of gravity acceleration, g=9.81 m/s^2, and the default measurement range is ±2 g. Therefore, to rescale raw values returned by the sensor, we divide raw data by `short.MaxValue / 2`, where 2 comes from the measurement range. Therefore, the resulting acceleration readings are in the range of ±1 g along each axis.

Angular speed samples are retrieved in a similar manner; see the definition of the `GetAngular-Acceleration` method from Listing 5-39. Angular speed measured by the STM inertial sensor is gathered by reading six registers and converting the resulting values to units of degrees per second. The resulting acceleration vector is stored using the `Vector3D` class. There are just two differences between retrieving linear and angular acceleration. Namely, in Listing 5-39, I use different registers and conversion scalers.

LISTING 5-39   The GetAngularAcceleration method

```
public Vector3D<float> GetAngularSpeed()
{
    var xAngularSpeedRegisterAddresses = new byte[] { 0x18, 0x19 };
    var yAngularSpeedRegisterAddresses = new byte[] { 0x1A, 0x1B };
    var zAngularSpeedRegisterAddresses = new byte[] { 0x1C, 0x1D };

    var xAngularSpeed = RegisterHelper.GetShort(device,
        xAngularSpeedRegisterAddresses);
    var yAngularSpeed = RegisterHelper.GetShort(device,
        yAngularSpeedRegisterAddresses);
    var zAngularSpeed = RegisterHelper.GetShort(device,
        zAngularSpeedRegisterAddresses);

    return new Vector3D<float>()
    {
        X = xAngularSpeed / angularSpeedScaler,
        Y = yAngularSpeed / angularSpeedScaler,
        Z = zAngularSpeed / angularSpeedScaler
    };
}
```

Angular speed measurements along each axis are stored in the following memory locations: 0x18 and 0x19 (R), 0x1A and 0x1B (P), and 0x1C and 0x1D (Y_w). Values gathered from these registers need to be converted to 16-bit signed integers, and then to a physically significant unit, which in this case is the degree per second (dps).

By default, the angular speed measurement range of the STM inertial sensor is ±245 degrees per second (dps), so the raw data is divided by `short.MaxValue / 245`.

Now, to display linear acceleration and angular speed measurements in the UI, all we need to do is to appropriately invoke the preceding public methods of the `InertialSensor` class in the MainPage.xaml.cs file as distinguished in Listing 5-40. (Note that readings from the inertial sensor are refreshed every 5 ms.)

LISTING 5-40 Selected fragments of the MainPage class definition

```
private SensorReadings sensorReadings = new SensorReadings();

private TemperatureAndPressureSensor temperatureAndPressureSensor =
    new TemperatureAndPressureSensor();
private HumidityAndTemperatureSensor humidityAndTemperatureSensor =
    new HumidityAndTemperatureSensor();
private InertialSensor inertialSensor = new InertialSensor();

public MainPage()
{
    InitializeComponent();

    InitSensors();
}

private async void InitSensors()
{
    // Temperature and pressure sensor
    if (await temperatureAndPressureSensor.Initialize())
    {
        BeginTempAndPressureAcquisition();
    }

    // Humidity
    if (await humidityAndTemperatureSensor.Initialize())
    {
        BeginHumidityAcquisition();
    }

    // Inertial
    if (await inertialSensor.Initialize())
    {
        BeginAccelerationAndAngularSpeedAcquisition();
    }
}

private void BeginAccelerationAndAngularSpeedAcquisition()
{
    const int msDelayTime = 5;

    BeginSensorReading(async () =>
    {
        // Get, and display sensors readings
        await Dispatcher.RunAsync(CoreDispatcherPriority.Normal, () =>
        {
            sensorReadings.Accelerometer = inertialSensor.GetLinearAcceleration();
            sensorReadings.Gyroscope = inertialSensor.GetAngularSpeed();
        });
    }, msDelayTime);
}
```

Now, you can run the SenseHat app to see readings from the inertial sensor. You should notice that, when the RPi2 or RPi3 with the Sense HAT on top, is not moving and is placed on its back surface, the accelerometer will simply measure the gravity. In that case, it will report a value of approximately 1 g along the Z axis. (See Figure 5-10.) However, when you start rotating your RPi2 device, the linear acceleration readings will change. Moreover, as depicted in Figure 5-11, you will notice changes of the angular speed, which will reflect how fast you shake or move your device.

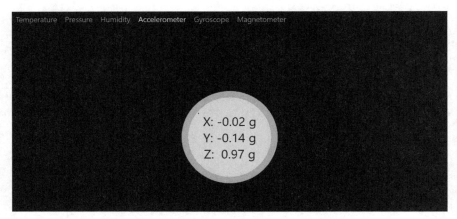

FIGURE 5-10   Sample accelerometer readings gathered using the SenseHat app.

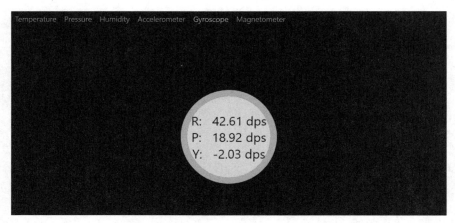

FIGURE 5-11   Sample angular IoT device speed measured using the MEMS gyroscope.

Magnetometer

The magnetometer is also a component of the LSM9DS1 module but it has a separate memory registers so we configure it independently. To enable and configure the magnetic field sensor we need to manipulate two registers. These are CTRL_REG1_M (0x20) and CTRL_REG3_M (0x22). The former, as shown in Figure 5-12, is used to configure the performance mode (bits 5, and 6) and ODR (bits 2-4). Moreover, the most significant bit (index of 7) allows you to enable the temperature compensation, while the least significant bit allows you to enable or disable the sensor self-test. In addition, the bit at index 1 allows you to enable fast ODR mode, allowing for sampling rates higher than 80 Hz. Otherwise, the magnetometer sampling rate (ODR) is parameterized by three bits as shown in Table 5-5. (ODR0, ODR1, and ODR2 denote bit values at indices 2–4 of the CTRL_REG1_M register, respectively; see Figure 5-12.) I implemented ODR configuration within the SetOdr method of the MagneticFieldSensorHelper class; see the companion code (Chapter 05/SenseHat/Helpers/MagneticFieldSensorHelper.cs). The implementation is based on the BitArray class, and uses already known techniques, so the specific description is omitted.

Bit index	0	1	2	3	4	5	6	7
Function	Self-test	Fast ODR	Output Data Rate (ODR)			Performance mode		Temperature compensation

FIGURE 5-12 A structure of the CTRL_REG1_M register of the Sense HAT magnetometer. This register, apart from enabling a sensor self-test, is used to configure sampling rate, performance, and temperature compensation.

TABLE 5-5 Output data rate configuration of the magnetometer of the STM LSM9DS1 inertial module

Register bit index			Sampling rate [Hz]
5 (ODR0)	6 (ODR1)	7 (ODR2)	
0	0	0	0.625
1	0	0	1.25
0	1	0	2.50
1	1	0	5.00
0	0	1	10.0
1	0	1	20.0
0	1	1	40.0
1	1	1	80.0

The magnetometer can work in several different modes: low-power (bit setting: 00), medium-performance (bit setting: 10), high-performance (bit setting: 01), and ultra-high performance (bit setting: 11). Performance configuration is implemented within the SetPerformance method. Definition of this method is analogous to SetOdr, and therefore its description is omitted.

Both methods, SetPerformance and SetOdr, are used within the ConfigureSensingParameters public method of the MagneticFieldSensorHelper class to configure the CTRL_REG1_M register.

The register, CTRL_REG1_M, described earlier does not allow you to enable the magnetometer. To this end, we need to use another register: CTRL_REG_3_M (0x22). Its structure is depicted in Figure 5-13. There are three bits (3, 4, and 6) that do not control any function, but must be set to 0 for proper magnetometer functioning. Bit 7 can disable the I2C interface. However, this is not desirable here, so we leave this bit at the default value. Next, the bit at index 5 controls the SPI mode. However, since we do not use the SPI interface, we do not change this bit either. The bit at index 2 can be used to turn the magnetometer into low-power mode, in which sampling is performed with the lowest ODR—that is, 0.625 Hz (every 1.6 s).

Bit index	0	1	2	3	4	5	6	7
Function	Operating mode		Low-power mode	-		SPI mode	-	Disable I²C

FIGURE 5-13 A structure of the CTRL_REG_M3 register of the Sense HAT magnetometer.

Lastly, the actual sensor operating mode is configured using two bits at indices of 0 and 1. As shown in Table 5-6, the magnetometer can work in three different modes: continuous-conversion (bit setting: 00), single-conversion (bit setting: 10), and power-down (bit setting: 11 or 10). In the continuous-conversion mode, the sensor continuously updates magnetic field readings at the sampling rate, specified by the CTRL_REG1_M register. Single-conversion mode is a single-shot mode, in which the magnetic field is updated just once. Finally, in power-down mode, the magnetic field is not measured at all. Although, you can read registers containing the magnetic field components in every mode, these values are not updated in the power-down mode, and are updated only once in the single-conversion mode.

TABLE 5-6 Magnetometer operating modes (OM) bit encoding of the CTRL_REG_M3 register (see Figure 5-13)

Register Bit Index		Operating Mode
0 (OM0)	1 (OM1)	
0	0	Continuous-conversion
1	0	Single-conversion
0	1	Power-down
0	1	

Again, to configure the operating-mode, I implemented the appropriate method, SetOperating-Mode, in the MagneticFieldSensorHelper class. The definition of this method is analogous to previous functions, and thus is not explicitly depicted here but can be found in the companion code. The SetOperatingMode method is invoked within the public member ConfigureOperatingMode of the MagneticFieldSensorHelper class.

To get magnetometer readings I implemented the MagneticFieldSensor class (see the companion code at Chapter 05/SenseHat/Sensors/MagneticFieldSensor.cs). As before, I have overridden the Configure method, which invokes two helper methods: ConfigureOperatingMode and Configure-SensingParameters. (See Listing 5-41.) Next, the actual sensor readings along each axis (X, Y, and Z) are gathered by reading six registers: 0x28 and 0x29 (X), 0x2A and 0x2B (Y), and 0x2C and 0x2D (Z). This functionality proceeds as in the case of acceleration reading, so the particular implementation depicted in Listing 5-42 is analogous, and does not require additional explanation—except the fact that the values reported by the magnetometer are given in gauss (G) units. So, for the default measurement range of ±4 G, the raw 16-bit signed integers are divided by short.MaxValue / 4.

LISTING 5-41   Magnetometer configuration

```
protected override void Configure()
{
    CheckInitialization();

    // Enable magnetometer
    const byte operatingModeControlRegisterAddress = 0x22;
    var operatingModeResiterValue = MagneticFieldSensorHelper.ConfigureOperatingMode();

    RegisterHelper.WriteByte(device, operatingModeControlRegisterAddress,
        operatingModeResiterValue);

    // Configure sensing parameters (ODR, performance)
    const byte controlRegisterAddress = 0x20;
    var controlRegisterByteValue = MagneticFieldSensorHelper.ConfigureSensingParameters();

    RegisterHelper.WriteByte(device, controlRegisterAddress, controlRegisterByteValue);
}
```

LISTING 5-42   Magnetic field is gathered by reading values from six registers: 0x28 – 0x2D

```
public Vector3D<float> GetMagneticField()
{
    var xMagneticFieldRegisterAddresses = new byte[] { 0x28, 0x29 };
    var yMagneticFieldRegisterAddresses = new byte[] { 0x2A, 0x2B };
    var zMagneticFieldRegisterAddresses = new byte[] { 0x2C, 0x2D };

    var xMagneticField = RegisterHelper.GetShort(device, xMagneticFieldRegisterAddresses);
    var yMagneticField = RegisterHelper.GetShort(device, yMagneticFieldRegisterAddresses);
    var zMagneticField = RegisterHelper.GetShort(device, zMagneticFieldRegisterAddresses);

    return new Vector3D<float>()
    {
        X = xMagneticField / scaler,
        Y = yMagneticField / scaler,
        Z = zMagneticField / scaler
    };
}
```

To put things together, the MagneticFieldSensor class is incorporated in MainPage.xaml.cs, as shown in Listing 5-43. Selected fragments of MainPage.xaml.cs show how to use the MagneticField-Sensor class. Magnetometer readings are updated every 13 ms, which roughly corresponds to the sampling rate of 80 Hz.

LISTING 5-43 Incorporating the MagneticFieldSensor class in the MainPage.xaml.cs file

```csharp
public sealed partial class MainPage : Page
{
    private MagneticFieldSensor magneticFieldSensor = new MagneticFieldSensor();

    private async void InitSensors()
    {
        // Temperature and pressure sensor
        if (await temperatureAndPressureSensor.Initialize())
        {
            BeginTempAndPressureAcquisition();
        }

        // Humidity
        if (await humidityAndTemperatureSensor.Initialize())
        {
            BeginHumidityAcquisition();
        }

        // Inertial
        if (await inertialSensor.Initialize())
        {
            BeginAccelerationAndAngularSpeedAcquisition();
        }

        // Magnetic field
        if (await magneticFieldSensor.Initialize())
        {
            BeginMagneticFieldAcquisition();
        }
    }

    private void BeginMagneticFieldAcquisition()
    {
        const int msDelayTime = 13;

        BeginSensorReading(async () =>
        {
            // Get, and display sensor readings
            await Dispatcher.RunAsync(CoreDispatcherPriority.Normal, () =>
            {
                sensorReadings.Magnetometer = magneticFieldSensor.GetMagneticField();
            });

        }, msDelayTime);
    }
}
```

In a typical room environment, the magnetometer should measure Earth's magnetic field. So the resulting readings, as shown in Figure 5-14, are in the range of 0.25–0.65 G, depending on your location.

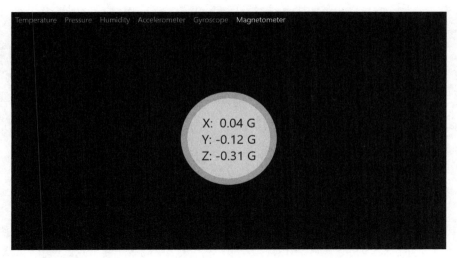

FIGURE 5-14 Sample magnetometer reading presented on the last tab of the SenseHat app UI.

Since measurements of linear acceleration and angular speed have straightforward applications, you may wonder, what do you need magnetic field measurements for? Magnetometers can be used to determine cardinal directions, and are widely used in smartphones to implement compasses. As you can see, the surface of the LSM9DS1 sensing module has just 3.5 by 3 millimeters, so this sensor can unnoticeably fit in every smartphone, smartwatch, or any other smart device.

Let me get back to cardinal direction determination using a magnetometer. To this end, I extended the definition of the `MagneticFieldSensorHelper` class by another public method, `GetDirectionAngle`. (See Listing 5-44.) This method determines an angle between X and Y components of the gathered magnetic field using the `Atan2` static method of the `Math` class. Subsequently, the resulting angle, given in radians, is converted to degrees using the `RadToDeg` helper method.

LISTING 5-44 Compass can be implemented using the magnetic field vector gathered from the magnetometer

```
public static double GetDirectionAngle(Vector3D<float> sensorReading)
{
    Check.IsNull(sensorReading);

    double directionAngle;

    if (sensorReading.Y != Constants.NorthAngle)
    {
        var radAngle = Math.Atan2(sensorReading.Y, sensorReading.X);
        var degAngle = RadToDeg(radAngle);

        directionAngle = degAngle < Constants.NorthAngle ?
            degAngle + Constants.MaxAngle : degAngle;
    }
    else
    {
```

```
            directionAngle = sensorReading.X > Constants.NorthAngle
                ? Constants.NorthAngle : Constants.SouthAngle;
    }

    return directionAngle;
}

private static double RadToDeg(double radAngle)
{
    return radAngle * 180.0 / Math.PI;
}
```

The angle value is in the range of –180° to +180°. Therefore, to turn this result into a range of 0 to 360°, required by cardinal directions, the value of 360° is added to negative angles.

In Listing 5-44, I also check if the Y component of the magnetic field is 0 G. In such a case, the direction angle can have two values: 0° (North), when the X magnetic field component is positive, or 180° (South), otherwise.

You can invoke GetDirectionAngle after obtaining the magnetic field vector, as shown in Listing 5-45. Then, after re-running the SenseHat app and rotating your device in the magnetic-field plane XY (device kept parallel to the ground), the direction angle will be displayed in the Output window of Visual Studio, provided you use the Debug configuration. You can compare the resulting values to the compass readings of your smartphone.

LISTING 5-45 Cardinal direction angle, calculated using the magnetometer, will be displayed in the Output window of Visual Studio

```
private void BeginMagneticFieldAcquisition()
{
    const int msDelayTime = 13;

    BeginSensorReading(async () =>
    {
        // Get, and display sensors readings
        await Dispatcher.RunAsync(CoreDispatcherPriority.Normal, () =>
        {
            sensorReadings.Magnetometer = magneticFieldSensor.GetMagneticField();

            var directionAngle = Helpers.MagneticFieldSensorHelper.
                GetDirectionAngle(sensorReadings.Magnetometer);
            System.Diagnostics.Debug.WriteLine(directionAngle.ToString("F2"));
        });

    }, msDelayTime);
}
```

However, during this testing, you may note inaccuracies of the magnetometer. This is because the magnetometer was not calibrated. This issue is further discussed in the next section.

For practice, you can independently implement another tab for the SenseHat app, in which you can display the direction angle.

Sensor calibration

Although modern sensing elements are all manufactured in the same way using microelectromechanical technology, precise measurements of various physical observables, including temperature, pressure, humidity, linear and angular acceleration, and magnetic field require sensor-specific calibration. That's why you typically need to calibrate the compass in your smartphone before the first use.

In general, the actual sensor readings may not be precise due to several reasons—for example, sensor sensitivity or sensor final mounting. These issues are most pronounced in the case of the inertial sensing module, because readings along each direction are non-symmetrical. To see this effect, you can record values reported by the magnetometer along the Z axis when your IoT device is placed on its bottom surface. In such a case, my sensor was reporting the average value of -0.428 G (Z1). Next, you need to put your IoT device upside down and note the magnetometer reading again. My device was reporting the average value of 0.368 G (Z2).

Ideally, these two values should be symmetrical—that is, differ by a sign only. However, in practice, we see that sensor readings are shifted by some constant offset, which can be determined by subtracting the absolute value of Z1 from Z2, and dividing the resulting number by 2. This yields the value of calibration offset along the Z axis, C_z

$$C_z = \frac{Z2 - |Z1|}{2} = -0.03$$

which must be subtracted from each magnetometer reading along the Z axis.

By repeating this procedure for other axes, you can determine your calibration vector, and use it to correct your readings, as shown in Listing 5-46. By doing so, you obtain symmetrical values.

LISTING 5-46 Sensor reading is corrected by the calibration offset

```
public Vector3D<float> GetMagneticField()
{
    var xMagneticFieldRegisterAddresses = new byte[] { 0x28, 0x29 };
    var yMagneticFieldRegisterAddresses = new byte[] { 0x2A, 0x2B };
    var zMagneticFieldRegisterAddresses = new byte[] { 0x2C, 0x2D };

    var xMagneticField = RegisterHelper.GetShort(device, xMagneticFieldRegisterAddresses);
    var yMagneticField = RegisterHelper.GetShort(device, yMagneticFieldRegisterAddresses);
    var zMagneticField = RegisterHelper.GetShort(device, zMagneticFieldRegisterAddresses);
```

```
    return new Vector3D<float>()
    {
        X = xMagneticField / scaler - calibrationOffset.X,
        Y = yMagneticField / scaler - calibrationOffset.Y,
        Z = zMagneticField / scaler - calibrationOffset.Z
    };
}
```

Perfect calibration would require one to apply to the sensor a magnetic field of the known value, and then verify the reading. Though this is not usually possible, the preceding procedure helps to correct sensor readings using fundamental physical insights about measurement symmetry.

After performing calibration, your LSM9DS1-based compass readings should agree with smartphone-based compass readings. Of course, the similar calibration can be performed for the linear and angular acceleration sensing components of the LSM9DS1 sensor.

Singleton pattern

Typically, the IoT device is equipped with just one sensor of a particular type. Namely, it has just one accelerometer, one gyroscope, and one magnetometer. Therefore, instantiating appropriate classes multiple times does not make too much sense. Instead, it is preferable to implement the so-called singleton pattern.

Generally, a thread-safe singleton pattern, is implemented in C# such that the class instance is available through the public static property, named `Instance` (see "Implementing Singleton in C#" at *http://bit.ly/singleton_cs*). Moreover, the class is instantiated using the private constructor within the critical section, so threads can access the `Instance` property sequentially.

To adopt such a design pattern in our sensor classes, all we need to do is the following. First, we need to extend the `SensorBase` class by an additional protected member:

```
protected static object syncRoot = new object();
```

Second, in each class implementing the sensor (`TemperatureAndPressureSensor`, `HumiditySensor`, `InertialSensor`, and `MagneticFieldSensor`) we change the constructor's access modifier to `private`, and implement the public `Instance` property. The sample implementation for the `TemperatureAnd-PressureSensor` class is given in Listing 5-47. Note that double-check locking is used to avoid thread concurrency problems. Moreover, the use of the volatile keyword ensures that the instance variable can be accessed after the variable instantiation completes.

LISTING 5-47 Thread-safe implementation of the singleton pattern in C#

```
public static TemperatureAndPressureSensor Instance
{
    get
    {
        if (instance == null)
        {
            lock (syncRoot)
            {
                if (instance == null)
                {
                    instance = new TemperatureAndPressureSensor();
                }
            }
        }

        return instance;
    }
}

private static volatile TemperatureAndPressureSensor instance;

private TemperatureAndPressureSensor()
{
    sensorAddress = 0x5C;

    whoAmIRegisterAddress = 0x0F;
    whoAmIDefaultValue = 0xBD;
}
```

Lastly, we modify MainPage.xaml.cs to use the `Instance` property of each sensor class. Classes, being abstract representations of each sensor, are instantiated only once when needed. (See Listing 5-48.)

LISTING 5-48 A singleton pattern in use

```
private TemperatureAndPressureSensor temperatureAndPressureSensor =
    TemperatureAndPressureSensor.Instance;

private HumidityAndTemperatureSensor humidityAndTemperatureSensor =
    HumidityAndTemperatureSensor.Instance;

private InertialSensor inertialSensor = InertialSensor.Instance;

private MagneticFieldSensor magneticFieldSensor = MagneticFieldSensor.Instance;
```

Though the preceding changes do not alter app functionality, they follow standard guidance patterns and practices for C# apps.

Summary

This chapter explored Windows 10 IoT Core capabilities in terms of acquiring and converting data from various sensors of the Sense HAT add-on board for RPi2 and RPi3. This board uses MEMS sensors, which can be found in many wearable and mobile devices, including smartphones, smartwatches, activity trackers, and so on. Therefore, knowledge you acquired by reading this chapter can be now used to build a mobile monitoring system for analyzing local weather conditions, a pedometer, or a gaming input device using an IoT device. Moreover, you are ready to implement software for smart devices for biomedical measurements, as used in activity trackers. Furthermore, In Chapter 7, I will show some advanced mathematical features, which may further help you analyze sensor data in the frequency domain. This can be particularly useful for pedometers or biomedical applications.

Throughout this chapter, I configured sensors with arbitrarily chosen fixed values of the sensor parameters. In general, I tend to minimize configuration, so the sensor reading is achieved with minimal effort. However, by using bitwise operators, the `BitConverter` class, and the `BitArray` class, you can extend presented classes by methods allowing you to configure other sensor parameters, like measurement range.

Finally, you learned how to calibrate your sensors and moreover how to adopt best design patterns.

You may wonder, why I used the add-on board. This is because, in real-world applications, the specific functionalities of the whole device, as in the programming of large software projects, are typically delegated to sub-boards to control the particular components. This chapter did something similar. The Sense HAT add-on board provides the functionality of sensing physical observables and serves basic I/O devices, which we will work with in the next chapter.

CHAPTER 6

Input and output

Often, an IoT device is accommodated in a small housing, in which there is no room for a full-size keyboard or a large display, and so it relies on a different form of input and output. For instance, the input device can be a set of buttons or a joystick, while the output can be a small LED display or touchscreen.

Such a device is the Sense HAT add-on board for the RPi2, which is equipped with an 8x8 array of RGB LEDs and a five-button joystick. (See Figure 6-1.) This joystick can control an IoT device, while the LED array can act as a simplified, low-resolution display.

FIGURE 6-1   Sense HAT add-on board installed on top of the RPi2. My finger is on the small joystick. Although this joystick has nothing to do with typical game controllers, it is built using very similar components, i.e. micro switches. These switches generate signals, which can be recorded through GPIO inputs and, as shown here, combined with other IoT elements, e.g. an LED array.

Because the joystick is formally a set of micro buttons (micro switches), I start this chapter with an example of how to handle the GPIO inputs generated by the tactile button. The tactile button is composed of a micro switch, which generates a signal when you press the button. Subsequently, I write a UWP app that utilizes the Sense HAT joystick and LED array, and I show how to handle gestures.

Tactile buttons

A tactile button, as you see in Figure 6-2, is part of the Windows 10 IoT Core Pack for the Raspberry Pi2. Pressing a button activates a micro switch, moving the internal circuit to the logical on state. Such a device can be used to switch on or off selected functions of the IoT device. In particular, you can use it to blink the green ACT LED of the RPi2. To do so, you first connect the button to the RPi2 through the solderless breadboard. The connection scheme is very similar to the one used in Chapter 2, "Universal Windows Platform on devices," to drive the external LED. However, you do not need to use an additional resistor, and you need to take off the Sense HAT add-on board to get access to the GPIO expansion header.

FIGURE 6-2   A tactile button, which is a very simple input device. Courtesy of *www.adafruit.com*.

The tactile button has four legs that you connect to the following breadboard points: D1, D3, G59, and G57 (see Figure 6-3). Use two jumper wires, one to connect the GPIO5 (pin 29 on the RPi2 GPIO header) with the J59 point of the breadboard, and the second to connect the H57 point with the ground port of the RPi2 (e.g. pin 25 or 39). This configuration is an active-low state.

FIGURE 6-3   A tactile button connected to the RPi2 using a solderless breadboard. The red jumper wire is connected to the ground (pin 39), while the brown jumper wire is attached to the GPIO5 (pin 29).

After the hardware components are connected, you can write the actual software. Here, the UI is not required, so you implement the headless app. Use the Background Application (IoT) C# project template. Create an app named ButtonInputBgApp, and then use that template to do the following: First, reference the Windows IoT Extensions for the UWP, and second, implement the logic responsible for changing the state of the GPIO pin of number 47. This pin controls the state of the green ACT LED of the RPi2.

 Note The RPi3 does not have this LED, so to run that sample, you can use the external LED circuit you built in Chapter 2.

As you saw in Chapter 3, "Windows IoT programming essentials," the default application logic of the headless app is implemented within the StartupTask class. You can find the complete implementation of this class, which handles the GPIO input in the companion code: Chapter 06/ButtonInputBgApp/StartupTask.cs. This implementation consists of similar methods for controlling the LED state as the ones I showed you in Chapters 2 and 3.

Listing 6-1 shows you how to handle the changes of the button's state attached to the GPIO pin by using members of the GpioPin class. First, you change the drive mode to InputPullUp so that the signal received when a button is pressed is the valid logic (high or low) state. Second, you attach the handler to the ValueChanged event. The event is fired when the button is pressed or released. When you press a button, the distance between two contact points in the micro switch decreases, and therefore the logic level may change because it is susceptible to noise. The ValueChanged event can be raised multiple times. To overcome this problem, you can filter out signals generated by noise using *debouncing*. Doing so ensures that only a single digital signal is registered by the GPIO controller during the specified time, which you configure through the DebounceTimeout property of the GpioPin class instance.

LISTING 6-1 Controlling the LED using an input device

```
public sealed class StartupTask : IBackgroundTask
{
    private const int buttonPinNumber = 5;
    private const int ledPinNumber = 47;

    private const int debounceTime = 20;

    private GpioPin ledPin;
    private BackgroundTaskDeferral bgTaskDeferral;

    public void Run(IBackgroundTaskInstance taskInstance)
    {
        bgTaskDeferral = taskInstance.GetDeferral();

        var buttonPin = ConfigureGpioPin(buttonPinNumber, GpioPinDriveMode.InputPullUp);
        if (buttonPin != null)
        {
            buttonPin.DebounceTimeout = TimeSpan.FromMilliseconds(debounceTime);
            buttonPin.ValueChanged += ButtonPin_ValueChanged;
```

```
            ledPin = ConfigureGpioPin(ledPinNumber, GpioPinDriveMode.Output);
            if (ledPin != null)
            {
                ledPin.Write(GpioPinValue.Low);
            }
        }
        else
        {
            bgTaskDeferral.Complete();
        }
    }

    private void ButtonPin_ValueChanged(GpioPin sender, GpioPinValueChangedEventArgs args)
    {
        if (ledPin != null)
        {
            var newValue = InvertGpioPinValue(ledPin);

            ledPin.Write(newValue);
        }
    }

    // Here are the ConfigureGpioPin, and InvertGpioPinValue methods; see companion code
}
```

 Note   If you use an external LED circuit you will need to update the value of ledPinNumber.

Note that in Listing 6-1 I use the BackgroundTaskDeferral object. It prevents the background task from being closed by the runtime until the Complete method of the BackgroundTaskDeferral class instance is invoked. This approach is necessary because any changes of the GPIO pin values are monitored using the worker thread that is created internally by the GpioPin class and reported using the ValueChanged event. Without deferring a background task, the application exits after a Run method completes, so the GpioPin class instance would not even have a chance to raise the ValueChanged event.

To test ButtonInputBgApp, deploy it to your IoT device. The green ACT LED (or external LED) turns on whenever you press the button. (See Figure 6-4.)

FIGURE 6-4   When the button is pressed, an interrupt is generated, and the green ACT on-board LED of the RPi2 is turned on; see the right corner of the IoT device. Compare this photograph with the one in Figure 6-3.

Joystick

A joystick of the Sense HAT add-on board is composed of five buttons (micro switches). When you move a stick toward one of the four available directions or press it down, the corresponding micro switch is activated, which in turn generates an interruption. This signal is registered and stored by the Atmel microcontroller of the Sense HAT add-on board. To read the current joystick state, you send a request to that microcontroller using the I²C bus and an address of 0x46. This works similarly to reading data from sensors. Therefore, you can use the previously developed helper classes as building blocks for your next IoT app.

Joystick micro switches correspond to the up, down, left, and right directions (see Figure 6-5). When your RPi2 board is located such that the Sense HAT is facing up, the left and right directions of a joystick are parallel to the longer side of the RPi2. Consequently, the up and down joystick directions are perpendicular to the longer RPi2 side. The right joystick button is directed toward the LAN and USB ports of the RPi2, while the left button is oriented toward an LED array.

An additional micro switch is activated when you press the joystick down. This button is defined as Enter (the letter E in Figure 6-5).

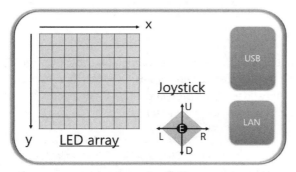

FIGURE 6-5 A sketch of the Sense HAT add-on board for the RPi2, assuming the device is facing up. L, U, D, R, and E denote the left, up, down, right, and enter joystick buttons, respectively. The figure also shows the coordinate system for LED indexing, which you use later in this chapter.

Sense HAT joystick buttons

I use the term *joystick buttons* when talking about the Sense HAT to be consistent with the official Raspberry Pi website. Although buttons on the Sense HAT joystick cannot be compared to buttons on a typical game controller, from the low-level point of view, they use similar concepts—specifically, they generate GPIO signals when micro switches are in contact. Hence, the terms *joystick button* and *micro switch* can be used interchangeably.

Middleware layer

Information about the joystick state is encoded using five bits of the single byte, which is stored by the Sense HAT add-on board. Each bit in this byte, starting from LSB, corresponds to the Down, Right, Up, Enter, and Left buttons; see Table 6-1. The particular bit is set to 1 when the appropriate micro switch is pressed. To decode information about currently pressed micro switches, you can use the BitArray class or bitwise operators described in Chapter 5, "Reading data from sensors."

I am going to implement the separate Joystick class, which is an abstract representation of the joystick. This class will send requests to the Sense HAT add-on board to get the current joystick status as the raw byte. This byte will be decoded using the BitArray class, and information about the currently pressed joystick micro switch will be propagated to any listeners using a custom event. Any app utilizing the joystick does not need to know anything about its internal functioning and can simply handle the appropriate event. All you need to do is implement the middleware layer, translating the low-level device functions to the high-level API.

TABLE 6-1   Joystick state encoding

Bit index	0	1	2	3	4
Button	Down	Right	Up	Enter	Left
Numerical value when a micro switch is active	1	2	4	8	16

The complete implementation of this functionality appears in the companion code: Chapter 06/SenseHatIO. I started by creating a new Blank UWP project called SenseHatIO. Next, I referenced the Windows IoT Extensions for the UWP, and then I added to the project the files I2cHelper.cs, Register-Helper.cs, and Check.cs, which I showed you how to develop in Chapter 5.

Subsequently, I wrote the class JoystickEventArgs, which represents the event arguments; see Listing 6-2 and the following file of the companion code: Chapter 06/SenseHatIO/SenseHatJoystick/Joystick-EventArgs.cs. The class implemented there uses two enumeration types: JoystickButton and JoystickButtonState. The former represents available joystick buttons: Down, Right, Up, Enter, and Left, while the JoystickButtonState corresponds to possible button states: Pressed, Holding, or Released. Additionally, JoystickButton and JoystickButtonState enumerations define a None element used to inform event listeners that the joystick is in the neutral position and thus is in the indeterminate state.

LISTING 6-2   The joystick button and its state will be passed using a dedicated class

```
public class JoystickEventArgs : EventArgs
{
    public JoystickButton Button { get; private set; }

    public JoystickButtonState State { get; private set; }

    public JoystickEventArgs(JoystickButton button, JoystickButtonState state)
    {
        Button = button;
        State = state;
```

```
    }
}

public enum JoystickButton : byte
{
    None = 0, Down = 1, Right = 2, Up = 4, Enter = 8, Left = 16
}

public enum JoystickButtonState : byte
{
    None = 0, Pressed, Holding, Released
}
```

After the enumeration types are defined, you prepare the helper class, `JoystickHelper`; see Chapter 06/SenseHatIO/SenseHatJoystick/JoystickHelper.cs. `JoystickHelper` includes two static methods: `GetJoystickButton` and `GetJoystickButtonState`. The first, `GetJoystickButton`, decodes information about the currently pressed joystick button according to the information obtained from the Sense HAT add-on board. I utilize the `BitArray` class and instantiate it using a single byte received from the Atmel microcontroller. Hence, the resulting array of Boolean variables will automatically tell which of the buttons is active. I iterate over this array to check which of the bits are set, and as shown in Listing 6-3, I use it to infer which of the joystick's buttons is currently pressed.

LISTING 6-3 Information about the currently pressed joystick button is decoded from the single byte obtained from the Sense HAT add-on board, using the BitArray class

```
public static JoystickButton GetJoystickButton(byte buttonInput)
{
    var bitArray = new BitArray(new byte[] { buttonInput });

    var joystickButton = JoystickButton.None;

    for (int i = 0; i < bitArray.Length; i++)
    {
        if (bitArray[i])
        {
            var numValue = Convert.ToByte(Math.Pow(2, i));

            if (Enum.IsDefined(typeof(JoystickButton), numValue))
            {
                joystickButton = (JoystickButton)numValue;
            }

            break;
        }
    }

    return joystickButton;
}
```

To deduce whether a button is pressed, held, or released, I wrote additional logic, in which I compare the currently active button state to the previous one. If the two are the same, the button is being held by the user (Holding state) or is inactive (None state). Subsequently, I check whether the previous state is None. If so, the joystick's state must be None (and Holding otherwise).

Similarly, you can probe for other joystick states when the currently pressed button differs from the previous one. In such a case the joystick is in the Pressed state, when the previous state was None. Consequently, a button is Released when the previous state was Pressed.

The preceding conditional checks are performed within the GetJoystickButtonState method of the JoystickHelper class, given in Listing 6-4.

LISTING 6-4 The current joystick state, described by one of the values of the JoystickButtonState enumeration, is inferred from the current and previous states

```
public static JoystickButtonState GetJoystickButtonState(JoystickButton currentButton,
    JoystickButton previousButton, JoystickButtonState previousButtonState =
JoystickButtonState.None)
{
    var buttonState = previousButtonState;

    if (currentButton != previousButton)
    {
        switch (previousButtonState)
        {
            case JoystickButtonState.None:
                buttonState = JoystickButtonState.Pressed;
                break;

            case JoystickButtonState.Holding:
                buttonState = JoystickButtonState.Released;
                break;
        }
    }
    else
    {
        if (currentButton == JoystickButton.None)
        {
            buttonState = JoystickButtonState.None;
        }
        else
        {
            buttonState = JoystickButtonState.Holding;
        }
    }

    return buttonState;
}
```

To obtain a byte encoding the joystick state, you need to send an appropriate request to the micro-controller of the Sense HAT add-on board, which requires reading one byte from the register of address 0xF2 using the static ReadByte method of the RegisterHelper class. The microcontroller of the Sense HAT add-on board samples the joystick's state with a frequency of 80 Hz. Accordingly, requests go to the Sense HAT every 12 ms using the DispatcherTimer class.

Every time the new byte is received from the Sense HAT add-on board, it's decoded by using static methods of the JoystickHelper class, and the resulting information passes to listeners using the custom event. Accordingly, the user of your middleware layer would have to handle only this event to detect joystick state changes.

This functionality is implemented within the Joystick class; see Chapter 06/SenseHatIO/SenseHat-Joystick/Joystick.cs. In this class, I configure DispatcherTimer to periodically send requests to the Sense HAT add-on board using the I2C interface by using the Interval event handler of the DispatcherTimer class instance; see the ConfigureTimer method from Listing 6-5.

LISTING 6-5   Selected fragments of the Joystick class

```
public class Joystick
{
    private const int msUpdateInterval = 12;
    private I2cDevice device;
    private DispatcherTimer joystickTimer;

    public Joystick(I2cDevice device)
    {
        Check.IsNull(device);

        this.device = device;

        ConfigureTimer();
    }

    private void ConfigureTimer()
    {
        joystickTimer = new DispatcherTimer();

        joystickTimer.Interval = TimeSpan.FromMilliseconds(msUpdateInterval);
        joystickTimer.Tick += JoystickTimer_Tick;

        joystickTimer.Start();
    }

    // JoystickTimer_Tick event handler is depicted in Listing 6-6
}
```

The response received from the Sense HAT is processed using the static methods of the JoystickHelper class, and the resulting values of the joystick's button and its state are stored using appropriate private members (previousButton and previousButtonState); see Listing 6-6. These values are stored be-cause they are used in subsequent processing to determine the current joystick state.

```csharp
public event EventHandler<JoystickEventArgs> ButtonPressed = delegate { };

private JoystickButton previousButton = JoystickButton.None;
private JoystickButtonState previousButtonState = JoystickButtonState.None;

private void JoystickTimer_Tick(object sender, object e)
{
    var rawInput = RegisterHelper.ReadByte(device, commandId);

    var buttonInfo = GetButtonInfo(rawInput);

    ButtonPressed(this, buttonInfo);
}

private JoystickEventArgs GetButtonInfo(byte buttonInfo)
{
    var currentJoystickButton = JoystickHelper.GetJoystickButton(buttonInfo);
    var currentJoystickButtonState = JoystickHelper.GetJoystickButtonState(
        currentJoystickButton, previousButton, previousButtonState);

    // Store the button value and its state
    previousButton = currentJoystickButton;
    previousButtonState = currentJoystickButtonState;

    return new JoystickEventArgs(currentJoystickButton, currentJoystickButtonState);
}
```

The preceding code described is reusable. Therefore, you can now use the Joystick class together with dependent classes in any other UWP app. You can distribute this functionality as the managed class library for the UWP; see Appendix D, "Class library for Sense HAT sensors," for details.

In general, such a separation of concerns helps you to organize, test, manage, and reuse your code between various apps. You can straightforwardly isolate your converters, controls, and logic into separate classes or libraries, and then share them between your desktop, mobile, holographic, and IoT UWP apps.

Joystick state visualization

Given the middleware layer, you can now build the actual high-level functionality exposed to the end-user. To this end, I am going to illustrate the joystick state in the default app view. This view will depict the currently pressed joystick button using five squares arranged in the quadratic cross within the Grid control. Each square will change its background color from gray to green when the corresponding joystick button is pressed by the user.

To explicitly separate independent view components, I prepared the custom control JoystickControl. You can find its complete implementation in the JoystickControl.xaml and JoystickControl.xaml.cs files under the folder Chapter 06/SenseHatIO/Controls of the companion code.

Figure 6-6 shows the visual part of the `JoystickControl`. This control uses a 3x3 `Grid` to arrange five `Rectangle` controls in the quadratic cross, based on the XAML layout techniques described in Chapter 4, "User interface design for headed devices."

FIGURE 6-6   The fill color of the square positioned in the center of a JoystickControl is green, indicating that the Enter button is active.

However, additional comments are necessary to explain the functionality of the code-behind associated with the JoystickControl, i.e., JoystickControl.xaml.cs. The class implemented in this file exposes the single public method named `UpdateView`. According to its definition, given in Listing 6-7, `UpdateView` accepts two arguments: `button` and `buttonState`. The first one is of type `JoystickButton`, while the second is of type `JoystickButtonState`. Therefore, both arguments of the `UpdateView` method fully describe the joystick's state. The `button` argument is associated with the particular `Rectangle` of the JoystickControl, while the `buttonState` is used to configure the `Fill` property of the given `Rectangle`.

LISTING 6-7   Rectangles change their background color to reflect the joystick's state

```
private SolidColorBrush inactiveColorBrush = new SolidColorBrush(Colors.LightGray);
private SolidColorBrush activeColorBrush = new SolidColorBrush(Colors.GreenYellow);

public void UpdateView(JoystickButton button, JoystickButtonState buttonState)
{
    ClearAll();

    if (button != JoystickButton.None)
    {
        var colorBrush = inactiveColorBrush;

        switch (buttonState)
        {
            case JoystickButtonState.Pressed:
            case JoystickButtonState.Holding:
                colorBrush = activeColorBrush;
                break;
        }

        buttonPads[button].Fill = colorBrush;
    }
}
```

Note   The definitions of the `ClearAll` method and the `buttonPads` dictionary are given in Listing 6-8.

To associate each `Rectangle` control with the joystick's buttons, I used the look-up table (LUT) named `buttonPads`, implemented using the `Dictionary` class. As shown in Listing 6-8, the keys of this dictionary are of type `JoystickButton`, and their values are of type `Rectangle`. Accordingly, an access to the `Rectangle`, accompanied by the particular joystick button, can be obtained very simply. For instance, to access the `Rectangle` representing the Up joystick button, you can use the following statement:

```
buttonPads[JoystickButton.Up].Fill = new SolidColorBrush(Colors.YellowGreen);
```

The `buttonPads` LUT is initialized within the constructor of the `JoystickControl` class; see Listing 6-8. In this constructor as well as in the `UpdateView` method, I am using a helper method, `ClearAll`. This method is used to set the default value of the `Fill` property of each `Rectangle` to gray.

LISTING 6-8   Selected fragments of the JoystickControl class

```
private Dictionary<JoystickButton, Rectangle> buttonPads;

public JoystickControl()
{
    InitializeComponent();

    ConfigureButtonPadsDictionary();

    ClearAll();
}

private void ConfigureButtonPadsDictionary()
{
    buttonPads = new Dictionary<JoystickButton, Rectangle>();

    buttonPads.Add(JoystickButton.Up, Up);
    buttonPads.Add(JoystickButton.Down, Down);
    buttonPads.Add(JoystickButton.Left, Left);
    buttonPads.Add(JoystickButton.Right, Right);
    buttonPads.Add(JoystickButton.Enter, Enter);
}

private void ClearAll()
{
    foreach (var buttonPad in buttonPads)
    {
        buttonPad.Value.Fill = inactiveColorBrush;
    }
}
```

 Note   A `buttonPads` dictionary is initialized within the class constructor, while `ClearAll` is a helper method for setting the `Fill` property of each rectangle to `inactiveColorBrush` (light gray).

Finally, after implementing the custom control, you can use it together with the `Joystick` class in the SenseHatIO app. First, modify the content of a MainPage.xaml file. This is simple, because you've already implemented the appropriate control. As Listing 6-9 shows, the MainPage.xaml declaration is very short. It contains only the markup declaring the `JoystickControl`, and the single anonymous style definition, which is responsible for centering the `JoystickControl` horizontally and vertically.

LISTING 6-9 XAML declarations of the MainPage

```xaml
<Page x:Class="SenseHatIO.MainPage"
    xmlns="http://schemas.microsoft.com/winfx/2006/xaml/presentation"
    xmlns:x="http://schemas.microsoft.com/winfx/2006/xaml"
    xmlns:local="using:SenseHatIO"
    xmlns:controls="using:SenseHatIO.Controls"
    xmlns:d="http://schemas.microsoft.com/expression/blend/2008"
    xmlns:mc="http://schemas.openxmlformats.org/markup-compatibility/2006"
    mc:Ignorable="d">

    <Page.Resources>
        <Style TargetType="controls:JoystickControl">
            <Setter Property="VerticalAlignment"
                    Value="Center" />
            <Setter Property="HorizontalAlignment"
                    Value="Center" />
        </Style>
    </Page.Resources>

    <Grid Background="{ThemeResource ApplicationPageBackgroundThemeBrush}">
        <controls:JoystickControl x:Name="SenseHatJoystickControl" />
    </Grid>
</Page>
```

Listing 6-10 shows the corresponding code-behind, which handles initializing the appropriate `I2cDevice` and using it to instantiate the `Joystick` class. Next, I handle the `ButtonPressed` event of the `Joystick` class instance. This event is processed by the `Joystick_ButtonPressed` method, which, as shown in Listing 6-10, invokes the `UpdateView` method of the `JoystickControl`. Thus, the background color of the appropriate square in the quadratic cross will change whenever you press an associated joystick's button. (Refer to Figure 6-6.)

LISTING 6-10 Selected elements of the MainPage code-behind

```csharp
public sealed partial class MainPage : Page
{
    private Joystick joystick;

    public MainPage()
    {
        InitializeComponent();
    }
```

```
        protected override async void OnNavigatedTo(NavigationEventArgs e)
        {
            base.OnNavigatedTo(e);

            await Initialize();
        }

        private async Task Initialize()
        {
            const byte address = 0x46;
            var device = await I2cHelper.GetI2cDevice(address);

            if (device != null)
            {
                joystick = new Joystick(device);
                joystick.ButtonPressed += Joystick_ButtonPressed;
            }
        }

        private void Joystick_ButtonPressed(object sender, JoystickEventArgs e)
        {
            SenseHatJoystickControl.UpdateView(e.Button, e.State);
        }
}
```

The `Joystick` class was easily incorporated into the UWP view since it exposes a convenient API. I isolated the code responsible for device interaction from view updating. Therefore, the code-behind of the `MainPage` looks simple and tidy.

LED array

You can use a colorful LED array of the Sense HAT as an output device. In particular, it can display information to the user using symbols or colors. You can use that feature if your IoT device is not connected to an external display. Together, an LED array and a joystick compose a pair of input-output devices that can control your IoT device.

Broadly speaking, the LED array is a low-resolution display because it is composed of just 64 pixels. Comparing this value to a modern Quad HD display, which has more than 8 million pixels, the Sense HAT add-on board has less than 0.001% of the modern display's capability. But the IoT is a special-purpose device, and those 64 pixels can be more than enough for many special functions.

Each pixel of the Sense HAT add-on board LED array is composed of the Surface Mounted Device (SMD) LED. These SMD LEDs include three red, green, and blue LEDs; mixing the wavelength (color) of the light emitted from each LED yields the final illumination color. (See *http://bit.ly/cree_plcc6*.)

The Sense HAT LEDs are arranged into an 8x8 array. The location of each LED is encoded using its row and column index. Row (x) and column (y) indices start from 0 and increase toward the USB ports (x) and HDMI port (y), respectively. (See Figure 6-5.) Accordingly, the LED in the top left corner has a position of (0,0).

The color of each LED is encoded using the set of three 5-bit values. Each specifies the contribution of the corresponding color channel (red, green, blue) to the resulting color. This 5-bit color scale uses 32 (2^5) discrete levels in a range of 0-31. For instance, a 5-bit RGB value of (31,0,0) will drive an LED to red illumination. On the other hand, colors in the UWP platform, defined as static members of the Colors class (Windows.UI namespace), use the 8-bit RGB color scale. Consequently, to relate 8-bit to 5-bit color scales, implement the conversion by using the LUT and the following equation:

$$C_5(C_8) = \left\lceil C_8 \frac{2^5 - 1}{2^8 - 1} \right\rceil$$

where C_5 and C_8 denote the channel value in the 5-bit and 8-bit color scales, respectively, and the symbol $\lceil x \rceil$ denotes the ceiling function. The values of the numerator and denominator of the scaling factor, $\frac{2^5 - 1}{2^8 - 1}$, come from the maximum values of the 5-bit and 8-bit unsigned integers, respectively.

Similarly, I implemented the logic responsible for controlling the LED array in a separate class named LedArray. You can find the complete definition of this class in the companion code: Chapter 06/Sense-Hatlo/LedArray/LedArray.cs.

To drive the LED array, you use the same I²C device as in the case of joystick. Therefore, the LedArray class constructor (see Listing 6-11) expects the single argument of the type I2cDevice. After storing a reference to this object, I initialize two arrays: Buffer and pixelByteBuffer. The first one, Buffer, is an 8x8 array, which is an abstract, high-level representation of the physical LED array. Each element of this array is of type Windows.UI.Color and therefore can be used to change the color of the particular LED identified by the appropriate array indices. The second array, pixelByteBuffer, internally converts 8-bit RGB color elements of the Buffer property to the corresponding 5-bit unsigned byte representation. Therefore, pixelByteBuffer has three times more elements than the Buffer array because three bytes are required to represent each RGB color. There is yet an additional element of the pixelByteBuffer, which I discuss later in this chapter.

LISTING 6-11 Properties, fields, and the constructor of the LedArray class

```
public static byte Length { get; private set; } = 8;

public static byte ColorChannelCount { get; private set; } = 3;

public Color[,] Buffer { get; private set; }

private I2cDevice device;

private byte[] pixelByteBuffer;
private byte[] color5BitLut;
```

```
public LedArray(I2cDevice device)
{
    Check.IsNull(device);

    this.device = device;

    Buffer = new Color[Length, Length];
    pixelByteBuffer = new byte[Length * Length * ColorChannelCount + 1];

    GenerateColorLut();
}
```

The last step performed inside the `LedArray` constructor invokes the `GenerateColorLut` method. The definition of this method appears in Listing 6-12, and initializes the LUT, composed of 256 elements (`color5BitLut` private field). Each element of this array is a discrete value, translating an 8-bit to a 5-bit single channel color level. For instance, to get the 5-bit representation of the red component of the UWP color, you can use the following statement:

```
var yellowColorRedComponent5bit = color5BitLut[Colors.Yellow.R];
```

LISTING 6-12 Initializing and generating the look-up table used for color scale conversion

```
private byte[] color5BitLut;

private void GenerateColorLut()
{
    const float maxValue5Bit = 31.0f; // 2^5 - 1

    int colorLutLength = byte.MaxValue + 1; // 256 discrete levels
    color5BitLut = new byte[colorLutLength];

    for (int i = 0; i < colorLutLength; i++)
    {
        var value5bit = Math.Ceiling(i * maxValue5Bit / byte.MaxValue);

        value5bit = Math.Min(value5bit, maxValue5Bit);

        color5BitLut[i] = Convert.ToByte(value5bit);
    }
}
```

In the `LedArray` class, I use the aforementioned possibility to get a three-element byte array, storing the 5-bit color values of each band of the particular UWP color. This functionality is implemented within the `ColorToByteArray` method of the `LedArray` class; see Listing 6-13.

```
private byte[] ColorToByteArray(Color color)
{
    return new byte[]
    {
        color5BitLut[color.R],
        color5BitLut[color.G],
        color5BitLut[color.B]
    };
}
```

Note   This method translates UWP colors to values understandable by the Sense HAT add-on board.

After the colors of each LED are converted to the 5-bit scale, you need to arrange them into a byte array consisting of 192 elements (64 LEDs and three values per LED). Subsequently, you write that buffer to the Sense HAT, which expects that a byte array is divided into eight blocks of 24 bytes. Each block corresponds to the particular row in the LED array. These rows are further divided into three sets of eight bytes. The first set encodes the red channel, while the other two correspond to the green and blue color bands. Such an LED buffer arrangement is schematically presented in Figure 6-7.

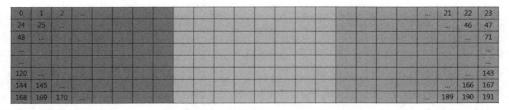

FIGURE 6-7   An LED buffer organization. Each cell corresponds to a single byte in the array, which controls the LEDs of the Sense HAT add-on board. A buffer is divided into three blocks, corresponding to each color channel: red, green, and blue.

The method `Serialize`, which is responsible for arranging the high-level `Buffer` property into the byte array, appears in Listing 6-14. There, I first clear the `pixelByteBuffer` field, and then iterate elements of the `Buffer` array using two loops. The first, loop variable x, is going through rows, while the second traverses the columns. At each iteration, the current element of the `Buffer` property is converted to a three-element byte array. Each element of the resulting array is copied to the appropriate location of the `pixelByteBuffer` array. (Refer to Figure 6-7.) At every loop iteration, the byte destination (`index` variable) is determined by using the following equation:

$$index = x + i * Length + y * Length * ColorChannelCount + 1$$

where *Length* is the LED array size, i.e. 8, *ColorChannelCount* is equal to 3 since I use RGB LEDs, *x* and *y* denote the row and column of the LED array, respectively, whereas 1 accounts for the synchronization byte, discussed momentarily.

LISTING 6-14 LED color buffer serialization

```
private void Serialize()
{
    int index;
    var widthStep = Length * ColorChannelCount;

    Array.Clear(pixelByteBuffer, 0, pixelByteBuffer.Length);

    for (int x = 0; x < Length; x++)
    {
        for (int y = 0; y < Length; y++)
        {
            var colorByteArray = ColorToByteArray(Buffer[x, y]);

            for (int i = 0; i < ColorChannelCount; i++)
            {
                index = x + i * Length + y * widthStep + 1;

                pixelByteBuffer[index] = colorByteArray[i];
            }
        }
    }
}
```

 Note The high-level `Buffer` property, composed of 64 UWP color values, is converted to a byte array, organized according to Figure 6-7.

The resulting byte buffer stored within the `pixelByteBuffer` member must be written to the I²C device of address 0x46. Do so by using the `Write` method of the `I2cDevice` class. A microcontroller of the Sense HAT internally uses the same shift register for the LED and a joystick control with the effective length of 193. Therefore, each time I request an LED update, I add an additional element to the transmitted array, which acts effectively as the synchronization byte. Note that the Sense HAT add-on board does not expose the API, which could be used to update the selected part of the buffer determining the LED state. You always need to send the whole array, even when you are updating the single pixel value.

To set the color of the single pixel, I wrote the `SetPixel` method; see Listing 6-15. It verifies the x and y arguments representing pixel location, and then updates the `Buffer` array. Subsequently, it writes to the device an updated byte buffer (`UpdateDevice` method).

LISTING 6-15 Setting the color of LED array located at x and y

```
public void SetPixel(int x, int y, Color color)
{
    CheckPixelLocation(x);
    CheckPixelLocation(y);
```

```
        ResetBuffer(Colors.Black);
        Buffer[x, y] = color;

        UpdateDevice();
}

private void UpdateDevice()
{
    Serialize();

    device.Write(pixelByteBuffer);
}
private void CheckPixelLocation(int location)
{
    if (location < 0 || location >= Length)
    {
        throw new ArgumentException("LED square array has maximum length of: " + Length);
    }
}
```

In summary, the API of LedArray is organized such that the color of a particular LED pixel is set by changing the corresponding value of the Buffer property. Next, the values stored in this property are converted to the byte array, containing 193 elements, which are later transferred to the Sense HAT add-on board through the I²C bus.

The LedArray class also implements two handy functions: Reset and RgbTest; see Listing 6-16. The first one, Reset, changes the color of all diodes to the uniform value, while RgbTest sequentially drives all LEDs to red, green, and blue. In particular, I use the RgbTest method to verify the functionality of the LedArray class. To this end, you can simply invoke this method in the MainPage.xaml.cs file of the SenseHatIO app as shown in Listing 6-17. Then, after deploying the SenseHatIO app and and running it, you will see that the LED array constantly changes its color from red to green and then to blue at approximately 1 second intervals.

LISTING 6-16 Two helper methods of the LedArray class

```
public void RgbTest(int msSleepTime)
{
    Color[] colors = new Color[] { Colors.Red, Colors.Green, Colors.Blue };

    foreach (var color in colors)
    {
        Reset(color);
        Task.Delay(msSleepTime).Wait();
    }
}

private void ResetBuffer(Color color)
{
    for (int x = 0; x < Length; x++)
```

```
    {
        for (int y = 0; y < Length; y++)
        {
            Buffer[x, y] = color;
        }
    }
}
```

LISTING 6-17 The LED array will be sequentially driven to the uniform color value of red, green, and blue

```
using SenseHatIO.SenseHatLedArray;

namespace SenseHatIO
{
    public sealed partial class MainPage : Page
    {
        private Joystick joystick;
        private LedArray ledArray;

        // This part is the same as in Listing 6-10

        private async Task Initialize()
        {
            const byte address = 0x46;
            var device = await I2cHelper.GetI2cDevice(address);

            if (device != null)
            {
                joystick = new Joystick(device);
                joystick.ButtonPressed += Joystick_ButtonPressed;

                ledArray = new LedArray(device);
                BeginRgbTest();
            }
        }

        private void Joystick_ButtonPressed(object sender, JoystickEventArgs e)
        {
            SenseHatJoystickControl.UpdateView(e.Button, e.State);
        }

        private void BeginRgbTest()
        {
            const int msDelayTime = 1000;

            while (true)
            {
                ledArray.RgbTest(msDelayTime);
            }
        }
    }
}
```

Figure 6-8, Figure 6-9, and Figure 6-10 show the LED array driven to red, green, and blue, respectively. For each color, different spatial LED locations light up. For instance, the red channel is generated by the sub-LED located on the left (assuming the GPIO header is located at the bottom), while the green LED is in the central part of the SMD LED. Consequently, the blue LED can be found on the right part of the SMD LED. You can now experiment with other colors to see how they affect the luminosity of each sub-LED.

FIGURE 6-8 An LED array driven to the uniform red color. In this case, the bottom left part of each LED lights up.

FIGURE 6-9 An LED array driven to the uniform green color. The central part of each LED is responsible for providing green channel contribution.

FIGURE 6-10 All LED pixels are driven to blue. In this case, only the right fragment of each SMD LED is active.

Joystick and LED array integration

After you confirm that the joystick and LED array work correctly, you can combine them. You now have all the tools to control the LED illumination using the joystick. In particular, the joystick can control the position and color of a single-pixel dot on the LED array. The Up, Down, Right, and Left buttons can change the pixel position, while the Enter button can modify the pixel color.

In Listing 6-18 I highlighted the changes required to implement the aforementioned functionality in the main view of the SenseHatIO app. After you re-run the app, a pixel at position (0,0) will be red. This color changes to green after you press the Enter button, and you can change the LED pixel position by moving the joystick.

To update the pixel position, 1 use the SetPixel method of the LedArray class and invoke it every time the ButtonPressed event of the Joystick class is raised, provided the joystick button state is Pressed; see the definition of the event handler Joystick_ButtonPressed from Listing 6-18. Then, I update the pixel location, stored using two private members: x and y. These members are incremented or decremented depending on which joystick button is pressed; see the UpdateDotPosition method from Listing 6-19. To ensure that the values of x and y are valid (i.e., positive and not greater than 7 [LED array length − 1]), I wrote the helper CorrectLedCoordinate method. It checks whether the new value for the x or y location of the LED is in the valid range and corrects the input value if necessary; see Listing 6-18. Figure 6-11 shows the program in action.

LISTING 6-18   Controlling the LED array using a joystick

```csharp
using SenseHatDisplay.Helpers;
using SenseHatIO.SenseHatJoystick;
using SenseHatIO.SenseHatLedArray;
using System;
using Windows.Devices.I2c;
using Windows.UI;
using Windows.UI.Xaml.Controls;
using Windows.UI.Xaml.Navigation;

namespace SenseHatIO
{
    public sealed partial class MainPage : Page
    {
        private Joystick joystick;
        private LedArray ledArray;

        private int x = 0;
        private int y = 0;

        private Color dotColor = Colors.Red;

        // This part is the same as in Listing 6-17

        private async void Initialize()
        {
            const byte address = 0x46;
            var device = await I2cHelper.GetI2cDevice(address);

            if (device != null)
            {
                joystick = new Joystick(device);
                joystick.ButtonPressed += Joystick_ButtonPressed;

                ledArray = new LedArray(device);
                //BeginRgbTest();
                UpdateDevice();
            }
        }

        private void Joystick_ButtonPressed(object sender, JoystickEventArgs e)
        {
            SenseHatJoystickControl.UpdateView(e.Button, e.State);

            if(e.State == JoystickButtonState.Pressed)
            {
                UpdateDotPosition(e.Button);
            }
        }

        // This part is the same as in Listing 6-17
```

```
        private void UpdateDotPosition(JoystickButton button)
        {
            switch (button)
            {
                case JoystickButton.Up:
                    y -= 1;
                    break;

                case JoystickButton.Down:
                    y += 1;
                    break;

                case JoystickButton.Left:
                    x -= 1;
                    break;

                case JoystickButton.Right:
                    x += 1;
                    break;

                case JoystickButton.Enter:
                    InvertDotColor();
                    break;
            }

            UpdateDevice();
        }

        private void UpdateDevice()
        {
            x = CorrectLedCoordinate(x);
            y = CorrectLedCoordinate(y);

            ledArray.SetPixel(x, y, dotColor);
        }

        private static int CorrectLedCoordinate(int inputCoordinate)
        {
            inputCoordinate = Math.Min(inputCoordinate, LedArray.Length - 1);
            inputCoordinate = Math.Max(inputCoordinate, 0);

            return inputCoordinate;
        }

        private void InvertDotColor()
        {
            dotColor = dotColor == Colors.Red ? Colors.Green : Colors.Red;
        }
    }
}
```

FIGURE 6-11 Controlling the LED array by using a joystick. When the SenseHatIO app is deployed to the device, the pixel located at (0,0) is red. You can change its position and color by using the joystick. (Refer to Figure 6-1.)

Integrating LED array with sensor readings

You can extend the sample app developed in the previous section in many ways—from implementing a simple arcade game to combining an LED array with sensor readings. For instance, the pixel can move according to the accelerometer readings. I implemented such functionality in the companion code: Chapter 06/SpaceDot. This app combines the functionality implemented in the `InertialSensor` class (refer to Chapter 5) with the `SetPixel` method of the `LedArray` class; see MainPage.xaml.cs of the SpaceDot app.

The structure of that file is worth noting: After instantiating the `LedArray` and `InertialSensor` classes, I acquire linear acceleration; see Listing 6-19. The constant scaler then multiplies the accelerometer readings along x and y axes. You can change the value of this scaler to control the speed of the LED pixel movement. The resulting values calculate the new pixel position, which is then sent to the device; see `UpdateDotPosition` from Listing 6-19. Hence, after you deploy and run the SpaceDot app to your IoT device, an active LED changes depending on how you move or shake your device. Most of the functionality implemented here is delegated to a separate class. You can easily incorporate it into your other IoT apps by referencing appropriate projects.

LISTING 6-19 LED array is controlled using the accelerometer

```
private void BeginAccelerationAcquisition()
{
    const int msDelayTime = 25;

    BeginSensorReading(() =>
    {
```

```
        var linearAcceleration = inertialSensor.GetLinearAcceleration();

        UpdateDotPosition(linearAcceleration);
    }, msDelayTime);
}

private void UpdateDotPosition(Vector3D<float> accelerometerReading)
{
    var stepX = Convert.ToInt32(accelerometerReading.X * accelerationScaler);
    var stepY = Convert.ToInt32(accelerometerReading.Y * accelerationScaler);

    x = CorrectLedCoordinate(x - stepX);
    y = CorrectLedCoordinate(y - stepY);

    ledArray.SetPixel(x, y, dotColor);
}
```

 Note   The LED pixel position changes depending on the position of the IoT device.

Touchscreen and gesture handling

Some embedded systems, e.g., ATMs and car audio systems, are equipped with touchscreens. Such devices can be controlled through touch gestures like tap, double tap, slide, or pinch. A UWP interface enables the device to respond to those gestures. The following discussion relates to the general UWP gesture handling. You can also use the methods presented here for tablets and phones. You can test the sample app described in this section using your IoT device connected to an external display. It can even be without a touch-sensitive layer. You can emulate gestures using a mouse hooked to one of the USB ports of the RPi2 (that is an option I used). Another possibility when testing gesture-handling is to use Windows IoT Remote Client (refer to Chapter 2). You can also hook up a dedicated touchscreen for the RPi2.

Your gesture-handling logic will depend on the gesture type and your particular application. Simple gestures are those in which the user simply touches the particular UI element (Tap event) or holds an element (Holding event). However, some applications can be controlled by complex gestures. Broadly speaking, placing one or multiple fingers on the UI element on the touchscreen works as a gesture and enables the user to manipulate the distinguished part of the UI to change its position, resize it, or rotate it. Figure 6-12 shows an example of the initial shape and position of the UI object being modified by a user's gesture.

To handle such complex gestures, you can use several manipulation events, raised by the UWP visual elements. In particular, when the user touches the UI element, the `ManipulationStarting` and `ManipulationStarted` events are triggered. Subsequently, the series of `ManipulationDelta` events is raised.

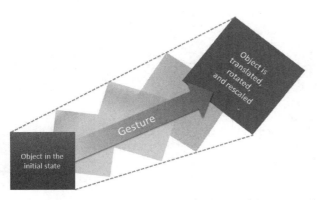

FIGURE 6-12 Object manipulation during a gesture. Most general-object manipulation includes translation, rotation, and scaling.

Each of them describes the instantaneous state of the UI element; note the light blue rectangles in Figure 6-12. Finally, when a gesture is finished, the `ManipulationCompleted` event is reported. This also provides information about the total manipulation made during a gesture.

During the manipulation, an object can be translated, rotated, and rescaled. Information about each of these transformations is passed to the appropriate event handlers using the instance of the `ManipulationDelta` class, declared in the `System.Windows.Input` namespace. `ManipulationDelta` has the properties `Translation`, `Rotation`, `Scale`, and `Expansion`, which tell you how the object was translated (`Translation`), rotated (`Rotation`), and rescaled (`Scale`). The `Expansion` field describes the scaling transformation but is expressed using units other than `Scale`. Namely, `Expansion` is given in device-independent units (1/96 of an inch), while `Scale` is given as a percentage. For instance, a `Scale` of 0.5 means that the distance between two contact points (e.g., fingers) was reduced by half.

In this section I further extend SenseHatIO app to incorporate two gestures associated with the `DoubleTapped` and `ManipulationDelta` events of the `Rectangle` control. The first event, `Double-Tapped`, is raised whenever a user touches the `Rectangle` control twice. I use this event to change the color of the LED pixel and the `Rectangle`'s background. It works essentially the same as the joystick's `Enter` button.

The second event, `ManipulationDelta`, is raised during the complex gesture. I use this event to update the pixel location on the LED array by using the translation vector obtained through the appropriate event arguments. These changes are synchronized with the updates made by using a joystick. So, when you press the joystick's `Enter` button, the `Rectangle` will change its color to green or red, depending on its current state. Any other joystick button will translate both the LED pixel on the LED array and the `Rectangle` position on the screen.

The implementation proceeds as follows: I modify the UI by introducing the `Pivot` control, composed of two tabs (`PivotItems`); see Listing 6-20. The first `PivotItem` contains the `JoystickControl`, while the second hosts a single `Rectangle` control, responding to touch manipulations.

LISTING 6-20 Manipulation-enabled Rectangle control

```xml
<Page x:Class="SenseHatIO.MainPage"
      xmlns="http://schemas.microsoft.com/winfx/2006/xaml/presentation"
      xmlns:x="http://schemas.microsoft.com/winfx/2006/xaml"
      xmlns:local="using:SenseHatIO"
      xmlns:controls="using:SenseHatIO.Controls"
      xmlns:converters="using:SenseHatIO.Converters"
      xmlns:d="http://schemas.microsoft.com/expression/blend/2008"
      xmlns:mc="http://schemas.openxmlformats.org/markup-compatibility/2006"
      mc:Ignorable="d">

    <Page.Resources>
        <Style TargetType="controls:JoystickControl">
            <Setter Property="VerticalAlignment"
                    Value="Center" />
            <Setter Property="HorizontalAlignment"
                    Value="Center" />
        </Style>

        <Style TargetType="Rectangle">
            <Setter Property="ManipulationMode"
                    Value="All" />
            <Setter Property="VerticalAlignment"
                    Value="Top" />
            <Setter Property="HorizontalAlignment"
                    Value="Left" />
            <Setter Property="Margin"
                    Value="0" />
        </Style>

        <converters:ColorToBrushConverter x:Key="ColorToBrushConverter" />
    </Page.Resources>

    <Pivot x:Name="MainPivot"
           Background="{ThemeResource ApplicationPageBackgroundThemeBrush}">
        <PivotItem Header="Joystick">
            <controls:JoystickControl x:Name="SenseHatJoystickControl" />
        </PivotItem>

        <PivotItem Header="Dot position">
            <Rectangle Fill="{x:Bind DotColor, Mode=OneWay, Converter={StaticResource
                          ColorToBrushConverter}}"
                       Width="{x:Bind rectangleWidth}"
                       Height="{x:Bind rectangleHeight}"
                       RenderTransform="{x:Bind rectangleTransform, Mode=OneWay}"
                       ManipulationDelta="Rectangle_ManipulationDelta"
                       DoubleTapped="Rectangle_DoubleTapped" />
        </PivotItem>
    </Pivot>
</Page>
```

In Listing 6-20 I use the custom converter ColorToBrushConverter; for its definition see the companion code at Chapter 06/SenseHatIO/Converters/ColorToBrushConverter.cs. This converter safely casts the UWP color to an instance of the SolidColorBrush class and updates the Fill property of the Rectangle control.

To enable manipulations for a particular visual element, configure the ManipulationMode property. It accepts values defined in the ManipulationModes enumeration (Windows.UI.Xaml.Input). Here, I enabled all possible manipulations, but you can restrict them so that the visual element responds only to translation, rotation, or scale changes.

Subsequently I modified the MainPage class. As you see in Listing 6-21, I implemented the INotifyPropertyChanged interface to update the Rectangle color using data binding. To this end, the Fill property of the Rectangle color is bound to the DotColor property of the MainPage; see Listings 6-20 and 6-21. To synchronize changes made using gesture manipulations and a joystick, I also modified the InvertDotColor method such that it updates the DotColor property instead of the associated dotColor private member.

LISTING 6-21   A Rectangle position and its current color are reflected on the LED array

```
public sealed partial class MainPage : Page, INotifyPropertyChanged
{
    public event PropertyChangedEventHandler PropertyChanged = delegate { };

    public Color DotColor
    {
        get { return dotColor; }
        set
        {
            dotColor = value;
            OnPropertyChanged();
        }
    }

    public void OnPropertyChanged([CallerMemberName] string propertyName = "")
    {
        PropertyChanged(this, new PropertyChangedEventArgs(propertyName));
    }

    private void InvertDotColor()
    {
        // dotColor = dotColor == Colors.Red ? Colors.Green : Colors.Red;
        DotColor = dotColor == Colors.Red ? Colors.Green : Colors.Red;
    }

    private void Rectangle_DoubleTapped(object sender, DoubleTappedRoutedEventArgs e)
    {
        InvertDotColor();

        UpdateDevice();
    }

    // The rest of implementation can be found in the companion code
}
```

I implemented the event handler `Rectangle_DoubleTapped`, which is invoked whenever a user performs a simple double-tap gesture. In such a case, I invert the color of the active LED so that it works as it would when you use the joystick's Enter button.

To update the `Rectangle` position on the screen, I used `TranslateTransform`, which is bound to the `RenderTransform` property of the `Rectangle`. `TranslateTransform` represents the translation vector composed of two components: X and Y. As shown in Listing 6-22, I update these properties by using the information obtained from the event arguments of the `Rectangle_ManipulationDelta` event handler. The second argument passed to this event handler is of type `ManipulationDeltaRoutedEventArgs`. This class exposes two members that describe gesture manipulation: `Cumulative` and `Delta`. The former stores the overall translation, rotation, and scaling changes since the beginning of the manipulation, while the `Delta` property contains the most recent transformation. Both `Cumulative` and `Delta` are of type `ManipulationDelta`. So, to translate the `Rectangle`, I use X and Y public members of the `ManipulationDelta.Translation` property. I simply add those values to the corresponding properties of the `TranslateTransform` class; see `Joystick_ButtonPressed` from Listing 6-22. Thus, the `Rectangle` will be shifted by the specified distance.

LISTING 6-22 Controlling the LED array using gesture manipulations

```
private TranslateTransform rectangleTransform = new TranslateTransform();

private void Joystick_ButtonPressed(object sender, JoystickEventArgs e)
{
    SenseHatJoystickControl.UpdateView(e.Button, e.State);

    if(e.State == JoystickButtonState.Pressed)
    {
        UpdateDotPosition(e.Button);

        rectangleTransform.X = x * rectangleWidth;
        rectangleTransform.Y = y * rectangleHeight;
    }
}

private void Rectangle_ManipulationDelta(object sender, ManipulationDeltaRoutedEventArgs e)
{
    if(!e.IsInertial)
    {
        rectangleTransform.X += e.Delta.Translation.X;
        rectangleTransform.Y += e.Delta.Translation.Y;

        UpdateDotPosition();
    }

    e.Handled = true;
}

private void UpdateDotPosition()
{
    x = Convert.ToInt32(rectangleTransform.X / rectangleWidth);
```

```
    y = Convert.ToInt32(rectangleTransform.Y / rectangleHeight);

    UpdateDevice();
}
```

After the manipulation is completed, a UWP can extrapolate—that is, continue the geometrical transformations of the visual element according to the previous input. This causes an illusion of the free (inertial) object movement, and for this reason is called the manipulation inertia. Such extrapolation is used to physically simulate a movement of the real object when the external force is applied. Namely, after you push an object, it moves for a while and does not stop immediately. Similarly, the visual element does not freeze promptly when the manipulation is completed.

To check whether the manipulation is inertial, you can use the `IsInertial` property of the `ManipulationDeltaRoutedEventArgs` class. As you can see in Listing 6-22, I update only the LED array and the `Rectangle` position when the manipulation is non-inertial.

To synchronize changes made using complex gestures with those made using a joystick, I implemented several methods. First, I use an overloaded parameterless method, `UpdateDotPosition`, which lights up the appropriate LED on the Sense HAT add-on board. Contrary to its parameterized counterpart, this method uses the `TranslateTransform` properties to select the appropriate LED.

This LED selection requires some additional calculations. When the `MainPage` is displayed, I adjust the size of the `Rectangle` according to the screen size and the LED array size; see Listing 6-23. The screen is then virtually divided into an 8x8 grid. Each cell of that grid corresponds to one LED of the Sense HAT add-on board. When you move the `Rectangle` using a gesture or joystick in an appropriate virtual cell, the corresponding LED array element becomes active. You can also note that the `Rectangle` is always snapped to the nearest grid's cell; see the definition of the parameterless version of the `UpdateDotPosition` method (see Listing 6-22).

LISTING 6-23 The rectangle width and height are dynamically adjusted to the actual screen and LED array dimensions

```
protected override async void OnNavigatedTo(NavigationEventArgs e)
{
    base.OnNavigatedTo(e);

    await Initialize();

    AdjustRectangleToScreenSize();
}

private void AdjustRectangleToScreenSize()
{
    const int headerHeight = 50;

    rectangleWidth = Window.Current.Bounds.Width / LedArray.Length;
    rectangleHeight = (Window.Current.Bounds.Height - headerHeight) / LedArray.Length;
}
```

Summary

In this chapter, I explored several I/O approaches, including button, joystick, and gesture manipulations. I showed you how to prepare various classes responsible for controlling the LED array and handling inputs from the joystick of the Sense HAT add-on board. I outlined how to combine those classes such that the LED array was controlled using the joystick and complex gesture manipulations. I have also shown how to combine accelerometer readings with the LED array such that LEDs light up depending on the IoT device position in 3D space.

In next chapters, the LedArray class developed here will be further combined with the UWP speech and face recognition engines, custom audio, image-processing routines, and artificial intelligence.

CHAPTER 7

Audio processing

This chapter explores the UWP's speech synthesis and recognition capabilities. You'll use them to build an app that will change the LED array color according to a user's voice commands. Subsequently, I will show how to read an audio signal from the audio file. A Fast Fourier Transformation (FFT) will digitally process this signal to find its frequency representation. The resulting frequency distribution divides into eight bands, and the contribution from each band to the overall spectrum displays on the LED array. Thus, the IoT device will work as a real-time audio spectrum analyzer, and the LEDs will blink in the rhythm of music.

These are more advanced aspects of the IoT programming. As described in Chapter 1, "Embedded devices programming," digital signal processing for controlling a specific process is one of the key ingredients in the IoT world. IoT devices constantly acquire temporal signals from external sensors, process them in the background, and use the resulting information to take specific control actions. An IoT device can monitor traction of your car or control a medical-imaging apparatus.

In this chapter I guide you toward an IoT device that will acquire audio signals from a microphone or read them from a file. It will process this signal and send the resulting information to drive the LED array. Your base IoT device, the RPi2 or RPi3, will use acquired and processed signals to drive another unit, the Sense HAT add-on board. Cars use similar devices; for instance, a traction-control IoT device acquires sensor signals to detect vehicle instability and eventually to drive the braking system to correct over- or understeer.

Speech synthesis

Speech synthesis (SS) is the method of converting text to human speech. Such artificial speech generation plays an important role in human-machine interfaces because it provides a natural way of expressing feedback to the user. On the other hand, speech recognition (SR) enables the machine to understand human voice commands. Together, SS and SR enable hands-free operation of computer systems. This is especially interesting, and useful for IoT applications where devices can be controlled by speech.

The UWP exposes a convenient programming interface for SS. In this section I explain how to implement a headed speech-enabled application named Speech. I also show you how to extend this example to include SR.

Speech capabilities of the UWP are universal. Therefore, I test the initial functionalities using a development PC. Next, this app will be tailored to RPi2 and RPi3 capabilities.

You can find the full code of the Speech app in the companion code: Chapter 07/Speech. Here, I summarize how I built this app. First, I implemented the reusable helper class. (See Listing 7-1 and the Speech-Helper.cs file, which is in the Helpers subfolder of the Speech app.) You can embed this class in the UWP Class Library project (see Appendix D, "Class library for Sense HAT sensors"), and then use it in any UWP app. However, the SpeechHelper class cannot be used on other platforms, such as iOS or Android.

LISTING 7-1   A definition of a reusable helper class

```
public class SpeechHelper
{
    private static SpeechSynthesizer speechSynthesizer;
    private static MediaElement mediaElement;

    static SpeechHelper()
    {
        speechSynthesizer = new SpeechSynthesizer();
        mediaElement = new MediaElement();
    }

    public static async void Speak(string textToSpeech, VoiceInformation voice = null)
    {
        if (!string.IsNullOrEmpty(textToSpeech))
        {
            ConfigureVoice(voice);

            var speechStream = await speechSynthesizer.
                SynthesizeTextToStreamAsync(textToSpeech);

            await mediaElement.Dispatcher.RunAsync(CoreDispatcherPriority.Normal, () =>
            {
                mediaElement.SetSource(speechStream, speechStream.ContentType);
                mediaElement.Play();
            });
        }
    }

    private static void ConfigureVoice(VoiceInformation voice)
    {
        if (voice != null)
        {
            speechSynthesizer.Voice = voice;
        }
        else
        {
            speechSynthesizer.Voice = SpeechSynthesizer.DefaultVoice;
        }
    }
}
```

Two main elements of the SpeechHelper class are important here: SpeechSynthesizer and Media-Element. The first, defined in the Windows.Media.SpeechSynthesis namespace, is the UWP implementation of the text to speech conversion. You can use either of two public methods to synthesize human speech: SynthesizeTextToStreamAsync and SynthesizeSsmlToStreamAsync. Both accept a single argument of type string. In the case of SynthesizeTextToStreamAsync, the argument is simply text to convert; SynthesizeSsmlToStreamAsync expects a string encoded using Speech Synthesis Markup Language (SSML). This is an XML-based markup language developed by the SS community. It provides the standard language for speech synthesis in Web applications. SSML offers more control of speech synthesis. However, SynthesizeTextToStreamAsync is much easier to use. Therefore, I omit SSML.

Regardless of the synthesis method, both functions generate a result of the same form—the artificial human voice stored as an instance of the SpeechSynthesisStream class. In particular, this object contains the byte array of the Waveform Audio File format (WAV). Therefore, it can be converted to a WAV file or played directly using the MediaElement class.

Given the SpeechHelper class, which contains all the functionality required for speech synthesis, I implemented the MainPage, which exposes SS functionality to the end user. I defined the UI with the Pivot control, in which I placed a text box, drop-down list, and button. (See Figure 7-1 and the companion code in Chapter 07/Speech/MainPage.xaml.) The user types into the text box; the text is converted to speech according to the speech engine selected in the drop-down list, which is activated by clicking the **Speak** button. The associated event handler then invokes an appropriate method of the SpeechHelper class. (See Listing 7-2, containing the code-behind of the Speech app.)

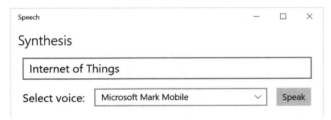

FIGURE 7-1 A user interface of the Speech application allows the user to specify the text to convert and the synthesis engine.

LISTING 7-2 Code-behind for MainPage contains data-bound fields and just one event handler

```
public sealed partial class MainPage : Page
{
    private string textToSpeak;

    private object allVoices = SpeechSynthesizer.AllVoices;
    private object voice;

    public MainPage()
    {
        InitializeComponent();
    }

    private void ButtonSpeak_Click(object sender, RoutedEventArgs e)
```

```
    {
        SpeechHelper.Speak(textToSpeak, voice as VoiceInformation);
    }
}
```

The UWP implements several SS engines, represented as instances of the `VoiceInformation` class. The list of available engines can be retrieved from the static property `AllVoices` of the `SpeechSynthesizer` class. In the Speech app, the list of available speech engines is bound to the drop-down control. You can use that control to choose any engine you want. It will automatically update the `Voice` property of the `Speech-Synthesizer` class instance. (Refer to Listing 7-1 and see the companion code in Chapter 07/Speech/Main-Page.xaml.) If you don't set this property explicitly, a default voice is used. In the desktop version of Windows 10, a default voice can be configured using the Settings app, as shown in Figure 7-2.

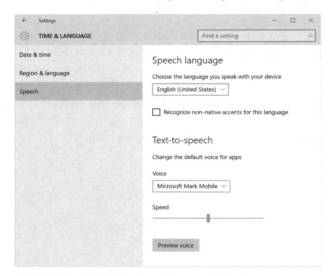

FIGURE 7-2   Default speech synthesis configuration.

Note also that the `textToSpeak` field of the `MainPage` class is bound to the `TextBox` control of the UI. Therefore, `textToSpeak` is updated automatically whenever the user types a string into the text box.

If you run the Speech app, you see that the list of voices is exactly the same as in the Settings app. Once you choose the synthesis engine using the **Select Voice** drop-down list and enter text, you click the **Speak** button. (See Figure 7-1.) As a consequence, text is converted to speech and played using a default sound playback device.

You can also deploy the Speech app to your RPi2 device. To fully test the Speech app, you need to connect the RPi2 to an external display and connect the USB mouse to use the UI. Then, to hear the artificial speech, connect an audio device like headphones to the A/V port of the RPi2. (See Figure 2-12.)

If you do not want to use the UI, you can always override the `OnNavigatedTo` method of the `Main-Page`, as shown in Listing 7-3. Doing so synthesizes the `Internet of Things` string using the `Speak` method of the `SpeechHelper` class right after navigating to the `MainPage`.

```
protected override void OnNavigatedTo(NavigationEventArgs e)
{
    base.OnNavigatedTo(e);

    SpeechHelper.Speak("Internet of Things");
}
```

Speech recognition

In general, you have three possible ways to perform SR: one-time recognition, one-time recognition with the UI, and continuous speech recognition session. One-time recognition with the UI isn't yet available in Windows 10 IoT Core. Before using these options, let's discuss the background of SR.

Background

Humans communicate every day using their voices. The speaker speaks, and his utterances are interpreted by the listener. During this interpretation, the listener matches recognized words to his vocabulary. Of course, this vocabulary develops over time; when you hear a new word, you can learn it and store it in your memory. Digital SR systems use similar methods. A modern speech recognizer—think of it as a virtual listener—analyzes raw voice input to extract its characteristic features in single phonemes, which are the fundamental blocks of words in each language. They are the shortest distinguishable parts of an utterance.

Such feature extraction reduces the complexity of a received audio signal; depending on recording quality, that signal may be very long—up to thousands of array elements in a few milliseconds—or may contain just dozens of elements. A decoder matches voice features to the model set of phonemes, and the results are combined into words and sentences.

The digital speech recognition system, the model set of phonemes, and the decoder correspond in some sense to a human brain, which processes sound received by the human auditory system. In the digital world, the model set of phonemes comprises a phoneme database. This model is accompanied by computational algorithms that match received phonemes to known, modeled signals to identify incoming utterances. These computational algorithms can be trained and tailored to the particular SR needs. Given the set of training data, the SR system optimizes its acoustic, pronunciation, or language-model parameters to achieve the best possible recognition performance.

In practice, modern SR finds the maximum likelihood between features representing actual and known features stored in appropriate models. This likelihood evaluation is typically performed based on Hidden Markov Models (HMM). Such models are widely used in many areas of science and engineering, and they were initially developed to model letter sequences.

HMM allows for very fast speech identification based on large models. Modern SRs are speaker-independent and thus do not require manual training, which was necessary in techniques based on template matching. SR systems significantly improved during the past few decades and, as you will see shortly, are now very robust.

App capability and system configuration

In the UWP, an SR module requires access to a microphone to record audio signals. Therefore, you need to enable the corresponding capability, which you do by using the package manifest editor. To run this editor, double-click **Package.appxmanifest** in the Solution Explorer of the Speech app. Select the **Microphone** check box in the Capabilities tab, as shown in Figure 7-3.

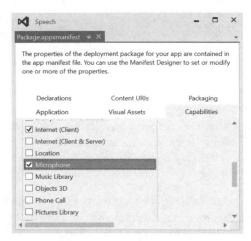

FIGURE 7-3 Providing access to a microphone.

Windows 10 IoT Core does not require any additional configuration to enable SR. However, on the desktop version of Windows 10, you need to appropriately configure privacy settings. To do so, click the **Get to Know Me** button in the Speech, inking, & typing tab of the Privacy Settings. (See Figure 7-4.) Confirm the use of your private info by clicking the **Turn On** button. Your development PC can now recognize your speech.

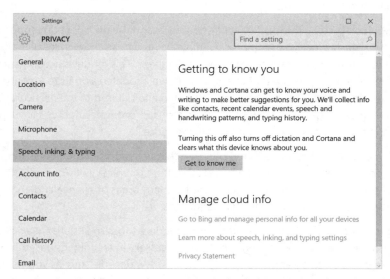

FIGURE 7-4 Enabling speech recognition in the desktop version of Windows 10.

UI changes

To provide controls for SR, I extended the UI of the Speech application by an additional `PivotItem` containing controls for running one time, continuous speech recognition, and displaying SR diagnostic info and its recognition results. In particular, as shown in Figure 7-5, the additional tab of the `Pivot` control is composed of the `ListBox` and three buttons: Recognize (One-Time), Start Continuous Recognition, and Clear. `ListBox` displays the status of the recognition process, and the first two button controls can enable or disable SR. The Clear button erases the `ListBox` contents. I built this UI using already known XAML declarations. (See the companion code in Chapter 07/Speech/MainPage.xaml.) Therefore, these declarations do not require additional comments.

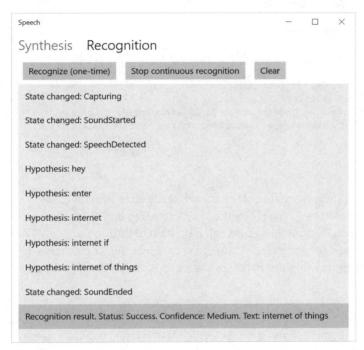

FIGURE 7-5 Speech recognition starts with audio capture and speech detection. A processing chain is then invoked.

One-time recognition

You can access UWP SR programmatically through the SpeechRecognizer class, defined in the `Windows.Media.SpeechRecognition` namespace. In the Speech app, I incorporated the SpeechRecognizer class in the MainPage.xaml.cs. (See the companion code in Chapter 07/Speech/MainPage.xaml.cs.)

The SpeechRecognizer class is initialized within a class constructor using the helper `Initialize-SpeechRecognizer` method. (See Listing 7-4.) This method instantiates the private member speech-Recognizer of the `MainPage`, using the parameterless constructor of the SpeechRecognizer class.

```
private SpeechRecognizer speechRecognizer;

public MainPage()
{
    InitializeComponent();

    InitializeSpeechRecognizer();
}

private async void InitializeSpeechRecognizer()
{
    speechRecognizer = new SpeechRecognizer();

    await speechRecognizer.CompileConstraintsAsync();

    speechRecognizer.RecognitionQualityDegrading +=
        SpeechRecognizer_RecognitionQualityDegrading;
    speechRecognizer.StateChanged += SpeechRecognizer_StateChanged;
    speechRecognizer.HypothesisGenerated += SpeechRecognizer_HypothesisGenerated;
}
```

 Note You can monitor the status of the speech recognizer by monitoring information generated by RecognitionQualityDegrading and StateChanged. Hypothetical speech recognition results can be obtained through a HypothesisGenerated event. RecognitionQualityDegrating, StateChanged, and HypothesisGenerated event handlers invoke the DisplayInfo method from Listing 7-5.

As you can imagine, SR can be computationally expensive. To make it faster, you can impose recognition restrictions by using a Constraints property of the SpeechRecognizer class. Confirm constraints using the CompileConstraintsAsync method. In the preceding example, I use default recognition constraints, so I invoke only the CompileConstraintsAsync method. Later in this chapter, I show a specific example of how to set custom constraints in the context of tailoring speech recognition to limited RPi2 and RPi3 capabilities.

As you can see, InitialzeSpeechRecognizer also attaches methods to the RecognitionQuality-Degrading, StateChanged, and HypothesisGenerated events of the SpeechRecognizer class. These events can be used to diagnose the SR process, and in this example, I simply display information obtained through the events in the UI. Every event handler looks the same and invokes the DisplayInfo method in Listing 7-5. In particular, the StateChanged event of SpeechRecognizer analyzes the particular steps performed by the SR system.

```
private void SpeechRecognizer_RecognitionQualityDegrading(SpeechRecognizer sender,
    SpeechRecognitionQualityDegradingEventArgs args)
{
    DisplayInfo("Quality degrading: " + args.Problem);
}

private async void DisplayInfo(string infoMessage)
{
    if (Dispatcher.HasThreadAccess)
    {
        ListBoxResults.Items.Add(infoMessage);
        ListBoxResults.SelectedIndex = ListBoxResults.Items.Count - 1;
    }
    else
    {
        await Dispatcher.RunAsync(CoreDispatcherPriority.Normal, () =>
        {
            DisplayInfo(infoMessage);
        });
    }
}
```

 Note Other event handlers used in Listing 7-4 have similar definitions, and therefore are omitted.

After initializing the speech recognizer, a one-time speech recognition session is started using the ButtonOneTimeRecognition_Click event handler. (See Listing 7-6.) There, I invoke the Recognize-Async method of the SpeechRecognizer class instance. However, a successful call to this method requires access to a microphone, configured recognition constraints, and appropriate privacy settings. If you do not grant access to a microphone, RecognizeAsync will throw an UnauthorizedAccess-Exception. Similarly, InvalidOperationException is thrown when constraints are not set. An Exception with the HResult property set to –2147199735 is generated when the privacy settings disable SR. To catch such eventual exceptions, a call to RecognizeAsync in the ButtonOneTimeRecognition_Click event handler is thus surrounded by an appropriate try catch block. Note that successful recognition results comprising recognized text, status, and confidence (likelihood estimation) are displayed in the UI.

LISTING 7-6 One-time speech recognition

```
private async void ButtonOneTimeRecognition_Click(object sender, RoutedEventArgs e)
{
    try
    {
        var recognitionResult = await speechRecognizer.RecognizeAsync();

        DisplayInfo(GetRecognitionResultInfo(recognitionResult));
```

```
        }
    catch (UnauthorizedAccessException)
    {
        DisplayInfo("Speech recognition requires an access to a microphone");
    }
    catch (Exception)
    {
        DisplayInfo("Speech recognition is disabled");
    }
}

private string GetRecognitionResultInfo(SpeechRecognitionResult speechRecognitionResult)
{
    return string.Format("Recognition result. Status: {0}. Confidence: {1}. Text: {2}",
        speechRecognitionResult.Status,
        speechRecognitionResult.Confidence,
        speechRecognitionResult.Text);
}
```

The ability of the computer system to automatically detect speech depends on the input signal quality. Recognition will fail if the audio input is noisy, the user speaks at an extreme volume or pace, or there is simply no valid audio signal. These problems are reported by the SpeechRecognizer using a RecognitionQualityDegrading event. The corresponding event handler can identify the eventual problem by reading a Problem property of the SpeechRecognitionQualityDegradingEventArgs class.

If the SR engine does not detect any problems with an input signal during the first Capturing state (see the first list entry in Figure 7-5), audio processing starts with detecting speech activity. (See the second [SoundStarted] and the third [SpeechDetected] list entries in Figure 7-5.) When valid speech is detected, the processing engine extracts its features and recognizes words. SpeechRecognizer can then generate several hypotheses. These hypothetical recognitions are reported by the Hypothesis-Generated event and displayed in the UI. (See entries 4–8 in the list in Figure 7-5.)

When the speech activity is finished, the SoundEnded state, which is the final recognition result, is generated. It is stored as an instance of the SpeechRecognitionResult class. You can use this object to obtain a recognized sentence (Text property), recognition confidence (Confidence or RawConfidence properties), and recognition status (Status property). Confidence and RawConfidence allow you to determine recognition quality, which measures how well current audio features are reflected in those stored in known models. In particular, you can reject recognized text when RawConfidence (given as a percentage) is below an arbitrarily chosen threshold.

To investigate SR yourself, you can run the Speech app, click the **Recognize (One-Time)** button, and then say whatever you like. The recognition module will process your voice input to detect words and sentences.

Your results should be similar to those in Figure 7-5. Namely, the speech recognition begins with audio capturing. Then the speech activity is isolated and processed to detect known words. Before a final result is generated, a few hypotheses are reported. A one-time speech recognition stops when it detects the end of sound. To continue speech recognition, you can invoke the RecognizeAsync method again or use continuous speech recognition.

Continuous recognition

For IoT applications, continuous recognition can be more suitable than one-time speech recognition, especially for controlling a device. In principle, continuous speech recognition is performed like a one-time recognition. Namely, the recognition engine processes the audio input to extract phonemes, match them to a model dataset, and generate results. The only difference is that you read recognition results using an event handler rather than by analyzing an object returned by the RecognizeAsync method.

To start continuous speech recognition, you make a call to the StartAsync method of the Speech-ContinuousRecognitionSession. I show you how in Listing 7-7, which depicts the event handler of the Start Continuous Recognition button. In this case, starting SR is very similar to one-time recognition. Specifically, to monitor recognizer state changes, input signal errors, and hypothesis generation, you use exactly the same events as in one-time recognition. Moreover, to stop a speech recognition session, you invoke a StopAsync method.

LISTING 7-7 Continuous speech recognition is started similarly to one-time recognition

```
private const string startCaption = "Start";
private const string stopCaption = "Stop";

private async void ButtonContinuousRecognition_Click(object sender, RoutedEventArgs e)
{
    var buttonCaption = ButtonContinuousRecognition.Content.ToString();

    if (buttonCaption.Contains(startCaption))
    {
        try
        {
            await speechRecognizer.ContinuousRecognitionSession.StartAsync();

            ButtonContinuousRecognition.Content =
                buttonCaption.Replace(startCaption, stopCaption);
        }
        catch (UnauthorizedAccessException)
        {
            DisplayInfo("Speech recognition requires an access to a microphone");
        }
        catch (Exception)
        {
            DisplayInfo("Speech recognition is disabled");
        }
    }
    else
    {
        await speechRecognizer.ContinuousRecognitionSession.StopAsync();

        ButtonContinuousRecognition.Content =
            buttonCaption.Replace(stopCaption, startCaption);
    }
}
```

However, to obtain recognition results you need to handle a SpeechContinuousRecognition-Session.ResultGenerated event. An instance of the SpeechContinuousRecognitionSession is available as a property of the SpeechRecognizer class. To handle the SpeechContinuousRecognition-Session.ResultGenerated event, I extend the definition of the InitializeSpeechRecognizer method, as shown in Listing 7-8. In this listing I also attach a method to the SpeechContinuousRecognition-Session.Completed event. This event is invoked when continuous speech recognition is finished. Typically, this happens when you invoke the ContinuousRecognitionSession.StopAsync method. (See Listing 7-7.)

LISTING 7-8 Obtaining and displaying results of continuous speech recognition

```
private async void InitializeSpeechRecognizer()
{
    speechRecognizer = new SpeechRecognizer();

    await speechRecognizer.CompileConstraintsAsync();

    speechRecognizer.RecognitionQualityDegrading +=
        SpeechRecognizer_RecognitionQualityDegrading;
    speechRecognizer.StateChanged += SpeechRecognizer_StateChanged;
    speechRecognizer.HypothesisGenerated += SpeechRecognizer_HypothesisGenerated;

    speechRecognizer.ContinuousRecognitionSession.ResultGenerated +=
        ContinuousRecognitionSession_ResultGenerated;
    speechRecognizer.ContinuousRecognitionSession.Completed +=
        ContinuousRecognitionSession_Completed;
}

private void ContinuousRecognitionSession_ResultGenerated(
    SpeechContinuousRecognitionSession sender,
    SpeechContinuousRecognitionResultGeneratedEventArgs args)
{
    DisplayInfo(GetRecognitionResultInfo(args.Result));
}

private void ContinuousRecognitionSession_Completed(
    SpeechContinuousRecognitionSession sender,
    SpeechContinuousRecognitionCompletedEventArgs args)
{
    DisplayInfo("Speech recognition completed. Status: " + args.Status);
}
```

To test continuous speech recognition, you need to run the Speech app, click the **Continuous Recognition** button, and then start talking. As in the one-time recognition, the UWP detects speech activity and then processes the voice input to identify words. Recognition steps and results are then displayed in the ListBox control. They are analogous to those depicted in Figure 7-5 except that you can continuously talk to your PC.

Device control using voice commands

This section shows you how to use the speech capabilities of the UWP to create the speech-controlled headed IoT app. It will change the color of the Sense HAT LED array according to a user's voice commands. The first step is to configure the audio input and output devices.

Setting up the hardware

A speech recognition engine of Windows 10 IoT Core requires a compatible microphone. I am using a built-in microphone of the Microsoft Life Cam HD-3000. This is an inexpensive ($20 to $30) and broadly available USB device that you can connect to one of the RPi2 or RPi3 USB ports. After you attach it (or any other compatible USB microphone) to your RPi2 or RPi3, you can configure it using a Device Portal. Navigate to the Audio tab, as shown in Figure 7-6, where you can control the microphone input level and the volume of the RPi2 speaker. Because an SR engine strongly depends on the input signal quality, you can adjust the microphone level if the recognition engine encounters any problems.

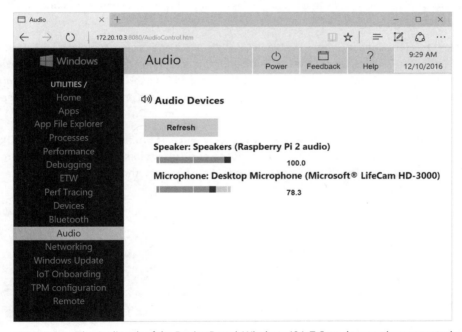

FIGURE 7-6 The Audio tab of the Device Portal. Windows 10 IoT Core does not have a control panel, so audio configuration is performed by using a Device Portal.

The app will also use SS to confirm commands and communicate any errors to the user. To hear your RPi2, you can connect headphones or earphones to the mini jack port of your RPi2 or RPi3. Alternatively, you can use a USB headset, but you need to connect it before powering up an IoT device; doing so ensures that the sound output is directed to the USB headset.

Coding

Now, I show you how to use SR in an IoT device. The switch from a development PC to an IoT requires specific considerations regarding IoT processing capabilities. SR based on complete speaker-independent models may require much more processing time, and so the IoT device may experience significant lags in responding to voice commands. To solve that problem, I use recognition constraints. They reduce computation time with a significantly smaller voice features model, which comes at the cost of a less-general SR system.

To present a sample usage of SS and SR in the IoT app, I prepared the SpeechControl project. (See the companion code in Chapter 07/SpeechControl.) After you deploy it to your IoT device, it initializes the LED array and the SpeechRecognizer class. If SpeechRecognizer cannot be initialized, the LED array starts blinking. Otherwise, a successful initialization is confirmed by a device using an artificial voice message that says "I'm ready. Choose a color." You can respond as follows: "Red," "Green," "Blue," or "None." Depending on your command, a device will drive all the Sense HAT LEDs to the specified color (Red, Green, or Blue) or turn the LED array off (None). The device confirms a correct command recognition by using the OK message. If, for some reason, a device cannot recognize your command, it will say, "I did not get that."

To implement this functionality, I used the blank UWP Visual C# app project template, and after referencing Windows IoT Extensions for the UWP and adding microphone capability, I included several files developed previously: Check.cs, I2cHelper.cs, LedArray.cs, and SpeechHelper.cs. Here, I am simply taking files from previous projects. However, a more general method is to embed those files in a separate class library project and then reference that project. (See Appendix D.)

Subsequently, I wrote the helper method InitializeCommandsDictionary. (See Listing 7-9.) This method instantiates an LUT that relates voice commands to particular colors, which are then used to drive the Sense HAT LED array. The InitializeCommandsDictionary method is invoked only once, in the MainPage constructor.

LISTING 7-9 Voice commands look up table initialization

```
private Dictionary<string, Color> commandsDictionary;

private void InitializeCommandsDictionary()
{
    commandsDictionary = new Dictionary<string, Color>();

    commandsDictionary.Add("Red", Colors.Red);
    commandsDictionary.Add("Green", Colors.Green);
    commandsDictionary.Add("Blue", Colors.Blue);
    commandsDictionary.Add("None", Colors.Black);
}
```

 Note Voice commands are mapped to colors, which are then used to control the LED array.

The next step is to initialize the LED array using the `InitializeLedArray` method. This proceeds exactly as in previous chapters, and thus does not require additional attention. I do need to explain the `InitializeSpeechRecognizer` method you see in Listing 7-10. This function initializes a continuous speech recognition session using the preceding methods. Additionally, I configured constraints so that the speech recognition module limits phoneme search to four words: Red, Green, Blue, and None. These restrictions are imposed using an instance of the `SpeechRecognitionListConstraint` class. A default constructor of that class expects a list of strings representing words or phrases. In the preceding example a list of commands was associated with colors using the `Dictionary` object. Therefore, to instantiate the `SpeechRecognitionListConstraint` class, I used a `Keys` property of the commands-`Dictionary` field.

LISTING 7-10 Initializing speech recognizer with constraints

```
private const string welcomeMessage = "I'm ready. Choose a color";

private async void InitializeSpeechRecognizer()
{
    try
    {
        speechRecognizer = new SpeechRecognizer();

        // Configure constraints
        var listConstraint = new SpeechRecognitionListConstraint(commandsDictionary.Keys);
        speechRecognizer.Constraints.Add(listConstraint);
        await speechRecognizer.CompileConstraintsAsync();

        // Attach event handler, and start continuous recognition
        speechRecognizer.ContinuousRecognitionSession.ResultGenerated +=
            ContinuousRecognitionSession_ResultGenerated;

        await speechRecognizer.ContinuousRecognitionSession.StartAsync();

        SpeechHelper.Speak(welcomeMessage);
    }
    catch (UnauthorizedAccessException)
    {
        StartBlinking();
    }
}

private void StartBlinking()
{
    const int msDelay = 100;

    while (true)
    {
        ledArray.Reset(Colors.Black);
        Task.Delay(msDelay).Wait();

        ledArray.Reset(Colors.Red);
        Task.Delay(msDelay).Wait();
    }
}
```

Note A definition of `ContinuousRecognitionSession_ResultGenerated` is given in Listing 7-11.

As you see in Listing 7-10, if the `SpeechRecognizer` cannot be initialized, the LED array will start blinking. Otherwise, the welcome message is generated by using the `SpeechHelper` class, and the continuous recognition processes voice input. When SR recognizes a correct command with an appropriate confidence level, the LED array color changes to the one requested by the user. (See Listing 7-11.) LED array colors are configured within the `SetColor` method. It simply checks whether the recognized text matches one of the keys in the `commandsDictionary` LUT. If so, the color corresponding to that key is passed to the `Reset` method of the `LedArray` class. Therefore, the LED array changes its color appropriately. The preceding app was built quite easily since we used several building blocks from previous sections and chapters.

LISTING 7-11 LED array changes its color according to voice input

```
private const string recognitionError = "I did not get that";
private const string confirmationMessage = "OK";

private void ContinuousRecognitionSession_ResultGenerated(
    SpeechContinuousRecognitionSession sender,
    SpeechContinuousRecognitionResultGeneratedEventArgs args)
{
    var message = recognitionError;

    if (args.Result.Confidence != SpeechRecognitionConfidence.Rejected)
    {
        message = SetColor(args);
    }

    SpeechHelper.Speak(message);
}

private string SetColor(SpeechContinuousRecognitionResultGeneratedEventArgs args)
{
    var message = recognitionError;

    var recognizedText = args.Result.Text;

    if (commandsDictionary.ContainsKey(recognizedText))
    {
        var color = commandsDictionary[recognizedText];

        message = confirmationMessage;

        ledArray.Reset(color);
    }

    return message;
}
```

Waves in time and frequency domain

SR is a complex task. Multiple approaches have been developed over time to make it fast and robust. Every speech recognition algorithm processes the raw audio signal to extract useful features, which are then compared to known or modeled audio characteristics. Since the UWP exposes a very robust SR system, you typically do not need to bother with low-level SR processing algorithms. However, if you would like to implement custom audio or signal-processing routines, which may happen in multiple automation solutions, then you need to know some fundamental aspects of signal processing. Specifically, almost every SR system begins processing by transforming temporal signal to a frequency domain.

An audio signal is a digital representation of sound generated by an acoustic wave. You can view this wave as a propagation of disturbances that include vibrations of particles or elastic bodies, which in turn become the sound sources. Broadly speaking, in the human auditory system, the particles composing an outer part of the human ear are vibrated by the incoming sound waves. These vibrations are detected by hair cells, which subsequently transmit that information to auditory neurons for processing. In the digital world, audio processing is inspired by that mechanism. However, hair cells are replaced by the microphone, and the signal is processed using a CPU, which analyzes the sound wave as it oscillates periodically in time with a frequency depending on the local medium vibrations.

A time course of the periodic phenomena (like wave or pendulum movement) is usually composed of many redundant data points. To reduce the amount of data required to represent this effect, use a frequency analysis. The mathematical tool that relates waves (or more general periodic phenomena) in time and frequency domains is the Fourier transform. As Figure 7-7 shows, it converts a temporal wave signal into a complex-valued frequency distribution (spectrum). In other words, it relates signals in time and frequency domains. The contribution from each frequency (which is related to a sound pitch) to the overall signal is then available and carried by the amplitude of a Fourier transformed signal.

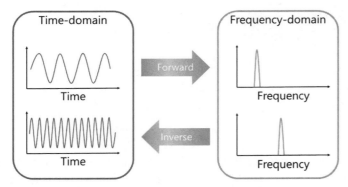

FIGURE 7-7 A Fourier transformation relates signals in time and frequency domains.

The Fourier transformation is typically the first step in SR algorithms. It provides the sound spectrum from which characteristic features for each phoneme are extracted. A detailed speech recognition processing chain would require a whole book. I refer interested readers to the Hidden Markov Model Toolkit (HTK) book at *http://bit.ly/htk_book*.

The Fourier transform is a powerful tool in many scientific and engineering applications, and it's usually a fundamental element of many existing numerical libraries. In the upcoming section, I show you how to write a sample UWP app, computing and displaying a magnitude of the Fourier transform of the simplest sine wave to determine its frequency distribution.

Fast Fourier Transformation

Fast Fourier Transformation (FFT) is an efficient and widely used numerical implementation of the Fourier transform. It's especially optimized for the input signals of which the length is a power of two. Many libraries implement FFT, so you can easily find its detailed description in several articles and books, e.g. *Numerical Recipes: The Art of Scientific Computing* (*http://numerical.recipes/*). Here, I leave out the history and show you how to use FFT in the UWP apps.

I developed a C# UWP app named FrequencyDistribution. (See the companion code in Chapter 07/ FrequencyDistribution.) After creating that project using a blank UWP C# project template as described in Chapter 2, "Universal Windows Platform on devices," I installed two NuGet packages. The first package, MathNet.Numerics (see Figure 7-8), implements many numerical algorithms, including FFT. The second, OxyPlot.Windows (see Figure 7-9) is used for plotting. When I was writing this chapter, the OxyPlot.Windows package was available only in its prerelease version, so I had to select the **Include Prerelease** check box in the NuGet package manager. (See Figure 7-9.) My choice for the FFT library was dictated by the number of downloads only; OxyPlot.Windows is a popular and easy-to-use plotting library.

FIGURE 7-8   NuGet package manager, presenting a list of FFT libraries.

After installing the packages, I referenced Windows IoT Extensions for the UWP and included three previously developed files: Check.cs, I2cHelper.cs, and LedArray.cs. I then implemented two static helper classes: PlotHelper and SpectrumHelper. You can find the full code for each one under the subfolder Helpers of the FrequencyDistribution app in the companion code.

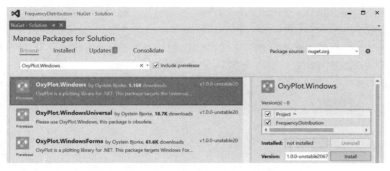

FIGURE 7-9 OxyPlot.Windows NuGet package installation.

In particular, PlotHelper has two public methods that are important here: GenerateSineWave and AddLineSeries. GenerateSineWave, shown in Listing 7-12, creates an array of signed 16-bit integers, representing a time course of the sine wave with an amplitude (height) of short.MaxValue and a given number of cycles (periods) in that array. This number of periods is controlled by the value of the frequency argument. Given that and the length of the array, I use the static Sin function of the Math class to set the value of each array element.

LISTING 7-12 Generating a sine wave

```
public static short[] GenerateSineWave(int length, double frequency)
{
    Check.IsPositive(length);

    var degToRadScaler = Math.PI / 180.0d;
    var lengthScaler = 360.0d / length;

    var sineWave = new short[length];

    for (int i = 0; i < length; i++)
    {
        var phase = i * degToRadScaler * frequency * lengthScaler;

        var sin = short.MaxValue * Math.Sin(phase);

        sineWave[i] = Convert.ToInt16(sin);
    }

    return sineWave;
}
```

Other public methods of the PlotHelper class, namely AddLineSeries and AddBarSeries, add (plot) an input vector to the given chart of the OxyPlot package. (See Listing 7-13.) In OxyPlot, the chart appearance is controlled through an instance of the PlotModel class. An instance of this class is bound to a PlotView control, which, as I show later in this chapter, can be declared in the XAML code. Accordingly, every change you make to PlotModel is automatically reflected in the UI after a call to the InvalidatePlot method.

LISTING 7-13 Plotting a line series using OxyPlot's chart

```
public static void AddLineSeries<T>(PlotModel plotModel, T[] inputData, OxyColor color)
{
    Check.IsNull(plotModel);
    Check.IsNull(inputData);

    var lineSeries = new LineSeries()
    {
        Color = color
    };

    AddDataPointSeries(plotModel, inputData, lineSeries);
}

private static void AddDataPointSeries<T>(PlotModel plotModel, T[] inputData,
    DataPointSeries dataPointSeries)
{
    for (int i = 0; i < inputData.Length; i++)
    {
        dataPointSeries.Points.Add(new DataPoint(i, Convert.ToDouble(inputData[i])));
    }

    plotModel.Series.Clear();
    plotModel.Series.Add(dataPointSeries);

    plotModel.InvalidatePlot(true);
}
```

The second helper class, `SpectrumHelper` (see Listing 7-14), implements one public method, `FourierMagnitude`. You invoke the `Forward` method of the `Fourier` class, declared in `MathNet.Numerics.IntegralTransforms`. Therefore, the signal is converted from the temporal to the frequency domain, and can be converted back to the time domain using an inverse FFT implemented in the `Inverse` method.

LISTING 7-14 A numerical Fourier transformation of the input temporal signal, represented as an array of shorts

```
public static class SpectrumHelper
{
    public static double[] FourierMagnitude(short[] inputData)
    {
        Check.IsNull(inputData);

        var complexInput = ShortToComplexArray(inputData);

        Fourier.Forward(complexInput);

        return GetMagnitude(complexInput);
    }
```

```
        private static Complex[] ShortToComplexArray(short[] inputData)
        {
            var elementsCount = inputData.Length;
            var complexData = new Complex[elementsCount];

            for(int i = 0; i < elementsCount; i++)
            {
                complexData[i] = new Complex(inputData[i], 0.0d);
            }

            return complexData;
        }

        private static double[] GetMagnitude(Complex[] fft)
        {
            var magnitude = new double[fft.Length];

            for (int i = 0; i < magnitude.Length; i++)
            {
                magnitude[i] = fft[i].Magnitude;
            }

            return magnitude;
        }
    }
```

The FourierMagnitude method of the SpectrumHelper class operates on signed 16-bit integers only; therefore, in subsequent sections, I use it to process audio signals in the WAV format. In most cases, this format uses 16-bit integers to digitally represent an audio signal.

I use a forward transformation here and convert the time-domain signal to the frequency-domain to reproduce the results you see in Figure 7-7. Namely, I plot an input signal modeled as the sine wave and then the magnitude of its Fourier transform.

In general, my goal is to explicitly show how various oscillations of temporal signals, e.g. audio waves, can be detected using the Fourier transform. I then employ this property to extract the spectrum of the audio wave, which in general is composed of many sine waves of different frequencies. These frequencies correspond to different tones.

As you see in Figure 7-10 and Figure 7-11, I declare the UI comprising a slider and two PlotView controls. The first chart displays a sine wave, while the second depicts a magnitude of the Fourier-transformed signal using an FFT.

You can use the slider to change input wave frequency. The Slider control is bound to the Frequency property of the MainPage class. (See Listing 7-15.) Whenever you change the slider position, the UpdatePlots method is invoked. It first generates an appropriate array, representing the sine wave. The length of the sine wave is controlled using the inputDataLength variable, which is set to 1024 points. (See Listing 7-15.) The generated sine wave is subsequently plotted in the PlotView control located on the left side of the UI. The second PlotView control plots the corresponding FFT magnitude, which is calculated using the SpectrumHelper class.

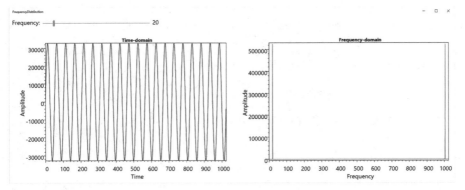

FIGURE 7-10   An idealized single-frequency sine wave (left) and the magnitude of the corresponding FFT.

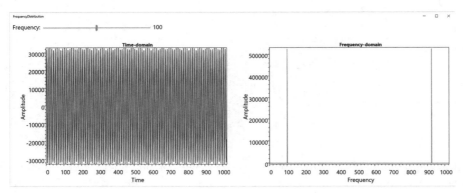

FIGURE 7-11   A magnitude of the FFT (right) reflects the frequency changes of the input signal; compare with Figure 7-10.

LISTING 7-15   Code-behind of MainPage

```
public sealed partial class MainPage : Page
{
    private const int inputDataLength = 1024;

    private PlotModel sineWavePlotModel;
    private PlotModel fftPlotModel;

    private double frequency;

    public double Frequency
    {
        get { return frequency; }
        set
        {
            frequency = value;
            UpdatePlots();
        }
    }
}
```

```
        public MainPage()
        {
            InitializeComponent();

            InitializePlots();

            Frequency = 1;
        }

        private void InitializePlots()
        {
            sineWavePlotModel = new PlotModel();
            fftPlotModel = new PlotModel();

            // Font size
            const int fontSize = 22;
            sineWavePlotModel.DefaultFontSize = fontSize;
            fftPlotModel.DefaultFontSize = fontSize;

            // Titles
            sineWavePlotModel.Title = "Time-domain";
            fftPlotModel.Title = "Frequency-domain";

            // Axes
            ConfigureAxes();
        }

    private void UpdatePlots()
    {
        var sineWave = PlotHelper.GenerateSineWave(inputDataLength, Frequency);
        var fourierMagnitude = SpectrumHelper.FourierMagnitude(sineWave);

        PlotHelper.AddLineSeries(sineWavePlotModel, sineWave, OxyColors.Blue);
        PlotHelper.AddLineSeries(fftPlotModel, fourierMagnitude, OxyColors.OrangeRed);
    }

    // ConfigureAxes method is given in the companion code.
    // It simply configures chart appearance, i.e. axes titles, ranges, etc.
}
```

In Listing 7-15, I also declare and initialize two instances of the PlotModel class. They are associated with two PlotView controls and are used to configure the chart appearance. In particular, I configure the font size, chart and axes titles, and axes ranges.

Figure 7-10 depicts sample results for a low-frequency sine wave, while Figure 7-11 shows the screenshot of a rapidly oscillating wave. For an idealized wave, the FFT magnitude contains two peaks. As you can see, the position of these peaks changes when you change the input wave frequency. Therefore, FFT decodes a frequency of the input temporal signal. The first peak of the FFT magnitude is located exactly at the wave frequency—20 in Figure 7-10, and 100 in Figure 7-11—while the second peak is located at index 1004 (see Figure 7-10) and at 924 (see Figure 7-11). The existence of the second peak is due to complex conjugate symmetry of the Fourier transform of real signals. I discuss this further in the next section.

Sampling rate and frequency scale

So far, I have not used physical units that describe the time scale of the input signals and the corresponding frequency range. In general, these depend on the acquisition device used to record a signal. Depending on the desirable recording quality, audio signals are typically sampled at rates of 3,000–44,100 samples per second. This sampling speed describes how well the recording device can probe (sample) the continuous audio wave. In practice, a recording device, e.g. microphone, cannot sample an audio signal without a small time delay, which is necessary for storing consecutive samples. Therefore, a recording device is incapable of ideally representing the continuous audio wave. The quality improves as the number of samples increases. The quality of a recorded signal increases with the sampling rate since higher frequencies carry more detailed information, i.e., higher tones. Therefore, telephony uses low sampling frequencies of 3–8 kHz, while CD quality requires a sampling rate of 44.1 kHz, where kHz denotes kilo hertz unit (kHz, 1 kHz = 1 ms^{-1}).

The sampling rate also determines the signal time scale and corresponding frequency range. Formally, the sampling rate f_s is an inverse of the time delay δt between consecutive recordings (samples): $f_s = \frac{1}{\delta t}$. Therefore, the sampling rate is expressed in hertz. Given the number of samples, n, one defines the record length $\Delta t = n \delta t$.

But how to relate those numbers to what was shown in the FrequencyDistribution app? This app uses discrete vectors without any time scale, which typically is set according to the recording capabilities of the particular audio device. In the FrequencyDistribution app, you just have the record length, which is controlled using the value of the inputDataLength field. (See Listing 7-15.)

Knowing the sampling rate enables you to determine δt and then convert indices of the input array containing audio samples to the physical time scale. Namely, for $f_s = 4$ kHz, $\delta t = 0.25$ ms, and then for $f_s = 44.1$ kHz, $\delta t \approx 0.023$ ms.

You use a record length to calculate the frequency range (or frequency band) $\Delta f = \frac{1}{\Delta t}$ of the temporal signal. This range is divided into equally spaced frequency bins:

$$f_i = i \times \frac{f_s}{n}, i = 0,1, \dots, n.$$

In general, FFT operates on complex numbers. However, when an input signal is real, the so-called Hermitian symmetry of the FFT reduces the number of useful points in the frequency distribution by a factor of two. As you see in Figure 7-10 and Figure 7-11, the second half of the Fourier-transformed array is a mirror image of the first half. Hence, one half of the FFT array contains useful information about the temporal signal. Therefore, the maximum usable frequency is $f_N = \frac{f_s}{2}$. This value is defined as the *Nyquist frequency*. One more FFT component, the zero or DC frequency, holds special meaning. From a mathematical point of view, the zero frequency is indefinite. Technically, it corresponds to the offset of the input wave, i.e., the value around which the signal is oscillating. In the preceding example, the sine waves vibrate around 0, so the DC component is 0. To investigate the effects of the DC offset, you can Fourier-transform a constant, non-zero vector, namely an array that's composed of the same constant value. You'll see that the DC component of the FFT magnitude increases with the increasing value you use to build an array.

As the preceding discussion indicates, you should exclude the DC component and frequencies higher than f_N from the calculated FFT magnitude. To this end, you modify the GetMagnitude method, whose original definition appears in Listing 7-14, as highlighted in Listing 7-16. Consequently, I also changed the abscissa range of the FFT plot in the MainPage.xaml.cs file. You see the results of these modifications in Figure 7-12.

LISTING 7-16 Use only the useful part of the FFT magnitude for further analysis

```
private static double[] GetMagnitude(Complex[] fft)
{
    var magnitude = new double[fft.Length / 2];

    for (int i = 0; i < magnitude.Length; i++)
    {
        // Skip the DC component and frequencies
        // higher than the Nyquist frequency
        magnitude[i] = fft[i + 1].Magnitude;
    }

    return magnitude;
}
```

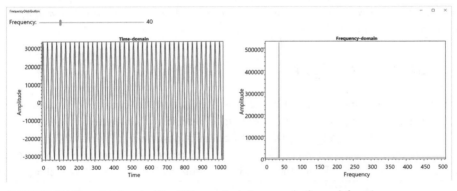

FIGURE 7-12 The useful part of the FFT magnitude is now a single-peak function.

The example in Figure 7-12 shows an idealized single-frequency wave corresponding to a particular tone. In practice, the audio signal, like speech or melody, is composed of many such elementary sine waves oscillating at different frequencies. In that case, the amplitude of the FFT contains many peaks, the height of which quantifies each tone's contribution to the audio signal.

Decibel scale

To compare FFT magnitudes of different signals, and for presentation purposes, FFT magnitude is often converted to the decibel scale using the following expression:

$$P = 20 \log_{10} \frac{A}{A_0}$$

where A and A_0 denote the FFT amplitude of the actual and reference signals. The value of A_0 depends on the particular application—for example, in the sound power measurements, $A_0 = 10^{-12} \, W$. However, for digital processing, applications can be assumed to have a value of 1, since a reference measurement is typically unavailable.

The decibel scale, when used for plotting the FFT magnitude, identifies low peaks, which can be dominated by high peaks on the linear scale. For this reason, I use the decibel scale in the waveform spectrum analyzer. I supplement a definition of the SpectrumHelper class by the method SetDbScale, implementing the preceding equation. (See Listing 7-17.)

LISTING 7-17   An input array is converted to the decibel scale

```
private static void SetDbScale(double[] input)
{
    for (int i = 0; i < input.Length; i++)
    {
        // Add epsilon to avoid infinity
        input[i] = 20.0 * Math.Log10(input[i] + double.Epsilon);
    }
}
```

In Listing 7-17, I add a numerical zero, i.e. $\varepsilon \approx 5 \times 10^{-324}$, to each element of the input array before calculating a logarithm. This does not significantly affect the final result and is done to avoid infinity, which arises when $x = 0$ in $\log_{10} x$.

Waveform spectrum analyzer

You're now familiar with FFT fundamentals and so can implement the real-time spectrum analyzer of the WAV audio file. Playing and processing the audio signal read from that file determines its frequency representation. Subsequently, the audio signal in the frequency domain is converted (binned) to an eight-bin histogram and displayed on the LED array. The signal processing is performed in the background, in parallel to audio playback such that LEDs blink to the rhythm of music. The audio analyzers in audio software inspired this functionality.

This implementation requires a few additional modules. I start with a helper method for reading the contents of a binary file and then implement a class for parsing WAV file data, followed by a Short Time Fourier Transform (STFT). Only a short fragment (20–40 ms) of the input signal is transformed in the FFT. The resulting frequency distribution is converted to the decibel scale, binned, and sent to the Sense HAT add-on board using the LedArray class, which you developed in the previous chapter.

Reading a file

In the UWP, a single file is represented by the StorageFile class, declared in the Windows.Storage namespace. In general, to open an existing file you can use the system file picker, implemented in the FileOpenPicker class (Windows.Storage.Pickers namespace). An instance of the FileOpenPicker class provides several methods for activating the file picker, which lets the user browse files. If you know the file path, you can use one of the following static methods of the `StorageFile` class: `GetFileFrom-PathAsync` or `GetFileFromApplicationUriAsync`. You can also open an existing file by using an instance method `GetFileAsync` of the `StorageFolder` class. The `StorageFolder` class is an object for managing folders. However, in Windows 10 IoT Core, file pickers are not available. Here, I use the `GetFileAsync` of the `StorageFolder`. I add a WAV file to the solution to deploy the audio file with the app to the IoT device.

Next, I show you how to add any 16-bit WAV file (*.wav extension) to the FrequencyDistribution project. First, open the Add Existing Item dialog box (choose **Project > Add Existing Item**), and then rename the file to audio.wav. You then need to change the build properties of the audio.wav such that it will be copied to the output directory. (See Figure 7-13.) Add to the FrequencyDistribution a Storage-FileHelper.cs file, which I show you in Listing 7-18. This listing shows you how to open a file located in the current app folder. You can obtain programmatic access to that folder through the `InstalledLocation` property of the Package class. Next, I asynchronously invoke the `GetFileAsync` method, which returns an instance of the `StorageFile` class. To open a file, I used the `OpenReadAsync` method, which returns an object implementing the `IRandomAccessStreamWithContentType` interface. To read file content, you need to read the stream. Implement this in the `StreamToBuffer` method of the `StorageFileHelper` class. (See Listing 7-18.) You use the methods of the `StorageFileHelper` class later in this chapter.

FIGURE 7-13   The Build Action configuration.

LISTING 7-18   A helper class for reading the file from the app folder

```
public static class StorageFileHelper
{
    public static async Task<IRandomAccessStreamWithContentType> OpenLocalFile(string
        fileName)
    {
        Check.IsNull(fileName);

        // Get app folder
        var storageFolder = Package.Current.InstalledLocation;

        // Get and open file
        var storageFile = await storageFolder.GetFileAsync(fileName);

        return await storageFile.OpenReadAsync();
    }
```

```
public static async Task<Windows.Storage.Streams.Buffer> StreamToBuffer(
    IRandomAccessStreamWithContentType stream)
{
    Check.IsNull(stream);

    var size = Convert.ToUInt32(stream.Size);

    var buffer = new Windows.Storage.Streams.Buffer(size);

    await stream.ReadAsync(buffer, size, InputStreamOptions.None);

    return buffer;
}
}
```

Waveform audio file format reader

The WAV file specification is based on the Resource Interchanged File Format (RIFF). RIFF divides a file into distinct structures, called chunks. Each chunk consists of the identifier, a four-length integer specifying chunk length, and the chunk data. The structure of the WAV file begins with the master chunk (see Table 7-1), which contains the RIFF identifier, followed by the size, and the WAVE string. The format (fmt) chunk follows. (See Table 7-2.) It begins with the identifier and is followed by the values describing the format and record parameters—number of audio channels, sample rate, etc.

TABLE 7-1   RIFF chunk structure

Field	Length (in bytes)	Offset from file beginning (in bytes)	Value
Chunk id	4	0	RIFF
Chunk length	4	4	Total file length – 8 bytes (containing Chunk id and Chunk length)
WAV identifier	4	8	WAVE

The format code in the format chunk specifies in detail how the registered analog samples are converted from analog to digital representation. This typically occurs through pulse-code modulation (PCM), which samples the amplitude of the input analog signal at constant intervals and then converts it to the linear scale (linear PCM). A-law or μ-law algorithms can also compound the audio amplitude to a non-linear scale. Communication protocols to enhance speech dynamic range typically utilize the non-linear scale. However, most computer WAV files are encoded using the linear PCM format; the WAV parser I implement here supports only the linear PCM format.

The format chunk also specifies the number of audio channels, a sample rate, and the bit depth of the audio samples, which are stored in the data chunk. The data chunk consists of the data identifier, followed by the byte array with audio samples. If the audio signal has two channels (left and right), then the samples of the left and right channels are interleaved.

TABLE 7-2   Format chunk structure

Field	Length (in bytes)	Offset from file beginning (in bytes)	Value / description
Chunk id	4	12	RIFF
Chunk length	4	16	16, 18 or 40
Format code	2	20	0x0001 (pulse-code modulation /PCM/) 0x0003 (IEEE float) 0x0006 PCM A-law algorithm 0x0007 PCM μ-law algorithm 0xFFEE extensible format
Number of audio channels	2	22	1 or 2
Sample rate	4	24	The sampling rate, depends on the record device
Bytes per second	4	28	Data rate, the averaged bytes per second
Block align	2	32	Data block size
Bits per sample	2	34	8, 16 (for PCM) and 32 or 64 (for non-PCM)
Extension length	4	36	Format extension is present only for a chunk length of 18, and have a size of 0 or 22

The complete implementation of the WaveData class, which parses the WAV byte array, appears in the companion code in Chapter 07/FrequencyDistribution/Helpers/WaveData.cs. Basically, the Wave-Data class exposes several public properties representing the WAV file. (See Table 7-2.) These properties include: ChunkLength, ChannelsCount, SampleRate, AverageBytesPerSecond, BlockAlign, BitsPerSample, SamplesPerChannel, and two arrays containing 16-bit samples. My implementation of the WaveData class is compatible with 16-bit PCM WAV files. I do not parse a fact chunk, which can be present in extended WAV file formats.

The properties of the WaveData are obtained from the raw byte array. This is achieved by reading the WAV file using the StoregeFileHelper class. Next, the result of the StorageFileHelper.Stream-ToBuffer method, which is of type Windows.Storage.Streams.Buffer, must be converted to the byte array. I'm using the instance ToArray extension method, declared in the WindowsRuntimeBuffer-Extensions static class from the System.Runtime.InteropServices.WindowsRuntime namespace.

The byte array is analyzed within the constructor of the WaveData class. (See Listing 7-19.) This constructor, after performing argument validation, invokes several helper functions that parse specific parts of the WAV file. Each of them uses the BitConverter class. Given the WAV format specifiers (Table 7-1 and Table 7-2), I simply invoke the appropriate methods of the BitConverter class to convert blocks of bytes at particular positions into meaningful values, representing a WAV file and audio samples. For example, see Listing 7-20, which shows how to read the format chunk of the WAV file.

LISTING 7-19 WaveData class reads RIFF format and data chunks of the byte array

```
public WaveData(byte[] rawData)
{
    Check.IsNull(rawData);
    Check.LengthNotLessThan(rawData.Length, minLength);

    var offset = ReadRiffChunk(rawData);

    offset = ReadFormatChunk(rawData, offset);

    ReadDataChunk(rawData, offset);
}
```

LISTING 7-20 Parsing the format chunk of the WAV file using the methods of the BitConverter class

```
private const string fmtChunk = "fmt ";
private const int pcmTag = 1;
private const int fmtExtendedSize = 18;
private const int supportedBitsPerSample = 16;

private int shortSize = sizeof(short);
private int intSize = sizeof(int);

private int ReadFormatChunk(byte[] rawData, int offset)
{
    VerifyChunkId(rawData, offset, fmtChunk);
    offset += chunkIdLength;

    var formatChunkLength = BitConverter.ToInt32(rawData, offset);
    offset += intSize;

    var formatTag = BitConverter.ToInt16(rawData, offset);
    VerifyFormatTag(formatTag);
    offset += shortSize;

    ChannelsCount = BitConverter.ToInt16(rawData, offset);
    offset += shortSize;

    SampleRate = BitConverter.ToInt32(rawData, offset);
    offset += intSize;

    AverageBytesPerSecond = BitConverter.ToInt32(rawData, offset);
    offset += intSize;

    BlockAlign = BitConverter.ToInt16(rawData, offset);
    offset += shortSize;

    BitsPerSample = BitConverter.ToInt16(rawData, offset);
    VerifyBps();
    offset += shortSize;
```

```
    if (formatChunkLength == fmtExtendedSize)
    {
        var extensionLength = BitConverter.ToInt16(rawData, offset);
        offset += extensionLength + shortSize;
    }

    return offset;
}

private void VerifyFormatTag(int formatTag)
{
    if (formatTag != pcmTag)
    {
        throw new ArgumentException("Unsupported data format");
    }
}

private void VerifyBps()
{
    if (BitsPerSample != supportedBitsPerSample)
    {
        throw new ArgumentException("Unsupported sample bit depth");
    }
}
```

Signal windowing and Short Time Fourier Transform

The length of a typical song is around 4–5 minutes, but to implement the real-time spectrum analyzer, I do not want to determine the spectral representation of the whole song. Instead, I want to process short song fragments of about a millisecond. Doing so means I divide a whole input signal into short frames and process only the frame that's playing. The resulting spectrum corresponds to the actual position of the audio file.

When the small frame is extracted from the longer signal, it might not contain the integral number of periods. In that case, the FFT would produce spurious frequencies. Usually, to reduce this effect, the signal is windowed before computing FFT. Windowing reduces the amplitude of the input signal at the boundaries. The Short Time Fourier Transform (STFT) is thus a method of extracting short fragments of the input signal, applying to them a window function, and calculating the FFT.

Several window functions are available. The most popular are Bartlett, Blackman, Hann, or Hamming. They are implemented in the Window class of the MathNet.Numerics NuGet package.

In this chapter, I use the Hamming window. In Listing 7-21, I show you how to use this function to window the input signal. As you can see, I first invoke the Hamming method and then multiply element-wise the resulting array by the input signal.

Spectrum Histogram

The LED array of the Sense HAT add-on board cannot display the full spectrum of the processed audio signal because it is just an 8x8 display. To reduce the length of the spectrum, neighboring frequency bins are combined to produce the histogram. (See Figure 7-14.) Although you can arbitrarily choose the frequency ranges for your audio histogram, several standardized methods are available, like organizing the frequencies as octaves. An octave is the frequency range; its upper limit is twice its lower limit. For example, the International Organization for Standardization (ISO) divides the audio spectrum into the following 10 octave bands: 31.5 Hz, 63 Hz, 125 Hz, 250 Hz, 500 Hz, 1 kHz, 2 kHz, 4 kHz, 8 kHz, and 16 kHz, assuming a sample rate of 44.1 kHz.

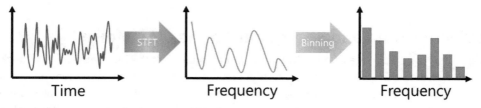

FIGURE 7-14 Spectrum binning for audio spectrum visualization.

A 10-bands histogram is not suitable here, because the Sense HAT has only 8 columns. Therefore, I divide the spectrum into eight octaves and threshold the spectrum at 14 kHz, since frequencies higher than this level contribute very little.

To implement spectrum binning, I extend the SpectrumHelper by one public method, Histogram, and two helper private methods: GetHistogram and GetFrequencyBins. See the companion code in Chapter 07/FrequencyDistribution/SpectrumHelper.cs. Two associated private members control the number of bins and the threshold frequency.

The GetFrequencyBins method, depending on the sampling rate, prepares the 8-component array of frequency bins. (See Listing 7-22.) This array specifies the lower and upper bounds of the frequency ranges used to build the histogram. (See Figure 7-12.) You construct these ranges by using the preceding octave method. Set the upper frequency range to the Nyquist frequency and the threshold to 14 kHz, if necessary. You compose subsequent frequency ranges by dividing the upper frequency from the previous step by a factor of 2.

LISTING 7-22   Octaves calculation

```
private const int binsCount = 8;

private static double[] GetFrequencyBins(double sampleRate)
{
    var bins = new double[binsCount];

    var startFrequency = sampleRate;

    for (int i = binsCount; i > 0; i--)
    {
        startFrequency /= 2;

        bins[i - 1] = Math.Min(startFrequency, maxFrequency);
    }

    return bins;
}
```

Given the frequency ranges, you can now assign each STFT amplitude to the appropriate frequency bin within the GetHistogram method from Listing 7-23. This method iterates over the Fourier-transformed frequency vector and adds decibel-scale magnitude values to the appropriate histogram element.

LISTING 7-23   Spectrum binning

```
private const double maxFrequency = 14000;

private static double[] GetHistogram(double[] dbFourierMagnitude, double sampleRate)
{
    var histogram = new double[binsCount];

    var bins = GetFrequencyBins(sampleRate);

    var signalLength = 2 * dbFourierMagnitude.Length;
    var frequencyScale = Fourier.FrequencyScale(signalLength, sampleRate);

    for (int i = 0, frequencyIndex = 0; i < histogram.Length; i++)
    {
        var binWidth = 0;
        while (frequencyScale[frequencyIndex] <= bins[i])
        {
            histogram[i] += dbFourierMagnitude[frequencyIndex];
            binWidth++;

            if (frequencyIndex++ == dbFourierMagnitude.Length - 1)
            {
                break;
            }
        }
    }
```

```
        histogram[i] = histogram[i] / binWidth;
    }

    return histogram;
}
```

The preceding methods are invoked within the Histogram function. This function first calculates the STFT and then converts its magnitude to the decibel scale. Subsequently, the GetHistogram method determines the spectral histogram. (See Listing 7-24.) To make the bar chart, I also supplemented the PlotHelper class by an additional method, AddBarSeries. Its definition is analogous to AddLineSeries and thus does not require additional comments.

LISTING 7-24   Implementation of the Short Time Fourier Transform and spectrum binning

```
public static double[] Histogram(short[] inputData, double sampleRate)
{
    Check.IsNull(inputData);

    // Windowing
    ApplyWindow(inputData);

    // FFT
    var fourierMagnitude = FourierMagnitude(inputData);

    // Db scale
    SetDbScale(fourierMagnitude);

    // Binning
    return GetHistogram(fourierMagnitude, sampleRate);
}
```

Spectrum display: putting things together

Incorporate the functionalities implemented in the previous sections to determine the histogram of the instantaneous audio spectrum. The audio frame and the histogram plot in the MainPage and an additional button trigger the signal processing. I supplemented the XAML code of the MainPage by an appropriate button declaration. This button begins custom audio processing, which is performed in the background to achieve results like those featured in Figure 7-15 and Figure 7-16.

This custom audio processing is based on the blocks developed in the preceding sections. You can find the complete implementation in the MainPage.xaml.cs file of the companion code in Chapter 07/ FrequencyDistribution/MainPage.xaml.cs.

The central part of the preceding functionality is embedded within the event handler, presented in Listing 7-25. Depending on the value of the IsMediaElementPlaying property, I either begin or stop audio processing. Before audio processing is started, I first open and parse the WAV file. Subsequently, I adjust the length of the processed audio frame to the sampling rate, such that the STFT window length is ~40 ms. (See AdjustWindowLength in the companion code.)

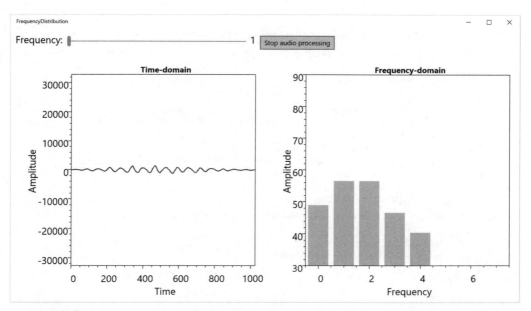

FIGURE 7-15 Low-frequency audio oscillations (left) and the corresponding spectral histogram. When the input frame is composed mainly of the low-frequency components, the histogram energy is distributed across the first few octaves only.

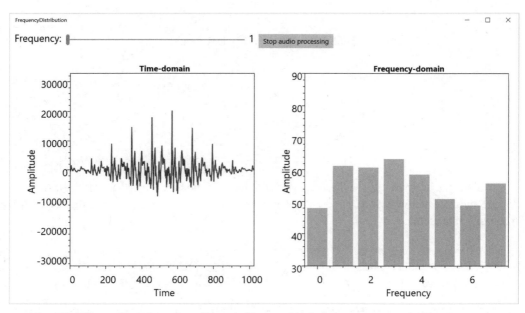

FIGURE 7-16 When an input frame is composed of low- and high-frequency waves, the histogram energy is distributed across all octaves.

LISTING 7-25 Event handler of the button, used to begin custom audio processing

```
private async void ButtonProcessAudio_Click(object sender, RoutedEventArgs e)
{
    if(!IsMediaElementPlaying)
    {
        // Get audio stream
        var audioStream = await StorageFileHelper.OpenLocalFile(fileName);

        // Get, and parse audio buffer
        var waveBuffer = await StorageFileHelper.StreamToBuffer(audioStream);
        var waveData = new WaveData(waveBuffer.ToArray());

        // Adjust window length to sample rate
        var windowLength = AdjustWindowLength(waveData.SampleRate);

        // Update plot display ranges
        ConfigureAxes(true, windowLength);

        // Play the stream
        IsMediaElementPlaying = true;

        mediaElement.SetSource(audioStream, audioStream.ContentType);
        mediaElement.Play();

        // Begin audio processing
        await Task.Run(() =>
        {
            DetermineAudioSpectrum(waveData, windowLength);
        });
    }
    else
    {
        mediaElement.Stop();
        IsMediaElementPlaying = false;
    }
}
```

I play the file using the MediaElement class and then run the task, which invokes the Determine-AudioSpectrum method. (See Listing 7-26.) The spectral histogram corresponds to the currently played fragment of the audio file.

LISTING 7-26 Processing an audio fragment to determine and display a spectral histogram

```
private async void DetermineAudioSpectrum(WaveData waveData, int windowLength)
{
    while (IsMediaElementPlaying)
    {
        var inputData = new short[windowLength];

        // Get MediaElement position
```

```
    var index = await GetWindowPosition(waveData.SampleRate, windowLength);

    if (index + windowLength < waveData.SamplesPerChannel)
    {
        // Get current frame
        Array.Copy(waveData.SamplesLeftChannel, index, inputData, 0, windowLength);

        // Determine histogram
        var hist = SpectrumHelper.Histogram(inputData, waveData.SampleRate);

        // Plot input frame, and spectrum histogram
        PlotHelper.AddLineSeries(sineWavePlotModel, inputData, OxyColors.Blue);
        PlotHelper.AddBarSeries(fftPlotModel, hist, OxyColors.Orange);
    }
    else
    {
        // File ended
        IsMediaElementPlaying = false;
    }
}
}
```

To synchronize the audio playback with signal processing, I process the frame according to the Position property of the MediaElement object. The value stored in this property is converted to seconds and then to the actual sample index of the audio buffer by knowing a sampling rate. (See the GetWindowPosition method from Listing 7-27.)

LISTING 7-27 Obtaining the sample index by using the position of the currently played fragment of an audio file

```
private async Task<int> GetWindowPosition(double sampleRate, int windowLength)
{
    int index = 0;

    await Dispatcher.RunAsync(CoreDispatcherPriority.Normal, () =>
    {
        var position = mediaElement.Position.TotalSeconds * sampleRate;
        index = Convert.ToInt32(position) - windowLength / 2;
        index = Math.Max(index, 0);
    });

    return index;
}
```

In the preceding example, I process the left channel only. A more general approach should process two channels separately, and then average the resulting spectral histograms or display them individually. I encourage you to implement such functionality on your own.

When you run the app and click the **Start Audio Processing** button, the app plays the sound, displays the input audio frame, and shows the corresponding binned frequency distribution in real time.

Two examples of captured instantaneous results of the FrequencyDistribution app appear in Figure 7-15 and Figure 7-16. Figure 7-15 shows an input frame consisting of low-frequency waves (low tones). As you can see, the corresponding spectral histogram does not contain high-frequency octaves. On the other hand, the audio frame in Figure 7-16 is composed of low-, medium-, and high-frequency fundamental waves (low, medium, and high tones, respectively). Consequently, you see all the octaves. The spectrum analyzer you just built can distinguish audio signals of different types and thus constitutes the simple machine hearing system.

The last aspect that requires additional comment is the histogram dynamic range controlled by using dbMinValue and dbMaxValue variables. Namely, all the histogram values smaller than 30 dB (dbMinValue) and larger than 90 dB (dbMaxValue) are not displayed. In other words, the histogram display range is fixed to 30–90 dB. You can modify this range empirically, depending on your audio file or the particular processing application.

Spectrum display on the LED array

In this section I show you how to incorporate the Sense HAT LED array and display the spectral histogram dynamically so that the LEDs will blink in the rhythm of the audio signal. See Figure 7-17 and Figure 7-18.

FIGURE 7-17   Spectral histogram displayed on the LED array.

FIGURE 7-18   Blinking changes dynamically on the LED array.

To achieve that functionality, you display the spectral histogram using the Sense HAT LED array instead of using the chart. Therefore, I first extended the definition of the LedArray class by an additional DrawHistogram method. (See Listing 7-28.) This method draws eight vertical lines, representing bars of the spectral histogram. The height of each line is adjusted to the histogram value.

LISTING 7-28   Colorful histogram drawing on the LED array

```
public void DrawHistogram(double[] histogram, double minValue, double maxValue)
{
    Check.IsNull(histogram);

    for (int i = 0; i < Length; i++)
    {
        var height = SetHeight(histogram[i], minValue, maxValue);

        DrawLine(Length - 1 - i, height);
    }

    UpdateDevice();
}

private int SetHeight(double histogramValue, double minValue, double maxValue)
{
    double step = (maxValue - minValue) / Length;

    var stretchedValue = Math.Floor((histogramValue - minValue) / step);
    var height = Convert.ToInt32(stretchedValue);

    height = Math.Max(height, 0);
    height = Math.Min(height, Length);

    return height;
}

private void DrawLine(int position, int height)
{
    for (int i = 0; i < Length; i++)
    {
        Buffer[position, i] = GetColor(i, height);
    }
}
```

 Note   The column color changes with increasing bar height.

To make the histogram more attractive, I implemented the GetColor method. (See Listing 7-29.) It creates a simple color ramp: the LED pixels on the top of the histogram column are red; the pixels in the middle are orange; and the lowest are green. (Refer to Figure 7-17 and Figure 7-18.)

LISTING 7-29 Implementation of the color ramp

```csharp
private Color GetColor(int level, int height)
{
    const int lowLevel = 3;
    const int mediumLevel = 6;

    var color = Colors.Black;

    if (level < height)
    {
        if (level < lowLevel)
        {
            color = Colors.Green;
        }
        else if (level < mediumLevel)
        {
            color = Colors.OrangeRed;
        }
        else
        {
            color = Colors.Red;
        }
    }

    return color;
}
```

Next, as Listing 7-30 shows, I associate a connection with the Sense HAT to control the LED array by using the I2cHelper class. I then invoke ButtonProcessAudio_Click. (See Listing 7-31.) I slightly modify this event handler to begin audio processing right after the app is deployed. When the IoT device starts, the sound is played and processed, and the resulting spectral histogram displays on the LED array. (Refer to Figure 7-17 and Figure 7-18.)

LISTING 7-30 LED array initialization and audio processing activation

```csharp
private LedArray ledArray;
private bool isIoTPlatform = false;

protected override void OnNavigatedTo(NavigationEventArgs e)
{
    base.OnNavigatedTo(e);

    InitializeLedArray();
}

private async void InitializeLedArray()
{
    const byte address = 0x46;
```

```
        var device = await I2cHelper.GetI2cDevice(address);

    if (device != null)
    {
        ledArray = new LedArray(device);
        isIoTPlatform = true;
        ButtonProcessAudio_Click(null, null);
    }
}
```

LISTING 7-31 If you run the FrequencyDistribution on the IoT device, the spectral histogram is drawn on the Sense HAT LED array

```
private async void DetermineAudioSpectrum(WaveData waveData, int windowLength)
{
    while (IsMediaElementPlaying)
    {
        var inputData = new short[windowLength];

        // Get MediaElement position
        var index = await GetWindowPosition(waveData.SampleRate, windowLength);

        if (index + windowLength < waveData.SamplesPerChannel)
        {
            // Get current frame
            Array.Copy(waveData.SamplesLeftChannel, index, inputData, 0, windowLength);

            // Determine histogram
            var hist = SpectrumHelper.Histogram(inputData, waveData.SampleRate);

            if (isIoTPlatform)
            {
                ledArray.DrawHistogram(hist, dbMinValue, dbMaxValue);
            }
            else
            {
                // Plot input frame, and histogram
                PlotHelper.AddLineSeries(sineWavePlotModel, inputData, OxyColors.Blue);
                PlotHelper.AddBarSeries(fftPlotModel, hist, OxyColors.Orange);
            }
        }
        else
        {
            // File ended
            IsMediaElementPlaying = false;
        }
    }
}
```

Summary

This chapter covered a broad range of audio processing aspects: speech synthesis, speech recognition, and custom digital signal processing routines. The UWP natively supports speech synthesis and recognition, but you can quite easily incorporate them into the IoT software for hands-free device control. Moreover, the fundamentals of digital signal processing I presented here serve as the basis for building custom and advanced IoT processing solutions or machine-hearing systems. For instance, you can combine FFT with sensor readings to detect periodic changes of a physically observable phenomenon monitored using an IoT device.

The signal-processing foundations presented here are not limited to audio processing. Some of them are widely used in many devices, ranging from wearable pedometers and heart rate counters to medical instruments measuring oxygen saturation in human blood.

CHAPTER 8

Image processing

The previous chapter covered one-dimensional audio signals. But IoT devices often process and analyze higher dimensional signals, in particular, two- or three-dimensional images. Embedded devices can acquire data from various cameras, including widely available USB web cams and more advanced cameras, e.g. infrared (thermal) cameras. Images are subsequently analyzed to control a specific process. An IoT device can monitor manufacturing by identifying damages in the component fabrication. A small camera mounted in your car can recognize traffic signs. An artificial intelligence (AI) module can use this information, along with data coming from sensors monitoring vehicle speed, to autonomously steer the car. IoT devices can also count cars passing on the highway, constitute robotic vision, or act as security modules.

In this chapter, we will build a machine vision system using the USB camera attached to the RPi2 or RPi3. Subsequently, we will combine this system with the UWP's facial recognition and tracking capabilities to detect and track human faces as shown in Figure 8-1.

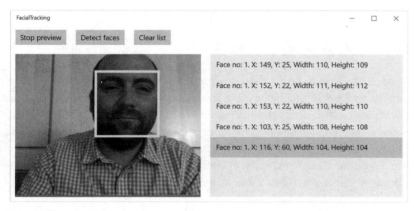

FIGURE 8-1   Facial recognition using the UWP.

Then I will present custom object recognition approaches with OpenCV libraries. When I was writing this chapter, OpenCV was marked on SourceForge as the top project in robotics. Therefore, OpenCV is a great tool for building custom IoT computer vision systems, which you can use to build robots. (For example, see the Air Hockey Robot project at *https://bit.ly/air_hockey_robot*.)

Similarly, as in the previous chapter, I will use the Microsoft Life Cam HD-3000. But this time, it will be employed for video capture only.

After reading this chapter you will know how to build a low-budget machine vision system that can be used to track human faces with the UWP API and indicate face movements on the Sense HAT LED array. Moreover, you will be able to turn your IoT device into an object detector that will indicate detected shapes on the LED array as depicted in Figure 8-2.

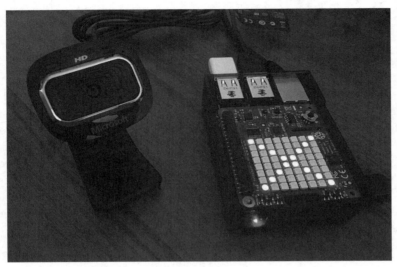

FIGURE 8-2   A photograph showing the RPi2 with the Sense HAT on top, connected to the Microsoft Life CAM HD-3000.

Image acquisition using a USB camera

The main part of every machine vision system is the video acquisition module. On the UWP, image acquisition is implemented within the MediaCapture class. To acquire a video sequence, you first initialize the MediaCapture object using an instance of the MediaCaptureInitializationSettings class, which exposes a field StreamingCaptureMode. This member configures the capture mode and can take one of the following values declared within the StreamingCaptureMode enumeration: AudioAndVideo, Audio, or Video. Depending on the streaming mode, either the audio and video will be acquired simultaneously or you can choose either the Audio or Video stream.

You will eventually use MediaCaptureInitializationSettings and MediaCapture to acquire a video sequence from a USB camera so that it can detect and track human faces. Hence, I create a project named FacialTracking using the Blank UWP Visual C# project. (See the companion code in Chapter 08/FacialTracking.) Then, I implement a helper class, CameraCapture (see the companion code in Chapter 08/FacialTracking/Helpers/CameraCapture.cs). CameraCapture is built on top of the MediaCapture class. As you see in Listing 8-1, I configure an instance of MediaCapture for video acquisition only by passing an appropriately prepared instance of MediaCaptureInitializationSettings to the MediaCapture.InitializeAsync method. This method initializes the capture device.

LISTING 8-1 MediaCapture initialization for video capture

```
public MediaCapture MediaCapture { get; private set; } = new MediaCapture();

public bool IsInitialized { get; private set; } = false;

public async Task Initialize(CaptureElement captureElement)
{
    if (!IsInitialized)
    {
        var settings = new MediaCaptureInitializationSettings()
        {
            StreamingCaptureMode = StreamingCaptureMode.Video
        };

        try
        {
            await MediaCapture.InitializeAsync(settings);

            GetVideoProperties();

            if (captureElement != null)
            {
                captureElement.Source = MediaCapture;

                IsInitialized = true;
            }
        }
        catch (Exception)
        {
            IsInitialized = false;
        }
    }
}
```

Subsequently, to display the video sequence you need to associate the `MedicaCapture` class with the `CaptureElement` control. `CaptureElement` is the UWP control that displays acquired images. To connect `MediaCapture` with a particular `CaptureElement`, you use the Source property of the `CaptureElement`. (See Listing 8-1.) As I show later, the `CaptureElement` is declared in the UI by using the standard XAML markup.

Within the `Initialize` method of the `CameraCapture` class, I also invoke the `GetVideoProperties` method. This method reads the width and height of the images acquired by using a `MediaCapture` class. As Listing 8-2 shows, these properties are obtained from the `VideoEncodingProperties` object. This object is returned by the `GetMediaStreamProperties` method of the `VideoDeviceController` class.

LISTING 8-2 Obtaining the width and height of the images acquired from the MediaCapture class

```
public uint FrameWidth { get; private set; }
public uint FrameHeight { get; private set; }
```

```
private void GetVideoProperties()
{
    if (MediaCapture != null)
    {
        var videoEncodingProperties = MediaCapture.VideoDeviceController.
            GetMediaStreamProperties(MediaStreamType.VideoPreview)
            as VideoEncodingProperties;

        FrameWidth = videoEncodingProperties.Width;
        FrameHeight = videoEncodingProperties.Height;
    }
}
```

After initializing `MediaCapture`, you can start and stop the preview by invoking the `StartPreview-Async` and `StopPreviewAsync` methods, respectively. As Listing 8-3 shows, the usage of those methods is straightforward. To check whether the preview is active, the `CameraCapture` class implements the `IsPreviewActive` property.

LISTING 8-3 Starting and stopping video acquisition

```
public bool IsPreviewActive { get; private set; } = false;

public async Task Start()
{
    if (IsInitialized)
    {
        if (!IsPreviewActive)
        {
            await MediaCapture.StartPreviewAsync();

            IsPreviewActive = true;
        }
    }
}

public async Task Stop()
{
    if (IsInitialized)
    {
        if (IsPreviewActive)
        {
            await MediaCapture.StopPreviewAsync();

            IsPreviewActive = false;
        }
    }
}
```

After implementing the CameraCapture class, I declare the UI, consisting of one button, and the CaptureElement control that displays images from a webcam. You find the corresponding XAML markup in Listing 8-4 (and the full declaration here: Chapter 08/FacialTracking/MainPage.xaml).

LISTING 8-4 The minimal UI declaration for video acquisition and display

```
<Page
    x:Class="FacialTracking.MainPage"
    xmlns="http://schemas.microsoft.com/winfx/2006/xaml/presentation"
    xmlns:x="http://schemas.microsoft.com/winfx/2006/xaml" >

    <Page.Resources>
        // See companion code for style definitions
    </Page.Resources>

    <Grid Background="{ThemeResource ApplicationPageBackgroundThemeBrush}"
          HorizontalAlignment="Stretch">
        <Grid.RowDefinitions>
            <RowDefinition Height="Auto" />
            <RowDefinition Height="*" />
        </Grid.RowDefinitions>

        <Button x:Name="ButtonPreview"
                Click="ButtonPreview_Click" />

        <CaptureElement x:Name="CaptureElementPreview"
                        Grid.Row="1" />
    </Grid>
</Page>
```

The logic associated with the UI performs two things:

- It configures the button caption, depending on the preview state. (See the UpdateUI method.)

- It configures the constant strings from Listing 8-5.

The UpdateUI method is invoked within the constructor and whenever the preview state changes.

LISTING 8-5 Button caption depends on the preview state

```
private const string previewStartDescription = "Start preview";
private const string previewStopDescription = "Stop preview";

private CameraCapture cameraCapture = new CameraCapture();

public MainPage()
{
    InitializeComponent();

    UpdateUI();
}
```

```csharp
private void UpdateUI()
{
    ButtonPreview.Content = cameraCapture.IsPreviewActive ? previewStopDescription :
        previewStartDescription;
}
```

Clicking a button can change the preview state. Doing so invokes the event handler from Listing 8-6. It initializes an instance of the CameraCapture class, and then starts or stops the preview depending on the IsPreviewActive flag of the CameraCapture class.

LISTING 8-6   Starting and stopping video sequence acquisition

```csharp
private async void ButtonPreview_Click(object sender, RoutedEventArgs e)
{
    await cameraCapture.Initialize(CaptureElementPreview);

    if (cameraCapture.IsInitialized)
    {
        await UpdatePreviewState();

        UpdateUI();
    }
    else
    {
        Debug.WriteLine("Video capture device could not be initialized");
    }
}

private async Task UpdatePreviewState()
{
    if (!cameraCapture.IsPreviewActive)
    {
        await cameraCapture.Start();
    }
    else
    {
        await cameraCapture.Stop();
    }
}
```

The FacialTracking app requires webcam capability. As in the previous chapter, this capability can be declared using the Package.appxmanifest. (See Figure 8-3.) You can then run the app on your development computer or an IoT device. If you choose the first option, enable the camera access by toggling the **Let Apps Use My Camera** button in the Camera Privacy Settings, as you see in Figure 8-4.

After you have deployed and launched the app, simply click the **Start Preview** button. The video stream from the USB camera displays in the MainPage within the CaptureElement control. You can stop the preview at any time by clicking a button again.

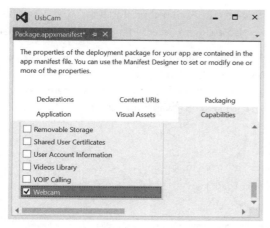

FIGURE 8-3 USB camera access requires webcam capability.

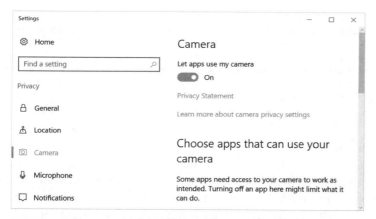

FIGURE 8-4 Camera tab of the Windows 10 Privacy Settings.

Face detection

Face detection (FD) is a branch of digital-image processing aimed at finding human faces in a given image. A face detection algorithm typically processes the image to find features characteristic of the human face. Face features may depend on the pose, age, or emotions. Some FD systems can even identify these parameters (see Chapter 11, "Device learning").

FD is conceptually similar to speech detection and recognition. Although speech recognition analyzes one-dimensional signals, it can be more difficult than FD because an image acquisition is usually synchronized—it starts at a specified time and lasts for a fixed duration. Moreover, each image in a video sequence has the same size. Audio signals can vary in length and are usually unsynchronized, which means that a speech processing algorithm must extract speech activity before processing. In general, an audio processing algorithm does not know *a priori* where the speech begins and ends.

Face detection is distinguished from face recognition (FR). Face recognition refers to the process that not only detects human faces in the image but also assigns a detected face to a particular person.

The UWP implements face detection within the Windows.Media.FaceAnalysis.FaceDetector class. FaceDetector enables you to detect multiple human faces in a given image, represented as the instance of the SoftwareBitmap class. To capture one such single frame from the webcam, I extend the CameraCapture class by the public CapturePhotoToSoftwareBitmap method. Its definition appears in Listing 8-7.

LISTING 8-7 Single image acquisition and conversion to SoftwareBitmap

```
public async Task<SoftwareBitmap> CapturePhotoToSoftwareBitmap()
{
    // Create bitmap-encoded image
    var imageEncodingProperties = ImageEncodingProperties.CreateBmp();

    // Capture photo
    var memoryStream = new InMemoryRandomAccessStream();
    await MediaCapture.CapturePhotoToStreamAsync(imageEncodingProperties, memoryStream);

    // Decode stream to bitmap
    var bitmapDecoder = await BitmapDecoder.CreateAsync(memoryStream);

    return await bitmapDecoder.GetSoftwareBitmapAsync();
}
```

To isolate the current frame from the video stream, I use the CapturePhotoToStreamAsync method of the MediaCapture class. This function writes the encoded image to the provided stream. The encoding format is specified using the instance of Windows.Media.MediaProperties.ImageEncodingParameters. In Listing 8-7, I convert an image to the BMP format by using the CreateBmp static method of the ImageEncodingParameters class. Other formats you can use include: JPEG (CreateJpg), JPEG XR (CreateJpgXR), PNG (CreatePng), NV12, and BGRA8 (CreateUncompressed). The CreateAsync static method of the BitmapDecoder class is later used to convert the bitmap stream to an instance of the SoftwareBitmap. This object can then be passed to the face-detection module for analysis.

To incorporate the FaceDetector class in the FacialTracking project, I first extend the UI by a list box and two additional buttons: Detect Faces and Clear List. The first button invokes computations to detect human faces in the image from the webcam, and the second simply clears the elements displayed in the list box.

The FaceDetector class does not implement any public constructors. Therefore, to obtain an instance of the FaceDetector class, I use the CreateAsync static method. This method is invoked within InitializeFaceDetection, as you see in Listing 8-8. Face detector initialization is performed only once, when the video preview is started for the first time. (See the bolded statement in the Button-Preview_Click event handler in Listing 8-8.)

LISTING 8-8   Face detection module initialization

```csharp
private FaceDetector faceDetector;
private BitmapPixelFormat faceDetectorSupportedPixelFormat;

private async void ButtonPreview_Click(object sender, RoutedEventArgs e)
{
    await cameraCapture.Initialize(CaptureElementPreview);

    await InitializeFaceDetection();

    if (cameraCapture.IsInitialized)
    {
        await UpdatePreviewState();

        UpdateUI();
    }
    else
    {
        Debug.WriteLine("Video capture device could not be initialized");
    }
}

private async Task InitializeFaceDetection()
{
    if (FaceDetector.IsSupported)
    {
        if (faceDetector == null)
        {
            faceDetector = await FaceDetector.CreateAsync();
            faceDetectorSupportedPixelFormat = FaceDetector.
                GetSupportedBitmapPixelFormats().FirstOrDefault();
        }
    }
    else
    {
        Debug.WriteLine("Warning. FaceDetector is not supported on this device");
    }
}
```

FaceDetector might not be available on every platform. To check whether a platform supports face detection, you use the FaceDetector.IsSupported static property.

The FaceDetector class can detect faces in images of a particular format. You can obtain the list of supported formats by using GetSupportedBitmapPixelFormats. In this example, I picked the first supported format. (See Listing 8-8.) To verify whether the format of an input image is compatible with the FaceDetector class, you can use the IsBitmapPixelFormatSupported static method. If the bitmap is incompatible, you can convert it to the supported pixel format using a Convert method of the SoftwareBitmap class, as shown in Listing 8-9.

```
private async Task<IList<DetectedFace>> DetectFaces(SoftwareBitmap inputBitmap)
{
    if (!FaceDetector.IsBitmapPixelFormatSupported(inputBitmap.BitmapPixelFormat))
    {
        inputBitmap = SoftwareBitmap.Convert(inputBitmap, faceDetectorSupportedPixelFormat);
    }

    return await faceDetector.DetectFacesAsync(inputBitmap);
}
```

Listing 8-9 also shows how to find faces using the DetectFacesAsync method. This function expects arguments of type SoftwareBitmap and optionally a BitmapBounds structure, which can be used to narrow the search area. After an image is processed, the DetectFacesAsync method returns a collection of DetectedFace objects. As Listing 8-10 shows, I use this collection inside the Detect Faces button event handler to display face locations in the list box through the DisplayFaceLocations method.

LISTING 8-10   Face detection processing chain consists of image acquisition, processing, and results display

```
private async void ButtonDetectFaces_Click(object sender, RoutedEventArgs e)
{
    if (faceDetector != null)
    {
        var inputBitmap = await cameraCapture.CapturePhotoToSoftwareBitmap();

        var facesDetected = await DetectFaces(inputBitmap);

        DisplayFaceLocations(facesDetected);
    }
}
```

DetectedFace consists of the public property FaceBox, which is of type BitmapBounds and stores four values, describing a face-bounding rectangle—that is, a face location in the given image. As you see in Listing 8-11, these values are displayed as consecutive rows in the list box.

LISTING 8-11   Displaying face locations in the list box

```
private void DisplayFaceLocations(IList<DetectedFace> facesDetected)
{
    for (int i = 0; i < facesDetected.Count; i++)
    {
        var detectedFace = facesDetected[i];
        var detectedFaceLocation = DetectedFaceToString(i + 1, detectedFace.FaceBox);

        AddItemToListBox(detectedFaceLocation);
    }
}
```

```
private string DetectedFaceToString(int index, BitmapBounds detectedFaceBox)
{
    return string.Format("Face no: {0}. X: {1}, Y: {2}, Width: {3}, Height: {4}",
        index,
        detectedFaceBox.X,
        detectedFaceBox.Y,
        detectedFaceBox.Width,
        detectedFaceBox.Height);
}

private void AddItemToListBox(object item)
{
    ListBoxInfo.Items.Add(item);
    ListBoxInfo.SelectedIndex = ListBoxInfo.Items.Count - 1;
}
```

Finally, I implement the event handler of the Clear List button, which invokes the Clear method of the list box items collection. (See Listing 8-12.)

LISTING 8-12 Event handler of the Clear List button

```
private void ButtonClearInfo_Click(object sender, RoutedEventArgs e)
{
    ListBoxInfo.Items.Clear();
}
```

To test the preceding functionality, run the FacialTracking app, start the preview, and then click the **Detect Faces** button. The position of detected faces will be displayed in the list box.

> **Note**   I need to start the preview because the single capture (from Listing 8-6) does not enable camera flash (illumination), which you might need in a dark environment.

Face tracking

The face detection module from the previous section detects faces in a single image. The UWP also implements another class, FaceTracker, which can be useful when you work with video sequences. You can use FaceTracker not only to detect faces in the video frames, but also to track them in real time.

Basically, the API of the FaceTracker class is very similar to that of the FaceDetector class. You obtain an instance of the FaceTracker class using the CreateAsync static method and then invoke ProcessNextFrameAsync to get the list of human faces in the acquired image. The main difference is that the ProcessNextFrameAsync expects an argument of type VideoFrame. This represents the single frame from the video sequence, and you obtain such an object using the GetPreviewFrameAsync method of the MediaCapture class.

Listing 8-13 shows that the FaceTracker initialization proceeds like FaceDetector (for the full code, see the companion code at Chapter 08/FacialTracking/MainPage.xaml.cs).

LISTING 8-13 FaceTracker initialization

```csharp
private FaceTracker faceTracker;
private BitmapPixelFormat faceTrackerSupportedPixelFormat;

private async Task InitializeFaceDetection()
{
    if (FaceDetector.IsSupported)
    {
        if (faceDetector == null)
        {
            faceDetector = await FaceDetector.CreateAsync();
            faceDetectorSupportedPixelFormat = FaceDetector.
                GetSupportedBitmapPixelFormats().FirstOrDefault();
        }
    }
    else
    {
        Debug.WriteLine("Warning. FaceDetector is not supported on this device");
    }

    if (FaceTracker.IsSupported)
    {
        if (faceTracker == null)
        {
            faceTracker = await FaceTracker.CreateAsync();
            faceTrackerSupportedPixelFormat = FaceTracker.
                GetSupportedBitmapPixelFormats().FirstOrDefault();
        }
    }
    else
    {
        Debug.WriteLine("Warning. FaceTracking is not supported on this device");
    }
}
```

As before, I first check whether face tracking is available on the current platform, invoke the asynchronous factory method, CreateAsync, and get the first available BitmapPixelFormat supported by the face tracking. I can the start the face tracking, for which I modify the UpdatePreviewState method (Listing 8-6) you see in Listing 8-14.

LISTING 8-14 Face tracking is run whenever the camera capture is active

```csharp
private async Task UpdatePreviewState()
{
    if (!cameraCapture.IsPreviewActive)
    {
```

```
        await cameraCapture.Start();

        BeginTracking();
    }
    else
    {
        await cameraCapture.Stop();

        CanvasFaceDisplay.Children.Clear();
    }
}
```

I invoke the BeginTracking method whenever the video preview starts. BeginTracking runs the background processing for tracking human faces. (See Listing 8-15.) Then, when the preview stops, I clear the Children collection of the CanvasFaceDisplay. This is declared in the UI, and I discuss it in more detail later in this chapter.

LISTING 8-15   Video frames are processed in the background to track human faces

```
private void BeginTracking()
{
    if (faceTracker != null)
    {
#pragma warning disable 4014

        Task.Run(async () =>
        {
            while (cameraCapture.IsPreviewActive)
            {
                await ProcessVideoFrame();
            }
        });

#pragma warning restore 4014
    }
}
```

Video sequence is processed in the background by using a separate worker thread. This processing is active whenever the camera capture is. Note that the background thread is started using a Run static method of the Task class.

FaceTracker can process video frames of the specified formats only. The supported format of VideoFrame is set during the frame acquisition. (See the ProcessVideoFrame method in Listing 8-16.) Note that this method also explicitly uses the FrameWidth and FrameHeight properties of the Camera-Capture class instance to create a VideoFrame object, which contains the acquired frame and is passed to ProcessNextFrameAsync of the FaceTracker class instance.

LISTING 8-16   Processing video frames

```
private LedArray ledArray;

private async Task ProcessVideoFrame()
{
    using (VideoFrame videoFrame = new VideoFrame(faceTrackerSupportedPixelFormat,
        (int)cameraCapture.FrameWidth, (int)cameraCapture.FrameHeight))
    {
        await cameraCapture.MediaCapture.GetPreviewFrameAsync(videoFrame);

        var faces = await faceTracker.ProcessNextFrameAsync(videoFrame);

        if (ledArray == null)
        {
            DisplayFaces(videoFrame.SoftwareBitmap, faces);
        }
        else
        {
            TrackFace(faces);
        }
    }
}
```

The face-tracking module, FaceDetector, returns a collection of DetectedFace objects. Here, rather than just displaying the values stored in the FaceBox property of each DetectedFace, I use them either to draw yellow rectangles over detected faces in the video stream or to indicate face movements on the Sense HAT LED array. I describe both modes in detail in the following sections. Which mode engages depends on whether the FacialTracking app runs on the IoT or desktop platform. I check this by verifying whether the appropriate I2cDevice was initialized. If so, I also start the preview and face-tracking automatically. (See Listing 8-17.)

LISTING 8-17   Sense HAT LED array initialization

```
private LedArray ledArray;

protected override async void OnNavigatedTo(NavigationEventArgs e)
{
    base.OnNavigatedTo(e);

    await InitializeLedArray();
}

private async Task InitializeLedArray()
{
    const byte address = 0x46;
    var device = await I2cHelper.GetI2cDevice(address);

    if (device != null)
    {
```

```
        ledArray = new LedArray(device);

        ButtonPreview_Click(null, null);
    }
}
```

Face location display in the UI

To indicate face location in the UI, I use the Canvas named CanvasFaceDisplay. This control is declared in the UI such that it hosts the CaptureElement (see the companion code in Chapter 08/FacialTracking/MainPage.xaml). Canvas is the container, in which you can absolutely position child objects with respect to the container position. You can also specify the order in which child objects are rendered. To this end, you use the Canvas.ZIndex attached property. (See Listing 8-18.)

LISTING 8-18 Using the Canvas.ZIndex attached property to specify that CaptureElement is rendered first, so face rectangles are displayed on top of it

```
<Canvas x:Name="CanvasFaceDisplay"
        Grid.Row="1" />

<CaptureElement x:Name="CaptureElementPreview"
                Grid.Row="1"
                Canvas.ZIndex="-1" />
```

I use Canvas.ZIndex to position the CaptureElement control such that the face rectangles are drawn on top of the camera image (refer to Figure 8-1). Therefore, I set the Canvas.ZIndex to -1. This ensures that CaptureElement is placed "below" the foreground in which face bounding rectangles are drawn.

Listing 8-19 shows the code responsible for drawing rectangles over detected faces. The method, DisplayFaces, first determines the horizontal (xScalingFactor) and vertical (yScalingFactor) scaling factors, which adjust the rectangle size to the actual size of the image displayed in the CaptureElement control. In general, this size can vary with the size of the app window. Then, DisplayFaces clears previous rectangles from the canvas and invokes the DrawFaceBox method for each DetectedFace object obtained from FaceTracker.

LISTING 8-19 Drawing face rectangles on top of the camera image

```
private async void DisplayFaces(SoftwareBitmap displayBitmap, IList<DetectedFace> faces)
{
    if (Dispatcher.HasThreadAccess)
    {
        var xScalingFactor = CanvasFaceDisplay.ActualWidth / displayBitmap.PixelWidth;
        var yScalingFactor = CanvasFaceDisplay.ActualHeight / displayBitmap.PixelHeight;

        CanvasFaceDisplay.Children.Clear();
```

```
        foreach (DetectedFace face in faces)
        {
            DrawFaceBox(face.FaceBox, xScalingFactor, yScalingFactor);
        }
    }
    else
    {
        await Dispatcher.RunAsync(CoreDispatcherPriority.Normal, () =>
        {
            DisplayFaces(displayBitmap, faces);
        });
    }
}
```

DrawFaceBox (see Listing 8-20) uses the Width and Height properties of the FaceBox along with scaling factors to dynamically create a yellow rectangle that corresponds in size to the detected face. Then, this rectangle is translated so it appears over the given face. To this end, I used the rescaled X and Y properties of the FaceBox. The rectangle is displayed in the Canvas by adding a Rectangle control to the Children collection of the CanvasFaceDisplay.

LISTING 8-20   Rectangles are constructed dynamically and added to the Children collection of the Canvas control

```
private void DrawFaceBox(BitmapBounds faceBox, double xScalingFactor, double yScalingFactor)
{
    // Prepare bounding rectangle
    var rectangle = new Rectangle()
    {
        Stroke = new SolidColorBrush(Colors.Yellow),
        StrokeThickness = 5,
        Width = faceBox.Width * xScalingFactor,
        Height = faceBox.Height * yScalingFactor
    };

    // Translate bounding rectangle
    var translateTransform = new TranslateTransform()
    {
        X = faceBox.X * xScalingFactor,
        Y = faceBox.Y * yScalingFactor
    };

    rectangle.RenderTransform = translateTransform;

    // Display bounding rectangle
    CanvasFaceDisplay.Children.Add(rectangle);
}
```

After running FacialTracking on your development PC, you will get results similar to those in Figure 8-1. Note that FacialTracking can detect multiple faces, in which case it draws several rectangles.

Face location display on the LED array

Here, I explain how to extend the FacialTracking app to indicate the actual position of the first detected face on the Sense HAT LED array. Because this array has only 64 pixels, I display the center position of the corresponding face box using a single LED. This pixel "moves" on the LED array according to the face displacements on the image.

Naturally, this functionality requires LED array interfacing and proper calculation of face displacements. To interface the LED array, I reference the Windows IoT Extensions for the UWP and supplement the FacialTracking project by the following files:

- **I2cHelper.cs**   See Listing 5-22 in Chapter 5, "Reading data from sensors."
- **Check.cs**   See Chapter 6, "Input and output."
- **LedArray.cs**   See Chapter 6, "Input and output," and Chapter 7, "Audio processing."

Subsequently, I implemented a helper struct LedPixelPosition (see the companion code in Chapter 08/FacialTracking/Helpers/LedPixelPosition.cs). This struct holds the X and Y coordinates of the LED pixel position and tracks human face displacements as implemented in the corresponding method from Listing 8-21.

LISTING 8-21   Displaying face displacements on the LED array

```
private LedPixelPosition previousLedPixelPosition;

private void TrackFace(IList<DetectedFace> faces)
{
    var face = faces.FirstOrDefault();

    if (face != null)
    {
        // Calculate LED pixel position
        var ledPixelPosition = CalculatePosition(face.FaceBox);

        // Display position
        ledArray.SetPixel(ledPixelPosition.X, ledPixelPosition.Y, Colors.Green);

        // Store position
        previousLedPixelPosition = ledPixelPosition;
    }
    else
    {
        // Switch color to red, when face is not detected
        ledArray.SetPixel(previousLedPixelPosition.X, previousLedPixelPosition.Y,
            Colors.Red);
    }
}
```

The preceding face tracking proceeds as follows: I take the first element from the collection of detected faces. If this element is valid (not null), I calculate the position of the LED pixel and then set its color to green. I also store this position in the previousLedPixelPosition field. I eventually use this value when no face was detected. In such a case, I set the pixel color to red.

Basically, to indicate the face position using an LED array, you map the position of the face bounding rectangle center to the corresponding pixel on the 8x8 LED grid. This mapping, implemented within the CalculatePosition method (Listing 8-22) occurs as follows. First, I calculate two scalers—one along the abscissa (xScaler) and the second along the ordinate (yScaler) of the coordinate system associated with the LED array. (See Figure 6-5.) Those scalers are calculated using the following equations:

$$xScaler = \frac{W - w}{L - 1}$$

$$yScaler = \frac{H - h}{L - 1}$$

where:

- W and H denote the width and height of the video frame, respectively.

- w and h stand for the width and height of the face bounding rectangle.

- L is the length of the LED array, i.e. 8.

I use the scalers to determine the LED pixel location by dividing the X and Y properties of the BitmapBounds struct by xScaler and yScaler, respectively.

LISTING 8-22   Mapping a face box to the LED pixel position

```
private LedPixelPosition CalculatePosition(BitmapBounds faceBox)
{
    // Determine bitmap-LED array scalers
    var xScaler = (cameraCapture.FrameWidth - faceBox.Width) / (LedArray.Length - 1);
    var yScaler = (cameraCapture.FrameHeight - faceBox.Height) / (LedArray.Length - 1);

    // Get LED pixel position
    var xPosition = Convert.ToInt32(faceBox.X / xScaler);
    var yPosition = Convert.ToInt32(faceBox.Y / yScaler);

    // Correct coordinates
    xPosition = CorrectLedCoordinate(LedArray.Length - 1 - xPosition);
    yPosition = CorrectLedCoordinate(yPosition);

    return new LedPixelPosition()
    {
        X = xPosition,
        Y = yPosition
    };
}
```

To ensure that LED pixel coordinates are in the valid range, corresponding to the dimensions of the LED array, I use the CorrectLedCoordinate from Listing 8-23. This method checks whether the calculated coordinate is positive and not larger than the length of the LED array minus 1.

LISTING 8-23 Ensuring that the LED coordinate is valid

```
private int CorrectLedCoordinate(int inputCoordinate)
{
    inputCoordinate = Math.Min(inputCoordinate, LedArray.Length - 1);
    inputCoordinate = Math.Max(inputCoordinate, 0);

    return inputCoordinate;
}
```

After FacialTracking launches on the IoT device, the app automatically begins video acquisition, facial recognition, and tracking. The position of the first detected face is displayed in the LED array.

The preceding examples prove that the UWP has very reliable facial detection and recognition capabilities. In Chapter 11, I further extend this functionality by the ability to recognize face emotions using Microsoft Cognitive Services.

OpenCV and native code interfacing

The UWP does not implement the API for custom image processing. Fortunately, for machine vision and robotics projects you can use one of the image-processing libraries. One toolkit that should be distinguished is OpenCV—a set of open-source computer vision libraries. OpenCV was started by Gary Bradsky at Intel Corporation and is currently maintained by Itseez company. OpenCV is a cross-platform tool with a large community reaching almost 50,000 developers. While I was writing this chapter, OpenCV was marked as the top project in robotics on the SourceForge page. Therefore, OpenCV is a good choice for your machine vision IoT applications.

OpenCV is cross-platform and exposes C/C++ interfaces. The C interface was used in the first versions of OpenCV. C++ is currently a suggested way to interface OpenCV. Though you cannot directly use such native libraries in the Visual C# UWP project, you can use them indirectly by using the Visual C++ Windows Runtime Component (WRC), which is written using C++ Component Extensions (C++/CX)—see Appendix E, "Visual C++ component extensions"—and can be used to interface with native code, including C/C++ libraries. An alternative way to interface with native code is the Platform Invoke (P/Invoke) feature of the .NET Framework. However, this requires you to manually import functions from a given DLL using Dl-lImportAttribute from the System.Runtime.InteropServices namespace.

After the WRC is referenced in the UWP project, it can be accessed easily. You just invoke methods from the WRC in the same way as with any other UWP API. This flexibility offers several advantages. One of them is that you can implement time-critical operations (like image or audio processing) within the WRC and then invoke them from the main project implemented in C# or Visual Basic. Such an approach is also beneficial when you need to interface with native drivers or control custom devices or sensors whose manufacturers provide C/C++ drivers or SDKs only. In addition, the WRC can interface with the Win32 and the COM API of the UWP, giving you access to low-level system features when you need to gain more control or access specific functions.

In this section I will show how to use OpenCV in the UWP projects using the preceding strategy. First, I implement several image processing algorithms within the WRC. The main UWP project will reference this component and employ it for object detection in a video sequence acquired from the USB camera. Finally, the information about the shape of a detected object will be presented using the Sense HAT LED array.

The companion code for this discussion includes three projects: ImageProcessingComponent, ImageProcessing, and MachineVision. Find each of them in the Chapter 08 folder of the companion code.

Solution configuration and OpenCV installation

To start, you need the Blank UWP Visual C# application, which references the Windows Runtime Component. Then you will configure project dependencies and install the required OpenCV NuGet packages. Here is the detailed procedure:

1. Create the new Blank UWP Visual C# project named ImageProcessing.

2. In the Solution Explorer, right-click **Solution 'Image Processing'** and from the context menu select **Add New Project**.

3. Type **C++ Windows Runtime Component** in the New Project dialog box's search box, as shown in Figure 8-5. Then choose **Windows Runtime Component (Universal Windows)**, change the project name to **ImageProcessingComponent**, and create the project targeting the 10.0.10586 Windows version.

FIGURE 8-5 A New Project dialog box showing the Windows Runtime Component (Universal Windows) project template.

4. Navigate back to the Solution Explorer, right-click the **References** node under the Image-ProcessingComponent project, and choose **Manage NuGet Packages** from the context menu. Doing so activates the NuGet Package Manager, from which you do the following:

    a. Select the **Include Prelease** check box.

    b. Click the **Browse** tab and type **opencv.uwp** in the search box.

    c. In the search results list, locate and install the OpenCV.UWP.native.imgproc package. (See Figure 8-6.) In addition, the NuGet Package Manager will also install one depending package, i.e. OpenCV.UWP.native.core.

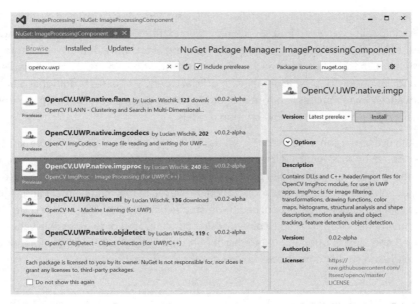

FIGURE 8-6 A NuGet Package Manager showing the OpenCV.UWP.native.imgproc package.

5. Reference the ImageProcessingComponent in the ImageProcessing project:

   a. Right-click **References** under the ImageProcessing project, and from the context menu select **Add Reference**. A Reference Manager dialog box will appear.

   b. Under Reference Manager, click the **Projects** tab, and as shown in Figure 8-7, select the **ImageProcessingComponent** check box.

FIGURE 8-7 A Reference Manager dialog box. Methods and classes declared in ImageProcessingComponent can be used as the main app after proper reference configuration.

I configured the solution such that there is a main application (ImageProcessing) and a proxy project (ImageProcessingComponent). The former references the latter, so every public member of the ImageProcessingComponent can be easily used in the main application.

You can download a stable OpenCV version from *http://opencv.org* and obtain the current source code from the following GitHub repository: *https://github.com/Itseez/opencv*. Alternatively, you can install the most popular OpenCV modules as NuGet packages, as shown above.

In the ImageProcessingComponent, I installed two OpenCV modules: core and imgproc. In general, the OpenCV functionality is divided into several main and extra modules. Main modules implement functionalities such as the well-established image processing algorithms, object and feature detection, image stitching, machine learning, and segmentation. Additional modules are implemented by contributors and are not distributed together with official OpenCV releases. Additional modules offer a variety of advanced image processing routines for face recognition, neural networks, image registration, object tracking, or biologically inspired vision models.

Every module uses common declarations from the core module. In particular, it contains the definition of the Mat object (matrix), which is used to represent images. Most of the OpenCV functions (e.g. methods defined in the imgproc module) process image data stored in matrices to generate an appropriate output, depending on the particular operation. However, many image-processing algorithms, especially those aiming at object detection, begin with image binarization. This is color scale conversion, in which an input image is transformed to binary scale and composed of two possible values. Typically, these levels are 0 and 255 for 8-bit and 0, 1 for higher bit-depth images. Such binary images can be obtained by image thresholding methods, which I discuss in the next section.

> ## A note on project building
>
> When implementing the Windows Runtime Components (WRC) referenced in the UWP projects, you want to rebuild the WRC component whenever you modify it, so the changes will be reflected in the UWP code. You do this manually because the background compiler might not automatically compile the Visual C++ code, which can be long. Visual Studio 2017 introduces improvements in the compilation time of C++ code, so the preceding issue can be more pronounced in Visual Studio 2015.

Image thresholding

Image thresholding is the operation in which all the pixels of an input image are modified when their value is below or above a threshold level, which is the fixed pixel value. It can be set arbitrarily or calculated specifically for a particular image. More formally, assuming that the image is represented as the two-dimensional array $I = [I_{ij}]$, the threshold algorithm processes the input image $I^{(in)}$ to generate the output (processed) image $I^{(out)}$ using the following formula:

$$I_{ij}^{(out)} = \begin{cases} v_1, & for\ I_{ij}^{(in)} > T \\ v_2, & otherwise \end{cases}$$

where T is the threshold level, v_1 and v_2 are values set by the particular threshold method, $i = 0$, $1,..., W-1$, $j = 0, 1,..., H-1$ with W and H denoting image width and height, respectively. Thus, image thresholding is the pixel-by-pixel operation that compares every pixel to T and then assigns the pixel either a v_1 or v_2 value.

For the simplest binary threshold of the 8-bit image, $v_1 = 255$ and $v_2 = 0$. Accordingly, all the pixels above the threshold level become white, while others will be black. The binary threshold can be easily inverted such that $v_1 = 0$ and $v_2 = 255$.

Image thresholding is implemented in the imgproc module of OpenCV as the `cv::threshold` function. This method operates on single-channel (grayscale) images and supports several threshold operations, which are defined in the `cv::ThresholdTypes` enumeration, from the imgproc.hpp file. Except for the simple binary and inverted binary thresholds, OpenCV also implements several pixel-truncation methods. They can be used to suppress noise by either excluding values below (`cv::ThresholdTypes::ToZero`) or above (`cv::ThresholdTypes::Trunc`, and `cv::ThresholdTypes::ToZeroInv`) the threshold level. Namely, these algorithms use the following v_1 and v_2 values:

- **cv::ThresholdTypes::ToZero** $v_1 = I_{ij}^{(in)}$, v_2

- **cv::ThresholdTypes::ToZeroInv** $v_1 = 0$, $v_2 = I_{ij}^{(in)}$

- **cv::ThresholdTypes::Trunc** $v_1 = T$, $v_2 = I_{ij}^{(in)}$

OpenCV also implements two algorithms for automatic threshold determination (`cv::ThresholdTypes::Otsu` and `cv::ThresholdTypes::Triangle`). They analyze the image histograms to find the optimal threshold level, which will classify pixel values into two distinguishable groups. The first includes pixels of the object, and the second contains the background pixels. Such automatic threshold determination is crucial for object detection since it helps to automatically distinguish objects from the background.

To present sample usage of the OpenCV thresholding algorithms, I implemented the ImageProcessing-Component in the following way: I defined the enumeration type that maps `cv::ThresholdTypes` from OpenCV to the enumeration type that can be used in the C# code (see the companion code in Chapter 08/ImageProcessingComponent/ThresholdType.h). To define such an enumeration type, you use the enum class keyword of C++/CX.

Then, I implemented the OpenCvWrapper class. This has the form of a typical C++ class, so the declaration is stored in the OpenCvWrapper.h file (Listing 8-24), while the definition is saved in OpenCvWrapper.cpp (see the companion code in Chapter 08/ImageProcessingComponent/OpenCvWrapper/OpenCvWrapper.cpp).

LISTING 8-24 OpenCvWrapper class declaration consists of one public method and four private helper functions

```
#pragma once

#include "ThresholdType.h"
#include <opencv2\core.hpp>
#include <opencv2\imgproc.hpp>

using namespace Windows::UI::Xaml::Media::Imaging;
using namespace Windows::Storage::Streams;

namespace ImageProcessingComponent
{
    [Windows::Foundation::Metadata::WebHostHidden]
    public ref class OpenCvWrapper sealed
    {
    public:
        static void Threshold(WriteableBitmap^ inputBitmap, int level, ThresholdType type);
```

```
    private:
        static const int pxMaxValue = 255;

        static void CheckInputParameters(WriteableBitmap^ inputBitmap);

        static cv::Mat ConvertWriteableBitmapToMat(WriteableBitmap^ inputBitmap);
        static cv::Mat ConvertMatToGrayScale(cv::Mat inputMat);

        static byte* GetPointerToPixelBuffer(IBuffer^ pixelBuffer);
    };
}
```

Several elements of the preceding declaration require explanation. First, note that the header file contains standard #include preprocessor directives and using namespace statements. Both are used to include specific instructions, defined elsewhere, but #include is used for native (unmanaged) code, while the other references the appropriate UWP API (managed code).

In the .NET Framework, the managed code is the intermediate code produced by the compiler. This intermediate code is then executed by the common language runtime (CLR). In particular, CLR converts the intermediate code to binary code and manages memory usage. A typical C/C++ native application is directly compiled to binary code, and you need to manually allocate and release memory.

With the advent of .NET Native, UWP apps, depending on the compilation mode (Debug or Release), are converted to intermediate code (Debug) or directly to binary code (Release). The second option improves the app performance but increases compilation time significantly.

Because the UWP app can be directly compiled to native code, the term *managed code* loses its full meaning. However, I will keep using this term here to refer to the UWP API, hoping that it won't introduce any confusion.

The OpenCvWrapper declaration is decorated with the WebHostHidden attribute and therefore cannot be used in the JavaScript UWP apps because the WriteableBitmap class is not available in the JavaScript UWP interface.

The declaration of the OpenCvWrapper class is composed of one public and four helper methods. The public method, Threshold, appears in Listing 8-25 and is used to process the input image using the OpenCV threshold function. However, before I can invoke any of the OpenCV functions, I need to perform several steps. First and foremost, I validate the inputBitmap argument (check if it's null; see the bottom part of Listing 8-25).

LISTING 8-25 Image thresholding with OpenCV

```
void OpenCvWrapper::Threshold(WriteableBitmap^ inputBitmap, int thresholdLevel,
    ThresholdType type)
{
    CheckInputParameters(inputBitmap);

    // Initialize Mat and convert it to gray scale
```

```
    auto inputMat = ConvertWriteableBitmapToMat(inputBitmap);
    auto workingMat = ConvertMatToGrayScale(inputMat);

    // Threshold image
    cv::threshold(workingMat, workingMat, thresholdLevel, pxMaxValue, (int) type);

    // Convert back to Bgra8
    cv::cvtColor(workingMat, inputMat, CV_GRAY2BGRA);

    // Release resources
    workingMat.release();
}

void OpenCvWrapper::CheckInputParameters(WriteableBitmap^ inputBitmap)
{
    if (inputBitmap == nullptr)
    {
        throw ref new NullReferenceException();
    }
}
```

Then, I appropriately convert the UWP WriteableBitmap object to an instance of the Mat class. Both the WriteableBitmap and Mat classes represent the bitmap-format raw image data using a two-dimensional array of bytes. The number of rows of this array corresponds to the image height, while the number of columns is determined by the image width, pixel bit-depth (pixel data type), and the number of color channels. In OpenCV, the pixel bit-depth and the number of image color channels are controlled using several predefined types of the form: CV_<B>_<T>_C<N>, where:

- <B> stands for the bit-depth (8, 16, 24, and 32).

- <T> defines one of the available pixel data types:

  - U   unsigned

  - S   signed

  - F   float

- <N> is the number of channels (1, 2, 3 or 4).

For instance, CV_8UC1 states that the raw image data is represented as the two-dimensional array (matrix), of which the elements are 8-bit unsigned integers. Moreover, the image has just one channel, so the number of columns will be equal to the image width. However, due to optimization, the width can be padded to a multiple of 4. Such padded width is typically denoted as the image width step—the distance between consecutive rows, measured in bytes.

On the other hand, WriteableBitmap operates on the bitmap-format images, in which pixel format is defined as the Bgra8 value from the BitmapPixelFormat enumeration, defined in the Windows. Graphics.Imaging namespace. The Bgra8 format uses four channels and 8-bit unsigned integers, while the channel order (column order) in the pixel data array (matrix) is the following: Blue, Green, Red, and Alpha (BGRA). Accordingly, such pixel data organization corresponds to the CV_8UC4 OpenCV type. I used this type in a definition of ConvertWriteableBitmapToMat. (See Listing 8-26.)

LISTING 8-26   WriteableBitmap to Mat conversion

```
cv::Mat OpenCvWrapper::ConvertWriteableBitmapToMat(WriteableBitmap^ inputBitmap)
{
    // Get a pointer to the raw pixel data
    auto imageData = GetPointerToPixelBuffer(inputBitmap->PixelBuffer);

    // Construct OpenCV image
    return cv::Mat(inputBitmap->PixelHeight, inputBitmap->PixelWidth, CV_8UC4, imageData);
}
```

Basically, I initialize the Mat object using the image data stored within the instance of the WriteableBitmap class. This contains the size of the image (PixelWidth and PixelHeight) and the raw image data. This can be accessed through the PixelBuffer property. However, the Mat object uses native, pointer-like methods to access the memory. Therefore, to retrieve the pointer to the PixelBuffer property of the WriteableBitmap, I use the IBufferByteAccess interface of the COM system. (See the GetPointerToPixelBuffer method in Listing 8-27.)

LISTING 8-27   Accessing the native pointer using the COM system

```
byte* OpenCvWrapper::GetPointerToPixelBuffer(IBuffer^ pixelBuffer)
{
    ComPtr<IBufferByteAccess> bufferByteAccess;

    reinterpret_cast<IInspectable*>(pixelBuffer)->QueryInterface(
        IID_PPV_ARGS(&bufferByteAccess));

    byte* pixels = nullptr;
    bufferByteAccess->Buffer(&pixels);

    return pixels;
}
```

I use the resulting pointer to the byte array to initialize the Mat class, after which I process the image using the OpenCV methods as shown in the definition of the Threshold method in Listing 8-25. This method first converts the image to grayscale using the cv::cvtColor function within the ConvertMat-ToGrayScale method from Listing 8-28. This conversion is required because cv::threshold operates on the single-channel images. Subsequently, I invoke the cv::threshold to get the processed image. Finally, I convert the image color scale back to 8-bit BGRA (BGRA8 for OpenCV or Bgra8 for UWP). The input instance of the WriteableBitmap class is thus updated and contains the processed image data.

LISTING 8-28 Color scale conversion

```
cv::Mat OpenCvWrapper::ConvertMatToGrayScale(cv::Mat inputMat)
{
    auto workingMat = cv::Mat(inputMat.rows, inputMat.cols, CV_8U);

    cv::cvtColor(inputMat, workingMat, CV_BGRA2GRAY);

    return workingMat;
}
```

Visualization of processing results

Here, you first experiment with several threshold values and run the ImageProcessing app on the desktop platform. Later, you will use this experience to implement an IoT app.

After you compile, deploy, and launch the ImageProcessing app, you can pick up any bitmap by using the **Browse** button. This activates the OS picker, which lets you choose any image in the JPG, PNG, or BMP format. Subsequently, the image is displayed within the Image control and processed when you change the slider position or the threshold algorithm using the drop-down list. The processed image will be displayed in the second Image control, as you see in Figure 8-8 and Figure 8-9.

I advise you to experiment with the ImageProcessing app and try different threshold types and levels to get an overall view of how they work. Note that by changing the threshold level you can extract more or fewer image features. Moreover, for Otsu and Triangle algorithms, the threshold level is calculated automatically, so changing the slider position does not affect the processed image.

FIGURE 8-8 An input and image processed using the binary inverted threshold of 127.

FIGURE 8-9 Otsu's method automatically determines an optimal threshold level, so many image features can be isolated.

To build the app, I started by declaring the UI. The main element there is the Browse button, located in the top left corner of the app window. When you click this button, a method from Listing 8-29 is executed. This method is used to load and display the image to process. For the companion code, see Chapter 08/ImageProcessing.

LISTING 8-29 Choosing an input image to process

```
private SoftwareBitmap inputSoftwareBitmap;

private async void ButtonLoadImage_Click(object sender, RoutedEventArgs e)
{
    var bitmapFile = await PickBitmap();

    if (bitmapFile != null)
    {
        inputSoftwareBitmap = await GetBitmapFromFile(bitmapFile);

        InputImage = inputSoftwareBitmap.ToWriteableBitmap();
    }
}
```

To load an image, I wrote the `PickBitmap` and `GetBitmapFromFile` methods, which I discuss later in the chapter. To display an image, you can use the XAML Image control, in which you at least need to set the Source property. In the ImageProcessing app, I defined a binding, which connects the `InputImage` field with the Source property of the first Image control in the UI (see the companion code in Chapter 08/ImageProcessing/MainPage.xaml). Hence, the Image control is updated whenever I modify the `InputImage` field. Note that I also defined the default style for Image controls, where I set the `Stretch` attribute to `Uniform`. `Stretch` property, which specifies how the image will be rendered to fill the rectangle spanned by the Image control. Uniform stretching means that image dimensions are rescaled to fit the Image control with the preserved image aspect ratio. Other stretching options include:

- **None**   The image preserves its original size, so when the size of the Image control does not match the image size, the image is clipped.

- **Fill**   The image is resized to fill the Image control without preserving the original image aspect ratio. The source image will not fill the Image control when sizes do not match.

- **UniformToFill**   This combines Uniform and Fill functionality such that the image is resized including the original aspect ratio. However, when the Image control dimensions do not match the original aspect ratio, the image is clipped before being displayed. When you resize the Image control, the source bitmap will be clipped only when its aspect ratio cannot be preserved.

I encourage you to test these rendering options yourself with different images. You can modify the style definition from the MainPage resources of the ImageProcessing app, load an image, and resize the app window. You will then see how various rendering options affect the image display.

To let the user choose the bitmap, I use the method from Listing 8-30. This function shows how you can use the FileOpenPicker class to activate the OS dialog box for choosing files. You can configure how the content of this dialog box will be displayed (ViewMode property), choose the initial folder (SuggestedStartLocation), and set up file search filters (FileTypeFilter collection). Then, you obtain the user-selected file using the PickSingleFileAsync method. It returns an instance of the StorageFile class, an abstract representation of files in the UWP. Note that the OS picker is not available on the IoT platform. I successfully tested the image picker on the desktop and mobile platforms.

LISTING 8-30   Picking a bitmap file

```
private string[] extensions = new string[] { ".jpg", ".jpeg", ".png", ".bmp" };

private IAsyncOperation<StorageFile> PickBitmap()
{
    var photoPicker = new FileOpenPicker()
    {
        ViewMode = PickerViewMode.Thumbnail,
        SuggestedStartLocation = PickerLocationId.PicturesLibrary
    };

    foreach (string extension in extensions)
    {
        photoPicker.FileTypeFilter.Add(extension);
    }

    return photoPicker.PickSingleFileAsync();
}
```

The instance of the StorageFile class is then used within the GetBitmapFromFile method from Listing 8-31. After opening the file, I read and then write its contents to the SoftwareBitmap object using BitmapDecoder. It automatically determines the bitmap properties (like pixel format and dimensions) from the file stream.

```
private async Task<SoftwareBitmap> GetBitmapFromFile(StorageFile bitmapFile)
{
    using (var fileStream = await bitmapFile.OpenAsync(FileAccessMode.Read))
    {
        var bitmapDecoder = await BitmapDecoder.CreateAsync(fileStream);

        return await bitmapDecoder.GetSoftwareBitmapAsync();
    }
}
```

SoftwareBitmap represents an uncompressed bitmap. To access raw pixel data for processing, you need to convert it to the WriteableBitmap. In the ImageProcessing app, this conversion is implemented as the extension method of the SoftwareBitmapExtensions class (Listing 8-32).

LISTING 8-32 Extension method for converting SoftwareBitmap to WriteableBitmap

```
public static class SoftwareBitmapExtensions
{
    private static BitmapPixelFormat bitmapPixelFormat = BitmapPixelFormat.Bgra8;

    public static WriteableBitmap ToWriteableBitmap(this SoftwareBitmap softwareBitmap)
    {
        if (softwareBitmap != null)
        {
            if (softwareBitmap.BitmapPixelFormat != bitmapPixelFormat)
            {
                softwareBitmap = SoftwareBitmap.Convert(softwareBitmap, bitmapPixelFormat);
            }

            var writeableBitmap = new WriteableBitmap(softwareBitmap.PixelWidth,
                softwareBitmap.PixelHeight);

            softwareBitmap.CopyToBuffer(writeableBitmap.PixelBuffer);

            return writeableBitmap;
        }
        else
        {
            return null;
        }
    }
}
```

SoftwareBitmapExtensions implements only one static method, ToWriteableBitmap. This function first converts the input object to the Bgra8 pixel format and then creates an instance of the Writeable-Bitmap. Finally, the raw pixel data is copied to WriteableBitmap using the CopyToBuffer method of the SoftwareBitmap class.

The `ToWriteableBitmap` extension method displays and processes an image. Image processing is invoked whenever you choose the binarization algorithm from the drop-down list or change the threshold level (T) using the slider control. (See Figure 8-8 and Figure 8-9.) The selected threshold value is also displayed in the text box.

The threshold type and threshold value are bound to the UI through the appropriate fields of the `MainPage` class. The list of all threshold algorithms is obtained from the `ThresholdType` enumeration as shown in Listing 8-33. By default, I use the first value of this enumeration, i.e. `Binary`.

LISTING 8-33 Configuring drop-down items, source and threshold type

```
private void ConfigureThresholdComboBox()
{
    thresholdTypes = Enum.GetValues(typeof(ThresholdType));
    ThresholdType = (ThresholdType)thresholdTypes.GetValue(0);
}

private object ThresholdType
{
    get { return thresholdType; }
    set
    {
        thresholdType = (ThresholdType)value;
        ThresholdImage();
    }
}
```

The `ThresholdType` property is bound to the UI, and it executes the `ThresholdImage` method whenever you change the threshold algorithm. The `ThresholdLevel` property, bound to the slider, works similarly.

The actual image processing occurs by invoking the `OpenCvWrapper.Threshold` method. As you see in Listing 8-34, you simply convert the input image to `WriteableBitmap` and then do an in-place threshold using the parameters obtained from the UI. The in-place operation means that the pixel buffer of the source image is overwritten.

LISTING 8-34 Interfacing native code from the OpenCvWrapper class

```
private void ThresholdImage()
{
    if (inputSoftwareBitmap != null)
    {
        processedImage = inputSoftwareBitmap.ToWriteableBitmap();

        OpenCvWrapper.Threshold(processedImage, thresholdLevel, thresholdType);

        OnPropertyChanged("ProcessedImage");
    }
}
```

In the next sample, I will extend this app for object detection.

Object detection

As I mentioned earlier, image thresholding is typically the first step of image processing algorithms aiming at object detection. So, after experimenting with thresholding, you can now move to more advanced stuff and implement object detection. OpenCV provides several algorithms for this purpose. In general, these algorithms analyze binary images to detect borders (rapid changes in the pixel values) and then arrange them into contours surrounding objects. One of the most convenient ways to find contours is the `cv::findContours` function. It requires the input binary image and returns detected contours. Accordingly, to detect the objects, all you need to do is to apply a threshold to the input image and then invoke the `cv::findContours` function. Moreover, to visualize detected contours, you can use the `cv::drawContours` function.

To show sample usage of these functions, I extend the ImageProcessing app by another button, Draw contours. It invokes object detection on the loaded image and displays results in the second Image control. (See Figure 8-10.)

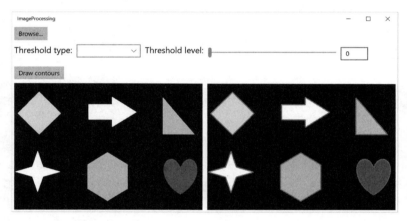

FIGURE 8-10 Object detection using the OpenCV toolkit.

An event handler of the Draw Contours button appears in Listing 8-35. This method's structure is similar to the `ThresholdImage` from Listing 8-34. Namely, I first convert the source `SoftwareBitmap` to `WriteableBitmap` and then pass the resulting object to the `OpenCvWrapper.DetectObjects` method.

LISTING 8-35 Contours detection

```
private void ButtonDrawContours_Click(object sender, RoutedEventArgs e)
{
    if (inputSoftwareBitmap != null)
    {
        processedImage = inputSoftwareBitmap.ToWriteableBitmap();

        OpenCvWrapper.DetectObjects(processedImage, true);

        OnPropertyChanged("ProcessedImage");
    }
}
```

To implement `OpenCvWrapper.DetectObjects`, I extend the declaration of `OpenCvWrapper` by the statements highlighted in Listing 8-36.

LISTING 8-36 OpenCvWrapper class declaration supplemented by one public and two private members for object detection

```
#pragma once

#include "ThresholdType.h"
#include <opencv2\core.hpp>
#include <opencv2\imgproc.hpp>

using namespace std;
using namespace Windows::UI::Xaml::Media::Imaging;
using namespace Windows::Storage::Streams;

namespace ImageProcessingComponent
{
    [Windows::Foundation::Metadata::WebHostHidden]
    public ref class OpenCvWrapper sealed
    {
    public:
        static void Threshold(WriteableBitmap^ inputBitmap, int level, ThresholdType type);
        static void DetectObjects(WriteableBitmap^ inputBitmap, bool drawContours);

    private:
        static const int pxMaxValue = 255;

        static void CheckInputParameters(WriteableBitmap^ inputBitmap);

        static cv::Mat ConvertWriteableBitmapToMat(WriteableBitmap ^inputBitmap);
        static cv::Mat ConvertMatToGrayScale(cv::Mat inputMat);

        static byte* GetPointerToPixelBuffer(IBuffer^ pixelBuffer);

        static vector<vector<cv::Point>> FindContours(cv::Mat inputMat);
        static void DrawContours(cv::Mat inputMat, vector<vector<cv::Point>> contours);
    };
}
```

There are two new private methods, FindContours and DrawContours, and one public method, DetectContours, which combines the functionality of those two private functions. The definition of FindContours appears in Listing 8-37. As you see there, I first threshold the input image using Otsu's algorithm and then pass the processed image to the `cv::findContours` method. It retrieves the contours stored using the `std::vector` container.

LISTING 8-37   Contour finding

```
vector<vector<cv::Point>> OpenCvWrapper::FindContours(cv::Mat inputMat)
{
    // Threshold image
    cv::threshold(inputMat, inputMat, 0, pxMaxValue, cv::ThresholdTypes::THRESH_OTSU);

    // Find contours
    vector<vector<cv::Point>> contours;
    cv::findContours(inputMat, contours, cv::RetrievalModes::RETR_LIST,
        cv::ContourApproximationModes::CHAIN_APPROX_SIMPLE);

    return contours;
}
```

The contour-finding algorithm implemented in the OpenCV toolkit can be controlled using the contour retrieval (mode) and approximation (method) modes. Available retrieval modes are declared within the cv::RetrievalModes enum (imgproc.hpp). This type controls how the contours hierarchy is constructed by the cv::findContours function. The contour hierarchy is the relation between objects (children) located inside the others (parents). Of course, child objects can be parents of other objects. So, the initial parents become grandparents, and so on.

If the retrieval mode is set to RETR_LIST (as in Listing 8-37), the hierarchy is not established. For RETR_CCOMP only parents and direct descendants are arranged into a hierarchy. The RETR_EXTERNAL flag instructs the cv::findContours function to pick the eldest objects only. In contrast, RETR_TREE retrieves a full contour hierarchy.

I did not use the contour hierarchy in the preceding example, but you can obtain it through the argument hierarchy of the second overloaded version of cv::findContours. Hierarchy is returned in the same way as contours.

Ultimately, detected contours can be compressed to reduce the number of points composing the contour. This is controlled by the method argument of the cv::findContours function. Possible contour compression methods are declared within cv::ContourApproximationModes (imgproc.hpp). You can either disable the compression feature (CHAIN_APPROX_NONE), compress horizontal, vertical, and diagonal segments only (CHAIN_APPROX_SIMPLE), or detect contour dominant points using the Teh-Chin algorithms (CHAIN_APPROX_TC89_L1, CHAIN_APPROX_TC89_KCOS), described in an article by Teh, C.H. and Chin, R.T., "On the Detection of Dominant Points on Digital Curve." PAMI 11 8, pp. 859–872 (1989). In Listing 8-37, I don't use contour hierarchy and I apply simple contour segment filtering. However, you can individually modify the cv::findContours options to see how they affect contour detection.

The contour collection can be drawn on the image using the cv::drawContours method. Listing 8-38 shows how to use this function. Basically, you define the color and line thickness and then iterate through contour collection. To define the RGB color in OpenCV, you use the cv::Scalar structure. It has four members, each of which specify color channels. They are arranged in the following order: blue, green, red, and alpha. Hence, in Listing 8-38, to define a red, non-transparent color, I set the red and alpha channels to 255.

LISTING 8-38 Contour drawing

```
void OpenCvWrapper::DrawContours(cv::Mat inputMat, vector<vector<cv::Point>> contours)
{
    // Line color and thickness
    cv::Scalar red = cv::Scalar(0, 0, 255, 255);
    int thickness = 5;

    // Draw contours
    for (uint i = 0; i < contours.size(); i++)
    {
        cv::drawContours(inputMat, contours, i, red, thickness);
    }
}
```

FindContours and DrawContours of OpenCvWrapper are used in the DetectObjects method from Listing 8-39. This method has two arguments: the bitmap to process (inputBitmap) and the Boolean parameter (drawContours). drawContours specifies whether detected contours should be depicted in the image. DetectObjects uses techniques that I already discussed, so its further description is not necessary.

LISTING 8-39 Object detection

```
void OpenCvWrapper::DetectObjects(WriteableBitmap^ inputBitmap, bool drawContours)
{
    CheckInputParameters(inputBitmap);

    auto inputMat = ConvertWriteableBitmapToMat(inputBitmap);
    auto workingMat = ConvertMatToGrayScale(inputMat);

    auto contours = FindContours(workingMat);

    if (drawContours)
    {
        DrawContours(inputMat, contours);
    }
}
```

Machine vision for object recognition

The previous sections have offered several insights on image processing fundamentals using OpenCV, and you can use that knowledge to build the IoT app. Here, I will combine USB camera acquisition with the OpenCV toolkit. The goal of the next project is to recognize objects in the video sequence by using an app that detects simple geometrical shapes: lines, triangles, and squares. I will utilize and extend contour detection routines so that all detected contours will be approximated by polygonal curves. The app will pick the object with the largest area and analyze its geometrical shape. The Sense HAT LED array will display the result of this analysis, as you see in Figure 8-2.

I divide the implementation of this example into two steps:

- I describe the contour approximation within the ImageProcessingComponent, showing you how to determine object area and the list of polygonal curves approximating the contour.

- I show you how to pass this data to the main IoT app, which will use it to drive the LED array. For this reason, I extend the definition of the LedArray class by methods for drawing shapes: triangles, squares, and X sign.

Contour approximation

To store the contour description (the area and contour surrounding the curve), I defined the Object-Descriptor class (see the companion code in Chapter 08/ImageProcessingComponent/ObjectDescriptor). This class has two properties: Area and Points.

The Area property stores the contour area, which I calculate using cv::contourArea. This function accepts two arguments: a contour, the input vector of cv::Point objects; and the Boolean flag, oriented. This flag specifies whether to determine the contour orientation (clockwise or counter-clockwise). Here, I do not use the contour orientation because I'm interested only in the absolute area. If required, the orientation is returned as the sign of the value returned by cv::contourArea.

The Points property of the ObjectDescriptor stores the contour surrounding curve as a collection of UWP 2D points, represented as a Windows::Foundation::Point structure. I convert the original contour surrounding curve, being a collection of cv::Point structures, within the ObjectDescriptor constructor. (See Listing 8-40.) This conversion simplifies access to the polygonal contour curve in the UWP app.

LISTING 8-40 ObjectDescriptor constructor

```
ObjectDescriptor::ObjectDescriptor(vector<cv::Point> contour, double area)
{
    auto contourSize = contour.size();
    if (contourSize > 0)
    {
        points = ref new Vector<Point>();

        for (int i = 0; i < contourSize; i++)
        {
            auto cvPoint = contour.at(i);

            points->Append(Point(cvPoint.x, cvPoint.y));
        }
    }

    this->area = area;
}
```

Given the ObjectDescriptor, I wrote the OpenCvWrapper::ContoursToObjectList in Listing 8-41. This method uses a collection of contours to generate object descriptors. By iterating through each contour (two-dimensional collection of cv::Point), it creates the ObjectDescriptor, storing the contour area and polygonal curve surrounding the contour.

LISTING 8-41   Generating a collection of object descriptors

```
IVector<ObjectDescriptor^>^ OpenCvWrapper::ContoursToObjectList(vector<vector<cv::Point>>
    contours)
{
    Vector<ObjectDescriptor^>^ objectsDetected = ref new Vector<ObjectDescriptor^>();

    const double epsilon = 5;

    for (uint i = 0; i < contours.size(); i++)
    {
        vector<cv::Point> polyLine;

        double contourArea = cv::contourArea(contours.at(i), false);

        if (contourArea > 0)
        {
            cv::approxPolyDP(contours.at(i), polyLine, epsilon, true);

            objectsDetected->Append(ref new ObjectDescriptor(polyLine, contourArea));
        }
    }

    return objectsDetected;
}
```

I previously described the calculation of the contour area, but the contour approximation bears further attention. You obtain the list of points constituting the polygonal curve approximating the contour by using the cv::approxPolyDP function. This function implements the Ramer-Douglas-Peucker algorithm for decreasing the number of points in a curve approximating the given object. That is, the original set of points (the first argument of the cv::approxPolyDP function) describing the contour is decreased to simplify contour representation. The simplified curve is obtained by using the second argument of the cv::approxPolyDP function. The accuracy of the cv::approxPolyDP function is controlled by the third argument (epsilon). It specifies the distance between the points of input and the reduced curve. Moreover, the cv::aproxPolyDP function will return the closed or open curves, depending on the value of the fourth argument (closed). In the preceding example, I set the accuracy to 5 and forced closed the polygonal curve approximating the contour.

Reducing the number of points representing the contour obtains the set of points that corresponds to the contour vertices. Therefore, calculating the number of these vertices reveals the shape kind. Namely, the line has just two vertices, the triangle has three, while the square has four. However, for bright images (e.g. images with a white background), the cv::findContours function returns a faked object, because it always fills the 1-pixel border of the image with zeros. After thresholding bright images, the border is detected as a rectangular object. You can easily check this behavior using the ImageProcessing app if you run the object detection algorithm on a white-background image.

Figure 8-11 illustrates the problem, showing the result of object detection in the color-inverted version of the image in Figure 8-10.

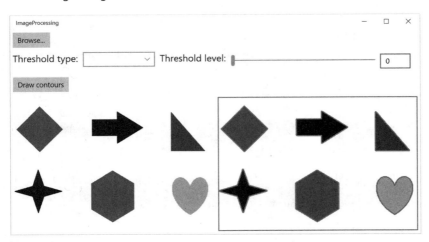

FIGURE 8-11 For bright images, contour finding incorrectly identifies the image border as the object. The input image contains six objects: diamond, right arrow, triangle, star, hexagon, and heart. However, the processed image presents seven objects. (The seventh shape is the large rectangle around the six detected shapes.)

To overcome this issue, I implement a function for determining image brightness. I simply calculate the average value of the pixels in the image converted to grayscale. (See Listing 8-42.) If the brightness is sufficiently high, I reject the largest object. This is implemented in the UWP app.

LISTING 8-42 Determining image brightness

```
double OpenCvWrapper::Brightness(WriteableBitmap^ inputBitmap)
{
    CheckInputParameters(inputBitmap);

    auto inputMat = ConvertWriteableBitmapToMat(inputBitmap);
    auto workingMat = ConvertMatToGrayScale(inputMat);

    return cv::mean(workingMat).val[0];
}
```

The OpenCvWrapper::DetectObjects method returns the list of object descriptors. An updated definition of this method appears in Listing 8-43. All changes compared to Listing 8-39 are highlighted.

LISTING 8-43 Returning the list of object descriptors

```
IVector<ObjectDescriptor^>^ OpenCvWrapper::DetectObjects(WriteableBitmap^
    inputBitmap, bool drawContours)
{
    CheckInputParameters(inputBitmap);
```

```
        auto inputMat = ConvertWriteableBitmapToMat(inputBitmap);
        auto workingMat = ConvertMatToGrayScale(inputMat);

        auto contours = FindContours(workingMat);

        if (drawContours)
        {
            DrawContours(inputMat, contours);
        }

        return ContoursToObjectList(contours);
}
```

Object identification

I used the functionality implemented above in the MachineVision app (see the companion code in Chapter 08/MachineVision). I created it in the same way as ImageProcessing. Namely, I used the Visual C# Blank UWP project template and referenced the Windows IoT Extensions for the UWP and Image-ProcessingComponent. Subsequently, I declared the Webcam capability, and supplemented the project by the following files: CameraCapture.cs, Check.cs, I2cHelper.cs, and LedArray.cs. All of them are stored under the Helpers folder for the MachineVision project.

After the MachineVision project launches, the video capture begins, and frames are processed in the background to recognize geometrical shapes by calculating vertices of detected and compressed contours. Based on the processing results, a corresponding shape is displayed on the Sense HAT LED array. (Refer to Figure 8-2.)

To acquire and process a video sequence, I use the same approach as in the ImageProcessing app. Namely, I start the preview within the OnNavigatedTo event handler. This event handler also initializes the LedArray class, which I use to drive the Sense HAT LED array.

The background image processing then proceeds as shown in Listing 8-44.

LISTING 8-44 Video frame processing for object recognition

```
private async Task ProcessVideoFrame()
{
    using (VideoFrame videoFrame = new VideoFrame(bitmapPixelFormat,
        (int)cameraCapture.FrameWidth, (int)cameraCapture.FrameHeight))
    {
        await cameraCapture.MediaCapture.GetPreviewFrameAsync(videoFrame);

        var objectDescriptor = await FindLargestObject(videoFrame);

        DisplayDetectedObject(objectDescriptor);
    }
}
```

After acquiring the video frame, I pass it to the `FindLargestObject` method from Listing 8-45. This method is dispatched in the UI thread, if necessary, and is responsible for preparing the `WriteableBitmap`, which is then processed by the `DetectObjects` method of the `OpenCvWrapper` class. Note that here I do not use the `ToWriteableBitmap` extension method because it generates a new instance of the `WriteableBitmap`. Because camera images can be large, such an approach would lead to huge memory usage, especially for high frame rates. To keep constant with memory demand, I use only one instance of the `WriteableBitmap` class, the `workingBitmap` field. It is instantiated before starting the background processing (see the `BeginProcessing` method in the companion code at Chapter 08/MachineVision/MainPage.xaml.cs).

LISTING 8-45 Finding the largest object in the image

```
private WriteableBitmap workingBitmap = null;

private async Task<ObjectDescriptor> FindLargestObject(VideoFrame videoFrame)
{
    if (Dispatcher.HasThreadAccess)
    {
        videoFrame.SoftwareBitmap.CopyToBuffer(workingBitmap.PixelBuffer);

        var objects = OpenCvWrapper.DetectObjects(workingBitmap, false);

        return GetLargestObject(objects);
    }
    else
    {
        ObjectDescriptor objectDescriptor = null;

        await Dispatcher.RunAsync(CoreDispatcherPriority.Normal, async () =>
        {
            objectDescriptor = await FindLargestObject(videoFrame);
        });

        return objectDescriptor;
    }
}
```

After the `OpenCvWrapper.DetectObjects` method returns the list of object descriptors, I pass it to `GetLargestObject`, which returns the object with the largest area. I use only one object because I do not have room on the LED array to display all the objects at once.

A definition of the `GetLargestObject` method appears in Listing 8-46. This method sorts the list of object descriptors by the contour area. It then invokes the `GetObjectIndex` method, which, depending on the image brightness (calculated by `OpenCvWrapper.Brightness`), indicates whether the first spurious object should be rejected. It rejects the object when the image brightness is larger than 100.

```
private ObjectDescriptor GetLargestObject(IList<ObjectDescriptor> objects)
{
    ObjectDescriptor largestObject = null;

    if (objects != null)
    {
        if (objects.Count() > 0)
        {
            var sorted = objects.OrderByDescending(s => s.Area);

            int objectIndex = GetObjectIndex();

            if (sorted.Count() >= objectIndex + 1)
            {
                largestObject = sorted.ElementAt(objectIndex);
            }
        }
    }

    return largestObject;
}

private const double minBrightness = 100.0d;

private int GetObjectIndex()
{
    double brightness = OpenCvWrapper.Brightness(workingBitmap);

    // The first spurious object is ignored
    // if the image brightness is sufficiently large
    return brightness > minBrightness ? 1 : 0;
}
```

The `DisplayDetectedObject` method (refer to Listing 8-44) utilizes the object descriptor returned by `GetLargestObject`. The `DisplayDetectedObject` method, shown in Listing 8-47, recognizes the shape kind, and then drives the LED array accordingly.

LISTING 8-47   Displaying the detected object

```
private void DisplayDetectedObject(ObjectDescriptor objectDescriptor)
{
    if (ledArray != null)
    {
        var shapeKind = GetShapeKind(objectDescriptor);

        ledArray.DrawShape(shapeKind);
    }
}
```

MachineVision can recognize objects with up to four vertices (this is specified by the `maxVertices-Count` field in the `MainPage` class). Single points or more complex shapes are indicated by the X sign, and if the image contains no object, all LEDs of the Sense HAT add-on board have a uniform red color.

The recognizable shapes are defined in the `ShapeKind` enum type from Listing 8-48 (the LedArray. cs file). The value of this type is returned by the `GetShapeKind` method from Listing 8-49. This method maps the number of vertices to the appropriate element of the `ShapeKind` enumeration.

LISTING 8-48 Detectable shapes enumeration

```
public enum ShapeKind
{
    None = 0, Line = 2, Triangle = 3, Square = 4, X = 5,
}
```

LISTING 8-49 Determining the shape kind based on the number of vertices

```
private ShapeKind GetShapeKind(ObjectDescriptor objectDescriptor)
{
    var shapeKind = ShapeKind.None;

    if (objectDescriptor != null)
    {
        var objectDescriptorPointsCount = objectDescriptor.Points.Count;

        if (objectDescriptorPointsCount > maxVerticesCount)
        {
            // Complex object is indicated as the X sign
            shapeKind = ShapeKind.X;
        }
        else
        {
            if (Enum.IsDefined(typeof(ShapeKind), objectDescriptorPointsCount))
            {
                shapeKind = (ShapeKind)objectDescriptorPointsCount;
            }
        }
    }

    return shapeKind;
}
```

After the shape kind is determined, the appropriate figure is displayed on the LED array. To this end, I extended the definition of the `LedArray` class by the public `DrawShape` method. (See Listing 8-50.) It includes a `switch` statement, which, depending on the input argument, invokes one of the private methods, `DrawLine`, `DrawTriangle`, `DrawSquare`, or `DrawX`, or it drives all the LEDs to red.

LISTING 8-50 Drawing shapes on the LED array

```
public void DrawShape(ShapeKind shapeKind)
{
    switch (shapeKind)
    {
        case ShapeKind.Line:
            DrawLine();
            break;

        case ShapeKind.Triangle:
            DrawTriangle(Colors.Red);
            break;

        case ShapeKind.Square:
            DrawSquare(Colors.Green);
            break;

        case ShapeKind.X:
            DrawX(Colors.Blue);
            break;

        case ShapeKind.None:
            Reset(Colors.Red);
            break;
    }
}
```

Drawing methods use the double for loop, in which I configure the `Buffer` property of the `LedArray` class. (See the companion code in Chapter 08/MachineVision/Helpers/LedArray.cs.) This method is based on quite standard techniques you most likely already know from programming labs or tutorials.

To test the MachineVision app, place a piece of paper with different geometric shapes in front of your USB camera. Depending on the recognition results, an appropriate shape will be displayed. I have successfully verified MachineVision using various black printed objects on white paper and using hand-drawn colorful objects.

Final notes

The preceding project can be a good start to implementing a real-world machine vision IoT app, e.g. for automatic road signs recognition. However, in real-world applications of object detection and recognition, you can face at least two problems:

- **Reduced signal-to-noise ratio** You can overcome this by applying appropriate image preprocessing. You can blur the image by using one of the functions implemented in OpenCV: `cv::blur`, `cv::GaussianBlur` or `cv::MedianBlur`. Or you can enhance the input image by histogram equalization (`cv::equalizeHist`).

- **Non-uniform image brightness** In such a case, the global thresholding algorithms (`cv::Threshold`) can't properly extract all the features, so not every object is detected. To solve this issue, use the adaptive thresholding implemented in the `cv::adaptiveThreshold` function.

OpenCV provides several techniques for object tracking and matching. For instance, you can match contours using the `cv::matchShapes` function or use a more general template matching approach implemented within the `cv::matchTemplate` method. All these components are available in the img-proc OpenCV module.

OpenCV is a very popular computer vision toolkit covered by a great number of books and articles—in particular, Gary Bradsky and Adrian Kaehler's *Learning OpenCV: Computer Vision with OpenCV Library* is a very comprehensive book. The original version published in 2008 describes the C interface of OpenCV. However, there is also an updated version of this book, which uses the C++ interface: *Learning OpenCV 3: Computer Vision in C++ with the OpenCV Library*.

Summary

This chapter investigated several machine vision capabilities of the UWP and OpenCV. You implemented image acquisition from the USB camera and used the UWP capabilities of facial detection and tracking. Subsequently, the custom digital image processing routines were created based on the OpenCV toolkit and integrated with the UWP application using the Windows Runtime Component written using C++ Component Extensions. You can use this approach to interface modern apps with unmanaged and legacy code. This possibility can be very useful for IoT programming—in particular, for integrating the UWP app with native libraries or drivers.

CHAPTER 9

Connecting devices

Connecting multiple embedded devices for data exchange and remote device control is one of the most important elements for implementing IoT solutions. You do not connect devices only to acquire readings from remote sensors. Complex embedded systems can include two or more internal subsystems, which control specific parts of the larger system. You typically use wired communication interfaces in those situations, and you're likely to use wireless interfaces, like Bluetooth or Wi-Fi, for remote device control and sensor readings.

Independent of the communication interface, you need the communication protocol—the language in which devices talk to each other. You can define custom protocols for custom control systems. Widely available small home automation devices communicate using standardized protocols.

In this chapter, I show you how to build UWP apps based on wired and wireless communication interfaces; I also show you how to implement and use custom and standardized communication protocols.

Serial communication

Serial communication (SC) is one of the most commonly used communication types in embedded programming. It transmits byte arrays sequentially; in other words, bits comprising each byte in the array move one by one. You used SC in previous chapters to read data from sensors or to control the LED array using the I²C bus. Typically, this communication interface enables intra-device communication, as between the CPU and peripherals. For inter-device communication, embedded devices generally use the Universal Asynchronous Receiver and Transmitter (UART), which is the interface for exchanging data using a serial port and RS-232, USB, or TTL interfaces.

Why do you need SC in your IoT solution? It's a relatively simple way to exchange data with other devices. Your IoT unit may include several boards controlling specific elements of the larger system. All of these sub-boards report their functioning status to the principal, global decision-making board. This board may also send appropriate requests to sub-boards, and it can communicate with other devices, like a desktop PC, to perform device maintenance, transfer sensor readings, update firmware of a particular sub-board, and so on.

In this section, I show you how to implement the SC using the `SerialDevice` class, defined in the `Windows.Devices.SerialCommunication` namespace. I use the RPi2 and the development PC. I set up communication by using the USB PC port and the RPi2 UART interface. This interface is accessible through two pins: 8 (transmitter, TX) and 10 (receiver, RX) on the expansion header. To connect the USB to those pins, I use the USB to TTL converter (roughly $10 at *https://www.adafruit.com/product/954*).

Next, I will write two apps: SerialCommunciation.Master and SerialCommunication.Blinky. The former will be deployed to a development PC, while the latter will be deployed to an IoT device, and will control the internal ACT LED status (if you use the RPi3, then you need to use an external LED circuit). The PC app will send requests to the IoT to update the LED blinking frequency.

The implementation of this example is quite complex and requires interoperability of several components. I first use the UART loopback mode and connect the TX and RX pins together. By doing so I can use the single IoT app to transmit byte arrays using the methods of the `SerialDevice` class. You can use this kind of loopback mode to test that individual components are working correctly.

UART loopback mode

First, prepare the hardware and connect the RX and TX pins of the RPi2/RPi3 together. You do this by using female-female or two female-male jumper wires connected to the RPi2/RPi3 through the solderless breadboard. As Figure 9-1 shows, I use the second option, because female-female jumper wires are unavailable in the Windows 10 IoT Pack.

FIGURE 9-1 UART loopback mode. TX (yellow wire) and RX (red wire) pins are connected using two female-male jumper wires and the solderless breadboard.

Project skeleton

You now start working on the software, building a sample that shows how to enumerate the serial ports of the current system. You then configure the selected port for SC. You use this functionality in the next, more comprehensive, project. I therefore implement core functions in a separate Class Library project, which is referenced by the main app executed on the IoT device. Follow these steps:

1. Bring up the New Project dialog box, and then pick up the new Blank App (Universal Windows) Visual C# project template.

2. Type **SerialCommunication.LoopBack** in the Name text box, and then change the solution name to **SerialCommunication**.

3. In the Solution Explorer, right-click **Solution 'SerialCommunication'**, and select **Add/New Project** from the context menu.

4. In the New Project dialog box, type **Class Library Universal** in the search box.

5. Select the **Class Library (Universal Windows) Visual C#** project template from the list of matching templates, and type **SerialCommunication.Common** in the Name text box.

6. Close the dialog box by clicking **OK**.

7. In the Solution Explorer, navigate to the SerialCommunication.Common project, and then rename Class1.cs to **SerialCommunicationHelper.cs**.

8. In the Solution Explorer, right-click a **References** node under SerialCommunication.LoopBack, and select **Add Reference** from the context menu.

9. In the Reference Manager, under SerialCommunication.LoopBack, navigate to the Projects/ Solution tab and select **SerialCommunication.Common**.

Serial device configuration

To enumerate and configure serial ports, use the SerialCommunicationHelper class; see Listing 9-1 and the companion code in Chapter 09/SerialCommunication.Common/Helpers/SerialCommunication-Helper.cs.

LISTING 9-1 Serial device enumeration

```
public static async Task<DeviceInformationCollection> FindSerialDevices()
{
    var defaultSelector = SerialDevice.GetDeviceSelector();

    return await DeviceInformation.FindAllAsync(defaultSelector);
}
```

In particular, this class implements the following public methods:

- FindSerialDevices
- GetFirstDeviceAvailable
- SetDefaultConfiguration

FindSerialDevices asks the UWP for the collection of all serial ports available in the current system; see Listing 9-1. This list represents an instance of the DeviceInformationCollection class and can be retrieved by using the static FindAllAsync method of the DeviceInformation class.

In general, the `DeviceInformation.FindAllAsync` method enables you to enumerate all devices. To narrow this search to serial devices, use the appropriate Advanced Query Syntax (AQS) selector by using the static `GetDeviceSelector` method of the `SerialDevice` class. Pass the resulting string as an argument of the `DeviceInformation.FindAllAsync` method. Doing so returns the collection of serial ports. (Note that I'm using the phrases "serial device" and "serial port" interchangeably. This is because in the UWP, a serial port is represented as the `SerialDevice` class.).

Listing 9-2 shows the AQS selector for serial devices. This selector filters and enables devices by using the globally unique identifier (GUID).

LISTING 9-2 Serial device selector

```
System.Devices.InterfaceClassGuid:="{86E0D1E0-8089-11D0-9CE4-08003E301F73}" AND
    System.Devices.InterfaceEnabled:=System.StructuredQueryType.Boolean#True
```

By default, the RPi2/RPi3 has just a single UART interface, so `DeviceInformationCollection` will contain just a single element: the instance of the `DeviceInformation` class. This is an abstract representation of a specified device, and thus contains properties identifying the system device. In particular, the `Id` property can be used to instantiate the `SerialDevice` class using the static `FromIdAsync` method. This procedure is used in the `GetFirstDeviceAvailable` method from Listing 9-3. This function first invokes `FindSerialDevices` (see Listing 9-1) and then obtains an `Id` of the first element of the resulting `DeviceInformationCollection` instance. Subsequently, the device identifier is used to obtain an instance of the `SerialDevice` class, which in the case of the RPi2/RPi3 will give you access to the UART interface.

LISTING 9-3 Returning the first available instance of the SerialDevice class

```
public static async Task<SerialDevice> GetFirstDeviceAvailable()
{
    var serialDeviceCollection = await FindSerialDevices();

    var serialDeviceInformation = serialDeviceCollection.FirstOrDefault();

    if (serialDeviceInformation != null)
    {
        return await SerialDevice.FromIdAsync(serialDeviceInformation.Id);
    }
    else
    {
        return null;
    }
}
```

I wrote the `SetDefaultConfiguration` method to configure an instance of the `SerialDevice`; see Listing 9-4. This function sets the default values of properties controlling SC. You can configure time-outs using the `WriteTimeout` and `ReadTimeout` properties. Moreover, you can specify the transmission speed (`BaudRate` property)—that is, how fast bits are transferred over the serial medium. The baud rate is expressed in bits per second (bps), and multiple standard baud rates are defined. (See Figure 9-2.)

LISTING 9-4 Serial port configuration

```
private const int msDefaultTimeOut = 1000;

public static void SetDefaultConfiguration(SerialDevice serialDevice)
{
    if(serialDevice != null)
    {
        serialDevice.WriteTimeout = TimeSpan.FromMilliseconds(msDefaultTimeOut);
        serialDevice.ReadTimeout = TimeSpan.FromMilliseconds(msDefaultTimeOut);

        serialDevice.BaudRate = 115200;
        serialDevice.Parity = SerialParity.None;
        serialDevice.DataBits = 8;
        serialDevice.Handshake = SerialHandshake.None;
        serialDevice.StopBits = SerialStopBitCount.One;
    }
}
```

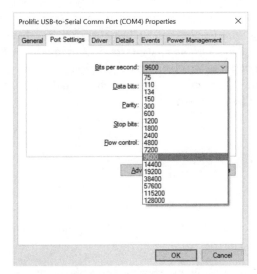

FIGURE 9-2 The list of baud rates supported by the USB to TTL converter.

In Listing 9-4, I set the default baud rate to 115200 bps and configure parity, data bits, handshake, and stop bits. In SC, bits to be transferred are partitioned into frames. In that approach, also known as character framing, the frame consists of a specified number of bits that carry the actual information (data bits) and additional bits used for synchronization and communication error detection. (See Figure 9-3.) Synchronization bits track the beginning and end of the frame being transferred. The parity bit is computed before transmitting the frame and then checked by the receiver. If the receiver detects an incorrect value of the parity bit, it can either reject an incorrect frame or request that the transmitter resend the given frame.

FIGURE 9-3   A structure of the frame character used in serial communication. 5-9 bits, carrying actual information (data bits), are surrounded by synchronization bits (start and stop) and an optional parity bit used for error detection.

In the default configuration (see Listing 9-4), I set the number of data bits to 8 (DataBits property), disable the parity bit (Parity) and handshake (Handshake), and use only one stop bit (StopBits).

Writing and reading data

After configuring the serial port, you can implement the actual functionality for transferring data. Figure 9-4 shows the UI layer I defined. You can find the corresponding XAML declaration in the companion code in Chapter 09/SerialCommunication.LoopBack/MainPage.xaml.

Basically, the app consists of the buttons Perform Test and Clear List and the ListBox control. The first button, Perform Test, sends the "UART transfer" string and reads that message by using methods of the SerialDevice class. The second button , Clear List, clears the contents of the list. Items displayed in this list are bounded to the field diagnosticData, which is declared by the generic Observable-Collection class. This class implements the INotifyPropertyChanged interface. Consequently, every change made to the diagnosticData field (adding or removing elements, for example) is automatically reflected in the UI. In other words, thanks to the ObservableCollection class, you do not need to independently implement the INotifyPropertyChanged interface.

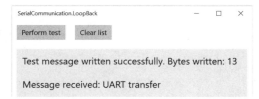

FIGURE 9-4   UART loopback mode. A test message "UART transfer" is sent through the TX pin, and the signal is immediately received on the RX pin.

To transfer data using methods of the SerialDevice class, implement the code-behind of the MainPage; see the companion code in Chapter 09/SerialCommunication.LoopBack/MainPage.xaml.cs. Three main methods exist:

- InitializeDevice
- WriteTestMessage
- ReadTestMessage

InitializeDevice (see Listing 9-5) is based on methods of the SerialCommunicationHelper class. It receives and then configures the first available serial port. Subsequently, the InitializeDevice method creates an instance of the DataWriter and DataReader classes by using the OutputStream and `InputStream` members of the `SerialDevice`. Think of `DataWriter` and `DataReader` as wrappers for the output and input streams of the serial port, respectively.

LISTING 9-5 An instance of the SerialDevice class used to configure the serial port and to instantiate the DataWriter and DataReader classes to further simplify serial communication; see Listing 9-6 and Listing 9-7

```
private SerialDevice serialDevice;

private DataWriter dataWriter;
private DataReader dataReader;

private async Task InitializeDevice()
{
    if (serialDevice == null)
    {
        serialDevice = await SerialCommunicationHelper.GetFirstDeviceAvailable();

        SerialCommunicationHelper.SetDefaultConfiguration(serialDevice);

        if (serialDevice != null)
        {
            dataWriter = new DataWriter(serialDevice.OutputStream);
            dataReader = new DataReader(serialDevice.InputStream);
        }
    }
}
```

To transmit data using the serial port, use the `WriteAsync` method of the `IOutputStream` interface, implemented by the `OutputStream` member of the `SerialDevice` class. However, the `WriteAsync` method accepts an argument of type `IBuffer`, representing a referenced byte array. Data you send thus has to be converted to that array. To simplify this operation, use the `DataWriter` class, which exposes several write methods that perform appropriate conversions automatically. `DataWriter` also takes care of an endianness that you can set by using the `ByteOrder` property.

Listing 9-6 shows a definition of the `WriteTestMessage` method, where an instance of the `DataWriter` class transmits the string "UART transfer" by using the `WriteString` method. This function writes the specified string to the output stream, which is an abstract representation of the serial port transmitter. To send data over the serial link, I call the `StoreAsync` method, which commits data to the underlying stream buffer asynchronously. As a result, the UART interface transmits a byte array containing the test message.

LISTING 9-6 Sending data using the serial port

```
private const string testMessage = "UART transfer";

private async Task WriteTestMessage()
{
    if (dataWriter != null)
    {
```

```
        dataWriter.WriteString(testMessage);

        var bytesWritten = await dataWriter.StoreAsync();

        DiagnosticInfo.Display(diagnosticData,
            "Test message written successfully. Bytes written: " + bytesWritten);
    }
    else
    {
        DiagnosticInfo.Display(diagnosticData, "Data writer has been not initialized");
    }
}
```

To read data received by the UART interface, I employ corresponding methods of the DataReader class rather than using methods of the DataWriter class; see Listing 9-7. First, data from the input stream is loaded into the internal store of the DataReader (LoadAsync method). Second, the received byte array is read as a string using the ReadString method. To use this method, specify a buffer length that you want to read. You can check the number of remaining (unread) bytes by reading the value of the UnconsumedBufferLength property.

LISTING 9-7   Reading a string received through the serial port

```
private async Task ReadTestMessage()
{
    if (dataReader != null)
    {
        var stringLength = dataWriter.MeasureString(testMessage);

        await dataReader.LoadAsync(stringLength);

        var messageReceived = dataReader.ReadString(dataReader.UnconsumedBufferLength);

        DiagnosticInfo.Display(diagnosticData, "Message received: " + messageReceived);
    }
    else
    {
        DiagnosticInfo.Display(diagnosticData, "Data reader has been not initialized");
    }
}
```

Alternatively, to read data from the serial port, you could use the InputStream member of the SerialDevice class. This member represents the receiver module of the UART interface and exposes a single ReadAsync method. This method reads the specified number of bytes to the given byte array. But again, this array is represented using the IBuffer interface, so you need to program the eventual conversion yourself.

Successful write and read operations are confirmed in the UI and debugging console (Output Window of Visual Studio) using methods of the helper class in Listing 9-8. To add the list item, simply invoke the Add method of the ICollection interface. The UI then updates automatically.

```
public static class DiagnosticInfo
{
    private const string timeFormat = "HH:mm:fff";

    public static void Display(ICollection<string> collection, string info)
    {
        if(collection != null)
        {
            collection.Add(info);
        }

        DisplayDebugMessage(info);
    }

    private static void DisplayDebugMessage(string message)
    {
        string debugString = string.Format("{0} | {1}",
            DateTime.Now.ToString(timeFormat), message);

        Debug.WriteLine(debugString);
    }
}
```

To run the preceding sample app, you also need to grant an app access to the serial port. Follow these steps:

1. Navigate to the Solution Explorer.

2. Right-click **Package.appxmanifest** under the SerialCommunication.LoopBack project, and select **View-Code** from the context menu.

3. Update the Capabilities tag as shown in Listing 9-9. You can now deploy an app to your IoT device.

LISTING 9-9 Serial port capability declaration

```
<Capabilities>
  <Capability Name="internetClient" />
  <DeviceCapability Name="serialcommunication">
    <Device Id="any">
      <Function Type="name:serialPort" />
    </Device>
  </DeviceCapability>
</Capabilities>
```

After you deploy the app, click the **Perform Test** button. The status of this operation appears in the UI. (See Figure 9-4.) If you do not want to use the UI, you can invoke ButtonPerformTest_Click in the class constructor or the OnNavigatedTo method as shown in Listing 9-10. You then see the write and read status in the Output Window (see Figure 9-5).

Invoking the communication test

```
public MainPage()
{
    InitializeComponent();

    ButtonPerformTest_Click(null, null);
}
```

```
Output                                              ▾ □ ×
Show output from:  Debug                    ▾     ⁝ ⁝ ⁝ ⁝
'SerialCommunication.LoopBack.exe' (CoreCLR: CoreCLR_UWP_Domain): Loaded 'C ▲
'SerialCommunication.LoopBack.exe' (CoreCLR: CoreCLR_UWP_Domain): Loaded 'C
'SerialCommunication.LoopBack.exe' (CoreCLR: CoreCLR_UWP_Domain): Loaded 'C
'SerialCommunication.LoopBack.exe' (CoreCLR: CoreCLR_UWP_Domain): Loaded 'C
07:13:891 | Test message written successfully. Bytes written: 13
07:13:938 | Message received: UART transfer
The thread 0x4dc has exited with code 0 (0x0).
                                                            ▼
◄ ▒▒▒▒▒▒                                            ►
```

FIGURE 9-5   Highlighted results of the UART loopback mode test in the debugging console.

Writing the app for intra-device communication

Before you write the app for intra-device communication, you need to connect the RPi2 to the USB port of the development PC. After that, you write two apps: one running on the PC and a second, a headless app, running on the IoT device. The PC app will remotely control the IoT device using SC.

Connecting a converter

I connect the UART interface of the RPi2 to the development PC by using a USB to TTL converter. (See Figure 9-6.) One end of this converter has the standard USB type A connector, and the other end has four wires: ground (black), power (red), RX (white), and TX (green).

FIGURE 9-6   A USB to TTL converter. Courtesy of *www.adafruit.org*.

Here's how to connect the jumper wires (see Figure 9-7):

- The white wire (RX) to the UART TX pin of the RPi2–pin 8 on the expansion header (GPIO 11).

- Green (TX) wire to UART RX pin of the RPi2–pin 10 (GPIO 13)

- The black wire (ground) to one of the GND pins on the RPi2 expansion header. These are: 6, 14, 20, 30 or 34. In Figure 9-7, I use pin 6.

- Red wire stays unconnected.

FIGURE 9-7   Wires of the USB to TTL converter connected to the RPi-2 pins. Note that the red (power) wire is unconnected, because the RPi-2 is powered through a micro-USB switch.

You can also use the loopback mode to verify that your USB to TTL converter works correctly. Simply connect the green and white wires by using female-female jumper wires. Use the SerialCommunication. LoopBack app or any other serial terminal, like Termite (*https://bit.ly/termite_terminal*). (See Figure 9-8.)

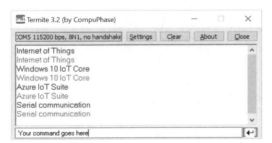

FIGURE 9-8   Testing the USB to TTL converter using the loopback mode and the serial terminal. Blue strings are sent through the TX pin. These messages are immediately received on the RX pin (green strings).

Controlling an IoT device remotely

To implement the headless IoT app, named SerialCommunication.Blinky, the code controls the ACT LED of the RPi2. (Again, if you use the RPi3, then you need to use an external LED circuit here.) This app continuously switches the ACT LED on and off. Moreover, SerialCommunication.Blinky exposes the communication API, which enables the remote app to change the LED blinking frequency and to disable and re-enable LED blinking.

To control LED blinking, client apps could simply send text commands to the SerialCommunication.Blinky app. However, in practice, bare string commands are very rarely used in favor of an application-specific communication protocol. Such a protocol typically assumes that byte arrays of a fixed length transmit between devices. This approach has several advantages over sending a pure string:

- The communication frame usually contains not only the command data but also additional bytes used for error detection and correction.

- Sending frames of a fixed length simplifies the data exchange because devices always expect the same number of bytes.

- A custom communication protocol helps you to hide actual information being transferred between devices.

Communication protocol

You can tailor a communication protocol to your specific needs. In this particular example I use two commands, one for changing blinking frequency and the second for disabling/enabling blinking. Moreover, I assume that blinking frequency is a `double`, spanned on eight bytes, and I need only one byte for disabling/enabling blinking. Therefore, I use frames comprised of 16 bytes.

Figure 9-9 shows the frame structure. The first (index of 0) and the last (index of 15) byte are used for synchronization. They mark the beginning and the end of the frame, so they have fixed values of 0xAA and 0xBB, respectively. Next, I have one byte at index 1, which specifies the command identifier. This byte is followed by 10 command bytes (indices 2–12), the error code (1 byte at index 13), and the check sum (1 byte at index 14).

Index	0	1	2-12	13	14	15
Description	Start byte	Command Id	Command data	Error code	Checksum	End byte
Value	0xAA		Variable			0xBB

FIGURE 9-9 The communication frame. A byte array used for communication contains 16 elements.

After designing the frame structure, I defined two enumeration types in the SerialCommunication. Common library. The first one, CommandId (see Listing 9-11), declares two commands: BlinkingFrequency and BlinkingStatus. The second enumeration type defines possible error codes; see Listing 9-12.

In general, a communication frame can contain multiple errors simultaneously. Namely, it can contain incorrect start, stop, or check sum bytes. To report all of them, the ErrorCode enumeration is decorated by the Flags attribute. This attribute indicates that enumeration is treated as a bit field. Accordingly, you can set multiple flags using bitwise operators.

LISTING 9-11   Command identifiers

```
public enum CommandId : byte
{
    BlinkingFrequency = 0x01,
    BlinkingStatus = 0x02,
}
```

LISTING 9-12   Error codes definition. .

```
[Flags]
public enum ErrorCode : byte
{
    OK = 0x00,
    UnexpectedStartByte = 0x01,
    UnexpectedStopByte = 0x02,
    UnexpectedCheckSum = 0x04,
}
```

I implemented the communication protocol within the CommandHelper class; see the companion code in Chapter 09/SerialCommunication.Common/Helpers/CommandHelper.cs. The properties and fields of this class, which appear in Listing 9-13, determine the frame length, indices of particular frame elements, and values of the start and stop bytes according to the communication frame design from Figure 9-9. These values are defined in one place. So whenever you need to change one of them, you do so only once.

LISTING 9-13   Properties and fields of the CommandHelper class

```
public static byte FrameLength { get; } = 16;
public static byte CommandIdIndex { get; } = 1;
public static byte CommandDataBeginIndex { get; } = 2;

public static byte StartByte { get; } = 0xAA;
public static byte StopByte { get; } = 0xBB;

private static byte startByteIndex = 0;
private static int errorByteIndex = FrameLength - 3;
private static int checkSumIndex = FrameLength - 2;
private static int stopByteIndex = FrameLength - 1;
```

The defined values can be used to write helper methods for preparing the frame skeleton. According to Figure 9-9, the start and stop bytes are fixed, as are the command identifier and check sum.

CommandHelper implements three helper functions: PrepareCommandStructure, SetChecksum, and CalculateChecksum; see Listing 9-14.

LISTING 9-14 Command skeleton and checksum calculation

```
private static byte[] PrepareCommandStructure(CommandId commandId)
{
    var command = new byte[FrameLength];

    command[startByteIndex] = StartByte;
    command[CommandIdIndex] = (byte)commandId;
    command[stopByteIndex] = StopByte;

    return command;
}

private static void SetChecksum(byte[] command)
{
    command[checkSumIndex] = CalculateChecksum(command);
}

private static byte CalculateChecksum(byte[] command)
{
    long sum = 0;

    for (int i = 0; i < FrameLength; i++)
    {
        if (i != checkSumIndex)
        {
            sum += command[i];
        }
    }

    return (byte)(sum % byte.MaxValue);
}
```

The first method, PrepareCommandStructure, instantiates the 16-element byte array and then sets the value of its first (start byte), second (command id), and last (stop byte) elements. The start and stop byte values are taken from the StartByte and StopByte properties, respectively, while the command identifier is obtained from the argument of the PrepareCommandStructure method.

SetChecksum simply sets the value of the checksum byte using the result of the CalculateChecksum function. This function implements a simple algorithm, which sums up all values of every frame element except the one carrying a checksum. The resulting value is then divided by 255 (Byte.MaxValue), and the remainder is used as a checksum. This relatively simple calculation helps to detect any communication errors.

The CommandHelper class also implements a private member VerifyCommand; see Listing 9-15. You use this method later in the IoT app to verify the correctness of incoming commands—that is, to check whether the frame has the proper structure and expected checksum. Thus, the VerifyCommand method, after checking the frame length, compares the start, stop, and checksum bytes to the expected values. An incorrect value of the start byte does not automatically imply that the stop byte is invalid. Therefore, in Listing 9-15 I use a bitwise alternative to set multiple error codes.

LISTING 9-15 Command structure verification

```
public static ErrorCode VerifyCommand(byte[] command)
{
    Check.IsNull(command);
    Check.IsLengthEqualTo(command.Length, FrameLength);

    var errorCode = ErrorCode.OK;

    var actualChecksum = command[checkSumIndex];
    var expectedChecksum = CalculateChecksum(command);

    errorCode = VerifyCommandByte(actualChecksum, expectedChecksum,
        ErrorCode.UnexpectedCheckSum);

    errorCode = VerifyCommandByte(command[startByteIndex], StartByte,
        ErrorCode.UnexpectedStartByte | errorCode);

    errorCode = VerifyCommandByte(command[startByteIndex], StartByte,
        ErrorCode.UnexpectedStopByte | errorCode);

    return errorCode;
}

private static ErrorCode VerifyCommandByte(byte actualValue, byte expectedValue,
    ErrorCode errorToSet)
{
    var errorCode = ErrorCode.OK;

    if (actualValue != expectedValue)
    {
        errorCode = errorToSet;
    }

    return errorCode;
}
```

The preceding helper methods make implementation of the actual commands straightforward. You need two commands; definitions of the corresponding methods appear in Listing 9-16. As you see there, I first invoke the PrepareCommandStructure method and then set the command data. Finally, the checksum fills the appropriate command byte.

LISTING 9-16 Final methods implementing commands of the communication protocol

```
public static byte[] PrepareSetFrequencyCommand(double hzBlinkFrequency)
{
    // Prepare command
```

```
        var command = PrepareCommandStructure(CommandId.BlinkingFrequency);

        // Set command data
        var commandData = BitConverter.GetBytes(hzBlinkFrequency);
        Array.Copy(commandData, 0, command, CommandDataBeginIndex, commandData.Length);

        // ... and checksum
        SetChecksum(command);

        return command;
}

public static byte[] PrepareBlinkingStatusCommand(bool? isBlinking)
{
        // Prepare command
        var command = PrepareCommandStructure(CommandId.BlinkingStatus);

        // Set command data
        command[CommandDataBeginIndex] = Convert.ToByte(isBlinking);

        // ... and checksum
        SetChecksum(command);

        return command;
}
```

The particular command data depends on the request. For a BlinkingFrequency command, the frame is filled with eight bytes representing a double. I obtain those bytes using the GetBytes method of the BitConverter class.

In the case of a BlinkingStatus command, the actual data consists of a single byte with a logical value. Therefore, setting the command data does not require additional comments.

Note that the CommandHelper class is implemented similarly to classes representing sensors. In both cases, you need to appropriately prepare the client app and consume the IoT app byte arrays. Unlike with sensors, you have full freedom to define the communication protocol.

Headless IoT app

You can find the full code of SerialCommunication.Blinky in the companion code in Chapter 09/Serial-Communication.Blinky. To build this app, I used the Visual C# Background Application (IoT) project template and implemented the LedControl class, which is responsible for blinking the green ACT LED of the RPi2 by driving the corresponding GPIO pin. You need to update the ledPinNumber member of the LedControl class to the appropriate GPIO pin if you use the RPi3 with an external LED circuit.

Internally, LedControl uses the Timer class described in Chapter 3, "Windows IoT programming essentials." The timer executes the BlinkLed callback at specified time intervals; see Listing 9-17. These intervals, represented as instances of the TimeSpan class, determine LED blinking frequency. To configure the timer, convert the blinking frequency (given in Hz) to TimeSpan within the HertzToTimeSpan function. This function divides 1000 by the frequency to show the value in milliseconds. I pass this value to the `FromMilliseconds` static method of the `TimeSpan`. (Note that definitions of the `ConfigureGpioPin` and `BlinkLed` methods referenced in Listing 9-17 appear in Listing 9-12.)

LISTING 9-17 Timer configuration and execution

```
private const int hzDefaultBlinkFrequency = 5;
private double hzBlinkFrequency = hzDefaultBlinkFrequency;

private Timer timer;

private TimeSpan timeSpanZero = TimeSpan.FromMilliseconds(0);

public LedControl()
{
    ConfigureTimer();

    ConfigureGpioPin();

    Start();
}

private void ConfigureTimer()
{
    var timerCallback = new TimerCallback((arg) => { BlinkLed(); });

    timer = new Timer(timerCallback, null, Timeout.InfiniteTimeSpan,
        HertzToTimeSpan(hzBlinkFrequency));
}

private static TimeSpan HertzToTimeSpan(double hzFrequency)
{
    var msDelay = (int)Math.Floor(1000.0 / hzFrequency);

    return TimeSpan.FromMilliseconds(msDelay);
}

public void Start()
{
    timer.Change(timeSpanZero, HertzToTimeSpan(hzBlinkFrequency));
}

public void Stop()
{
    timer.Change(Timeout.InfiniteTimeSpan, timeSpanZero);
}
```

To control the ACT LED, I use the same methods described in Chapter 2, "Universal Windows Platform on devices," and Chapter 3. Namely, I first open and configure the GPIO drive mode pin; see the ConfigureGpioPin method in Listing 9-18. Subsequently, I invert the value of the GPIO pin associated with the green ACT LED; see the BlinkLed method from Listing 9-18.

LISTING 9-18 GPIO configuration and LED blinking

```csharp
private const int ledPinNumber = 47;
private GpioPin ledGpioPin;

private void ConfigureGpioPin()
{
    var gpioController = GpioController.GetDefault();

    if (gpioController != null)
    {
        ledGpioPin = gpioController.OpenPin(ledPinNumber);

        if (ledGpioPin != null)
        {
            ledGpioPin.SetDriveMode(GpioPinDriveMode.Output);
            ledGpioPin.Write(GpioPinValue.Low);
        }
    }
}

private void BlinkLed()
{
    GpioPinValue invertedGpioPinValue;

    var currentPinValue = ledGpioPin.Read();

    if (currentPinValue == GpioPinValue.High)
    {
        invertedGpioPinValue = GpioPinValue.Low;
    }
    else
    {
        invertedGpioPinValue = GpioPinValue.High;
    }

    ledGpioPin.Write(invertedGpioPinValue);
}
```

I implemented the LedControl class to explicitly separate the actual hardware control from SC. The LedControl class "hides" the implementation of the GPIO pin control from the other layer and exposes only several public members, which are used to control the blinking frequency and status (disabled/enabled). The LedControl class implements Start, Stop, SetFrequency, and Update methods. Listing 9-19 defines these members.

LISTING 9-19 Controlling LED blinking status and frequency

```csharp
public static double MinFrequency { get; } = 1;
public static double MaxFrequency { get; } = 50;

public static bool IsValidFrequency(double hzFrequency)
```

```
{
    return hzFrequency >= MinFrequency && hzFrequency <= MaxFrequency;
}

public void SetFrequency(double hzBlinkFrequency)
{
    if (IsValidFrequency(hzBlinkFrequency))
    {
        this.hzBlinkFrequency = hzBlinkFrequency;

        timer.Change(timeSpanZero, HertzToTimeSpan(hzBlinkFrequency));
    }
}

public void Update(bool isBlinkingActive)
{
    if(isBlinkingActive)
    {
        Start();
    }
    else
    {
        Stop();
    }
}

public void Start()
{
    timer.Change(timeSpanZero, HertzToTimeSpan(hzBlinkFrequency));
}

public void Stop()
{
    timer.Change(Timeout.InfiniteTimeSpan, timeSpanZero);
}
```

SetFrequency simply invokes the Change method of the Timer class instance in order to update the time intervals at which the BlinkLed function is invoked—to change the LED blinking frequency. I use the additional static method IsValidFrequency to validate the frequency value passed to the SetFrequency method. Doing so ensures that the user cannot set the frequency below minimum or above maximum levels. I define these levels by using two read-only public properties: MinFrequency and MaxFrequency.

The Update method, depending on its argument value, either starts (isBlinkingActive is true) or stops (isBlinkingActive is false) the timer. To this end, the Update method invokes the Start and Stop functions, both of which are based on the Change instance function of the Timer class. They also configure the dueTime parameter of the Timer; see Chapter 3.

After implementing the LedControl class, I supplement the SerialCommunicationHelper class by two static methods, which you see in Listing 9-20. The first, WriteBytes, transmits the byte array over the serial port. I use the analogous techniques described earlier in the section "Writing and reading data." However, because DataWriter is instantiated every time, I need to detach the underlying output stream of the serial port after transmitting data. I do so by using the DetachStream method of the DataWriter class instance.

LISTING 9-20 Helper methods for writing and reading byte arrays to and from the serial port

```
public static async Task<uint> WriteBytes(SerialDevice serialDevice, byte[] commandToWrite)
{
    Check.IsNull(serialDevice);
    Check.IsNull(commandToWrite);

    uint bytesWritten = 0;

    using (var dataWriter = new DataWriter(serialDevice.OutputStream))
    {
        dataWriter.WriteBytes(commandToWrite);
        bytesWritten = await dataWriter.StoreAsync();

        dataWriter.DetachStream();
    }

    return bytesWritten;
}

public static async Task<byte[]> ReadBytes(SerialDevice serialDevice)
{
    Check.IsNull(serialDevice);

    byte[] dataReceived = null;

    using (var dataReader = new DataReader(serialDevice.InputStream))
    {
        await dataReader.LoadAsync(CommandHelper.FrameLength);

        dataReceived = new byte[dataReader.UnconsumedBufferLength];

        dataReader.ReadBytes(dataReceived);

        dataReader.DetachStream();
    }

    return dataReceived;
}
```

I implement the second method from Listing 9-20, ReadBytes, in a similar way with the one exception of using DataReader instead of DataWriter. Note that in Listing 9-20 I refer to the static property FrameLength of the CommandHelper class. Thus, an IoT app always expects a byte array of constant length; that is, the ReadByte method always tries to read 16 bytes.

Reading data received through the serial port is a bit tricky, because you need to know the exact frame length. You find two common solutions to this problem. In the first, used here, the communication protocol specifies that each byte frame transferred between devices has a fixed length. In the second, every message transferred contains a header of the known length. This header carries the value, specifying the length of the rest of the data frame being transferred. The client application first reads the header and then the rest of the message.

Next, I extend the default StartupTask class so it can handle requests of the client apps. To that end I write the SetupCommunication method in Listing 9-21 to be invoked within the Run method of the StartupTask. SetupCommunication first configures the serial port and then runs the additional task, which listens for incoming commands. As Listing 9-22 shows, this CommunicationListener method reads the byte array from the serial port, parses it according to the predefined communication protocol, and updates the LED blinking status.

LISTING 9-21 An entry point of the headless app instantiates the LedControl class and, after configuring the serial port, listens for incoming data

```
private BackgroundTaskDeferral taskDeferral;
private LedControl ledControl;
private SerialDevice serialDevice;

public async void Run(IBackgroundTaskInstance taskInstance)
{
    taskDeferral = taskInstance.GetDeferral();

    ledControl = new LedControl();

    await SetupCommunication();
}

private async Task SetupCommunication()
{
    serialDevice = await SerialCommunicationHelper.GetFirstDeviceAvailable();

    SerialCommunicationHelper.SetDefaultConfiguration(serialDevice);

    new Task(CommunicationListener).Start();
}
```

LISTING 9-22 Incoming requests are read using the ReadBytes method of the SerialCommunicationHelper

```
private async void CommunicationListener()
{
    while (true)
    {
        var commandReceived = await SerialCommunicationHelper.ReadBytes(serialDevice);

        try
        {
```

```
            ParseCommand(commandReceived);
        }
        catch (Exception ex)
        {
            DiagnosticInfo.Display(null, ex.Message);
        }
    }
}
```

The ParseCommand definition (see Listing 9-23) relies on the communication protocol. After validating the received command, ParseCommand checks the request identifier and subsequently sets the frequency or updates the status of LED blinking. To this end, I use the previously developed methods of the LedControl class. Explicitly separating areas of concern keeps the definition of the ParseCommand clear and easy to read.

LISTING 9-23 Incoming requests are interpreted in order to update blinking frequency and status

```
private void ParseCommand(byte[] command)
{
    var errorCode = CommandHelper.VerifyCommand(command);

    if (errorCode == ErrorCode.OK)
    {
        var commandId = (CommandId)command[CommandHelper.CommandIdIndex];

        switch (commandId)
        {
            case CommandId.BlinkingFrequency:
                HandleBlinkingFrequencyCommand(command);
                break;

            case CommandId.BlinkingStatus:
                HandleBlinkingStatusCommand(command);
                break;
        }
    }
}

private void HandleBlinkingFrequencyCommand(byte[] command)
{
    var frequency = BitConverter.ToDouble(command, CommandHelper.CommandDataBeginIndex);

    ledControl.SetFrequency(frequency);
}

private void HandleBlinkingStatusCommand(byte[] command)
{
    var isLedBlinking = Convert.ToBoolean(command[CommandHelper.CommandDataBeginIndex]);

    ledControl.Update(isLedBlinking);
}
```

You can now deploy SerialCommunication.Blinky to your IoT device. To choose which of the solution projects to deploy or execute, use the Startup Projects drop-down list of Visual Studio. (See Figure 9-10.) After you deploy and run your app, you'll quickly see that the green ACT LED (or external LED) blinks at the default frequency, that is, 5 Hz.

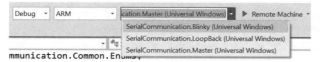

```
mmunication.Common.En
```

FIGURE 9-10 Selecting the startup project.

Headed client app

The headed client app will remotely control an IoT device from your development PC. Find the related source code under the following folder of the companion code: Chapter 09/SerialCommunication.Master. Building this app moves quickly because I implemented most of the underlying functionality within the Class Library project SerialCommunication.Common.

I first declare the UI, as you see in Figure 9-11. This UI has a drop-down list that allows you to choose the serial device. Click the **Connect** button to associate the connection. After you connect to the device, you can use the slider and the check box to update the blinking frequency. Confirm your selections by clicking the Send button. This sends the appropriate frames to the IoT device and displays them in the list box. Every time the frame successfully transmits, the IoT device responds by updating the status of its green LED.

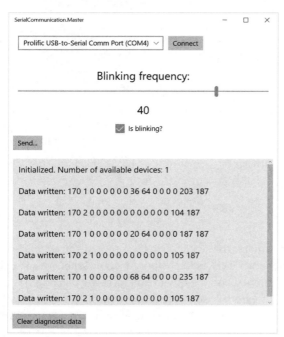

FIGURE 9-11 Main headed app used to remotely control an IoT device. A list box presents raw byte arrays transmitted to the IoT device.

The default event handler of the Connect button appears in Listing 9-24. This method uses already known techniques and methods of the `SerialCommunicationHelper` class. The only new element is that I close the active connection before associating the new one. You close the connection by disposing of an instance of the `SerialDevice` class; see the `CloseConnection` method from Listing 9-24.

LISTING 9-24 An event handler of the Connect button

```
private async void ButtonConnect_Click(object sender, RoutedEventArgs e)
{
    try
    {
        await SetupConnection();
    }
    catch(Exception ex)
    {
        DiagnosticInfo.Display(diagnosticData, ex.Message);
    }
}

private async Task SetupConnection()
{
    // Close any previous connections before associating the new one
    CloseConnection();

    serialDevice = await SerialDevice.FromIdAsync(serialDeviceId);

    if (serialDevice != null)
    {
        // Configure connection
        SerialCommunicationHelper.SetDefaultConfiguration(serialDevice);
    }
}

private void CloseConnection()
{
    if (serialDevice != null)
    {
        serialDevice.Dispose();
        serialDevice = null;
    }
}
```

The SerialCommunication.Master app also requires that you define the Send button event handler, which you see in Listing 9-25. This event handler invokes the helper function `SendCommand` twice. Here, I'm sending two frames: One sets the frequency, and the other configures the blinking status. Of course, I could use only one frame; however, I intentionally separate those requests to have at least two different commands in the communication protocol. Listing 9-26 shows a definition of `CommandToString`.

LISTING 9-25 Sending control commands to the IoT device (both commands are sent sequentially)

```csharp
private async void ButtonSendData_Click(object sender, RoutedEventArgs e)
{
    await SendCommand(CommandId.BlinkingFrequency);
    await SendCommand(CommandId.BlinkingStatus);
}

private async Task SendCommand(CommandId commandId)
{
    if (serialDevice != null)
    {
        byte[] command = null;

        switch (commandId)
        {
            case CommandId.BlinkingFrequency:
                command = CommandHelper.PrepareSetFrequencyCommand(hzBlinkingFrequency);
                break;

            case CommandId.BlinkingStatus:
                command = CommandHelper.PrepareBlinkingStatusCommand(isLedBlinking);
                break;
        }

        await SerialCommunicationHelper.WriteBytes(serialDevice, command);
        DiagnosticInfo.Display(diagnosticData, "Data written: " + CommandHelper.
            CommandToString(command));
    }
    else
    {
        DiagnosticInfo.Display(diagnosticData, "No active connection");
    }
}
```

LISTING 9-26 A definition of the helper function CommandToString, which converts the communication frame to a string for debugging purposes

```csharp
public static string CommandToString(byte[] commandData)
{
    string commandString = string.Empty;

    if (commandData != null)
    {
        foreach (byte b in commandData)
        {
            commandString += " " + b;
        }
    }

    return commandString.Trim();
}
```

Bluetooth

Bluetooth (BT) is a wireless technology for transmitting data between devices using radio waves. BT communication is used in many modern sensors. A group of low energy BT-enabled sensors, which are very energy efficient, can monitor remote processes for several months on a single battery. Longevity like that makes BT and other wireless communication critical within the IoT world.

In this section I show you how to utilize BT communication in two UWP apps. The first, Bluetooth-Communication.Leds is a headless app deployed to the RPi2/RPi3 and controls the color of the LED array of the Sense HAT add-on board. Moreover, this headless app exposes the wireless radio frequency communication (RFCOMM) BT protocol, enabling other apps to remotely change the color of the LED array.

I also write the headed UWP app, BluetoothCommunication.Master, to run on the development PC. The UI of this app appears in Figure 9-12. Basically, it consists of three sliders for setting particular components of the color, which is transmitted to the IoT device. For this purpose, I extend the communication protocol developed in the previous section by one additional command. The first step is to configure hardware components and pair Bluetooth devices.

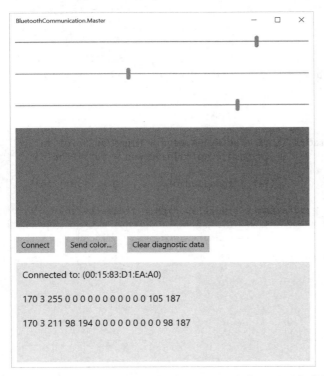

FIGURE 9-12   A UWP headed app for remote, wireless control of LED array color. Sliders compose the color, displayed in the rectangle. Color is then sent to the IoT device by clicking the Send Color button.

Setting up the connection

The Raspberry Pi 2 does not have an internal BT module. However, you can get an inexpensive USB BT adapter. I use the BT adapter built on the CSR8510 BT USB Host. (See Figure 9-13.) This module is easily available for about $12 at *https://www.adafruit.com/product/1327*. It does not require any special configuration or installation. You just plug it into one of the RPi2 USB ports. Then, after you navigate to the Bluetooth tab of the Device Portal, you will see the available devices list of nearby BT devices. (See Figure 9-14.)

FIGURE 9-13   Bluetooth 4.0 CSR USB module. Courtesy of *www.adafruit.com*.

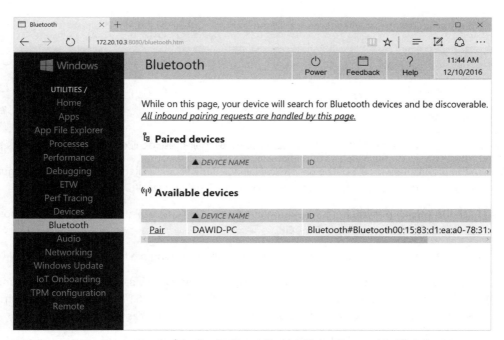

FIGURE 9-14   The Bluetooth tab of the Device Portal displays all the discoverable BT devices.

If you do not see your development PC on the list of nearby BT devices, you need to ensure that your PC is discoverable. You can do this as follows:

1. Open Settings Trusted Store App.

2. Navigate to Devices/Bluetooth, and then click the **More Bluetooth Options** link. A Bluetooth Settings window opens.

3. In the Bluetooth Settings window (see Figure 9-15), ensure that **Allow Bluetooth Devices to Find This PC** is checked. You might want to also choose **Alert Me When a New Bluetooth Device Wants to Connect**.

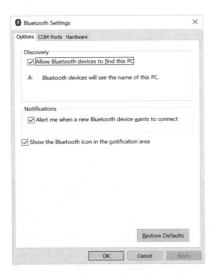

FIGURE 9-15   Bluetooth settings allow you to make your PC discoverable.

After ensuring that your RPi2/RPi3 recognizes your PC BT, pair those devices by following these steps:

1. In the Bluetooth window of the Device Portal, go to the list of available devices (refer to Figure 9-14), and then find your IoT device. Here, I pair my RPi2 with DAWID-PC.

2. Click the **Pair Hyperlink** button next to your device. Device Portal displays a pop-up window asking you to confirm pairing. Click **OK**.

3. Device Portal displays another pop-up window with the pairing pin number. Click OK.

4. The action center of your development PC displays the Add a Device notification. Click it, and the Compare Passcodes pop-up window appears. (See Figure 9-16.) This pop-up window should display the same pin number as the Device Portal. If so, click the **Yes** button.

5. Your devices pair, and your development PC appears on the list of paired devices of the Device Portal as shown in Figure 9-17.

FIGURE 9-16 A Compare the passcodes pop-up window appears on your development PC during pairing.

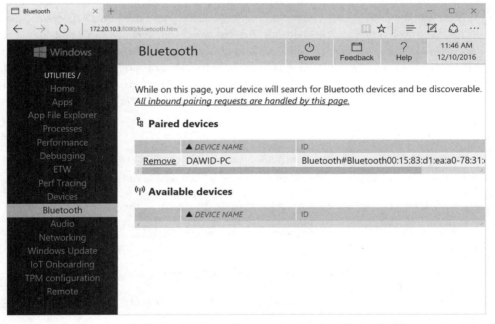

FIGURE 9-17 The name of your development PC appears in the Paired devices list after a successful pairing procedure. Compare with Figure 9-14.

Bluetooth bonding and pairing

When you pair Bluetooth devices, a bond between the two is established. So, devices can reconnect automatically when they are again placed within the communication range. Pairing is also used to secure the connection. Specifically, the PIN number is used to generate cryptographic secrets, encrypting data sent through the BT interface.

Project architecture and Bluetooth device enumeration

The project architecture relies on the same structure and communication protocol developed in previous sections; see projects in the companion code in Chapter 09/BluetoothCommunication. As there, I have three projects:

- A headless IoT app, BluetoothCommunication.Leds

- A headed UWP app named BluetoothCommunication.Master

- The Class Library implementing shared functionality, BluetoothCommunication.Common

Both BluetoothCommunication.Leds and BluetoothCommunication.Master reference Bluetooth-Communication.Common. In addition, BluetoothCommunication.Leds references the Windows IoT Extensions for the UWP.

Start with the Class Library. This project implements the single static class BluetoothCommunication-Helper, containing three public methods. The first two, FindPairedDevices and GetFirstPaired-DeviceAvailable, appear in Listing 9-27. They are analogous to FindSerialDevices and GetFirst-DeviceAvailable of the SerialCommunicationHelper. The only difference is that instead of Serial-Device I use the BluetoothDevice class. Moreover, in the FindPairedDevices method I use the AQS selector specific for paired BT devices by using the static GetDeviceSelector method of the Bluetooth-Device class.

LISTING 9-27 Bluetooth devices' enumeration proceeds analogously as in the case of serial ports.

```
public static async Task<DeviceInformationCollection> FindPairedDevices()
{
    var defaultSelector = BluetoothDevice.GetDeviceSelector();

    return await DeviceInformation.FindAllAsync(defaultSelector);
}

public static async Task<BluetoothDevice> GetFirstPairedDeviceAvailable()
{
    var serialDeviceCollection = await FindPairedDevices();

    var serialDeviceInformation = serialDeviceCollection.FirstOrDefault();

    if (serialDeviceInformation != null)
    {
        return await BluetoothDevice.FromIdAsync(serialDeviceInformation.Id);
    }
    else
    {
        return null;
    }
}
```

I next implement the Connect method, which associates the connection with the selected BT device, represented as an instance of the BluetoothDevice class. According to Listing 9-28, the Connect method gets the first available RFCOMM service exposed by the BT device and then connects to that service using the ConnectAsync method of the StreamSocket class. The StreamSocket class is used for network communication based on the stream socket over TCP and BT RFCOMM protocols. Connecting to the socket enables you to transfer data among devices just as with SC. To that end, you use the InputStream and OutputStream properties of the StreamSocket class instance. Everything then proceeds just as in the previous example. Namely, to read and write data you use the static ReadBytes and WriteBytes methods of the SerialCommunicationHelper class. But before transmitting data, you need to extend the communication protocol by an additional command.

LISTING 9-28 Connecting to the RFCOMM

```
public static async Task<StreamSocket> Connect(BluetoothDevice bluetoothDevice)
{
    Check.IsNull(bluetoothDevice);

    var rfcommService = bluetoothDevice.RfcommServices.FirstOrDefault();

    if (rfcommService != null)
    {
        return await ConnectToStreamSocket(bluetoothDevice, rfcommService.
            ConnectionServiceName);
    }
    else
    {
        throw new Exception(
            "Selected bluetooth device does not advertise any RFCOMM service");
    }
}

private async static Task<StreamSocket> ConnectToStreamSocket(
    BluetoothDevice bluetoothDevice,
    string connectionServiceName)
{
    try
    {
        var streamSocket = new StreamSocket();

        await streamSocket.ConnectAsync(bluetoothDevice.HostName, connectionServiceName);

        return streamSocket;
    }
    catch (Exception)
    {
        throw new Exception(
            "Connection cannot be established. Verify that device is paired");
    }
}
```

LED color command

In order to set the LED array color remotely, send the RGB components to the remote device. The data part of the communication protocol defined in the section "Controlling an IoT device remotely" contains three bytes, each carrying the value of a color channel. As Listing 9-29 shows, the method `PrepareLedColorCommand` fills the data part of the command using the RGB properties of the `Color` class instance. I also use an additional value `LedColor` of the `CommandId` enumeration.

LISTING 9-29   Command data carries RGB color components

```
public static byte[] PrepareLedColorCommand(Color color)
{
    // Prepare command
    var command = PrepareCommandStructure(CommandId.LedColor);

    // Set command data
    command[CommandDataBeginIndex] = color.R;
    command[CommandDataBeginIndex + 1] = color.G;
    command[CommandDataBeginIndex + 2] = color.B;

    // ... and checksum
    SetChecksum(command);

    return command;
}
```

LedArray class adopted to Windows Runtime requirements

I used the BT communication grounds laid in the previous sections to construct the headless IoT app, which enables the remote control of the LED array of the Sense HAT add-on board. Find sources in the companion code at Chapter 09/BluetoothCommunication/BluetoothCommunication.Leds. This app has a structure similar to that of SerialCommunication.Blinky. Namely, the Run method of the StartupTask initializes the LedArray class and then starts the RFCOMM service; see Listing 9-30.

LISTING 9-30   An entry point of BluetoothCommunication.Leds

```
public async void Run(IBackgroundTaskInstance taskInstance)
{
    taskDeferral = taskInstance.GetDeferral();

    InitializeLedArray();

    await StartRfcommService();
}
```

The LedArray initialization does not require special comments because I've covered it in earlier listings. However, the original version of the LedArray class and the I2cHelper used for communication with the Sense HAT add-on board were adjusted to the requirements of the Windows Runtime (WinRT) components. This is the basis of the IoT Background Application project template. I modified the following elements of the LedArray class:

- The declaration of the Buffer member was changed from a property to a private field. WinRT components cannot export multi-dimensional public arrays. An attempt to do so generates the compilation error WME1035.

- The namespace was changed to BluetoothCommunication.Leds.SenseHatLedArray. WinRT components require that exported classes are declared within the namespace, whose name is implied by the file name. If you do not satisfy this requirement, the compilation error WME1044 will be reported.

- The definition of the LedArray class was supplemented by the sealed keyword, so this type cannot be inherited. Exporting unsealed classes is not supported by the WinRT components (compilation error: WME1086).

- WinRT components also require you to explicitly set array arguments as read- or write-only (compilation error: WME1106). To that end you use either [ReadOnlyArray] or [WriteOnly-Array] attributes. In declaring the DrawHistogram method, I used the [ReadOnlyArray] attribute; see Listing 9-31.

LISTING 9-31 Array arguments of the WinRT component can be either readable or writeable

```
public void DrawHistogram([ReadOnlyArray] double[] histogram, double minValue,
    double maxValue)
```

- I introduced similar changes in the I2cHelper class. I first modified the namespace and then changed the declaration of the GetI2cDevice such that it uses IAsyncOperation<I2cDevice> rather than async Task<I2cDevice>; see Listing 9-32. You do this because you cannot export public members from the WinRT components. Instead, your declarations should use one of the following interfaces, defined in the Windows.Foundation namespace:

  - IAsyncAction

  - IAsyncActionWithProgress<TProgress>

  - IAsyncOperation<TResult>

  - IAsyncOperationWithProgress<TResult, TProgress>

In terms of dependent code, this change is insignificant, because the standard .NET await pattern also applies for WinRT asynchronous interfaces.

LISTING 9-32 Public methods of the WinRT components cannot use the Task<T> asynchronous API

```
using System;
using System.Linq;
using System.Threading.Tasks;
```

```
using Windows.Devices.Enumeration;
using Windows.Devices.I2c;
using Windows.Foundation;

namespace BluetoothCommunication.Leds.Helpers
{
    public static class I2cHelper
    {
        public static IAsyncOperation<I2cDevice> GetI2cDevice(byte address)
        {
            return GetI2cDeviceHelper(address).AsAsyncOperation();
        }

        private static async Task<I2cDevice> GetI2cDeviceHelper(byte address)
        {
            I2cDevice device = null;

            var settings = new I2cConnectionSettings(address);

            string deviceSelectorString = I2cDevice.GetDeviceSelector();

            var matchedDevicesList = await DeviceInformation.FindAllAsync(
                deviceSelector-String);
            if (matchedDevicesList.Count > 0)
            {
                var deviceInformation = matchedDevicesList.First();

                device = await I2cDevice.FromIdAsync(deviceInformation.Id, settings);
            }

            return device;
        }
    }
}
```

Listing 9-33 shows you how to start the BT RFCOMM device service and handle requests incoming from remote clients. To start the RFCOMM service, you need two ingredients: RfcommServiceProvider and StreamSocketListener. The first class creates the BT service, detectable by client devices. The second, StreamSocketListener, handles actual socket communication. To relate RfcommService-Provider with the particular StreamSocketListener, use the BindServiceNameAsync method of the StreamSocketListener class.

LISTING 9-33 Starting BT RFCOMM service advertisement and binding that service to the StreamSocketListener

```
private RfcommServiceProvider rfcommProvider;
private StreamSocketListener;

private async Task StartRfcommService()
{
    var serviceGuid = Guid.Parse("34B1CF4D-1069-4AD6-89B6-E161D79BE4D8");
```

```
        var serviceId = RfcommServiceId.FromUuid(serviceGuid);

        rfcommProvider = await RfcommServiceProvider.CreateAsync(serviceId);

        streamSocketListener = new StreamSocketListener();
        streamSocketListener.ConnectionReceived += StreamSocketListener_ConnectionReceived;

        try
        {
            await streamSocketListener.BindServiceNameAsync(
                rfcommProvider.ServiceId.AsString(),
                SocketProtectionLevel.BluetoothEncryptionAllowNullAuthentication);

            rfcommProvider.StartAdvertising(streamSocketListener);

            DiagnosticInfo.Display(null, "RFCOMM service started. Waiting for clients...");
        }
        catch (Exception ex)
        {
            DiagnosticInfo.Display(null, ex.Message);
        }
}
```

When a remote client connects to your RFCOMM service, the instance of an associated Stream-SocketListener class raises the ConnectionReceived event. You use that event to obtain an instance of the StreamSocket. Given that instance, you can perform the actual communication between your device and a remote device. You can also implement additional logic to handle a ConnectionReceived event. Here, I'm using such an event handler to start the worker thread, which apart from storing the reference to the StreamSocket class, handles all incoming requests; see Listing 9-34.

LISTING 9-34 The ConnectionReceived event handler obtains a reference to the StreamSocket class and starts the worker thread, consuming incoming requests

```
private bool isCommunicationListenerStarted = false;

private void StreamSocketListener_ConnectionReceived(StreamSocketListener sender,
    StreamSocketListenerConnectionReceivedEventArgs args)
{
    DiagnosticInfo.Display(null, "Client has been connected");

    streamSocket = args.Socket;

    StartCommunicationListener();
}

private void StartCommunicationListener()
{
    if (!isCommunicationListenerStarted)
    {
        new Task(CommunicationListener).Start();
```

```
            isCommunicationListenerStarted = true;
    }
}

private async void CommunicationListener()
{
    const int msSleepTime = 50;

    while(true)
    {
        var commandReceived = await SerialCommunicationHelper.ReadBytes(
            streamSocket.InputStream);

        try
        {
            if (commandReceived.Length > 0)
            {
                ParseCommand(commandReceived);
            }
        }
        catch (Exception ex)
        {
            DiagnosticInfo.Display(null, ex.Message);
        }

        Task.Delay(msSleepTime).Wait();
    }
}
```

As Listing 9-35 shows, the incoming requests are parsed similarly to the wired SC. Namely, I first verify the command structure and then check the command identifier. If it is equal to CommandId.LedColor, I read the color components from the command data and then update the LED array color using the Reset method of the LedArray class instance; see HandleLedColorCommand from Listing 9-35.

LISTING 9-35 LedColor command parsing

```
private void ParseCommand(byte[] command)
{
    var errorCode = CommandHelper.VerifyCommand(command);

    if (errorCode == ErrorCode.OK)
    {
        var commandId = (CommandId)command[CommandHelper.CommandIdIndex];

        switch (commandId)
        {
            case CommandId.LedColor:
                HandleLedColorCommand(command);
                break;
        }
```

```
        }
    }

    private void HandleLedColorCommand(byte[] command)
    {
        var redChannel = command[CommandHelper.CommandDataBeginIndex];
        var greenChannel = command[CommandHelper.CommandDataBeginIndex + 1];
        var blueChannel = command[CommandHelper.CommandDataBeginIndex + 2];

        var color = Color.FromArgb(0, redChannel, greenChannel, blueChannel);

        if (ledArray != null)
        {
            ledArray.Reset(color);
        }

        DiagnosticInfo.Display(null, color.ToString() + " " + redChannel
            + " " + greenChannel + " " + blueChannel);
    }
```

The headless IoT app is almost exactly the same as in the previous example. The main difference is that you use different procedures for initiating the communication. Transferring data between devices is the same. It is also important to note that BT communication shares socket communication procedures with the TCP protocol. So, if you want to transfer data using sockets and TCP, perform exactly the same steps.

The last element declares Bluetooth capability. Supplement the Capabilities section of the Package.appxmanifest according to Listing 9-36.

LISTING 9-36   Bluetooth device capability

```
<Capabilities>
  <Capability Name="internetClient" />
  <Capabilities>
    <Capability Name="internetClient" />
    <DeviceCapability Name="bluetooth" />
  </Capabilities>
</Capabilities>
```

Headed client app

The headed client app controls the IoT device remotely; see the companion code in Chapter 09/BluetoothCommunication/BluetoothCommunication.Master. As you saw in Figure 9-12, the view of this app has three sliders—used to configure the RGB channels of the color, which are sent to the IoT device. You can preview the color in the rectangular panel. The sliders and the rectangle are bound to the code-behind through the helper class SenseHatColor; see Listing 9-37. I used the additional object because the UWP does not support multi-binding, which is required here. Eventually you could use binding with methods.

LISTING 9-37 A definition of the helper class used for data binding

```csharp
public class SenseHatColor {

    public SolidColorBrush Brush { get; private set; }

    public double R
    {
        get { return colorComponents[0]; }
        set { UpdateColorComponent(0, Convert.ToByte(value)); }
    }

    public double G
    {
        get { return colorComponents[1]; }
        set { UpdateColorComponent(1, Convert.ToByte(value)); }
    }

    public double B
    {
        get { return colorComponents[2]; }
        set { UpdateColorComponent(2, Convert.ToByte(value)); }
    }

    private byte[] colorComponents;

    private void UpdateColorComponent(int index, byte value)
    {
        colorComponents[index] = value;
        UpdateBrush();
    }

    private void UpdateBrush()
    {
        Brush.Color = Color.FromArgb(255, colorComponents[0],
            colorComponents[1], colorComponents[2]);
    }

    public SenseHatColor()
    {
        var defaultColor = Colors.Black;

        colorComponents = new byte[]
        {
            defaultColor.R, defaultColor.G, defaultColor.B
        };

        Brush = new SolidColorBrush(defaultColor);
    }
}
```

Basically, SenseHatColor contains four properties: Brush, R, G, and B. The first, Brush, is bound to the Rectangle.Fill property; the R, G, and B properties are associated with corresponding sliders.

Whenever the user changes the slider position, the color channel value is updated. This value is then used to update the Brush property. To that end, I use the UpdateColorComponent private method. The rectangle fill reflects the color according to the mix of RGB components.

To send your selected color to the IoT device through BT, BluetoothCommunication.Master needs an active BT connection. Obtain a connection within the Click event handler of the Connect button. In this method, I associate the connection with the first available paired device. Here, I use the static GetFirstPairedDeviceAvailable and Connect methods of the BluetoothCommunication class; see Listing 9-38.

LISTING 9-38 Connecting to the paired Bluetooth device

```
private ObservableCollection<string> diagnosticData = new ObservableCollection<string>();
private StreamSocket streamSocket;

private async void ButtonConnect_Click(object sender, RoutedEventArgs e)
{
    try
    {
        var device = await BluetoothCommunicationHelper.GetFirstPairedDeviceAvailable();

        await CloseConnection();

        streamSocket = await BluetoothCommunicationHelper.Connect(device);

        DiagnosticInfo.Display(diagnosticData, "Connected to: " + device.HostName);
    }
    catch (Exception ex)
    {
        DiagnosticInfo.Display(diagnosticData, ex.Message);
    }
}

private async Task CloseConnection()
{
    if (streamSocket != null)
    {
        await streamSocket.CancelIOAsync();

        streamSocket.Dispose();
        streamSocket = null;
    }
}
```

After you connect to the remote device, the LedColor commands transfer information by using the Send button event handler; see Listing 9-39. The definition of that method is based on the blocks implemented previously. Namely, you first generate the byte array containing the RGB color channels by using the PrepareLedColorCommand of the CommandHelper class. Subsequently, you write the bytes to the OutputStream of the StreamSocket using the WriteBytes method of the SerialCommunication-Helper class.

LISTING 9-39 Sending the LedColor command to the IoT device using the Bluetooth RFCOMM protocol

```
private async void ButtonSendColor_Click(object sender, RoutedEventArgs e)
{
    if (streamSocket != null)
    {
        var commandData = CommandHelper.PrepareLedColorCommand(senseHatColor.Brush.Color);

        await SerialCommunicationHelper.WriteBytes(streamSocket.OutputStream, commandData);

        DiagnosticInfo.Display(diagnosticData, CommandHelper.
            CommandToString(commandData));
    }
    else
    {
        DiagnosticInfo.Display(diagnosticData, "No active connection");
    }
}
```

When you run the BluetoothCommunication.Master app and click the Connect button for the first time, Windows 10 will display a dialog box asking you to grant access to your RPi2/RPi3 device. (See Figure 9-18.) After confirming this access, you can use the sliders to generate any color you want. When you send that value to the IoT device, the LED array changes its color accordingly.

FIGURE 9-18 Accessing your Bluetooth device

Bluetooth communication based on the RFCOMM protocol works like the wired SC. Accordingly, you can easily implement both techniques based on the common, shared logic you find in this chapter. This shortens development time and helps you to expose the functionality of the IoT device using multiple network interfaces.

Wi-Fi

Wireless local area networks, commonly known as Wi-Fi, are widely used and can be easily adopted for IoT applications. In this section, I show you how to programmatically enumerate Wi-Fi adapters, scan Wi-Fi networks, and connect to and authenticate the selected Wi-Fi network. Subsequently, I connect a development PC and then an IoT device to the same local network. Given that connection, the headed UWP app running on the development PC will remotely control the IoT device.

The headed app will have the same UI as the BluetoothCommunication.Master and will let you change the color of the Sense HAT LED array. However, I'll use the Wi-Fi instead of Bluetooth as the communication medium. For testing Wi-Fi samples, I set up a personal hotspot named Dawid-WiFi with WPA2-Personal security using my smartphone.

Find the sources supporting this discussion in the following folder of the companion code: Chapter 09/WiFiCommunication. The Class Library project WiFiCommunication.Common implements the shared functionality. WiFiCommunication.Common utilizes the single static class WiFiCommunicationHelper, which in turn implements two public methods: ConnectToWiFiNetwork and ConnectToHost.

The first method connects to a network of a given service set identifier (SSID) using the provided passphrase. The SSID and the network password are obtained from the ConnectToWiFiNetwork arguments; see Listing 9-40.

LISTING 9-40 Connecting to a Wi-Fi network

```
public const string DefaultSsid = "Dawid-WiFi";
public const string DefaultPassword = "P@ssw0rD";

public static async Task<WiFiConnectionStatus> ConnectToWiFiNetwork(
    string ssid = DefaultSsid, string password = DefaultPassword)
{
    var connectionStatus = WiFiConnectionStatus.NetworkNotAvailable;

    // Verify SSID, and password
    if (!string.IsNullOrEmpty(ssid) && !string.IsNullOrEmpty(password))
    {
        // Verify that app has an access to WiFi functionality
        var hasAccess = await WiFiAdapter.RequestAccessAsync();

        // If so, scan available networks using the first WiFi adapter
        if (hasAccess == WiFiAccessStatus.Allowed)
        {
            // Get first WiFi adapter available
            var wiFiAdapters = await WiFiAdapter.FindAllAdaptersAsync();
            var firstWiFiAdapterAvailable = wiFiAdapters.FirstOrDefault();

            if (firstWiFiAdapterAvailable != null)
            {
                // Scan networks
                await firstWiFiAdapterAvailable.ScanAsync();

                // Filter the list of available networks by the SSID,
                var wiFiNetwork = firstWiFiAdapterAvailable.NetworkReport.
                    AvailableNetworks.Where(network => network.Ssid == ssid).FirstOrDefault();

                if (wiFiNetwork != null)
                {
                    // Try to connect to network using password provided
                    var passwordCredential = new PasswordCredential()
                    {
```

```
                    Password = password
            };

            var connectionResult = await firstWiFiAdapterAvailable.
                ConnectAsync(wiFiNetwork,
                WiFiReconnectionKind.Automatic, passwordCredential);

            // Return connection status
            connectionStatus = connectionResult.ConnectionStatus;
        }
      }
    }
  }

  return connectionStatus;
}
```

To connect to the Wi-Fi network, your app needs access to the Wi-Fi adapter, which in the UWP is represented by the WiFiAdapter class. The members of this class allow you to enumerate the local Wi-Fi adapters, scan available networks, and connect to the selected network.

First, invoke the FindAllAdaptersAsync method to get the list of Wi-Fi adapters. In this example, I get the first available adapter. Next, I initiate the network scan using the ScanAsync method. Obtain the results of that scan through the NetworkReport property of the WiFiAdapter class. NetworkReport is of type WiFiNetworkReport and includes the Timestamp property containing the date and time when the network scan operation ended and the AvailableNetworks property, which is the list of available networks. In Listing 9-40, I filter that list by the SSID to find the selected network, represented as an instance of the WiFiNetwork class. I obtain a reference to that class and then connect to the network using the ConnectAsync method of the WiFiAdapter class.

The ConnectAsync method lets you specify the network key. You pass that value through the Password property of the PasswordCredential class instance. You can also configure an automatic network reconnection by using the reconnectionKind argument of the ConnectAsync method. This argument can have one of the values defined in the WiFiReconnectionKind enumeration: Automatic or Manual. The first specifies that the OS will automatically reconnect, while the second allows the user to manually reconnect to the Wi-Fi network. Here, I use an automatic reconnection. The SSID and passwords are defined by DefaultSsid and DefaultPassword, which are constant members of the WiFiCommunicationHelper class.

After associating the Wi-Fi connection, you can connect to any host in that network. To this end, in WiFiCommunicationHelper, I implemented the ConnectToHost static method. As you see in Listing 9-41, the ConnectToHost method instantiates the StreamSocket class and then invokes the Stream-Socket.ConnectAsync method. Remote service connection looks much like Bluetooth communication, but now you explicitly specify the remote host name and the port number. The host name is the string containing either the host network name or its IP address.

LISTING 9-41 Connecting to a remote host

```
public const string Rpi2HostName = "Dawid-RPi2";
public const int DefaultPort = 9090;

public static async Task<StreamSocket> ConnectToHost(string hostName = Rpi2HostName,
    int port = DefaultPort)
{
    var socket = new StreamSocket();

    await socket.ConnectAsync(new HostName(hostName), port.ToString());

    return socket;
}
```

Proceed as you did in the previous section and prepare the headless app such that it will listen for incoming connections over the TCP protocol; see the companion code in Chapter 09/WiFiCommunication/WiFiCommunication.Leds. As before, you need to create an instance of the `StreamSocketListener` class and then bind it to the selected TCP port; see Listing 9-42.

LISTING 9-42 Initiating StreamSocketListener, bound to the selected TCP port

```
private StreamSocketListener;

private async void StartTcpService()
{
    var connectionStatus = await WiFiCommunicationHelper.ConnectToWiFiNetwork();

    if (connectionStatus == WiFiConnectionStatus.Success)
    {
        streamSocketListener = new StreamSocketListener();

        await streamSocketListener.BindServiceNameAsync(
            WiFiCommunicationHelper.DefaultPort.ToString());

        streamSocketListener.ConnectionReceived +=
            StreamSocketListener_ConnectionReceived;
    }
    else
    {
        DiagnosticInfo.Display(null, "WiFi connection failed: "
            + connectionStatus.ToString());
    }
}
```

To access the hardware Wi-Fi adapters and create network servers, your app requires a `wiFiControl` device and `internetClientServer` capabilities. You configure them in Package.appxmanifest, as shown in Listing 9-43. All other elements of the headless IoT app stay unchanged with respect to BluetoothCommunication.Leds.

LISTING 9-43 Capabilities of the WiFiCommunication.Leds project

```
<Capabilities>
  <Capability Name="internetClient" />
  <Capability Name="internetClientServer" />
  <DeviceCapability Name="wifiControl" />
</Capabilities>
```

In the client app, the only thing you need is to use the helper methods of the WiFiCommunication-Helper within the default event handler of the Connect button; see Listing 9-44 and the companion code in Chapter 09/WiFiCommunication /WiFiCommunication.Master. Again, all other aspects of the headed app are the same as in the previous section about Bluetooth.

LISTING 9-44 Connecting to a remote client using a Wi-Fi network

```
private async void ButtonConnect_Click(object sender, RoutedEventArgs e)
{
    try
    {
        await CloseStreamSocket();

        var connectionStatus = await WiFiCommunicationHelper.ConnectToWiFiNetwork();

        if (connectionStatus == WiFiConnectionStatus.Success)
        {
            streamSocket = await WiFiCommunicationHelper.ConnectToHost();

            DiagnosticInfo.Display(diagnosticData, "Connected to: " +
                WiFiCommunicationHelper.Rpi2HostName);
        }
    }
    catch (Exception ex)
    {
        DiagnosticInfo.Display(diagnosticData, ex.Message);
    }
}

private async Task CloseStreamSocket()
{
    if (streamSocket != null)
    {
        await streamSocket.CancelIOAsync();

        streamSocket.Dispose();
        streamSocket = null;
    }
}
```

When you deploy and run WiFiCommunication.Leds in your IoT device, it will start a web server waiting for incoming requests. You send those requests using the WiFiCommunication.Master app. As before, you use the sliders to set the color, which can be sent to update the LED array of the Sense HAT add-on board remotely.

To summarize, the UWP offers a very convenient interface for implementing wireless communication. You use the same procedures to handle various wireless communication protocols. The only difference is that each wireless connection requires specific routines to enumerate adapters and to connect to the particular network or service. However, the actual process of transferring data is exactly the same.

AllJoyn

All the previous examples used a custom communication protocol. Such an approach is completely fine when you need custom solutions. However, when you build a communication system that includes various sensors or devices, you typically want to utilize a unified, standardized communication protocol so that you can freely extend your IoT network by new devices. Several projects provide such universal communication protocols, for example, AllJoyn, IoTivity, and Open Interconnect Consortium. Here, I describe AllJoyn, because it is natively supported by the UWP.

The AllJoyn framework (*https://bit.ly/all_joyn*) enables interoperability among connected devices by providing a core set of services and communication protocols based on a D-Bus message bus (*https://bit.ly/d-bus*). D-Bus was originally developed as an inter-process communication protocol (IPC) and provided remote procedure call (RPC) mechanisms for Linux desktop environments. Its goal was to simplify the IPC and RPC mechanisms by introducing a single virtual channel, gathering all the communication among various processes and machines. (See Figure 9-19.) Since the IoT functions as a grid of interconnected devices that exchange data like system processes, the D-Bus approach works well for implementing universal IoT communication. D-Bus is transport agnostic, so it does not depend on the communication medium.

AllJoyn devices communicate in a producer-consumer model. Producers advertise their capabilities using predefined "introspection" XML files described in the next section. These files define methods, properties, and signals exposed by producers. Accordingly, based on the introspection XML files, client devices (consumers) know what kind of requests they can send to producers. This was not possible in the custom communication protocol we used in previous samples. The IoT background apps, acting as producers, were not advertising their capabilities. Client apps were supposed to know the communication protocol.

The D-Bus context is identified by the bus (or interface) name, which is the set of two or more dot-separated strings, for example, com.microsoft.iot. Each client in the D-Bus network context can be recognized by its unique connection name. To connect to the existing AllJoyn network and exchange data with devices, the simplest answer is to connect to the particular interface and then use methods, properties, or signals implemented by producers.

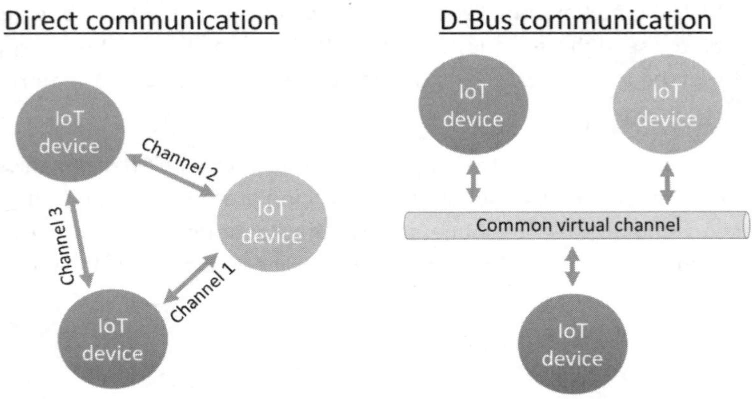

Direct communication   **D-Bus communication**

FIGURE 9-19 Comparison of direct and D-Bus communication. In direct communication, devices use one-to-one communication, so all of them communicate over dedicated channels. In contrast, D-Bus communication uses the common virtual channel, which every device writes to and reads messages from.

In the following sections, I guide you through the process of creating an introspection XML file and then generating the AllJoyn producer and consumer. Subsequently, I implement the headless IoT app, which will expose the remote functionality of drawing shapes on the LED array over the AllJoyn network. Next, I enumerate the AllJoyn devices using the IoT Explorer for the AllJoyn UWP app. Finally, I explain how to implement the AllJoyn consumer individually.

Introspection XML file

An introspection XML file (*https://bit.ly/d-bus-api*) has the root node tag, which contains a child `description` tag and one or more `interface` tags. Each `interface` tag defines the name, description, methods, properties, and signals implemented by the producer. Listing 9-45 shows the custom introspection XML file I defined for the AllJoyn producer and enables remote drawing of shapes on the Sense HAT LED array. This protocol has two methods: `DrawShape` and `TurnOff`. The first method accepts the single argument, which specifies the shape to be drawn, while `TurnOff` disables all LEDs. There is also one read-only property, `Shape`, which allows the consumer to read the value describing the currently displayed shape.

LISTING 9-45 Introspection XML file, defining a single interface com.iot.SenseHatLedArray

```
<node>
  <description>AllJoyn introspection XML for the Sense HAT LED array </description>

  <interface name="com.iot.SenseHatLedArray">
    <description>Provides basic LED array control functionality</description>

    <method name="DrawShape">
      <description>Draws selected shape on the LED array</description>
      <arg name="shapeKind" type="i" direction="in">
        <description>A value to specify the shape to be drawn</description>
      </arg>
```

```
    </method>

    <method name="TurnOff">
      <description>Turns the LED array off</description>
    </method>

    <property name="Shape" type="y" access="read">
      <description>The current shape drawn on the LED array</description>
    </property>
  </interface>
</node>
```

To define an interface method, you use the method tag, whose name attribute describes the method name. Under the method tag you can include the description tag and the set of arg tags, which define the method formal parameters. Every arg tag can be parameterized using the name, type, and direction attributes. The first one determines the argument name seen by the consumers, while the type attribute specifies the argument type. D-Bus identifies types by non-straightforward ASCII type-codes. For instance, y represents byte, while i is the 32-bit signed integer (int C# counterpart). Other commonly used argument types appear in Table 9-1. Lastly, the direction can be either in for input arguments or out for output parameters.

TABLE 9-1   Selected ASCII codes of argument types (find complete D-Bus specification at *https://dbus.freedesktop.org/doc/dbus-specification.html*)

Type Name	ASCII Code
Byte	y
Boolean	b
Int16	n
UInt16	q
Int32	i
UInt32	u
Int64	x
UInt64	t
Double	d
String	s
Array	a

Properties are defined using the property tag. You define the property name and type as in the case of methods, namely, by using name and type attributes. In the case of properties, there is yet another attribute, access, which specifies the read-write access level. Each property can be read-only (access="read"), write-only (access="write"), or readable and writeable (access="readwrite").

AllJoyn Studio

You can implement the AllJoyn producer and consumer by using the AllJoyn Standard Client API, which is the native C library (*https://bit.ly/all_joyn_windows*). To shorten that process, Microsoft introduced the AllJoyn Studio extension for Visual Studio. AllJoyn Studio automatically generates the Visual C++ Windows Runtime Component, implementing producer and consumer classes based on the introspection XML file. Therefore, you do not need to manually implement the middleware Visual C++ layer that connects the AllJoyn Standard Client API with the UWP project as when working with the OpenCV libraries in the previous chapter.

You can install AllJoyn Studio by using the Extensions and Updates dialog box of Visual Studio. In this dialog box, you type **alljoyn** in the search text box, and then select **AllJoyn Studio**. (See Figure 9-20.) After installation, restart your Visual Studio. The Visual Studio menu is now supplemented by an additional entry, AllJoyn. Moreover, AllJoyn Studio installs the AllJoyn App (Universal Windows) project templates for C#, Visual C++, Visual Basic, and JavaScript.

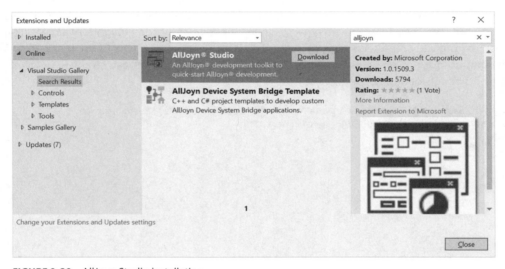

FIGURE 9-20   AllJoyn Studio installation.

Next, in order to generate the producer and consumer classes, create the new UWP app—either headed or headless. Here, I use the headless UWP Background IoT app, named AllJoynCommunication. Producer; see the companion code in Chapter 09/AllJoynCommunication. After creating the project, choose **Add/Remove Interfaces** from the **AllJoyn** menu. As a result, the Add/Remove AllJoyn interfaces dialog box appears; click the **Browse** button, and then select the introspection XML file. Here, I use the LedArray-introspection.xml file, which contains the declarations from Listing 9-45.

After parsing the introspection XML file, AllJoyn Studio will detect interfaces and display them in the list. Choose the **com.iot.SenseHatLedArray** interface, change the project name to **AllJoynCommunication.SenseHatLedArrayInterface**, and click the **OK** button. (See Figure 9-21.) Windows Runtime Component is generated and added to the solution. However, you need to manually reference that project in AllJoynCommunication.Producer.

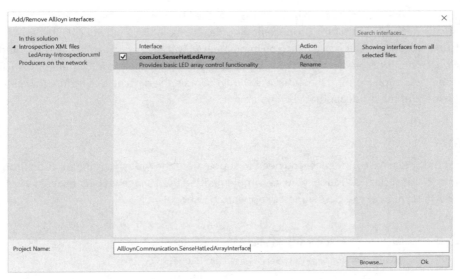

FIGURE 9-21 Adding AllJoyn interface parsed from the introspection XML file.

A quick glance at the structure of the generated project shows that it includes several classes, which, apart from implementing the AllJoyn producer (SenseHatLedArrayProducer) and consumer (SenseHatLedArrayConsumer), have a logic for managing the AllJoyn bus (AllJoynBusObjectManager) and implementing the service interface (ISenseHatLedArrayService), device watcher (SenseHatLed-ArrayWatcher), and helper classes. (See Figure 9-22.)

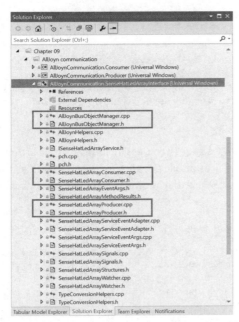

FIGURE 9-22 A structure of the automatically generated project, implementing AllJoyn bus manager, consumer, and producer. Files containing implementation of these objects are highlighted.

Typically, you do not explicitly use the helper classes or the bus manager. The device watcher in the consumer app detects whether the producer joins or leaves the AllJoyn network, while the actual ISenseHatLedArrayService interface has to be implemented within the producer layer. This interface contains the declarations of the methods whose signatures are specified in the introspection XML file. Accordingly, the class implementing that interface should contain the device-specific functionality. This is the main element of the producer that you implement.

Producer

To implement the actual AllJoyn service, you need to supplement the AllJoynCommunication.Producer project by an additional class, AllJoynLedArray, implementing the ISenseHatLedArrayService interface. The AllJoynLedArray class signature appears in Listing 9-46.

LISTING 9-46 Declaration of the class implementing the AllJoyn interface

```
public sealed class AllJoynLedArray : ISenseHatLedArrayService
```

I generated the definition of the ISenseHatLedArrayService interface (see Listing 9-47) according to the introspection XML file from Listing 9-46. Therefore, ISenseHatLedArrayService has three members: DrawShapeAsync, GetShapeAsync, and TurnOffAsync. They are asynchronous, except for the argument of AllJoynMessageInfo, and return the status of the asynchronous operation by using dedicated, automatically generated classes.

LISTING 9-47 ISenseHatLedArrayService interface was generated according to the introspection XML file

```
public interface ISenseHatLedArrayService
{
    IAsyncOperation<SenseHatLedArrayDrawShapeResult> DrawShapeAsync(AllJoynMessageInfo info,
        int interfaceMemberShapeKind);
    IAsyncOperation<SenseHatLedArrayGetShapeResult> GetShapeAsync(AllJoynMessageInfo info);
    IAsyncOperation<SenseHatLedArrayTurnOffResult> TurnOffAsync(AllJoynMessageInfo info);
}
```

As Listing 9-48 shows, the declaration of the AllJoynMessageInfo class includes a single argument constructor and the public property SenderUniqueName. This public property uniquely identifies the consumer (the client app) that sent the actual request. You can use that information for writing consumer-dependent logic.

LISTING 9-48 Declaration of the AllJoynMessageInfo class

```
public sealed class AllJoynMessageInfo : IAllJoynMessageInfo
{
    public AllJoynMessageInfo(System.String senderUniqueName);
    public System.String SenderUniqueName { get; }
}
```

The declarations of the return types of the ISenseHatLedArrayService methods have two static methods, CreateFailureResult and CreateSuccessResult, and the read-only Status property. The producer uses these methods to inform the consumer whether the particular request was fulfilled. The consumer then gets that information by reading the Status property.

As you see in Listing 9-49, I used the LedArray class to implement the DrawShapeAsync method in the AllJoynLedArray class. (The DrawShapeAsync method is used to draw shapes on the LED array, which are requested by AllJoyn consumers.)

LISTING 9-49 Selected fragments of the AllJoynLedArray class

```
private ShapeKind currentShape = ShapeKind.None;

private LedArray;

public AllJoynLedArray(LedArray ledArray)
{
    this.ledArray = ledArray;
}

public IAsyncOperation<SenseHatLedArrayDrawShapeResult> DrawShapeAsync(
    AllJoynMessageInfo info, int interfaceMemberShapeKind)
{
    Task<SenseHatLedArrayDrawShapeResult> task =
        new Task<SenseHatLedArrayDrawShapeResult>(() =>
    {
        if (ledArray != null)
        {
            currentShape = GetShapeKind(interfaceMemberShapeKind);

            ledArray.DrawShape(currentShape);

            return SenseHatLedArrayDrawShapeResult.CreateSuccessResult();
        }
        else
        {
            return SenseHatLedArrayDrawShapeResult.CreateFailureResult(
                (int)ErrorCodes.LedInitializationError);
        }
    });

    task.Start();

    return task.AsAsyncOperation();
}

private ShapeKind GetShapeKind(int intShapeKind)
{
    var shapeKind = ShapeKind.None;

    if (Enum.IsDefined(typeof(ShapeKind), intShapeKind))
```

```
    {
        shapeKind = (ShapeKind)intShapeKind;
    }

    return shapeKind;
}
```

I first verify that the LedArray class was correctly initialized. If not, I create the failure result with the status of ErrorCodes.LedInitialzationError; see the companion code in Chapter 09/AllJoynCommunication/AllJoynCommunication.Producer/ErrorCodes.cs. If AllJoynLedArray accesses a properly initialized LedArray class, I do the following:

1. I convert the integral argument received from the consumer (interfaceMemberShapeKind) to one of the values specified by the ShapeKind enumeration; see Chapter 8, "Image processing."

2. Subsequently, I store that value in the private field and then pass it to the DrawShape method of the LedArray class.

3. Finally, I create and return the success result. This logic is run asynchronously using the Task class.

Other methods of the ISenseHatLedArrayService interface are implemented analogously in the AllJoynLedArray class, and therefore do not warrant additional comments; see the companion code in Chapter 09/AllJoynCommunication/AllJoynCommunication.Producer/AllJoynLedArray.cs

To advertise in the AllJoyn devices, you first need to instantiate the AllJoynBusAttachment class and then pass that object to the SenseHatLedArrayProducer constructor. Second, you create the actual producer service by setting the Service property of the SenseHatLedArrayProducer class instance. The last step is to start the advertisement using the Start method of the producer class. This procedure is implemented within the StartAllJoynService method of the StartupTask; see Listing 9-50 and the companion code in Chapter 09/AllJoynCommunication /AllJoynCommunication. Producer/StartupTask.cs. (Note that the InitializeLedArray method is omitted because it performs only already-known LED array initialization.)

LISTING 9-50 Running the AllJoyn producer
```
private LedArray ledArray;
private BackgroundTaskDeferral taskDeferral;

private AllJoynBusAttachment allJoynBusAttachment;

public async void Run(IBackgroundTaskInstance taskInstance)
{
    taskDeferral = taskInstance.GetDeferral();

    await InitializeLedArray();

    StartAllJoynService();
}

 private void StartAllJoynService()
```

```
{
    allJoynBusAttachment = new AllJoynBusAttachment();

    SenseHatLedArrayProducer senseHatAllJoynProducer =
        new SenseHatLedArrayProducer(allJoynBusAttachment);
    senseHatAllJoynProducer.Service = new AllJoynLedArray(ledArray);
    senseHatAllJoynProducer.Start();
}
```

To access the AllJoyn API, you need to declare the AllJoyn capability in the Package.appxmanifest as Listing 9-51 shows. Afterward, you can deploy and run AllJoynCommunication.Producer in your IoT device. You can send requests to that app either by using the IoT Explorer for the AllJoyn app or writing a custom consumer. I show you each possibility in the next two sections.

LISTING 9-51 Declaration of the AllJoyn capability

```
<Capabilities>
  <Capability Name="internetClient" />
  <Capability Name="allJoyn" />
</Capabilities>
```

IoT Explorer for AllJoyn

The IoT Explorer for AllJoyn (IoT Explorer) is a free UWP app distributed through the Windows Store (*https://www.microsoft.com/store/apps/9nblggh6gpxl*). The IoT Explorer helps you easily enumerate AllJoyn devices in your local network, investigate their interfaces, invoke remote methods, and access properties.

After you install and run this app, it will display three AllJoyn producers. (See Figure 9-23.) The default producer is IoT Core Onboarding. You can use it to change description of your IoT board and also control the Wi-Fi module. You configure this default AllJoyn using an IoT Onboarding tab of the Device Portal. (See Figure 9-24.)

FIGURE 9-23 AllJoyn producers discovered in the local network.

FIGURE 9-24 The IoT Onboarding tab of the Device Portal.

In the IoT Explorer you will also see the custom producer implemented in the previous section. Its description reflects values defined in the Packaging section of the app manifest. In my case this entry has the value of CN=Dawid. When you click the rectangle representing your custom producer, the IoT Explorer will display a single service comprising of five interfaces. You can click that service, and then choose the com.iot.SenseHatLedArray interface. As a result, methods and properties of that interface are displayed. You can use the corresponding rectangles to invoke selected methods and read property values as shown in Figure 9-25 and Figure 9-26. Your requests are transmitted to the IoT device, and appropriate shapes appear on the LED array.

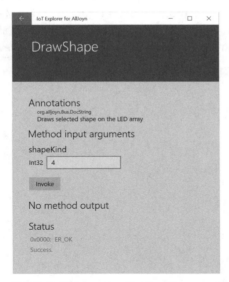

FIGURE 9-25 Invoking the DrawShape method to remotely draw a selected shape on the LED array.

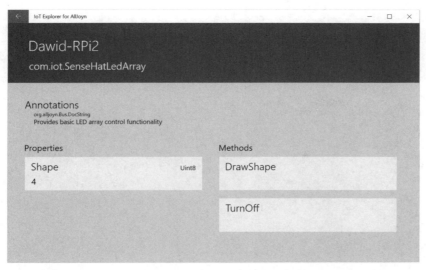

FIGURE 9-26 Properties and methods of the com.iot.SenseHatLedArray AllJoyn interface. The Shape property shows the value corresponding to the currently displayed shape.

Custom Consumer

The IoT Explorer offers a quick and convenient way to test your AllJoyn interface for general use. For custom solutions, you can write your own consumer using an appropriate UWP API. In this section, I show how to implement the headed UWP app consuming the com.iot.SenseHatLedArray interface.

Use either the AllJoyn (Universal Windows) project template or a Blank App UWP template. In the former case, the AllJoyn capability is automatically configured, and in the latter case, the Blank App UWP template, you need to manually declare AllJoyn capability in the app manifest.

To build the consumer app, AllJoynCommunication.Consumer, I use the AllJoyn (Universal Windows) project template and then reference the AllJoynCommunication.SenseHatLedArrayInterface project along with SerialCommunication.Common and AllJoynCommunication.Producer. I use the `Diagnostic-Info` class from the first project and `ShapeKind` enumeration from the second one.

Next, I define the simple UI—see Figure 9-27—composed of a drop-down list that enables the user to pick a shape, three buttons for sending requests to the AllJoyn producer, and the list box for displaying diagnostic messages.

Given the UI, the implementation of the AllJoyn consumer logic typically proceeds as in Listing 9-52. As in the case of producer, you need to instantiate the `AllJoynBusAttachment` class; you use this object to construct the AllJoyn device watcher, `SenseHatLedArrayWatcher`; see Listing 9-52.

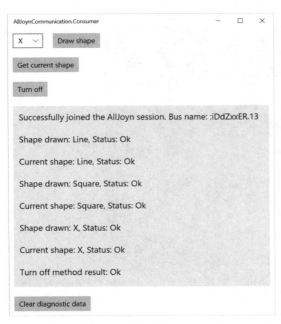

FIGURE 9-27 User interface of the custom AllJoyn consumer. Buttons invoke remote methods exposed by the AllJoyn producer, while the list displays results of remote requests, as well as diagnostic data.

LISTING 9-52 AllJoyn device watcher initialization

```
private AllJoynBusAttachment allJoynBusAttachment;
private SenseHatLedArrayWatcher senseHatLedArrayWatcher;

public MainPage()
{
    InitializeComponent();

    InitializeWatcher();
}

private void InitializeWatcher()
{
    allJoynBusAttachment = new AllJoynBusAttachment();

    senseHatLedArrayWatcher = new SenseHatLedArrayWatcher(allJoynBusAttachment);

    senseHatLedArrayWatcher.Added += SenseHatLedArrayWatcher_Added;
    senseHatLedArrayWatcher.Stopped += SenseHatLedArrayWatcher_Stopped;

    senseHatLedArrayWatcher.Start();
}
```

Subsequently, you use the Added and Stopped events of the watcher class to detect whether the particular producer joins or leaves the network. Once the producer is found in the network, you need to join the session using JoinAsync. After a successful call to that method, you also obtain the reference to the actual consumer class; see Listing 9-53.

LISTING 9-53 Connecting to and disconnecting from the producer

```
private SenseHatLedArrayConsumer senseHatLedArrayConsumer;
private bool isSenseHatAvailable = false;

private ObservableCollection<string> diagnosticData = new ObservableCollection<string>();

private async void SenseHatLedArrayWatcher_Added(SenseHatLedArrayWatcher sender,
    AllJoynServiceInfo args)
{
    var result = await SenseHatLedArrayConsumer.JoinSessionAsync(args,
        senseHatLedArrayWatcher);

    if (result.Status == AllJoynStatus.Ok)
    {
        isSenseHatAvailable = true;

        senseHatLedArrayConsumer = result.Consumer;

        DiagnosticInfo.Display(diagnosticData,
            "Successfully joined the AllJoyn session. Bus name: " + args.UniqueName);
    }
}

private void SenseHatLedArrayWatcher_Stopped(SenseHatLedArrayWatcher sender,
    AllJoynProducerStoppedEventArgs args)
{
    isSenseHatAvailable = false;

    senseHatLedArrayConsumer.Dispose();
    senseHatLedArrayConsumer = null;

    DiagnosticInfo.Display(diagnosticData,
        "SenseHatLedArray AllJoyn device left the network");
}
```

The reference to the consumer class lets you access methods and properties of the particular AllJoyn interface. As Listing 9-54 shows, to draw the shape on the LED array or turn it off, you invoke the Draw-ShapeAsync and TurnOff methods, respectively.

LISTING 9-54 Invoking the producer's methods

```
private object selectedShape = ShapeKind.None;
private const string deviceUnavailable = "Device unavailable";
```

```
private async void ButtonDrawShape_Click(object sender, RoutedEventArgs e)
{
    if (isSenseHatAvailable)
    {
        var drawShapeResult = await senseHatLedArrayConsumer.DrawShapeAsync(
            (int)selectedShape);

        var allJoynStatus = AllJoynStatusHelper.GetStatusCodeName(
            drawShapeResult.Status);

        var info = string.Format("Shape drawn: {0}, Status: {1}",
            selectedShape, allJoynStatus);

        DiagnosticInfo.Display(diagnosticData, info);
    }
    else
    {
        DiagnosticInfo.Display(diagnosticData, deviceUnavailable);
    }
}

private async void ButtonTurnOff_Click(object sender, RoutedEventArgs e)
{
    if (isSenseHatAvailable)
    {
        var turnOffResult = await senseHatLedArrayConsumer.TurnOffAsync();

        var allJoynStatus = AllJoynStatusHelper.GetStatusCodeName(turnOffResult.Status);

        DiagnosticInfo.Display(diagnosticData, "Turn off method result: " + allJoynStatus);
    }
    else
    {
        DiagnosticInfo.Display(diagnosticData, deviceUnavailable);
    }
}
```

To check whether your request was successfully fulfilled, you can read the Status property of the object returned by the DrawShapeAsync or TurnOff methods. These are instances of the SenseHat-LedArrayGetShapeResult and SenseHatLedArrayTurnOffResult classes. Both of them expose the Status property, which is the 32-bit signed integer. The collection of possible status codes is defined within the static class AllJoynStatus, implemented in the Windows.Devices.AllJoyn namespace. However, AllJoynStatus does not provide a convenient way for casting integral status codes to strings, which can be then easily interpreted during debugging. To solve that problem, I wrote the AllJoynStatusHelper class. It uses the C# reflection mechanism to dynamically enumerate values and names of AllJoynStatus static properties; see the GetNamedStatusCodes method from Listing 9-55. On these grounds, I built the lookup table, returning the name of the particular AllJoyn status; see GetStatusCodeName from Listing 9-55. Then, I can easily get the string representation of the particular AllJoyn status code by simply reading the value from the look-up table.

```
public static class AllJoynStatusHelper
{
    private static Dictionary<int, string> namedAllJoynStatusDictionary =
        GetNamedStatusCodes();

    private const string unknownStatus = "Unknown status";

    public static string GetStatusCodeName(int statusCode)
    {
        var statusName = unknownStatus;

        if(namedAllJoynStatusDictionary.ContainsKey(statusCode))
        {
            statusName = namedAllJoynStatusDictionary[statusCode];
        }

        return statusName;
    }

    private static Dictionary<int, string> GetNamedStatusCodes()
    {
        var namedStatusCodes = typeof(AllJoynStatus).GetRuntimeProperties().Select(
            r => new RequestStatus()
            {
                Name = r.Name,
                Value = (int)r.GetValue(null)
            });

        var result = new Dictionary<int, string>();

        foreach (var namedStatusCode in namedStatusCodes)
        {
            if (!result.ContainsKey(namedStatusCode.Value))
            {
                result.Add(namedStatusCode.Value, namedStatusCode.Name);
            }
        }

        return result;
    }
}
```

To read property values you proceed according to an example from Listing 9-56. The procedure is similar to invoking methods. First, you call the appropriate asynchronous method (GetShapeAsync in this case). Then, to check whether your request was successfully fulfilled, you can read the Status property of the object returned by the GetShapeAsync method (that is SenseHatLedArrayGetShape Result). Finally, the actual property value can be obtained by reading an appropriate member of the SenseHatLedArrayGetShapeResult, that is, Shape.

LISTING 9-56 Reading properties of the AllJoyn interface

```csharp
private async void ButtonGetShape_Click(object sender, RoutedEventArgs e)
{
    if (isSenseHatAvailable)
    {
        var getShapeResult = await senseHatLedArrayConsumer.GetShapeAsync();

        var allJoynStatus = AllJoynStatusHelper.GetStatusCodeName(getShapeResult.Status);

        var info = string.Format("Current shape: {0}, Status: {1}",
            (ShapeKind)getShapeResult.Shape, allJoynStatus);

        DiagnosticInfo.Display(diagnosticData, info);
    }
    else
    {
        DiagnosticInfo.Display(diagnosticData, deviceUnavailable);
    }
}
```

After running the AllJoynCommunication.Consumer app, you can remotely control your IoT device similarly to using the IoT Explorer. However, AllJoynCommunication.Consumer exposes the UI tailored to the com.iot.SenseHatLedArray AllJoyn interface, so instead of typing integers, you can choose the particular shape to be drawn from the drop-down list.

In the preceding AllJoyn interface, consumers are not signaled whenever the particular property changes; they need to read properties in the specified time intervals. To solve this problem, the D-Bus specification introduces the concept of signals. They are defined in the introspection XML file using the `signal` tag; see Listing 9-57.

When you define signals in your introspection XML file, the AllJoyn studio will map them to events. You raise the events to broadcast the signal to the session-specific consumers. Signals can be also sessionless. In that case, they are advertised to all apps in the proximity AllJoyn network, and not only to the connected consumers.

LISTING 9-57 AllJoyn signal declarations

```xml
<signal name="LedArrayOn" sessionless="false">
    <description>Emitted when the LED array turns on</description>

    <arg name="turnedOffInternally" type="b"/>
</signal>

<signal name="LedArrayOff" sessionless="true">
    <description>Emitted when the LED array turns off</description>
</signal>
```

By comparing AllJoyn with the custom communication interface, you do not need to deal with low-level data conversion or other aspects like error detection. AllJoyn takes care of such low-level operations, so you can focus on implementing your logic, and you can use remote methods and properties of producers as regular methods of C# objects. Hence, AllJoyn together with AllJoyn Studio serves you the basis for quick IoT development. However, when you build a custom and comprehensive control system, you will most likely need to define your own protocol.

Windows Remote Arduino

There is yet another library related to device communication that bears mentioning: Windows Remote Arduino. It uses the Firmata communication protocol (*https://bit.ly/firmata*) to remotely control Arduino boards using various communication protocols, including Bluetooth, USB, Wi-Fi, and Ethernet. I omitted a detailed example of Windows Remote Arduino because the complete guide is available online at *https://bit.ly/windows_remote_arduino*.

Summary

This chapter explored several UWP communication APIs for transferring data between devices. We started with wired communication. I showed how to test wired communication interfaces in the loopback mode and implement custom communication protocol, which was then used to remotely control IoT devices. Subsequently, we explored wireless interfaces such as Bluetooth and Wi-Fi. Lastly, you learned how to implement and use the standardized AllJoyn communication protocol. These various capabilities let you build standardized or completely custom IoT communication systems.

CHAPTER 10

Motors

Electronic motor systems are a very important element in robotics and moveable automation systems. They may include a direct current (DC), a stepper, and servo motors. In this chapter I will tell you how they differ and also introduce the PID controller. Then, I will tell you how to control motors using the RPi2/RPi3 through dedicated motor HATs. The central element of these HATs is the pulse-width modulation (PWM) module. Accordingly, I first explain how to write a driver for controlling PWM. Subsequently, I use it to steer DC and stepper motors. Finally, I control a wheel attached to the servo-mechanisms. I also discuss automatic motor speed adjustments similar to those used in PID. After completing this chapter, you will be able to build control systems for robot positioning.

Motors and device control fundamentals

DC motors are widely used in toys, tools, and home appliances. In the simplest case, a DC motor is composed of two stationary magnets with opposite polarities, so that the magnets generate a magnetic field. A conducting coil is located between the magnets and connected to the DC power source. The current rotates the coil. The more current, the faster the rotation. Hence, to control the DC motor using an IoT device you need to provide an appropriate voltage.

A stepper motor is a DC motor in which the full rotation is divided into a specific number of steps (discrete angles). You can use a stepper motor for more precise positioning applications, in which you can set the motor position (rotation) by rotating a motor shaft to a given angle. Stepper motors typically do not use any feedback control, so you do not know whether the motor is in the requested position, which occurs when the motor parameters are mismatched with the torque or you move the motor too fast.

Servo motors ensure the correct position (or rotation) based on the feedback coming from additional components that measure motor speed and position. Such a closed-feedback loop is one of the most important aspects of the control systems. Traditionally, a closed-feedback loop is implemented within the proportional-integrated-derivative (PID) controller.

A PID controller minimizes the error between the actual and requested motor position. It does so by calculating the time-dependent error function using proportional (P), integral (I), and derivative (D) components:

- P-component   This describes the instantaneous error.
- I-component   This describes accumulated errors.
- D-component   This predicts future position differences.

By combining information from each component, a PID controller provides smooth motor positioning; large instantaneous errors therefore do not yield rapid changes in motor position. Speed is adjusted to the past, present, and predicted position changes.

As a practical example, consider the cruise control in your car. After you turn on this system, the speed of your car stays at the fixed value. When you drive on a flat road, your car keeps a constant speed. When you drive over a hill, the PID controller embedded in the cruise control system detects that your car slows down or accelerates. The PID controller then gently corrects the speed of your car according to the past and present speed changes. Namely, when the speed starts to decrease (going uphill), the PID controller slowly starts to accelerate to reach the requested speed. It provides a smooth acceleration, so your car does not twitch. This is possible because the PID controller stores previous speed readings and can predict short-term speed changes.

Motor HATs

To control the motor position, you typically need to output an appropriate voltage or current to the motor. In practice, you use a dedicated driver, which translates your programmatic requests to low-level electronic signals.

There are several HATs for the RPi2/RPi3 that support motor control. Here, I'm using a DC and stepper motor HAT (*https://bit.ly/dc_stepper_motor_hat*) (see Figure 10-1) and a servo/PWM Pi HAT (*https://bit.ly/servo_hat*) (see Figure 10-2). Both HATs can be easily attached to the RPi2/RPi3 through the GPIO header. However, they require some soldering. You can find detailed assembly instructions here: *https://bit.ly/hat_soldering*.

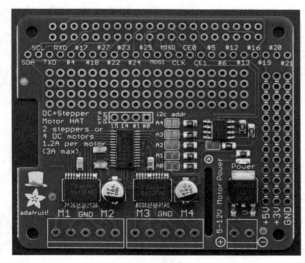

FIGURE 10-1 DC and stepper motor HAT for Raspberry Pi 2. (Courtesy of *https://www.adafruit.com/*).

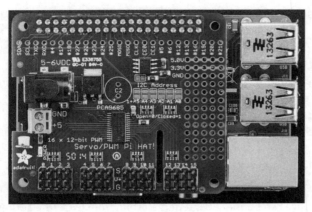

FIGURE 10-2 A servo/PWM Pi HAT attached to the Raspberry Pi 2. (Courtesy of *https://www.adafruit.com/*).

Pulse-width modulation

The central part of both motor HATs described earlier is the PCA9685 module (*https://bit.ly/PCA9685*). It's an I²C-controlled, 16-channel, 12-bit resolution pulse-width modulation (PWM) controller. PWM encodes information using a pulsing signal. The pulse duration (or width) is modulated in time with a specified period and thus determines the duration of active (on) and inactive (off) states and the pulse repetition rate, or how often the pulses are generated. Duration of an active state is defined as the PWM duty cycle, D. For example, D = 30% means that PWM is in an active state for 30% and in an inactive state for 70% of the modulation period.

The basic idea of PWM is depicted in Figure 10-3. Short pulse duration corresponds to short high states and long low states. Long pulse width yields long on states and short off states. You can reverse this by swapping active and inactive states. PWM devices (including PCA9685) typically achieve such modulation using an internal oscillator, generating the PWM signal.

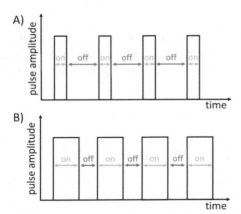

FIGURE 10-3 Pulse-width modulation. Pulse width (or duration) determines the duration of on and off states. (A) Short pulses yield short and long durations of on and off states, respectively. (B) On the contrary, long pulses correspond to long off and short on states.

You can control the PCA9685 PWM duty cycle by using appropriate control registers. PCA9685 has 64 dedicated control registers with four 13-bit registers per channel and two registers per state. In the PCA9685 datasheet, these registers are denoted as LEDx_ON_L, LEDx_ON_H (active) and LEDx_OFF_L, LEDx_OFF_H (inactive), where x denotes the channel index, that is, the integral value from 0 to 15. L, and H suffices correspond to low and high bytes of the 13-bit unsigned integer with a value from the range of 0–4096. PWM channels have a 12-bit resolution, so the maximum value you typically use is 4095. The value of 4096 has a special meaning. By setting the minimum value of 0 for the on register and a value of 4096 for the off register, you achieve the special fully off PWM mode with a duty cycle of 0%. If you swap those values—that is, use 4096 for the on register and 0 for the off register—you achieve the opposite case. Namely, the PWM is fully on with the duty cycle of 100%. Though PCA9685 was designed for controlling LEDs, it can be also used, as shown here, for other applications.

LED registers are addressed by successive 8-bit unsigned integers starting from 0x06 (the address of LED0_ON_L) and ending at 0x45 (LED15_OFF_H). There are also four registers: ALL_LED_ON_L (0xFA), ALL_LED_ON_H (0xFB), ALL_LED_OFF_L (0xFC), and ALL_LED_OFF_H (0xFD), which allow you to control all LED channels simultaneously.

You configure the PWM duty cycle much like you do sensors. You just need to write appropriate values to the control registers after associating the connection with PCA9685 through the I2C bus. However, to enable PCA9685, you need to turn on an internal oscillator, which generates a PWM signal. To that end you use the MODE1 register with an address of 0x00.

The MODE1 register stores the single byte value, in which the bit at index 4 controls the oscillator state. You set that bit to 0 to enable the oscillator, and hence the PWM output. To disable the PWM signal, set that bit to 1. By default, the PCA9685 oscillator is disabled, that is, the device is in the sleep (low-power) mode. Each time you change the power mode, you need to wait at least 500 µs for the oscillator to stabilize.

Finally, to control the PWM signal frequency, you use the PRE_SCALE register with an address of 0xFE. PCA9685 can generate PWM signals of frequencies between 24 to 1526 Hz.

Driver

I implemented the PWM control described earlier within the PcaRegisterValue, PcaRegisters, and PcaPwmDriver classes. (See the companion code at Chapter 10/Motors/MotorsControl/PWM). These classes constitute the common implementation for controlling the PWM module, so I implemented them in the separate MotorsControl class library.

PcaRegisterValue is an object for storing unsigned shorts of the on and off registers. (See Listing 10-1.)

LISTING 10-1   A helper class for storing on and off register values of the PCA9685 PWM module

```
public class PcaRegisterValue
{
    public ushort On { get; set; }

    public ushort Off { get; set; }
}
```

The PcaRegisters class serves as the helper, whose public properties store addresses of MODE1, PRESCALE registers, and the sleep mode bit index. (See Listing 10-2.) Additionally, the PcaRegisters class implements the helper static GetRegisterAddressList method, which returns a two-dimensional byte array of register addresses for the given LED channel. GetRegisterAddressList returns an address list depending on the register type, which can be either on or off. An abstract representation of those values is an enumeration type RegisterType from Listing 10-3.

LISTING 10-2 Definition of the PcaRegisters class dedicated for determining addresses of PCA9685 registers

```csharp
public static class PcaRegisters
{
    public static byte Mode1 { get; } = 0x00;
    public static byte Prescale { get; } = 0xFE;

    public static byte SleepModeBitIndex { get; } = 4;

    private const byte ledAddressBeginIndex = 0x06;
    private const byte channelOffset = 4;
    private const byte registerLength = 2;
    private const byte maxChannelIndex = 15;

    public static byte[] GetRegisterAddressList(byte channelIndex, RegisterType registerType)
    {
        // Verify channel index
        if(channelIndex > maxChannelIndex)
        {
            throw new ArgumentException("Channel index cannot be larger than " +
                maxChannelIndex);
        }

        // Get start address by jumping 4 * channelIndex from the LED begin index of 6
        var registerStartAddress = Convert.ToByte(ledAddressBeginIndex
            + channelIndex * channelOffset);

        // If register type is off, then add an additional offset of 2
        if(registerType == RegisterType.Off)
        {
            registerStartAddress += Convert.ToByte((byte)registerType * registerLength);
        }

        // Construct the address list
        var addressList = new byte[registerLength];

        for(byte i = 0; i < registerLength; i++)
        {
            addressList[i] = Convert.ToByte(registerStartAddress + i);
        }

        return addressList;
    }
}
```

LISTING 10-3   An abstract representation of the on and off LED registers

```
public enum RegisterType : byte
{
    On = 0, Off
}
```

The `PcaPwmDriver` class is the actual class that exposes the functionality of the controlling PCA9685 module. First, the `PcaPwmDriver` initializes an I²C connection within the `Init` method. (See Listing 10-4.) This method uses the I²C address of 0x60.

LISTING 10-4   PcaPwmDriver class initialization

```
public bool IsInitialized { get; private set; } = false;

private const byte defaultAddress = 0x60;

public async Task Init(byte address = defaultAddress)
{
    device = await I2cHelper.GetI2cDevice(address);

    IsInitialized = device != null;
}
```

Second, the `PcaPwmDriver` implements actual methods for interfacing LED registers. These are `GetChannelValue` and `SetChannelValue`. (See Listing 10-5.) Both methods employ the `GetRegisterAddressList` method of the `PcaRegisters` and then either the `GetUShort` method (to read register values) or `WriteUShort` method (to set register values). The `GetUShort` and `WriteUShort` methods extend the previous definition of the `RegisterHelper` class. (See the companion code at Chapter 10/Motors/MotorsControl/Helpers/RegisterHelper.cs.) These are implemented analogously to other methods of the `RegisterHelper` class, which aims at transferring data through the I²C bus and therefore does not require additional discussion.

LISTING 10-5   Reading and writing values to PCA9685 registers for configuring PWM output

```
public PcaRegisterValue GetChannelValue(byte index)
{
    CheckInitialization();

    var onRegisterAddressList = PcaRegisters.GetRegisterAddressList(index, RegisterType.On);
    var offRegisterAddressList = PcaRegisters.GetRegisterAddressList(index, RegisterType.Off);

    return new PcaRegisterValue()
    {
        On = RegisterHelper.GetUShort(device, onRegisterAddressList),
        Off = RegisterHelper.GetUShort(device, offRegisterAddressList)
    };
```

```
}

public void SetChannelValue(byte index, PcaRegisterValue pcaRegisterValue)
{
    CheckInitialization();

    var onRegisterAddressList = PcaRegisters.GetRegisterAddressList(index, RegisterType.On);
    var offRegisterAddressList = PcaRegisters.GetRegisterAddressList(index, RegisterType.Off);

    RegisterHelper.WriteUShort(device, onRegisterAddressList, pcaRegisterValue.On);
    RegisterHelper.WriteUShort(device, offRegisterAddressList, pcaRegisterValue.Off);
}

private void CheckInitialization()
{
    if (!IsInitialized)
    {
        throw new Exception("Device is not initialized");
    }
}
```

The PCA9685 sleep mode configuration is implemented within the SetSleepMode method of the PcaPwmDriver class. (See Listing 10-6.) This function accepts one argument of an enumeration type SleepMode. Subsequently, SetSleepMode reads the current value from the MODE1 register and then updates the fourth bit of that register. This bit is either 1, if SleepMode == SleepMode.LowPower, or 0 otherwise. SetSleepMode updates the value of the MODE1 register. Note that to convert an instance of the BitArray class to byte, I'm using the GetByteValueFromBitArray method, described in Chapter 5, "Reading data from sensors." Moreover, the internal oscillator requires 0.5 ms for initialization. This delay is accounted for by the last statement of the SetSleepMode method.

LISTING 10-6   Configuring the PCA9685 power mode

```
public void SetSleepMode(SleepMode mode)
{
    CheckInitialization();

    // Read current mode
    var currentMode = RegisterHelper.ReadByte(device, PcaRegisters.Mode1);

    // Update sleep mode bit to true, if PwmMode == LowPower
    var currentModeBits = new BitArray(new byte[] { currentMode });
    currentModeBits[PcaRegisters.SleepModeBitIndex] = mode == SleepMode.LowPower;

    // Write updated byte value to Mode1 register
    RegisterHelper.WriteByte(device, PcaRegisters.Mode1,
        RegisterHelper.GetByteValueFromBitArray(currentModeBits));

    // Delay required by the internal oscillator
    Task.Delay(1).Wait();
```

```
}

public enum SleepMode
{
    Normal, LowPower
}
```

To update the PWM signal frequency, you can use the SetFrequency method of the PcaPwmDriver. (See Listing 10-7.) This function proceeds as follows. First, it turns the PWM module into the sleep mode, that is, disables an internal oscillator. Subsequently, given the required PWM frequency (the hzFrequency argument of the SetFrequency method), f_{PWM}, and the fixed internal oscillator frequency, f_0 = 25 MHz, the PRE_SCALE register value, p_v is calculated using the following equation:

$$p_v = \text{round}\left[\frac{f_O}{2^{12} \times f_{PWM}}\right] - 1$$

where 2^{12} = 4096 and denotes the resolution of the PCA9685 PWM module. This equation is implemented within the UpdateFrequency method from Listing 10-7. The value of p_v calculated in this way is stored in the prescale variable and then written to the PRE_SCALE register. Finally, the SetFrequency method re-enables the internal oscillator of the PCA9685.

LISTING 10-7   PWM signal frequency configuration

```
public static ushort Range { get; } = 4096;

public static int HzMinFrequency { get; } = 24;
public static int HzMaxFrequency { get; } = 1526;

private const int hzOscillatorFrequency = (int)25e+6; // 25 MHz

public void SetFrequency(int hzFrequency)
{
    // Validate argument
    Check.IsLengthInValidRange(hzFrequency, HzMinFrequency, HzMaxFrequency);

    // Verify that device is initialized
    CheckInitialization();

    // Set low-power mode
    SetSleepMode(SleepMode.LowPower);

    // Update frequency
    UdpateFrequency(hzFrequency);

    // Set normal power mode again
    SetSleepMode(SleepMode.Normal);
}
```

```
private void UdpateFrequency(int hzFrequency)
{
    var prescale = Math.Round(1.0 * hzOscillatorFrequency / (hzFrequency * Range), 0) - 1;

    RegisterHelper.WriteByte(device, PcaRegisters.Prescale, Convert.ToByte(prescale));
}
```

To obtain the current PWM frequency, you need to read the PRE_SCALE register value and then convert it to the actual frequency by inverting the previous equation for the f_{PWM} variable:

$$f_{PWM} = \text{round}\left[\frac{f_0}{2^{12} \times (p_v + 1)}\right]$$

The preceding equation is implemented in the GetFrequency method of the PcaPwmDriver. (See Listing 10-8.)

LISTING 10-8 Reading PWM frequency

```
public int GetFrequency()
{
    CheckInitialization();

    var prescale = RegisterHelper.ReadByte(device, PcaRegisters.Prescale);

    return (int)Math.Round(1.0 * hzOscillatorFrequency / (Range * (prescale + 1)), 0);
}
```

PcaPwmDriver implements two public, static, read-only properties: FullyOn and FullyOff. Their definitions are given in Listing 10-9. Both properties will be used later to either fully enable or disable the particular LED channel—in other words, to set the PWM duty cycle to 100% (FullyOn) or 0% (FullyOff). These special values will be used to control the DC motor.

LISTING 10-9 Special LED register values

```
public static ushort Range { get; } = 4096;

public static PcaRegisterValue FullyOn { get; } = new PcaRegisterValue()
{
    On = Range,
    Off = 0
};

public static PcaRegisterValue FullyOff { get; } = new PcaRegisterValue()
{
    On = 0,
    Off = Range
};
```

In this section, we prepared the PWM driver, which is the fundamental element for controlling the DC, stepper, and servo motors using motor and servo HATs for the RPi2/RPi3. Most of the basic programmatic work is already done, so let's now use the PcaPwmDriver class to drive motors.

DC motor

Before we can drive a DC motor, we need to connect it to the motor HAT, which has to be powered up. Here, I'm using the very cheap ($2) DC toy motor (*https://bit.ly/dc_toy_motor*). (See Figure 10-4.) As a power supply, I decided to use the 9 V 1 A power adapter (*https://bit.ly/hat_power_adapter*), which is connected to the motor HAT through the female DC power adapter (*https://bit.ly/dc_power_adapter*).

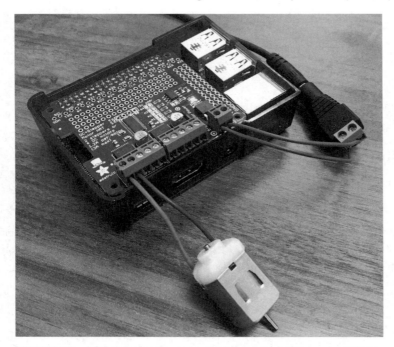

FIGURE 10-4 A DC motor connected to the M1 terminal of the motor HAT.

When you attach the motor HAT to the RPi2/RPi3 you need to make sure that the motor HAT is not in contact with the HDMI port of the RPi2/RPi3. To ensure that, you can use the insulating tape and put it on the HDMI port or use dedicated standoffs (*https://bit.ly/hat_standoffs*).

Once the motor HAT is in place, you can connect the DC motor wires to the appropriate terminal blocks denoted as M1, M2, M3, and M4. (See Figure 10-1.) Here, I'm using the M1 terminal blocks, so the final hardware assembly looks as shown in Figure 10-4. Note that you can reverse the red and blue wires. By doing so, you change the direction of the motor rotation.

Additionally, to power up your motors you need to connect the + and − HAT terminals to the DC power adapter and then to a power supply. The lit green power LED shows your connection is correct. The LED is located right above the + and − terminals of the HAT. (See Figure 10-1.)

Implementation of the motor control with PWM signals

The full implementation of the DcMotor class for controlling DC motors using the motor HAT can be found in the companion code at Chapter 10/MotorsControl/MotorHat/DcMotor.cs. This class internally uses PcaPwmDriver since the motor HAT drives DC motors using the PWM module. Each DC motor is driven by three PWM signals. Two are connected to the DC motor input pins (denoted as In1 and In2), which control the direction of the motor rotation. The third PWM channel is used to control the motor speed. The PWM channel association with particular motor terminal blocks on the motor HAT is given in Table 10-1. Note that I used a different naming convention for indicating DC motors (DC1–DC4 instead of M1–M4) because the motor HAT uses one terminal block for DC motors and two terminal blocks for each stepper motor. Accordingly, a motor HAT can control up to four DC motors and up to two stepper motors simultaneously.

TABLE 10-1 PWM channel mapping for the DC motor control

DC motor index	In1	In2	Speed
DC1	10	9	8
DC2	11	12	13
DC3	4	3	2
DC4	5	6	7

The PWM channels used to control the DC motor are represented as the DcMotorPwmChannels structure, the definition of which is given in Listing 10-10. Subsequently, I use this structure to configure the PWM channel mapping according to Table 10-1. This procedure is implemented within the ConfigureChannels method of the DcMotor class. (See Listing 10-11.) ConfigureChannels sets the Speed, In1, and In2 properties of the DcMotorPwmChannels structure, depending on the motorIndex argument.

LISTING 10-10 Definition of the DcMotorPwmChannels

```
public struct DcMotorPwmChannels
{
    public byte Speed { get; set; }

    public byte In1 { get; set; }

    public byte In2 { get; set; }
}
```

```
private DcMotorPwmChannels channels;

private void ConfigureChannels(DcMotorIndex motorIndex)
{
    switch (motorIndex)
    {
        case DcMotorIndex.DC1:
            channels.In1 = 10;
            channels.In2 = 9;
            channels.Speed = 8;
            break;

        case DcMotorIndex.DC2:
            channels.In1 = 11;
            channels.In2 = 12;
            channels.Speed = 13;
            break;

        case DcMotorIndex.DC3:
            channels.In1 = 4;
            channels.In2 = 3;
            channels.Speed = 2;
            break;

        case DcMotorIndex.DC4:
            channels.In1 = 5;
            channels.In2 = 6;
            channels.Speed = 7;
            break;
    }
}
```

To set the motor speed you configure the duty cycle of the corresponding PWM channel. As described in the "Pulse-width modulation" section, you achieve this using the SetChannelValue of the PcaPwmDriver. The definition of the SetSpeed appears in Listing 10-12. Namely, this method first configures the PWM channels and then writes the speed value to the appropriate On register.

LISTING 10-12   DC motor speed configuration

```
public void SetSpeed(DcMotorIndex motorIndex, ushort speed)
{
    Check.IsLengthInValidRange(speed, 0, PcaPwmDriver.Range - 1);

    ConfigureChannels(motorIndex);

    var speedRegisterValue = new PcaRegisterValue()
    {
```

```
    On = speed
};

pcaPwmDriver.SetChannelValue(channels.Speed, speedRegisterValue);
}
```

Finally, the DcMotor class implements two methods for starting (Start) and stopping (Stop) a DC motor. (See Listing 10-13.) To run the DC motor in a forward direction, you write 4096 to the On register and 0 to the Off register (100% PWM duty cycle) of the In2 PWM channel. At the same time, the duty cycle of the In1 PWM Channel has to be 0%, that is, you write 0 for the On and 4096 for the Off register. In contrast, if you want the DC motor to rotate in the opposite (backward) direction, you reverse the values of the In1 and In2 channels. (See the Start method from Listing 10-13.)

LISTING 10-13 DC motor is started and stopped by controlling the duty cycle of the In1 and In2 PWM channels

```
public void Start(DcMotorIndex motorIndex, MotorDirection direction)
{
    ConfigureChannels(motorIndex);

    if (direction == MotorDirection.Forward)
    {
        pcaPwmDriver.SetChannelValue(channels.In1, PcaPwmDriver.FullyOn);
        pcaPwmDriver.SetChannelValue(channels.In2, PcaPwmDriver.FullyOff);
    }
    else
    {
        pcaPwmDriver.SetChannelValue(channels.In1, PcaPwmDriver.FullyOff);
        pcaPwmDriver.SetChannelValue(channels.In2, PcaPwmDriver.FullyOn);
    }
}

public void Stop(DcMotorIndex motorIndex)
{
    ConfigureChannels(motorIndex);

    pcaPwmDriver.SetChannelValue(channels.In1, PcaPwmDriver.FullyOff);
    pcaPwmDriver.SetChannelValue(channels.In2, PcaPwmDriver.FullyOff);
}
```

Such a control circuit is defined as the H bridge. Enabling one channel and disabling the other applies a positive voltage to the DC motor. Voltage polarity can be inverted when channels are swapped, and then the DC motor rotates in the opposite direction. Physical H bridges of the DC and stepper HAT are two TB6612 chipsets, located above the M1–M4 terminals. (See Figure 10-1.) By controlling the duty cycle of the PWM channels, we effectively transfer signals to the H bridges, which then apply the appropriate voltages to the DC motor.

Finally, to stop the DC motor, you set the duty cycle of the `In1` and `In2` PWM channels to 0%—that is, you close both channels of the H bridge to keep voltage from the DC motor. (See the `Stop` method from Listing 10-3.)

In Listing 10-13, I use the `DcMotorIndex` and `MotorDirection` enumeration types, which are implemented in the `MotorControl` class library. (See the companion code at Chapter 10/Motors/ MotorControl/Enums.) The motor index can take one of the following values: DC1, DC2, DC3, or DC4, whereas motor direction can be either `Forward` or `Backward`.

Headed app

With the hardware components in place and the `DcMotor` class, you can write the headed app for controlling the DC motor. To that end I use the Blank UWP headed app C# project template to create the Motors app. The default view of this app appears in Figure 10-5. The full definition of the UI can be found in the companion code at Chapter 10/Motors/DcMotor/MainPage.

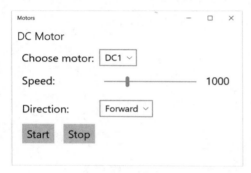

FIGURE 10-5   UI of the Motors app.

The UI of the Motors app includes a pivot control whose first item is dedicated to DC motors, and two drop-down lists, which let you choose the DC motor index and motor direction. There is also one `Slider`, which lets you set the motor speed—the value from range 0 to 4095. Finally, the UI of DC Motor has two buttons, Start and Stop, which you use to start or stop the selected DC motor. Hence, to run the motor you just need to deploy the Motors app to your IoT device, then choose DC1, set the motor speed and rotation direction, and click the Start button. You use the Stop button to disable the motor.

All UI elements are bound to the code-behind, while the required initialization of the PWM driver, followed by enabling the PWM oscillator and the `DcMotor` class instantiation, is done within the `OnNavigatedTo` event handler. (See Listing 10-14.) As shown there, if you do not want to use the UI to control the DC motor, you can simply invoke the `DcMotorTest` method. Just uncomment the last statement of the `InitializeDcMotor` method, which invokes the `DcMotorTest` function. This function runs the DC motor for 5 seconds with a fixed speed and a given direction.

LISTING 10-14 DcMotor class initialization and sleep mode configuration

```
private PcaPwmDriver pwmDriver;

private ushort speed;

private DcMotor dcMotor;

public double Speed
{
    get { return speed; }
    set
    {
        speed = Convert.ToUInt16(value);

        if (dcMotor.IsInitialized)
        {
            dcMotor.SetSpeed(dcMotorIndex, speed);
        }
    }
}

protected async override void OnNavigatedTo(NavigationEventArgs e)
{
    base.OnNavigatedTo(e);

    await InitializePwmDriver();

    InitializeDcMotor();
}

private async Task InitializePwmDriver()
{
    pwmDriver = new PcaPwmDriver();

    await pwmDriver.Init();

    if(pwmDriver.IsInitialized)
    {
        // Enable oscillator
        pwmDriver.SetSleepMode(SleepMode.Normal);
    }
}

private void InitializeDcMotor()
{
    dcMotor = new DcMotor(pwmDriver);

    // Set default speed
    Speed = 1000;

    // Uncomment the following line to run DC1 motor for 5 seconds without using UI.
```

```
    // DcMotorTest(DcMotorIndex.DC1, MotorDirection.Backward, speed);
}

private void DcMotorTest(DcMotorIndex motorIndex, MotorDirection direction, ushort speed)
{
    if (dcMotor.IsInitialized)
    {
        const int msDelay = 5000;

        // Set speed, and run motor
        dcMotor.SetSpeed(motorIndex, speed);
        dcMotor.Start(motorIndex, direction);

        // Wait a specified delay
        Task.Delay(msDelay).Wait();

        // Stop motor
        dcMotor.Stop(motorIndex);
    }
}
```

To complement the preceding description, Listing 10-15 shows the button event handlers. These methods are based on the Start and Stop methods of the DcMotor class. Similarly, as before, by separating concerns, the button event handlers look very clean since the actual motor control was delegated to a separate class.

LISTING 10-15 Starting and stopping the DC motor

```
private void ButtonStart_Click(object sender, RoutedEventArgs e)
{
    if (dcMotor.IsInitialized)
    {
        dcMotor.Start(dcMotorIndex, motorDirection);
    }
}

private void ButtonStop_Click(object sender, RoutedEventArgs e)
{
    if (dcMotor.IsInitialized)
    {
        dcMotor.Stop(dcMotorIndex);
    }
}
```

Stepper motor

There are many various stepper motors available, but I use the popular NEMA-17 motor (*https://bit.ly/nema_17*). Similar motors were also used in the Air Hockey Robot project. The NEMA-17 motor divides a full rotation into 200 full steps, so each step corresponds to a motor shaft rotation of 1.8°. Each full step can be further divided into 256 micro-steps, so NEMA-17 can be used for precise positioning.

In contrast to the DC motor, NEMA-17 has two coils that control the shaft position. Each coil is controlled by two PWM signals, so there are four PWM channels needed to control the stepper motor. Accordingly, to connect NEMA-17 to the DC and stepper motor HAT, you need to connect four motor wires to two HAT terminals. As Figure 10-6 shows, you connect the red and yellow wires of the stepper motor to either the M1 or M3 terminal. Then you connect the green and gray (or brown) wire to the M2 or M4 terminal. Note that you need to use two consecutive terminals, that is, M1 and M2 or M3 and M4. I used the second option because I have a DC motor connected to the M1 terminal. Unipolar stepper motors are also available and have five wires. In such a case, you connect an additional wire to the GND terminal.

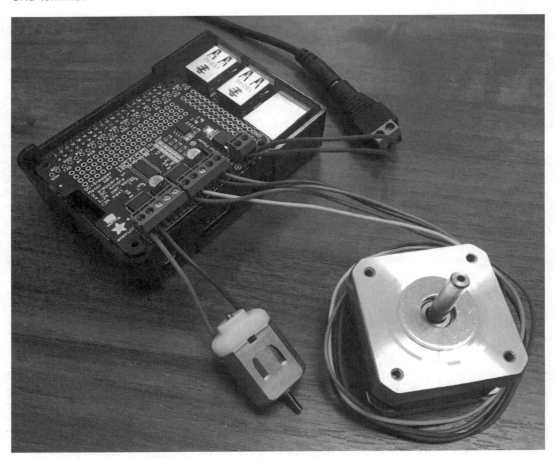

FIGURE 10-6 A stepper motor connected to the M3 and M4 DC and stepper motor HAT terminals.

There are several common techniques for controlling stepper motors. In the simplest case of full-stepping, you set the stepper motor position by utilizing four signals. These signals are commonly denoted as a, $\bar{a}$, b, and $\bar{b}$. As in the case of the DC motor, each signal can be either in a high (PWM fully on) or low (PWM fully off) state. I will denote the combination of signal states as the control phase.

In the full-step motor control, each phase has one high-state signal and three low-state signals. The high-state signal changes sequentially between phases, as shown in Table 10-2. To rotate a stepper motor, you use a variable storing an index of the current control phase. Using that index, you pick the necessary control phase and then use the appropriate signal states to drive the motor. For the full stepping, your control phase index is an integer in the range 0–3. So, after you reach the fourth control phase, you need to go back to the first one. For instance, to make a full revolution of the NEMA-17, you need to use the control phase sequence from Table 10-2 50 times, since NEMA-17 has 200 steps. The stepper motor will rotate forwards. To rotate it backwards, you reverse the control phase sequence, that is, decrement the current control phase index. Such incrementing/decrementing can be envisioned as the motor step counting.

TABLE 10-2   Stepper motor control phases for full-stepping

Control phase	State of signal a	State of signal $\bar{a}$	State of signal b	State of signal $\bar{b}$
0	High	Low	Low	Low
1	Low	High	Low	Low
2	Low	Low	High	Low
3	Low	Low	Low	High

A little bit more effort is necessary for half- and micro-stepping. Your control phase sequence will look like the one in Table 10-3 or Table 10-4, respectively. Each control phase rotates the motor by a half step (see Table 10-3) or specifies the particular full step, which is further divided into micro-steps. As I show later, micro-stepping requires the use of two additional signals.

TABLE 10-3   Stepper motor control phases for half-stepping. Note that, contrary to full-stepping, intermediate control phases have two signals in a high state.

Control phase	State of signal a	State of signal $\bar{a}$	State of signal b	State of signal $\bar{b}$
0	High	Low	Low	Low
1	High	High	Low	Low
2	Low	High	Low	Low
3	Low	High	High	Low
4	Low	Low	High	Low
5	Low	Low	High	High
6	Low	Low	Low	High
7	High	Low	Low	High

TABLE 10-4 Stepper motor control phases for micro-stepping

Control phase	State of signal a	State of signal $\overline{a}$	State of signal b	State of signal $\overline{b}$
0	High	High	Low	Low
1	Low	High	High	Low
2	Low	Low	High	High
3	High	Low	Low	High

Full-step mode control

I implement the stepper motor control using the StepperMotorPwmChannels structure and two classes: StepperMotorPhase and StepperMotor. (See the companion code at Chapter 10/MotorsControl/MotorHat.) The first class, StepperMotorPwmChannels, is used to associate PWM channels to motor coils. StepperMotorPwmChannels has six properties. (See Listing 10-16.) AIn1 and AIn2 correspond to the first $(a, \overline{a})$, while BIn1 and BIn2 are related to the second $(b, \overline{b})$ coil, whereas PwmA and PwmB are used for micro-stepping only. (See Table 10-5.) Since PCA9685 has 16 PWM channels, the DC and stepper motor HAT can control up to two steppers at a time. Thus, steppers are identified by SM1 and SM2 values defined in the StepperMotorIndex enumeration. (See the companion code at Chapter 10/MotorsControl/Enums/StepperMotorIndex.cs.)

LISTING 10-16 The stepper motor is driven by six PWM channels

```
public struct StepperMotorPwmChannels
{
    public byte AIn1 { get; set; }
    public byte AIn2 { get; set; }

    public byte BIn1 { get; set; }
    public byte BIn2 { get; set; }

    public byte PwmA { get; set; }
    public byte PwmB { get; set; }
}
```

TABLE 10-5 PWM channel mapping for the stepper motor control

DC motor index	AIn1	AIn2	BIn1	BIn2	PwmA	PwmB
SM1	10	9	11	12	8	13
SM2	4	3	5	6	2	7

StepperMotorPhase, whose definition is presented in Listing 10-17, is a class related to StepperMotor-PwmChannels and stores PWM channel values for a particular control phase. By default, the PwmA and PwmB channels are fully on—they change only in the case of the micro-stepping control.

```
public class StepperMotorPhase
{
    public PcaRegisterValue AIn1 { get; set; }
    public PcaRegisterValue AIn2 { get; set; }

    public PcaRegisterValue BIn1 { get; set; }
    public PcaRegisterValue BIn2 { get; set; }

    public PcaRegisterValue PwmA { get; set; } = PcaPwmDriver.FullyOn;
    public PcaRegisterValue PwmB { get; set; } = PcaPwmDriver.FullyOn;
}
```

Similar to the DcMotor, the StepperMotor class is also based on the PWM control implemented within the PcaPwmDriver class. An instance of this class is passed as an argument of the StepperMotor class constructor. (See Listing 10-18.) Additionally, this constructor accepts another argument, steps, which is used to configure the number of steps per revolution. By default, this value is 200 but can be adjusted to the particular stepper motor.

LISTING 10-18   StepperMotor class constructor

```
public uint Steps { get; private set; }

public byte Rpm { get; private set; } = 30;

private List<StepperMotorPhase> fullStepControlPhases;

public StepperMotor(PcaPwmDriver pcaPwmDriver, uint steps = 200)
{
    Check.IsNull(pcaPwmDriver);

    this.pcaPwmDriver = pcaPwmDriver;

    Steps = steps;

    SetSpeed(Rpm);

    fullStepControlPhases = ControlPhaseHelper.GetFullStepSequence();
}
```

As shown in Listing 10-18, the StepperMotor class also sets the motor speed, which is the delay in driving the stepper motor, that is, incrementing or decrementing the current step. Speed configuration is implemented within the SetSpeed method from Listing 10-19. This function accepts a single argument rpm, which determines the motor revolutions per minute (RPM).

LISTING 10-19   Stepping speed configuration

```
public byte MinRpm { get; } = 1;
public byte MaxRpm { get; } = 60;
public byte Rpm { get; private set; } = 30;

public void SetSpeed(byte rpm)
{
    Check.IsLengthInValidRange(rpm, MinRpm, MaxRpm);

    Rpm = rpm;
}
```

Lastly, the StepperMotor class constructor invokes the GetFullStepSequence static method of the ControlPhaseHelper class. (See Listing 10-20.) This method creates the four-element collection, controlPhases, comprising of StepperMotorPhase objects. Hence, controlPhases is a signal sequence used to drive a stepper motor. Each of its elements implements the consecutive control phase used to move the stepper by a single step.

LISTING 10-20   Full-step control sequence

```
public static List<StepperMotorPhase> GetFullStepSequence()
{
    var controlPhases = new List<StepperMotorPhase>();

    controlPhases.Add(new StepperMotorPhase()
    {
        AIn2 = PcaPwmDriver.FullyOn,
        BIn1 = PcaPwmDriver.FullyOff,
        AIn1 = PcaPwmDriver.FullyOff,
        BIn2 = PcaPwmDriver.FullyOff
    });

    controlPhases.Add(new StepperMotorPhase()
    {
        AIn2 = PcaPwmDriver.FullyOff,
        BIn1 = PcaPwmDriver.FullyOn,
        AIn1 = PcaPwmDriver.FullyOff,
        BIn2 = PcaPwmDriver.FullyOff
    });

    controlPhases.Add(new StepperMotorPhase()
    {
        AIn2 = PcaPwmDriver.FullyOff,
        BIn1 = PcaPwmDriver.FullyOff,
        AIn1 = PcaPwmDriver.FullyOn,
        BIn2 = PcaPwmDriver.FullyOff
    });

    controlPhases.Add(new StepperMotorPhase()
```

```
    {
        AIn2 = PcaPwmDriver.FullyOff,
        BIn1 = PcaPwmDriver.FullyOff,
        AIn1 = PcaPwmDriver.FullyOff,
        BIn2 = PcaPwmDriver.FullyOn
    });

    return controlPhases;
}
```

You use values stored in the particular control phase depending on the motor index and the current step value. First, you configure the PWM channel mapping, and then either increment (for forward motor rotation) or decrement (for backward movement) a variable, storing the current step value. Subsequently, you write the control phase to an appropriate PCA9685 register.

The preceding procedure is implemented within the MakeStep method. (See Listing 10-21.) This function associates the PWM channel mapping using the ConfigureChannels private method. This method implements the mapping from Table 10-5 and works exactly the same as the analogous method ConfigureChannels of the DcMotor class. Thus, I omit a detailed description of this method.

LISTING 10-21 A procedure for rotating a motor by one step

```
public void MakeStep(StepperMotorIndex motorIndex, MotorDirection direction)
{
    ConfigureChannels(motorIndex);

    UpdateCurrentStep(direction);

    UpdateChannels();
}
```

Next, MakeStep invokes the UpdateCurrentStep function. (See Listing 10-22.) This method, depending on the parameter value, direction, either increments (direction = MotorDirection. Forward) or decrements (otherwise) the value stored in the CurrentStep property. Moreover, the UpdateCurrentStep method ensures that the CurrentStep property falls in the range of 0 to Steps − 1. Naturally, CurrentStep cannot be negative nor exceed the maximum number of steps specified using the StepperMotor class constructor.

LISTING 10-22 Updating current step value

```
public int CurrentStep { get; private set; } = 0;

private void UpdateCurrentStep(MotorDirection direction)
{
    if (direction == MotorDirection.Forward)
    {
```

```
        CurrentStep++;
    }
    else
    {
        CurrentStep--;
    }

    if(CurrentStep < 0)
    {
        CurrentStep = (int)Steps - 1;
    }

    if(CurrentStep >= Steps)
    {
        CurrentStep = 0;
    }
}
```

After calculating the step value, you update the PCA9685 registers using an appropriate control phase. You do this within the UpdateChannels private method. (See Listing 10-23.) The UpdateChannels function first determines the current control phase index, which is the remainder after the division of the CurrentStep value by the total number of control phases. For the full-step control, this value is 4. Next, the resulting PWM values are written to PCA9685 using the SetChannelValue of the PcaPwmDriver class. (Note that the fullStepControlPhases collection is initialized in the StepperMotor class constructor using the GetFullStepSequence method from Listing 10-20.)

LISTING 10-23   Updating PWM channels to drive a stepper motor

```
private List<StepperMotorPhase> fullStepControlPhases;

private void UpdateChannels()
{
    var phaseIndex = CurrentStep % fullStepControlPhases.Count;

    var currentPhase = fullStepControlPhases[phaseIndex];

    pcaPwmDriver.SetChannelValue(channels.PwmA, currentPhase.PwmA);
    pcaPwmDriver.SetChannelValue(channels.PwmB, currentPhase.PwmB);

    pcaPwmDriver.SetChannelValue(channels.AIn1, currentPhase.AIn1);
    pcaPwmDriver.SetChannelValue(channels.AIn2, currentPhase.AIn2);

    pcaPwmDriver.SetChannelValue(channels.BIn1, currentPhase.BIn1);
    pcaPwmDriver.SetChannelValue(channels.BIn2, currentPhase.BIn2);
}
```

The StepperMotor class also implements the public Move method, which lets you rotate the stepper motor by a specified number of steps in the given direction. As shown in Listing 10-24, the Move method internally uses the MakeStep function. Subsequent calls to MakeStep are delayed by a millisecond delay (msDelay), which is passed to the Task.Delay method. To determine a value of msDelay, I divide 60,000 (60 seconds times 1000 milliseconds) by a product of motor steps and the RPM.

LISTING 10-24 Rotating the stepper by a specified number of steps

```
public void Move(StepperMotorIndex motorIndex, MotorDirection direction, uint steps)
{
    var msDelay = RpmToMsDelay(Rpm);

    for (uint i = 0; i < steps; i++)
    {
        MakeStep(motorIndex, direction);

        Task.Delay(msDelay).Wait();
    }
}

private int RpmToMsDelay(byte rpm)
{
    const double minToMsScaler = 60000.0;

    return Convert.ToInt32(minToMsScaler / (Steps * rpm));
}
```

Headed app

To use the StepperMotor class, I extend the UI of the Motors app by an additional pivot item, stepper motor. (See the companion code at Chapter 10/Motors/MainPage.xaml.) As shown in Figure 10-7, this tab contains two drop-down lists, two sliders, and one button. The drop-down lists let you choose the motor index and set the motor rotation direction, while the sliders configure the RPM and the number of steps (rotation angle). A button invokes the StepperMotor.Move method, with the arguments configured using the visual controls of the Stepper Motor tab.

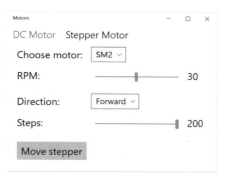

FIGURE 10-7 A pivot item for controlling the stepper motor.

I next extend the code-behind, saved in the MainPage.xaml.cs. Then, I supplement the OnNavigatedTo event handler by the statement invoking the InitializeStepperMotor function. (See Listing 10-25.) This function instantiates the StepperMotor class using a previously created instance of the PcaPwmDriver class and then sets the default motor RPM, that is, 30 revolutions per minute.

LISTING 10-25 Stepper motor initialization

```
protected async override void OnNavigatedTo(NavigationEventArgs e)
{
    base.OnNavigatedTo(e);

    await InitializePwmDriver();

    InitializeDcMotor();

    InitializeStepperMotor();
}

private void InitializeStepperMotor()
{
    stepperMotor = new StepperMotor(pwmDriver);

    StepperRpm = stepperMotor.Rpm;

    // Uncomment the following line to move stepper motor
    // by 200 steps forward, and then backwards.
    // StepperMotorTest(StepperMotorIndex.SM2);
}
```

The commented statement of the InitializeStepperMotor method can be used to test a stepper motor without using the UI. After you uncomment that line, the StepperMotorTest will be invoked. As shown in Listing 10-26, this method performs the full motor rotation in the forward direction and then rotates the motor backward to the initial position.

LISTING 10-26 Testing a stepper motor by performing a full forward and backward rotation

```
private void StepperMotorTest(StepperMotorIndex motorIndex)
{
    if (stepperMotor.IsInitialized)
    {
        // Configure steps, and RPM
        const uint steps = 200;
        const byte rpm = 50;

        // Set speed
        stepperMotor.SetSpeed(rpm);

        // Move motor forward
        stepperMotor.Move(motorIndex, MotorDirection.Forward, steps);
```

```
            // ... and go back to initial position
            stepperMotor.Move(motorIndex, MotorDirection.Backward, steps);
    }
}
```

When you test the stepper motor, it may not rotate accurately, especially when you use high speed and a larger number of steps. For instance, if you move a stepper by 200 steps with the maximum RPM in a forward direction and then do the same in the opposite direction, the motor will most likely not go back to its initial position. This effect is known as step loss, and it can be solved by automatic motor speed adjustment. Namely, you need to smoothly accelerate the stepper motor to avoid step loss. You cannot drive the stepper motor with an arbitrary speed.

Automatic speed adjustment

Physical constraints disable abrupt changes of the stepper motor position. As pointed out in the previous section, the stepper motor can lose steps if you drive the motor too fast. To solve this issue, we adopt automatic speed adjustment, which is also known as the speed ramp. Namely, we will control the motor speed such that at the beginning and end of the motor stepping trajectory, we smoothly accelerate and decelerate the stepper motor, respectively. Moreover, we will enable the max speed for large motor rotations (that is, a large number of steps) only.

In this section I use a simple trapezoidal speed ramp, shown in Figure 10-8. The motor will be linearly accelerated (ACC) from the minimum to maximum RPM. When the maximum speed is reached, the motor will be stepping at that constant speed, and subsequently it will decelerate (DEC) to the minimum speed. In general, ACC and DEC slopes can have different lengths: s_1 and s_2. For simplicity, I use slopes of the same length.

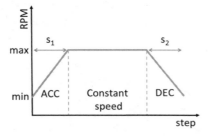

FIGURE 10-8   Sketch of the trapezoidal speed ramp. First, the speed is increased (ACC) linearly from the minimum to maximum value. Then, the motor is driven at a constant speed. Subsequently, a motor is linearly decelerated (DEC). s_1 and s_2 denote the length of acceleration and deceleration slopes, respectively.

To implement the trapezoidal ramp, I supplement the MotorsControl project by the SpeedRampHelper. This class exposes a single public method, GenerateTrapezoidalRamp. (See Listing 10-27.) This method first determines the ramp slope length by increasing the total steps by 15%. If the slope length is too small, I use the flat ramp with a minimum RPM. (See Listing 10-28.) In such a case, the motor will step at the constant lowest possible RPM—in this example, 10 RPM. Note that I'm adjusting the ramp slope length to the total number of steps. The slope length increases with the step length.

LISTING 10-27   Trapezoidal speed ramp generation

```
private const float rampSlope = 0.15f;
private const byte minRampSlopeLength = 5;

private const byte minRpm = 10;
private const byte maxRpm = 60;

public static byte[] GenerateTrapezoidalRamp(uint steps)
{
    byte[] speedRamp;

    var rampSlopeLength = Convert.ToInt32(rampSlope * steps);

    if (rampSlopeLength >= minRampSlopeLength)
    {
        speedRamp = TrapezoidalRamp(steps, rampSlopeLength);
    }
    else
    {
        speedRamp = FlatRamp(steps, minRpm);
    }

    return speedRamp;
}
```

LISTING 10-28   Flat ramp generation

```
private static byte[] FlatRamp(uint steps, byte rpm)
{
    var speedRamp = new byte[steps];

    for (int i = 0; i < steps; i++)
    {
        speedRamp[i] = rpm;
    }

    return speedRamp;
}
```

For large enough rotations, the trapezoidal ramp can be used. To generate such a ramp, I use the code from Listing 10-29. I first determine the speed step used for accelerating and decelerating a motor. This step is calculated by dividing the difference between the maximum and minimum RPM by the slope length. I use this step to generate the ACC and DEC parts of the ramp using the LinearSlope helper method. This function ensures that the speed does not exceed a valid RPM range. Then, the ACC and DEC parts are joined with the line of constant speed generated by using the FlatRamp method. Finally, I obtain the ramp depicted in Figure 10-8.

LISTING 10-29   The trapezoidal speed ramp is prepared by joining the ACC and DCC linear slopes with the flat speed ramp, that is, horizontal line of constant speed

```csharp
private static byte[] TrapezoidalRamp(uint steps, int rampSlopeLength)
{
    var speedRamp = new byte[steps];

    // Determine speed step (linear increase)
    var speedStep = Math.Ceiling(1.0 * (maxRpm - minRpm) / rampSlopeLength);

    // Acceleration (ACC)
    var acceleration = LinearSlope(rampSlopeLength, minRpm, speedStep);
    acceleration.CopyTo(speedRamp, 0);

    // Flat part
    var flatPartLength = (uint)(steps - 2 * rampSlopeLength);
    var flatPart = FlatRamp(flatPartLength, maxRpm);
    flatPart.CopyTo(speedRamp, rampSlopeLength);

    // Deacceleration (DEC)
    var deacceleration = LinearSlope(rampSlopeLength, maxRpm, -speedStep);
    deacceleration.CopyTo(speedRamp, (int)(steps - rampSlopeLength));

    return speedRamp;
}

private static byte[] LinearSlope(int rampSlopeLength, byte startRpm, double speedStep)
{
    var slope = new byte[rampSlopeLength];

    for (var i = 0; i < rampSlopeLength; i++)
    {
        var speed = startRpm + i * speedStep;

        // Ensure that speed is between min, and max RPM
        speed = Math.Min(speed, maxRpm);
        speed = Math.Max(speed, minRpm);

        slope[i] = (byte)speed;
    }

    return slope;
}
```

The trapezoidal speed ramp is then used to drive the stepper motor. In the StepperMotor class, I defined an additional method, MoveWithSpeedAdjustment, which is shown in Listing 10-30. This function uses the consecutive RPMs stored in the speed ramp to determine an actual millisecond delay between sending subsequent requests to the stepper motor. Accordingly, a motor will not lose steps. If it does, which might happen for a smaller number of total steps, you can empirically adjust the linear slope length by modifying the value stored in the rampSlope field of the SpeedRampHelper class. (See Listing 10-27.)

LISTING 10-30   An automatic adjusted delay between subsequent calls to the MakeStep function

```
public void MoveWithSpeedAdjustment(StepperMotorIndex motorIndex,
    MotorDirection direction, uint steps)
{
    var speedRamp = SpeedRampHelper.GenerateTrapezoidalRamp(steps);

    for (uint i = 0; i < steps; i++)
    {
        MakeStep(motorIndex, direction);

        var msAutoDelay = RpmToMsDelay(speedRamp[i]);

        Task.Delay(msAutoDelay).Wait();
    }
}
```

To test the preceding code, I have supplemented the stepper motor tab of the Motors app by an additional button. Its click event handler lets you move the motor with auto-speed adjustment. (See Listing 10-31.) Note that to achieve similar functionality you can also replace the Move method with MoveWithSpeedAdjustment in the StepperMotorTest function from Listing 10-26.

LISTING 10-31   Rotating a motor with automatic speed adjustment to avoid step loss

```
private void ButtonStepperMoveAutoSpeedAdjustment_Click(object sender, RoutedEventArgs e)
{
    if (stepperMotor.IsInitialized)
    {
        stepperMotor.MoveWithSpeedAdjustment(stepperMotorIndex, motorDirection,
            stepperMotorSteps);
    }
}
```

You can now easily extend the trapezoidal ramp to obtain even smoother control of your stepper motor. Replace the linear ACC and DEC RPM lines by sinusoidal or other nonlinear curves. You can also independently implement a ramp with different lengths of s_1 and s_2 slopes.

Micro-stepping

Micro-stepping is used for precise motor positioning. In micro-stepping, the full step is divided by the specific number of micro-steps. For instance, the full-step NEMA 17 rotation of 1.8° can be divided by 8 micro-steps to obtain a positioning accuracy of 0.225°.

To change the motor shaft position with micro-stepping accuracy, use a control phase sequence from Table 10-4 to drive channels AIn1, AIn2, BIn1, and BIn2, and also the micro-stepping curve for the PwmA and PwmB channels. The first four channels are used to make a full step. You use them similarly as in the case of the full-step motor control. However, you change the full-step control phase after rotating a motor by a given number of micro-steps, M_s. For instance, for $M_s = 8$, you use a subsequent full-step control phase after rotating a motor by eight micro-steps, that is, after rotating a motor by a full-step.

For a fixed full-step control phase, you adjust the PwmA and PwmB channels by using a micro-stepping monotonically increasing curve, f_m. This curve is represented as the one-dimensional array of length $M_s + 1$. For PCA9685, each value of that array is the register value—an instance of the PcaRegisterValue class. In the simplest case, this array is just a linear ramp of the Off registers, but you can also use non-linear curves, for example, sinusoidal.

Subsequently, you need to determine a pair of values from f_m, which you then write to the PwmA and PwmB registers. The particular values you use depend on the current micro-step index, μ_i, a number of micro-steps, and also the micro-step index in the micro-step control cycle, v_i.

The micro-step index is calculated by taking a modulo of the current motor step, c_s, by using M_s: $\mu_i = c_s \bmod M_s$. Now, the value of the current step is incremented or decremented whenever you change the motor position by a micro-step. Accordingly, the total number of motor steps is multiplied by M_s. For instance, for 200 full-steps and eight micro-steps, you get 1600 total motor steps.

The micro-step control cycle, which you repeatedly send to a stepper driver, contains $4 \times M_s$ elements. This follows from the fact that the full-step control cycle contains four elements (see Table 10-4), and for each full-step control phase you have M_s micro-step phases. Accordingly, to determine the value of v_i, you take a modulo of the current motor step, c_s by using $4 \times M_s$: $v_i = c_s \bmod 4 \times M_s$.

Given the values of M_s, c_s, μ_i, and v_i, you obtain the PwmA and PwmB using the following equations:

$$\mathrm{PwmA} = f_m(\mu_i), \ \mathrm{PwmB} = f_m(M_s - \mu_i)$$

when $0 \leq v_i < M_s$ or $2 M_s \leq v_i < 3M_s$, and

$$\mathrm{PwmA} = f_m(M_s - \mu_i), \ \mathrm{PwmB} = f_m(\mu_i)$$

for other values of v_i.

To give a numerical example, let's assume that you have eight micro-steps, $M_s = 8$. Then, for the current motor step of $c_s = 1$, we get $\mu_i = v_i = 1$, which yields PwmA $= f_m(1)$, and PwmB $= f_m(7)$. Similarly, for $c_s = 12$, we have $\mu_i = 4$, $v_i = 12$, so PwmA $= f_m(4)$, and PwmB $= f_m(4)$.

To implement such a micro-stepping control, I introduce the following changes in the MotorsControl library. I supplement the ControlPhaseHelper class by a static method, GetMicroStepSequence, implementing stepper motor control phases as described in Table 10-4. This method is analogous to ControlPhaseHelper.GetFullStepSequence, so its description is omitted.

Next, I implement the MicrosteppingHelper class. (See the companion code at Chapter 10/ MotorsControl/Helpers/MicroSteppingHelper.cs.) This class has three static methods: GetLinearRamp, GetPhaseIndex, and AdjustMicroStepPhase. The first method, shown in Listing 10-32, implements a linear ramp, that is, the f_m function used to drive the PwmA and PwmB channels. As you can see, I create the PcaRegisterValue collection. Each element of that collection has a linearly increasing value of the Off property. The linear slope is calculated by dividing the maximum register value by the number of micro-steps.

```
LISTING 10-32   A linear ramp for micro-stepping

public static List<PcaRegisterValue> GetLinearRamp(uint microstepCount)
{
    Check.IsPositive(microstepCount);

    var ramp = new List<PcaRegisterValue>();

    var increment = PcaPwmDriver.Range / microstepCount;

    for (var i = 0; i <= microstepCount; i++)
    {
        ramp.Add(new PcaRegisterValue()
        {
            On = 0,
            Off = Convert.ToUInt16(i * increment)
        });
    }

    return ramp;
}
```

The next method, GetPhaseIndex, calculates the index of the full-step control phase using conditional checks. The resulting index is used to determine the control phase of the AIn1, AIn2, BIn1, and BIn2 properties of the StepperMotorPhase class instance. Finally, AdjustMicroStepPhase sets the PwmA and PwmB values using the two equations on the preceding page the f_m function (microStepCurve argument), and the values of M_s (microStepCount), μ_i (microStepIndex), and v_i (microStepPhaseIndex). (See Listing 10-33.)

```
LISTING 10-33   Adjusting PwmA and PwmB properties of the micro-step control phase

public static void AdjustMicroStepPhase(StepperMotorPhase phase,
    List<PcaRegisterValue> microStepCurve, uint microstepCount,
    int microStepIndex, int microStepPhaseIndex)
{
    Check.IsNull(phase);
    Check.IsNull(microStepCurve);

    Check.IsPositive(microStepIndex);
    Check.IsPositive(microStepPhaseIndex);

    Check.LengthNotLessThan(microStepCurve.Count, (int)(microstepCount + 1));

    var microStepPhase1 = microStepCurve[(int)(microstepCount - microStepIndex)];
    var microStepPhase2 = microStepCurve[microStepIndex];

    if (microStepPhaseIndex >= 0 && microStepPhaseIndex < microstepCount
        || microStepPhaseIndex >= 2 * microstepCount && microStepPhaseIndex < 3 * microstepCount)
    {
```

```
        phase.PwmA = microStepPhase1;
        phase.PwmB = microStepPhase2;
    }
    else
    {
        phase.PwmA = microStepPhase2;
        phase.PwmB = microStepPhase1;
    }
}
```

Static methods of the `ControlPhaseHelper` and `MicrosteppingHelper` classes are then employed in the `StepperMotor` class. The class definition was supplemented by a public read-only property, `MicroStepCount`, and two private fields storing a micro-step control phase sequence (`microStep-ControlPhase`) and an f_m function (`microStepCurve`). Those fields are configured, along with the total number of steps, in the class constructor, as shown in Listing 10-34. As you can see, I set the number of micro-steps to 8.

LISTING 10-34 An updated StepperMotor class constructor accounting for the micro-stepping control

```
public uint MicroStepCount { get; } = 8;

private List<StepperMotorPhase> microStepControlPhases;
private List<PcaRegisterValue> microStepCurve;

public StepperMotor(PcaPwmDriver pcaPwmDriver, uint steps = 200)
{
    Check.IsNull(pcaPwmDriver);

    this.pcaPwmDriver = pcaPwmDriver;

    Steps = steps * MicroStepCount;

    SetSpeed(Rpm);

    fullStepControlPhases = ControlPhaseHelper.GetFullStepSequence();

    // Micro-stepping control phase, and linear ramp
    microStepControlPhases = ControlPhaseHelper.GetMicroStepSequence();
    microStepCurve = MicrosteppingHelper.GetLinearRamp(MicroStepCount);
}
```

To distinguish between full steps and micro-steps, I declare the `SteppingMode` enumeration type. It contains two values: `FullSteps` and `MicroSteps`. Given that type I modify the declarations of the `Move`, `MoveWithSpeedAdjustment`, `MakeStep`, `UpdateChannels`, and `RpmToMsDelay` methods by the additional argument `steppingMode`, with a default value of `SteppingMode.FullSteps`. This helps me to make the stepper motor control logic dependent on the stepping mode.

By analyzing the original version of the MakeStep method responsible for moving a stepper motor (Listing 10-21), we see that the actual changes are required in the UpdateChannels method, which sets register values. Accordingly, I modify that function to make it dependent on the stepping mode as shown in Listing 10-35. Namely, I first check the steppingMode argument value and then get an appropriate control phase, which is subsequently written to the PCA9685.

LISTING 10-35 Updating PWM channels, depending on the stepping mode

```
private void UpdateChannels(SteppingMode steppingMode = SteppingMode.FullSteps)
{
    StepperMotorPhase currentPhase = null;

    switch (steppingMode)
    {
        case SteppingMode.MicroSteps:
            currentPhase = GetMicroStepControlPhase();
            break;

        default:
            currentPhase = GetFullStepControlPhase();
            break;
    }

    pcaPwmDriver.SetChannelValue(channels.PwmA, currentPhase.PwmA);
    pcaPwmDriver.SetChannelValue(channels.PwmB, currentPhase.PwmB);

    pcaPwmDriver.SetChannelValue(channels.AIn1, currentPhase.AIn1);
    pcaPwmDriver.SetChannelValue(channels.AIn2, currentPhase.AIn2);

    pcaPwmDriver.SetChannelValue(channels.BIn1, currentPhase.BIn1);
    pcaPwmDriver.SetChannelValue(channels.BIn2, currentPhase.BIn2);
}

private StepperMotorPhase GetMicroStepControlPhase()
{
    // mu_i
    var microStepIndex = (int)(CurrentStep % MicroStepCount);

    // nu_i
    var microStepPhaseIndex = (int)(CurrentStep % (MicroStepCount *
        fullStepControlPhases.Count));

    // Full-step control phase index
    var mainPhaseIndex = MicrosteppingHelper.GetPhaseIndex(microStepPhaseIndex,
        MicroStepCount);

    // Control phase for AIn1, AIn2, BIn1, BIn2 signals
    var phase = microStepControlPhases[mainPhaseIndex];

    // PwmA, PwmB signals
    MicrosteppingHelper.AdjustMicroStepPhase(phase, microStepCurve,
```

```
          MicroStepCount, microStepIndex, microStepPhaseIndex);

     return phase;
}

private StepperMotorPhase GetFullStepControlPhase()
{
     var phaseIndex = CurrentStep % fullStepControlPhases.Count;

     return fullStepControlPhases[phaseIndex];
}
```

I also update the RpmToMsDelay method to adjust the millisecond delay between consecutive calls to the MakeStep method.

To determine the total steps to make, I supplement the StepperMotor class by the GetTotalStep-Count method. Depending on the stepping mode, this function returns either the full-step count (SteppingMode.FullSteps) or the full-step count times micro-steps (SteppingMode.MicroSteps). The GetTotalStepCount method is used in the Move and MoveWithSpeedAdjustment methods to update the total number of steps to make (Listing 10-36).

LISTING 10-36   Step value is updated according to the stepping mode

```
public void Move(StepperMotorIndex motorIndex, MotorDirection direction, uint steps,
    SteppingMode steppingMode = SteppingMode.FullSteps)
{
    var msDelay = RpmToMsDelay(Rpm, steppingMode);

    steps = GetTotalStepCount(steppingMode, steps);

    for (uint i = 0; i < steps; i++)
    {
        MakeStep(motorIndex, direction, steppingMode);

        Task.Delay(msDelay).Wait();
    }
}

private uint GetTotalStepCount(SteppingMode steppingMode, uint steps)
{
    if (steppingMode == SteppingMode.MicroSteps)
    {
        steps *= MicroStepCount;
    }

    return steps;
}
```

Finally, to control the stepping mode from the UI, I add a check box. When it is checked, the stepper motor will rotate with a micro-stepping accuracy. I make a similar change in the `StepperMotorTest` method. To test micro-stepping, you can use the UI or just invoke the `StepperMotorTest` method.

Servo motor

Servos are controlled by using the PWM pulse duration. This changes the servo position or rotation speed (for continuous servos). For instance, a 2 ms pulse can force a servo to continuously rotate forward at full speed.

Our PCA9685 control driver, implemented within the `PcaPwmDriver` class, only allows for setting the `On` and `Off` registers of the PCA9685. We do not have a conversion method that would set the `On` and `Off` registers to generate a pulse of specified width because it was not required for controlling the DC and stepper motors.

To implement such a procedure, you first invert the frequency to determine the pulse repetition rate and then divide the resulting value by 4096, the PWM resolution. This gives a time per tick of the internal PCA9685 oscillator. Lastly, to create `PcaRegisterValue`, generating a pulse of specified width, we set the `On` value to 0 and the `Off` value to the pulse duration divided by time per tick.

For instance, assuming that the PCA9685 frequency is 100 Hz and we want to generate a pulse duration of 2 ms = 2000 μs, the PWM signal duration is $1/100$ Hz = 10 ms. The resulting time per tick is $10/4096$ ms = 2.44 μs. Hence, the `Off` value of the PCA9685 register would be 2000 μs/2.44 μs = 820.

I implemented the preceding calculations in the `PcaPwmDriver` as the `PulseDurationToRegister-Value` static method. Its definition is given in Listing 10-37.

LISTING 10-37   Adjusting the PCA9685 register value to the required pulse width

```
public static int HzMinFrequency { get; } = 24;
public static int HzMaxFrequency { get; } = 1526;

public static PcaRegisterValue PulseDurationToRegisterValue(double msPulseDuration,
    int hzFrequency)
{
    Check.IsLengthInValidRange(hzFrequency, HzMinFrequency, HzMaxFrequency);
    Check.IsPositive(msPulseDuration);

    var msCycleDuration = 1000.0 / hzFrequency;

    var msTimePerOscillatorTick = msCycleDuration / Range;

    return new PcaRegisterValue()
    {
        On = 0,
        Off = Convert.ToUInt16(msPulseDuration / msTimePerOscillatorTick)
    };
}
```

Hardware assembly

To demonstrate servo motor usage for robotics, I use the micro-continuous rotation servo FS390R (*https://bit.ly/FS390R*) with an attached wheel (*https://bit.ly/servo_wheel*). Such elements can serve as the basis for building a tiny moving robot.

According to the FS390R datasheet (*https://bit.ly/FS390R_datasheet*), this servo will rotate forward when the PWM pulse is wider than 1.5 ms and doesn't exceed 2.3 ms. The wider the pulse, the faster the motor rotates. The motor will stop if its pulse duration is 1.5 ms and start to rotate backward when you further narrow the pulse. Backward rotation speed increases with decreasing pulse width and reaches its maximum value for a width of 0.7 ms. To control this servo using the described modulation, we need to attach the servo HAT to the RPi2/RPi3 and then provide a sufficient power supply to the HAT. In this case, you have several options. You can either use a 5 V power supply (*https://bit.ly/power_supply_5V*) or provide power using a terminal located next to the power plug. Here, I'm using the second option and I attach a HAT to the lab power supply, generating 5 V. Subsequently, I connect a servo to the first PWM channel (indexed as 0) as shown in Figure 10-9.

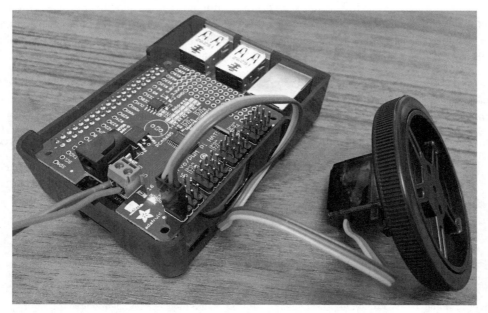

FIGURE 10-9 A wheel controlled by the servo motor is attached to the Raspberry Pi 2 through the first PWM channel of the servo HAT.

Headed app

You can now prepare the servo control software. To this end, I implement the headed app using the Blank UWP Visual C# project template. (See the companion code at Chapter 10/Servo.) As shown in Figure 10-10, this app lets you choose the PWM channel and control the pulse width generated by that channel. You can also stop signal generation by clicking a Stop button. This will write the fully off value to the selected PCA9685 register.

FIGURE 10-10 UI of the Servo app for controlling the servo motors.

When you click the Update button, the corresponding method from Listing 10-38 will be invoked. This simply uses the SetChannelValue of the PcaPwmDriver class instance. First you need to prepare several things. The requested pulse width has to be converted to the register value (or more precisely to the duty cycle), which you do by using the PulseDurationToRegisterValue static method of the PcaPwmDriver class within the MsPulseDuration property. (See Listing 10-39.) This is bound to the slider of the Servo app UI. The register value (the pwmValue member of the MainPage) is updated whenever the slider value changes.

LISTING 10-38 Updating the PWM channel

```
private PcaPwmDriver pwmDriver;
private PcaRegisterValue pwmValue = new PcaRegisterValue();

private void ButtonUpdateChannel_Click(object sender, RoutedEventArgs e)
{
    if(pwmDriver.IsInitialized)
    {
        pwmDriver.SetChannelValue(pwmChannel, pwmValue);
    }
}
```

LISTING 10-39 Converting a millisecond pulse duration to the PCA9685 register value

```
private double msPulseDuration;

private double MsPulseDuration
{
    get { return msPulseDuration; }
    set
    {
        msPulseDuration = value;
        pwmValue = PcaPwmDriver.PulseDurationToRegisterValue(msPulseDuration, hzFrequency);
    }
}
```

Next, to associate a connection with the servo HAT, I use the `InitializePwmDriver` method from Listing 10-40. This method, which is invoked within the `OnNavigatedTo` event handler, uses the I²C address of 0x40 and sets the default PWM frequency to 100 Hz. After initializing and configuring the `PcaPwmDriver` class, you can control the servo motor with the UI.

LISTING 10-40 PWM driver initialization with an address of 0x40 and frequency of 100 Hz

```
private const byte pwmAddress = 0x40;
private const int hzFrequency = 100;

protected async override void OnNavigatedTo(NavigationEventArgs e)
{
    base.OnNavigatedTo(e);

    await InitializePwmDriver();

    // Uncomment the following line to run servo test without using UI
    // ServoTest()
}

private async Task InitializePwmDriver()
{
    pwmDriver = new PcaPwmDriver();

    await pwmDriver.Init(pwmAddress);

    if (pwmDriver.IsInitialized)
    {
        // Enable oscillator
        pwmDriver.SetSleepMode(SleepMode.Normal);

        // Set frequency
        pwmDriver.SetFrequency(hzFrequency);
    }
}
```

Alternatively, in the `OnNavigatedTo` event handler, you can uncomment a statement invoking the `ServoTest` method. The method sequentially changes a pulse duration between the maximum and minimum values recognized by FS390R. (See Listing 10-41.) Thus, after running `ServoTest`, the wheel attached to the servo motor will rotate forward with the maximum speed. The motor speed will decrease, and then the wheel will change the rotation direction to backward and start to accelerate to the maximum speed. Lastly, the wheel will stop according to the last statement of the `ServoTest` method.

LISTING 10-41 Testing a servo connected to the PWM first channel without using the UI

```
private void ServoTest()
{
    if (pwmDriver.IsInitialized)
    {
```

```
        const byte channel = 0;

        const int msSleepTime = 1000;

        const double minPulseDuration = 0.7;
        const double maxPulseDuration = 2.3;
        const double step = 0.1;

        for (var pulseDuration = maxPulseDuration;
            pulseDuration >= minPulseDuration - step;
            pulseDuration -= step)
        {
            var registerValue = PcaPwmDriver.PulseDurationToRegisterValue(
                pulseDuration, hzFrequency);

            pwmDriver.SetChannelValue(channel, registerValue);

            Task.Delay(msSleepTime).Wait();
        }

        // Disable PWM channel
        pwmDriver.SetChannelValue(pwmChannel, PcaPwmDriver.FullyOff);
    }
}
```

Providers

Hardware submodules, such as the motor HAT or Sense HAT, comprise a convenient way to extend the functionality of the IoT system. To simplify programming of such submodules with the common UWP API, Windows 10 IoT Core introduces the concept of the provider model (*https://bit.ly/lightning_provider*).

The provider model delivers a set of programming interfaces, which you implement to give your users a uniform API that conforms to the UWP and offers access to hardware components. One example of such a solution is the Microsoft.IoT.Lightning library. It gives you access to onboard features like GPIO, I²C, and SPI through the Direct Memory Mapped driver. However, the actual code for accessing hardware components is almost exactly the same as with the inbox default driver. You only need to explicitly change the provider to that delivered by Microsoft.IoT.Lightning. Such an approach is convenient because, when you update the hardware component, you change only the corresponding software provider without having to modify the source code of other parts of your app.

All controller classes of the IoT UWP API implement the interface, which has members common to all controllers of a specific type. For instance, GpioController implements the IGpioController interface, while I2cDeviceController derives from I2cController.

In this section, I will show you how to use Lightning providers. Subsequently I will tell you how to write your own custom provider to control the PCA9685 PWM module and then utilize it to drive the DC motor.

Lightning providers

To employ Microsoft.IoT.Lightning I create the BlinkyApp.Lightning app using the Visual C# Blank App (Universal Windows) project template. Then, I install the Microsoft.IoT.Lightning NuGet package and implement the app exactly the same as in BlinkyApp, discussed in Chapter 3, "Windows IoT programming essentials." BlinkyApp.Lightning simply drives the GPIO pin to sequentially turn on and off an LED.

I then implement the method from Listing 10-42. This method checks if the Lightning driver is enabled and then sets the default provider to that delivered by the Microsoft.IoT.Lightning.

LISTING 10-42   Configuring low level devices controller

```
private void ConfigureLightningController()
{
    if(LightningProvider.IsLightningEnabled)
    {
        LowLevelDevicesController.DefaultProvider = LightningProvider.GetAggregateProvider();
    }
}
```

A `ConfigureLightningController` controller is invoked within the `MainPage` constructor, before accessing the GPIO pins for controlling an LED. (See Listing 10-43.)

LISTING 10-43   Invoking a ConfigureLightningController

```
public MainPage()
{
    InitializeComponent();

    ConfigureLightningController();

    ConfigureGpioPin();
    ConfigureMainButton();
    ConfigureTimer();
}
```

To use the Lightning provider, you need to enable the Direct Memory Mapped driver through the Device Portal and, as shown in Listing 10-44, declare appropriate capabilities in the app manifest. Note that these declarations use the `iot` namespace importing declarations from *http://schemas.microsoft. com/appx/manifest/iot/windows10*. The first capability is necessary to access the low-level device controller, while the second capability corresponds to the global unique identifier of the Lightning interface.

LISTING 10-44   A fragment of the BlinkyApp.Lightning app manifest

```
<Package
  xmlns="http://schemas.microsoft.com/appx/manifest/foundation/windows10"
  xmlns:mp="http://schemas.microsoft.com/appx/2014/phone/manifest"
  xmlns:uap="http://schemas.microsoft.com/appx/manifest/uap/windows10"
  xmlns:iot="http://schemas.microsoft.com/appx/manifest/iot/windows10"
  IgnorableNamespaces="uap mp iot">

  <Capabilities>
    <Capability Name="internetClient" />
    <iot:Capability Name="lowLevelDevices" />
    <DeviceCapability Name="109b86ad-f53d-4b76-aa5f-821e2ddf2141"/>
  </Capabilities>

  <!--Other declarations stay unchanged-->

</Package>
```

PCA9685 controller provider

To show you how to implement a custom provider, I create a new project, Motors.PwmProvider, with the Visual C# Blank App (Universal Windows) project template. Then I reference the MotorsControl class library to gain access to the PcaPwmDriver class and other helpers we developed previously.

Subsequently, I implement the PcaPwmControllerProvider. (See the companion code at Chapter 10/ Motors.PwmProvider/ControllerProviders/PcaPwmControllerProvider.cs.) This class wraps the functionality of PcaPwmDriver to adapt it to the provider model. Therefore, PcaPwmController-Provider implements the IPwmControllerProvider interface. This interface, declared in the Windows.Devices.Pwm.Provider namespace, has several public methods and properties, which are common to all PWM controllers, including the PCA9685, which we use here.

In particular, to set the frequency of the PWM output, your controller class has to implement the SetDesiredFrequency method. PcaPwmDriver already implements such a functionality in the SetFrequency method. As Listing 10-45 shows, I can straightforwardly use this function to update the PWM frequency. SetDesiredFrequency should return the actual PWM frequency. In general, the desired value can be different from the actual one (due to incompatibilities in number representation, for example). To return the actual PWM frequency I use the GetFrequency method of the PcaPwmDriver.

LISTING 10-45   A fragment of the PcaPwmControllerProvider class

```
public class PcaPwmControllerProvider : IPwmControllerProvider
{
    private PcaPwmDriver pcaPwmDriver = new PcaPwmDriver();

    public double SetDesiredFrequency(double frequency)
```

```
    {
        pcaPwmDriver.SetFrequency(Convert.ToInt32(frequency));

        return pcaPwmDriver.GetFrequency();
    }

    // The rest of class definition

}
```

To control the duty cycle of the particular PWM channel, the `PcaPwmControllerProvider` class implements `SetPulseParameters`, shown in Listing 10-46. Again, I use the corresponding functionality from the `PcaPwmDrive`—that is, the `SetChannelValue` method. This method, instead of duty cycle (given in percent), uses instances of the `PcaRegisterValue` class. To convert duty cycle to `PcaRegisterValue`, I write the helper static method, `DutyCycleToRegisterValue`.

LISTING 10-46 Setting PWM pulse parameters

```
public void SetPulseParameters(int pin, double dutyCycle, bool invertPolarity)
{
    var pcaRegisterValue = PcaPwmDriver.DutyCycleToRegisterValue(dutyCycle, invertPolarity);

    pcaPwmDriver.SetChannelValue(Convert.ToByte(pin), pcaRegisterValue);
}
```

`DutyCycleToRegisterValue` is defined in the `PcaPwmDriver` class and, as shown in Listing 10-47, calculates the `On` value of the `PcaRegisterValue` by simply multiplying a duty cycle by 4096 (PWM resolution/Range property) and then dividing the resulting value by 100 (`PercentageScaler` property).

LISTING 10-47 Converting a duty cycle to the register value

```
public static double PercentageScaler { get; } = 100.0;

public static PcaRegisterValue DutyCycleToRegisterValue(double dutyCycle, bool invertPolarity)
{
    var registerValue = dutyCycle * Range / PercentageScaler;
    registerValue = Math.Min(registerValue, Range);

    ushort offValue = 0;
    ushort onValue = Convert.ToUInt16(registerValue);

    return new PcaRegisterValue()
    {
        On = !invertPolarity ? onValue : offValue,
        Off = !invertPolarity ? offValue : onValue
    };
}
```

IPwmControllerProvider has another four methods: AcquirePin, ReleasePin, EnablePin, and DisablePin. They are used to get (AcquirePin) or release (ReleasePin) exclusive access to the PWM pin and to enable (EnablePin) or disable (DisablePin) pulse generation from the corresponding channel. However, the PCA9685 PWM driver does not have any API for acquiring, releasing, enabling, or disabling channels. Thus, PcaPwmControllerProvider has empty definitions for the AcquirePin, ReleasePin, EnablePin, and DisablePin methods.

Going further, PcaPwmControllerProvider has four read-only properties imposed by the IPwmControllerProvider interface. These are ActualFrequency, MaxFrequency, MinFrequency, and PinCount. To define all of them, I used corresponding members of the PcaPwmDriver class (see the companion code).

Finally, PcaPwmControllerProvider has a private constructor, in which I initialize the PcaPwmDriver and disable the driver sleep mode. This initialization uses the asynchronous method Init of the PcaPwmDriver class. However, the C# class constructors cannot be asynchronous, nor use a wait modifier. Hence, I need to invoke the Init method synchronously with the Wait method. Such waiting would block the UI thread, so I invoke asynchronous code in a separate background thread with the Task.Run method. (See Listing 10-48.) If the initialization could not be performed, I raise a custom DeviceInitializationException, implemented in DeviceInitializationException.cs under the Exceptions folder of the Motors.PwmProvider project.

LISTING 10-48   PcaPwmDriver initialization

```
private PcaPwmControllerProvider(byte address = 0x60)
{
    // Initialize PcaPwmDriver in a background
    // thread to prevent blocking of the UI
    Task.Run(async () =>
    {
        await pcaPwmDriver.Init(address);

        pcaPwmDriver.SetSleepMode(SleepMode.Normal);
    }).Wait();

    if (!pcaPwmDriver.IsInitialized)
    {
        throw DeviceInitializationException.Default(address);
    }
}
```

To get an actual instance of PcaPwmControllerProvider, you use the public GetDefault method, which appears in Listing 10-49.

```
public static PcaPwmControllerProvider GetDefault()
{
    return new PcaPwmControllerProvider();
}
```

DC motor control

Now I tell you how I incorporate the PWM controller provider to control a DC motor. (See the DcMotor.cs file under the MotorsControl folder of the Motors.PwmProvider project.) I leave the implementation of the stepper motor and servo as a task for you.

First, I modify the DcMotor class constructor such that it now uses an argument that is the concrete implementation of the IPwmControllerProvider interface. (See Listing 10-50.) Consequently, I also change the type of the private member storing a reference to that argument.

LISTING 10-50 A modified DcMotor class constructor

```
private IPwmControllerProvider pwmControllerProvider;

public DcMotor(IPwmControllerProvider pwmControllerProvider)
{
    Check.IsNull(pwmControllerProvider);

    this.pwmControllerProvider = pwmControllerProvider;
}
```

Second, I change the Start and Stop methods, so they now use the SetPulseParameters of the IPwmControllerProvider interface. (See Listing 10-51.)

LISTING 10-51 Starting and stopping a DC motor (compare these methods to those from Listing 10-13)

```
private const double dutyCycleFullyOn = 100.0;
private const double dutyCycleFullyOff = 0.0;

public void Start(DcMotorIndex motorIndex, MotorDirection direction)
{
    ConfigureChannels(motorIndex);

    if (direction == MotorDirection.Forward)
    {
        pwmControllerProvider.SetPulseParameters(channels.In1, dutyCycleFullyOn, false);
        pwmControllerProvider.SetPulseParameters(channels.In2, dutyCycleFullyOff, false);
    }
    else
    {
```

```
                pwmControllerProvider.SetPulseParameters(channels.In1, dutyCycleFullyOff, false);
                pwmControllerProvider.SetPulseParameters(channels.In2, dutyCycleFullyOn, false);
        }
}

public void Stop(DcMotorIndex motorIndex)
{
    ConfigureChannels(motorIndex);

    pwmControllerProvider.SetPulseParameters(channels.In1, dutyCycleFullyOff, true);
    pwmControllerProvider.SetPulseParameters(channels.In2, dutyCycleFullyOff, true);
}
```

Last, I modify the SetSpeed method as shown in Listing 10-52.

LISTING 10-52 Setting the DC motor speed with the PcaPwmControllerProvider (compare this method to that from Listing 10-12)

```
public void SetSpeed(DcMotorIndex motorIndex, ushort speed)
{
    ConfigureChannels(motorIndex);

    var dutyCycle = PcaPwmDriver.PercentageScaler * speed / PcaPwmDriver.Range;

    dutyCycle = Math.Min(dutyCycle, PcaPwmDriver.PercentageScaler);

    pwmControllerProvider.SetPulseParameters(channels.Speed, dutyCycle, false);
}
```

Given the modified DcMotor class, I define the UI as shown in Figure 10-5, and implement code-behind. However, most of the logic is the same as in the Motors app. The only thing that differs is the initialization of the modified DcMotor class. As Listing 10-53 shows, this initialization now requires the PcaPwmControllerProvider.

LISTING 10-53 PcaPwmControllerProvider and DcMotor initialization

```
private void InitializeDcMotor()
{
    var pcaPwmControllerProvider = PcaPwmControllerProvider.GetDefault();

    dcMotor = new DcMotor(pcaPwmControllerProvider);

    // Set default speed
    Speed = 1000;

    // Uncomment the following line to run DC1 motor for 5 seconds without using UI.
    // DcMotorTest(DcMotorIndex.DC1, MotorDirection.Backward, speed);
}
```

To test the app, you need to revert your device back to use the Inbox driver and deploy the app to your device. You can then either use the UI to start and stop the DC motor or uncomment the last line of the `InitializeDcMotor` method.

The functionality of the app does not change with respect to the Motors app. However, we increase the maintainability of the source code. When building an app that conforms to specific interfaces from the provider model, you can just replace the concrete implementations of your drivers. Specifically, if you need to upgrade some hardware module, and thus modify the driver, you change only the underlying classes. Other software modules using your driver do not need to "know" anything about your changes since they invoke methods delivered by specific interfaces. This approach resembles the code-sharing strategies from mobile and web programming.

Summary

In this chapter, you developed the control driver for the PCA9685 PWM module, which is the key element of the motor RPi2/RPi3 HATs. You learned how to use that driver to implement H bridges for controlling DC motors, changing position of the stepper motor with the full- and micro-stepping techniques, and modulating the pulse-width for driving servo motor. Along the way, you developed three headed apps for testing your control software. I also discussed methods for implementing automatic stepper motor speed adjustment and provider model.

CHAPTER 11

Device learning

N ow that I've covered implementing artificial sensing, auditory, vision, and motor functions, in this chapter I show you how to prepare an artificial intelligence (AI) module, which can combine signals acquired by other artificial modules to reason, make decisions, and predict outcomes like a human.

An AI module can memorize data such as sensor readings, voice commands, or images. It can evaluate this data and use it to take specific action. For instance, an AI module can analyze sensor readings to detect an anomaly and process voice commands to turn on or off a particular function. AI can also use images to perform automated technical inspection. You already use AI every day. Your e-mail client "reads" your emails to detect spam. Your bank analyzes your credit card transactions to identify possible fraud. Your favorite web store suggests products you may be interested in based on your shopping history.

AI is also of great importance for the IoT because interconnected sensors and devices can produce large datasets. As processes monitored by those sensors and devices become more and more complex, manual data handling becomes time consuming, difficult, and sometimes simply impossible. To solve this issue, you can teach the machine to automatically process and analyze data for you.

Broadly, AI is the ability of a computer system (machine) to perform functions that emulate human cognition—knowledge, memory, evaluation, and reasoning. Humans memorize patterns (features), which can be sensed (like weather changes), visualized (letters, signs), or voiced (speech) along with their meaning (labels). Humans evaluate those patterns based on their experience, knowledge, and emotions to draw conclusions—in other words, to generalize what they already learned.

AI uses a similar concept. Specifically, the data from artificial sensing modules is processed to extract characteristic features, which then feed the Machine Learning (ML) algorithm. The ML algorithm, based on the previously trained model—the set of mathematical objects that describe the process being monitored—predicts trends in data, classifies datasets, and searches for patterns and correlations. The outcome of the ML algorithm can guide specific actions or decisions.

You can approach ML training in several ways. In supervised learning, training datasets include labeled inputs and known outcomes—for instance, sensor readings labeled as normal (0) or abnormal (1). This dataset trains the ML algorithm (adjusts its intrinsic parameters), so that it can generalize what it has learned and becomes able to independently apply labels (0 or 1) for a given temperature. As a result, ML can automatically detect anomalies in the sensor readings.

ML algorithms can also evaluate unlabeled data in unsupervised learning. ML identifies similarities in data to classify them or predict trends. Unsupervised learning may automatically find boundaries between normal and abnormal values in sensor readings by analyzing the distance of each sensor reading from the mean value.

You can combine supervised and unsupervised learning to process datasets containing labeled and unlabeled data.

Another way of approaching ML is through reinforcement learning, in which external feedback (a reinforcement signal) identifies correct machine decisions after the machine performs some action, e.g. classifying input data. The reinforcement system is inspired by a behavior where awards and penalties correlate with successes and failures, respectively.

I have shown you several AI techniques for tasks such as processing voice input, detecting faces in images, and controlling stepper motors. In this chapter, I show you how to explicitly use selected AI algorithms available through the REST APIs of Microsoft Cognitive Services and how to build a custom AI module using Azure Machine Learning Studio.

Microsoft Cognitive Services

Microsoft Cognitive Services (MCS), also known as Project Oxford, is a set of REST APIs providing access to the cloud-based artificial intelligence (AI) algorithms for vision, speech, language, knowledge, and search applications (*http://bit.ly/mcs_api*). MCS is platform-independent and lets you extend any of your apps with AI features by using just a few lines of code.

For instance, the set of vision APIs implements complex algorithms for comprehensive image processing. These include extracting information describing image content (Vision API); optical character recognition (OCR) for image, text, and video moderation (Content Moderator API); human face detection and verification (Face API); human emotions detection (Emotion API); and digital stabilization, face tracking, and motion detection for video processing (Video API). The functionality offered by these algorithms is comprehensive. For example, the Face API can be used not only to detect human faces as the FaceDetector class but to extract human face features like age, gender, pose, and facial landmarks. Moreover, the Face API can automatically classify a face image and identify similar faces from a provided image collection.

You access all MCS APIs similarly. In the upcoming section, I implement a sample app based on the Emotion API. It's the basis for building UWP apps that utilize MCS. You can also use MCS on other platforms—you just need your favorite class implementing the REST client and JSON parsing.

Emotions detector

Here, I show you how to use the Emotion API of MCS to develop an app that can detect and indicate human emotions in faces. I first build a UWP app, capturing photos from the webcam to be sent to the Emotion API for analysis. The analysis eventually displays along with the image; see Figure 11-1. I combine this functionality with the Sense HAT LED array driver, enabling the human emotion to be indicated as a uniform LED color.

In order to implement this AI-enabled app, I use the blank UWP project template for Visual C# to create an EmotionsDetector app; see the companion code at Chapter 11/EmotionsDetector. Then I install the Microsoft.ProjectOxford.Emotion NuGet package. (See Figure 11.2.) It implements the EmotionsServiceClient class, which is the REST client, simplifying access to the Emotion API. Microsoft.ProjectOxford.Emotion also implements classes wrapping JSON responses from the Emotion API.

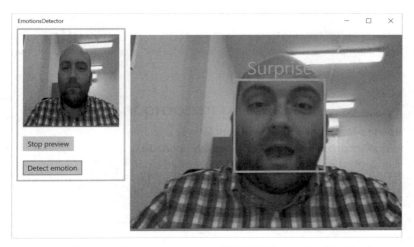

FIGURE 11-1 EmotionsDetector app uses artificial intelligence for detecting human emotions.

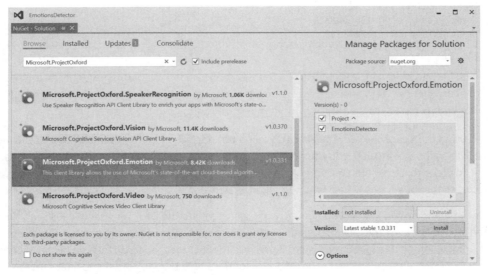

FIGURE 11-2 The Emotion API client installation

The request URL for the Emotion API is *https://api.projectoxford.ai/emotion/v1.0/recognize*. In the request body, you specify either the URL or binary data of the face image to be analyzed. The response from the Emotion API is the JSON array; see Listing 11-1. Each element of this array is wrapped as the Microsoft.ProjectOxford.Emotion.Contract.Emotion and includes two objects: the face rectangle, represented as the `Microsoft.ProjectOxford.Common.Rectangle` class, and scores (the `Microsoft.ProjectOxford.Emotion.Contract.Scores` class). The face rectangle indicates the bounding box of the detected face, while scores is the collection of confidence (or probability) values—that is, the real number in the range of 0–1. The higher the score, the higher the probability that a given emotion is expressed in the analyzed face.

The Emotion API can detect the following emotions: anger, contempt, disgust, fear, happiness, neutral, sadness, and surprise. The sample Emotion API response from Listing 11-1 contains scores for the face image from Figure 11-1, so the largest value was assigned to surprise, and the other scores are negligible.

LISTING 11-1   JSON response from the Emotion API

```
[
  {
    "faceRectangle": {
      "left": 109,
      "top": 136,
      "width": 61,
      "height": 109
    },
    "scores": {
      "anger": 0.000804054,
      "contempt": 7.84957047E-06,
      "disgust": 0.000139290976,
      "fear": 0.000154535242,
      "happiness": 0.000134000831,
      "neutral": 0.00167221332,
      "sadness": 1.17382831E-06,
      "surprise": 0.9970869
    }
  }
]
```

When using the `EmotionsServiceClient`, you do not need to manually define a request URL nor parse a JSON response. Instead, you use dedicated methods of the `EmotionsServiceClient` class. However, in order to access the Emotion API as well as other cognitive services of Project Oxford, you need to subscribe for a free API key: *https://bit.ly/mcs_sign-up*.

After obtaining an API key, all you need to do is to instantiate the `EmotionsServiceClient` class and then invoke `RecognizeAsync` or `RecognizeInVideoAsync`, depending on whether you are processing a single image or a video sequence. Here, I use the first method to process an instance of the `SoftwareBitmap` class—an abstract representation of the single bitmap containing a face image.

As you saw in Figure 11-1, the app consists of two modules: a webcam preview and a display of processing results. The webcam preview is based on the `CameraCapture` class (see Chapter 8, "Image processing") and is activated after you click the **Start Preview** button. The caption of the button will then change to Stop Preview.

When the preview is active, you can invoke image processing by clicking the **Detect Emotion** button, which invokes an event handler from Listing 11-2.

LISTING 11-2   A video frame captured from the webcam is analyzed using the Emotion API

```
private CameraCapture cameraCapture = new CameraCapture();

private async void ButtonDetectEmotion_Click(object sender, RoutedEventArgs e)
{
    if (cameraCapture.IsPreviewActive)
    {
        // Capture, and display bitmap
        var softwareBitmap = await cameraCapture.CapturePhotoToSoftwareBitmap();
        DisplayBitmap(softwareBitmap);

        // Get, and display emotion
        var emotion = await GetEmotion(softwareBitmap);
        DisplayEmotion(softwareBitmap, emotion);
    }
}
```

The Detect Emotion button click event handler captures the video frame using the CapturePhotoTo-SoftwareBitmap method of the CameraCapture class and then displays this frame in the Image control using the DisplayBitmap method you find in Listing 11-3. This happens indirectly using a databinding between two properties: Image.Source and MainPage.FaceBitmap. In the DisplayBitmap method, I copy the pixel buffer from the acquired frame to an instance of the WriteableBitmap class, which can then be assigned to Image.Source and displayed as an image in the UI.

LISTING 11-3   An instance of the WriteableBitmap class is displayed in the Image control bound to the FaceBitmap property

```
private WriteableBitmap faceBitmap;

private WriteableBitmap FaceBitmap
{
    get { return faceBitmap; }
    set
    {
        faceBitmap = value;
        OnPropertyChanged();
    }
}

private void DisplayBitmap(SoftwareBitmap softwareBitmap)
{
    if (softwareBitmap != null)
    {
```

```
        var writeableBitmap = new WriteableBitmap(softwareBitmap.PixelWidth,
            softwareBitmap.PixelHeight);

        softwareBitmap.CopyToBuffer(writeableBitmap.PixelBuffer);

        FaceBitmap = writeableBitmap;
    }
}
```

Subsequently, the emotion service receives the bitmap for analysis. The emotion service REST client expects image data to be represented using the `Windows.IO.Stream` object. Hence, in Listing 11-4, an instance of the `SoftwareBitmap` class is converted to the `Stream` class instance before it is sent to the Emotion API using the `RecognizeAsync` method of the `EmotionServiceClient` class instance.

LISTING 11-4   Processing a face image using the Emotion API

```
private EmotionServiceClient emotionServiceClient = new EmotionServiceClient("TYPE_YOUR_
API_KEY_HERE");

private const string emotionsApiError = "Emotion API error: ";

private async Task<Emotion> GetEmotion(SoftwareBitmap softwareBitmap)
{
    Emotion emotion = null;

    try
    {
        var bitmapImageStream = await SoftwareBitmapHelper.GetBitmapStream(softwareBitmap);

        var recognitionResult = await emotionServiceClient.RecognizeAsync(bitmapImageStream);

        emotion = recognitionResult.FirstOrDefault();
    }
    catch (Exception ex)
    {
        DisplayMessage(emotionsApiError + ex.Message);
    }

    return emotion;
}
```

I implement the above conversion within the `GetBitmapStream` method of the `SoftwareBitmapHelper` class; see Listing 11-5. After validating the argument value, I encode a pixel buffer to the bitmap format using methods of the `BitmapEncoder` class and the `InMemoryRandomAccessStream`. First, the `BitmapEncoder.CreateAsync` static method achieves an instance of the `BitmapEncoder`. It accepts two arguments: an identifier of the image format and the instance of the object implementing the `IRandomAccessStream` interface, e.g. `InMemoryRandomAccessStream`. Optionally, you can specify encoding options using a key-value pair collection (`encodingOptions` argument).

BitmapEncoder exposes the following static fields representing available image formats: BmpEncoderId, GifEncoderId, JpegEncoderId, JpegXREncoderId, PngEncoderId, and TiffEncoderId. In Listing 11-5, I use BmpEncoderId to indicate that the image format is BMP. Then, I invoke SetSoftware-Bitmap to set the pixel data and FlushAsync to asynchronously commit image data (copy it to the object) that conforms to the IRandomAccessStream interface.

Basically, the BitmapEncoder class supplements the raw pixel buffer by the header, which contains an image description. The Emotion API uses this header, together with the pixel buffer, to identify image dimensions, bit depth, color encoding, and so on, to appropriately interpret the pixel buffer and thus properly detect face location and emotion.

LISTING 11-5   SoftwareBitmap conversion to an instance of the System.IO.Stream class

```
public static class SoftwareBitmapHelper
{
    public static async Task<Stream> GetBitmapStream(SoftwareBitmap softwareBitmap)
    {
        Check.IsNull(softwareBitmap);

        var bitmapImageInMemoryRandomAccessStream = new InMemoryRandomAccessStream();

        var bitmapEncoder = await BitmapEncoder.CreateAsync(
            BitmapEncoder.BmpEncoderId, bitmapImageInMemoryRandomAccessStream);

        bitmapEncoder.SetSoftwareBitmap(softwareBitmap);

        await bitmapEncoder.FlushAsync();

        return bitmapImageInMemoryRandomAccessStream.AsStream();
    }
}
```

The response of the Emotion API, obtained from the RecognizeAsync method, is the collection of Emotion objects. Each of them corresponds to each face detected in the provided image. Here, I use the first Emotion class instance; see Listing 11-4. Namely, using the DisplayEmotion method from Listing 11-6, I get the primarily expressed emotion, convert it to its string representation, and display it above the rectangle bounding the detected face; see Figure 11-1.

LISTING 11-6   Most apparent detected emotion is displayed on the captured frame right above the face-bounding rectangle

```
private void DisplayEmotion(SoftwareBitmap softwareBitmap, Emotion emotion)
{
    if (emotion != null)
    {
```

```
        var emotionName = EmotionHelper.GetTopEmotionName(emotion);

        DrawFaceBox(softwareBitmap, emotion.FaceRectangle, emotionName);
    }
}
```

As you see in Listing 11-7, to sort emotion scores, you can use the ToRankedList method of the Scores class instance. It produces the collection of key-value pairs, where keys identify emotion names and values are their scores. Then, to get an emotion name you simply read the Key property of the first element from the emotions ranked list.

LISTING 11-7   String representation of the most pronounced emotion is obtained by using the ToRankedList method of the Scores class instance

```
public static string GetTopEmotionName(Emotion emotion)
{
    Check.IsNull(emotion);

    var rankedList = emotion.Scores.ToRankedList();

    return rankedList.First().Key;
}
```

I use the face-bounding box stored in the FaceRectangle property of the Emotion class to draw a rectangle on top of the captured video frame; see Listing 11-8. This proceeds the same way it did in Chapter 8. However, here I'm also adjusting the rectangle color to the particular emotion using the GetEmotionColor method of the EmotionHelper class; see Listing 11-9 and the companion code at Chapter 11/EmotionsDetector/EmotionHelper.cs.

LISTING 11-8   Face box and emotion description display on top of the acquired video frame

```
private double xScalingFactor;
private double yScalingFactor;

private void DrawFaceBox(SoftwareBitmap softwareBitmap,
    Microsoft.ProjectOxford.Common.Rectangle faceRectangle, string emotionName)
{
    // Clear any previous face rectangles
    CanvasFaceDisplay.Children.Clear();

    // Update scaling factors for displaying face rectangle
    GetScalingFactors(softwareBitmap);

    // Adjust color to emotion
    var emotionColor = EmotionHelper.GetEmotionColor(emotionName);

    // Prepare face box
```

```
    var faceBox = EmotionHelper.PrepareFaceBox(faceRectangle, emotionColor,
        xScalingFactor, yScalingFactor);

    // Prepare emotion description
    var emotionTextBlock = EmotionHelper.PrepareEmotionTextBlock(faceBox,
        emotionColor, emotionName);

    // Display bounding rectangle, and emotion description
    CanvasFaceDisplay.Children.Add(faceBox);
    CanvasFaceDisplay.Children.Add(emotionTextBlock);
}
```

To relate colors to emotions, I use the switch statement, where each switch label is obtained as the name of the appropriate field of the Scores class instance. To this end, I construct a dummy Scores object and invoke the nameof operator for each emotion field of the Scores class instance. By doing so I do not need to hardcode emotion names.

LISTING 11-9 Each emotion has a specific color, which is then used to format the face rectangle and the emotion description

```
public static Color GetEmotionColor(string emotionName)
{
    Check.IsNull(emotionName);

    // Dummy object for reading emotion names
    var scores = new Scores();

    switch (emotionName)
    {
        case nameof(scores.Happiness):
            return Colors.GreenYellow;

        // and so on...

        default:
        case nameof(scores.Neutral):
            return Colors.White;
    }
}
```

Next, I display the name of the most exposed emotion above the face rectangle. This is implemented in the EmotionHelper.PrepareEmotionTextBlock; see Listing 11-10. This method works similarly to PrepareFaceBox of the EmotionHelper class. Namely, it creates the TextBlock control, sets its Foreground, FontSize, and Text properties, and then translates the control using the Translate-Transform class. To calculate the value of the X property, I divide the difference between the face box and the text block widths by a factor of 2. The corresponding Y property is set to -textBlock. ActualHeight, so the text block will be located above the face box.

Sample results of EmotionsDetector appear in Figures 11-1, 11-3, and 11-4. As you can see, the Emotion API successfully detected surprise, happiness, and sadness.

LISTING 11-10 Configuring a text block used to indicate the emotion name

```
public static TextBlock PrepareEmotionTextBlock(Rectangle faceBox, Color emotionColor,
    string emotionName)
{
    Check.IsNull(faceBox);
    Check.IsNull(emotionColor);
    Check.IsNull(emotionName);

    var textBlock = new TextBlock()
    {
        Foreground = new SolidColorBrush(emotionColor),
        FontSize = 38,
        Text = emotionName
    };

    // Measure text block
    textBlock.Measure(Size.Empty);

    // Calculate offsets
    var xTextBlockOffset = (faceBox.ActualWidth - textBlock.ActualWidth) / 2.0;
    var yTextBlockOffset = -textBlock.ActualHeight;

    // Ignore negative horizontal offset
    xTextBlockOffset = Math.Max(0, xTextBlockOffset);

    // Translate text block, so it is centered with respect to face box
    var faceBoxTranslateTransform = faceBox.RenderTransform as TranslateTransform;

    textBlock.RenderTransform = new TranslateTransform()
    {
        X = faceBoxTranslateTransform.X + xTextBlockOffset,
        Y = faceBoxTranslateTransform.Y + yTextBlockOffset
    };

    return textBlock;
}
```

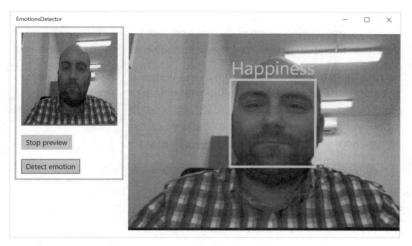

FIGURE 11-3 EmotionsDetector detected happiness.

FIGURE 11-4 EmotionsDetector indicates sadness

Indicating emotions on the LED array

You can combine the above functionality with the LedArray class from Chapter 8. This example shows you how the IoT machine vision can be supported by artificial intelligence to automatically recognize various objects and take appropriate actions on these grounds. Here, these actions indicate recognized emotions on the LED array attached to the RPi2/RPi3, but they can be extended for various purposes.

To implement the above functionality, I use the building blocks developed previously. Naturally, I need the LedArray class and dependent modules, i.e. I2cHelper and RegisterHelper. I use the Joystick class (see Chapter 6, "Input and output") to control the webcam preview and initiate the emotions detector. The Up joystick button will start or stop the preview, and the Enter button will invoke the appropriate method of the Emotion API, so the app can be controlled without using the UI.

After adding the necessary classes to the EmotionsDetector project, I write the Initialize method; see Listing 11-11. It is invoked within the OnNavigatedTo event handler and is used to associate a connection with the Sense HAT and then to initialize camera capture. Additionally, I set the isIoTPlatform flag to check whether the platform is supported, so I can use the MessageDialog class for displaying errors; see the DisplayMessage method in the MainPage.xaml.cs of the companion code at Chapter 11/ EmotionsDetector.

LISTING 11-11   Hardware components initialization

```
private bool isIoTPlatform = false;

private Joystick joystick;
private LedArray ledArray;

private async Task Initialize()
{
    const byte address = 0x46;
    var device = await I2cHelper.GetI2cDevice(address);

    if (device != null)
    {
        joystick = new Joystick(device);
        joystick.ButtonPressed += Joystick_ButtonPressed;

        ledArray = new LedArray(device);

        await cameraCapture.Initialize(CaptureElementPreview);

        isIoTPlatform = true;
    }
}
```

I implement the Joystick.ButtonPressed event handler you see in Listing 11-12. This method checks whether a button is in a pressed state, and if so, the Joystick_ButtonPressed either updates the preview state (for the Up joystick button) or captures an image to process it using the Emotion API (for the Enter joystick button).

To start and stop the webcam preview, I use the UpdatePreviewState method. It internally uses the Start and Stop methods of the CameraCapture class instance, depending on the value of the IsPreviewActive property of that class; see the companion code at Chapter 11/EmotionsDetector/ MainPage.xaml.cs.

Subsequently, I display the preview status to the user; see Listing 11-13. I use the Sense HAT LED array, blinking all LEDs twice by using the specified uniform color. I use the following color convention: Green indicates an active preview; blue indicates an inactive preview; red indicates an error—a lack of Internet connection, for example.

LISTING 11-12 An event handler invoked when the Sense HAT joystick's buttons are pressed

```
private async void Joystick_ButtonPressed(object sender, JoystickEventArgs e)
{
    if (e.State == JoystickButtonState.Pressed)
    {
        switch (e.Button)
        {
            case JoystickButton.Up:
                await UpdatePreviewState();
                DisplayPreviewStatus();
                break;

            case JoystickButton.Enter:
                await IndicateEmotionOnTheLedArray();
                break;
        }
    }
}
```

LISTING 11-13 LED array is used to communicate the preview status and any errors

```
private void DisplayPreviewStatus()
{
    var color = cameraCapture.IsPreviewActive ? Colors.Green : Colors.Blue;

    Blink(color);
}

private void Blink(Color color)
{
    const int msDelayTime = 100;
    const int blinkCount = 2;

    for (int i = 0; i < blinkCount; i++)
    {
        ledArray.Reset(Colors.Black);
        Task.Delay(msDelayTime).Wait();

        ledArray.Reset(color);
        Task.Delay(msDelayTime).Wait();

        ledArray.Reset(Colors.Black);
        Task.Delay(msDelayTime).Wait();
    }
}
```

Pressing the **Enter** button invokes the IndicateEmotionOnTheLedArray method you see in Listing 11-14. When the webcam preview is active, this function works like the ButtonDetectEmotion_Click event handler to capture the bitmap and send it to the Emotion API for processing. A result of this processing is used to determine the emotion name, which is later converted to an appropriate color displayed on the Sense HAT LED array.

To test this app, deploy and run it in your IoT device. Then, after enabling the webcam preview using the Up joystick button, send requests to the Emotion API using the Enter joystick button. The LED array shows the processing results and any errors.

LISTING 11-14   Indicating the recognized emotion on the LED array

```
private async Task IndicateEmotionOnTheLedArray()
{
    if (cameraCapture.IsPreviewActive)
    {
        try
        {
            // Capture bitmap
            var softwareBitmap = await cameraCapture.CapturePhotoToSoftwareBitmap();

            // Get emotion, and its name
            var emotion = await GetEmotion(softwareBitmap);
            var emotionName = EmotionHelper.GetTopEmotionName(emotion);

            // Display emotion color on the LED array
            var color = EmotionHelper.GetEmotionColor(emotionName);
            ledArray.Reset(color);
        }
        catch (Exception)
        {
            Blink(Colors.Red);
        }
    }
    else
    {
        Blink(Colors.Blue);
    }
}
```

Here you have combined the functionality of an embedded device—that is, machine vision with AI algorithms available through the cloud system. So you effectively build the IoT solution in which untapped data (an image) from the credit-card-sized computer is turned into useful information—recognized human emotions.

Computer Vision API

The Computer Vision API is another component of MCS (*https://bit.ly/mcs_cv*), and you can access it similarly to the Emotion API—by using the Microsoft.ProjectOxford.Vision NuGet package. It implements a VisionServiceClient class, which can be used almost exactly like EmotionServiceClient.

Interestingly, VisionServiceClient exposes several methods for analyzing image content (AnalyzeImageAsync), describing an image (DescribeAsync), and even providing optical character recognition (OCR) (`RecognizeTextAsync`). You can use these methods to further extend the sample app in the previous sections. For instance, you can employ OCR to recognize text and display it on the LED array or use an image description to get insights on your app users or images seen by the camera.

Figure 11-5 and Figure 11-6 depict sample results generated using a UWP app utilizing the Computer Vision API to recognize text and analyze image content. I strongly encourage you to independently build your own project based on the Computer Vision API.

FIGURE 11-5 Optical character recognition with Computer Vision API. The analyzed image is displayed on the left, and detected sentences are shown in the list box on the right.

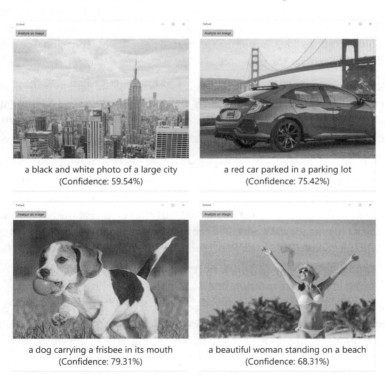

a black and white photo of a large city
(Confidence: 59.54%)

a red car parked in a parking lot
(Confidence: 75.42%)

a dog carrying a frisbee in its mouth
(Confidence: 79.31%)

a beautiful woman standing on a beach
(Confidence: 68.31%)

FIGURE 11-6 Detecting image content with the Computer Vision API.

Custom artificial intelligence

Though the AI algorithms presented above are very exciting, they may not be suitable for all IoT applications. In such cases, you can build your own AI system. Fortunately, you do not need to start from scratch because you can use a cloud-based machine learning system from Microsoft—Azure Machine Learning Studio (*https://studio.azureml.net/*). This offers a variety of ready-to-use ML algorithms and tools. To choose a suitable algorithm for particular needs, you first need to understand some basic concepts behind ML.

Motivation and concepts

In order to execute weather monitoring and forecasting, you can read and record thermometer values every day (data acquisition). You can then determine average temperatures for each month (data accumulation and processing). By plotting such data, you will find yearly temperature trends (data visualization). Given those plots you can easily discover patterns in your data, e.g. warm and hot months.

The next step is to use temperature data to predict weather for the next few days (extrapolation and prediction), which you can accomplish by modeling temperature using a specific mathematical function. In this case, the model will depend on a single variable (temperature) and a set of parameters. For example, a linear regression model would have two parameters (slope and intercept), while an nth degree polynomial model would have n+1 parameters (n coefficients and one constant). You adjust these parameters to your data by fitting a model function—that is, by finding parameter values, which minimizes the error function between a model and data (mathematical optimization). The model becomes an object that adequately approximates the true (recorded) data. Simply speaking, the data is what you actually see and the model is what you expect to see.

In general, many models can describe the same process. You choose the particular model by evaluation. Namely, you analyze how well your model fits the data by calculating the so-called coefficient of determination, R^2 (the larger the value, the better), and most importantly, whether the model can efficiently predict future temperature readings to perform simple weather forecasting.

In Figure 11-7, I plotted synthesized temperature readings for 24 days (black dots) and then fit this data in Microsoft Excel with two models: linear regression (green line) and 4th degree polynomial (red curve). Additionally, the models predict temperatures for the next seven days. As you can see, the polynomial model fits better to the data (it has a much higher R^2), but it predicts that the temperature will increase above reasonable values. In contrast, although the linear trend has a lower coefficient of determination, it seems to better forecast temperature on a short time-scale. However, it will also fail at a long time-scale, because it tends to predict a linearly decreasing temperature. At some point, it will approach unrealistic values.

The above evaluation, apart from helping to choose the model function, reveals several issues. We see that although both models fit well to the data, at some point they lead to unrealistic temperature values, and in turn, incorrectly predict temperature. Extending the training dataset (the number of temperature readings) and decreasing the prediction time-scale can solve this problem. In Figure 11-8, I show an extended dataset (more black dots) and a prediction limited to a single data point. Although

R^2 decreased for both models, the prediction improved. The observed decrease in R^2 should not be correlated with prediction efficiency. It just measures how well the model function fits to the data. The better the agreement, the larger R^2 values are, which in turn, improves the prediction rate.

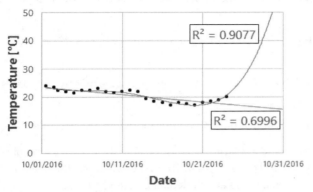

FIGURE 11-7 Predicting temperature using linear (green line) and nonlinear (red curve) regression. The linear regression fits less closely to the data than the nonlinear (4th order polynomial) model but yields more reasonable predictions.

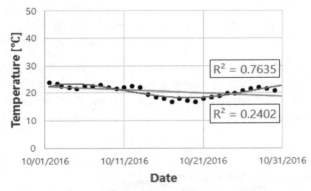

FIGURE 11-8 Accumulating data improves prediction.

Greater data accumulation improved prediction. For ML purposes, this translates as "the better the training set, the better the future predictions and analysis." If you do not provide enough input data, your model will most likely fail to provide correct outcomes, even though you use the best possible model. Note that in the above analysis I used unsupervised learning, because I provided unlabeled data. This simple example also explains why weather forecasting is unstable and strongly varies in time. Usually, a weather forecast can be considered "good" for short time scales only.

To generate a large dataset, you can record more temperatures at a higher frequency—maybe a few times a day—and then store them in an Excel spreadsheet. Excel will automatically readjust model parameters. However, extending this procedure for more thermometers becomes problematic: You need to manually enter temperatures, and you do not have access to more comprehensive algorithms that can process big datasets. To solve these problems, you can use digital sensors (like those from the Sense HAT) to automate temperature measurements and then employ ML algorithms to automatically process this data. At the end of the day, you will turn raw, untapped data into meaningful information, which helps you to understand temperature changes in your area.

The above discussion serves as the basis to start working with ML algorithms, providing a general idea of how the ML works:

- First, you need an input dataset, which is used to prepare one or more models by adjusting their parameters.

- Second, you need to evaluate models to validate whether they provide expected outcomes for test datasets.

- Last, you can employ models to make predictions and detect anomalies or patterns in data.

ML is not limited to the two-dimensional datasets I used here. ML is suitable for processing big multi-dimensional datasets. You can use as many dimensions as you want. ML will do the rest for you, providing useful information that can help you analyze and understand your processes.

Microsoft Azure Machine Learning Studio

Microsoft Azure Machine Learning Studio is a web app that lets you quickly create, evaluate, and deploy scalable ML solutions as web services with just a few mouse clicks. Hence, you can build AI-enabled apps fully tailored to your needs and access ML functionality much like you did with Microsoft Cognitive Services.

To start using Azure Machine Learning Studio, sign up for a free workspace at *https://studio.azureml.net* by using an existing or new Microsoft account. After you log in to Azure Machine Learning Studio, you see the screen shown in Figure 11-9. Like Azure Portal, it includes tabs on the left that let you explore your projects, ML experiments, web services, notebooks, datasets, and trained models.

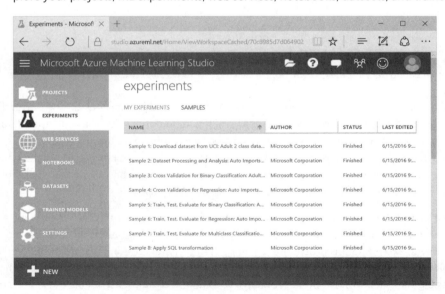

FIGURE 11-9 The list of sample ML experiments available in Microsoft Azure Machine Learning Studio.

To develop your ML solution, first create a new experiment (or use an existing experiment). There you will drag and drop to connect data to preprocessing and model training modules and then to trained models, model evaluators, model scorers, and web services.

You can use data preprocessing modules to "clean up" your data, which some models require. Namely, you can remove repetitive entries, split your data, remove entries without labels, and so on.

Use the resulting datasets to train the model—to adjust the model's intrinsic parameters to the given data. Basically, this proceeds like fitting data to a line or polynomial in Excel, but it uses more complex math.

Model evaluators assess the model accuracy and help you to choose the model. The model accuracy typically tells you how good your model is for unseen (test) data. There are several measures of this accuracy. Azure Machine Learning Studio calculates the coefficient of determination (R^2) and other metrics: Negative Log Likelihood, Mean Absolute Error, Root Mean Squared Error, Relative Absolute Error, and Relative Squared Error. All these metrics, except R^2, should be as small as possible, while R^2 should come as close to 1 as possible.

You use model scorers to make predictions. Given the trained model, a scorer evaluates test data and gives you the outcome—prediction, anomaly detection, or classification. With respect to temperature predictions, the test data could be the date for which you want to find an expected temperature. In terms of anomaly detection, you provide data, and the scorer decides whether it is normal or abnormal (e.g., whether a temperature is outside the expected range). The scorer can also classify your data into further groups. For instance, it can decide whether the given face image expresses happiness, sadness, or surprise.

You can get predictions from your model scorer in two ways.

- Connect test data to the scorer, so you get your predictions directly in Azure Machine Learning Studio.

- Deploy the scorer as the web service and access the trained model by a custom REST client. Azure Machine Learning Studio assists you by generating sample C# code based on your data.

Data preparation

Although Azure Machine Learning Studio comes with a number of predefined datasets, I use the temperature dataset I discussed previously so that you can easily compare Excel capabilities with Azure Machine Learning Studio. I attached the referenced dataset as the CSV spreadsheet to the companion code at Chapter 11/Machine Learning/TemperatureData.csv.

To upload this dataset to Azure Machine Learning Studio, you click the **New** button, located in the bottom left corner of the UI, and then choose **Dataset/From Local File**; see Figure 11-10. In the Upload a New Dataset pop-up, which you see in Figure 11-11, browse for the TemperatureData.csv file and make sure the **Select a Type for the New Dataset** drop-down list is set to **Generic CSV File with a Header (.csv)**. Finally, click the check box and wait for your file upload to be finished. The status of this operation displays in the bottom part of the UI. Once the dataset is uploaded, you will see the new entry under the datasets tab (my datasets group).

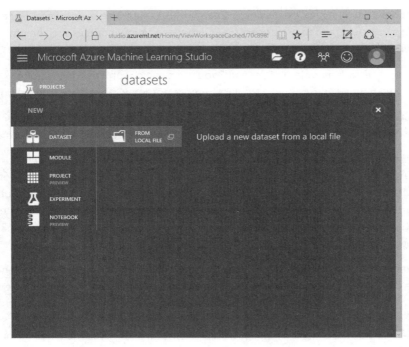

FIGURE 11-10 An expanded New menu of the Microsoft Azure Machine Learning Studio. Dataset/From Local File option is highlighted.

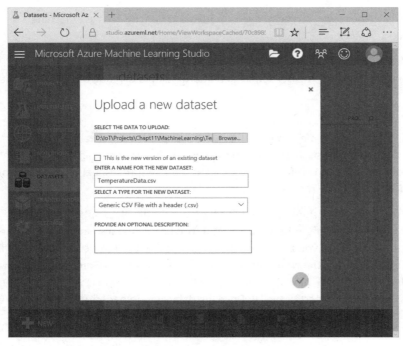

FIGURE 11-11 Uploading a CSV file to Azure Machine Learning Studio.

Model training

I now show you how to create a new blank experiment in which you will train, evaluate, and score two models implemented in Azure Machine Learning Studio: Linear Regression and Decision Forest Regression. I use regression models because the goal of this example is to prepare a temperature predictive system analogous to our previous experiment made in Excel.

Expand the **New** menu and choose the **Experiment** node. Click the **Blank Experiment** option; see Figure 11-12. You will see a graphical sketch of an experiment consisting of several dashed line rectangles where you can put your ML objects (datasets, models, scorers, etc.). The list of these objects is on the left hand side.

Expand the **Saved Datasets** node, look up **TemperatureData.csv** under **My Datasets**, and then drag it in the experiment working area. The graphical sketch will disappear, and you will only have a single rectangle representing your dataset. Now you need models. Find them under the Machine Learning/Initialize Model/Regression node. After expanding this node, drag and drop to the experiment two objects: **Linear Regression** and **Decision Forest Regression**. Subsequently, add two **Train Model** objects (one for each model), which are located under the following node: Machine Learning/Train.

Note that each object you place in the experiment has a specific number of input and output nodes. For instance, the dataset has just an output node, which you connect to one of the input nodes of the model trainers. The second input node of the model trainer is the untrained model, Linear Regression or Decision Forest Regression. Now, you connect all objects as shown in Figure 11-13. An arrow indicates the direction of data flow between the nodes.

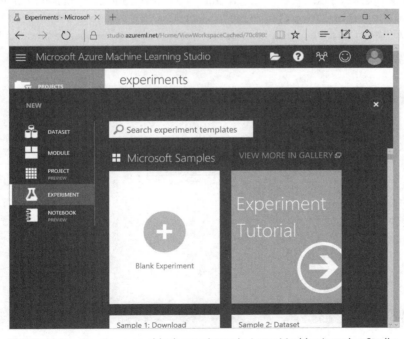

FIGURE 11-12   Creating a new blank experiment in Azure Machine Learning Studio.

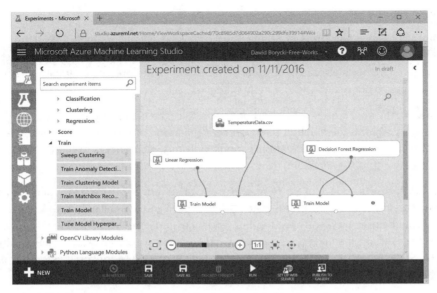

FIGURE 11-13 Regression models training in Azure Machine Learning Studio.

After you connect the nodes, the Train Model objects require additional action—indicated by an exclamation mark. Specifically, model trainers require you to choose a dataset column that shall be used for training. To do so, click the **Train Model** object and then expand the menu on the right; see Figure 11-14. Under the Properties group, press **Launch Column Selector**, and in the Select a Single Column pop-up, move **Temperature [deg C]** from the Available Columns section to the Selected Columns area; see Figure 11-15. Close the pop-up, and repeat this procedure for the second model trainer.

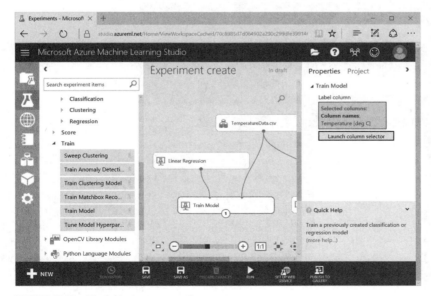

FIGURE 11-14 Model trainer properties.

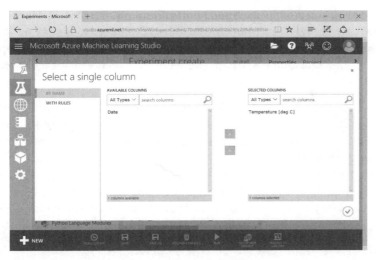

FIGURE 11-15 Selecting dataset columns for training.

Model scoring and evaluation

You can now run the experiment you prepared; it will train two models using the provided data. Next, you assess the trained models by scoring both models using a training dataset (Score Model) and then evaluating them using the Evaluate Model object. Scoring a trained model to a training dataset means that you compare reality (recorded temperatures) to some mathematical theory (temperatures expected by the model). Evaluate Model then quantifies differences between the two.

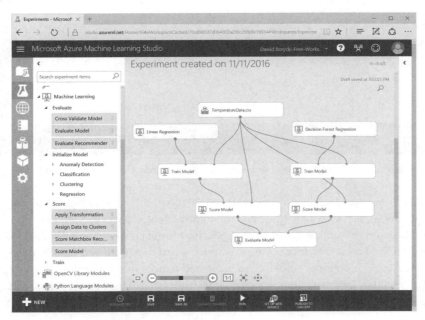

FIGURE 11-16 Model evaluation experiment.

To evaluate trained models, drag and drop to the experiment two Score Model objects (**Machine Learning/Score**) and one Evaluate Model object (**Machine Learning/Evaluate**). Subsequently, you need to connect the output nodes of the dataset and trained models with the appropriate input nodes of the Score Model objects. Finally, you associate the output nodes of the scorers with the input nodes of the evaluator; see Figure 11-16.

To obtain evaluation results, run the experiment by clicking the appropriate button in the bottom part of Azure Machine Learning Studio. An experiment will be completed after several seconds. Right-click the output node of the Evaluate Model object and select **Evaluation Results/Visualize** from the context menu. Azure Machine Learning Studio then presents evaluation results in a graphical form, as you see in Figure 11-17. The first row shows the metrics of the Linear Regression model and the second shows the Decision Forest Regression. This resembles reality (our data) much better than the Linear Regression model. Decision Forest Regression has a much higher Coefficient of Determination, while minimizing other metrics.

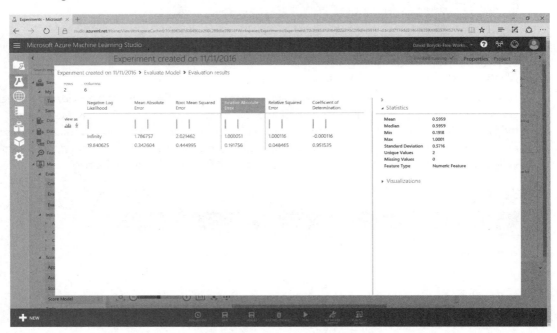

FIGURE 11-17   Model evaluation results of the Linear Regression model (first row) and Decision Forest Regression.

The Excel experiments also visualized data along with model scores (fit); refer to Figure 11-9 and Figure 11-10. Azure Machine Learning Studio gives you this information, and you can retrieve it by selecting the **Scored Dataset/Visualize** option from the **Score Model** context menu. Figure 11-18 shows scores of the Decision Forest with four columns, where the first two (Date and Temperature [deg C]) show data. The third column presents model labels, expected temperatures (fitted values), and the last column contains label standard deviations, which quantify the distance between real data and our expectations (values produced by the model).

In scores visualization, you can also plot data from a selected column. In Figure 11-18, I plotted temperatures and compared them to Scored Labels. In an ideal case (perfect agreement), dots on this scatter plot make a line. Naturally, it is almost impossible to get perfect agreement between a model and data because many processes have a nondeterministic character. Machine Learning tends to only approximate these processes.

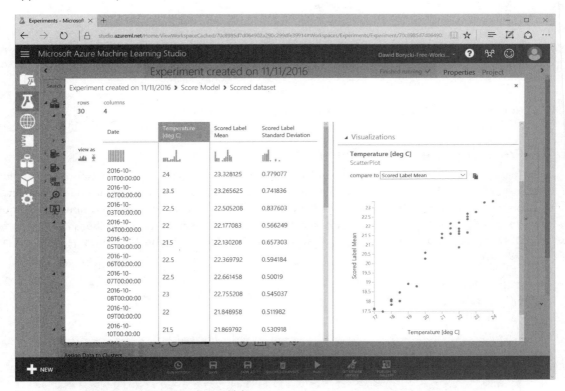

FIGURE 11-18   Decision Forest Regression model scores.

In Figure 11-19, I plotted scores of Linear Regression and Decision Forest Regression along with temperature data. As in the earlier section "Motivation and concepts," I copied data from Azure Machine Learning Studio to an Excel spreadsheet and then used its plotting capabilities.

Decision Forest Regression approximates the data pretty well and, importantly, does so better than the polynomial model used previously in the Excel experiment. In this case, ML noticeably resembles reality better than the polynomial fit. Hence, I can also expect predictions made by this model to be more accurate. As you see in Figure 11-19, the temperature predicted for the next day relates closely to the previous data. There is no rapid change as seen in the Excel experiments.

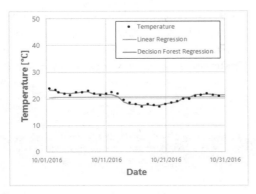

FIGURE 11-19 Visual comparison of two ML regression models with the actual data.

Predictions based on trained model

To use your trained model to make predictions, run the scorer against the test dataset. You can upload test data in a CSV file, but doing so may be cumbersome for providing just a single date. You might prefer to enter it manually by using the Enter Data Manually object under the Data Input and Output node. After dragging this object, make sure that its Properties window is visible, choose **CSV** from the **DataFormat** drop-down list, select the **HasHeader** check box, and type the following lines in the Data text box (see Figure 11-20):

> **Date, Temperature [deg C]**
> **2016-10-20T00:00:00,**
> **2016-10-31T00:00:00,**

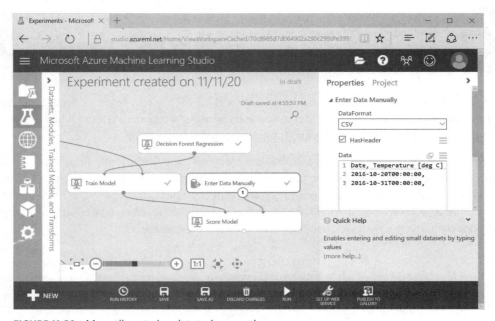

FIGURE 11-20 Manually entering data to be scored.

Connect the trained model to another Score Model and test the dataset as Figure 11-20 shows, and rerun the experiment. You can access predicted (scored) values (Figure 11-21) by using the **Scored Dataset/Visualize** option from the **Score Model** context menu.

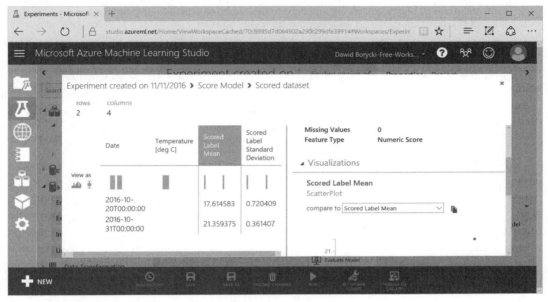

FIGURE 11-21   Scoring a model on using a test dataset.

Anomaly detection

You can build an AnomalyDetection app by using an ML experiment published as a web service to detect anomalous temperature readings and indicate them by LED array. Anomalies appear as red; normal temperature readings appear in green.

To prepare the model, you need an input training dataset, which you acquire from the temperature sensor of the Sense HAT add-on board. The training dataset will be stored as a CSV file, so you can easily upload it to Microsoft Azure Machine Learning and then train the ML algorithm in supervised mode. The provided temperatures will constitute the normal or expected values, assuming that temperatures will not vary over time. Based on this input data, the ML algorithm will be able to recognize abnormal readings by comparing them to normal values from a training dataset.

Training dataset acquisition

Figure 11-22 depicts the UI of the AnomalyDetection app; see the companion code at: Chapter 11/AnomalyDetection/MainPage.xaml. There are three buttons and a text block showing the temperature reading. Abnormal values appear in red. Data binding controls this color, the temperature value, and the status of each button (disabled or enabled). Buttons and text block properties are bound to the corresponding fields of the AnomalyViewModel class instance. This class implements the INotifyPropertyChanged interface, so appropriate changes in the code-behind can be automatically reflected in the UI. Here, unlike in previous examples, I moved data-bound properties to a separate class, so they do not interfere with main aspects of this sample app—the custom Azure Machine Learning predictive web service.

The Acquire Training Dataset button records temperatures from the Sense HAT for the specified time and then saves them in the CSV file. To read temperatures, I supplemented the AnomalyDetection app with the TemperatureAndPressureSensorHelper class from Chapter 5 and with other objects required by that class. Then, I wrote the TemperatureFileStorage class (Chapter 11/AnomalyDetection/Storage/TemperatureFileStorage.cs). This class creates the SenseHatTemperatureData.csv file under the app temporary folder. The CSV file contains one column of temperatures obtained from the Sense HAT sensor.

FIGURE 11-22 Abnormal temperatures appear in red.

The structure of the TemperatureFileStorage class requires several comments since it uses the UWP API related to storage, which we have not dealt with yet. First, note that TemperatureFileStorage does not implement a public constructor. Instead, it has a factory-like method, CreateAsync, which returns an instance of the TemperatureFileStorage class; see Listing 11-15.

LISTING 11-15 Asynchronous creation of the TemperatureFileStorage class

```
public static async Task<TemperatureFileStorage> CreateAsync()
{
    var temperatureFileStorage = new TemperatureFileStorage();

    await temperatureFileStorage.PrepareFolder();
    await temperatureFileStorage.PrepareFile();

    return temperatureFileStorage;
}

// Create an empty constructor, so it's not publicly accessible
private TemperatureFileStorage() { }
```

Typically, you use such an approach to creating objects when you need asynchronous methods during class initialization. Here, I use such methods to prepare the folder and a file, to which I'm writing recorded temperatures.

Listing 11-16 shows how to access the temporary folder of the app by using the TemporaryFolder property of the ApplicationData class. The ApplicationData class does not implement a public constructor. However it exposes the static field Current, which lets you access the current application data store, including the temporary, local cache, local, and roaming folders. All of them are represented as instances of the StorageFolder class. This class implements a number of methods and fields for reading folder parameters (like name or path) and their contents and for managing folders. To get a subfolder, I use the TryGetItemAsync method. It accepts a single argument, name, and then either returns null (if an object of the given name does not exist) or an object conforming to the IStorageItem interface. IStorageItem is an interface implemented by both StorageFolder and StorageFile (representing a file in the UWP). Hence, TryGetItemAsync can also get access to the specific file.

LISTING 11-16   Methods used to prepare the SenseHatTemperatureData.csv file

```
private string folderName = Package.Current.DisplayName;

private StorageFolder workingFolder;
private const string fileName = "SenseHatTemperatureData.csv";

private StorageFile workingFile;

private async Task PrepareFolder()
{
    var storageFolder = ApplicationData.Current.TemporaryFolder;

    // Check if folder already exists
    var storageItem = await storageFolder.TryGetItemAsync(folderName);

    if (storageItem == null)
    {
        // ... if not, create one
        storageFolder = await storageFolder.CreateFolderAsync(folderName);
    }
    else
    {
        storageFolder = (StorageFolder)storageItem;
    }

    workingFolder = storageFolder;
}

private async Task PrepareFile()
{
    // Create file, overwriting the previous one
    workingFile = await workingFolder.CreateFileAsync(fileName,
        CreationCollisionOption.ReplaceExisting);
}
```

As Listing 11-16 shows, when TryGetItemAsync returns null, I create the subfolder using the CreateFolderAsync method of the StorageFolder class instance. On the other hand, if TryGetItemAsync returns the valid reference to the storage item, I cast it to the StorageFolder.

Given access to the destination folder, I create there a SenseHatTemperatureData.csv file using CreateFileAsync of the StorageFolder class; see PrepareFile from Listing 11-16. Note that CreateFile-Async is configured to overwrite the existing file. A reference to SenseHatTemperatureData.csv is then stored in the workingFile field. This file is of type StorageFile, which has an analogous meaning and purpose to StorageFolder but refers to physical files instead of folders.

In order to write the list of temperature values to the CSV file, I implemented the WriteData method. As shown in Listing 11-17, this method opens the SenseHatTemperatureData.csv in the read/write mode using the OpenAsync method. This method returns the reference to the object implementing IRandomAccessStream. Given that object you simply use DataWriter to put formatted values into the stream.

LISTING 11-17 Writing temperatures to a dedicated CSV file

```
private const string columnName = "Temperature";

public async Task WriteData(List<float> temperatureDataset)
{
    var randomAccessStream = await workingFile.OpenAsync(FileAccessMode.ReadWrite);

    using (var dataWriter = new DataWriter(randomAccessStream))
    {
        WriteLine(dataWriter, columnName);

        foreach (float temperature in temperatureDataset)
        {
            WriteLine(dataWriter, temperature.ToString());
        }

        await dataWriter.StoreAsync();
    }
}

private void WriteLine(DataWriter dataWriter, string value)
{
    dataWriter.WriteString(value);
    dataWriter.WriteString("\r\n");
}
```

Here, I use DataWriter to write each entry from the temperature list as the new line in the CSV file, followed by writing the column name, Temperature. Note that I have just a single column. If you want to write data to additional columns, separate them with commas. Accordingly, you would need to modify the WriteLine method from Listing 11-17 to write additional comma-separated values before using the carriage return (\r) and new line feed (\n), e.g.:

```
private void WriteLine(DataWriter dataWriter, string value1, float value2)
{
    dataWriter.WriteString(value1);
    dataWriter.WriteString(",");
    dataWriter.WriteString(value2.ToString());
    dataWriter.WriteString("\r\n");
}
```

In the next step, I use the TemperatureFileStorage and TemperatureAndPressureSensor classes inside TrainingDatasetAcquisition; see the companion code at Chapter 11/AnomalyDetection/Training/TrainingDatasetAcquisition.cs. The TrainingDatasetAcquisition class implements one public method, Acquire. As shown in Listing 11-18, this method accepts two arguments: msDelayTime and duration. The first, msDelayTime, specifies the delay between consecutive temperature readings (sampling rate), while the second, duration, determines how long the acquisition lasts.

Given these parameters, the Acquire method continuously reads temperature data from a sensor, writes the resulting dataset to the CSV file, and returns the location of this file so you can easily find it.

LISTING 11-18   Recording a training dataset

```
private TemperatureAndPressureSensor sensor = TemperatureAndPressureSensor.Instance;

public async Task<string> Acquire(int msDelayTime, TimeSpan duration)
{
    // Prepare storage
    var storage = await TemperatureFileStorage.CreateAsync();
    // Initialize sensor
    await sensor.Initialize();

    // Begin asynchronuous sensor reading
    var temperatureDataset = new List<float>();

    await BeginSensorReading(() =>
    {
        var temp = sensor.GetTemperature();
        temperatureDataset.Add(temp);
    }, msDelayTime, duration);

    // and write resulting dataset to CSV file
    await storage.WriteData(temperatureDataset);

    return storage.FilePath;
}
```

The BeginSensorReading (Listing 11-19) used internally in the Acquire method repeatedly runs the block of code passed by using the periodicAction argument. The execution of this action is separated in time by the msDelayTime, and BeginSensorReading invokes the periodicAction as long as the total execution time does not exceed the time span specified by the duration argument.

LISTING 11-19   Implement continuous sensor reading by repeating a specific action as long as the specified period of time has not passed

```
private async Task BeginSensorReading(Action periodicAction, int msDelayTime, TimeSpan duration)
{
    await Task.Run(() =>
    {
        var beginTime = DateTime.Now.ToUniversalTime();
        var currentTime = beginTime;

        // Perform action unless specified period of time has passed
        while (currentTime - beginTime <= duration)
        {
            periodicAction();

            Task.Delay(msDelayTime).Wait();

            currentTime = DateTime.Now.ToUniversalTime();
        };
    });
}
```

The Acquire method of the TrainingDataSetAcquisition class instance is used in the event handler of the Acquire Training Dataset button in the AnomalyDetection app; see Listing 11-20. As you see there, I record a training dataset for 30 seconds at the approximate sampling rate of 25 samples per second. Therefore, the resulting dataset should contain 750 items. However, this number is reduced because some specific time is needed to get and process each sensor reading. In my case, the actual training dataset contained approximately 610 elements.

LISTING 11-20   Training dataset acquisition

```
private async void ButtonAcquireTrainingDataset_Click(object sender, RoutedEventArgs e)
{
    const int msDelay = 40;
    const int secDuration = 30;

    anomalyViewModel.IsAcquisitionInProgress = true;

    anomalyViewModel.FilePath = await trainingDatasetAcquisition.Acquire(msDelay,
        TimeSpan.FromSeconds(secDuration));

    anomalyViewModel.IsAcquisitionInProgress = false;
}
```

When you run the AnomalyDetection app on your IoT device and then click the Acquire Training Dataset button, the temperature dataset acquisition begins. All buttons are disabled during this operation, and you also see the orange progress ring; see Figure 11-23. The progress ring disappears after the temperature dataset is acquired. The location of the dataset is then displayed in the bottom of the UI. In my case it was: C:\Data\Users\DefaultAccount\AppData\Local\Packages\72c9e91f-f30a-42f2-a088-e0b4fd4463c9_9h3w8f2j4szm6\TempState\AnomalyDetection\SenseHatTemperatureData.csv.

You get this file by associating the FTP connection with your IoT device (see Chapter 2, "Universal Windows Platform on devices") and copying it to your development PC. Use this dataset to train the ML algorithm.

FIGURE 11-23 An orange process ring shows the progress of asynchronous training dataset acquisition.

Anomaly detection using a one-class support vector machine

Anomaly detection algorithms work differently than regression. Regression algorithms belong to the unsupervised group of ML techniques; anomaly detection algorithms constitute supervised ML. In regression, you provide a training dataset, and then the ML algorithm adjusts its internal parameters to this data. You typically use such an approach for predicting trends. For anomaly detection ML, you provide a training dataset containing values along with their labels (known outcomes). Labels tell the ML algorithm which class the associated value belongs to. In the simplest case, you have one class of normal values and want to check whether new values of the observables (e.g., temperature) belong to that class. Anomaly detection finds statistical outliers—observation values distinct from other elements in the dataset. ML checks whether the new value generated by some process (e.g., reading data from a sensor, credit card transaction, or human face image) matches the known dataset. If so, the value is classified as normal. Of course, such supervised ML can work with several classes. For instance, for human emotion recognition, the Emotion API uses eight classes (one class per emotion).

In Azure Machine Learning Studio, two ML algorithms exist for anomaly detection: One-Class Support Vector Machine (SVM) and PCA-Based Anomaly Detection. Both of them are used in scenarios where you can easily obtain normal (expected) values and generating abnormal values is difficult. Temperature monitoring is a good example of such a scenario because you do not expect this observable to significantly vary over time, you basically do not know how much temperature can change during a failure, and you can very easily obtain a "normal" dataset.

The SVM algorithms represent values from the training dataset as points in space and map them to specific classes (categories). This mapping is performed to maximize the distances between each category, so new values can be easily assigned to the particular class. For one-class SVM you provide only normal datasets and then measure the specific distance between a current value and known examples.

PCA-Based Anomaly Detection works similarly. In PCA-Based Anomaly Detection, you also provide a "normal" dataset. However, this algorithm first converts the set of provided observations to the set of variables called principal components. Namely, the original dataset is approximated by a linear combination of principal components (PCs). Such Principal Component Analysis (PCA) excludes redundant or statistically insignificant information. Typically, you have many fewer PCs than values in your training dataset. In PCA-Based Anomaly Detection, new observables are projected (mapped) to a space spanned by PCs to determine the anomaly score—the error between a mapping of new observables to PC-based space. This error is small for the "normal" dataset, since the ML algorithm finds an optimal representation of the training dataset in the PC's space. Hence, abnormal values increase the error and thus the anomaly score.

Here, I show you how to train the One-Class SVM for detecting anomalies in temperature readings from the Sense HAT add-on board. Start by uploading the training dataset (SenseHatTemperatureData.csv) as a Generic CSV File with a header to Azure Machine Learning Studio (Figure 11-11) and then creating the new Blank Experiment. Next, drag the training dataset to the experiment along with the One-Class Support Vector Machine Model (Machine Learning/Initialize Model/Anomaly Detection node), Train Anomaly Detection Model (Machine Learning/Train), Score Model, and Enter Data Manually objects; see Figure 11-24.

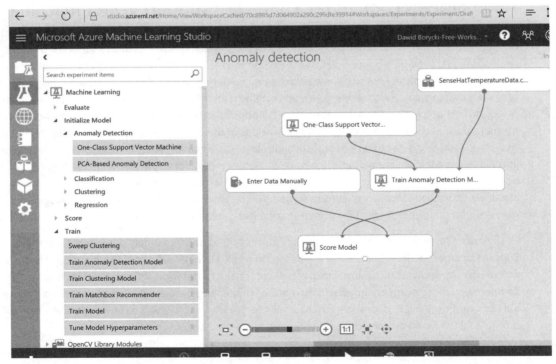

FIGURE 11-24 One-Class Support Vector Machine anomaly detection experiment in Azure Machine Learning Studio.

Note that I changed the experiment name. By default, each experiment is named as *Experiment created on mm/dd/yyyy*. You can change this value by simply clicking it and typing a new name.

I used the Enter Data Manually object to empirically test the anomaly detector and eventually adjust its parameters. Based on my training dataset, I created a test dataset by providing values that conform to and differ from an average temperature within my training dataset—36.55 ± 0.03 °C. Basically, I wanted to check whether the anomaly detector correctly recognizes abnormal values and find its tolerance margin. Typically, you don't want to attribute small temperature variations to anomaly.

The test dataset I used appears in the Temperature column in Figure 11-25. The Scored Labels column shows labels applied by the anomaly detector (0 for normal and 1 for abnormal), while the Scored Probabilities column is the anomaly measure. The larger the value, the larger the probability that the particular test value is abnormal. The results from Figure 11-25 show that the ML algorithm is not very tolerant. Even a slight deviation from the average temperature is considered an anomaly. To increase the anomaly detector tolerance, use the η parameter of the One-Class Support Vector Machine. Formally, this parameter controls the fraction of outliers to normal cases. The larger the value of this fraction, the larger the tolerance for outliers. As Figure 11-26 shows, the One-Class Support Vector Machine has another parameter, ε, which is the stopping tolerance and thus determines the number of iterations used internally to optimize the model.

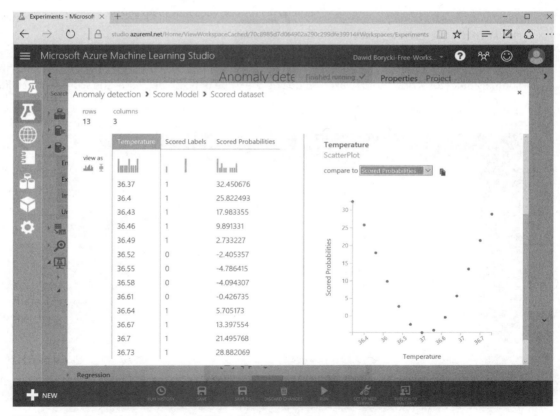

FIGURE 11-25   Scored labels and probabilities of the anomaly detector for the test dataset.

By default, η = 0.1, and ε = 0.001. You can manually change these parameters to optimize your model. You can also specify parameter ranges by using the **Parameter Range** option from the **Create Trainer Mode** drop-down list. In that case, Azure Machine Learning Studio will try to find an optimal parameter value. However, it may not be the most suitable value for your application. Typically, you need to manually adjust these parameters to your needs. That's why the module of Azure Machine Learning Studio is called an experiment. We experiment with our data and model in order to match reality (data) to expectations (model).

Usually there is no consensus of how to find parameter values. Hence, I rerun the experiment using several different values of η—0.1, 0.01, 0.005, and 0.0025—leaving the default value for ε. Then, for each η, I check the anomaly detector scores and decide to use the smallest value of η. It yields the scores you see in Figure 11-27. Your training dataset will most likely be different from mine, so I encourage you to independently experiment with your η value.

Properties   Project

◢ One-Class Support Vector Machine

Create trainer mode

| Single Parameter | ▾ |

η

| 0.1 |

ε

| 0.001 |

FIGURE 11-26   One-Class Support Vector Machine properties.

By comparing results from Figure 11-27 to the corresponding table in Figure 11-25, you see that the anomaly detector is now more relaxed. Reducing the value of η also decreases the scored probabilities.

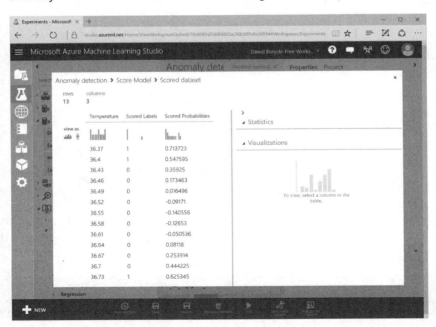

FIGURE 11-27   Scored labels and probabilities of an anomaly detector for a test dataset and η of 0.0025.

Preparing and publishing a Web service

To publish your trained and adjusted anomaly detector experiment as a web service, you need to drag four additional objects to your experiment: Web Service Input and Web Service Output (Web Service node), Score Model, and Edit Metadata (Data Transformation/Manipulation). You then connect the input and output nodes of these objects; see Figure 11-28.

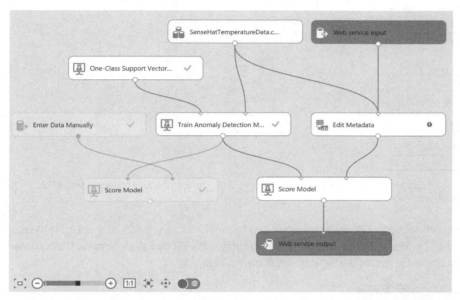

FIGURE 11-28   Adding the web service interface to an anomaly detection experiment.

Input and output nodes of a web service denote the JSON-formatted requests and responses sent to (sent by the client app) and from the service (received by the client app). The request contains input test data (one or many temperatures), while the response will give you the scored labels and corresponding probabilities. In general, the training and input datasets can have multiple columns. To specify which column (or columns) the web service uses, you use the Edit Metadata object. Before you select a column, Edit Metadata displays an exclamation mark.

Choose the column from the Edit Metadata properties window, where you click the **Launch Column Selector** button. This opens a new window, Select Columns (as you see in Figure 11-15), where you pick the Temperature column. After closing that dialog box, your Edit Metadata properties window will look like the one in Figure 11-29.

I use an additional Score Model to score data from the web service input. The web service output returns the resulting scored labels and probabilities to the client app.

Note that, after I add the web service nodes, the experiment toolbar you see in the bottom part of Figure 11-28 contains an additional toggle button. It is used to switch between the experiment display modes: experiment and web service view. In the web service view, Enter Data Manually and the associated Score Model are ignored, since data to be tested is taken from the web service input. In the experiment view, the web service nodes are ignored.

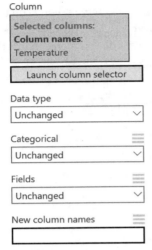

▲ Edit Metadata

Column

Selected columns:
Column names:
Temperature

Launch column selector

Data type
Unchanged ⌄

Categorical ☰
Unchanged ⌄

Fields ☰
Unchanged ⌄

New column names ☰

FIGURE 11-29 The Edit Metadata properties window with the Single Temperature column selected. No further data transformations are used.

Before you can set up the web service, you need to run the experiment. Then, as Figure 11-30 shows, you click the **Set Up Web Service** button and then choose **Predictive Web Service [Recommended]**. Doing so generates the predictive experiment shown in Figure 11-31.

Predictive Web Service [Recommended]

Deploy Web Service

▶ RUN | 🔧 SET UP WEB SERVICE | PUBLISH TO GALLERY

FIGURE 11-30 Setting up web service.

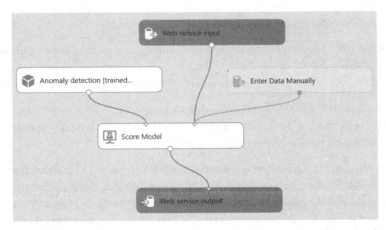

Web service input

Anomaly detection [trained...

Enter Data Manually

Score Model

Web service output

FIGURE 11-31 Anomaly detection predictive experiment in the web service view.

The One-Class SVM Anomaly Detector Model along with the Train Anomaly Detection Model, training dataset, and one Score Model were converted to a single object: Anomaly detection [trained model]. Again, the predictive experiment has two preview modes: experiment, in which Enter Data Manually is enabled, and web service view, where this object becomes unused and disabled.

As a final touch, using the properties window of the Web service input and output, I change the input name to temperatureInput and the output name to anomalyDetectionResult; see Figure 11-32.

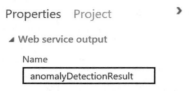

FIGURE 11-32 Web service output name configuration. The corresponding name of the web service input can be set analogously.

You can now rerun the predictive experiment to validate it. Subsequently, to deploy the web service you use the Deploy Web Service button in the bottom menu of Azure Machine Learning Studio. You will be redirected to the web service dashboard; see Figure 11-33. Specifically, this dashboard displays the API key required to access the web service. You also find links to the API help pages, which show how to construct and send requests. You will use all this information in the next section as you implement the web service client.

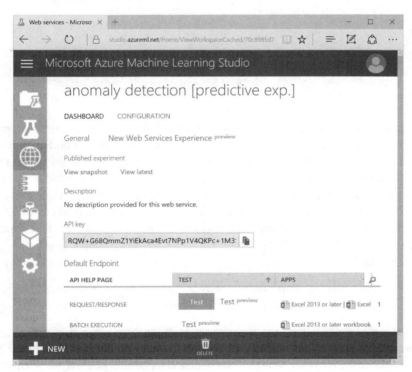

FIGURE 11-33 Web service dashboard.

Implementing a Web service client

A web service, which we prepared above, can be accessed much like the Emotion API, through the dedicated REST client class. However, you need to manually implement this class based on the web service API. In the cloud-first, mobile-first world, such a task is typical for web and mobile developers, and many tools accelerate the development of custom REST clients.

The first thing you need is the Microsoft.AspNet.WebApi.Client NuGet package. I installed it in the AnomalyDetection app using the package manager; see Figure 11-34. You can also use the package manager console (Tools/NuGet Package Manager/Package Manager console), where you type **Install-Package Microsoft.AspNet.WebApi.Client**.

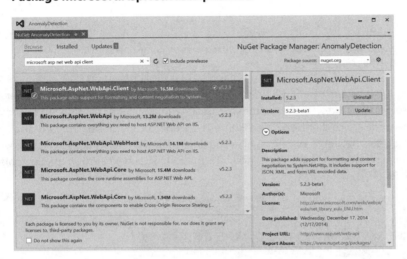

FIGURE 11-34 A NuGet package manager of the AnomalyDetection app shows an installed version of the Microsoft.AspNet.WebApi.Client package.

Next, find the web service API by clicking the **Request/Response** link under the web service dash-board (Figure 11-33). The API documentation shows you the request URI, headers, and body, along with a sample response. You can also find there sample code snippets written in C#, Python, and R that show you how to access the web service. However, the C# example, which we are most interested in, does not explicitly show how to easily read the most desirable information, i.e. the scored label. To that end you need to transform the JSON response into a C# object. You can do so nearly automatically by using the HttpClient extension methods implemented in the Microsoft.AspNet.WebApi.Client NuGet package and an additional tool for mapping the JSON structure to a C# class—for example, json2csharp (*http://json2csharp.com/*), which, given the JSON object, generates the corresponding C# class for you.

To use json2csharp you simply copy the sample request or response JSON to the json2csharp input text box and then click the **Generate** button. It will make the C# class, which you can then copy to your project.

Listing 11-21 contains a sample json2csharp result generated from the sample request from the anomaly detection [predictive exp.] web service (Listing 11-22). As you can see, the C# class reflects the JSON structure. Thereafter, the anomaly detection [predictive exp.] web service will be denoted as the predictive web service.

C# mapping of the sample predictive experiment web service request

```csharp
public class TemperatureInput
{
    public List<string> ColumnNames { get; set; }
    public List<List<string>> Values { get; set; }
}

public class Inputs
{
    public TemperatureInput temperatureInput { get; set; }
}

public class GlobalParameters { }

public class RootObject
{
    public Inputs Inputs { get; set; }
    public GlobalParameters GlobalParameters { get; set; }
}
```

LISTING 11-22   Sample body of the predictive experiment

```json
{
  "Inputs": {
    "temperatureInput": {
      "ColumnNames": [
        "Temperature"
      ],
      "Values": [
        [
          "0"
        ],
        [
          "0"
        ]
      ]
    }
  },
  "GlobalParameters": {}
}
```

To implement the REST client for a predictive web service, I started by converting a JSON request and response to C# classes using json2csharp. Then, I slightly modified the auto-generated definitions; see the companion code at Chapter 11/AnomalyDetection/PredictiveService. First, I saved an auto-generated request class in the PredictionRequest.cs file, and then I modified types of TemperatureInput from string lists to string arrays. Subsequently, I modified the name of the TemperatureInput property of the Inputs class, and I renamed RootObject to PredictionRequest. Finally, I implemented the PredictionRequest class constructor as shown in Listing 11-23. This constructor has one argument, temperature, used to prepare the request. That is the only information required from the user. In this way, the user does not need to take care of the internal request structure. This pattern is similar to that used in the Emotion API client: Provide the image data, and the client class does the job.

LISTING 11-23 PredictionRequest class wraps the web service request body

```
public class PredictionRequest
{
    public Inputs Inputs { get; set; }
    public GlobalParameters GlobalParameters { get; set; }

    public PredictionRequest(double temperature)
    {
        Inputs = new Inputs()
        {
            TemperatureInput = new TemperatureInput()
            {
                ColumnNames = new string[]
                {
                    "Temperature"
                },
                Values = new string[,]
                {
                    { temperature.ToString() },
                    { "0" },
                }
            }
        };
    }
}
```

The C# classes wrapping the web service response are in the PredictionResponse.cs file. As before, I changed the types of the Value class from List<string> to string[], and List<List<string>> to string[,]. Then, I made some name adjustments. Specifically, I renamed the auto-generated class RootObject to PredictionResponse; see the companion code at Chapter 11/AnomalyDetection/ PredictiveService/PredictionResponse.cs.

The response from the predictive web service is a data table that organizes data similarly to the Azure Machine Learning Studio scored data visualizer; refer to Figure 11-27. Namely, there are three columns: temperature, scored labels, and scored probabilities. This data is packed in the JSON string array, which you can access through the AnomalyDetectionResult.Value.Values property. This is the two-dimensional string array. To easily interpret each row from this array, I wrote the PredictionScore class; see Listing 11-24. This class implements a constructor, accepting an argument of type PredictionResponse, and then automatically takes the temperature, label, and probability from the first row of the data table received from a web service. These are converted and then exposed as appropriate properties of the PredictionScore class. PredictionScore uses the first data row only because our request is designed to send only one temperature at a time. However, you can easily generalize this to multiple temperatures. You would just need to generalize the constructor from

Listing 11-23 to add subsequent temperatures to the `Values` array and then iterate through rows of the received data table.

PredictionScore also implements the `IsNormal` property, which converts the scored label to straightforward information and implements the `ToString` method, which can be used for debugging. I'm using string interpolation, a feature of C# 6.0.

LISTING 11-24 PredictionScore simplifies web service response

```
public class PredictionScore
{
    public double Temperature { get; set; }
    public double Label { get; set; }
    public double Probability { get; set; }

    public bool IsNormal
    {
        get { return !Convert.ToBoolean(Label); }
    }

    public PredictionScore() { }

    public PredictionScore(PredictionResponse predictiveServiceResponse)
    {
        Check.IsNull(predictiveServiceResponse);

        var values = predictiveServiceResponse.Results.AnomalyDetectionResult.Value.Values;

        if (values.Length > 0)
        {
            Temperature = Convert.ToDouble(values[0, 0]);
            Label = Convert.ToDouble(values[0, 1]);
            Probability = Convert.ToDouble(values[0, 2]);
        }
    }

    public override string ToString()
    {
        return $"Temperature: {Temperature:F2}, label: {Label}, Probability: {Probability:F3}";
    }
}
```

Given the above, I implemented the `PredictiveServiceClient` class, which is the actual REST client. This class is based on the `HttpClient` declared in the `System.Net.Http` namespace. `HttpClient` provides basic functionality for sending and receiving data using the HTTP protocol from a resource identified by the URI. In Listing 11-25, I show you how to configure the `HttpClient` to work with the predictive web service. Namely, you first write the request URI (from a web service API help) to the `BaseAddress` property of the `HttpClient` class. The request URI has the following form:

```
https://ussouthcentral.services.azureml.net/workspaces/<workspaceId>/
services/<serviceId>/execute?api-version=2.0&details=true
```

where `<workspaceId>` and `<serviceId>` are GUIDs of your Azure Machine Learning Studio workspace and your web service, respectively. Next, you pass your API key as the bearer token, or simply bearer. You add this to the HTTP request header using an instance of the `AuthenticationHeaderValue` class.

LISTING 11-25   Minimal HttpClient configuration for accessing the predictive web service

```
private const string postAddress = "TYPE_YOUR_REQUEST_URI_HERE";
private const string apiKey = "TYPE_YOUR_API_KEY_HERE";

private HttpClient httpClient;

public PredictiveServiceClient()
{
    httpClient = new HttpClient()
    {
        BaseAddress = new Uri(postAddress),
    };

    httpClient.DefaultRequestHeaders.Authorization = new AuthenticationHeaderValue("Bearer",
        apiKey);
}
```

To send the score request, I supplemented the `PredictiveServiceClient` class by the asynchronous method `PredictAnomalyAsync`; see Listing 11-26. It accepts a single argument, temperature. This value is first used to instantiate the `PredictionRequest` class and then sent to a web service as a JSON POST request using `PostAsJsonAsync` (defined in `System.Net.Http.HttpClientExtensions`). The resulting response is automatically parsed to an instance of the `PredictionResponse` class within the `ReadAsAsync` extension method (defined in `System.Net.Http.HttpContentExtensions`). The `PredictionResponse` class is wrapped by `PredictionScore` and returned to the caller.

LISTING 11-26   Predicting anomaly in temperature using the predictive web service

```
public async Task<PredictionScore> PredictAnomalyAsync(double temperature)
{
    var predictionRequest = new PredictionRequest(temperature);

    var response = await httpClient.PostAsJsonAsync(string.Empty, predictionRequest);

    PredictionScore predictionScore;

    if (response.IsSuccessStatusCode)
    {
        var scoreResponse = await response.Content.ReadAsAsync<PredictionResponse>();

        predictionScore = new PredictionScore(scoreResponse);
    }
    else
```

```
    {
        throw new Exception(response.ReasonPhrase);
    }

    return predictionScore;
}
```

Putting it all together

You have now all the tools to dynamically probe temperature readings from the Sense HAT sensor to detect anomalies. To put them together, you need the asynchronous operation (Task), which will read the temperature from the sensor, send it to the web service, and drive the LED array, depending on the scored label.

I implemented such functionality in the code-behind of the MainPage in the AnomalyDetection app; see the companion code at Chapter 11/AnomalyDetection/MainPage.xaml.cs.

In particular, Listing 11-27 shows the event handler of the Start Temperature Monitoring button (refer to Figure 11-22). I use this handler to disable a button and then to create and run the background operation, which processes data from a sensor. The corresponding temperatureMonitoringTask is instantiated every time, and the associated anonymous method is active as long as the user clicks the Stop Temperature Monitoring button. This invokes the event handler from Listing 11-28. In particular, it sends the signal to stop the temperatureMonitoringTask and subsequently re-enables the Start Temperature Monitoring button.

To send a signal to break a task, I use the CancellationTokenSource class. Specifically, IsCancellationRequested is used to control the while loop in the anonymous task method (Listing 11-27). IsCancellationRequested changes from false to true after invoking the Cancel method of the CancellationTokenSource class instance; see Listing 11-28. This method can be invoked after checking the while loop condition, so I additionally wait for the temperatureMonitoringTask to be finished. Then I update the UI through the appropriate field of the AnomalyViewModel.

LISTING 11-27 Asynchronous temperature processing

```
private Task temperatureMonitoringTask;
private CancellationTokenSource temperatureMonitoringCancellationTokenSource;

private void ButtonStartTemperatureMonitoring_Click(object sender, RoutedEventArgs e)
{
    anomalyViewModel.IsTemperatureMonitoringEnabled = true;

    temperatureMonitoringCancellationTokenSource = new CancellationTokenSource();

    temperatureMonitoringTask = new Task(() =>
    {
```

```
        const int msDelay = 500;

        while (!temperatureMonitoringCancellationTokenSource.IsCancellationRequested)
        {
            GetAndProcessTemperature();

            Task.Delay(msDelay).Wait();
        }
    }, temperatureMonitoringCancellationTokenSource.Token);

    temperatureMonitoringTask.Start();
}
```

LISTING 11-28 Stopping temperature monitoring

```
private void ButtonStopTemperatureMonitoring_Click(object sender, RoutedEventArgs e)
{
    temperatureMonitoringCancellationTokenSource.Cancel();
    temperatureMonitoringTask.Wait();

    anomalyViewModel.IsTemperatureMonitoringEnabled = false;
}
```

The actual temperature processing is implemented in the GetAndProcessTemperature method from Listing 11-29. A temperature either is obtained from a sensor if the field isSensorEmulationMode is false or is generated randomly; see Listing 11-30. I implemented this simple sensor emulation mode to be able to test communication with a web service independently from sensor readings.

The resulting temperature is sent to the predictive web service using the PredictAnomalyAsync method of the PredictiveServiceClient. The prediction score is then used to update the UI and the LED array.

LISTING 11-29 Detecting temperature anomaly

```
private bool isSensorEmulationMode = false;
private TemperatureAndPressureSensor sensor = TemperatureAndPressureSensor.Instance;
private PredictiveServiceClient predictiveServiceClient = new PredictiveServiceClient();

private async void GetAndProcessTemperature()
{
    try
    {
        var temperature = GetTemperature();

        var result = await predictiveServiceClient.PredictAnomalyAsync(temperature);

        UpdateTemperatureDisplay(temperature, result.IsNormal);
    }
```

```
        catch(Exception ex)
        {
            Debug.WriteLine(ex.Message);
        }
    }
}

private float GetTemperature()
{
    if (isSensorEmulationMode)
    {
        return GetRandomTemperature();
    }
    else
    {
        return sensor.GetTemperature();
    }
}

private float GetRandomTemperature(float baseTemperature = 36.55f)

{
    var random = new Random();

    const double scaler = 0.5;

    return (float)(baseTemperature + random.NextDouble() * scaler);
}
```

As you see in Listing 11-30, the UI is updated within the UI thread through the properties of the AnomalyViewModel class. The temperature is then displayed in the text box. Its foreground color is green for normal and red for abnormal temperatures. The LED array color changes analogously using UpdateLedArray, which has an effect only if there's an associated Sense HAT connection. If so, the isLedArrayAvailable is true.

LISTING 11-30   Updating temperature display

```
private bool isLedArrayAvailable = false;

private async void UpdateTemperatureDisplay(float temperature, bool isNormalLevel)
{
    if (Dispatcher.HasThreadAccess)
    {
        anomalyViewModel.Temperature = temperature;
        anomalyViewModel.TemperatureStatusColorBrush =
            isNormalLevel ? normalTemperatureLevelColorBrush :
            abnormalTemperatureLevelColorBrush;

        UpdateLedArray();
```

```
    }
    else
    {
        await Dispatcher.RunAsync(CoreDispatcherPriority.Normal,
            () => { UpdateTemperatureDisplay(temperature, isNormalLevel); });
    }
}

private void UpdateLedArray()
{
    if (isLedArrayAvailable)
    {
        ledArray.Reset(anomalyViewModel.TemperatureStatusColorBrush.Color);
    }
}
```

If you now rerun the app and click the **Start Temperature Monitoring** button, you will see results similar to those depicted in Figure 11-22. Note that by changing a value of isSensorEmulationMode, you can test the app in two modes: with (isSensorEmulationMode = false) and without (isSensorEmulationMode = true) the real IoT device. In the sensor emulation mode, randomly generated temperatures are sent to the predictive service, while in the nonemulation mode actual temperature readings are used for that purpose.

You can adjust the nonemulation mode to your training dataset by changing the baseTemperature argument of the GetRandomTemperature method to the average value of your training dataset. You can also modify the scaler, which specifies how much the random temperature changes over time; see the GetRandomTemperature method from Listing 11-29. By decreasing a scaler you can make your temperatures "more normal." Conversely, temperatures become "less normal" when you increase the scaler. In the nonemulation mode you can induce temperature changes by covering your IoT device, which should increase temperature.

As a final note, please keep in mind that your device warms up during operation. So if you rerun the AnomalyDetection the next day with a cold IoT device, you will most likely need to retrain the ML model, because the "normal" temperature has changed. To solve this issue you can also modify the SVM model tolerance. Another option is to set some arbitrary threshold for the scored label probability. You can then ignore anomalies with probabilities below that threshold.

Summary

In this chapter, you learned how to supplement UWP apps by using an artificial intelligence module. You started by using the AI module from Microsoft Cognitive Services, i.e. the Emotion API. Then, you learned how to build and train custom AI using Azure Machine Learning Studio. You developed regression and classification models. Regression was used to predict temperature, while classification was employed for anomaly detection. You then combined the anomaly detector with an IoT app through the web by using HTTP protocol.

PART III

Azure IoT Suite

The machine learning solution developed in the previous chapter required manual acquisition of the training dataset and data upload to the cloud. We stored a training dataset in CSV format, downloaded it from the IoT device, and then uploaded it to the cloud. This works fine when you have a single device or do not retrain your ML model very often. However, when the number of devices increases (which is typical for IoT systems) or you want to frequently update the ML model with new data, the services that would automate these operations become more attractive.

Azure IoT provides multiple services that enable you to collect and aggregate data from devices. Specifically, you can use these services to automatically send data from your device to the cloud and then update your ML model. You can also use Azure IoT services to visualize sensor data in real time and even remotely control your smart devices.

The Microsoft Azure IoT Suite combines multiple Azure IoT services along with the solution back end. The solution back end is the web app – the control panel of an IoT solution. The control panel deployed to Azure can be accessible from any place in the world and, having direct access to the Azure IoT and ML services, can process data to find trends or repeatable patterns or to predict device malfunction. Hence, the Azure IoT Suite is the *Internet* component of the IoT definition (see Chapter 1, "Embedded devices programming").

In the last part of the book, I describe two preconfigured IoT solutions delivered by the Microsoft Azure IoT Suite. These are remote monitoring and predictive maintenance. The remote monitoring IoT solution, described in Chapter 12, "Remote devices monitoring," shows how to collect, process, and visualize data from remote devices. The predictive maintenance solution, characterized in Chapter 13, "Predictive maintenance," extends this functionality through intelligence implemented using Machine Learning. In Chapter 14, "Custom solution," I describe Azure IoT services in more detail to show how you can build an IoT solution yourself.

CHAPTER 12

Remote device monitoring

In this chapter, you create the remote device monitoring Azure IoT Suite solution, which consists of a cloud-based system to accumulate data coming from remote devices using the Azure IoT Hub and Azure Storage. Based on several other Azure services, like Azure Event Hubs, Azure Stream Analytics, and Microsoft Power BI, remote devices monitor solution processes and visualize sensor data and device location on the Bing map through the web app. (See Figure 12-1.) This portal also enables remote control of devices. You can send messages to a remote device to instruct the device to take a particular action.

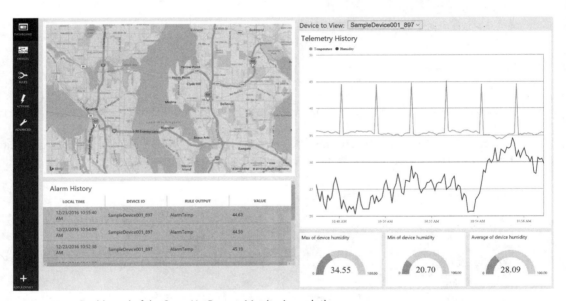

FIGURE 12-1   Dashboard of the SenseHatRemoteMonitoring solution.

I first set up a preconfigured Azure IoT Suite solution for remote devices monitoring and then write the software, which will run on the RPi2/RPi3 with the Sense HAT add-on board so that both apps will communicate. The client IoT device will send sensor data to the cloud, which will run the SenseHatRemoteMonitoring solution to process and visualize sensor data in real time. I also define commands for the remote control of the Sense HAT telemetry.

Setting up a preconfigured solution

To create a preconfigured solution in Microsoft Azure IoT Suite solutions, you use the *http://azureiotsuite.com* website. After logging in and configuring your subscription (you can use the one-month free trial), you will be redirected to a page where you click the **+** icon shown in Figure 12-2.

FIGURE 12-2 Microsoft Azure IoT Suite Provisioned Solutions screen.

After clicking **Create a New Solution**, you have two options: **Predictive Maintenance** or **Remote Monitoring**. (See Figure 12-3.) Pick the second one.

FIGURE 12-3 Microsoft Azure IoT Suite solution types.

Azure IoT Suite will display a page where you set the solution name, Azure subscription, and region. As shown in Figure 12-4, I set my solution name to SenseHatRemoteMonitoring, and used the Free Trial subscription.

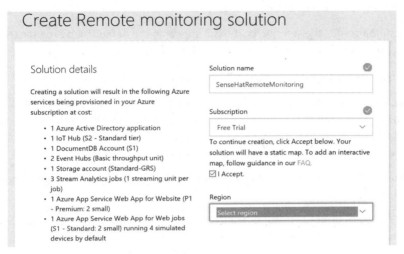

FIGURE 12-4   Creating a remote monitoring solution.

Choose the region depending on your geographical location. It will adjust the location of physical Azure servers accordingly. Note that the solution name is unique, so you will need to use a different solution name than SenseHatRemoteMonitoring.

After clicking the **Create Solution** button (at the bottom of the page), solution provisioning begins. It will take a while to complete this process. A successful creation will be confirmed by a Ready label with a green check mark. (See Figure 12-5.) In this page, you can also preview all the details about the solution you just created and navigate to the portal source code on GitHub.

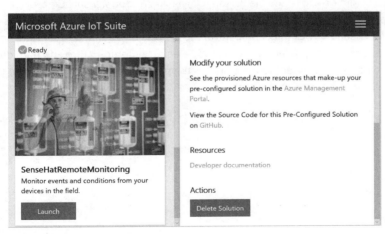

FIGURE 12-5   The SenseHatRemoteMonitoring solution created using an Azure IoT Suite preconfigured solution.

For now, just launch the solution by clicking the **Launch** button, and confirm it is running by clicking the solution dashboard link. It has the following form: *<your-solution-name>.azurewebsites.net*. In my case, that is *sensehatremotemonitoring.azurewebsites.net*. The dashboard URL can be also found on top of the solution details pane (the right part of Figure 12-5).

After clicking the dashboard URL, the solution portal will appear in the default web browser and will look similar to the one you see in Figure 12-1. Get to know each tab of the portal:

- **Dashboard**   This displays a map of connected devices, alarms, and telemetry data.

- **Devices**   This is a list of remote devices, including their status, identifiers, hardware capabilities, and description. Currently, there should be four emulated devices. Device details for each appear in the right pane. Note that this pane also includes a Commands link. Clicking this link shows a form that lets you send remote requests to the particular device.

- **Rules and actions**   This is used to define alarm rules and actions taken when telemetry values exceed threshold values.

- **Advanced**   This enables optional features. For example, it lets you connect your solution to the Jasper Control Center (*http://www.jasper.com*).

Provisioning a device

To enable the Azure IoT Hub to receive telemetry data from IoT hardware, you need to provision a device in the SenseHatRemoteMonitoring dashboard. Then your IoT device can send telemetry data, which in the following example consists of the temperature and humidity obtained from the Sense HAT add-on board.

I implement this functionality in the SenseHatTelemeter app (see the companion code at Chapter 12/SenseHatTelemeter), which I build on top of the Blank App (Universal Windows) Visual C# project template. The UI of this app appears in Figure 12-6. It consists of four buttons and two labels. Buttons are used connect to the cloud, send device info, and control the process of reading temperature and humidity from appropriate sensors (Start Telemetry and Stop Telemetry). Temperature and humidity values are displayed in labels and are also sent to the cloud. In the next few sections I tell you how to implement each functionality associated with the buttons.

27.13 °C   43.10 %

FIGURE 12-6   User interface of the SenseHatTelemeter app.

Registering a new device

First, you need to register a device in the SenseHatRemoteMonitoring dashboard. Do so by using the **Add a Device** button, which is located in the bottom left corner of the portal. After you click this button, a new page displays.

You can choose either Simulated Device or Custom Device. (See Figure 12-7.) Because you are going to use the real hardware, pick the **Custom Device** option.

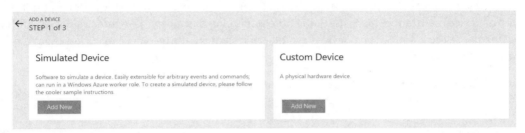

FIGURE 12-7 Adding a device.

Then, as shown in Figure 12-8, you define the device identifier manually or let SenseHatRemote-Monitoring generate it for you automatically. I will be using a manual device ID, which I set to SenseHAT. After verifying that this identifier is available, you click the **Create** button. Device credentials will display after a while. Copy these values. You'll need them in your code. Finally, click the **Done** button. A new device appears in the Device List. (See Figure 12-9.) Note that this device has Pending status. It will change to Running after you send the device information to the cloud.

ADD A CUSTOM DEVICE
STEP 2 of 3

How would you like to define the Device ID?
(DeviceID is case-sensitive)

○ **Generate a Device ID for me**

◉ **Let me define my own Device ID**

SenseHAT   Check ID

✓ Device ID is available

☐ **Attach a SIM ICCID to the device**

Create   Cancel

FIGURE 12-8 Generating a device identifier.

Device List (5)

STATUS	DEVICE ID	MANUFACTURER
● Running	SampleDevice001_897	Contoso Inc.
● Running	SampleDevice002_897	Contoso Inc.
● Running	SampleDevice003_897	Contoso Inc.
● Running	SampleDevice004_897	Contoso Inc.
○ Pending	SenseHAT	

FIGURE 12-9 A device list now includes the newly provisioned SenseHAT device.

Sending device info

The device registered in the SenseHatRemoteMonitoring dashboard becomes active when you send the message describing the hardware capabilities (device info). To enable communication between your IoT device and Microsoft Azure, you use the Microsoft.Azure.Devices.Client NuGet package. It provides the DeviceClient class. This is used communicate with the IoT Hub.

DeviceClient does not implement any public constructor. To instantiate DeviceClient you use specific overrides of either the Create or CreateFromConnectionString method. During the last step of device registration, the SenseHatRemoteMonitoring dashboard gave three values: an IoT Hub hostname, device identifier, and device key. You can instantiate the DeviceClient class using the first version of the Create method:

```
public static DeviceClient Create(string hostname, IAuthenticationMethod
    authenticationMethod);
```

This method accepts a hostname and an object implementing the IAuthenticationMethod interface. For a hostname you simply pass the string with the IoT Hub hostname; it has the following form: <iot-hub-identifier>.azure-devices.net, e.g. sensehatremotemonitoring28a04.azure-devices.net.

For the authentication method you can pass an instance of the DeviceAuthenticationWith-RegistrySymmetricKey class. Its public constructor accepts two string arguments: deviceId and key. They directly correspond to values provided during device registration. Note that these values are case sensitive.

After you create DeviceClient, open the connection by invoking an OpenAsync method. The complete code snippet for associating communication with the IoT Hub will look like the code in Listing 12-1.

LISTING 12-1   Connecting to the Azure IoT Suite

```
private const string deviceId = "SenseHAT";
private const string hostname = "<TYPE_YOUR_IOT_HUB_ID_HERE>.azure-devices.net";
private const string deviceKey = "<TYPE_YOUR_KEY_HERE>";

private DeviceClient deviceClient;

private async Task InitializeDeviceClient()
{
    var authentication = new DeviceAuthenticationWithRegistrySymmetricKey(deviceId, deviceKey);

    deviceClient = DeviceClient.Create(hostname, authentication);

    await deviceClient.OpenAsync();
}
```

As shown in Listing 12-2, the `InitializeDeviceClient` method is invoked within the click event handler of the Connect button of SenseHatTelemeter. You can see that I'm also using two objects there: `TelemetryViewModel` and `Telemetry`. Select public properties of the first object are bound to properties of visual controls, and are used to update the UI. Designation of the `TelemetryViewModel` is similar to `AnomalyViewModel` in Chapter 11, "Device learning." The second object, `Telemetry`, implements all the logic related to periodic sensor readings. Unlike with the AnomalyDetection app, I delegate functionality of sensor handling to a separate class to better distinguish the code related to the Azure IoT Suite. A `Telemetry` class is discussed in detail in the next section. Here, I focus on sending device info.

LISTING 12-2 Connecting to the cloud and setting up a Telemetry class for reading data from sensors

```
private const int secReadoutDelay = 5;

private TelemetryViewModel telemetryViewModel = new TelemetryViewModel();
private Telemetry telemetry;

private async void ButtonConnect_Click(object sender, RoutedEventArgs e)
{
    if (!telemetryViewModel.IsConnected)
    {
        try
        {
            // Connect to the cloud
            await InitializeDeviceClient();

            // Setup telemetry
            telemetry = await Telemetry.CreateAsync(TimeSpan.
                FromSeconds(secReadoutDelay));
            telemetry.DataReady += Telemetry_DataReady;

            telemetryViewModel.IsConnected = true;
        }
        catch (Exception ex)
        {
            Debug.WriteLine(ex.Message);
        }
    }
}
```

To send the device info, you construct an appropriate JSON object by following an approach similar to the one in Chapter 11. Namely, you construct C# classes, which reflect the JSON object structure. Then you configure their properties. Finally, you serialize these objects and send resulting data to the cloud.

An abstract C# representation of the device info object appears in Listing 12-3. It consists of five properties. The first two specify whether a device is real or simulated (`IsSimulatedDevice`) and device info version (`Version`). For the third property, `ObjectType`, you use a constant string `DeviceInfo`. These three members are clear.

LISTING 12-3   A C# class mapping JSON DeviceInfo object

```
public class DeviceInfo
{
    public bool IsSimulatedDevice;

    public string Version;

    public string ObjectType;

    public DeviceProperties DeviceProperties;

    public Command[] Commands;
}
```

More attention is needed for last two properties. The first of them, `DeviceProperties`, is implemented in the class of the same name. (See the companion code at Chapter 12/SenseHatTelemeter/AzureHelpers/DeviceProperties.cs.) The `DeviceProperties` class maps the complete device description, which appears in the SenseHatRemoteMonitoring dashboard. This description characterizes the capabilities of your hardware. In the default dashboard, they're used only for presentation purposes. Hence, you can specify any values you want, noting that `Latitude` and `Longitude` will be used to mark a geolocation of your hardware on the dashboard map.

To configure fields of the `DeviceProperties` class, I write a `SetDefaultValues` method, given in Listing 12-4. This method is invoked in the `DeviceProperties` class constructor. For most of the fields, `SetDefaultValues` uses constant strings. Only three fields can vary: `Manufacturer`, `FirmwareVersion`, and `Platform`. The first, `Manufacturer`, is taken from the publisher display name. As shown in Figure 12-10, you configure this value through the package manifest editor (Packaging tab). To determine the `FirmwareVersion` and the `Platform` properties, I write a static class, `VersionHelper`.

LISTING 12-4   Default device properties

```
private void SetDefaultValues()
{
    HubEnabledState = true;
    DeviceState = "normal";
    Manufacturer = Package.Current.PublisherDisplayName;
    ModelNumber = "Sense HAT #1";
    SerialNumber = "0123456789";
    FirmwareVersion = VersionHelper.GetPackageVersion();
    AvailablePowerSources = "1";
    PowerSourceVoltage = "5 V";
    BatteryLevel = "N/A";
    MemoryFree = "N/A";
    Platform = "Windows 10 IoT Core " + VersionHelper.GetWindowsVersion();
    Processor = "ARM";
    InstalledRAM = "1 GB";
```

```
        Latitude = 47.6063889;
        Longitude = -122.3308333;
}
```

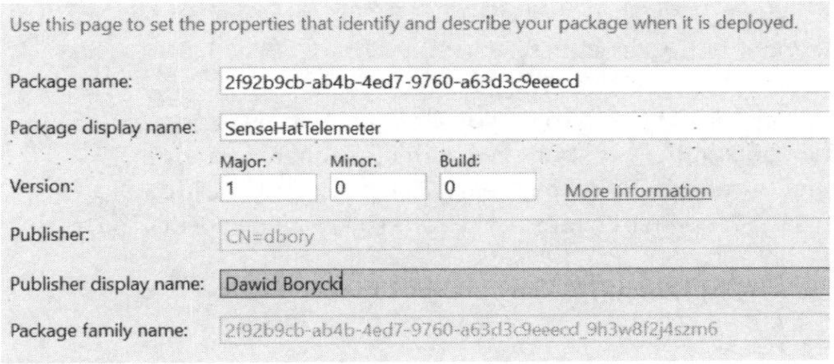

Use this page to set the properties that identify and describe your package when it is deployed.

Package name:	2f92b9cb-ab4b-4ed7-9760-a63d3c9eeecd
Package display name:	SenseHatTelemeter
Version:	Major: 1 Minor: 0 Build: 0 More information
Publisher:	CN=dbory
Publisher display name:	Dawid Borycki
Package family name:	2f92b9cb-ab4b-4ed7-9760-a63d3c9eeecd_9h3w8f2j4szm6

FIGURE 12-10 Configuring a publisher display name.

The VersionHelper class has two public methods: GetPackageVersion and GetWindowsVersion. The former, given in Listing 12-5, transforms the struct PackageVersion into a string. PackageVersion has four members, corresponding to each version component: Major, Minor, Build, and Revision. GetPackageVersion combines all of them into a single, dot-separated string. You can configure major, minor, and build values using the package manifest. If you want to set the revision value, you need to use the Assembly Information window. You can activate it by navigating to the Application tab of the project properties (in Visual Studio, open the **Project** menu and choose **Properties**) and then by clicking the **Assembly Information** button.

LISTING 12-5 Determining and formatting package version

```
public static string GetPackageVersion()
{
    var packageVersion = Package.Current.Id.Version;

    return $"{packageVersion.Major}.{packageVersion.Minor}.{packageVersion.Build}.
        {packageVersion.Revision}";
}
```

The second public method of the VersionHelper class, GetWindowsVersion, parses the DeviceFamilyVersion string. (See Listing 12-6.) DeviceFamilyVersion is obtained from the VersionInfo property of the AnalyticsInfo static class. The DeviceFamilyVersion string is first converted to a 64-bit integer, which is then partitioned into four 16-bit integers using the bitwise AND and bit shifts. Depending on the version component (major, minor, build, or revision) you want to get, you distinguish the appropriate 16 bits. For instance, the revision component is encoded using the first 16 bits (starting from the LSB), while the build component can be obtained from the next 16 bits, and so on.

```
public static string GetWindowsVersion()
{
    var deviceFamilyVersion = AnalyticsInfo.VersionInfo.DeviceFamilyVersion;

    var version = ulong.Parse(deviceFamilyVersion);

    var major = GetWindowsVersionComponent(version, VersionComponent.Major);
    var minor = GetWindowsVersionComponent(version, VersionComponent.Minor);
    var build = GetWindowsVersionComponent(version, VersionComponent.Build);
    var revision = GetWindowsVersionComponent(version, VersionCompone.Revision);

    return $"{major}.{minor}.{build}.{revision}";
}
```

To simplify version component decoding, I write the GetWindowsVersionComponent method and define the VersionComponent enumeration type. (See Listing 12-7.) The VersionComponent enumeration type defines four elements: Major, Minor, Build, and Revision. Each is assigned a value, which corresponds to the offset from the LSB. This offset is then used to isolate appropriate 16 bits, which are subsequently converted to a meaningful integer value using GetWindowsVersionComponent.

```
public enum VersionComponent
{
    Major = 48, Minor = 32, Build = 16, Revision = 0
}

private static ulong GetWindowsVersionComponent(ulong version,
    VersionComponent versionComponent)
{
    var shift = (int)versionComponent;

    return (version & (0xFFFFUL << shift)) >> shift;
}
```

The very last property of the DeviceInfo class, Commands, lets you define the collection of commands accepted by your device. Based on this information, SenseHatRemoteMonitoring will create a form for sending remote messages. As shown in Listing 12-8, each command consists of the command name and a set of command parameters. These consist of the name-type pairs and specify the command argument list. At this point, you don't need to define any commands, so keep it empty until you get to the "Receiving and handling remote commands" section later in this chapter.

LISTING 12-8   Classes used for command configuration

```
public class Command
{
    public string Name;

    public CommandParameter[] Parameters;
}

public class CommandParameter
{
    public string Name;

    public string Type;
}
```

Given the `DeviceInfo` and `DeviceProperties` classes, you can now register a device in the Azure IoT Suite portal. This is implemented in the SenseHatTelemeter app within the default event handler of the Send Device Info button. (See Listing 12-9.) This method first instantiates the `DeviceInfo` class. Then, this object is serialized and wrapped into a `Message` object (see Listing 12-10) and subsequently sent to the Azure IoT Hub using the `SendEventAsync` method of the `DeviceClient` class.

LISTING 12-9   Sending device info to the Azure IoT Hub

```
private async void ButtonSendDeviceInfo_Click(object sender, RoutedEventArgs e)
{
    var deviceInfo = new DeviceInfo()
    {
        IsSimulatedDevice = false,
        ObjectType = "DeviceInfo",
        Version = "1.0",
        DeviceProperties = new DeviceProperties(deviceId)
    };

    var deviceInfoMessage = MessageHelper.Serialize(deviceInfo);

    try
    {
        await deviceClient.SendEventAsync(deviceInfoMessage);
    }
    catch(Exception ex)
    {
        Debug.WriteLine(ex.Message);
    }
}
```

LISTING 12-10 Serializing an object to JSON format and wrapping it into the Message data structure

```
public static Message Serialize(object obj)
{
    Check.IsNull(obj)

    var jsonData = JsonConvert.SerializeObject(obj);

    return new Message(Encoding.UTF8.GetBytes(jsonData));
}
```

The `Message` class implements the data structure used to interact with the Azure IoT Hub. Basically, it supplements raw data (a JSON file being transferred) with additional properties. These properties help to track messages (`CorrelationId`), monitor the time when a message was received by the server (`DeliveryCount`), and set the message expiration time (`ExpiryTimeUtc`).

If you now run the SenseHatTelemeter app, click the **Connect** button, and then click the **Send Device Info** button, a detailed device description will be sent to the SenseHatRemoteMonitoring solution. You'll see your device running in the dashboard in the Device List. (See Figure 12-11.)

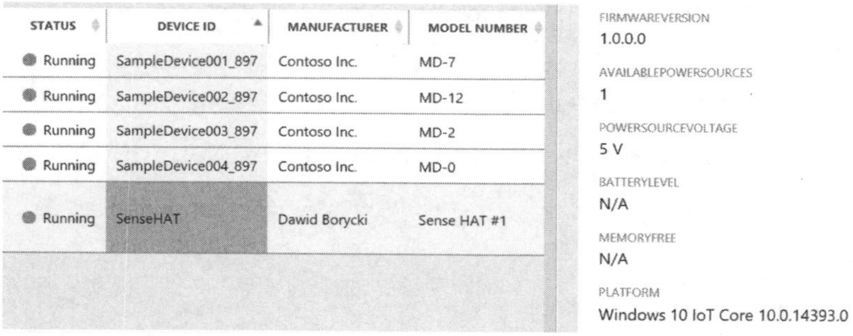

FIGURE 12-11 Updated status of the SenseHAT device. Compare this device status with that from Figure 12-9.

Because the device info was correctly interpreted by the solution back end, our custom IoT hardware can now interact with the cloud, sending telemetry data to and handling commands from the cloud.

You had to explicitly set the `ObjectType` property to `DeviceInfo` because the remote monitoring solution uses this value to distinguish device info from telemetry data. More specifically, the data stream received from remote devices is filtered by the appropriate Stream Analytics job. You can see the query of this job after logging into the Azure portal (*https://portal.azure.com*). By default, the name of the particular Stream Analytics job is *<solution-name>-DeviceInfo*. In my case that is *SenseHatRemoteMonitoring-DeviceInfo*. After clicking this job, a list of options appears on the right. Go to Query in the Job Topology pane, and then click **Inputs/DeviceDataStream**. The following query will appear:

```
SELECT * FROM DeviceDataStream Partition By PartitionId WHERE ObjectType = 'DeviceInfo'
```

Sending telemetry data

To send telemetry data, you first need to acquire temperature and humidity values from the Sense HAT sensors. I implement sensor data acquisition within the Telemetry class. (See the companion code at Chapter 12/SenseHatTelemeter/TelemetryControl/Telemetry.cs.) This class does not have any public constructors, but you can instantiate it using the static asynchronous factory method, CreateAsync, as shown in Listing 12-11.

LISTING 12-11   Creating the Telemetry object

```
private TimeSpan readoutDelay;

public static async Task<Telemetry> CreateAsync(TimeSpan readoutDelay)
{
    Check.IsNull(readoutDelay);

    var telemetry = new Telemetry(readoutDelay);

    await telemetry.InitializeSensors();

    return telemetry;
}

private Telemetry(TimeSpan readoutDelay)
{
    this.readoutDelay = readoutDelay;
}
```

First, CreateAsync validates the input argument, readoutDelay, which specifies a delay between consecutive sensor readings. Then, CreateAsync invokes a private Telemetry constructor and subsequently the InitializeSensors method. The latter associates the I^{2}C connection with the temperature and humidity sensors. (See Listing 12-12.) I'm using two separate sensors, but you can extend the HumidityAndTemperatureSensor class to handle temperature readings as discussed in Chapter 5, "Reading data from sensors." Then you could obtain both temperature and humidity readings using a single sensor.

LISTING 12-12   Sensor initialization within the Telemetry class

```
private TemperatureAndPressureSensor temperatureAndPressureSensor =
    TemperatureAndPressureSensor.Instance;
private HumidityAndTemperatureSensor humidityAndTemperatureSensor =
    HumidityAndTemperatureSensor.Instance;

private async Task InitializeSensors()
{
    await temperatureAndPressureSensor.Initialize();
    VerifyInitialization(temperatureAndPressureSensor,
```

```
            "Temperature and pressure sensor is unavailable");

    await humidityAndTemperatureSensor.Initialize();
    VerifyInitialization(humidityAndTemperatureSensor,
        "Humidity sensor is unavailable");
}

private void VerifyInitialization(SensorBase sensorBase, string exceptionMessage)
{
    if (!sensorBase.IsInitialized)
    {
        throw new Exception(exceptionMessage);
    }
}
```

To start and stop periodic sensor readings, the Telemetry class implements corresponding methods from Listing 12-13. Depending on the value of the IsActive property, these methods either initialize and start the appropriate background operation (Start) or break its execution (Stop).

LISTING 12-13 Starting and stopping sensor data acquisition

```
public bool IsActive { get; private set; } = false;

private Task telemetryTask;
private CancellationTokenSource telemetryCancellationTokenSource;

public void Start()
{
    if (!IsActive)
    {
        InitializeTelemetryTask();

        telemetryTask.Start();

        IsActive = true;
    }
}

public void Stop()
{
    if (IsActive)
    {
        telemetryCancellationTokenSource.Cancel();

        IsActive = false;
    }
}
```

To run a background operation, I use an approach similar to the one in the AnomalyDetection app. I create the `while` loop, in which I obtain temperature and humidity readings. These values are wrapped into an instance of TelemetryEventArgs (see the companion code at Chapter 12/ SenseHatTelemetry/TelemetryControl/TelemetryEventArgs.cs), and reported to listeners using the DataReady event. (See Listing 12-14.) This procedure is repeated as long as the cancellation token is not signaled.

LISTING 12-14   Initialization of the telemetry background operation

```
public event EventHandler<TelemetryEventArgs> DataReady = delegate { };

private void InitializeTelemetryTask()
{
    telemetryCancellationTokenSource = new CancellationTokenSource();

    telemetryTask = new Task(() =>
    {
        while (!telemetryCancellationTokenSource.IsCancellationRequested)
        {
            if (IsActive)
            {
                var temperature = temperatureAndPressureSensor.GetTemperature();
                var humidity = humidityAndTemperatureSensor.GetHumidity();

                DataReady(this, new TelemetryEventArgs(temperature, humidity));

                Task.Delay(readoutDelay).Wait();
            }
        }
    }, telemetryCancellationTokenSource.Token);
}
```

Note that in the Start and Stop methods, I could use `telemetryCancellationTokenSource.IsCancellationRequested` instead of the `IsActive` flag. But this would require additional conditional checks, verifying that `telemetryCancellationTokenSource` is not `null`.

Sensor readings are then sent to the cloud. This is implemented in the MainPage.xaml.cs file of SenseHatTelemeter within the `Telemetry.DataReady` event handler. As shown in Listing 12-15, this event handler first displays the sensor readings locally in the UI using the `DisplaySensorReadings` method (see Listing 12-16). Then temperature and humidity values, along with the device identifier, are wrapped into the `TelemetryData` object (see the companion code at Chapter 12/SenseHatTelemeter/ AzureHelpers/TelemetryData.cs), serialized, structured, and finally sent to the cloud. After the data is received, it is processed in the cloud, and displayed in the SenseHatRemoteMonitoring dashboard in real time as depicted in Figure 12-12.

LISTING 12-15 Data obtained from sensors is displayed in the UI and sent to the cloud

```
private void Telemetry_DataReady(object sender, TelemetryEventArgs e)
{
    DisplaySensorReadings(e);

    var telemetryData = new TelemetryData()
    {
        DeviceId = deviceId,
        Temperature = e.Temperature,
        Humidity = e.Humidity
    };

    var telemetryMessage = MessageHelper.Serialize(telemetryData);
    deviceClient.SendEventAsync(telemetryMessage);
}
```

LISTING 12-16   The UI is updated indirectly through TelemetryViewModel

```
private async void DisplaySensorReadings(TelemetryEventArgs telemetryEventArgs)
{
    await Dispatcher.RunAsync(CoreDispatcherPriority.Normal, () =>
        {
            telemetryViewModel.Temperature = telemetryEventArgs.Temperature;
            telemetryViewModel.Humidity = telemetryEventArgs.Humidity;
        });
}
```

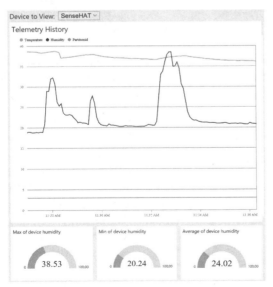

FIGURE 12-12   Telemetry data acquired from the Sense HAT sensors displayed in the SenseHatRemoteMonitoring dashboard.

You see that data obtained from the local sensor was sent to the cloud and processed there. The SenseHatRemoteMonitoring solution calculates the minimum, maximum, and average values of the humidity and presents the telemetry history in a chart. The end user obtains useful information without bothering with how the data was acquired. You can easily imagine that, by extending this example to multiple Sense HAT sensors, you can build a distributed sensor network. Data from these sensors can be transferred to the central system for processing and storage, so end users can access this data anytime from any place in the world using their favorite web browser.

Receiving and handling remote commands

A SenseHatRemoteMonitoring user might remotely control your IoT hardware using commands you define. Command definition is a two-step process. First, you resend the extended device info, which includes the collection of commands accepted by your device. Then you write additional logic, which parses requests sent from the cloud. Let's see how to do it in the SenseHatTelemeter app.

Updating device info

The single command UpdateTelemetryStatus enables the SenseHatRemoteMonitoring operator to remotely invoke Start and Stop methods of the Telemetry class. The UpdateTelemetryStatus command accepts a single Boolean argument, IsOn. Depending on its value, it either enables (true) or disables (false) the telemetry of the SenseHatTelemeter app.

To construct the UpdateTelemetryStatus command, I write a CommandHelper helper class. (See the companion code at Chapter 12/SenseHatTelemeter/Helpers/CommandHelper.cs.) This class implements one public method, CreateUpdateTelemetryStatusCommand. As shown in Listing 12-17, this method instantiates a Command object, and configures its properties: Name and Parameters. The Parameters collection has only one Boolean parameter, named IsOn.

LISTING 12-17   Defining the UpdateTelemetryStatusCommand

```
public static string UpdateTelemetryStatusCommandName { get; } = "UpdateTelemetryStatus";
private static string updateTelemetryStatusCommandParameterName = "IsOn";

public static Command CreateUpdateTelemetryStatusCommand()
{
    return new Command()
    {
        Name = UpdateTelemetryStatusCommandName,
        Parameters = new CommandParameter[] {
            new CommandParameter()
            {
                Name = updateTelemetryStatusCommandParameterName,
                Type = "Boolean"
            }
        }
    };
}
```

I modify the `DeviceInfo` object sent to the Azure IoT Suite to include an `UpdateTelemetryStatus` command. All the necessary changes are highlighted in Listing 12-18.

LISTING 12-18   Sending the commands collection as a part of the DeviceInfo message

```
private async void ButtonSendDeviceInfo_Click(object sender, RoutedEventArgs e)
{
    var deviceInfo = new DeviceInfo()
    {
        IsSimulatedDevice = false,
        ObjectType = "DeviceInfo",
        Version = "1.1",
        DeviceProperties = new DeviceProperties(deviceId),
        // Configure commands
        Commands = new Command[]
        {
            CommandHelper.CreateUpdateTelemetryStatusCommand()
        }
    };

    var deviceInfoMessage = MessageHelper.Serialize(deviceInfo);

    try
    {
        await deviceClient.SendEventAsync(deviceInfoMessage);
    }
    catch(Exception ex)
    {
        Debug.WriteLine(ex.Message);
    }
}
```

After sending an updated `DeviceInfo` object, the SenseHatRemoteMonitoring portal will display the form, which lets you transmit commands to your device. (See Figure 12-13.) The list of commands appears in the drop-down list. After you select one of available commands, its parameters will appear below the list.

FIGURE 12-13   A part of the SenseHatRemoteMonitoring portal for sending commands to a remote IoT device.

Commands can be invoked remotely from any place, at any time. The only requirement is that the IoT device and the end user have access to the Internet. SenseHatRemoteMonitoring implements the *Internet* component of the *Internet of Things* term.

Responding to remote commands

The remote commands invoked using the appropriate form of SenseHatRemoteMonitoring are transmitted to the Azure IoT Hub. To read them, you use the same DeviceClient class as for sending data to the cloud. In particular, you use the ReceiveAsync method. This method returns an instance of the Message class, which again comprises the JSON object, containing the remote command and additional values characterizing the message. To encode the remote command, all you need to do is map the JSON object to the corresponding C# class.

The JSON data can be obtained using the GetBytes method of the Message class instance. First, I read the result of this method (after sending a remote command) during debugging using the Watch window (in Visual Studio, open the **Debug** menu, choose **Windows**, and select **Watch 1**). To see the value of any variable, type its name in the Watch window. You can also type whole statements.

I use this capability to see the JSON structure received from the cloud. While debugging the SenseHatTelemeter, I place a breakpoint right after the execution of the ReceiveAsync method and read the JSON string using the following statement: Encoding.UTF8.GetString(message. GetBytes()). I copy the JSON string to the text box of the json2csharp.com website, and save the generated C# classes in the SenseHatTelemeter project. (See the companion code at Chapter 12/ SenseHatTelemeter/AzureHelpers/RemoteCommand.cs.) Finally, I rename the default RootObject class to RemoteCommand.

Given the RemoteCommand class, I extend the MessageHelper static class by the Deserialize method shown in Listing 12-19. This method reads the JSON string received from the cloud and converts it to the RemoteCommand class instance using the DeserializeObject static method of the JsonConvert class. The latter comes from the Newtonsoft.Json NuGet package, which was installed with the Microsoft.Azure.Devices.Client package.

LISTING 12-19   Converting JSON data received from the cloud to the RemoteCommand class instance

```
public static RemoteCommand Deserialize(Message message)
{
    Check.IsNull(message);

    var jsonData = Encoding.UTF8.GetString(message.GetBytes());

    return JsonConvert.DeserializeObject<RemoteCommand>(jsonData);
}
```

You now have code for interpreting the received commands. To go further, you need a background task to listen for incoming requests. It can be implemented as the infinite while loop. Such an approach is used in my sample implementation in Listing 12-20. The method, BeginRemoteCommandHandling, runs a Task instance, which repeatedly invokes the ReceiveAsync method of the DeviceClient class instance.

LISTING 12-20   Cloud message listener

```
private void BeginRemoteCommandHandling()
{
    Task.Run(async () =>
    {
        while (true)
        {
            var message = await deviceClient.ReceiveAsync();

            if (message != null)
            {
                await HandleMessage(message);
            }
        }
    });
}
```

Every time a valid message is received, it is processed using the HandleMessage method. As shown in Listing 12-21, this function first converts the Message class instance to the RemoteCommand object using the Deserialize method from Listing 12-19. Then, the RemoteCommand is interpreted and, if everything goes correctly, a confirmation is sent to the cloud using the CompleteAsync method of the DeviceClient class. If an error occurs, the message is rejected. The cloud is informed about such an event by invoking the RejectAsync method of the DeviceClient.

LISTING 12-21   Remote command handling

```
private async Task HandleMessage(Message message)
{
    try
    {
        // Deserialize message to remote command
        var remoteCommand = MessageHelper.Deserialize(message);

        // Parse command
        await ParseCommand(remoteCommand);

        // Send confirmation to the cloud
        await deviceClient.CompleteAsync(message);
    }
    catch (Exception ex)
    {
        Debug.WriteLine(ex.Message);

        // Reject message, if it was not parsed correctly
        await deviceClient.RejectAsync(message);
    }
}
```

The procedure of remote command parsing appears in Listing 12-22. I implement it to work as follows:

1. I check the name of the received command by comparing it to the `UpdateTelemetryStatus-CommandName` static property of the `CommandHelper` class (see Listing 12-17).

2. If the command name agrees, I either invoke the click event handler of the Start Telemetry or Stop Telemetry buttons, depending on the `IsOn` command parameter value.

3. The UI will also reflect the current status of the telemetry process. Note that button event handlers are invoked within the UI thread because `ParseCommand` is called from the worker thread.

LISTING 12-22 The remote command either starts or stops telemetry, depending on the IsOn parameter value

```
private async Task ParseCommand(RemoteCommand remoteCommand) {
    // Verify remote command name
    if (string.Compare(remoteCommand.Name, CommandHelper.
        UpdateTelemetryStatusCommandName) == 0)
    {
        // Update telemetry status depending on the IsOn parameter value
        await Dispatcher.RunAsync(CoreDispatcherPriority.Normal, () =>
        {
            if (remoteCommand.Parameters.IsOn)
            {
                ButtonStartTelemetry_Click(this, null);
            }
            else
            {
                ButtonStopTelemetry_Click(this, null);
            }
        });
    }
}
```

Test the whole IoT solution by deploying SenseHatTelemeter to your device and sending remote commands. The status of each command will be displayed in the Command History of the SenseHatRemoteMonitoring portal. (See Figure 12-14.) Initially, each command has a status of Pending. It changes to Success when the IoT device sends the appropriate confirmation.

Command History

COMMAND NAME	RESULT	VALUES SENT	LOCAL TIME CREATED	LOCAL TIME UPDATED	
UpdateTelemetryStatus	Pending	{"IsOn":false}	12/23/2016, 12:13:50 PM	Invalid date	Resend
UpdateTelemetryStatus	Success	{"IsOn":true}	12/23/2016, 12:13:37 PM	12/23/2016, 12:13:37 PM	Resend
UpdateTelemetryStatus	Success	{"IsOn":false}	12/23/2016, 12:13:20 PM	12/23/2016, 12:13:20 PM	Resend
UpdateTelemetryStatus	Success	{"IsOn":true}	12/23/2016, 12:12:17 PM	12/23/2016, 12:12:17 PM	Resend

FIGURE 12-14 The list of commands sent to the remote IoT device. The commands appear as Pending until the device sends the confirmation of handling it.

Azure IoT services

There are several IoT services behind the solution we developed here. The most important is the IoT Hub. It acts as the gateway, connecting devices with the cloud. The IoT Hub receives telemetry data and distributes commands sent from the cloud to device end points.

Messages received from devices are then filtered by Azure Stream Analytics jobs. In the preconfigured remote monitoring solution, three jobs are defined:

- **DeviceInfo job**   This handles messages containing device information objects, which are used to register new hardware or update its state. Device information is stored in a DocumentDB database, which is defined here as the device registry. The device registry is updated using the dedicated Azure Event Hub.

- **Telemetry job**   This is responsible for storing and aggregating untapped telemetry data. In particular, sensor readings are saved in the Azure Storage and then displayed in the solution portal (Dashboard tab).

- **Rules job**   This analyzes telemetry data to find anomaly values that exceed threshold values. Such data is output to the Azure Event Hub and displayed in the alarm history table, which is located under the map of the solution dashboard.

The messages from the Azure Event Hubs are delivered to the event processor. It either updates the device registry (DeviceInfo) or updates the web app display (Rules).

You will see how to use these services for custom solutions in Chapter 14, "Custom solution."

Summary

In this chapter, you got to know the remote monitoring solution of the Azure IoT Suite. You set up the solution and provisioned a custom hardware. Then, you sent telemetry data to the cloud and implemented logic for remote control of the RPi2/RPi3 with the Sense HAT add-on board.

CHAPTER 13

Predictive maintenance

In this chapter I discuss the predictive maintenance preconfigured solution of the Azure IoT Suite. This solution uses telemetry data from four simulated sensors to predict the remaining useful life (RUL) of an aircraft engine. A predictive maintenance preconfigured solution works much like a remote monitoring solution but extends that functionality by a regression machine learning model, which predicts the failure of the simulated aircraft's engine.

You control the predictive maintenance solution using the IoT portal (or dashboard), shown in Figure 13-1. However, there is no straightforward way to incorporate your custom hardware to this solution without source code modifications. Therefore, this discussion is limited to simulated devices.

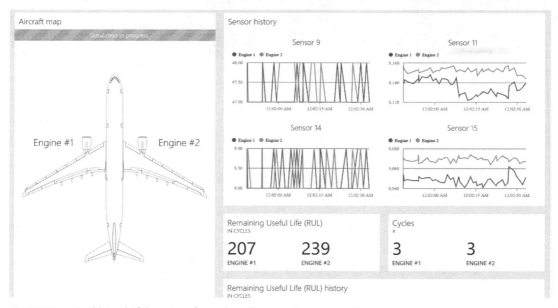

FIGURE 13-1 Dashboard of the preconfigured predictive maintenance solution.

After I show you how to set up the solution, I will discuss solution components and explain how they work. I will also discuss the internal source code so you will be able to modify the solution as needed. You put all this information to use in the next chapter for creating a custom IoT solution from scratch.

Preconfigured solution

The predictive maintenance solution can be set up like the remote monitoring solution. First, you navigate to *https://www.azureiotsuite.com*, where you click the **Create a New Solution** button. Next, you choose **Predictive Maintenance**, and use the wizard to set the solution name (here I'm using PredictiveMaintenanceSolutionDemo), select your Azure subscription, and choose the region. Finally, you click the **Create Solution** button and wait until provisioning is finished, which is confirmed as shown in Figure 13-2.

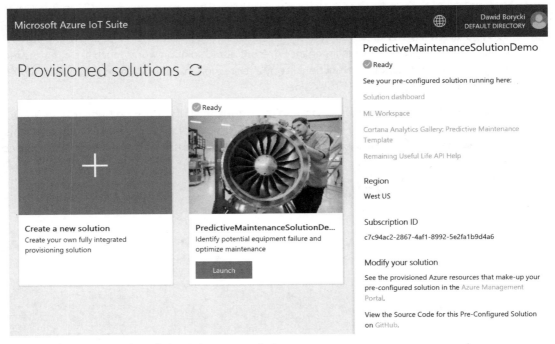

FIGURE 13-2   Provisioned predictive maintenance solution.

Once you've created the solution, there are several links available on the right panel of the Azure IoT Suite screen:

- **Solution Dashboard**   This gets you to the web app, which can be used to control the telemetry and display simulated sensor readings.

- **ML Workspace**   This is a link to the Machine Learning Workspace, which contains predictive maintenance experiments.

- **Cortana Analytics Gallery: Predictive Maintenance Template**   This directs you to a website containing a detailed explanation of the predictive ML models, which you can use for building ML solutions for predicting asset failures.

- **Remaining Useful Life API Help**   This is the REST API documentation for the predictive maintenance model.

Apart from the preceding links, you can find two additional elements under Modify Your Solution:

- **Azure Management Portal** This is a link to the Azure Portal, showing Azure resources used by PredictiveMaintenanceSolutionDemo.

- **GitHub** This directs you to the source code of the predictive maintenance preconfigured solution.

In the next sections, I discuss all these elements in more detail.

Solution dashboard

Once you go to the dashboard, you see the screen in Figure 13-3. The aircraft map with two engines is shown on the left. On the right, there is telemetry data from each sensor, and RUL information for both engines. The RUL comes from the ML model, which uses accumulated sensor data to calculate when engines are expected to fail.

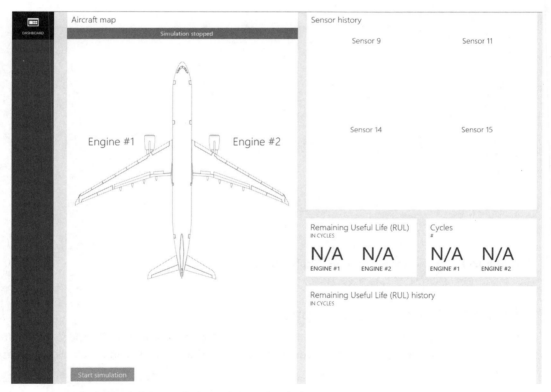

FIGURE 13-3 Dashboard of the predictive maintenance solution.

There are two sensors per engine. They are labeled Sensor 9, Sensor 11, Sensor 14, and Sensor 15. Sensor readings are captured every half hour during the flight, which lasts from 2 to 10 hours. The total flight duration is denoted as the cycle. The data used for simulation purposes comes from the real engine sensors and, as you see shortly, is stored in the CSV spreadsheet.

To see the solution running, you simply click the **Start Simulation** button. After a short while you will see sensor readings and the calculated RUL as shown in Figure 13-1 and Figure 13-4. These displays work the same as in the remote telemetry solution. You can stop the simulation at any time by clicking the **Stop Simulation** button. If you keep the simulation running for about half an hour, you will see a warning indicating that the RUL of one of the engines has reached its critical value.

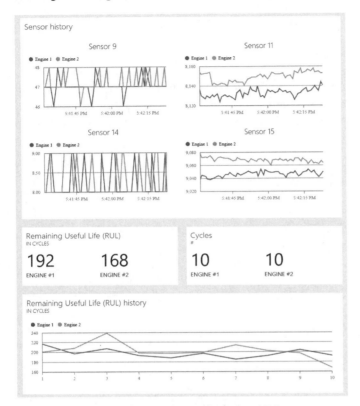

FIGURE 13-4   Simulated sensor data and calculated RUL.

Machine Learning Workspace

If you click the **ML Workspace** link, the Microsoft Azure Machine Learning Studio opens. A default screen will display the Experiments tab, containing two experiments: Remaining Useful Life Engines and Remaining Useful Life [Predictive Exp.].

The first experiment uses three datasets from the following spreadsheets: CMAPPS_train.csv, CMAPPS_test.csv, and CMAPPS_ground.csv. They are used to train (CMAPPS_train.csv), and then evaluate the machine learning models. Input data, which is a single string column with multiple numerical values, is pre-processed using several R scripts. You can see the source code of these scripts using the Properties window, where you click what looks like a Restore icon. It will open the editor window, where you can view and modify the source code of the script (see Figure 13-5).

R Script

```
1 # This module parse the input data into multiple column data frame
2 # with appropriate column names
3
4 # Map 1-based optional input ports to variables
5 dataset <- maml.mapInputPort(1) # class: data.frame
6 names(dataset) <- "V1"
7
8 # delete the extra space at the end of the lines
9 dataset$V1 <- gsub(" +$","",dataset$V1)
```

FIGURE 13-5 A fragment of the R Script Editor in Microsoft Azure Machine Learning Studio.

By analyzing the description and source code of each script, you see that the first one parses each row into multiple columns. The second script adds labels to training data, and the last script generates additional data features—that is, it calculates the moving average of the most recent sensor values.

Once the data is processed, it is used to train two machine learning regression models: Decision Forest Regression and Boosted Decision Tree Regression (see Figure 13-6). Subsequently, the models are scored and evaluated using the test data. You can see evaluation results by running the experiment (as shown in Chapter 11, "Device learning"), and then right-clicking the **Evaluate Model** component, choosing **Evaluation**, and selecting **Visualize**. You should get results similar to those in Figure 13-7. The second regression model (Boosted Decision Tree) leads to a slightly better coefficient of determination than the Decision Forest model. As explained in Chapter 11, Boosted Decision Tree fits to real data better than Decision Forest Regression.

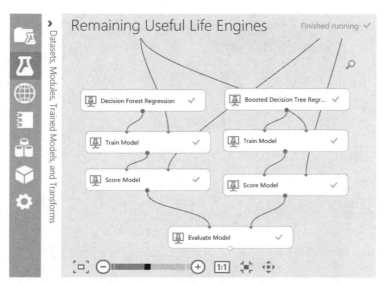

FIGURE 13-6 A fragment of the Remaining Useful Life Engines experiment. The upper part of experiment diagram, with datasets and R scripts, is omitted to improve readability.

rows columns
2 6

	Negative Log Likelihood	Mean Absolute Error	Root Mean Squared Error	Relative Absolute Error	Relative Squared Error	Coefficient of Determination
view as						
	468.264518	21.254563	29.140027	0.578085	0.491723	0.508277
	Infinity	21.312586	28.892966	0.579663	0.48342	0.51658

FIGURE 13-7 The models' evaluation of the Remaining Useful Life Engines experiment.

You now see that the Remaining Useful Life Engines experiment was constructed in a very similar way to our temperature experiment from Chapter 11. The training dataset is used to train two models, which are then evaluated and used to predict RUL.

The second ML experiment, Remaining Useful Life [Predictive Exp.], referred to hereinafter as RUL web service, is the trained version of the RUL. As shown in Figure 13-8, this predictive experiment is composed of the Remaining Useful Life [trained model], Score Model, Web Service Input and Web Service Output nodes, Enter Data Manually, and two components for data formatting (Select Columns in Dataset and Edit Metadata).

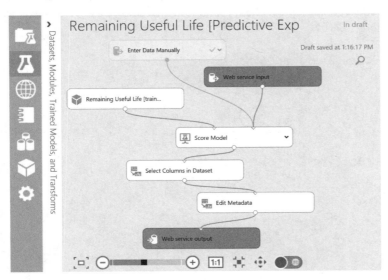

FIGURE 13-8 Remaining Useful Life [Predictive Exp.].

As in Chapter 11, Enter Data Manually can be used in the experiment view to manually score the model or, in the other words, to check the output of the trained model. To see the test data, you can use the Properties window of Enter Data Manually. You should get following values:

```
id, cycle, s9, s11, s14, s15
36, 1,9060.36, 47.91, 8140.46, 8.451
```

The first value, id, is the unique indentifier, cycle is the time unit, while s9, s11, s14, and s15 are sensor measurements. After running the experiment, you will see that the predicted RUL for this test data is about 180 cycles, which means that engine should work without failure for the next 180 flights. You can change the s9, s11, s14, and s15 values (sensor data) to see how this affects the predicted RUL. Note that the Enter Data Manually node is used here much like it was in our custom experiments from Chapter 11.

In the web service view, the Enter Data Manually node becomes inactive, while the Web Service Input and Web Service Output nodes are active. These nodes are used to represent web service requests and responses, respectively. According to the Remaining Useful Life API Help, the sample request has the form shown in Listing 13-1. This is a JSON file, containing two objects: Inputs and GlobalParameters. The second one is empty and thus not discussed. The Inputs object has one child object, which is the data table with six columns: id, cycle, s9, s11, s14, and s15. They represent a unique identifier, cycle number, and data from each sensor. You pass values for these columns using the two-dimensional array, Values. In the sample request, all sensor values are set to 0.

LISTING 13-1 Sample request of the RUL predictive experiment

```
{
  "Inputs": {
    "data": {
      "ColumnNames": [
        "id", "cycle", "s9", "s11", "s14", "s15"
      ],
      "Values": [
        [ "0", "0", "0", "0", "0", "0" ],
        [ "0", "0", "0", "0", "0", "0"]
      ]
    }
  },
  "GlobalParameters": {}
}
```

The responses of the RUL web service are also JSON files of the form shown in Listing 13-2. There is one Results object, which contains a data table with three numeric columns: id, cycle, and rul. The last one contains the actual prediction result of the regression model, which is displayed in the dashboard.

LISTING 13-2 Sample response of the RUL predictive experiment

```
{
  "Results": {
    "[Default]": {
      "type": "DataTable",
      "value": {
        "ColumnNames": [
          "id", "cycle", "rul"
        ],
```

```
        "ColumnTypes": [
          "Numeric", "Numeric", "Numeric"
        ],
        "Values": [
          [ "0", "0", "0" ],
          [ "0", "0", "0" ]
        ]
      }
    }
  }
}
```

Cortana Analytics Gallery

The Cortana Analytics Gallery: Predictive Maintenance Template link takes you to a website containing a detailed description of the predictive maintenance experiments, which you can use for predicting assets failure. In general, this Cortana template has three preconfigured models:

- **Regression**   This predicts the RUL or time to failure (TTF). This model is used in the predictive Azure IoT solution discussed here.

- **Binary classification**   This can be used to predict whether an asset is expected to fail within a certain time.

- **Multi-class classification**   This is dedicated to scenarios where you need to determine whether the asset is expected to fail within different time windows. It works similarly to binary classification but partitions the total time window into sub-windows.

All these experiments show you the complete machine learning process, starting from data preparation using R scripts, feature engineering, and up to training and evaluating your models. You can use these preconfigured models as a starting point for your custom solutions.

Azure resources

To see the resources used by PredictiveMaintenanceSolutionDemo, you use the dedicated link shown in the Azure IoT Suite. It directs you to the Azure Management Portal, as shown in Figure 13-9. These resources fall into the following categories:

- **Storage accounts mlpredictivemainten and predictivemaintenan<n1> (where <n1> is uniquely generated during solution creation)**   These store data for predictive experiment (CSV) files to manage partitions of the Event Hub processor (discussed later) and to collect sensor data and predicted RUL values.

- **IoT Hub predictivemaintenancesolutiondemo<n2> (where <n2> is uniquely generated during solution creation)** This service provides a bidirectional communication channel.

- **Stream Analytics job** This is PredictiveMaintenanceSolutionDemo-Telemetry.

- **Event Hub** This is PredictiveMaintenanceSolutionDemo.

- **App Services** These are PredictiveMaintenanceSolutionDemo and PredictiveMaintenanceSolutionDemo-jobhost.

- **App Service plans** PredictiveMaintenanceSolutionDemo-plan and PredictiveMaintenance-SolutionDemo-jobsplan determine the App Service plan. As shown in Figure 13-10, you can change the plan using the Scale Up (App Service Plan) option and adjust it to your needs. You can find a comparison of various price tiers here: *https://bit.ly/azure_service_plans*. To reduce the solution cost, I change the service plans to F1 Free. I first disable the PredictiveMaintenanceSolutionDemo App Service Always On feature. I do so by going to the Application settings (Settings group) of the PredictiveMaintenanceSolutionDemo App Service, toggling the Always On button to Off, and clicking the Save button at the top to save the changes.

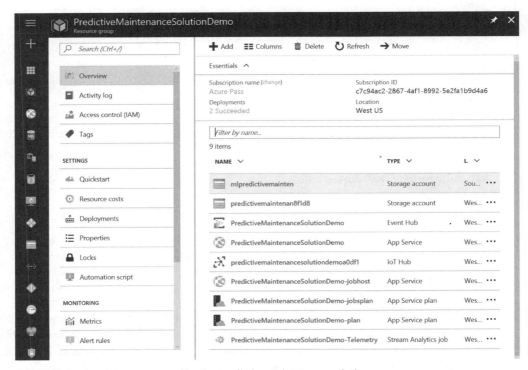

FIGURE 13-9 Azure resources used by the predictive maintenance solution.

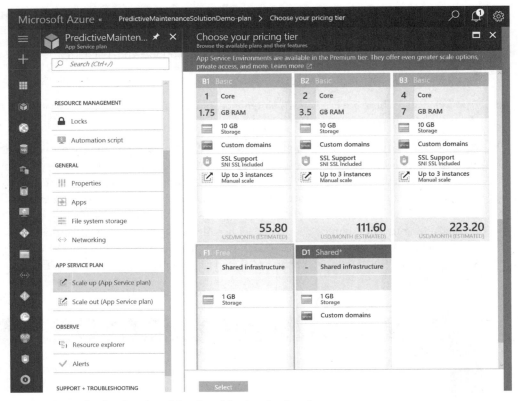

FIGURE 13-10 Configuring the pricing tier of the App Service plan.

I now show you how the preceding elements constitute the entire solution. I'll use the Cloud Explorer from Visual Studio (see Figure 13-11).

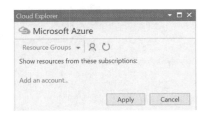

FIGURE 13-11 Cloud Explorer

To activate the Cloud Explorer, open the **View** menu and choose **Cloud Explorer**. Enter your account information and choose **Azure Subscription**. Go to the Azure Account settings tab (represented using the icon that looks like the top half of a snowman), and then click the **Add an Account** link. After you provide your credentials, the available Azure subscriptions will appear. Choose the correct one, and click the **Apply** button. A list of Azure resources appears after a short while (see Figure 13-12). The list contains same elements as listed in Figure 13-9. However, now you can actually see the storage data and all the files used by WebJobs and web apps.

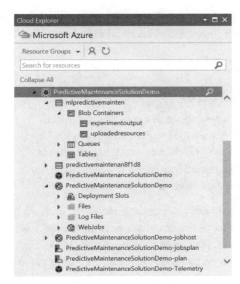

FIGURE 13-12 Azure resources listed in the Cloud Explorer.

Azure Storage

Start by inspecting the storage resources. Azure Storage is the cloud storage solution that supports big data scenarios required by many applications, including IoT solutions (see *https://bit.ly/azure_storage*). Azure Storage can be accessed from anywhere using a variety of programming languages through dedicated clients or REST APIs.

Four storage services are available for accessing Azure Storage:

- **Blob storage**   This is used for unstructured data, for example, text or binary files.

- **Table storage**   This stores structured data.

- **Queue storage**   This is dedicated to the asynchronous transfer of data between various application components.

- **File storage**   This provides cloud-based SMB storage.

As you will quickly see, the predictive maintenance solution uses blob and table storage only.

Predictive maintenance storage

The first storage account, mlpredictivemainten, is dedicated to storing training, test datasets, and experiment outputs. After expanding child nodes of mlpredictivemainten in the Cloud Explorer, you will see that all nodes except the Blob Containers node are empty. Blob Containers has two children: experimentoutput and uploadedresources. When you click either node, Visual Studio will display its contents. For instance, experimentoutput contains plain text files, while uploadedresources has two

CSV files and one plain text file. You can open each file by double-clicking on it in Visual Studio. If you open one of the CSV files, you will see that they contain a single column with plenty of numbers. These are parsed and preprocessed by the R scripts.

Telemetry and prediction results storage

The second storage, predictivemaintenan<n1>, is more interesting, since it contains the actual data coming from the simulated sensors (device telemetry), the list of registered devices, and also the output of the RUL Predictive Experiment web service. This data can be found under the predictivemaintenan<n1>/Tables node. There are four data tables: DeviceList, devicemlresult, devicetelemetry, and simulatorstate. Clicking one of them shows the data they contain.

As shown in Figure 13-13, the table in Azure Storage contains rows of data. However, unlike a relational data store, the Azure Table service does not enforce the schema for tables. Hence, rows in such a NoSQL table can have different sets of properties. For this reason, horizontal table entries are defined as entities (or table entities). Each property is defined by its name, value, and value data type.

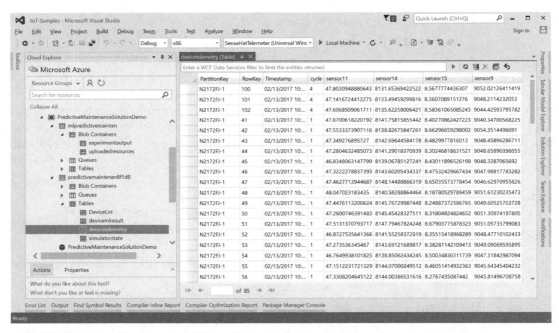

FIGURE 13-13 Device telemetry data of the predictive maintenance solution.

Each entity must define three system properties: PartitionKey, RowKey, and TimeStamp. PartitionKey and RowKey constitute the table primary key, while TimeStamp is automatically maintained by the Azure Table service to mark when the entity was last modified. TimeStamp is used to handle concurrency issues.

The whole Azure Table is divided into partitions for scalability purposes. Each entity in the partition is uniquely identified by `PartitionKey`. Then, each entity in the partition can be identified by RowKey. Both values are needed to uniquely identify the particular entity.

By analyzing the `PartitionKey` property of the devicetelemetrydata table, you can note that values there are either N2172FJ-1 or N2172FJ-2. These directly correspond to the aircraft's engines. The engine data is partitioned with respect to the engine identifier. Then, each entity in the partition is identified by increasing integral values starting from 100. Finally, there are five properties storing engine cycle and sensor data. In this case, every entity has the same schema. However, in general, the Azure Table can handle entities of different schemas. The only requirement is that they define three system properties: `PartitionKey`, RowKey, and `TimeStamp`.

You will later see where the actual sensor data comes from. For now, open the devicemlresult table. As shown in Figure 13-14, this table holds the predicted RUL values for each engine. Apart from the property storing these values, devicemlresult also has three Azure-required properties: `PartitionKey`, RowKey, and `Timestamp`. Partitions are identified by using two strings, N2172FJ-1 and N2172FJ-2, while RowKey is an integral number starting from 1.

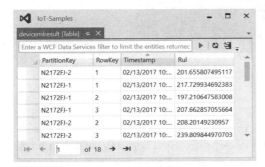

FIGURE 13-14   A few entities of the devicemlresult Azure Table.

DeviceList

Entities in the DeviceList table represent registered devices (see Figure 13-15). Again, there are three system properties, and one additional property, Key. It is used to access the IoT Hub by the particular device. The device can send and receive commands to and from the cloud.

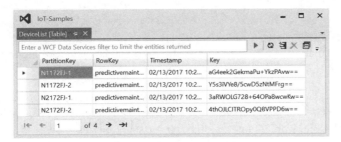

FIGURE 13-15   Contents of the DeviceList Azure Table.

The list of registered devices can be also accessed through the Azure Portal. Click the predictive maintenance IoT Hub in the Azure resources list, and then go to the Devices tab (a link is located in the top part, right under the IoT Hub name). The list of registered devices will appear as shown in Figure 13-16. Keys and connection strings for the particular device appear in the right panel, after you click the corresponding entry in the Device Explorer.

FIGURE 13-16   The Device Explorer of the Azure Portal showing the list of devices registered in the IoT Hub.

Azure Stream Analytics

Azure Stream Analytics refers to the real-time cloud stream processing unit, designed to rapidly analyze data incoming from many remote devices or sensors to get real-time insights on the process being monitored (see *https://bit.ly/azure_stream_analytics*).

In the predictive maintenance solution, there is one Azure Stream Analytics job, Predictive-MaintenanceSolutionDemo-Telemetry. To analyze this job, check its topology by choosing **PredictiveMaintenanceSolutionDemo-Telemetry** in the Azure Resources list, and then clicking **Job Diagram** from the Support + Troubleshooting group, which is located at the very bottom.

As shown in Figure 13-17, the PredictiveMaintenanceSolutionDemo-Telemetry job has one input, IoTHubStream, and two outputs, Telemetry Table Storage and TelemetrySummary Event Hub. The analytics job queries the data stream from the IoT Hub to extract sensor data, which is subsequently stored in the Telemetry data table (devicetelemetrydata). Additionally, the PredictiveMaintenanceSolutionDemo-Telemetry Azure Stream job calculates the average sensor data using a sliding window and then passes the resulting data to the Event Hub.

To filter and process data, the job uses queries, displayed in the right panel of the Azure Portal. To see the query code, you simply click rectangles marked using brackets: <>. According to Figure 13-17, the PredictiveMaintenanceSolutionDemo-Telemetry job has three such queries: `streamdata`, `telemetry`, and `telemetrysummary`. These queries use Stream Analytics Query Language (see *https://bit.ly/stream_analytics_QL*), which resembles SQL syntax.

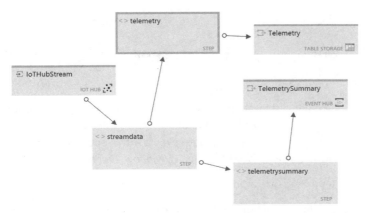

FIGURE 13-17 A job diagram of PredictiveMaintenanceSolutionDemo-Telemetry.

The `streamdata` query shows you how to filter out non-telemetry data coming from the IoT Hub. To this end, the `where` clause checks whether the `ObjectType` property is `null`. If so, the incoming message is interpreted as telemetry data. (See Listing 13-3.)

LISTING 13-3 The streamdata query filters out non-telemetry data

```
WITH
    [StreamData] AS (
        SELECT
            *
        FROM
            [IoTHubStream]
        WHERE
            [ObjectType] IS NULL -- Filter out device info and command responses
    )
```

As shown in Listing 13-4, the `telemetry` query selects seven properties from each `telemetry` command and inserts them into the Telemetry table. These properties are `DeviceId`, `Counter`, `Cycle`, `Sensor9`, `Sensor11`, `Sensor14`, and `Sensor15`. We saw these values in the devicetelemetry table, except that `DeviceId` was `PartitionKey`, and `Counter` was RowKey.

LISTING 13-4 The telemetry query selects seven properties from the telemetry command and then inserts them into the Telemetry table

```
SELECT
    DeviceId,
    Counter,
    Cycle,
    Sensor9,
    Sensor11,
    Sensor14,
    Sensor15
```

```
INTO
    [Telemetry]
FROM
    [StreamData]
```

Finally, the query of `telemetrysummary`, displayed in Listing 13-5, calculates averages of the sensor data from the telemetry events that fall within a specific period of time, the engine cycle. To do so, `telemetrysummary` uses windows. Namely, the window arranges events with respect to their time stamp. There are three types of windows available (see *https://bit.ly/window_functions*):

- **Tumbling window**   This uses a fixed-size, non-overlapping series of events.

- **Hopping window**   This uses a fixed-size but overlapping series of events.

- **Sliding window**   This outputs a series of events only when the values within the window actually change, enter, or leave the time window. In this demo, sliding window is used to catch the start and end events of the cycle.

LISTING 13-5   The telemetrysummary query aggregates sensor data

```
SELECT
    DeviceId,
    Cycle,
    AVG(Sensor9) AS Sensor9,
    AVG(Sensor11) AS Sensor11,
    AVG(Sensor14) AS Sensor14,
    AVG(Sensor15) AS Sensor15
INTO
    [TelemetrySummary]
FROM
    [StreamData]
GROUP BY
    DeviceId,
    Cycle,
    SLIDINGWINDOW(minute, 2) -- Duration must cover the longest possible cycle
HAVING
    SUM(EndOfCycle) = 2 -- Sum when EndOfCycle contains both start and end events
```

The real-time Azure Stream Analytics allows you to store data coming from sensors in the Azure Table without writing the actual logic. You define the input and output and then declare the query, which tells Azure Stream Analytics which data you want to store. You can also declare additional logic to preprocess your data and stream it further to Event Hub for extra processing. In the next chapter, I show you that you can also transfer your data to Power BI for visualization.

Solution source code

Here, I show you what happens to the actual data coming to the TelemetrySummary Event Hub, and where telemetry data comes from. I start by analyzing the source code of the preconfigured solution.

You can download the source code of the Azure IoT predictive maintenance preconfigured solution from the following GitHub repository: *https://bit.ly/iot_predictive_maintenance*. I also include the version of the code I work on with the companion code in the Chapter 13 folder. After downloading the source code from GitHub, I make the following modifications:

1. I rename projects and outputs by adding to their original names the "PredictiveMaintenance." prefix. I rename projects using the Solution Explorer. To change assembly names, I use the Assembly Name text box, which you can find under the Application tab of the project's properties.

2. I update or reinstall dependent NuGet packages using the NuGet package manager. This is the easiest way to revolve any NuGet issues you may find when downloading the source code from a repository.

The source code of the Azure IoT predictive maintenanced preconfigured solution from the companion code includes the following projects:

*   **PredictiveMaintenance.Common**   This class library project contains common helpers for configuration, device schemas, exceptions, models, and so on. The functionality implemented in this class library project is referenced by other components of the predictive maintenance solution.

*   **PredictiveMaintenance.EventProcessor.WebJob**   This console application processes events received by the Event Hub.

*   **PredictiveMaintenance.Simulator.WebJob**   Another console application, which implements sensor simulation. This project synthesizes sensor readings and inserts them in the dedicated Azure Table storage.

*   **PredictiveMaintenance.Web**   This ASP.NET MVC web application implements the solution dashboard.

*   **PredictiveMaintenance.WebJobHost**   This console application hosts the PredictiveMaintenance.EventProcessor.WebJob and PredictiveMaintenance.Simulator. WebJob WebJobs.

Event Hub and the machine learning event processor

In Azure, the Event Hub is a large-scale service dedicated to big data and IoT solutions (see *https://bit.ly/azure_event_hubs*). Event Hub collects, rapidly transforms, and processes large amounts of information. Event Hub uses partitions, which define how many concurrent consumers and producers can access the data pipe.

To process data received by the Event Hub, you create a class that implements the IEventProcessor interface. Then you instantiate the EventProcessorHost class, which hosts event processors. EventProcessorHost associates your event processor with the particular Event Hub. The IEventProcessor interface and EventProcessorHost class are both available through the client, implemented within the Microsoft.Azure.ServiceBus.EventProcessorHost NuGet package. Basically, this package handles partition-related functionality and simplifies implementation of event processors.

In the Azure IoT predictive maintenance example, the Event Hub receives preprocessed telemetry data. To see what is then happening with this data, let's open the PredictiveMaintenance.EventProcessor. WebJob project. The entry point of this app is the static Main method of the Program class. (See the companion code at Chapter 13/PredictiveMaintenance.EventProcessor.WebJob/Program.cs.) The Main method uses the inversion of control (IoC) design pattern, implemented on top of the Autofac NuGet package, to create the MLDataProcessorHost, which hosts event processors.

The IoC design pattern is extensively used in cross-platform programming, where the application depends on components or services and concrete implementation is resolved at compilation or run time. The app uses the platform functionality abstractions, exposed via interfaces, which are then mapped to platform-specific functionality (see *https://bit.ly/code_sharing*). In the Autofac, this mapping is performed using an instance of the ContainerBuilder class, which you use to register modules and concrete type implementations of the abstraction layer.

As shown in Listing 13-6, the Autofac IoC container is created under the try catch statements of the Program.Main method. Next, the EventProcessorModule class is registered (the BuildContainer method from Listing 13-6).

LISTING 13-6   A fragment of the Main method, where the IoC container is created

```
static readonly CancellationTokenSource CancellationTokenSource = new
CancellationTokenSource();
static IContainer eventProcessorContainer;

static void Main(string[] args)
{
    try
    {
        BuildContainer();
        eventProcessorContainer
            .Resolve<IShutdownFileWatcher>()
            .Run(StartMLDataProcessorHost, CancellationTokenSource);
    }
    catch (Exception ex)
    {
        CancellationTokenSource.Cancel();
        Trace.TraceError("Webjob terminating: {0}", ex.ToString());
    }
}

static void BuildContainer()
```

```
{
    var builder = new ContainerBuilder();
    builder.RegisterModule(new EventProcessorModule());
    eventProcessorContainer = builder.Build();
}
```

In Listing 13-7, `EventProcessorModule` derives from the Autofac's `Module` class and overrides its `Load` method to register three types: `ShutdownFileWatcher`, `ConfigurationProvider`, and `MLDataProcessorHost`. They implement the following abstractions: `IShutdownFileWatcher`, `IConfigurationProvider`, and `IMLDataProcessorHost`, respectively. Instead of accessing concrete implementations directly, the app then invokes interface methods. The actual mapping between interfaces and concrete types is done by the IoC container.

LISTING 13-7   EventProcessorModule registers three types

```
public sealed class EventProcessorModule : Module
{
    protected override void Load(ContainerBuilder builder)
    {
        builder.RegisterType<ShutdownFileWatcher>()
            .As<IShutdownFileWatcher>()
            .SingleInstance();

        builder.RegisterType<ConfigurationProvider>()
            .As<IConfigurationProvider>()
            .SingleInstance();

        builder.RegisterType<MLDataProcessorHost>()
            .As<IMLDataProcessorHost>()
            .SingleInstance();
    }
}
```

The `ShutdownFileWatcher` and `ConfigurationProvider` classes are implemented in the PredictiveMaintenance.Common project. The first class is used to monitor the cloud environment variable `WEBJOBS_SHUTDOWN_FILE` to listen for file shutdown signals. Detailed usage of this variable is described in the source code. (See ShutdownFileWatcher.cs of the PredictiveMaintenance.Common project).

The `ConfigurationProvider` class is used to determine environment and application settings. For further details see ConfigurationProvider.cs of the PredictiveMaintenance.Common.

Here, the most important part is the last registered type, `MLDataProcessorHost`. (See the companion code at Chapter 13/PredictiveMaintenance.EventProcessor.WebJob/Processors/MLDataProcessorHost.cs.) This type derives from the generic `EventProcessorHost` class. (See the companion code at Chapter 13/ PredictiveMaintenance.EventProcessor.WebJob/Processors/Generic/EventProcessorHost.cs.) The latter internally uses the `EventProcessorHost` class from Microsoft.Azure.ServiceBus.EventProcessorHost and thus is directly related to processing Event Hub's data.

Next, I analyze the EventProcessorHost.cs file to see how to create EventProcessorHost and register particular event processors. This functionality is implemented within the StartProcessor method, shown in Listing 13-8. This method instantiates EventProcessorHost using the five-argument constructor. This constructor takes the hostname, a path to the Event Hub, the event's consumer group name, a connection string to the Event Hub, and the connection string to the blob storage used for partition distribution.

LISTING 13-8 Creation of the event processor host and event processor registration

```
public async Task StartProcessor(CancellationToken token)
{
    try
    {
        // Initialize
        _eventProcessorHost = new EventProcessorHost(
            Environment.MachineName,
            _eventHubName.ToLowerInvariant(),
            EventHubConsumerGroup.DefaultGroupName,
            _eventHubConnectionString,
            _storageConnectionString);

        _factory = Activator.CreateInstance(typeof(TEventProcessorFactory), _arguments)
            as TEventProcessorFactory;

        Trace.TraceInformation("{0}: Registering host...", GetType().Name);

        EventProcessorOptions options = new EventProcessorOptions();
        options.ExceptionReceived += OptionsOnExceptionReceived;
        await _eventProcessorHost.RegisterEventProcessorFactoryAsync(_factory);

        // processing loop
        while (!token.IsCancellationRequested)
        {
            Trace.TraceInformation("{0}: Processing...", GetType().Name);
            await Task.Delay(TimeSpan.FromMinutes(5), token);
        }

        // cleanup
        await _eventProcessorHost.UnregisterEventProcessorAsync();
    }
    catch (Exception e)
    {
        Trace.TraceInformation("Error in {0}.StartProcessor, Exception: {1}",
            GetType().Name, e.Message);
    }
    _running = false;
}

void OptionsOnExceptionReceived(object sender, ExceptionReceivedEventArgs
    exceptionReceivedEventArgs)
{
```

```
      Trace.TraceError("Received exception, action: {0}, message: {1}",
          exceptionReceivedEventArgs.Action, exceptionReceivedEventArgs.Exception.ToString());
}
```

The actual values of these arguments are set automatically during solution deployment. If you want to see connection strings, use the Azure Portal. The Event Hub connection string can be found under the Shared Access Policies (Settings group). By default, there is only one policy, RootManageSharedAccessKey. You can see that this policy allows you to manage, send, and list events of the PredictiveMaintenanceSolutionDemo Event Hub. After you click the RootManageSharedAccessKey policy, you will see access keys and the primary and secondary connection strings, which have the following form:

```
Endpoint=sb://predictivemaintenancesolutiondemo.servicebus.windows.net
/;SharedAccessKeyName=RootManageSharedAccessKey;SharedAccessKey=xwCZgzjLhA
/KYIdq16ova4UFTyHzF/R4HhjBRa7R+jg=
```

The general form of the blob storage connection string is:

```
DefaultEndpointsProtocol=https;AccountName=<your_storage_account_name>;AccountKey=<your_key>;
BlobEndpoint=<endpoint>
```

You get the account name, account key, and blob endpoint from the Azure Portal. In the PredictiveMaintenanceSolutionDemo, the blob storage of interest is predictivemaintenance-solutiondemo-ehdata. It is contained in the predictivemaintenan<n1> storage account, under Blobs (Figure 13-18). This list also displays endpoints, which are contained in the URL column.

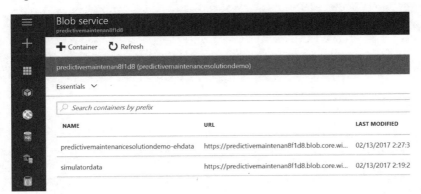

FIGURE 13-18   Blob service of the storage account.

To get access keys, you click the **Access Keys** link under the Settings group of the predictivemaintenan<n1> storage account in the Azure Portal. Two keys appear along with the storage account name.

You may wonder why you need this blob storage, and indeed at first glance it looks peculiar. The blob storage is used internally by EventProcessorHost to manage concurrent access to the Event Hub.

After the `EventProcessorHost` is instantiated, the `StartProcessor` method creates the instance of `TEventProcessorFactory`—the argument of the generic `EventProcessorHost` class. It can work with different objects. However, in the PredictiveMaintenanceSolutionDemo the actual class used is `EventProcessorFactory<MLDataProcessor>` (see MLDataProcessorHost.cs). This object implements a factory of event processors represented by the `MLDataProcessor` class. As shown in Listing 13-8, this factory is registered in the event processor host using `EventProcessorHost.RegisterEventProcessorFactoryAsync`. We thus see that the actual event data is processed using `MLDataProcessor`, which is discussed further in the next section.

Machine learning data processor

You can find the implementation of the machine learning data processor, `MLDataProcessor`, in the MLDataProcessor.cs file of the PredictiveMaintenance.EventProcessor.WebJob project. After opening this file, you will see that the `MLDataProcessor` class derives from `EventProcessor`, implementing the `IEventProcessor` interface. The latter comes from Microsoft.Azure.ServiceBus.EventProcessorHost.

`IEventProcessor` has three methods: `OpenAsync`, `CloseAsync`, and `ProcessItemsAsync`. The first two are invoked when the event processor is initialized and right before it is closed or unregistered. The last method, `ProcessItemsAsync`, is invoked whenever new messages are delivered to the Event Hub stream. `ProcessItemsAsync` is the actual place where averaged sensor data is consumed.

The `ProcessItemsAsync` method of the `EventProcessor` class appears in Listing 13-9. As you see, `ProcessItemsAsync` sequentially processes elements of the message collection. Each element of this collection is of type `EventData`, which represents data sent to and from the Event Hub.

LISTING 13-9   Sequential message processing

```
public async Task ProcessEventsAsync(PartitionContext context,
IEnumerable<EventData> messages)
{
    Trace.TraceInformation("{0}: In ProcessEventsAsync", GetType().Name);

    foreach (EventData message in messages)
    {
        try
        {
            // Write out message
            Trace.TraceInformation("{0}: {1} - Partition {2}", GetType().Name,
                message.Offset, context.Lease.PartitionId);
            LastMessageOffset = message.Offset;

            string jsonString = Encoding.UTF8.GetString(message.GetBytes());
            dynamic result = JsonConvert.DeserializeObject(jsonString);
            JArray resultAsArray = result as JArray;

            if (resultAsArray != null)
            {
```

```
                foreach (dynamic resultItem in resultAsArray)
                {
                    await ProcessItem(resultItem);
                }
            }
            else
            {
                await ProcessItem(result);
            }

            _totalMessages++;
        }
        catch (Exception e)
        {
            Trace.TraceError("{0}: Error in ProcessEventAsync -- {1}",
                GetType().Name, e.Message);
        }
    }

    // batch has been processed, checkpoint
    try
    {
        await context.CheckpointAsync();
    }
    catch (Exception ex)
    {
        Trace.TraceError(
            "{0}{0}*** CheckpointAsync Exception - {1}.ProcessEventsAsync ***{0}{0}{2}{0}{0}",
            Console.Out.NewLine,
            GetType().Name,
            ex);
    }

    if (IsClosed)
    {
        IsReceivedMessageAfterClose = true;
    }
}

public abstract Task ProcessItem(dynamic data);
```

Similar to the `Message` class used in Chapter 12, "Remote device monitoring," `EventData` wraps the actual binary data with additional properties, which helps you to track events. To get the actual event data you use the `GetBytes` method and then parse it depending on your needs. In PredictiveMaintenanceSolutionDemo, the raw byte array is a JSON object, which is deserialized using the `JsonConvert` class. The resulting object is passed to the abstract `ProcessItem` method.

The concrete implementation of the `ProcessItem` method is contained in the `MLDataProcessor` class (the `ProcessItem` method from Listing 13-10). The logical structure of the `MLDataProcessor.ProcessItem` method can be divided into two parts. The first one verifies the structure of the event data to see whether the device identifier, cycle, and sensor data are not null. If so, they are wrapped into the MLRequest object (see the MLRequest.cs file of the PredictiveMaintenance.EventProcessor. WebJob project), which is then posted as a JSON file to the RUL web service. The response of this request is then used to construct a RulTableEntity object, which is subsequently inserted into the dedicated Azure table, devicemlresult.

LISTING 13-10 The ProcessItem method of the MLDataProcessor class

```
const string ML_ENDPOINT = "/execute?api-version=2.0&details=true";
readonly string[] ML_REQUEST_COLUMNS = { "id", "cycle", "s9", "s11", "s14", "s15" };
const int RUL_COLUMN = 2;

readonly IConfigurationProvider _configurationProvider;
public override async Task ProcessItem(dynamic eventData)
{
    // Ensure this is a correctly formatted event for ML; ignore it otherwise
    if (eventData == null || eventData.deviceid == null || eventData.cycle == null ||
        eventData.sensor9 == null || eventData.sensor11 == null ||
        eventData.sensor14 == null || eventData.sensor15 == null)
    {
        return;
    }

    // The experiment theoretically supports multiple inputs at once,
    // even though we only get one value at a time, so the request
    // requires an array of inputs
    MLRequest mlRequest = new MLRequest(ML_REQUEST_COLUMNS, new string[,]
    {
        {
            // The id is required to be numeric, so we hash the actual device id
            eventData.deviceid.ToString().GetHashCode().ToString(),
            // The remaining entries are string representations of the numeric values
            eventData.cycle.ToString(),
            eventData.sensor9.ToString(),
            eventData.sensor11.ToString(),
            eventData.sensor14.ToString(),
            eventData.sensor15.ToString()
        }
    });

    HttpClient http = new HttpClient();
    http.DefaultRequestHeaders.Authorization = new AuthenticationHeaderValue("Bearer",
        _configurationProvider.GetConfigurationSettingValue("MLApiKey"));
    http.BaseAddress = new Uri(_configurationProvider.GetConfigurationSettingValue(
        "MLApiUrl") + ML_ENDPOINT);

    HttpResponseMessage response = await http.PostAsJsonAsync("", mlRequest);

    if (response.IsSuccessStatusCode)
    {
```

```
        MLResponse result = JsonConvert.DeserializeObject<MLResponse>(
            await response.Content.ReadAsStringAsync());

        RulTableEntity entry = new RulTableEntity
        {
            PartitionKey = eventData.deviceid.ToString(),
            RowKey = eventData.cycle.ToString(),
            // Extract the single relevant RUL value from the JSON output
            Rul = result.Results["data"].value.Values[0, RUL_COLUMN],
            // Since the simulator might replay data, ensure we can overwrite table values
            ETag = "*"
        };

        // We don't need a data model to represent the result of this operation,
        // so we use a stub table/model converter
        await AzureTableStorageHelper.DoTableInsertOrReplaceAsync<object,
            RulTableEntity>(entry, (RulTableEntity e) => null,
            _configurationProvider.GetConfigurationSettingValue("eventHub.
            StorageConnectionString"),
            _configurationProvider.GetConfigurationSettingValue("MLResultTableName"));
    }
    else
    {
        throw new Exception(string.Format("The ML request failed with status code: {0}",
            response.StatusCode));
    }
}
```

The programmatic access to the ML web service proceeds as in Chapter 11. However, accessing the Azure Table storage requires more attention.

Azure Table storage

PredictiveMaintenanceSolutionDemo uses two helper classes to handle Azure Table storage: AzureRetryHelper and AzureTableStorageHelper. Implementation of both classes can be found in the companion code at Chapter 13/PredictiveMaintenanceDemo.Common/Helpers.

AzureRetryHelper implements retry logic, which runs a particular operation like entity insertion, update, or deletion for the specified number of times. There are several methods implemented in AzureRetryHelper, but the most important one is OperationWithBasicRetryAsync. As shown in Listing 13-11, this method invokes asynchronous operation passed using an asyncOperation argument within the while loop. Each call to this method is followed by incrementing the local currentRetry variable. The while loop is terminated when currentRetry reaches the RETRY_COUNT value. By default, the RETRY_COUNT value is 2, so the OperationWithBasicRetryAsync method tries to perform the specific operation twice. The internal while loop of the OperationWithBasicRetryAsync is also terminated in case of transient errors. AzureRetryHelper checks for transient errors using the IsTransient method, which is well-commented in the source code.

LISTING 13-11   Retry logic of the AzureRetryHelper class

```
const int RETRY_COUNT = 2;

public static async Task<T> OperationWithBasicRetryAsync<T>(Func<Task<T>> asyncOperation)
{
    int currentRetry = 0;

    while (true)
    {
        try
        {
            return await asyncOperation();
        }
        catch (Exception ex)
        {
            currentRetry++;

            if (currentRetry > RETRY_COUNT || !IsTransient(ex))
            {
                // If this is not a transient error
                // or we should not retry re-throw the exception.
                throw;
            }
        }

        // Wait to retry the operation.
        await Task.Delay(100 * currentRetry);
    }
}
```

AzureTableStorageHelper has three public methods: GetTableAsync,
DoTableInsertOrReplaceAsync, and DoDeleteAsync. It also has one internal method,
PerformTableOperation.

The definition of the GetTableAsync method appears in Listing 13-12 and shows how to access
the table in Azure Storage using classes and methods implemented in the WindowsAzure.Storage
NuGet package (or Azure Storage client). You first instantiate the CloudStorageAccount class using a storage connection string. Then, you create CloudTableClient using an appropriate method
of the CloudStorageAccount class instance. Finally, you get access to the selected table using the
GetTableReference method of the CloudTableClient class instance. As shown in Listing 13-12,
GetTableReference identifies tables by their names.

LISTING 13-12   Accessing the Azure Table

```
public static async Task<CloudTable> GetTableAsync(string storageConnectionString,
    string tableName)
{
```

```
        CloudStorageAccount storageAccount = CloudStorageAccount.Parse(storageConnectionString);
        CloudTableClient tableClient = storageAccount.CreateCloudTableClient();
        CloudTable table = tableClient.GetTableReference(tableName);
        await table.CreateIfNotExistsAsync();
        return table;
}
```

DoTableInsertOrReplaceAsync, shown in Listing 13-13, updates or inserts the entity to the Azure Table. The entity is updated, if it already exists. Otherwise, the entity is inserted into the table. To distinguish table operations, Azure Storage implements the TableOperation class. It exposes several static methods that represent a particular operation, like Delete, Insert, Replace, Merge, and Retrieve. Listing 13-13 shows how to use Replace and Insert operations. The Delete operation is used in the DoDeleteAsync method from Listing 13-14. It simply takes the table and then removes the selected entity. The Retrieve operation is employed in PerformTableOperation, shown in Listing 13-15.

LISTING 13-13 Inserting and replacing entities

```
public static async Task<TableStorageResponse<TResult>> DoTableInsertOrReplaceAsync<
    TResult, TInput>(TInput incomingEntity,
    Func<TInput, TResult> tableEntityToModelConverter,
    string storageAccountConnectionString, string tableName) where TInput : TableEntity
{
    var table = await GetTableAsync(storageAccountConnectionString, tableName);

    // Simply doing an InsertOrReplace will not do any concurrency checking, according to
    // http://azure.microsoft.com/en-us/blog/managing-concurrency-in-microsoft-azure-storage-2/
    // So we will not use InsertOrReplace. Instead we will look to see if we have a rule like this.
    // If so, then we'll do a concurrency-safe update, otherwise simply insert
    TableOperation retrieveOperation =
        TableOperation.Retrieve<TInput>(incomingEntity.PartitionKey, incomingEntity.RowKey);
    TableResult retrievedEntity = await table.ExecuteAsync(retrieveOperation);

    TableOperation operation = null;
    if (retrievedEntity.Result != null)
    {
        operation = TableOperation.Replace(incomingEntity);
    }
    else
    {
        operation = TableOperation.Insert(incomingEntity);
    }

    return await PerformTableOperation(table, operation, incomingEntity,
        tableEntityToModelConverter);
}
```

LISTING 13-14 Delete operation

```
public static async Task<TableStorageResponse<TResult>> DoDeleteAsync<
    TResult, TInput>(TInput incomingEntity,
    Func<TInput, TResult> tableEntityToModelConverter,
    string storageAccountConnectionString, string tableName) where TInput : TableEntity
{
    var azureTable = await GetTableAsync(storageAccountConnectionString, tableName);
    TableOperation operation = TableOperation.Delete(incomingEntity);
    return await PerformTableOperation(azureTable, operation,
        incomingEntity, tableEntityToModelConverter);
}
```

Once the table operation is specified, you execute it using either the Execute or ExecuteAsync method of the CloudTable class. The bolded statements from Listing 13-15 show how to use both methods.

LISTING 13-15 Performing table operation

```
static async Task<TableStorageResponse<TResult>> PerformTableOperation<
    TResult, TInput>(CloudTable table,
    TableOperation operation, TInput incomingEntity,
    Func<TInput, TResult> tableEntityToModelConverter) where TInput : TableEntity
{
    var result = new TableStorageResponse<TResult>();

    try
    {
        await table.ExecuteAsync(operation);

        var nullModel = tableEntityToModelConverter(null);
        result.Entity = nullModel;
        result.Status = TableStorageResponseStatus.Successful;
    }
    catch (Exception ex)
    {
        TableOperation retrieveOperation = TableOperation.
            Retrieve<TInput>(incomingEntity.PartitionKey, incomingEntity.RowKey);
        TableResult retrievedEntity = table.Execute(retrieveOperation);

        if (retrievedEntity != null)
        {
            // Return the found version of this rule in case
            // it had been modified by someone else since our last read.
            var retrievedModel = tableEntityToModelConverter(
                (TInput)retrievedEntity.Result);
            result.Entity = retrievedModel;
        }
        else
        {
```

```
            // We didn't find an existing rule, probably creating new,
            // so we'll just return what was sent in
            result.Entity = tableEntityToModelConverter(incomingEntity);
        }

        if (ex.GetType() == typeof(StorageException)
            && (((StorageException)ex).RequestInformation.HttpStatusCode ==
        (int)HttpStatusCode.PreconditionFailed
            || ((StorageException)ex).RequestInformation.HttpStatusCode ==
            (int)HttpStatusCode.Conflict))
        {
            result.Status = TableStorageResponseStatus.ConflictError;
        }
        else
        {
            result.Status = TableStorageResponseStatus.UnknownError;
        }
    }

    return result;
}
```

The result of table operation execution is represented by the TableResult class. It has three properties: Result, HttpStatusCode, and Etag. The first two are quite obvious. Result represents the status of the table operation, while HttpStatusCode stores the HTTP status of the service request. The last property, Etag, is used for handling concurrency. In general, the cloud table can be accessed concurrently by multiple clients. For instance, you use Etag to implement additional logic to ensure that you do not overwrite changes made by other clients. Various concurrency approaches are explained in this article: *https://bit.ly/storage_concurrency*.

Simulator WebJob

The source code of the simulator WebJob can be found within the PredictiveMaintenance.Simulator. WebJob project. (See the companion code in the Chapter 13 folder.) In particular, this project implements logic simulating sensor readings from the aircraft's engines. Emulated engines are represented by the EngineDevice class. Its full implementation can be found under the following file of the WebJob's project: Engine/Devices/EngineDevice.cs.

Listing 13-16 shows three methods of the EngineDevice class. Accordingly, we see that this device handles three commands: Start, Stop, and Ping. The first two are used to either start or stop the telemetry, while the last one verifies the connection with a device. The actual structure of these commands and the device properties are governed by methods of the SampleDeviceFactory class. (See the companion code at Chapter 13/PredictiveMaintenance.Common/Factory/SampleDeviceFactory.cs.)

LISTING 13-16   A fragment of the EngineDevice class

```
protected override void InitCommandProcessors()
{
    var pingDeviceProcessor = new PingDeviceProcessor(this);
    var startCommandProcessor = new StartCommandProcessor(this);
    var stopCommandProcessor = new StopCommandProcessor(this);

    pingDeviceProcessor.NextCommandProcessor = startCommandProcessor;
    startCommandProcessor.NextCommandProcessor = stopCommandProcessor;

    RootCommandProcessor = pingDeviceProcessor;
}

public void StartTelemetryData()
{
    var predictiveMaintenanceTelemetry = (PredictiveMaintenanceTelemetry)TelemetryController;
    predictiveMaintenanceTelemetry.TelemetryActive = true;
    Logger.LogInfo("Device {0}: Telemetry has started", DeviceID);
}

public void StopTelemetryData()
{
    var predictiveMaintenanceTelemetry = (PredictiveMaintenanceTelemetry)TelemetryController;
    predictiveMaintenanceTelemetry.TelemetryActive = false;
    Logger.LogInfo("Device {0}: Telemetry has stopped", DeviceID);
}
```

StartTelemetryData and StopTelemetryData control the status of the telemetry process, which sends simulated sensor readings to the cloud. This telemetry is implemented within the PredictiveMaintenanceTelemetry class (Engine/Telemetry/PredictiveMaintenanceTelemetry.cs). In particular, PredictiveMaintenanceTelemetry implements the SendEventsAsync method (see Listing 13-17). It sends messages to the IoT Hub every second. PredictiveMaintenanceTelemetry uses the IoC design pattern, so the concrete implementation of data transfer is in a different class, IoTHubTransport (SimulatorCore/Transport/IoTHubTransport.cs).

LISTING 13-17   Implementing the SendEventsAsync method

```
const int REPORT_FREQUENCY_IN_SECONDS = 1;

public async Task SendEventsAsync(CancellationToken token, Func<object, Task> sendMessageAsync)
{
    while (!token.IsCancellationRequested)
    {
        if (_active)
        {
            try
            {
```

```
                // Search the data for the next row that contains this device ID
                while (_data.MoveNext() && !_data.Current.Values.Contains(_deviceId)) { }

                if (_data.Current != null)
                {
                    _logger.LogInfo(_deviceId + " =>\n\t" + string.Join("\n\t",
                        _data.Current.Select(m => m.Key + ": " + m.Value.ToString()).ToArray()));

                    await sendMessageAsync(_data.Current);
                }
                else
                {
                    // End of the data; stop replaying
                    TelemetryActive = false;
                }
            }
            catch (InvalidOperationException)
            {
                // The data has been modified; stop replaying
                TelemetryActive = false;
            }
        }
        await Task.Delay(TimeSpan.FromSeconds(REPORT_FREQUENCY_IN_SECONDS), token);
    }
}
```

To send messages to the cloud, IoTHubTransport uses the same DeviceClient class I used in Chapter 12. As shown in Listing 13-18, the SendEventAsync method of IoTHubTransport invokes the DeviceClient.SendEventAsync method within the AzureRetryHelper.OperationWithBasicRetry-Async. Note that IoTHubTransport tries to send messages twice.

LISTING 13-18 Sending events to the cloud

```
DeviceClient _deviceClient;

public async Task SendEventAsync(Guid eventId, dynamic eventData)
{
    string objectType = EventSchemaHelper.GetObjectType(eventData);
    var objectTypePrefix = _configurationProvider.GetConfigurationSettingValue(
        "ObjectTypePrefix");

    if (!string.IsNullOrWhiteSpace(objectType) && !string.IsNullOrEmpty(objectTypePrefix))
    {
        eventData.ObjectType = objectTypePrefix + objectType;
    }

    // sample code to trace the raw JSON that is being sent
    //string rawJson = JsonConvert.SerializeObject(eventData);
```

```
//Trace.TraceInformation(rawJson);

byte[] bytes = _serializer.SerializeObject(eventData);

var message = new Message(bytes);
message.Properties["EventId"] = eventId.ToString();

await AzureRetryHelper.OperationWithBasicRetryAsync(async () =>
{
    try
    {
        await _deviceClient.SendEventAsync(message);
    }
    catch (Exception ex)
    {
        _logger.LogError(
            "{0}{0}*** Exception: SendEventAsync ***{0}{0}EventId: {1}{0}Event Data:
            {2}{0}Exception: {3}{0}{0}",
            Console.Out.NewLine,
            eventId,
            eventData,
            ex);
    }
});
}
```

Sensor data is stored in the CSV file, which can be found under the blob container in Azure Storage. The CSV file is read and parsed within the constructor of the EngineTelemetryFactory class, shown in Listing 13-19. You can find the full code of this class in Engine/Telemetry/Factory/EngineTelemetryFactory. cs of the PredictiveMaintenance.Simulator.WebJob project. Listing 13-19 shows how to read data from the blob object. Use CreateCloudBlobClient from the CloudStorageAccount class. You obtain the blob container reference (GetContainerReference in the CloudBlobClient class) and finally access your blob using the CloudBlobContainer.GetBlockBlobReference method. The latter returns the instance of the CloudBlockBlob class. To read binary data of this blob, you obtain the reference to the underlying stream using the Open method and pass the stream to the StreamReader class constructor. Then you can parse this data using methods of the StreamReader class.

LISTING 13-19 Obtaining simulated sensor data

```
readonly IList<ExpandoObject> _dataset;

public EngineTelemetryFactory(ILogger logger, IConfigurationProvider config)
{
    _logger = logger;
    _config = config;

    // This will load the CSV data from the specified file in blob storage;
    // any failure in accessing or reading the data will be handled as an exception
```

```
Stream dataStream = CloudStorageAccount
    .Parse(config.GetConfigurationSettingValue("device.StorageConnectionString"))
    .CreateCloudBlobClient()
    .GetContainerReference(config.GetConfigurationSettingValue("SimulatorDataContainer"))
    .GetBlockBlobReference(config.GetConfigurationSettingValue("SimulatorDataFileName"))
    .OpenRead();

_dataset = ParsingHelper.ParseCsv(new StreamReader(dataStream)).ToExpandoObjects().ToList();
}
```

The binary data is parsed using the `ParseCsv` method of the `ParsingHelper` class. (See the companion code at Chapter 13/PredictiveMaintenance.Common/Helpers/ParsingHelper.cs.)

Predictive Maintenance web application

The Predictive Maintenance web application (see the companion code at Chapter 13/ PredictiveMaintenance.Web) implements the solution dashboard. As shown in Figure 13-1, this dashboard controls the simulator state and displays the telemetry data and RUL prediction results. To accomplish these tasks, the web app uses two services: simulation service and prediction service.

Simulation service

Simulation service is implemented within the `SimulationService` class (Services/SimulationService.cs). This class is used to remotely start and stop a simulation when the appropriate button is clicked by the user. As shown in Listing 13-20, the simulator is started or stopped by sending an appropriate command to the IoT Hub.

LISTING 13-20 Starting and stopping simulation

```
public async Task<string> StartSimulation()
{
    ClearTables();

    await WriteState(StartStopConstants.STARTING);
    await SendCommand("StartTelemetry");

    return StartStopConstants.STARTING;
}

public async Task<string> StopSimulation()
{
    await WriteState(StartStopConstants.STOPPING);
    await SendCommand("StopTelemetry");

    return StartStopConstants.STOPPING;
```

```
}

async Task SendCommand(string commandName)
{
    var command = CommandSchemaHelper.CreateNewCommand(commandName);

    foreach (var partitionKey in _deviceService.GetDeviceIds())
    {
        await _iotHubRepository.SendCommand(partitionKey, command);
    }
}
```

Additionally, the SimulationService class implements methods clearing tables with telemetry and prediction data (ClearTables), and writing the simulation state to the Azure Table (WriteState).

Telemetry service

The telemetry service, represented as the TelemetryService class (Services/TelemetryService.cs), implements two public methods: GetLatestTelemetry and GetLatestPrediction.

GetLatestTelemetry, shown in Listing 13-21, queries the Azure Table to retrieve telemetry entities by using the TableQuery class. This class implements methods which let you create the property filters. Here, two filters are used. The first filters the PartitionKey property to get telemetry data for the specific device using the GenerateFilterCondition method. The second takes the telemetry entities for which Timestamp is not older than 2 minutes (the TimeOffsetInSeconds constant). This is done using the GenerateFilterConditionForDate method. Subsequently, both filters are combined using the TableQuery.CombineFilters method. Additionally, the LINQ syntax is utilized to gather the following entity properties only: sensor11, sensor14, sensor15, and sensor9. The query is executed against the cloud table using the CloudTable.ExecuteQuery method. The list of resulting entities is then limited to 200 records (MaxRecordsToReceive) and transformed into a collection of Telemetry objects. The data is then passed to the front end for display.

LISTING 13-21   Retrieving telemetry data

```
const int TimeOffsetInSeconds = 120;
const int MaxRecordsToSend = 50;
const int MaxRecordsToReceive = 200;

public async Task<IEnumerable<Telemetry>> GetLatestTelemetry(string deviceId)
{
    var storageConnectionString = _settings.StorageConnectionString;
    var table = await AzureTableStorageHelper.GetTableAsync(storageConnectionString,
        _settings.TelemetryTableName);
    var startTime = DateTimeOffset.Now.AddSeconds(-TimeOffsetInSeconds).DateTime;

    var deviceFilter = TableQuery.GenerateFilterCondition("PartitionKey",
        QueryComparisons.Equal, deviceId);
```

```
    var timestampFilter = TableQuery.GenerateFilterConditionForDate("Timestamp",
        QueryComparisons.GreaterThanOrEqual, startTime);
    var filter = TableQuery.CombineFilters(deviceFilter, TableOperators.And,
        timestampFilter);

    TableQuery<TelemetryEntity> query = new TableQuery<TelemetryEntity>()
        .Where(filter)
        .Take(MaxRecordsToReceive)
        .Select(new[] { "sensor11", "sensor14", "sensor15", "sensor9" });

    var result = new Collection<Telemetry>();
    var entities = table.ExecuteQuery(query)
        .OrderByDescending(x => x.Timestamp)
        .Take(MaxRecordsToSend);

    foreach (var entity in entities)
    {
        var telemetry = new Telemetry
        {
            DeviceId = entity.PartitionKey,
            RecordId = entity.RowKey,
            Timestamp = entity.Timestamp.DateTime,
            Sensor1 = Math.Round(double.Parse(entity.sensor11, CultureInfo.InvariantCulture)),
            Sensor2 = Math.Round(double.Parse(entity.sensor14, CultureInfo.InvariantCulture)),
            Sensor3 = Math.Round(double.Parse(entity.sensor15, CultureInfo.InvariantCulture)),
            Sensor4 = Math.Round(double.Parse(entity.sensor9, CultureInfo.InvariantCulture))
        };
        result.Add(telemetry);
    }

    return result.OrderBy(x => x.Timestamp);
}
```

GetLatestPrediction works similarly but queries the table, which contains prediction data (see Listing 13-22) and wraps the resulting data into the collection of Prediction objects.

LISTING 13-22 Retrieving RUL prediction data

```
public async Task<IEnumerable<Prediction>> GetLatestPrediction(string deviceId)
{
    var storageConnectionString = _settings.StorageConnectionString;
    var table = await AzureTableStorageHelper.GetTableAsync(storageConnectionString,
        _settings.PredictionTableName);
    var startTime = DateTimeOffset.Now.AddSeconds(-TimeOffsetInSeconds).DateTime;

    var deviceFilter = TableQuery.GenerateFilterCondition("PartitionKey",
        QueryComparisons.Equal, deviceId);
    var timestampFilter = TableQuery.GenerateFilterConditionForDate("Timestamp",
        QueryComparisons.GreaterThanOrEqual, startTime);
```

```
        var filter = TableQuery.CombineFilters(deviceFilter, TableOperators.And,
            timestampFilter);

        TableQuery<PredictionRecord> query = new TableQuery<PredictionRecord>()
            .Where(filter)
            .Take(MaxRecordsToReceive)
            .Select(new[] { "Timestamp", "Rul" });

        var result = new Collection<Prediction>();
        var entities = table.ExecuteQuery(query)
            .OrderByDescending(x => x.RowKey)
            .Take(MaxRecordsToSend);

        foreach (var entity in entities)
        {
            var prediction = new Prediction
            {
                DeviceId = entity.PartitionKey,
                Timestamp = entity.Timestamp.DateTime,
                RemainingUsefulLife = (int)double.Parse(entity.Rul, CultureInfo.InvariantCulture),
                Cycles = int.Parse(entity.RowKey, CultureInfo.InvariantCulture)
            };
            result.Add(prediction);
        }

        return result.OrderBy(x => x.Cycles);
}
```

Summary

This chapter explored the capabilities and source code of the Azure IoT predictive maintenance preconfigured solution. I started by creating the solution, and then I analyzed its components and Azure resources: Azure Storage, Azure Stream Analytics, and Azure Event Hub. I analyzed the source code of the solution. You learned how to programmatically access cloud data storage and process data received by the Event Hub. Finally, I explained how telemetry data is generated by the simulator WebJob and accessed by the solution dashboard. Fueled by this knowledge, you will build your own IoT solution in next chapter.

CHAPTER 14

Custom solution

I n this chapter, I combine multiple functionalities implemented in previous chapters of this book to create a custom IoT solution. This solution will utilize the Windows 10 IoT Core app running on the remote
devices, Universal Windows App for desktop and mobile Windows 10 platforms, Azure IoT Hub, Azure
Stream Analytics, the Azure Event Hub, Power BI, and the Azure Notification Hub. I start from scratch and
guide you through a detailed implementation process. This information, along with advanced topics used
by preconfigured Azure IoT solutions, will enable you to build complete, sophisticated IoT systems.

The solution I develop here will work as follows: The remote device will stream sensor data to the
cloud through the IoT Hub. This data will be analyzed in real time by an Azure Stream Analytics job.
The job will have three outputs. The first output is directed to an Azure Table for storing telemetry
data. The second output contains time-averaged sensor data, which will be transferred and analyzed
by the Event Hub processor. If this processor determines that a sensor reading is abnormal, it will send
a toast notification to the mobile UWP app with the Azure Notification Hub. Hence, the information
about abnormal values will be directly delivered to the mobile user, even when the app is not running.
Moreover, the mobile app will be able to get the most recent sensor readings along with the information
about which device raised the alarm (see Figure 14-1). The last output of the analytics job will transfer
sensor data to the Power BI dashboard to visualize them in real time as shown in Figure 14-2.

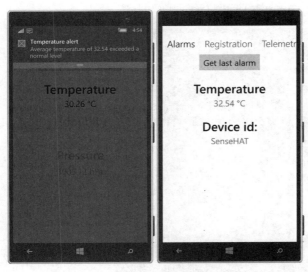

FIGURE 14-1   The mobile app receives notifications from the Event Hub about abnormal sensor readings.
The mobile client also reads sensor data and the alarm history from the cloud.

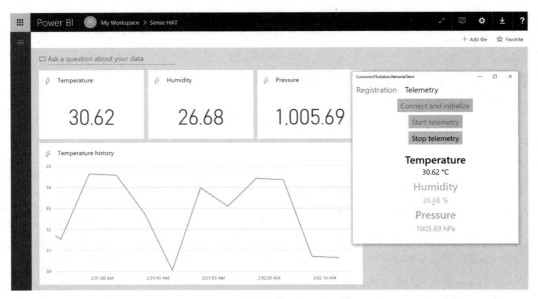

FIGURE 14-2 A custom IoT solution displays remote sensor readings in the Power BI dashboard. Note that data is analyzed in real time, so sensor readings are displayed almost immediately after they are sent to the cloud from the remote client app.

IoT Hub

We start by creating the IoT Hub, which will act as a connection gate to the cloud. You create the IoT Hub using the Azure Portal, where you click the **New** button (it features a plus sign), and then go to the **Internet of Things** node, where you choose **IoT Hub**. (See Figure 14-3.)

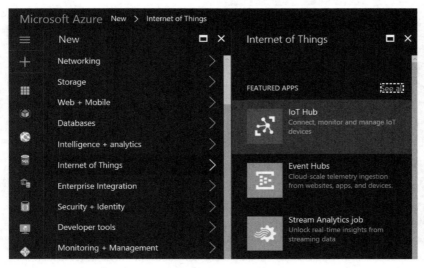

FIGURE 14-3 Creating the IoT Hub in the Azure Portal.

In the next screen, you can specify basic parameters of your IoT Hub, like name, pricing and scale tier, subscription, resource group, and location. As shown in Figure 14-4, I set the IoT Hub name to *sense-hat-iot-hub*, picked the S1-Standard pricing tier, created the new resource group, Sense-HAT, and selected West US as my location.

FIGURE 14-4 IoT Hub configuration.

Depending on the pricing tier, you can also specify the number of IoT Hub units and device-to-cloud partitions. You adjust both numbers depending on the scale of your solution. IoT Hub units depend on the size of your remote devices. The more messages you send, the more units you need. Similarly, if you want to stream data in multiple parallel channels, you can use more device-to-cloud partitions. They specify a number of parallel channels you use to stream data.

When you click the **Create** button, your configuration will be validated, and IoT Hub deployment will start. You will be notified about the completion of this process. Notifications are displayed in the top right corner of the Azure window (see Figure 14-5). Wait for the IoT Hub to be deployed.

FIGURE 14-5 Notification area of the Azure Portal.

Client app

Once the IoT Hub is ready, you can write the client app. This will run on the remote IoT device and stream data to the cloud. To create the client app, CustomIoTSolution.RemoteClient, I use the Blank App (Windows Universal) Visual C# project template. The complete source of this app is with the companion code at Chapter 14/CustomIoTSolution.RemoteClient.

As shown in Figure 14-6, the UI of the app consists of two tabs. The first one, Registration, lets you register and unregister your IoT device from the identity registry using two dedicated buttons. When you register a device, its primary authentication key appears in the text box. The second tab, Telemetry, contains three buttons. As in Chapter 12, "Remote devices monitoring," they are used to associate a connection with the cloud and sensors (Connect and Initialize), and then to either start (Start Telemetry) or stop (Stop Telemetry) the background operation, which periodically reads and then sends sensor data to the cloud.

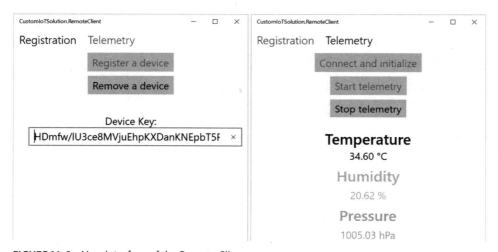

FIGURE 14-6 User interface of the Remote Client app.

The logical layer of the client app was implemented using several blocks developed in other chapters or appendixes. Specifically, to interact with sensors, I use sensor classes from the referenced class libraries SenseHat.Portable and SenseHat.UWP. (See Appendix D, "Sense HAT class library.") To periodically read and report sensor data, I use a slightly extended version of the Telemetry class from Chapter 12. I extend this class to obtain barometric pressure apart from temperature and humidity. (See the companion code at Chapter 14/CustomIoTSolution.RemoteClient/TelemetryControl/Telemetry.cs.)

Consequently, I supplement the definition of the TelemetryData class (see the companion code at Chapter 14/CustomIoTSolution.RemoteClient/Models/TelemetryData.cs) with three properties: RowId, Time, and Pressure. RowId. The RowId property will be used to fill the RowKey property of the appropriate Azure Table, storing telemetry data. As shown in Listing 14-1, RowId is globally unique, and is generated using the NewGuid static method of the System.Guid class. RowId and Time are set in the TelemetryData class constructor. Other properties are set within the Telemetry_DataReady event handler, which appears in Listing 14-2.

LISTING 14-1 TelemetryData class constructor

```
public TelemetryData()
{
    RowId = Guid.NewGuid().ToString();
    Time = DateTime.Now;
}
```

LISTING 14-2 Sending telemetry data

```
private void Telemetry_DataReady(object sender, TelemetryEventArgs e)
{
    DisplaySensorReadings(e);

    var telemetryData = new TelemetryData()
    {
        DeviceId = deviceId,
        Temperature = e.Temperature,
        Humidity = e.Humidity,
        Pressure = e.Pressure
    };

    var telemetryMessage = MessageHelper.Serialize(telemetryData);
    deviceClient.SendEventAsync(telemetryMessage);
}
```

To connect a device to the cloud, I employ the DeviceClient class from the Device SDK for Azure IoT Devices. The main API elements of DeviceClient appear in Chapter 12. Here, I'm using DeviceClient and other helper classes (like MessageHelper and RemoteCommand) in exactly the same way.

As in previous examples, I use data binding to control the UI and display sensor readings. The ClientViewModel class, deriving from the INotifyPropertyChanged interface, is used here. ClientViewModel implements several properties, which are bound to the UI with the help of several converters: TemperatureToStringConverter, HumidityToStringConverter, PressureToStringConverter, and LogicalNegationConverter. The first three converters are implemented in the SenseHat.UWP class library (see Appendix D), and are used to format sensor values. The last converter, LogicalNegationConverter, is implemented locally in CustomIoTSolution.RemoteClient. (See the companion code at Chapter 14/CustomIoTSolution. RemoteClient/Converters/LogicalNegationConverter.cs.) I use this converter to disable the Register a Device button when the IsDeviceRegistered property of the ClientViewModel is true:

```
<Button x:Name="ButtonRegisterDevice"
        Content="Register a device"
        Click="ButtonRegisterDevice_Click"
        IsEnabled="{x:Bind clientViewModel.IsDeviceRegistered, Mode=OneWay,
            Converter={StaticResource LogicalNegationConverter}}" />
```

To import converters (and other resources) from the class libraries, proceed as you would with local converters. As shown in Listing 14-3, you use the xmlns attribute, pointing the appropriate namespace, and then declare converters in the resource dictionary.

LISTING 14-3   Application-scoped resources of CustomIoTSolution.RemoteClient

```xml
<Application
    x:Class="CustomIoTSolution.RemoteClient.App"
    xmlns="http://schemas.microsoft.com/winfx/2006/xaml/presentation"
    xmlns:x="http://schemas.microsoft.com/winfx/2006/xaml"
    xmlns:converters="using:CustomIoTSolution.RemoteClient.Converters"
    xmlns:contertersSenseHat="using:SenseHat.UWP.Converters"
    RequestedTheme="Light">

    <Application.Resources>
        <converters:LogicalNegationConverter x:Key="LogicalNegationConverter" />
        <contertersSenseHat:HumidityToStringConverter x:Key="HumidityToStringConverter" />
        <contertersSenseHat:PressureToStringConverter x:Key="PressureToStringConverter" />
        <contertersSenseHat:TemperatureToStringConverter x:Key="TemperatureToStringConverter" />
    </Application.Resources>
</Application>
```

Device registry

To connect your client app to the cloud, you need to register your device in the IoT Hub. In Chapter 12, you used the IoT portal to register the device. Here, I will tell you how you can register your device programmatically using the Service SDK for Azure IoT Devices, implemented within the Microsoft.Azure. Devices NuGet package. This package delivers the RegistryManager class and implements two methods: AddDeviceAsync and GetDeviceAsync. You use the first one to add the IoT unit to the device registry (or identity registry) of the IoT Hub. The second one, GetDeviceAsync, is used to retrieve the device from the registry. Typically, you first invoke the GetDeviceAsync method to check whether the device of a specific identifier already exists in the registry. Then, if necessary, you invoke the AddDeviceAsync method.

RegistryManager does not implement public constructors. To instantiate this class, you use the static CreateFromConnectionString method. It requires one argument, connectionString. To obtain the connection string, you use the Azure Portal, where you go to the shared access policies (under the Settings group) of your IoT Hub. The list of policies will be displayed. A policy defines the permission level for the IoT Hub endpoint—which actions can be done by the client (for more details, see *https://bit.ly/iot_hub_security*). As shown in Figure 14-7, there are five default policies:

- **iothubowner**   This gives the full permission set. The IoT Hub endpoint can read and write to the identity registry, send and receive messages from the cloud-side endpoint (for example, the Event Hub processor), and do the same from the device-side endpoint.

- **service**   This enables service connect permission, which sends and receives messages from the cloud endpoints.

- **device** This enables device connect permission, which sends and receives messages from the device endpoints.

- **registryRead** This enables registry read permission, so the endpoint can list only registered devices.

- **registryReadWrite** This enables registry read/write permission to list and register new devices.

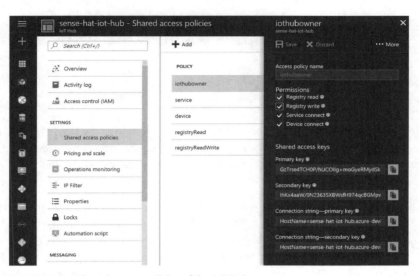

FIGURE 14-7 Shared access policies of the IoT Hub.

When you click each policy, the permission set, access keys, and connection strings appear on the right. Here, I'll be using the iothubowner connection string to get full access to the IoT Hub.

Listing 14-4 depicts the `RegisterDevice` method of the `DeviceRegistrationHelper` static class. (See the companion code at Chapter 14/CustomIoTSolution.RemoteClient/Helpers/DeviceRegistration-Helper.cs.) `RegisterDevice` shows the complete example of the device registration process. First, I instantiate the `RegistryManager` class using the provided connection string. Then, I invoke the `GetDeviceAsync` method to check whether the device already exists in the identity registry. If not, I register the device using the `AddDeviceAsync` method.

LISTING 14-4 Registering a device

```
public static async Task<Device> RegisterDevice(string connectionString, string deviceId)
{
    // Associate connection with the IoT Hub
    var registryManager = RegistryManager.CreateFromConnectionString(connectionString);

    Device device;

    try
```

```
    {
        // Check if device already exists?
        device = await registryManager.GetDeviceAsync(deviceId);
    }
    catch(DeviceAlreadyExistsException)
    {
        // If not, register a device
        device = await registryManager.AddDeviceAsync(new Device(deviceId));

        // ... and store device key in the local settings
        StoreDeviceKey(device.Authentication.SymmetricKey.PrimaryKey);
    }

    return device;
}
```

You can unregister a device using the RemoveDeviceAsync method of the RegistryManager class. The latter can perform batch operations on the identity registry. You can get, add, and remove multiple devices with a single method. To do this, you use GetDevicesAsync, AddDevicesAsync, and RemoveDevicesAsync, respectively.

After successful device registration, I store the device key in the local app settings. So, I can retrieve this key after the app is restarted. As shown in Listing 14-5, to access the app settings, you use the Values property of the ApplicationDataContainer class. The Values property implements the IPropertySet interface and is the collection of key-value pairs. Hence, you access each setting using its key. To get an instance of ApplicationDataContainer containing local app settings, you read the LocalSettings property of the current application data: ApplicationData.Current.LocalSettings.

LISTING 14-5 Storing values in local app settings

```
private static string DeviceKeyString = "DeviceKey";

public static string RetrieveDeviceKey()
{
    var localSettings = ApplicationData.Current.LocalSettings;

    return localSettings.Values[DeviceKeyString] as string;
}

private static void StoreDeviceKey(string deviceKey)
{
    var localSettings = ApplicationData.Current.LocalSettings;

    localSettings.Values[DeviceKeyString] = deviceKey;
}
```

To register a device with CustomIoTSolution.ClientApp, click the **Register a Device** button. It invokes the event handler from Listing 14-6. This method first registers the device and then displays the generated primary access key in a text box. You can also see this key in the Azure Portal with the Devices tab of the IoT Hub properties.

LISTING 14-6 Device registration in CustomIoTSolution.ClientApp

```
private const string connectionString = "<TYPE_YOUR_CONNECTION_STRING_HERE>";
private const string deviceId = "SenseHAT";

private ClientViewModel clientViewModel = new ClientViewModel();

private async void ButtonRegisterDevice_Click(object sender, RoutedEventArgs e)
{
    var device = await DeviceRegistrationHelper.RegisterDevice(connectionString, deviceId);

    UpdateDeviceRegistrationDisplay(device.Authentication.SymmetricKey.PrimaryKey);
}

private void UpdateDeviceRegistrationDisplay(string deviceKey)
{
    // Device is assumed to be registered when the deviceKey is valid
    if (!string.IsNullOrEmpty(deviceKey))
    {
        clientViewModel.IsDeviceRegistered = true;
    }
    else
    {
        clientViewModel.IsDeviceRegistered = false;
    }

    clientViewModel.DeviceKey = deviceKey;
}
```

As shown in Listing 14-7, the device key is restored from local settings every time `MainPage` is created. If the device key is successfully restored, the Register a Device button becomes disabled, while the Remove a Device button becomes active. You can use the second button to remove a device from the identity registry.

LISTING 14-7 Retrieving the device key from the app settings

```
public MainPage()
{
    InitializeComponent();

    CheckDeviceRegistration();
}

private void CheckDeviceRegistration()
{
```

```
    var deviceKey = DeviceRegistrationHelper.RetrieveDeviceKey();

    UpdateDeviceRegistrationDisplay(deviceKey);
}
```

The click event handler of the Remove a Device button appears in Listing 14-8. This method removes the device from the identity registry, clears the device key from the local settings, and then updates the view. The Remove a Device button becomes disabled, and the other button becomes enabled. Consequently, the text box displaying a device key is cleared, and the telemetry is stopped. Finally, the IsConnected flag of ClientViewModel is set to false. This means that the connection with the cloud cannot be established using the previous device key.

LISTING 14-8 Click event handler of the Remove a Device button

```
private async void ButtonRemoveDevice_Click(object sender, RoutedEventArgs e)
{
    await DeviceRegistrationHelper.RemoveDevice(connectionString, deviceId);

    UpdateDeviceRegistrationDisplay(null);

    if(telemetry != null)
    {
        telemetry.Stop();
    }

    clientViewModel.IsConnected = false;
}
```

To remove a device, I extend the definition of the DeviceRegistrationHelper class by the RemoveDevice method, shown in Listing 14-9.

LISTING 14-9 Removing a device from identity registry

```
public static async Task RemoveDevice(string connectionString, string deviceId)
{
    // Associate connection with the IoT Hub
    var registryManager = RegistryManager.CreateFromConnectionString(connectionString);

    // Check if device exists
    var device = await registryManager.GetDeviceAsync(deviceId);
    if (device != null)
    {
        // If so, remove a device
        await registryManager.RemoveDeviceAsync(deviceId);

        // Clear device key in the app settings
        StoreDeviceKey(null);
    }
}
```

Sending telemetry data

To start sending data to your IoT Hub with CustomIoTSolution.RemoteClient, deploy this app to your IoT device, and when the app runs, click the **Register a Device** button. After device registration, you go to the Telemetry tab, where you use the **Connect and Initialize** option to connect to the IoT Hub and configure sensors. Then you can run telemetry using the **Start Telemetry** button. To confirm that the IoT Hub receives messages, go to Azure Portal, where you click the **Overview** option of your IoT Hub. (See Figure 14-8.) The number of received messages and registered devices appears in the Usage pane.

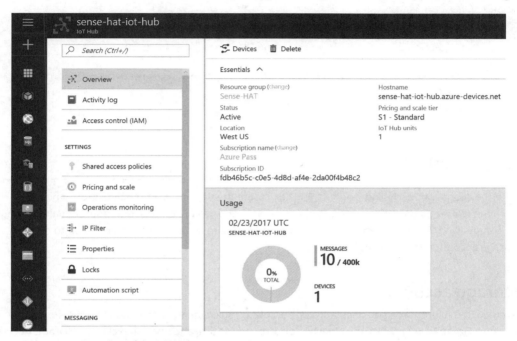

FIGURE 14-8   Overview of the IoT Hub.

You can also emulate sensor readings with CustomIoTSolution.RemoteClient. Change the isEmulationMode flag of the Telemetry class to true. The sensor values will randomly fluctuate around hard-coded values (see Listing 14-10), and you can run the client app at your development PC to quickly test all examples presented here.

LISTING 14-10   Sensor readings can be emulated with CustomIoTSolution.RemoteClient

```
private bool isEmulationMode = true; // Set this value to false to get data from real sensors

private TelemetryEventArgs GetSensorReadings()
{
    if (!isEmulationMode)
    {
        var temperature = temperatureAndPressureSensor.GetTemperature();
```

```
            var humidity = humidityAndTemperatureSensor.GetHumidity();
            var pressure = temperatureAndPressureSensor.GetPressure();

            return new TelemetryEventArgs(temperature, humidity, pressure);
    }
    else
    {
        var random = new Random();

        var temperature = (float)(30.0 + random.NextDouble() * 5.0);
        var humidity = (float)(20.0 + random.NextDouble() * 10.0);
        var pressure = (float)(1005.0 + random.NextDouble() * 2.5);

        return new TelemetryEventArgs(temperature, humidity, pressure);
    }
}
```

Stream analytics

With the client app ready and working, you can create the Azure Stream Analytics job, which will store the telemetry data in the dedicated Azure Table and calculate the average sensor values using a hopping window, and then send those values to the Azure Event Hub. First, you need to create a storage account and the Event Hub.

Storage account

To create the Azure Table, you need a storage account. You create the one using the Azure Portal. As shown in Figure 14-9, you click the **New** button, expand the **Storage** node, and choose **Storage Account**.

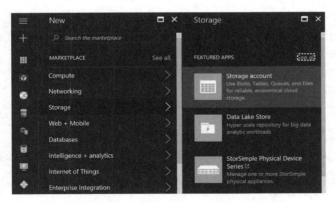

FIGURE 14-9   Creating a storage account in the Azure Portal.

The Create Storage Account screen appears (see Figure 14-10). Use this screen to define your storage account. Set its name, and then choose the deployment model, performance, replication, encryption,

Azure subscription, resource group, and location. Click the **Create** button, and wait until the storage account is deployed.

FIGURE 14-10 Storage account configuration.

I set the name of my storage account to sensehatstorage, used Resource Manager as the deployment model, picked the general purpose account kind, set the performance to standard, used locally-redundant storage (LRS), and disabled storage encryption. In addition, I'm using Azure Pass (subscription), the previously created resource group (Sense HAT), and the West US location.

While name, location, resource group, and subscription do not require special attention, a discussion about other parameters of the storage account is warranted.

The deployment model (Resource Manager or Classic) specifies how your resources are deployed and managed. The Azure Portal recommends using Resource Manager for new applications. The Classic model remained for compatibility with Azure resources deployed in a Classic virtual model. Both models are compared and discussed in detail here: *https://bit.ly/azure_deployment_models*.

You can choose from two account types: general purpose and blob storage. The general purpose storage account provides a unified account for blobs, files, tables, and queues, while the blob storage account is optimized for blobs only. If you set the account type to blob storage, then you choose one of two access tiers: cool or hot. The cool access tier is optimized for infrequently accessed blobs, and the hot access tier is specialized for frequently accessed blobs. The cool access tier is less expensive than the hot one. A more detailed description of the various storage types is provided in this article: *https://bit.ly/storage_account_kind*.

You use the Storage Performance option to choose between storing your data on a magnetic (standard) or solid-state (premium) drives. The premium storage can only be used with Azure virtual machine disks and is dedicated for I/O-intensive applications.

Replication is used to copy your storage account data to other physical locations, depending on the replication option you choose. There are four replication options available (*https://bit.ly/storage_replication*):

- **Locally Redundant Storage (LRS)**   This copies data three times within the datacenter in the specified location.

- **Zone-Redundant Storage (ZRS)**   This replicates your data in a local datacenter as the LRS. Additionally, your data is replicated to one or two datacenters in different regions, which are relatively close to your primary datacenter.

- **Geo-Redundant Storage (GRS)**   This works similarly to the ZRS, but replicates data to a secondary region, located far away from the primary one. This ensures that your data is safe even if it isn't recoverable from the primary region.

- **Read-Access Geo-Redundant Storage (RA-GRS)**   In addition to GRS, this provides read-only access to the data in the secondary location.

Azure Tables

The created storage account does not contain any Azure Tables yet. Now, create two tables: telemetrydata and alerthistory. The first stores telemetry data, while the second contains the alert history.

To create the Azure Table, you use the Cloud Explorer, where you navigate to the appropriate storage (sensehatstorage in this case) and click the **Tables** node (see Figure 14-11). Then you use the **Create Table** link shown on the Actions pane of the Cloud Explorer. When you click this link a text box appears, in which you type the table name: **telemetrydata**. Do the same for the second table, **alerthistory**.

FIGURE 14-11   Cloud Explorer showing items of the SenseHAT Azure resource group.

Event Hub

To create the Event Hub, you proceed similarly as with the IoT Hub. Go to the Azure Portal, click the **New** button, select the **Internet of Things** node, and then pick the **Event Hubs** app (refer to Figure 14-3). A screen to create the Event Hub namespace will appear, as shown in Figure 14-12. You use this screen to specify a namespace for your Event Hubs, pricing tier, subscription, and resource group. Here, I'm using sense-hat-event-hub for the namespace, Sense HAT for the resource group, and the Basic pricing tier.

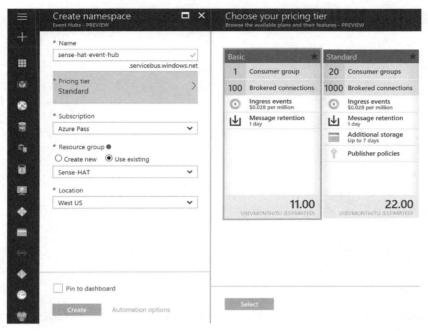

FIGURE 14-12   Event Hub namespace configuration.

You create the actual Event Hub by navigating to the Event Hub namespace you just created (it can be found under the Sense-HAT resource group in the Azure Portal). Click the **+ Event Hub** button on the Overview pane (see Figure 14-13). The Create Event Hub screen appears.

FIGURE 4-13   A fragment of the Overview pane of the sense-hat-event-hub namespace.

As shown in Figure 14-14, to create the Event Hub, you need to specify its name and partition count, and eventually configure how messages are retained and archived, which can be changed in the standard pricing tier. Retention specifies the lifetime of messages sent to the Event Hub. By default, each message expires after one day. A message is no longer available after this time. You can increase message retention when using a standard pricing tier (refer to Figure 14-10). You use the Event Hubs archive to automatically back up received data in the blob storage (for more details see *https://bit.ly/event_hub_archive*). You will most likely consider enabling this feature for data-critical applications.

FIGURE 14-14   Event Hub configuration.

Stream Analytics Job

Components required by the Stream Analytics Job are ready, so you can create the actual job with the Azure Portal. The corresponding app template can be found under the Internet of Things node (refer to Figure 14-3). After you choose **Stream Analytics Job**, a new screen appears (see Figure 14-15). Use this screen to set the job name, configure the Azure subscription, and select the resource group. Finally, click the **Create** button, and wait until Stream Analytics Job deployment is done.

FIGURE 14-15   Stream Analytics job configuration.

Inputs

As mentioned in the previous chapter, the Stream Analytics Job processes input data using queries, and their results are directed to the job output. In the other words, outputs are related to inputs through queries. All three objects constitute the job topology. You define the job topology using the Overview pane of the Stream Analytics Job (see Figure 14-16). This pane also lets you start and stop the job using dedicated buttons (top panel) once the topology is defined.

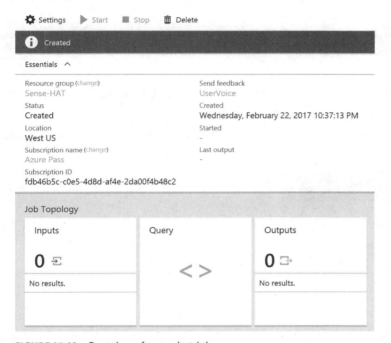

FIGURE 14-16 Overview of sense-hat-job.

Now create the input. Click **Inputs** in the Job Topology pane. When the list of inputs appears, click the **Add** button. A New Input screen appears. Use this screen to configure the input by specifying the following options (see Figure 14-17):

- **Input Alias**   This identifies input in the job queries. I set its value to **datastream**.

- **Source Type**   This can be either Data Stream or Reference Data. The first one is a continuous sequence of messages to be consumed or transformed by the job. Reference data is optional, used for correlations and lookup. So, use **Data Stream**.

- **Source**   This specifies the input sink. You have three options here: Event Hub, Blob Storage, and IoT Hub. Choose the last option since our input will come from sense-hat-iot-hub. Once you do that, two other list boxes, Subscription and IoT Hub, will be automatically populated. Using the first one, choose **Use IoT Hub from Current Subscription**. Then use the second one to choose **sense-hat-iot-hub**.

- **Endpoint** This can have one of two possible values: Messaging or Operations Monitoring. You use Messaging for sending device telemetry and device info to the cloud. Operations Monitoring is used for sending remote commands from the cloud to the device. Here, we analyze data sent from the remote device and thus use **Messaging**.

- **Shared Access Policy Name** This lets you select the access policy. There are two available options: iothubowner and service. We do not need full access here, so pick the **service** policy name.

- **Event Serialization Format** This defines the input format of your data stream. Here we use **JSON**, since `DeviceClient` uses this format to transmit messages from the remote device to the cloud.

- **Encoding** This specifies the encoding format. When I was writing this chapter, only UTF-8 encoding was available.

After configuring an input, you click the **Create** button. Your new input will appear on the inputs list and in the Overview pane.

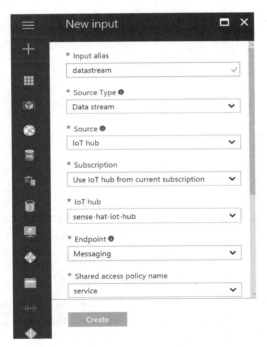

FIGURE 14-17 New input configuration.

Outputs

You now create two outputs—one associated with the telemetrydata table storage, so query results can be directly stored in this Azure Table, and a second one transferred to the Event Hub, which will consume average temperature values.

To create the job output, you proceed in the same way as with inputs. Click **Outputs** in the Job Topology pane. A list of job outputs appears, and you click the **Add** button. The New Output screen will be displayed. You use this screen to create and configure the first job output, telemetrydata. The list of options includes the following items:

- **Output Alias**　This identifies the output in the job query. I set this value to **telemetrytable**.

- **Sink**　This specifies the output sink, that is, where the query result will be directed. There are multiple options here: SQL Database, Blob Storage, Event Hub, Table Storage, Service Bus Queue, Service Bus Topic, DocumentDB, Power BI, and Data Lake Store. Here, we direct the query output to table storage, so choose **Table Storage**. After choosing that option, another two list boxes will be populated. Configure them as follows:

  - **Subscription**　Choose **Use Table Storage from Current Subscription**.

  - **Storage Account**　Choose **sensehatstorage**.

- **Partition Key**　Choose **DeviceId**.

- **Row Key**　Choose **RowId**.

- **Batch Size**　This can be a value between 1 and 100. It specifies the number of batch transactions. Let's set it to the maximum value of **100**.

Partition and Row Key text boxes enable you to enter names of output columns containing the partition and row key of the entity. In case of any mismatch between values you specify and query outputs, the job will output an error.

The second output can be created in the same way. You use the following configuration:

- **Output Alias**　Choose **averagetemperature**.

- **Sink**　Choose **Event Hub**.

- **Subscription**　Choose **Use Event Hub from Current Subscription**.

- **Service Bus Namespace**　Choose **sense-hat-event-hub**.

- **Event Hub Name**　Choose **alerts-hub** (or whatever you typed in the screen in Figure 14-13).

- **Event Hub Policy Name**　Choose **RootManageSharedAccessKey**.

- **Partition Key Column**　Either leave this empty or set it to **DeviceId**.

- **Event Serialization Format**　Choose **JSON**.

- **Encoding**　Choose **UTF-8**.

- **Format**　Choose **Line Separated**.

Changing the sink type also changes the list of available options. In case of the Event Hub, unlike with table storage, you can now define the serialization format, encoding, and format. Here, I leave these options at the default values, which are most common.

After defining inputs and outputs, your job topology should look like the one in Figure 14-18. Note that the Overview pane of the Azure Stream Analytics job will be supplemented by an additional chart, Monitoring. It displays input and output event metrics for the past hour. Moreover, the Start button will be enabled.

FIGURE 14-18   Updated job topology.

Query

Having defined inputs and outputs, let's write the first query, which will extract sensor data from the incoming data stream, and then write them to the Azure Table. The temperature values will be averaged using a hopping window, and transferred to the Event Hub sink.

To define that query, click Query in the Job Topology pane. The query editor, shown in Figure 14-19, will appear. The list of available inputs and outputs is displayed on the left, while the right shows the query code. Replace the default query with the one from Listing 14-11.

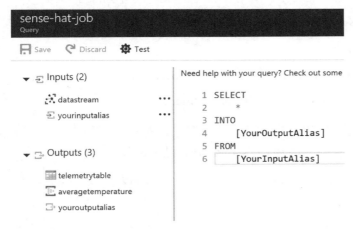

FIGURE 14-19   Job query editor.

LISTING 14-11 Query definition

```
SELECT
    DeviceId,
    RowId,
    Temperature,
    Humidity,
    Pressure
INTO
    [telemetrytable]
FROM
    [datastream]

SELECT
    DeviceId,
    AVG(Temperature) AS AvgTemperature
INTO
    [averagetemperature]
FROM
    [datastream]
GROUP BY
    DeviceId,
    HOPPINGWINDOW(minute, 10, 5)
```

Let's analyze how our query transforms every message received by the IoT Hub. First, the query selects DeviceId, RowId, Temperature, Humidity, and Pressure values from every message, and then combines them into entities, which are inserted into the telemetrydata Azure Table. You do not need to write any code that updates the Azure Table. You just configure your output so the query knows which value to use for row and partition keys.

The second part of the query calculates average temperature values and groups them by DeviceId. The query uses a hopping window (see *https://bit.ly/window_functions*). You define such a window using the HoppingWindow function. This function accepts three arguments:

- **timeunit** This is the unit of time used to describe the window and hop size. It can take one of the following values: microsecond, millisecond, second, minute, hour, or day.

- **windowsize** This is the window size (length) given in timeunit. The maximum windowsize is 7 days.

- **hopsize** This determines the time delay between generating events.

You use windowsize to specify how long streamed data will be analyzed, while hopsize specifies the overlap between windows. For instance, assuming a windowsize of 10, and a hopsize of 5 minutes (as in Listing 14-11), the query will give you the average temperature calculated from messages received over the last 10 minutes. Since the hopsize is 5 minutes, the average value will be generated every 5 minutes. If you use a 10-minute tumbling window, average temperatures would be reported every 10 minutes.

The data stream of the job we've just created is summarized in the diagram in Figure 14-20.

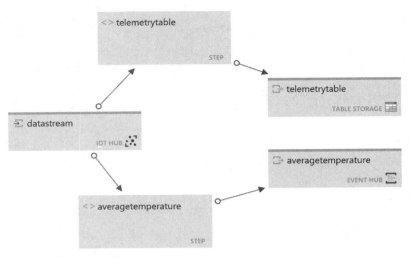

FIGURE 14-20 A job diagram.

Running a job and streaming data

Let's now see how the Azure Stream Analytics job works. Start the job using the appropriate button on the job's Overview pane. Then run the CustomIoTSolution.RemoteClient app, register a device (if necessary), connect to the cloud, and start telemetry. Stream data for at least several minutes, so the average temperature can be output.

You can preview the streamed data at any time using the Cloud Explorer. If you open telemetrydata, you will see that it was populated with multiple entities containing your sensor data (see Figure 14-21). This confirms that the first part of the query from Listing 14-11 works correctly.

	PartitionKey	RowKey	Timestamp	humidity	pressure	temperature
▶	SenseHAT	025aa5f9-8...	02/23/2017 1...	25.8257579803467	1007.42034912109	30.0019836425...
	SenseHAT	0932a684-...	02/23/2017 1...	22.2770195007324	1005.82342529297	30.8790836334...
	SenseHAT	0c2e0423-7...	02/23/2017 1...	22.941478729248	1007.05651855469	30.4680995941...
	SenseHAT	0d4f042a-7...	02/23/2017 1...	20.4152603149414	1006.12365722656	34.6133766174...
	SenseHAT	1d2f691d-...	02/23/2017 1...	22.5248775482178	1006.85162353516	33.8375473022...
	SenseHAT	29aab19a-...	02/23/2017 1...	25.0718040466309	1006.926663574219	34.0382804870...
	SenseHAT	2c9dbae2-...	02/23/2017 1...	27.8830051422119	1006.56481933594	34.0222206115...
	SenseHAT	31e4576b-...	02/23/2017 1...	26.2483959197998	1006.25115966797	31.3689651489...
	SenseHAT	31e89a38-a...	02/23/2017 1...	23.9639987945557	1005.22058105469	33.7362747192...
	SenseHAT	34309fc7-f...	02/23/2017 1...	28.1308631896973	1005.09307861328	31.9806842803...
	SenseHAT	3d4b747e-...	02/23/2017 1...	29.5699844360352	1005.96203613281	31.8794116973...

FIGURE 14-21 Telemetry table filled with sensor data.

Let's now ensure that the second part of the query also works. Go to the Azure Portal and navigate to the Overview pane of sense-hat-event-hub. You will see there a chart displaying metrics. You can customize this chart using the **Edit** link, located in the top right corner of the metrics chart. Once you activate the Edit Chart pane, you can adjust the time range and data, which will be plotted in the metrics chart. I use this to display only incoming messages from the past hour (see Figure 14-22).

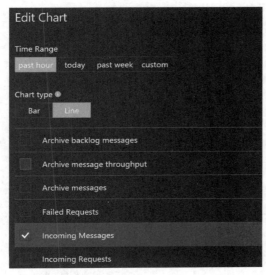

FIGURE 14-22 The Edit Chart screen enables you to specify the time range and chart type and to choose which metrics will be displayed.

My metrics plot looks as shown in Figure 14-23. Incoming messages appear precisely every 5 minutes according to the job's query. The custom Azure Stream Analytics job works correctly, and you can move forward to write a custom event processor, which will analyze average temperatures.

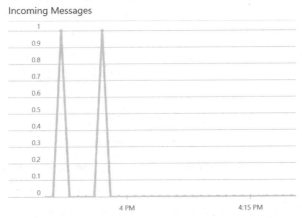

FIGURE 14-23 A plot of the number of messages received by the Event Hub.

Event processor

To implement a custom event processor, which processes average temperature readings transmitted to the Event Hub, I create CustomIoTSolution.EventProcessor. I make this app using the Visual C# Console Application project template (see Figure 14-24). Then I reference the SenseHat.Portable class library and install the Microsoft.Azure.ServiceBus.EventProcessorHost NuGet package.

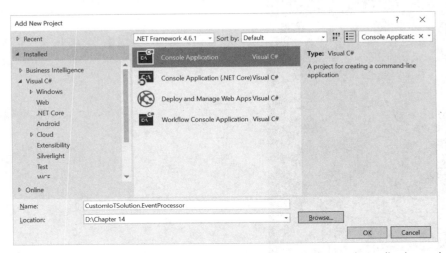

FIGURE 14-24   The New Project dialog box showing the Visual C# Console Application project template.

Subsequently, I write the helper class `Configuration`, which stores several values necessary to associate a connection with the Event Hub and dependent resources, like table storage. Since several of these values, like Azure Table names or credentials for Azure Storage, will be also used in subsequent projects, I saved the `Configuration` class in a PCL project, CustomIoTSolution.Common. Note that this project references the WindowsAzure.Storage NuGet package. Before you can install this package in the PCL, you need to install two other packages: Microsoft.NETCore.Platforms and System.Runtime.InteropServices.RuntimeInformation.

The `Configuration` class (see the companion code at Chapter 14/CustomIoTSolution.Common/Config/Configuration.cs) has the following public properties, which you adjust according to values you obtain from the Azure Portal:

- **AccountName**   This is the name of the storage account (sensehatstorage).

- **AccountKey**   This is either the primary or secondary key to your storage account.

- **BlobEndPoint**   This is the endpoint URL of the blob storage (https://<storage_account_name>.blob.core.windows.net/).

- **EventHubPath**   This is the name of event hub you configured in the previous section (alerts-hub).

- **ConsumerGroupName**   This is the consumer group name. Its default value is $Default. You can verify it in the Azure Portal in the alerts-hub Overview pane.

- **EventHubConnectionString**   This is a connection string to the event hub. You get this value from the RootManageSharedAccesKey policy of sense-hat-event-hub (in the Shared Access Policies pane).

- **AlertsTableName**   This is the name of the Azure Table, where alerts data will be inserted. Earlier, you set this name to alerthistory.

Additionally, the Configuration class implements the GetStorageCredentials method, which combines AccountName and AccountKey and returns them as the instance of the StorageCredentials class. This will be used later to connect to the Azure Table.

To simplify creation of the blob connection string, which is required by EventProcessorHost (see Chapter 13, "Predictive maintenance"), I implement the ConnectionStringHelper class (stored in the CustomIoTSolution.Common project under the Helpers folder). The full source code of this class appears in Listing 14-12. ConnectionStringHelper has four public properties, which are related to particular components of the connection string: DefaultEndpointsProtocol, AccountName, AccountKey, and BlobEndpoint. Values for last three components are configured with respect to parameters passed to the GetBlobConnectionString method. Then, I merge particular components of the connection string with their parameters using the System.Text.StringBuilder class.

LISTING 14-12   Definition of ConnectionStringHelper

```
public static class ConnectionStringHelper
{
    public static string EndpointsProtocolProperty { get; private set; } =
        "DefaultEndpointsProtocol=https;";
    public static string AccountNameProperty { get; private set; } = "AccountName=";
    public static string AccountKeyProperty { get; private set; } = "AccountKey=";
    public static string BlobEndpointProperty { get; private set; } = "BlobEndpoint=";

    public static string GetBlobConnectionString(string accountName,
        string accountKey, string blobEndpoint)
    {
        Check.IsNull(accountName);
        Check.IsNull(accountKey);
        Check.IsNull(blobEndpoint);

        var stringBuilder = new StringBuilder(EndpointsProtocolProperty);

        // Set account name
        stringBuilder.Append(AccountNameProperty);
        stringBuilder.Append(accountName);
        stringBuilder.Append(";");

        // Set account key
        stringBuilder.Append(AccountKeyProperty);
```

```
            stringBuilder.Append(accountKey);
            stringBuilder.Append(";");

            // Set blob endpoint
            stringBuilder.Append(BlobEndpointProperty);
            stringBuilder.Append(blobEndpoint);
            stringBuilder.Append(";");

            return stringBuilder.ToString();
    }
}
```

In the next step, I implement the `AlertEntity` class, depicted in Listing 14-13 (CustomIoTSolution.Common/Models). `AlertEntity` is an abstract representation of the entities stored in the alerthistory Azure Table. Apart from system properties derived from the `TableEntity` class, it has only one additional public property, `AlertTemperature`. It carries a temperature value that exceeds "normal" values. Note that `AlertTemperature` is of type `double`. This is because Azure Tables support the following types only: `byte[]`, `bool`, `DateTime`, `double`, `Guid`, `int`, `long`, and `string`. Properties of different types are ignored by the Azure Storage Service, and thus will not be inserted into the Azure Table.

LISTING 14-13 Abstract representation of entities of the alerthistory Azure Table

```
public class AlertEntity : TableEntity
{
    public double AlertTemperature { get; set; }
}
```

As Chapter 13 showed, messages received by the Event Hub processor are represented as raw byte arrays. However, according to the configuration of the averagetemperature Stream Analytics output, data generated by the Stream Analytics query will have a JSON format. Hence, to easily deserialize JSON objects, I define the `TemperatureEventData` class (see Listing 14-14). It maps avgtemperature and deviceid fields from the Stream Analytics output to the `AverageValue` and `DeviceId` properties, respectively. `TemperatureEventData` also implements the static method `FromEventData`, which converts instances of `EventData` to `TemperatureEventData` objects.

LISTING 14-14 Definition of the TemperatureEventData class

```
public class TemperatureEventData
{
    [JsonProperty(PropertyName = "avgtemperature")]
    public float AverageValue { get; set; }

    public string DeviceId { get; set; }

    public static TemperatureEventData FromEventData(EventData eventData)
    {
```

```
          Check.IsNull(eventData);

          TemperatureEventData result = null;

          try
          {
              var jsonString = Encoding.UTF8.GetString(eventData.GetBytes());

              result = JsonConvert.DeserializeObject<TemperatureEventData>(jsonString);
          }
          catch (Exception) { }

          return result;
      }
}
```

Finally, I create the TemperatureEventDataProcessor class, responsible for processing events received by the Event Hub. (See the companion code at Chapter 14/CustomIoTSolution. EventProcessor/Processors/TemperatureEventDataProcessor.cs.) As explained in Chapter 13, TemperatureEventDataProcessor has to implement the IEventProcessor interface. Therefore, TemperatureEventDataProcessor has three public methods: OpenAsync, CloseAsync, and ProcessEventAsync. The first two methods appear in Listing 14-15. They do not implement any significant logic and only output to the console selected in the properties of the PartitionContext class instance representing the Event Hubs partition.

LISTING 14-15 OpenAsync and CloseAsync methods of the TemperatureEventDataProcessor class

```
public Task OpenAsync(PartitionContext context)
{
    Console.WriteLine($"Open: {context.EventHubPath}, Partition Id: {context.Lease.
        PartitionId}");

    return Task.FromResult<object>(null);
}

public Task CloseAsync(PartitionContext context, CloseReason reason)
{
    Console.WriteLine($"Close: {context.EventHubPath}, Reason: {reason}");

    return Task.FromResult<object>(null);
}
```

Much more logic is contained within ProcessEventsAsync, shown in Listing 14-16. This method iterates through a collection of EventData objects. Each of them is converted to an instance of TemperatureEventData displayed in the console. Lastly, I check whether the temperature value is above the threshold. If so, the alert entity is created and written to the alerthistory Azure Table.

LISTING 14-16   Processing messages received by the Event Hub

```
public Task ProcessEventsAsync(PartitionContext context, IEnumerable<EventData> messages)
{
    foreach (var message in messages)
    {
        try
        {
            var temperatureEventData = TemperatureEventData.FromEventData(message);

            DisplayTemperature(temperatureEventData);

            CheckTemperature(temperatureEventData);
        }
        catch (Exception ex)
        {
            Console.WriteLine(ex.Message);
        }
    }

    return Task.FromResult<object>(null);
}
```

To display temperature values in the console, I use the DisplayTemperature method, which appears in Listing 14-17. This method checks whether the TemperatureEventData instance passed as the argument is not null. If so, it displays a value stored in the AverageValue property. Otherwise, the constant string Unknown structure of the event data is output.

LISTING 14-17   Displaying average temperature values

```
private void DisplayTemperature(TemperatureEventData temperatureEventData)
{
    if (temperatureEventData != null)
    {
        Console.WriteLine(temperatureEventData.AverageValue);
    }
    else
    {
        Console.WriteLine("Unknown structure of the event data");
    }
}
```

In this example, to check whether the average temperature is at normal level, I simply compare it to the fixed value stored in the temperatureThreshold constant (see Listing 14-18). You can easily extend this app by sending requests to the anomaly detection web service developed in Chapter 11, "Device learning."

LISTING 14-18 Checking whether average temperature is above a specified threshold

```
private const double temperatureThreshold = 32.5;

private async void CheckTemperature(TemperatureEventData temperatureEventData)
{
    if (temperatureEventData.AverageValue >= temperatureThreshold)
    {
        await AzureStorageHelper.WriteAlertToAzureTable(new AlertEntity()
        {
            AlertTemperature = temperatureEventData.AverageValue,
            PartitionKey = temperatureEventData.DeviceId,
            RowKey = Guid.NewGuid().ToString(),
            Timestamp = DateTime.Now,
            ETag = "*"
        });

        NotificationHelper.SendToast(temperatureEventData.AverageValue);
    }
}
```

If the average temperature is detected as abnormal, I store it along with the identifier of the device that reported the value in the alerthistory Azure Table. To write entities to that table, I implement the AzureStorageHelper class (CustomIoTSolution.Common/Helpers/AzureStorageHelper.cs). This class has a static constructor, in which I create an instance of the CloudTableClient class, used to perform operations on Azure Tables. Specifically, I use this object to write data to the alerthistory table, as shown in Listing 14-19.

LISTING 14-19 Writing entities to the alerthistory Azure Table

```
public static async Task WriteAlertToAzureTable(AlertEntity alertEntity)
{
    // Verify input arguments
    Check.IsNull(alertEntity);

    // Get table reference
    var cloudTable = cloudTableClient.GetTableReference(Configuration.AlertsTableName);

    // Configure table operation to insert AlertEntity
    var tableOperation = TableOperation.Insert(alertEntity);

    // Execute request
    await cloudTable.ExecuteAsync(tableOperation);
}
```

TemperatureEventDataProcessor is associated with alerts-hub in the Main method of the Program class (see Listing 14-20). First, I prepare the blob storage connection string and then instantiate EventProcessorHost. Finally, I register TemperatureEventDataProcessor using the RegisterEventProcessorAsync method of the EventProcessorHost class.

LISTING 14-20 An entry point of the CustomIoTSolution.EventProcessor

```
static void Main(string[] args)
{
    try
    {
        // Prepare storage connection string
        var storageConnectionString = ConnectionStringHelper.GetBlobConnectionString(
            Configuration.AccountName,
            Configuration.AccountKey,
            Configuration.BlobEndPoint);

        // Instantiate EventProcessorHost
        var eventProcessorHost = new EventProcessorHost(
            Configuration.EventHubPath,
            Configuration.ConsumerGroupName,
            Configuration.EventHubConnectionString,
            storageConnectionString);

        // Register event processor
        // Note that Wait is necessary here since an entry point method cannot be marked
        // as async
        eventProcessorHost.RegisterEventProcessorAsync<TemperatureEventDataProcessor>().
            Wait();
    }
    catch (Exception ex)
    {
        Console.WriteLine(ex.Message);
    }

    Console.Read();
}
```

To test, the event processing procedure, run CustomIoTSolution.EventProcessor on the development PC. The string containing a partition identifier will be displayed after a short while, followed by a series of strings with average temperature values (see Figure 14-25). The number of these items will depend on the number of telemetry messages you sent previously with CustomIoTSolution.RemoteClient.

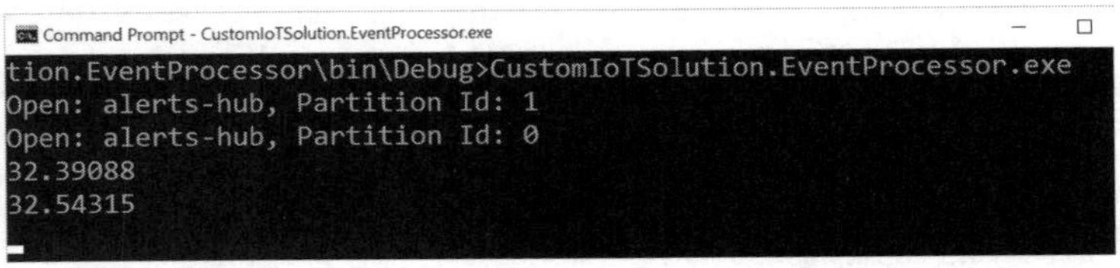

FIGURE 14-25 Sample outputs of CustomIoTSolution.EventProcessor.

You can now use Cloud Explorer to see whether the alerthistory Azure Table contains any new values. If not, you can adjust the temperatureThreshold (refer to Listing 14-18) value to your real or simulated sensor readings.

The CustomIoTSolution.EventProcessor app works as long as you press the Enter key, which will also close the event processor.

A final note on message retention: Azure Event Hub stores messages for the specified amount of time until they expire. So, if you rerun CustomIoTSolution.EventProcessor, all unexpired messages will be processed again. To skip messages that you already processed, you can use the Offset property of the EventData class instance. The offset is a marker for an event within the Event Hubs stream and has unique value.

Data visualization with Power BI

Both preconfigured Azure IoT Suite solutions I discussed in the two previous chapters display data in a graphical form on nice-looking plots. In this chapter, I show you how you can achieve such functionality with Microsoft Power BI.

Microsoft Power BI is a set of tools for data analytics and visualization. You can use Power BI to quickly create dashboards, presenting your sensors' data along with their metrics. Dashboards can be updated in real time and are available for any device, from any place.

Here, I show you how to use an Azure Stream Analytics job to transfer data from a remote device to the Power BI. Then, I create a dashboard displaying temperature, humidity, and pressure acquired with the Sense HAT add-on board for Raspberry Pi.

To start, you need to sign up for a free Power BI account here: *https://bit.ly/power_BI*. After creating your account, you use it to sign in to Power BI. You should then see the screen shown in Figure 14-26. There is nothing apart from the empty workspace. To prepare a dashboard, we need a data stream.

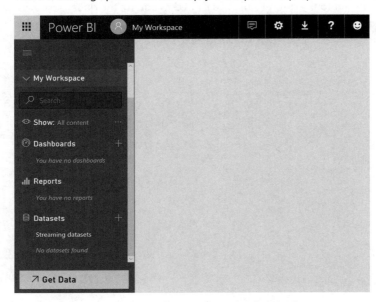

FIGURE 14-26   Default view of the Power BI right after sign in.

To prepare a data source for Power BI, go back to the Azure Portal and navigate to the Azure Stream Analytics job where you stop the job. Then, define a new output for the Power BI sink and set its alias to **telemetryplots** (see Figure 14-27). You will need to authorize your Azure account to access Power BI, so click the **Authorize** button. It will display a new browser window, where you enter your credentials to the Power BI account. One list box and two text boxes appear. Use the list box to choose the Power BI workspaces. By default, there is only one such workspace, My Workspace, so choose a default option. Then, in the Dataset and Table Names text boxes, type **Sense HAT** and **Telemetry**, respectively. Finally, click the **Create** button, and let Azure Portal validate your new output.

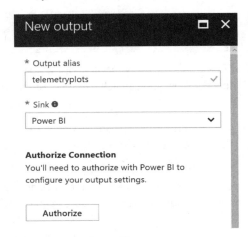

FIGURE 14-27 Power BI output.

You've just created the new output associated with your Power BI dataset. Tell the Stream Analytics Job which data you want to transmit to the output sink. You'll need to update the query, so navigate to the query editor, and supplement the query with the statements highlighted in Listing 14-21. After saving the query, your job topology will be updated as shown in Figure 14-28.

LISTING 14-21 Sending telemetry data to the Power BI sink

```
SELECT
    DeviceId,
    RowId,
    Temperature,
    Humidity,
    Pressure
INTO
    [telemetrytable]
FROM
    [datastream]

SELECT
    DeviceId,
    AVG(Temperature) AS AvgTemperature
INTO
```

```
        [averagetemperature]
FROM
        [datastream]
GROUP BY
        DeviceId,
        HOPPINGWINDOW(minute, 10, 5)

SELECT
        Time,
        DeviceId,
        Temperature,
        Humidity,
        Pressure
INTO
        [telemetryplots]
FROM
        [datastream]
```

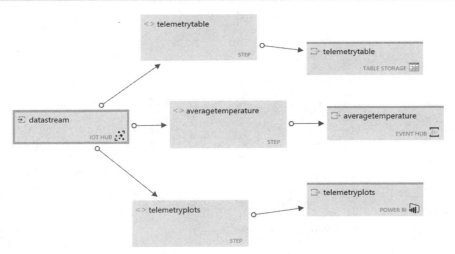

FIGURE 14-28 Updated job topology.

After the topology is configured, you need to stream new data. Restart the Stream Analytics job. Then, run CustomIoTSolution.RemoteClient, connect to the cloud, and start telemetry. Keep the app running to make sure you will have enough data points to display in the Power BI dashboard.

Navigate back to Power BI and, using the menu on the left, create a new dashboard named Sense HAT. Then click the plus (**+**) sign in the right corner of the dashboard window. The Add Tile screen will be displayed. Scroll down to the Real-Time Data group and click **Custom Streaming Data** (see Figure 14-29). The list of available datasets appears. According to the output sink configuration, you should have a single item there: Sense HAT. Choose it and click the **Next** button. This will open the Add a Custom Streaming Data Tile screen, depicted in Figure 14-30.

Add tile

Select source

FIGURE 14-29 The Add Tile screen highlighting a custom streaming data source.

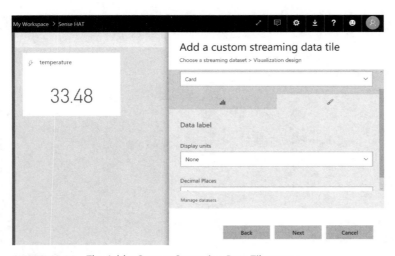

FIGURE 14-30 The Add a Custom Streaming Data Tile screen.

You use the new screen to choose data to display and determine how your data will be formatted and visualized. First you use the Visualization Type list box to choose from the following:

- **Card**   This displays a single value. You typically use it to depict the most recent value from some sensor, for example, current temperature reading.

- **Line Chart**   This is a two-dimensional plot, displaying a data series. You use this kind of visualization to plot temporal changes of a column in your dataset—for instance, how temperature changes over time.

- **Clustered Bar and Column Charts**   You can use these charts to visualize sensor data for different devices (or different categories).

- **Gauge**   This displays a gauge chart, used typically for visualizing aggregated values—for example, average temperature, along with its minimum and maximum possible value.

Then, you select the data to display and its formatting. Use the controls displayed below the Visualization Type list box. The particular options depend on the visual you choose.

We will now create three cards to display sensor readings in real time and one line chart for presenting historical temperatures. To do so, set Visualization Type to **Card**. You will see a tab control below the Visualization Type list box. This has two tabs: one for choosing a value to display, and the second for format configuration. Use the **Add Value** link from the first tab and choose **Temperature**. Then, go to the second tab and set Display Units to **none** and Decimal Places to **2**. Click the **Next** button and set the title of your tile to Temperature, and click the **Apply** button. Your tile will now display a current temperature reading in the Sense HAT dashboard.

Using the same procedure, create two additional tiles for your humidity and pressure values. Finally, create a line chart tile. For this visualization, you can configure the following options:

- **Axis** This is used to choose the column, whose data will be used for abscissa. Set it to **Time**.

- **Legend** This is the legend for your dataset. This is useful when you display several lines on a single chart—for example, temperatures from different devices. Set this value to **deviceid**.

- **Values** This is used to select data for the ordinate. Set it to **Temperature**.

- **Time Window** This is used to specify the time interval for displaying your data. Set it to **1 Minute**.

After configuring these parameters, you click the **Next** button. You have an option to set the title of your chart. Change the title to **Temperature History**, and then click the **Apply** button. A line chart will appear in the Sense HAT dashboard. Note that you can easily move your tiles around the dashboard. I place the cards next to each other, and the line chart below them. So, my final dashboard looks as shown in Figure 14-2.

Power BI features are much more advanced than what I present here. You can build really comprehensive reports with this tool. Power BI has very detailed documentation (see *https://bit.ly/power_BI_docs*), including many podcasts and tutorials, so detailed discussion is omitted here.

Notification Hub

In a final step, we implement the UWP app, which enables mobile clients to get the latest sensor readings and temperature alarms, as shown in Figure 14-1. We will also create the Azure Notification Hub, which will send notifications to mobile clients whenever the Event Hub processor detects an abnormal temperature. This procedure requires several elements. First, to enable your app to receive notifications from the cloud, you need to associate the app with the Windows Store, and then register the app with this particular instance of the Notification Hub. Second, we'll use a UWP app I created called CustomIoTSolution.NotificationClient to receive notifications and read sensor readings stored in the cloud. Third, we'll create and configure the Notification Hub in the Azure Portal. Finally, we'll send Toast notifications to mobile clients with such a Hub through the Event Hub processor.

Figure 14-31 shows the structure of your custom IoT solution. Remote IoT devices are controlled by the CustomIoTSolution.RemoteClient app, which transmits sensor readings to the cloud through the Azure IoT Hub. Then, the incoming data stream is analyzed at the cloud-side by the Azure Stream Analytics job, which transforms and outputs the data to three sinks: Power BI, Azure Table Storage, and Azure Event Hub. Power BI displays sensor data in real time on the dedicated dashboard. Azure Table Storage is used to store sensor data and information about abnormal sensor readings. These are detected by the Azure Event Hub, which analyzes the average temperature received from the Azure Stream Analytics job. Although in this case I use a fixed temperature threshold to detect abnormalities, nothing is blocking you from extending this solution by the custom Machine Learning web service, developed in Chapter 11.

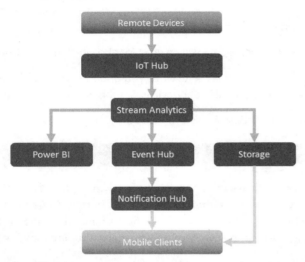

FIGURE 14-31 A diagram summarizing the data flow and structure of the custom IoT solution.

At the bottom of the solution diagram are mobile clients. These are UWP devices running CustomIoTSolution.NotificationClient. Mobile clients can send requests to the cloud to obtain recent sensor readings and temperature alarms. Additionally, mobile clients automatically receive notifications about abnormal readings.

Azure IoT Suite objects are used to obtain data from remote sensors and then process it in real time. Moreover, Azure is employed to store data and even send notifications to the mobile clients. It's an exciting and powerful data stream. Though I am using simple sensor data here, you can easily adjust this solution to monitor practically any process. In particular, you can move signal processing functionality to the event processor and analyze data in the cloud, possibly using the Machine Learning algorithms.

Store association

To associate the app with the Windows Store, register as an app developer (see *http://bit.ly/ app_dev_registration*). Then create a new Blank UWP (Universal Windows) Visual C# project named CustomIoTSolution.NotificationClient. Next, navigate to the Solution Explorer, right-click the project, choose **Store**, and select **Associate App with the Store** from the menu that appears. This opens the Associate Your App with the Windows Store wizard. In the first tab of this wizard, click the **Next** button. Then, you need to log in to your Microsoft account, which you used to register as an app developer. Finally, you type the app name in the Reserve a New App Name text box and click **Next**. This takes you to the last wizard step, which displays package information. Click the **Associate** button.

Store two parameters of your app: package SID and app secret. You obtain both of from *https:// apps.dev.microsoft.com*, where you click the **My Applications** button located in the top right corner. Then you need to enter your credentials, and the registered app will appear in the Live SDK Applications list. Click a link with your app name, and on the next webpage you will see the app secret and package SID (in the Windows Store group). Save these values. You will need them later to configure the Notification Hub.

Notification client app

To implement the notification client (see the companion code at Chapter 14/CustomIoTSolution. NotificationClient), I reference two solution projects: CustomIoTSolution.Common and SenseHAT.UWP. Then, I install two NuGet packages:

- **WindowsAzure.Messaging.Managed**   This implements the API for subscribing your app to the notification channel.

- **WindowsAzure.Storage**   This is required by CustomIoTSolution.Common.

Given this skeleton, I define the app UI, composed of three tabs: Registration, Telemetry, and Alarms (see Figure 14-32). The Registration tab has one button and two labels. You use the button to register the app for the Windows Push Notification Service (WNS) channel. When registration is complete, the label displays a registration identifier. The Telemetry tab looks similar to the corresponding tab of CustomIoTSolution.RemoteClient. It has a Get Sensor Reading button and labels with recent temperature, humidity, and pressure readings obtained from the Sense HAT add-on board. The last tab, Alarms, has one button and four labels. After the button is clicked, a request is sent to the cloud to retrieve the most recent information about the temperature alarm (from the alertshistory Azure Table). The appropriate values from this entity are then displayed in labels.

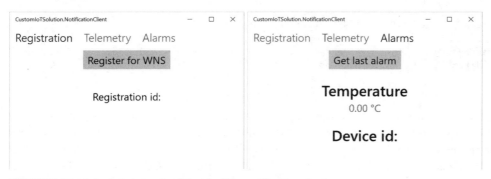

FIGURE 14-32   Selected elements of the UI of the notification client app.

To update values displayed in the UI, I implement the `NotificationClientViewModel` class. (See the companion code at Chapter 14/CustomIoTSolution.NotificationClient/ViewModels/ NotificationClientViewModel.cs.) Public members of this class are bound to appropriate objects of the UI.

Then, I write event handlers for the buttons. The event handler of the Register for WNS button appears in Listing 14-22. It shows how to register your app for the WNS notification channel. Namely, you first create the push notification channel for the application using the dedicated static method of the `PushNotificationChannelManager` class. Then, you associate this channel with the Notification Hub using the `RegisterNativeAsync` method of the `NotificationHub` class instance. The latter comes from the WindowsAzure.Messaging.Managed NuGet package.

LISTING 14-22   Registering an app for WNS notifications

```
private PushNotificationChannel pushNotificationChannel;

private async void ButtonRegister_Click(object sender, RoutedEventArgs e)
{
    try
    {
        pushNotificationChannel = await PushNotificationChannelManager.
            CreatePushNotificationChannelForApplicationAsync();

        var notificationHub = new NotificationHub(Configuration.NotificationHubPath,
            Configuration.DefaultListenSharedAccessSignatureConnectionString);

        var registration = await notificationHub.RegisterNativeAsync(
            pushNotificationChannel.Uri);

        notificationClientViewModel.RegistrationId = registration.RegistrationId;
    }
    catch (Exception ex)
    {
        await DisplayMessage("Registration error: " + ex.Message);
    }
}

private async Task DisplayMessage(string message)
{
    var messageDialog = new MessageDialog(message, Name);
    await messageDialog.ShowAsync();
}
```

`PushNotificationChannelManager` implements another public method, `CreatePush-NotificationChannelForSecondaryTileAsync`. It enables you to create a notification channel for the secondary tile of your app. This tile is displayed in the start menu of the mobile or desktop device. Naturally, this functionality is not available for Windows IoT 10 Core devices, which do not have a start menu.

To instantiate the `NotificationHub` class, you need a path to the Notification Hub and a connection string with the listen access policy. As I show you later in this chapter, there are two default connection strings to the Azure Notification Hub: `DefaultListenSharedAcceesSignatureConnectionString` and `DefaultFullSharedAccessSignatureConnectionString`. You use the first one in the client apps, which listen to notifications. The other connection string is utilized in the server- or cloud-side apps to send notifications.

To store the Notification Hub path and connection strings, I extend the definition of the `Configuration` class with the following properties: `NotificationHubPath`, `DefaultListenSharedAccessSignature-ConnectionString`, and `DefaultFullSharedAccessSignatureConnectionString`. I'll show where to find values for these properties.

As shown in Listing 14-23, event handlers for two other buttons are very similar. Both use the `GetMost-RecentEntity` method of the `AzureStorageHelper` class (see the companion code at Chapter 14/ CustomIoTSolution.Common/Helpers/AzureStorageHelper.cs) and then convert the Azure entity to either `SensorReadings` or `TemperatureAlertInfo`. Instances of these two classes are bound to labels of the Telemetry and Alerts tabs of the app UI.

LISTING 14-23 Obtaining sensor readings and alert information from Azure Storage

```
private async void ButtonGetSensorReadings_Click(object sender, RoutedEventArgs e)
{
    var mostRecentEntity = await AzureStorageHelper.GetMostRecentEntity(
        Configuration.TelemetryTableName, notificationClientViewModel.Offset);

    notificationClientViewModel.SensorReadings =
        EntityConverter.DynamicTableEntityToSensorReadings(mostRecentEntity);
}

private async void ButtonGetLastAlarmInfo_Click(object sender, RoutedEventArgs e)
{
    var mostRecentEntity = await AzureStorageHelper.GetMostRecentEntity(
        Configuration.AlertsTableName, notificationClientViewModel.Offset);

    notificationClientViewModel.TemperatureAlertInfo =
        EntityConverter.DynamicTableEntityToTemperatureAlertInfo(mostRecentEntity);
}
```

The `GetMostRecentEntity` method, which appears in Listing 14-24, proceeds as follows. After verifying input parameters, I obtain the Azure Table reference and create a filter, which selects only the most recent entities. Therefore, this filter uses a timestamp property greater than the specified date time offset. You can change this offset using the `Offset` property of the `NotificationClientViewModel` class. By default, I set this value to `DateTime.Now.AddDays(-1)`. Only entities updated within the last 24 hours will be selected.

LISTING 14-24   Retrieving most recent entity from the Azure Table

```
public static async Task<DynamicTableEntity> GetMostRecentEntity(string tableName,
    DateTimeOffset dateTimeOffset)
{
    // Verify input arguments
    Check.IsNull(tableName);
    Check.IsNull(dateTimeOffset);

    // Get cloud table client
    var cloudTable = cloudTableClient.GetTableReference(tableName);

    // Create timestamp filter
    var timestampFilter = TableQuery.GenerateFilterConditionForDate("Timestamp", "gt",
        dateTimeOffset);

    // Create and execute query
    var tableQuery = new TableQuery()
    {
        FilterString = timestampFilter.ToString()
    };

    // Execute query and filter to get the most recent entity
    return (await cloudTable.ExecuteQuerySegmentedAsync(tableQuery,
        dynamicTableEntityResolver, null))
        .OrderByDescending(x => x.Timestamp)
        .FirstOrDefault();
}

private static EntityResolver<DynamicTableEntity> dynamicTableEntityResolver =
    (partitionKey, rowKey, timestamp, properties, etag) =>
{
    return new DynamicTableEntity(partitionKey, rowKey, etag, properties);
};
```

This filter is then used to create a table query, which is subsequently executed using the
ExecuteQueryAsyncSegmented method of the CloudTable class instance. To use this method, you
need to provide the EntityResolver object. It is used to project entity properties to C# objects.
Here, I create a simple EntityResolver that maps entity properties to the DynamicTableEntity
object and then performs conversion using static methods of EntityConverter (see Listing 14-25).
I decided to use this approach because the SensorReadings class is defined in the UWP project,
while CustomIoTSolution.Common is a portable class library, which will also be referenced later in
the CustomIoTSolution.EventProcessor.

LISTING 14-25 Converting DynamicTableEntity to SensorReadings and TemperatureAlertInfo

```
public static SensorReadings DynamicTableEntityToSensorReadings(
    DynamicTableEntity dynamicTableEntity)
{
    SensorReadings sensorReadings = null;

    if (dynamicTableEntity != null)
    {
        sensorReadings = new SensorReadings()
        {
            Temperature = Convert.ToSingle(dynamicTableEntity.Properties["temperature"].
                PropertyAsObject),
            Humidity = Convert.ToSingle(dynamicTableEntity.Properties["humidity"].
                PropertyAsObject),
            Pressure = Convert.ToSingle(dynamicTableEntity.Properties["pressure"].
                PropertyAsObject)
        };
    }

    return sensorReadings;
}

public static TemperatureAlertInfo DynamicTableEntityToTemperatureAlertInfo(
    DynamicTableEntity dynamicTableEntity)
{
    TemperatureAlertInfo temperatureAlertInfo = null;

    if (dynamicTableEntity != null)
    {
        temperatureAlertInfo = new TemperatureAlertInfo()
        {
            DeviceId = dynamicTableEntity.PartitionKey,
            Temperature = dynamicTableEntity.Properties["AlertTemperature"].DoubleValue.
                Value
        };
    }

    return temperatureAlertInfo;
}
```

The particular API of the WindowsAzure.Storage NuGet package depends on the targets of the project using this package. Here, my PCL targets are set to .NET Framework, Windows 8.1, and Windows Phone 8.1 (see Appendix D). If your app or class library targets UWP, then ExecuteQueryAsyncSegmented does not require you to use EntityResolver. Instead, it returns a collection of DynamicTableEntity objects. Moreover, in the WindowsAzure.Storage NuGet package dedicated for PCLs, I need to use strings representing query comparisons, while in the corresponding NuGet package used in the PredictiveMaintenance.Web project, discussed in the previous chapter, those comparisons were defined in the QueryComparisons class, shown in Listing 14-26. I am explicitly stating those differences to indicate that various APIs of the NuGet packages might not be unified between platforms.

LISTING 14-26 QueryComparisons class from the WindowsAzure.Storage targeting

```
public static class QueryComparisons
{
    //
    // Summary:
    //     Represents the Equal operator.
    public const string Equal = "eq";
    //
    // Summary:
    //     Represents the Greater Than operator.
    public const string GreaterThan = "gt";
    //
    // Summary:
    //     Represents the Greater Than or Equal operator.
    public const string GreaterThanOrEqual = "ge";
    //
    // Summary:
    //     Represents the Less Than operator.
    public const string LessThan = "lt";
    //
    // Summary:
    //     Represents the Less Than or Equal operator.
    public const string LessThanOrEqual = "le";
    //
    // Summary:
    //     Represents the Not Equal operator.
    public const string NotEqual = "ne";
}
```

You can now run the app to read recent sensor readings and temperature alert information. The app can run on your development PC, mobile phone, or emulator. You choose the target device using the drop-down list in Figure 14-33. (Note that if you do not have any emulators available, you can install them using the Download New Emulators option.)

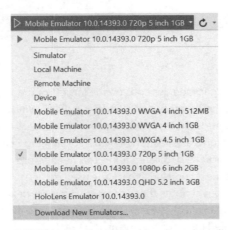

FIGURE 14-33 Target Machine drop-down list.

When you try to register the app for push notifications, it will not work, because no Notification Hub has been created. You prepare one in the next section.

Notification Hub creation and configuration

You create the Notification Hub with the Azure Portal the same way you do other Azure IoT Suite objects. As shown in Figure 14-34, you click the **New** button (the one with a plus sign), choose the **Internet of Things** node, and choose the **Notification Hub** option. The New Notification Hub screen appears.

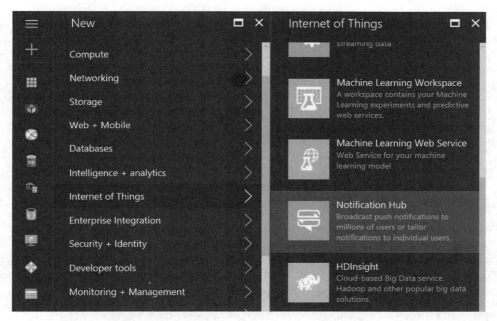

FIGURE 14-34 Creating a Notification Hub.

Using the New Notification Hub screen you configure basic properties of the Notification Hub, like the name, namespace, location, and so on. As shown in Figure 14-35, I changed the hub name to sense-hat-notification-hub, and its namespace to sense-hat-notifications. Choose **Sense-HAT** as the resource group and choose the **Free** pricing tier. Finally, click the **Create** button.

The Notification Hub you just created can send notifications to apps running on various platforms including iOS, Android, Windows Universal, and Windows Phone. Each platform has its own native notification system, which requires specific configuration. Here, I'm using WNS, which requires a package SID and the security key I obtained previously with the app developer portal.

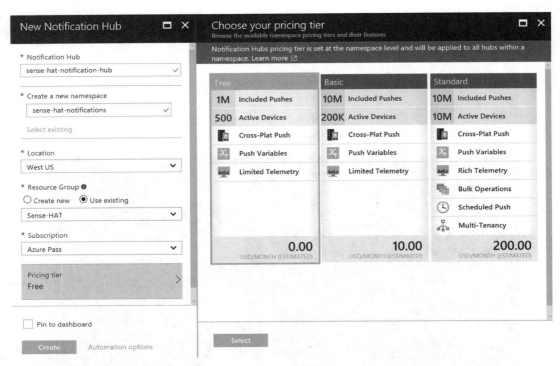

FIGURE 14-35 Notification Hub configuration.

To configure notification services, click **Push Notification Services** in the sense-hat-notification-hub Overview pane and choose **Windows (WNS)**. Finally, type your package SID and security key in the corresponding text boxes and save your changes (see Figure 14-36).

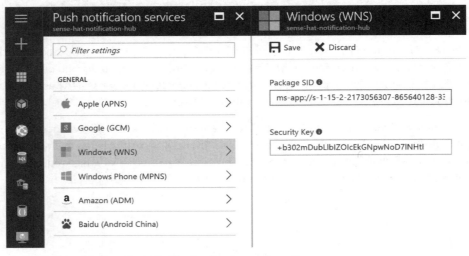

FIGURE 14-36 Windows Push Notification Service configuration.

The last thing you need to register your app with the Notification Hub are connection strings. As shown in Figure 14-37, you obtain them from the Access Policies pane of sense-hat-notification-hub. Subsequently, you use them to set corresponding properties of the Configuration class from the CustomIoTSolution.Common project.

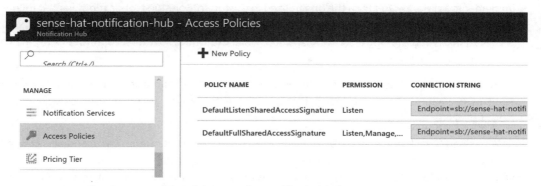

FIGURE 14-37 A list of access policies of the sense-hat-notification-hub.

Sending toast notifications with the event processor

With the Notification Hub ready and configured, you can extend the CustomIoTSolution.EventProcessor project by adding methods to send toast notifications to mobile clients. In the UWP, the visual appearance of the toast notification depends on the actual device the app is running on. On your desktop, the notification is pushed from the right part of the screen; on a mobile phone, the notification is pushed from the top part of the screen. Then, the toast notification stays active in the center. Typically, when you click the toast notification, the app is activated. You can write logic that may alter normal startup of your app to respond to the notification. To check whether your app was activated from the toast notification, read the Kind property of the LaunchActivatedEventArgs class, whose instance is passed to the OnLaunched event of the App class (refer to Chapter 4, "User interface design for headed devices"). For instance, you can automatically navigate to the Alarms tab and retrieve recent information about the temperature alarm.

To create a toast notification, you prepare a notification payload. This is an XML file that defines the visual appearance of the toast notification. You can install the payload file manually or using the dedicated NuGet package: Microsof.Toolkit.Uwp.Notifications.

Here, I show you how to create a simple toast notification with a title and literal content. You can further extend your toast using the detailed syntax description from the following article: *https://bit.ly/toast_payload*.

To send toast notifications from the CustomIoTSolution.EventProcessor project, I first install two packages:

- **Microsoft.Toolkit.Uwp.Notifications**   This helps to dynamically create the toast payload.

- **Microsoft.Azure.NotificationHubs**   This is used to connect to the Notification Hub and send actual push notifications.

Subsequently, I implement the `NotificationHelper` class, whose full definition is depicted in Listing 14-26. The static constructor of this class creates an instance of `NotificationHubClient`. Unlike in Listing 14-22, I'm using the `DefaultFullSharedAccesssSignature` policy because I need to send notifications to clients. It should be also noted that the `NotificationHubClient` class used here implements a different API than the one utilized in CustomIoTSolution.NotificationClient. It follows that both apps use different NuGet packages since they target different platforms. CustomIoTSolution. NotificationClient is the Universal Windows app, while CustomIoTSolution.EventProcessor is the console app, using the full .NET Framework.

To create and send notifications, I use the `SendToast` method of the `NotificationHelper` class. SendToast creates the toast payload using several objects from the Microsoft.Toolkit.Uwp.Notifications NuGet package.

A payload has a hierarchical structure with the `<toast>` element on top. This element is created with the ToastContent class. Then, you define a `<visual>` node using the `ToastVisual` class. Subsequently, you define a binding template, which determines the structure of your toast notification. To this end, I use the `ToastBindingGeneric` class. Finally, set the `Children` property of the `ToastBindingGeneric` class instance to set up a toast title and its content. Once the `ToastContent` object is created, you get its underlying XML payload using a GetContent method. For the ToastContent I create in Listing 14-27, the GetContent method outputs the XML shown in Listing 14-28. The hierarchy of the ToastContent class directly corresponds to the structure of the XML payload.

LISTING 14-27   Full definition of the NotificationHelper class

```
public static class NotificationHelper
{
    private static NotificationHubClient notificationHubClient;

    static NotificationHelper()
    {
        notificationHubClient = NotificationHubClient.CreateClientFromConnectionString(
            Configuration.DefaultFullSharedAccessSignatureConnectionString,
            Configuration.NotificationHubPath);
    }

    public static void SendToast(float temperature)
    {
        // Create toast notification
        var toastContent = new ToastContent()
        {
            Visual = new ToastVisual()
            {
                BindingGeneric = new ToastBindingGeneric()
                {
                    Children =
                    {
                        new AdaptiveText()
                        {
```

```
                    Text = "Temperature alert"
                },
                new AdaptiveText()
                {
                    Text = $"Average temperature of {temperature:F2} exceeded a
                        normal level"
                }
            }
        }
    }
};

// Send toast to mobile clients
notificationHubClient.SendWindowsNativeNotificationAsync(toastContent.
    GetContent()).Wait();
    }
}
```

LISTING 14-28 Payload created by the SendToast method from Listing 14-27

```
<?xml version="1.0" encoding="utf-8"?>
<toast>
    <visual>
        <binding template="ToastGeneric">
            <text>Temperature alert</text>
            <text>Average temperature of 32.54 exceeded a normal level</text>
        </binding>
    </visual>
</toast>
```

Once the payload is ready, I pass it as the argument of the SendWindowsNativeNotificationAsync method of the NotificationHubClient class instance. This will send the actual toast to the registered app whenever temperature is detected to be abnormal. Hence, I invoke NotificationHelper.SendToast within the CheckTemperature method of TemperatureEventDataProcessor (see Listing 14-29).

LISTING 14-29 Sending toast notification from the event processor

```
private async void CheckTemperature(TemperatureEventData temperatureEventData)
{
    if (temperatureEventData.AverageValue >= temperatureThreshold)
    {
        await AzureStorageHelper.WriteAlertToAzureTable(new AlertEntity()
        {
            AlertTemperature = temperatureEventData.AverageValue,
            PartitionKey = temperatureEventData.DeviceId,
            RowKey = Guid.NewGuid().ToString(),
            Timestamp = DateTime.Now,
```

```
          ETag = "*"
     });

     NotificationHelper.SendToast(temperatureEventData.AverageValue);
  }
}
```

To run the solution, you need to run CustomIoTSolution.NotificationClient, associate it with the Notification Hub by clicking the **Register for WNS** button on the Registration tab, and then run CustomIoTSolution.EventProcessor. If the latter finds any abnormal temperatures, it will send an appropriate notification to the UWP app, as shown in Figure 14-1.

You still need to run the event processor independently. However, it can be deployed to the cloud and run continuously. I'll show you how to achieve this in the next section.

Deploying the Event Hub processor to the cloud

To deploy the Event Hub processor to the cloud, you create an Azure web app. Physically, such an app runs within the virtual machine hosted by the Windows Server operating system and is typically written with ASP.NET MVC. Apart from that, web apps can run background operations, called WebJobs. These can be implemented as executable files or scripts written with Windows Command Line (batch files), Windows PowerShell, Bash, PHP, Python, or Java Script (Node.js). Additionally, WebJobs can execute Java jar files.

I utilize this possibility to deploy CustomIoTSolution.EventProcessor, which is an executable file, as a WebJob. To prepare the package to deploy, build that project and then the build output directory, typically located under the bin folder. Depending on your build configuration, you will find there two subfolders: Debug and Release. Open the appropriate one and create a ZIP archive, CustomIoTSolution.EventProcessor.zip, using the following files:

- CustomIoTSolution.EventProcessor.exe

- CustomIoTSolution.Common.dll

- Microsoft.Azure.KeyVault.Core.dll

- Microsoft.Azure.NotificationHubs.dll

- Microsoft.Data.Edm.dll

- Microsoft.Data.OData.dll

- Microsoft.Data.Services.Client.dll

- Microsoft.ServiceBus.dll

- Microsoft.ServiceBus.Messaging.EventProcessorHost.dll

- Microsoft.Toolkit.Uwp.Notifications.dll

- Microsoft.WindowsAzure.Configuration.dll

- Microsoft.WindowsAzure.Storage.dll

- Newtonsoft.Json.dll

- SenseHat.Portable.dll

- System.Spatial.dll

The first file on this list is the executable file. All others are its dependents provided by CustomIoTSolution.Common, SenseHat.Portable projects, or NuGet packages.

Once the WebJob package is ready, create the actual web app. Navigate to the Azure Portal, click the **New** button, and choose the **Web App** template. Then, as shown in Figure 14-38, set the app name to **sense-hat**, choose **Sense-HAT Resource Group**, and then create a new app service plan using **Free-F1** pricing tier. Once this is done, click the **Create** button.

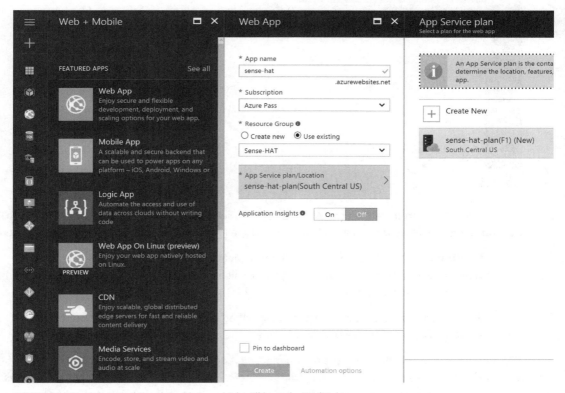

FIGURE 14-38 Creating the new web app, which will host the WebJob.

After deploying a web app, navigate to its WebJobs pane. As shown in Figure 14-39, this pane has several buttons, which enable you to create and control your WebJobs. At the moment, you do not have a WebJob. Click the **Add** button. The Add WebJob screen, shown in Figure 14-40, appears.

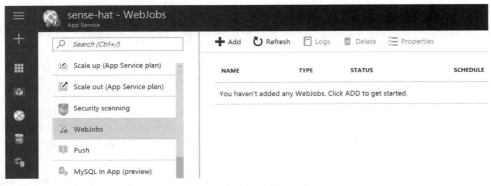

FIGURE 14-39   The WebJobs pane of the sense-hat web app.

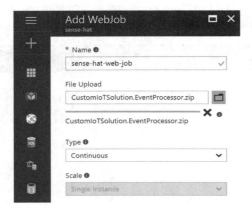

FIGURE 14-40   Adding a WebJob.

In the Add WebJob screen, set the WebJob name to **sense-hat-web-job**, upload the **CustomIoT-Solution.EventProcessor.zip** file, and choose the type for your WebJob. You have two options here:

- **Continuous**   The WebJob runs continuously until it crashes or is manually stopped. You typically use continuous WebJobs when you wait for data to process, and you do not know when data can be delivered.

- **Scheduled**   The WebJob is executed at specified times. Such WebJobs are used to run scheduled operations (like backups), or are triggered on demand.

The event processor shall process data whenever it is delivered to the Event Hub, so the WebJob should run in the background and wait for data. Therefore, we set the WebJob type to **Continuous**. Confirm the WebJob configuration with the **OK** button. The sense-hat-web-job WebJob will appear on the list of WebJobs, where you can run it using the **Start** button. The CustomIoTSolution. EventProcessor.exe file will be executed. To see its output, you click the **Logs** button. It will open a new window showing the output of the WebJob (see Figure 14-41).

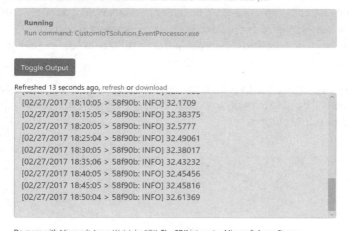

Continuous WebJob Details sense-hat-web-job

Running
Run command: CustomIoTSolution.EventProcessor.exe

Toggle Output

Refreshed 13 seconds ago, refresh or download

```
[02/27/2017 18:10:05 > 58f90b: INFO] 32.1709
[02/27/2017 18:15:05 > 58f90b: INFO] 32.38375
[02/27/2017 18:20:05 > 58f90b: INFO] 32.5777
[02/27/2017 18:25:04 > 58f90b: INFO] 32.49061
[02/27/2017 18:30:05 > 58f90b: INFO] 32.38017
[02/27/2017 18:35:06 > 58f90b: INFO] 32.43232
[02/27/2017 18:40:05 > 58f90b: INFO] 32.45456
[02/27/2017 18:45:05 > 58f90b: INFO] 32.45816
[02/27/2017 18:50:04 > 58f90b: INFO] 32.61369
```

Do more with Microsoft Azure WebJobs SDK. The SDK integrates Microsoft Azure Storage, triggering a function in your program when items are added to Queues, Blobs, or Tables.

FIGURE 14-41 Output of the sense-hat-web-job.

The event processor now runs in the Azure cloud. You can concurrently run CustomIoTSolution. RemoteClient and CustomIoTSolution.NotificationClient apps to stream data and receive notifications whenever abnormal temperatures are detected.

Summary

In this chapter I guided you through a detailed process of creating a fully customized IoT solution using Windows 10 IoT Core, Universal Windows Platform, and Azure IoT Suite. You created a comprehensive solution in which remote IoT devices stream data to the Azure cloud, which stores, presents, transforms, and processes data to detect abnormal readings. Information about anomaly detection was also delivered to UWP apps with Windows Push Notification Service.

As shown throughout this book, Windows 10 IoT Core, Universal Windows Platform, and Azure cloud offer a very exciting combination of tools, which you can use to build complicated IoT systems whose functionality is limited only by your imagination.

Most of the examples use easily available add-on boards for the popular Raspberry Pi IoT device. You started from scratch and then developed the relatively simple functionality of reading data from sensors. Then you worked with much more advanced signal and image processing, which helped you to develop artificial senses of hearing and vision. Then, you learned how to implement communication and control methods of various motors, which you can use to construct artificial motor functions. I presented Microsoft Cognitive Services and Azure Machine Learning tools to show how they can be used to create an artificial intelligence module for the IoT device.

In the last part of the book, I dealt with two preconfigured Azure IoT solutions for remote devices monitoring and predictive maintenance. Fueled by this knowledge, you created a fully customized IoT solution.

The preceding material is supplemented by six appendixes, which show how to start IoT development with JavaScript and Visual Basic, explain basic properties of bit-encoding, the creation of portable class libraries, and code sharing strategies between different projects. I also present select aspects of C++ component extensions (C++/CX) and show you how to set up Visual Studio 2017 for IoT development. These appendixes are available online at *https://aka.ms/IoT/downloads*.

I hope that what you've learned here will significantly help to boost development of your IoT solutions, and I strongly believe that you will be able to easily implement any IoT solution you can imagine. I'm looking forward to seeing your next IoT solution.

Index

Appendixes are presented in this index using the letter of the appendix followed by the number of the page within the appendix. For example, A4–A6 would indicate that an entry's information appears on pages 4–6 of Appendix A.

Symbols